Historic Events
for Students
The Great Depression

Historic Events

for Students

The Great Depression
Volume 2: F-Po

Richard C. Hanes, Editor
Sharon M. Hanes, Associate Editor

GALE®

THOMSON
GALE

Detroit • New York • San Diego • San Francisco • Cleveland • New Haven, Conn. • Waterville, Maine • London • Munich

THOMSON

GALE

Historic Events for Students: The Great Depression

Richard C. Hanes and Sharon M. Hanes

Project Editor
Nancy Matuszak

Editorial
Jason M. Everett, Rachel J. Kain

Permissions
Debra J. Freitas, Lori Hines

Imaging and Multimedia
Dean Dauphinais, Christine O'Bryan

Product Design
Pamela A. E. Galbreath

Composition and Electronic Capture
Evi Seoud

Manufacturing
Rita Wimberley

LIBRARY OF CONGRESS CATALOGING-IN-PUBLICATION DATA

The Great Depression / Richard C. Hanes, editor; Sharon Hanes, associate editor.
    p. cm. — (Historic events for students)
        Includes bibliographical references and index.
        ISBN 0-7876-5701-8 (set)—ISBN 0-7876-5702-6 (v. 1)—ISBN
    0-7876-5703-4 (v. 2)—ISBN 0-7876-5704-2 (v. 3)
        1. United States—History—1933-1945. 2. United States—History—1919-1933.
        3. Depressions—1929—United States. 4. New Deal, 1933-1939.
        5. United States—History—1933-1945—Sources.
        6. United States—History—1919-1933—Sources.
        7. Depressions—1929—United States—Sources.
        8. New Deal, 1933-1939—Sources. I. Hanes, Richard Clay, 1946- II. Series.

E806 .G827 2002
973.917—dc21
2001007712

Printed in the United States of America
10 9 8 7 6 5 4 3 2 1

Table of Contents

Chronological Contents vii

Advisory Board ix

Credits x

About the Series xv

Introduction xvi

Chronology xix

A
American Indians **v1,** 1
Arts Programs **v1,** 24

B
Banking **v1,** 40
Black Americans **v1,** 66

C
Causes of the Crash **v1,** 87
Civilian Conservation Corps **v1,** 109
Crime **v1,** 123

D
Democratic Coalition **v1,** 146
Dust Bowl **v1,** 168

E

Education **v1,** 186
Effects of the Great Depression—LBJ's
  Great Society **v1,** 215
Employment **v1,** 239
Escapism and Leisure Time **v1,** 262
Ethnic Relations **v1,** 284
Everyday Life **v1,** 305

F

Farm Relief **v2,** 1
Food **v2,** 21

G

Global Impact **v2,** 50

H

Hollywood **v2,** 70
Housing **v2,** 97

I

Interwar Era **v2,** 117
Isolationism **v2,** 138

J

Journalism **v2,** 159

L

Labor and Industry **v2,** 189
Literature **v2,** 207

N

National Industrial Recovery Act **v2,** 228
New Deal (First, and Its Critics) **v2,** 252

New Deal (Second) **v2,** 274

P

Photography **v2,** 295
Political Ideologies: Leaning Left . . . **v2,** 315
Prohibition Repealed **v3,** 1
Public Health **v3,** 33

R

Radio **v3,** 57
(Rails) Riding the Rails **v3,** 76
Reconstruction Finance Corporation . . . **v3,** 92
Religion **v3,** 118
Rural Electrification Administration . . . **v3,** 153

S

Social Security **v3,** 177
Supreme Court **v3,** 202

T

Tennessee Valley Authority **v3,** 229

W

Water and Power **v3,** 257
Women in Public Life **v3,** 282
Works Progress Administration **v3,** 306
World War II Mobilization **v3,** 325
World's Fairs **v3,** 352

Glossary **v1,** 333; **v2,** 337; **v3,** 369

Bibliography **v1,** 349; **v2,** 353; **v3,** 385

Index **v1,** 355; **v2,** 359; **v3,** 391

Chronological Table of Contents

1920–1929
Causes of the Crash **v1,** 87

1929–1941
Arts Programs **v1,** 24
Black Americans **v1,** 66
Crime **v1,** 123
Education **v1,** 186
Employment **v1,** 239
Escapism and Leisure Time **v1,** 262
Ethnic Relations **v1,** 284
Everyday Life **v1,** 305
Food **v2,** 21
Global Impact **v2,** 50
Hollywood **v2,** 70
Interwar Era **v2,** 117
Journalism **v2,** 159
Labor and Industry **v2,** 189
Literature **v2,** 207
Political Ideologies: Leaning Left . . . **v2,** 315
Public Health **v3,** 33
Radio **v3,** 57
Rails (Riding the Rails) **v3,** 76
Religion **v3,** 118

1930–1941
Water and Power **v3,** 257

1932–1939

World's Fairs **v3,** 352

1932–1941

Reconstruction Finance Corporation . . . **v3,** 92

March 1933–June 1934

New Deal (First, and Its Critics) **v2,** 252

1933–1941

Women in Public Life **v3,** 282

March 1933

Banking **v1,** 40
Civilian Conservation Corps **v1,** 109

May 1933

Farm Relief **v2,** 1
Tennessee Valley Authority **v3,** 229

June 1933

National Industrial Recovery Act **v2,** 228

June 1933–1941

Housing **v2,** 97

December 1933

Prohibition Repealed **v3,** 1

1934–1939

Dust Bowl **v1,** 168

1934–1941

American Indians **v1,** 1
Isolationism **v2,** 138

April 1935–June 1938

New Deal (Second) **v2,** 274

April 1935–1941

Photography **v2,** 295

May 1935

Rural Electrification Administration . . . **v3,** 153
Works Progress Administration **v3,** 306

August 1935

Social Security **v3,** 177

1935–1939

Supreme Court **v3,** 202

1936–1968

Democratic Coalition **v1,** 146

1940–1944

World War II Mobilization **v3,** 325

1964–1968

Effects of the Great Depression—LBJ's
Great Society **v1,** 215

Advisory Board

Credits

Copywrited excerpts in *Historic Events for Students: The Great Depression,* were reproduced from the following books:

A., G. From **Recipes & Remembrances of the Great Depression** by Emily Thacker. Tresco Publishers, 1993. Copyright 1993 Tresco Publishers. All rights reserved. Reproduced by permission.

Adamic, Louis. From **My America: 1928–1938.** Harper & Brothers Publishers, 1938. Copyright, 1938, by Louis Adamic. All rights reserved. Reproduced by permission.

Agee, James and Walker Evans. From **Let Us Now Praise Famous Men.** Ballantine Books, 1960. © 1941 by James Agee and Walker Evans. © renewed 1969 by Mia Fritsch Agee and Walker Evans. All rights reserved. Reprinted by permission of Houghton Mifflin Company.

Asbury, Herbert. From **The Great Illusion: An Informal History of Prohibition.** Doubleday & Company, Inc., 1950. Copyright, 1950, by Herbert Asbury. All rights reserved. Reproduced by permission.

B., Mildred. From **Recipes & Remembrances of the Great Depression** by Emily Thacker. Tresco Publishers, 1993. Copyright 1993 Tresco Publishers. All rights reserved. Reproduced by permission.

Balderrama, Francisco E. and Raymond Rodriguez. From *Decade of Betrayal: Mexican Repatriation in the 1930s.* University of New Mexico Press, 1995. © 1995 by the University of New Mexico Press. All rights reserved. Reproduced by permission.

Baldwin, C. B. (Beanie). From "Concerning the New Deal," in **Hard Times: An Oral History of the Great Depression** by Studs Terkel. Pantheon Books, 1986. © 1970, 1986 by Studs Terkel. All rights reserved. Reproduced by permission.

Bolino, August C. From **From Depression to War: American Society in Transition—1939.** Praeger Publishers, 1998. © 1998 by August C. Bolino. All rights reserved.

Bonnifield, Paul. From **The Dust Bowl: Men, Dirt, and Depression.** University of New Mexico Press, 1979. © 1979 by the University of New Mexico Press. All rights reserved. Reproduced by permission.

Brown, D. Clayton. From **Electricity for Rural America: The Fight for REA.** Greenwood Press, 1980. All rights reserved.

Brown, Josephine Chapin. From **Public Relief 1929–1939. Henry Holt and Company, 1940.** Copyright, 1940, by Henry Holt and Company, Inc.

Burke, Clifford. From "Man and Boy," in **Hard Times: An Oral History of the Great Depression** by Studs Terkel. Pantheon Books, 1986. © 1970, 1986 by Studs Terkel. All rights reserved. Reproduced by permission.

Burns, Helen M. From **The American Banking Community and New Deal Banking Reforms, 1933–1935.** Greenwood Press, 1974. © 1974 by Helen M. Burns. All rights reserved.

Colbert, David. From "Crash," in **We Saw It Happen.** Simon and Schuster, 1938. Reproduced by permission.

Daniels, Roger. From **Asian America: Chinese and Japanese in the United States since 1850.** University of Washington Press, 1988. © 1988 by the University of Washington Press. All rights reserved. Reproduced by permission.

Deutsch, Sarah Jane. From "From Ballots to Breadlines, 1920–1940," in **No Small Courage: A History of Women in the United States.** Edited by Nancy F. Cott. Oxford University Press, 2000.

Deutsch, Sarah Jane. From "From Ballots to Breadlines: Taking Matters into Their Own Hands," in **No Small Courage: A History of Women in the United States.** Edited by Nancy F. Cott. Oxford University Press, 2000.

Edsforth, Ronald. From **The New Deal: America's Response to the Great Depression.** Blackwell Publishers, 2000.

Farrell, James T. From "Introduction," in **Studs Lonigan: A Trilogy.** The Modern Library, 1938.

Meltzer, Milton. From **Violins & Shovels: The WPA Arts Projects.** Delacorte Press, 1976. © 1976 by Milton Meltzer. All rights reserved.

Montella, Frank. From **Memories of a CCC Boy,** in an interview with Kim Stewart. Cal State Fullerton and Utah State Historical Society Oral History Project, July 9, 1971.

Oettinger, Hank. From "Bonnie Laboring Boy," in **Hard Times: An Oral History of the Great Depression** by Studs Terkel. Pantheon Books, 1986. © 1970, 1986 by Studs Terkel. All rights reserved. Reproduced by permission.

Parran, Thomas. From "Shadow on the Land," in **Tuskegee's Truths: Rethinking the Tuskegee Syphilis Study.** Edited by Susan M. Reverby. University of North Carolina Press, 2000. © 2000 by The University of North Carolina Press. All rights reserved. Used by permission of the publisher.

Perkins, Frances. From **The Roosevelt I Knew.** The Viking Press, 1946. Copyright 1946 by Frances Perkins. Reproduced by permission.

Phillips, Cabell. From **From the Crash to the Blitz 1929–1939.** The Macmillan Company, 1969. © The New York Times Company 1969. All rights reserved. Reproduced by permission.

Plotke, David. From **Building A Democratic Political Order.** Cambridge University Press, 1996. © Cambridge University Press 1996. Reproduced by permission of the publisher and author.

Rauch, Basil. From **The History of the New Deal, 1933-1938.** Creative Age Press, Inc., 1944. Copyright 1944 by Basil Rauch. All rights reserved. Reproduced by permission.

Reid, Robert L. From "Introduction," in **Back Home Again: Indiana in the Farm Security Administration Photographs, 1935–1943.** Edited by Robert L. Reid. Indiana University Press, 1987. © 1987 by Robert L. Reid. All rights reserved. Reproduced by permission.

Roosevelt, Eleanor. From "Women in Politics," in **What I Hope to Leave Behind.** Edited by Allida M. Black. Carlson Publishing, Inc., 1995. Reproduced by permission.

Roosevelt, Franklin D. From "Hopkins Before 1941," in **Roosevelt and Hopkins: An Intimate History** by Robert E. Sherwood. Harper & Brothers Publishers, 1950. © 1948, 1950 by Robert E. Sherwood; copyright renewed © 1976, 1978 by Madeline H. Sherwood. All rights reserved. Reprinted by permission of Brandt & Hochman Literary Agents, Inc.

Rothstein, Arthur. From **Just Before the War** by Thomas H. Garver and Arthur Rothstein. October House Inc., 1968. Copyright 1968, Newport Harbor Art Museum, Balboa, California. Reproduced by permission.

Russo, Anthony. From "Prologue," in **Capone: The Man and the Era** by Laurence Bergreen. Simon & Schuster, 1994. © 1994 by Laurence Bergreen. All rights reserved. Reproduced by permission.

S., K. From **Recipes & Remembrances of the Great Depression** by Emily Thacker. Tresco Publishers, 1993. Copyright 1993 Tresco Publishers. All rights reserved. Reproduced by permission.

Schieber, Sylvester J. and John B. Brown. From **The Real Deal: The History and Future of Social Security.** Yale University Press, 1999. © 1999 by Yale University. All rights reserved.

Schlesinger, Jr., Arthur M. From **The Age of Roosevelt: The Coming of the New Deal.** Houghton Mifflin Company, 1988. © 1958, renewed 1986 by Arthur M. Schlesinger, Jr. All rights reserved. Reprinted by permission of Houghton Mifflin Company.

Steichen, Edward. From "Introduction," in **The Bitter Years: 1935–1941.** Edited by Edward Steichen. The Museum of Modern Art, 1962. © 1962, The Museum of Modern Art, New York.

Steinbeck, John. From **I Remember the Thirties.** Copyright 1960 by John Steinbeck.

Steinbeck, John. From **The Grapes of Wrath.** The Viking Press, 1939. Copyright, 1939, John Steinbeck. All rights reserved.

Stockard, George. From **Stories and Recipes of the Great Depression of the 1930's, Volume II.** Edited by Rita Van Amber. Van Amber Publishers, 1999. © Library of Congress. All rights reserved. Reproduced by permission of the author.

Stryker, R. E. From a letter in **Portrait of a Decade: Roy Stryker and the Development of Documentary Photography in the Thirties** by F. Jack Hurley. Louisiana State University Press, 1972. Copyright 1972 by Louisiana State University Press. All rights reserved.

Sueur, Meridel Le. From **Women on the Breadlines.** West End Press, 1984. © 1977, 1984 by West End Press. Reproduced by permission.

Sundquist, James. From **Dynamics of the Party System: Alignment and Realignment of Political Parties in the United States.** Brookings Institution, 1983.

Svobida, Lawrence. From **Farming the Dust Bowl: A First-Hand Account from Kansas.** University Press of Kansas, 1986. Copyright 1940 by The Caxton Printers, Ltd.; 1968 by Lawrence Svobida. All rights reserved. Reproduced by permission.

Swados, Harvey. From "Introduction," in **The American Writer and the Great Depression.** Edited by Harvey Swados. The Bobbs-Merrill Company, Inc., 1966. © 1966 by The Bobbs-Merrill Company, Inc.

Terkel, Studs. From "Concerning the New Deal," in **Hard Times: An Oral History of the Great Depression.** Pantheon Books, 1986. © 1970, 1986 by Studs Terkel. All rights reserved. Reproduced by permission.

Terkel, Studs. From "Three Strikes: Mike Widman," in **Hard Times: An Oral History of the Great Depression.** Pantheon Books, 1986. © 1970, 1986 by Studs Terkel. All rights reserved. Reproduced by permission.

Terrell, Harry. From "The Farmer is the Man," in **Hard Times: An Oral History of the Great Depression** by Studs Terkel. Pantheon Books, 1986. © 1970, 1986 by Studs Terkel. All rights reserved. Reproduced by permission.

Tugwell, Rexford Guy. From **The Bitter Years: 1935–1941.** Edited by Edward Steichen. The Museum of Modern Art, 1962. © 1962, The Museum of Modern Art, New York. Reproduced by permission.

Tully, Grace. From "Pearl Harbor News Reaches FDR," in **We Saw It Happen.** Simon and Schuster, 1938. Reproduced by permission.

Tyack, David, Robert Lowe, and Elisabeth Hansot. From "A Black School in East Texas," in **Public Schools in Hard Times: The Great Depression and Recent Years.** Harvard University Press, 1984. © 1984 by the President and Fellows of Harvard College. All rights reserved. Reproduced by permission.

Tyack, David, Robert Lowe, and Elisabeth Hansot. From **Public Schools in Hard Times: The Great Depression and Recent Years.** Harvard University Press, 1984. © 1984 by the President and Fellows of Harvard College. All rights reserved. Reproduced by permission.

Uys, Errol Lincoln. From **Riding the Rails: Teenagers on the Move During the Great Depression.** TV Books, 2000. © 1999, 2000 Errol Lincoln Uys. All rights reserved. Reproduced by permission of the author.

Van Amber, Rita. From **Stories and Recipes During the Great Depression of the 1930's.** Van Amber Publishers, 1999. © Library of Congress. All rights reserved. Reproduced by permission.

Wasserman, Dale. From "Troubles and Triumphs," in **Free, Adult, Uncensored: The Living History of the Federal Theatre Project.** Edited by John O'Connor and Lorraine Brown. New Republic Books, 1978. Reproduced by permission.

Watkins, T. H. From **The Hungry Years: A Narrative History of the Great Depression in America.** Henry Holt and Company, 1999. © 1999 by T. H. Watkins. All rights reserved. Reprinted by permission of Henry Holt and Company, LLC.

Weinberg, Sidney J. From "The Big Money," in **Hard Times: An Oral History of the Great Depression** by Studs Terkel. Pantheon Books, 1986. © 1970, 1986 by Studs Terkel. All rights reserved. Reproduced by permission.

Winslow, Susan. From **Brother, Can You Spare A Dime?: America from the Wall Street Crash to Pearl Harbor.** Paddington Press Ltd., 1976. © 1976 by Susan Winslow.

Wright, Richard. From "How 'Bigger' Was Born," in **Native Son.** Harper & Row, Publishers, 1940. Copyright 1940 by Richard Wright. Renewed in 1967 by Ellen Wright.

Wright, Richard. From **Uncle Tom's Children: Five Long Stories.** Harper & Brothers, 1938. Copyright 1936, 1937, 1938 by Richard Wright. All rights reserved.

Song lyrics appearing in *Historic Events for Students: The Great Depression,* were received from the following sources:

Guthrie, Woody. From "Talking Dust Bowl." © Copyright 1961 and 1963 Ludlow Music, Inc., New York, N. Y.

Warren, Harry and Al Dubin, lyrics from "We're In the Money." Music and lyrics by Harry Warren and Al Dubin. Copyright 1933, Remick Music, Inc. Reproduced by permission.

About the Series

Historic Events for Students (HES) is a new addition to the Gale Group's *for Students* line, presenting users with the complete picture of an important event in world history. With standardized rubrics throughout each entry, for which the *for Students* line is well-known, and a variety of complementary elements including illustrations, sidebars, and suggestions for further research, *HES* will examine all of the components that contributed to or sprung from a significant period of time, from ideologies and politics to contemporary opinions and popular culture.

A new one- to three-volume set of forty-five to sixty entries will appear each year. The topics are evaluated by an advisory board of teachers and librarians familiar with the information needed by students in today's classrooms. Essays contain consistent rubrics for easy reference as well as comparison across entries and volumes, and each volume contains a complete glossary, general bibliography, and subject index. Additionally, approximately one hundred images are included per volume, including photos, maps, and statistics to enhance the text and add visual depictions of the event.

The standardized headings found throughout *HES* let users choose to what depth they want to explore the subject matter. Take a quick glance at the topic via the Introduction, Chronology, and Issue Summary rubrics, or delve deeper and get a more inclusive view through the Contributing Forces, Perspectives, and Impact sections. A who's who for a particular issue can be found under the heading of Notable People, while excerpts of speeches, personal accounts, and news clippings can be located under Primary Sources. Ideas for further study can be found with Suggested Research Topics and the Bibliography, while numerous sidebars provide additional information on material associated with the issue being discussed.

Historic Events for Students is different from other history texts in that it doesn't just narrate the facts of an event from the past. It traces the social, cultural, political, religious, and ideological threads that combined to create an historic event. *HES* follows these threads to the end of the event and beyond it to discern how it shaped the history that followed it. The result is a comprehensive examination of the causes of and effects from a significant event in history and a greater understanding of how it influenced where we are today.

Introduction

Technologies and accepted behavioral norms comprising the human experience are constantly changing. Such change in society, however, does not occur at a consistent pace. Sometimes change may be slow and barely perceptible to the average person. At other times, extraordinary events spur change much more quickly. While such events most often involve times of war (the American Civil War, World War I, World War II, and the Vietnam War all resulted in fundamental changes to American society), other watershed events may be no less dramatic. The Great Depression was one such event.

Historical Overview—The Great Depression

Though signs of pending economic problems were surfacing in the United States throughout the 1920s, hardly anyone took notice as most people in the country enjoyed prosperity like never before. The dramatic stock market crash in October 1929, however, captured the attention of the American public. Many feared for the first time that the economic health of the United States might not be as good as it had seemed just a year or two previously. The period that followed, known as the Great Depression, may not have actually resulted from the stock market crash, but it is frequently linked to it in the public's mind.

The Great Depression was an extended period of severe economic hard times, first for the United States and then for many of the world's nations. Though the depression was rooted in earlier economic undercurrents, a cascade of economic events followed the stock

market crash and exacerbated the problem. Many investors, including banks, lost their fortunes in the Wall Street crash as the value of stocks tumbled. This loss meant less money was available to invest in businesses, which led companies, now short on cash, to layoff workers. The rise in unemployment meant that the public had less money to buy consumer goods and pay back the bank loans it had accumulated in the liberal spending times of the 1920s. As a result, thousands of banks closed and more layoffs resulted from decreased purchases by consumers as inventories of goods mounted. By 1933 almost 25 percent of the U.S. workforce was unemployed, amounting to more than twelve million people. Those who kept their jobs saw their incomes decrease significantly.

The arrival of Franklin Delano Roosevelt to the White House as the thirty-second president of the United States in March 1933 significantly changed the relationship between Americans and their government. Through Congress, Roosevelt orchestrated numerous and diverse pieces of legislation designed to bring economic relief and recovery, and later reform, to the desperate nation. These laws and the resulting government programs are collectively known as the New Deal.

Though the New Deal would not lead to significant recovery, it did end the dramatic economic plunge Americans experienced through the early 1930s. It gave those most affected by the Great Depression food and shelter. For many more it reestablished hope for the future and faith in the U.S. economic system. Historically the federal government had largely been detached from the public's everyday life. The severity of the depression, however, made many Americans consider the possibility—and even to expect—that the government would take action to assure the wellbeing of the people it governed. Significant differences of opinion emerged over how far government should go in regulating business and guaranteeing the financial security of its citizens.

All of this took place at a time when American popular culture was gaining its own distinct character, unique from its predominant European roots. It also occurred in the midst of new mass production technologies in business, mass media, and mass consumerism. The United States would emerge as a profoundly different nation in 1940 than it had been in 1930.

Content

These volumes specifically address the actual event of the Great Depression rather than presenting a general treatment of the 1930s. They describe the events and issues surrounding the economic depression and the New Deal. The authors, editors, and advisors selected forty-five issues that take an inclusive look at the Great Depression as it affected such diverse elements of American society as economics, the arts, literature, mass media, ethnic and gender relations, the functioning of government, international relations, religion, politics, crime, public health, education, and everyday life.

The writers of these volumes, well-versed in the relevant historical issues, sought to provide a comprehensive treatment of each issue, yet in a concise, readily digestible format. They strove to provide an objective overview of each issue, helping the reader to experience and evaluate the diverse perspectives of often-controversial events. The reader is provided with sufficient background information to encourage the formation of his or her own opinions of the complex events and the contemporary reactions to them. In addition to in-depth text, this premier set of *Historic Events for Students* includes maps, statistics, photographs, sidebars, bibliographic sources, and suggestions for further research, designed to meet the curriculum needs of high school students, undergraduate college students, and their teachers.

How Each Entry is Organized

Each of the forty-five issue entries are divided into multiple headings for easy and complete reference:

- **Introduction:** briefly introduces the reader to the topic. Its connection to the Great Depression is established and some of the key concepts and events that will be addressed are presented.

- **Chronology:** a brief timeline is provided for each topic to place the various key events related to it into an easy-to-understand time-frame for the reader.

- **Issue Summary:** the primary source of information describing the topic, firmly set in the context of the Great Depression. The topic is thoroughly discussed, including governmental efforts made to resolve economic and social problems associated with it. The student will gain a keen sense of just how dynamic the topic was and the major consequences of the individual issues at the time. This summary is divided into subheadings that are unique to each issue.

- **Contributing Forces:** identifies the key social, economic, and political currents in U.S. history leading up to the topic. The section explores how the events and prevailing attitudes contributed to the particular issue and how they influenced the New Deal's response to the issue.

- **Perspectives:** prevailing and competing notions and opinions of the day are detailed and, where feasible, the varying viewpoints are distinguished at the local community level or among the general public; at the national level, including the country's political leaders; and internationally as the Great Depression became an increasingly global event. The discussion includes the perspectives of what should be done, if anything, by the federal government and what the implications were of government action or inaction.

- **Impact:** the long-term consequences of the issue and resulting government action are discussed. The New Deal's response to the Great Depression posed dramatic changes to American society. The events of the depression shaped the evolution of the social, economic, and political foundation of the nation after the 1930s and into the twenty-first century. This section highlights the lasting effects for that particular issue.

- **Notable People:** describes the lives and accomplishments of some of key individuals in the context of the specific issue. Each issue commonly has several key people associated with it, including people who advocated for or against government action and those who administered the New Deal programs.

- **Primary Sources:** provide first-hand accounts from the common citizen and notable people such as Franklin Roosevelt and Herbert Hoover. The Great Depression was a traumatic time. As a result emotions were openly displayed and opinions and solutions hotly debated. There is no better way to experience the depression days than through the words of those caught in the turmoil.

- **Suggested Research Topics:** guide students to explore matters further. Many suggested topics ask the student to examine his or her own communities more closely and how New Deal programs might still influence their lives today.

- **Bibliography:** lists key sources used by the writer in researching the topic and also includes suggestions for further reading. The list of further readings is predominantly aimed at the reading level of the high school and undergraduate student and targets sources most likely found in public libraries and book stores.

Additionally, each entry is also accompanied by several sidebars presenting insights into various facets of the issue. The sidebars focus on different kinds of topics related to the particular issue, including descriptions of concepts, extensive biographies of the most important figures to play a role, or more thorough descriptions of particular agencies or other organizations involved in the issue.

Additional Features

In an attempt to create a comprehensive reference tool for the study of the Great Depression, this set also includes:

- A general chronology covers the Great Depression from its start to its finish to place the various issues and events into a historical context, including some key national and international events to underscore what the citizens and leaders of other countries were experiencing at the same time.

- A general bibliography consolidates the numerous and significant research on the Great Depression and offers an easy reference for users, with material divided into books, periodicals, novels, and websites.

- A glossary presents a number of terms and phrases introduced in the entries that may be unfamiliar to readers.

- A subject index provides easy reference to topics, people, and places.

Acknowledgments

A number of writers contributed to these volumes in addition to the lead authors, including Michael Vergamini, Dr. Richard Pettigrew, Dr. Doug Blandy, Dr. Stephen Dow Beckham, Linda Irvin, and Meghan O'Meara. Catherine Filip typed much of the manuscript. Much gratitude also goes to the advisors who guided the project throughout its course.

Comments on these volumes and suggestions for future sets are welcome. Please direct all correspondence to:

Editor, *Historic Events for Students*
Gale Group
27500 Drake Rd.
Farmington Hills, MI 48331-3535
(800) 877-4253

Chronology

1914 Industrialist Henry Ford introduces the moving assembly line to manufacture automobiles; the production technique will revolutionize U.S. industry over the next decade.

1914 World War I begins in Europe, placing a high demand of U.S. goods, though the United States does not itself enter the war for another three years; high wartime production levels will continue following the war, leading to a long term agricultural economic downturn.

1919 The peace treaty of Versailles ends World War I and leads to excessive economic demands on Germany.

1919 The General Motors automobile company introduces a consumer credit program that makes loans available to purchase cars; this program begins the popular installment plan for many other industries producing consumer goods.

1920 The Nineteenth Amendment to the U.S. Constitution is ratified, granting women the right to vote; women voters will become an important element of the Democratic Coalition 15 years later.

January 16, 1920 The Eighteenth Amendment, or the Prohibition Amendment, goes into effect nationwide, prohibiting the sale, transport, and consumption of alcoholic beverages in the United States.

1920s Continued expansion of farming production leads to soil exhaustion in some areas of the United States and expansion into marginal agricultural areas, setting the stage for future topsoil problems; record production causes continued decline in farm prices.

1922 Benito Mussolini takes over Italy, which becomes a fascist nation under his leadership.

1923 The U.S. stock market begins a six-year expansion as the value of stocks begins to climb.

1924 Congress passes the National Origins Act, reducing the number of immigrants allowed to enter the country to only 150,000 per year, and sets quotas favoring northwestern and southeastern Europeans.

October 6, 1927 The first talking motion picture is released, *The Jazz Singer,* starring Al Jolson.

November 7, 1928 Republican Herbert Hoover, an engineer with a reputation as a humanitarian, is elected to the U.S. presidency over Democrat Al Smith, the first Catholic to run for the U.S. presidency.

October 24, 1929 Known as "Black Thursday," the value of stocks plummets on Wall Street, costing many investors vast sums of money, and raises public concern over the health of the U.S. economy.

1930 As economic conditions in the United States continue to worsen following the stock market crash, Congress passes the Smoot-Hawley Tariff Act, which greatly raises taxes on foreign goods to boost sales of domestic goods. In application, however, the act instead causes foreign trade to greatly decline, decreasing the demand for U.S. goods.

1931 The U.S. economic crisis spreads to Europe as American investments decline and trade decreases; the United States pulls back from international affairs and looks increasingly inward.

May 1, 1931 The Empire State Building in New York City, the world's tallest building, is opened.

July 14, 1931 The German banking system fails as all banks in Germany close.

September 18, 1931 Japan begins a military expansion in the Pacific by invading Manchuria and seizing the Manchurian railroad.

1932 With the farm economy in desperate condition, the Farmers' Holiday Association is formed in Iowa, which leads to farmer protests seeking government assistance.

January 22, 1932 To help an economy in crisis President Herbert Hoover creates the Reconstruction Finance Corporation, a federal agency designed to provide loans to struggling banks and businesses.

July 28 1932 Thousands of unemployed and financially strapped World War I veterans and their families, known as the Bonus Army, march on Washington, DC, seeking early payment of previously promised bonus pay. They are denied by Congress and routed violently by U.S. army troops.

October 24, 1932 Gangster Al Capone is sentenced to 11 years in prison for tax evasion.

November 8, 1932 Pledging a "New Deal" for Americans, Democratic candidate Franklin Delano Roosevelt is overwhelmingly elected president over the highly unpopular Hoover; Roosevelt will not be inaugurated until the following March.

February 1933 The U.S. banking crisis deepens as almost five thousand banks have closed and panic spreads among depositors; faith in the U.S. banking system hits an all-time low.

January 30, 1933 Adolf Hitler becomes Chancellor of Germany.

March 4, 1933 Roosevelt is inaugurated as president promising hope to American citizens, claiming the "only thing to fear is fear itself" and beginning a dramatic surge of legislation during his first one hundred days in office forming the New Deal.

March 6, 1933 President Roosevelt closes all U.S. banks, declaring a Banking Holiday, and Congress passes the Emergency Banking Act three days later in a successful effort to restore public confidence in the banking system; most banks reopen on March 13.

March 23, 1933 The legislature is dismissed in Germany and Hitler assumes dictatorial powers of the country.

March 31, 1933 The U.S. Congress passes the Civilian Conservation Corps Reforestation Act, creating the Civilian Conservation Corps (CCC) to provide jobs for young males.

May 12, 1933 Congress passes the Agricultural Adjustment Act and Emergency Farm Mortgage Act to bring economic relief to farmers, and the Federal Emergency Relief Act to provide relief for the needy.

May 17, 1933 The Tennessee Valley Authority (TVA) is created to establish a massive program of regional economic development for a broad region of the American Southeast.

June 16, 1933 Congress passes the Banking Act, reforming the U.S. banking system. The Federal Deposit Insurance Corporation (FDIC) is established to insure depositors' money; the National Industrial Recovery Act (NIRA) is created to regulate industry; and the Public Works Administration begins to provide funding for large public projects.

December 5, 1933 Prohibition ends in the United States after a nearly 14-year ban on the sale of all alcoholic beverages.

1934 Great dust storms sweep across the Plains of the United States; the hardest hit region of the southern Plains becomes known as the Dust Bowl. The drought persists for several years.

June 6, 1934 Congress passes the Securities Exchange Act to regulate the stock market and protect investors.

June 28, 1934 Congress passes the National Housing Act, creating the Federal Housing Administration to provide loans to home buyers and setting national standards for house construction; this marks the end of the First New Deal under the Roosevelt administration.

April 8, 1935 Kicking off the Second New Deal, Congress passes the Emergency Relief Appropriation Act, authorizing the creation of the Resettlement Administration and the Works Progress Administration.

May 11, 1935 Roosevelt creates the Rural Electrification Administration to provide electricity to rural areas through federal partnership with private farming cooperatives.

May 27, 1935 The U.S. Supreme Court issues several rulings against New Deal programs, including *Schechter Poultry Corporation v. United States,* striking down the National Industrial Recovery Act; the day becomes known as "Black Monday."

July 5, 1935 In reaction to the Schechter decision, Congress passes the National Labor Relations Act, recognizing the right of workers to organize in unions and conduct collective bargaining with employers.

August 2, 1935 Roosevelt establishes the Federal Art Project, Federal Music Project, Federal Theatre Project, and Federal Writers' Project to provide work relief for people involved in the arts.

August 14, 1935 Congress passes the Social Security Act, providing old age and unemployment benefits to American workers.

August 28, 1935 The Public Utility Holding Company Act is enacted by Congress, prohibiting the use of multiple layers of holding companies in the utility industry.

October 1935 Italy sends 35,000 troops and volunteers to Ethiopia, seeking to expand its rule into Africa.

November 9, 1935 In organizing unions for semi-skilled workers of mass production industries, John L. Lewis begins to break with the craft-oriented American Federation of Labor (AFL) and creates the Committee of Industrial Organizations (CIO), which later becomes known as the Congress of Industrial Organizations.

January 6, 1936 The Supreme Court rules the Agricultural Adjustment Act unconstitutional in *United States v. Butler.*

March 7, 1936 German troops retake the Rhineland region of Europe without conflict, beginning the German expansion through Europe.

August 1936 Athlete Jesse Owens, a black American, wins four gold medals at the Berlin Summer Olympics, conflicting with Adolf Hitler's white supremacy beliefs.

November 1936 Franklin Roosevelt wins reelection to the U.S. presidency by a landslide, winning a record 61 percent of the vote.

December 30, 1936 Seven General Motors plants in Flint, Michigan, are shut down by sit-down strikes; the company gives in to worker demands on February 11, 1937.

February 5, 1937 Roosevelt introduces a plan to reorganize the U.S. judiciary system. It becomes known as the "court packing" plan and attracts substantial opposition in Congress and the public.

June 22, 1937 Black American Joe Louis defeats Briton James Braddock to become the new world heavyweight boxing champion.

July 30, 1937 Japan invades China and begins a major offensive toward other countries in the Far East.

April 12, 1937 The Supreme Court begins making decisions supportive of New Deal programs by ruling in favor of the National Labor Relations Act in *National Labor Relations Board v. Jones & Laughlin Steel Corporation.*

May 1937 A steelworkers' strike at Republic Steel leads to a violent confrontation between striking workers and Chicago police, leaving ten people dead and 90 injured.

June 25, 1938 Marking the end of the Second New Deal, Congress passes the Fair Labor Standards Act, setting minimum wage and maximum hour regulations.

April 30, 1939 The New York World's Fair opens.

September 30, 1939 Germany invades Poland, starting World War II as France and Great Britain declare war on Germany.

May 1940 Germany invades Western Europe; France surrenders in June.

December 29, 1940 In a "fireside chat" over the radio, Franklin Roosevelt describes the United States as the "arsenal of democracy" to provide war supplies to those nations fighting German expansion. The country's war mobilization efforts help the economy and spur recovery from the Great Depression.

1941 A. Philip Randolph threatens to lead a march of black Americans on Washington, DC, protesting racial discrimination in the war industry; Roosevelt establishes the Fair Employment Practices Commission in response to the pressure.

December 7, 1941 Japan bombs U.S. military facilities in Pearl Harbor, Hawaii; the United States declares war on Japan and later Germany, entering World War II.

April 12, 1945 Franklin Roosevelt dies suddenly from a cerebral hemorrhage at 63 years of age.

April 30, 1945 With defeat imminent, Adolf Hitler commits suicide in Germany.

Farm Relief

Introduction

Perhaps more than anyone else in the United States, farmers experienced the greatest swings between prosperity and poverty through the first half of the twentieth century. Just before and during World War I (1914–1918), farmers enjoyed prosperity at levels never seen before in rural America. Unexpectedly, good times suddenly turned bad as worldwide demand for U.S. produce sharply dropped following the war. Farmers suffered through economically lean times during the 1920s, while other parts of the U.S. economy prospered. Surpluses of key crops mounted as produce prices plummeted. In addition, the increased mechanization of arms made the typical small family farm far less competitive than the increasingly larger commercial operations. And just when farmers believed the farm economy could not get worse, it did. The 1929 stock market crash and resulting Great Depression added to the problems of an economically struggling rural America.

Through the lean times of the 1920s, farmers became frustrated over the policies of Republican presidents Calvin Coolidge (served 1923–1929) and Herbert Hoover (served 1929–1933). Coolidge and Hoover believed it was not the government's role to provide direct relief. Franklin Delano Roosevelt's (served 1933–1945) presidency brought a new perspective. Roosevelt's administration immediately placed a high priority on federal assistance to the farmer as part of his New Deal programs, but calm on the farm proved elusive. Complex farming problems resulted in com-

Chronology:

1909–1914: American farmers enjoy a period of record prosperity marked by high market prices for their produce.

1914–1919: The U.S. government encourages farmers to further increase production, making up for European shortages in food production during World War I.

1920s: Farmers suffer more than any other industry from a postwar decline in demand for U.S. products.

1932: Prices for farm produce hit bottom as farmer unrest rises.

1933: Congress passes the Farm Credit Act, making loans available to farmers and creating a banking system for farming cooperatives.

1933: Congress passes the Agricultural Adjustment Act, one of Roosevelt's first major New Deal programs, aimed at increasing the prices of agricultural products by reducing production.

1933: Roosevelt creates the Commodity Credit Corporation to help farmers market their produce to gain year-round price stability and minimize price changes from year to year.

1935: The Soil Conservation Service is established to assist farmers to conserve their farmlands through improved farming practices.

1935: The Resettlement Administration, later known as the Farm Security Administration, provides loans to small farm operators to purchase better farmland.

1936: The U.S. Supreme Court in *United States v. Butler* rules the 1933 Agricultural Adjustment Act unconstitutional due to its provisions for taxing food-processing businesses.

1938: Congress passes the new Agricultural Adjustment Act revising and expanding the earlier 1933 act and becoming the foundation for U.S. agricultural policy for the remainder of the twentieth century.

1941: The United States enters World War II against Japan and Germany, increasing the demand once again for farm products and ending agricultural economic strife.

plex New Deal agricultural relief programs. Uncommon problems led to uncommon solutions, such as government payments for not planting, that farmers might have not accepted in less desperate times.

Critics of these programs came from all directions. Some charged that the newly created federal programs favored large commercial operations and ignored those hurt most by the Depression—the small-scale farmer. Others believed the federal government had overreached its legal authority to enter the private farm marketplace. The public, however, seemed generally pleased with Roosevelt's New Deal programs. He was handily reelected in 1936.

Not only did new government farm programs appear in the 1930s, it was also a period of major social and technological change in America's hinterland. New machines allowed for the planting and harvesting of larger acreages. Such technological advancements encouraged small farms to combine into larger farms (consolidation). This trend resulted in fewer but larger, more efficient farms. Small farmers were often at a disadvantage. Even as the farmer population declined, production increased. Many farm families moved to cities to escape the bleakness of a depressed agricultural economy, spurring the continued transition of the United States from a largely rural society to an urban one.

It would take another global war, World War II (1939–1945), to finally end the farmland plight. The New Deal programs did make economic survival possible for many farmers who were able to keep their land during hard times. The decade of the 1930s was indeed a unique period in American rural life.

Issue Summary

Prosperity in the Farm Belt

Throughout U.S. history farming has been very important to the nation's economy. Most Americans have viewed farming as a distinctive and superior way of life. These beliefs are based on Jeffersonian ideals. These ideals bestow great respect on those nobly working the soil to gain economic self-sufficiency and independence.

As late as 1900, 60 percent of the U.S. population lived in rural areas. Horsepower and manpower remained the key means of performing farm work. Kerosene lamps, wood and coal stoves, and outhouses were typical of farm life. Few rural homes had electricity. Those that did have electricity received it from a steam engine, windmill, or water wheel that was used to generate it.

The distinctive agricultural character of the various regions in the country had become well established. Dairy and poultry farms were dominate in the Northeast, cotton and tobacco farms in the South, corn and hog production in the Midwest, wheat farms in the Great Plains and Northwest, open grassland livestock grazing in the West, and vegetable fields, cotton, and orchards in California. Sharecroppers and tenant farmers were commonly found in the South, and migrant farmers in the West.

Prior to 1900 Congress had come to the assistance of farmers on occasion. In 1862 alone three laws were passed making cheap land available through the Homestead Act, establishing agricultural colleges through land grants to states, and creating the U.S. Department of Agriculture. Typically for this period, none of the laws passed were designed to provide direct monetary assistance to U.S. farmers or to raise their economic status in society. For example, the 1862 Morrill Act was important to future agricultural development in the United States. The act granted certain amounts of federal lands to each state. The states were to sell the lands to raise funds for establishing colleges to teach agriculture and engineering. This was designed to help meet the needs of a rapidly industrializing nation.

During the first two decades of the twentieth century, American farmers enjoyed considerable economic growth and prosperity. In fact, the period from 1909 to 1914 has been called the golden age of agriculture in the United States. Increased prices for farm products and increased farmland values raised the purchasing power of farmers above that of many other U.S. workers. This period created the expectation that farmers should enjoy incomes and a standard of living equal to workers in other parts of the national economy.

Good Times Turn Hard

The conclusion of World War I in 1918 brought a rapid decline in the demand for farm products. The

Number and Value of Farms, 1880-1940

Year	Percent of farm population from total population	Number of Farms (1,000)	Average value of farm land and buildings ($)
1880	43.8%	4,009	$2,544
1890	42.3	4,565	2,909
1900	41.9	5,740	2,895
1910	34.9	6,366	5,480
1915	32.4	6,458	6,130
1920	30.1	6,454	10,295
1925	27.0	6,372	7,764
1930	24.9	6,295	7,624
1931	24.9	6,608	6,618
1932	25.2	6,687	5,560
1933	25.8	6,741	4,569
1934	25.6	6,776	4,752
1935	25.3	6,812	4,823
1936	24.8	6,739	5,084
1937	24.3	6,636	5,306
1938	23.9	6,527	5,388
1939	23.6	6,441	5,290
1940	23.2	6,102	5,532

The average value of farms declined steadily from its high in 1920 to its low in 1933. (The Gale Group.)

decline led to large surpluses and falling prices as farmers kept producing at their World War I levels, trying to cover expenses. Years of angry debate focused on federal agricultural policies. As a result, the 1920s proved a harsh period for American farmers. Times were only to get harder, however, with the 1929 stock market crash.

President Herbert Hoover took office in early 1929 when the nation's economy appeared healthy and growing, except in the area of agriculture. In 1929 one-fourth of all workers in the United States were farmers. Though having a reputation as a humanitarian, Hoover, like Coolidge before him, firmly believed government should not take an active role in social and economic reform. Under pressure from agricultural interests, however, Hoover established the Federal Farm Board. The board was to help farmers sell their produce through farm organizations known as cooperatives, and to increase farm prices. Hoover believed voluntary production controls and modest support for farm cooperatives would help. Farmers, still trying to cover costs, continued to keep overall production high, however, and as a result prices remained low.

Following the stock market crash in October 1929, Congress took action again. It passed the Hawley-Smoot Tariff Act in 1930 to help both farmers and manufacturers. The act established the highest tax on imports, known as a protective tariff, in U.S. history. The tariff would shield agricultural products from foreign competition. The effects of the act, however, backfired by greatly reducing foreign trade and farm exports. Other countries did not have the cash to buy U.S. products since they could not easily sell their own products in the United States. Foreign countries also retaliated by raising their tariffs on U.S. goods. These tariffs soon decreased world trade by 40 percent. Th export of farming products had previously provided one fourth of all farm income. To make matters even worse for U.S. farmers, European and Russian farm production increases created a greater worldwide glut in produce, further reducing prices. Farming income was devastated.

One of the most famous depictions of rural life in the United States came from this time period. Grant Wood's 1930 painting *American Gothic* shows two stern-faced people, a father and daughter, standing stiffly in front of their farmhouse with the father holding a pitchfork.

The Farmer's Revolt

In 1932, aside from black Americans, farmers were the hardest hit by the economic turmoil. In 1932 farmers' income was less than one-third of what it was in 1929. Farm prices had bottomed out at half of what they were only a few years earlier. That meant the farmer, with his money made from wheat, corn, hogs, and cotton, could only purchase half as many goods as before. As a result, many farmers were going broke. Between 1929 and 1932 approximately 400,000 farms were lost through foreclosure. A foreclosure is where a bank that holds a mortgage on a farm seeks to take possession of the farm when the farmer could not meet his mortgage payments. Many who lost their land turned to tenant farming, an arrangement in which the farmer pays a landowner for use of the land to farm.

With the nation's economy worsening, anger over Hoover's limited efforts in raising low crop prices led to farmer protests. Rural poverty was leading to despair and desperate action. Farmers burned their corn and wheat and dumped their milk on highways rather than sell for a loss. In May 1932 farmers met in a national convention organized by the Iowan Farmers' Union to decide what they could do to pressure for change. They created the Farmers Holiday Association, with well-known farmer advocate Milo Reno as president. The association aimed to organize a strike, or "farmers' holiday," in which farmers would refuse to sell their produce for several weeks. The farmers hoped that by reducing the supply of farm produce to markets that prices would increase. The action became so popular among farmers that it lasted more than a month. Roads were often blocked, preventing food from reaching market. On August 25, 1,200 pickets blocked five highways leading to a large produce market in Omaha, Nebraska. Occasional violence broke out, including a gun battle that erupted near Sioux City, Iowa. The onset of winter weather in late 1932 brought a break in these actions.

During the winter efforts turned to blocking farm foreclosures. "Penny auctions" occurred in which farmers would pack the auction sale and bid only pennies for the foreclosed farm, equipment, and livestock. They would then give it back to the owner after the auction. In February 1933 Iowa passed a law reducing the number of foreclosures. Other Midwest and Plains states followed. Force was also used to stop authorities from foreclosing on farms. In early 1933 farmers took over a Nebraska sheriff's office until they were driven out by tear gas. Others faced off with authorities in an Iowan courthouse.

A New Deal for Farmers: Relief Takes Shape

With the nation's economy steadily in decline following the 1929 stock market crash, Franklin D. Roosevelt ran on the 1932 Democratic presidential ticket promising a "new deal" for the American citizen. Roosevelt handily defeated the unpopular Hoover in the November 1932 elections, and an overwhelming majority of Democrats won seats in Congress. Roosevelt believed Hoover's policies were clearly insufficient for solving the farm crisis. Revolutionary changes in federal farm policies to aid the farmer were soon to appear.

Given the urgency of the agricultural situation, Roosevelt believed he could not wait until he moved into the White House in March 1933 to begin action. While Hoover was serving out the remainder of his term, Roosevelt identified new agricultural legislation as a priority. He wanted to take action before the spring planting began. Meetings were held in December 1932 between farm representatives and Roosevelt's key advisors, including Henry Morgenthau, Jr., and Rexford Tugwell. Soon, Roosevelt nominated Henry Wallace, a highly knowledgeable Iowan, as his secretary of agriculture and Tugwell as the assistant secretary of agriculture. Wallace was dedicated to restoring the farmer as a key part of the U.S. economy and to bring back "parity" for farm goods. Parity meant that farm goods would have the same value relative to manufactured goods as they did during the golden years of the 1910s. This would mean farmers would have the same purchasing power to buy goods as they did during the period of 1909 to 1914.

Biography:

Henry A. Wallace

1888, October 7–1965, November 18

> Of course, Henry Wallace ... was the man who saved the farmer. The farmer would have passed clear out of the picture. They took this corn and paid for it and stored it. They put a price on it that was above the miserable going price.

This statement was made by Iowan Harry Terrell decades later in remembering the difficult times of the 1930s and the key role Secretary Henry A. Wallace played in helping farmers. (quoted in Terkel, 1988, p. 216).

Wallace filled the important role of President Franklin Roosevelt's secretary of agriculture during the New Deal years. Wallace was born on a farm near Orient, Iowa. His father also served as U.S. secretary of agriculture from 1921 to 1924, under presidents Warren Harding and Calvin Coolidge. Wallace's contribution to the agriculture field was notable before joining Roosevelt's administration. He was editor of the influential *Wallace's Farmer* publication, originally founded by his grandfather, from 1924 to 1933. A keen interest in plant breeding led Henry to experiment with corn. He eventually became head of the largest hybrid seed company in the nation.

As farm economic woes grew in the 1920s, Henry Wallace was a spokesman for increased mechanization of farms. He also lobbied for government price support and production control programs. Wallace's views attracted the attention of Franklin Roosevelt, who appointed him secretary in March 1933. Wallace became the architect of the New Deal agricultural programs and policies. He is considered one of the most

knowledgeable secretaries of agriculture in U.S. history. Wallace was ambitious and outspoken on farm issues. As a result, he attracted considerable criticism as well as praise. Wallace served as secretary of agriculture until 1940.

In 1940 Wallace became Roosevelt's running mate for vice-president in the presidential elections. He served as vice-president through the war years of 1941 to 1945. Later he was the presidential candidate of the Progressive Party in 1948. He died in 1975. Wallace has been one of the most influential people associated with U.S. agricultural programs. He began policies that remained in place for the rest of the twentieth century.

Throughout the New Deal era, Wallace had proven highly popular with many farmers in the nation. Coming from a farm family himself and with his father having been a former secretary of agriculture in the early 1920s, Wallace had a firm grasp of the complex economic issues farmers faced. He also had a great deal of sympathy with their plight. Though he would not go as far as some farm activists wanted in terms of government aid, he was highly respected by most. This respect was evident in a note written by U.S. Senator Louis Murphy of Iowa to President Roosevelt (Schlesinger, *The Coming of the New Deal*, p. 71)

> Corn is 70 cents on the farms in Iowa. Two years ago it was 10 cents. Top hogs sold at Iowa plants yesterday at $7.40, or $4.50 to $5.00 better than a year ago. Farmers are very happy and convinced of the virtue of planning ... Secretary Wallace can have whatever he wants from Iowa farmers.

Roosevelt and his advisors realized that to have any chance of success, new government programs would have to first gain farmer acceptance. Supporters for agricultural assistance stressed to Roosevelt that programs would have to be locally operated, rather than by federal bureaucrats in Washington, DC. Therefore, on March 16, 1933, shortly after Roosevelt's inauguration, Wallace gathered farm leaders again in Washington at Roosevelt's invitation to draft a revolutionary farm bill. Their goal was an "agricultural adjustment" of farmer income. These leaders came up with highly inventive solutions that clearly

went beyond the traditional limits of governmental action known at that time.

Four types of actions were proposed in early 1933: (1) enticing farmers to reduce the amount of crops they grew; (2) reducing the amount of farm debt; (3) increasing the prices for crops; and (4) developing new foreign trade agreements to expand markets for American farm produce.

Decreasing farm production was a priority. Those crops being produced in greatest surplus included wheat, hogs, cotton, and corn. The desire was to establish a

Henry Wallace in his garden in 1942. Wallace served as President Franklin Roosevelt's secretary of agriculture during the New Deal years, and from 1941 to 1945 his vice president. (The Library of Congress.)

reorganizing existing federal credit agencies and forming the Farm Credit Administration (FCA). The FCA replaced Hoover's Federal Farm Board. Roosevelt appointed Henry Morgenthau Jr. to its head. Congress provided funding for the agency by first passing the Emergency Farm Mortgage Act in April, followed by the Farm Credit Act in June. The FCA began moving quickly to provide financial assistance to farmers in danger of losing their farms. The FCA also established a banking system to support farming cooperatives in marketing their crops and purchasing supplies.

The FCA issued considerably more loans than Hoover's Federal Farm Board. In 1932 the board made 7,800 loans for $28 million. The FCA in its first twelve-month period approved 541,000 loans for $1.4 billion. To give an example of its high activity, in one day the FCA once approved 3,174 loans for $8.3 million.

Birth of the Agricultural Adjustment Administration (AAA)

The key benefit of the AAA and FCA programs was that money would be placed directly into the hands of farm households. This direct aid would allow them to avoid bankruptcy, keep their land, and buy goods, thus helping other industries. Due to the desperate economic condition of farms, many farmers had little choice but to participate in the AAA production control program. For them, AAA checks became their chief source of income.

To achieve local control, the AAA's production control program was placed in the hands of county agents from the Agricultural Extension Service and local farmer committees. The committees were often organized with the assistance of local farm bureaus that were members of the national American Farm Bureau Federation. State agricultural colleges were used for technical assistance to farmers.

With the passage of the Agricultural Adjustment Act, problems in reducing crop surplus immediately arose. With the act not passed until May, 40 million acres of cotton had already been planted for another season. To raise cotton prices as quickly as possible, the AAA offered to pay farmers to plow under more than 10 million acres of cotton in the summer of 1933. The local agents and committees recruited hundreds of thousands of farmers to participate. Over $112 million dollars in government benefits were paid. Secretary Wallace, in recognizing the historic nature of this crop reduction effort, sincerely hoped it would be the last time farmers would be asked to destroy standing crops, as the very notion was so much against that in which farmers believed.

voluntary production control system. If a farmer agreed to control his crop production according to an established government plan, he would receive government payments. Those farmers not participating would still benefit from the anticipated higher market prices, but not as much as those who volunteered to participate. To raise the funds to pay farmers for reducing the acreage they were farming, a tax would be placed on companies processing farm products. Processors included flour mills, textile mills, and meat packing houses. This strategy of production control became the heart of the adjustment bill. The proposed legislation took two critical months during spring planting season before finally passing in the U.S. Senate by a vote of 64 to 20. On May 12, 1933, President Roosevelt signed the Agricultural Adjustment Act into law. The act created the Agricultural Adjustment Administration (AAA), which would pay farmers to limit their crop production. The AAA was Roosevelt's first New Deal economic recovery program.

Reducing farm debt was another key concern identified in March 1933. To make loans more available to farmers, Roosevelt issued an executive order

Corn and hogs presented another surplus urgency much like cotton. Most of the corn was not sold at markets, but rather was fed to hogs which appeared at market as pork. A National Corn-Hog Committee composed of farmers from around the country was assembled in the summer of 1933 to consider solutions to the surplus of hogs. To the surprise of many, the committee recommended the government purchase and slaughter six million hogs that fall. The recommendation was adopted by Wallace and carried out in September 1933.

The AAA policy of produce destruction brought out many critics. They were angered by the destruction of farm produce while many in the nation were going hungry. In defense of the pig killing campaign, Wallace complained that the public seemed to believe that "every little pig has the right to attain before slaughter the full pigginess of his pigness. To hear them talk, you would have thought that pigs were raised for pets." (Schlesinger, *The Coming of the New Deal: The Age of Roosevelt,* 1988, p. 63) Responding to the uproar, Wallace agreed to purchase some surplus agricultural produce and give it to the needy. The Federal Surplus Relief Corporation, created in October 1933, purchased over 100 million pounds of baby pork and gave it to hungry people enrolled in various relief programs.

Drought on the Plains

New Dealers on the Great Plains faced a different situation. Because of increasingly dry weather conditions, drought had largely solved wheat overproduction problems by 1933. The AAA made a three-year program available to wheat farmers. Those who agreed to reduce wheat crops in 1934 and 1935 to levels set by the government would receive government payments. The annual average of 864 million bushels of wheat produced between 1928 and 1932 fell to 567 million bushels from 1933 to 1935. Only twenty million bushels of the decrease, however, resulted from AAA programs. Most of the decrease was due to drought.

Though drought solved overproduction problems, it did create others. Soil erosion became critical as hot winds stirred up massive clouds of dry topsoil. The Dust Bowl was born. Soil conservation became an additional concern of federal farm programs. To increase federal support of farmland conservation, in 1935 the Roosevelt administration transferred the Soil Erosion Service from the Department of Interior to the Department of Agriculture and renamed it the Soil Conservation Service (SCS). The SCS provided both technical assistance and loans to farmers to promote soil conservation measures. Such measures included the new methods of terracing, contour plowing, and reseeding with native grasses. The Civilian Conservation Corps (CCC), created in 1935, assisted these conservation activities. In 1936 Roosevelt assembled the Great Plains Drought Area Committee to recommend measures for improving conditions in the region. The committee recommended taking agriculturally marginal lands out of production and reseeding them with natural grasses.

The success of the New Deal agricultural aid programs on the Great Plains was limited. Many farmers lost their farms and moved to cities. An overall improvement in farming techniques did occur, however, during this period of extraordinary drought and severe economic conditions. These methods would serve the surviving farmers well in following decades. Only federal aid allowed many of these farmers to keep their farms. In the northern and central Great Plains, between 40 and 75 percent of farmers' incomes came from AAA and other New Deal programs. Still, approximately 500,000 people left the rural life of the Great Plains in the 1930s, seeking economic relief in the cities. Increased rainfall, as well as the increased demands of World War II, finally pulled the region out of economic hard times. The Dust Bowl left scars for decades, however. Farmers felt more vulnerable than ever to the forces of nature on the Great Plains. This traumatic period became the backdrop for one of the era's most popular Hollywood movies. The 1939 movie *The Wizard of Oz,* in which actress Judy Garland starred, told a fantasy tale of a young girl's escape from the bleak life in Kansas in the 1930s to the colorful land of Oz.

The Desert West

Conservation concerns of the New Dealers also extended further west. Ranchers had grazed livestock on open range public lands since the mid-nineteenth century without controls. Public lands consist of the millions of acres of land in the West that were never settled due to lack of water, remoteness, or other reasons. Cattle and sheep had overgrazed much of the land. Congress passed the Taylor Grazing Act in 1934, regulating the use of the range lands. Like on the Plains, the Civilian Conservation Corps built fences and made other range improvements. At the end of the New Deal era, over 11 million head of livestock grazed on 142 million public lands. Much tighter control of public land use became the policy of the federal government from that point on.

Farmers Want More

By late 1933 a comprehensive agricultural relief program had become well established in much of the

Many farms were reduced to dirt and dust due to drought and unsound farming techniques during the Great Depression. (UPI/Corbis-Bettmann. Reproduced by permission.)

nation. However, the AAA, the cornerstone of the program, was not bringing results quick enough to satisfy everyone. Some farmers continued arguing for more radical policies that would guarantee farm incomes and fix produce prices. Wallace and the Roosevelt administration resisted such proposals and stuck with the program of benefit payments and loans.

In an effort to satisfy the critics, Roosevelt created the Commodity Credit Corporation by presidential executive order in October 1933. The Commodity Credit Corporation provided loans at low interest rates to farmers who agreed to production controls. The loan rates were set so that farmers would receive somewhat more money than the market value of their crops. This measure was a price support. The program was first applied to the surplus of crops stored in 1934, such as cotton, wheat, and corn. The goal was to make sure these surpluses would not further decrease market prices. The Commodity Credit Corporation loan program served the United States well, supporting farm prices at higher levels and substantially expanding operation after World War II.

Though the AAA production control measures were largely voluntary, Congress did apply some pressure in 1934 on farmers to participate. The Bankhead

Cotton Control Act, the Kerr-Smith Tobacco Control Act, and the Potato Act imposed substantial taxes on those farmers not cooperating.

The Problem of Small Farm Operators

Despite vital relief provided to many farmers, by the mid-1930s thousands of small farmers had lost their farms. Their land went to the mortgage holders, such as banks and insurance companies, and eventually became parts of large mechanized farms. Corporate agriculture was replacing the family farm.

This trend brought more criticism of New Deal programs. People complained the programs strongly favored large landowners. In an effort to answer these complaints, Roosevelt created the Resettlement Administration (RA) in 1935. The RA was designed to provide direct assistance to sharecroppers, migrant laborers, and other poor families. Sharecroppers were small farmers who did not own land, but rather rented from large landowners. The goal was to resettle impoverished farm families away from poor land and place them on more productive land. Besides providing a loan to purchase new land, the RA would provide tools and technical advice so that the resettled farmers would have a chance of economic survival. Rex Tugwell, a close adviser to Roosevelt, assumed lead of the agency.

Critics of the RA were uncomfortable with promoting small subsistence family farms. Even Tugwell had second thoughts. Many within Roosevelt's administration firmly believed large commercial farms were the future of American agriculture. They argued federal government efforts to preserve small family farms would likely be more costly than their social value justified. They feared that creating areas of small farms would be establishing isolated pockets of lasting poverty. Most New Dealers strongly believed the application of new technological innovations to large commercial farms was the only real future for the agriculture industry.

Given these concerns, the RA soon evolved into the Farm Security Administration (FSA) in 1937. Rather than resettling poor farmers, the FSA loaned money so farm families could afford such necessities as food, clothing, feed, seed, and fertilizer. This loan system was a last resort for farmers who did not qualify for loans or credit from regular banks or other credit institutions.

The Court Strikes Down AAA

The U.S. Supreme Court played a major role in the New Deal era and agricultural issues proved no exception. Roosevelt had proclaimed in 1933 when introducing the AAA and other initial New Deal programs that the U.S. Constitution was sufficiently flexible and practical to allow new approaches during extraordinary times. The food processing companies being taxed to support the AAA's program, however, charged the farm relief system was unfair. They went to court to challenge the AAA. As a result, in January 1936 the U.S. Supreme Court ruled in *United States v. Butler* that the processor tax was unconstitutional. Using a narrow definition of federal powers, the Court claimed Congress had no legal authority to control their businesses, hence striking down the AAA. That authority, according to the Court's majority, was reserved in the Constitution for state governments.

Congress responded quickly to the Court decision with passage of the Soil Conservation and Domestic Allotment Act. The new act changed the way in which farmers were paid. Now farmers were paid for soil conservation rather than for reducing acreage of crops. They focused on planting crops that caused the least amount of soil depletion. Also, payments to farmers would come from general government revenues rather than special taxes on processors. Farmers were encouraged to decrease production through voluntary means.

Following his reelection, Roosevelt responded in early 1937 to the *Butler* decision and to other unfavorable Court rulings by proposing to restructure the Supreme Court. Though his proposal met with great resistance, it did serve to put pressure on the Court. New Deal programs began receiving more favorable rulings. The Court issued rulings supporting the New Deal tax plans in *Steward Machine Co. v. Davis* (1937) and the regulation of agriculture in *Mulford v. Smith* (1939) and *Wickard v. Filburn* (1941). The Court finally affirmed that the federal government held the power to regulate agriculture under the Constitution's interstate commerce clause.

The problem of crop overproduction still continued through 1936 and 1937. Not enough farmers volunteered to cut back their crop production. Pressure mounted again from farmers for government financial assistance. In 1938 Congress passed a new Agricultural Adjustment Act. The new act kept the conservation measures of the Soil Conservation and Domestic Allotment Act. It also added a new method for price supports for farmers when oversupply of produce led to lower prices. The act was very broad and set up research stations and other means of aiding farmers. Unfortunately, overproduction would continue to be a major problem until World War II.

Power to the Farmer

The New Deal brought another revolutionary improvement to rural farm life—electric power. In 1933 most rural areas had no electric service. Congress created the Tennessee Valley Authority (TVA) to bring inexpensive electric service to the farm regions of Mississippi, Alabama, Georgia, and Tennessee. TVA provided hydroelectric power below private industry rates. Roosevelt also created the Electric Home and Farm Authority (EHFA). EHFA provided low-interest loans to farmers for the purchase of electric appliances. At last farmers could enjoy the benefits of refrigerators, cooking ranges, and water heaters and businesses selling such items rebounded. Sales of appliances in the Tennessee River basin tripled.

With the successes of TVA and EHFA programs, Roosevelt created the Rural Electrification Administration (REA) to bring electrical power to other rural regions. The REA provided loans to rural farming cooperatives to finance the wiring of homes, the stringing of power lines, and the purchasing or generating of electricity. Private utility companies contended the demand for electricity in rural farm areas was insufficient to make it profitable to provide power. Consequently, long-standing farming cooperatives became the primary avenue for bringing power to their areas. By 1939 more than 350 REA projects in 45 states provided electric service to nearly 1.5 million rural residents and 40 percent of U.S. farms. The REA proved one of the most successful New Deal programs. Most immediately these programs provided farmers power to operate barn machinery, irrigation water pumps, and other labor saving devices. The availability of electrical power led to later development of more mechanical and electrical equipment.

Immediate Benefits of Agricultural Relief

Despite criticisms and shortcomings, the AAA and other farm programs helped many farmers. No strong recovery resulted from the programs but the decline was halted. Gross farm income in the nation rose from a low of $6.4 billion in 1932 to $8.5 billion in 1934. Income increased 50 percent between 1932 and 1936. Prices of farm produce rose 67 percent. Benefit payments of $577 million were paid out in 1933 and 1934 to several million farmers. Farm debt decreased by $1 billion. The federal government replaced private banks and insurance companies as key creditors. The government held 40 percent of farm mortgage debt by the end of the 1930s. Human suffering was eased, and the future outlook for many improved. Some considered this rural economic recovery remarkable since the U.S. economy in general was struggling.

Problems faced by the New Dealers were numerous: (1) the complexity of the problem was large with

The Agricultural Adjustment Agency (AAA) encouraged farmers to limit or destroy their crops in order to raise prices and create more demand. (© Bettmann/Corbis. Reproduced by permission.)

many diverse regions and crops affected; (2) the difficult challenge of convincing people to produce less product than they were capable of; and (3) dealing with a traditionally highly independent segment of U.S. society. Desperation no doubt played an important role in fostering acceptance of new proposed programs and unusual solutions. Despite these obstacles and many more, the AAA and other programs operated surprisingly smoothly for a large bureaucracy. Having a well-trained corps of specialists coming from

the land-grant agricultural colleges and working in cooperation with state and county extension service agents helped. Every state has an extension service and almost every county have extension agents to help farmers. The service and agents, part of the Cooperative Extension System formed by federal, state, and county governments, provide farmers with up-to-date information on farming techniques. Above all, reliance on local grassroots guidance proved critical. Letting farmers make important decisions and using county farmer committees to oversee production control programs guided by their own elected leaders was crucial. Nearly four thousand local committees existed in 1934. Programs were largely voluntary with most pressure to participate coming from local farmers themselves. In 1935 Presidential advisor Raymond Moley, looking back at the first three years of the New Deal's effort to improve the economy, considered the AAA one of the more successful and popular programs adopted.

Contributing Forces

Several major long-term trends leading up to 1929 contributed to the U.S. farm crisis. These factors involved overproduction, world trade, technological farm innovations, the government's role in regulating business, and weather. The American farmer was more vulnerable to the economic hard times of the Great Depression than most other segments of U.S. society. By the time of the 1929 stock market crash, farmers had large debts, lowered incomes, and farms of reduced value.

American Overproduction

Ironically, a major factor leading to hard times on the farm in the 1930s was farm prosperity of the 1910s. During the earlier period, an unparalleled high demand for U.S. farm produce existed. This demand resulted in higher prices the farmer could get for his crops and livestock. During World War I, the U.S. government encouraged greater farm production to make up for European shortages and help in the war effort. To meet these growing demands, farmers purchased more land, livestock, and new equipment. They often borrowed money to make these purchases, assuming the good times would continue. As a result, farm debt substantially increased as farmers rushed to take advantage of the high prices. Unexpectedly, the demand for U.S. farm produce plummeted after 1919 when European farms began producing again. Farmers were left with big bills to pay and substantially less income. Farm debt was $3.3 billion in the nation in 1910. It doubled to $6.7 billion in 1920 and increased further to $9.4 billion by 1925. American farmers were ill prepared to weather a depression.

By 1920 World War I was over. Europe began an economic recovery, including the revival of its agricultural production to feed its population. In addition, Russia, Australia, Argentina, and Canada began increasing their exports of beef and wheat. Suddenly, international competition was much stiffer for U.S. farmers. As a result, demand for U.S. products began declining. As the 1920s progressed, farmers continued producing more food than could be sold for profit. As prices fell for farm products, farmers increased production to sell more, causing even greater surpluses and consequently even lower prices. Farmers were unable to pay off loans, leading many rural banks to fail. Agriculture became perhaps the weakest part of the American economy during that decade.

Farm Modernization and Limited Government

The foundation for new commercial agriculture in the United States was laid between 1900 and 1930. Science and technology breakthroughs began to transform American agriculture. Gasoline-powered tractors first came into use in the 1890s, replacing the impractical steam-driven tractors, but they had insufficient power for everyday farm use. The first all-purpose tractors that could power a variety of farm implements appeared in the 1920s. More and more acreage could be planted and harvested by a farmer. With these technological advances, the small family farm become increasingly less cost efficient and competitive with growing commercial farms. Production costs on the newly mechanized farms were cut in half or more. This new tractor-powered machinery brought increased efficiency and productivity. It also contributed to overproduction, declining prices, and increased operating expenses. In addition, 25 million acres previously used to grow feed for horses and mules were converted to other crops, adding further to overproduction.

A continued high level of farm production in the United States through the 1920s led to a drastic decline in prices. Many farmers began losing their farms and equipment to foreclosure as they could not meet their loan payments. Meaningful government relief was not coming to the rescue. Prior to the 1930s, the federal government played a small role in the private social and economic affairs of its citizens. This political tradition was embraced by Coolidge's Republican administrations of the 1920s.

Farm advocates began campaigning for federal farm relief. They argued that farmers were suffering the most of all Americans from postwar economic changes. In response to the clamor, Congress took action by passing the McNary-Haugen Bill calling for federal price supports. As proposed in the bill, the government would buy the surplus of key crops at guaranteed higher prices than the going open market rate. It would then sell them on the world market at normally lower prices. The government would regain the

More About...

Sharecropping

Prior to the American Civil War (1861–1865), most black Americans worked as slaves on farmlands and plantations in the southern states. Following emancipation in 1865, blacks were free but had no money or land. The war-torn South was going through traumatic social and economic change. White landowners sought a stable, low-cost work force, and newly freed slaves sought to reestablish long-broken family ties. A new farming system emerged in which landowners divided up their land and assigned each unit to a family. The owner would furnish sharecroppers with shelter, fuel, implements, feed for stock, seed, and one-half of the needed fertilizers. The sharecroppers, who were predominantly black but included many poor white Americans as well, provided their own labor and the remainder of the fertilizer. The sharecropper would pay rent with up to half of his harvest. Food, clothing, and some supplies had to be purchased from local merchants on credit.

Under the sharecropping system, blacks, often only semiliterate, were at the mercy of both landlords and merchants. Merchants would frequently charge excessive rates of interest on their credit. Deceitful landowners shortchanged them in assessing the value of their harvests each year. The system basically guaranteed the families would remain in substantial debt for many years. This indebtedness was a form of involuntary slavery. Blacks were legally bound to continue working for landlords as long as their debt persisted. Sharecroppers attempting to flee debt were frequently caught and returned by law authorities to face severe whippings.

Poverty and discrimination permeated the sharecroppers' world. Typically, sharecroppers lived in crowded, flimsy shacks, had worn clothes, and ate poor diets of corn bread, molasses, potatoes, and "fatback," which is fat from the back of a hog carcass often cooked with greens. They frequently were victims of violence as white society maintained its social and political dominance. Black families commonly operated forty-acre parcels, whereas white tenant farmers averaged over ninety acres.

In 1930 over 776,000 black sharecroppers worked the soil, but by 1959 only 121,000 remained. Increased mechanization of farms, erosion and exhaustion of the land, and New Deal policies took their toll through the 1930s. Sharecroppers' plots had become too small to be profitable, and many left for wage labor in the industrialized northern cities.

---

money through a tax placed on domestic food sales. In that way the cost of the proposed farm program would be passed along to the consumer. The bill never became law, however, as President Calvin Coolidge twice vetoed it. Coolidge believed farmers had always been poor and there was little the government could do about it.

Herbert Hoover was more sympathetic. He set up Farm Boards to guide farm recovery. The board nationally organized local farm associations. The number of independent local cooperative marketing associations had grown rapidly after 1915. The cooperatives were local organizations owned and operated by the farmers and others involved in processing and marketing farm produce. Over eleven thousand cooperatives existed by the mid-1920s. Hoover's action, however, was insufficient to respond to the added effects of the stock market crash.

Dust Bowl in the Wheat Lands

Natural factors also played a role in making farmers particularly vulnerable to the economic hardships of the Great Depression. These factors were particularly evident on the wheat farms of the Great Plains. Years of ample rainfall in the 1920s and new technology enabled wheat farmers to steadily expand operations. They spread into marginal farming areas previously thought too dry for farming. With this overexpansion wheat became yet another surplus crop of the decade.

Generations of careless cultivation practices had plowed up protective ground cover, such as thick native grasses. Many farmers had plowed up and down hills, making the fields vulnerable to water erosion, rather than contour plowing horizontally across hillsides. Removal of the native ground cover also made soils susceptible to wind erosion when rows of trees were not planted along the edges of fields for windbreaks. When the soils dried out and winds stirred up across the broad flat expanse of the region, massive dust clouds resulted.

By the 1930s the combination of large wheat crops, exposed topsoil, prolonged drought, declining world demand for U.S. crops, increased foreign competition, the Great Depression, and too little government assistance brought economic disaster to the region. In the following several years, a five-state area of the southern Great Plains became known as the Dust Bowl. Wheat prices plummeted as the changing climate and poor farming practices added further economic misery to the effects of the Great Depression.

Perspectives

Local Perspectives

At the local level, reception of the New Deal's agricultural programs was largely positive. This approval by the rural populace no doubt contributed to Roosevelt's major victory in his 1936 reelection.

Farmers were traditionally very independent persons. They commonly strove to be free of government control. Not surprisingly, resistance was strong to initial suggestions for the government production control measures during the 1920s. By late 1932 desperation was finally leading farmers to be more receptive.

Still, farmers were suspicious of plans to cut back production. They wanted something more immediately concrete. Farm advocates wanted the government to guarantee that farmers would recover the costs of production. They also wanted increased farm prices but believed Roosevelt's proposed New Deal farm bill was too weak in that regard.

By late April 1933, the sweeping farm bill was still bogged down in Congress with considerable debate over its elements. With financial relief not coming quickly, farmers in the rural regions began taking action on their own. They interrupted eviction sales, intimidated bank and insurance agents, and combated foreclosures.

One of the more dramatic local actions by farmers took place in Le Mars, Iowa, on April 27, 1933. Over five hundred farmers angrily crowded into a courtroom to request that Judge Charles C. Bradley suspend further farm foreclosure hearings. They wanted the courts to hold off further hearings until proposed state laws could be passed helping the farmers. When Bradley refused, the crowd forcibly took him out of the courtroom blindfolded and placed him in the back of a truck in which he was driven out of town. The crowd threw a rope over a telephone pole, placing one end around the judge's neck. Grease was poured over his head, and his trousers were torn off and tossed in a nearby ditch. Bradley was left alive but badly shaken.

A few days later, another crowd of farmers attacked agents and deputies trying to enforce a foreclosure on a farm. Iowa governor Clyde L. Herring, alarmed by the rise in violence, called in the Iowan National Guard and declared martial law in several counties. Nearly 150 men were arrested and detained in a fenced enclosure. While watching trucks filled with soldiers dressed in khaki and holding rifles pass, one Iowan farmer likened the scene to something in Russia with the oppressive communist government there.

In California agricultural workers sought improved working and living conditions. Efforts by migrant workers to organize and fight for better working conditions met with militant reaction by the growers and others. Large farms replaced the earlier small-scale operations. Corporations gained tighter control over the food production and processing industry. The Associated Farmers of California, an organization of large-scale growers supported by investment corporations and large packing, transportation, and utility companies, wielded considerable influence. With few other options available, as early as 1931 workers began joining the newly established communist-controlled union of United Cannery, Agricultural, Packing and Allied Workers of America. Workers made some gains in improving conditions. Perhaps their biggest gain was raising public awareness of their plight.

Passage of the Agricultural Adjustment Act in May 1933 still did not bring local tranquility. Many charged the crop reduction program favored large-scale farmers who had plenty of land to set aside. Smaller-scale farmers did not have enough land to set aside to qualify for financial aid. Without access to financial aid, many small farmers were essentially run out of business. Large land companies would purchase these small farms. The small farms were combined, the fences removed, and mechanized equipment such as tractors purchased. This trend contributed to the decline of small family farms, an integral part of early U.S. economic history. The larger farms, however, proved more competitive in the increasingly mechanized agricultural era of the 1930s. Sharecroppers and tenant farmers suffered as well. With southern landowners paid to farm fewer acres, they simply took AAA checks and let sharecroppers go.

President Franklin Roosevelt visits with a North Dakota farmer who is receiving drought relief. In the northern and central Great Plains, between 40 and 75 percent of farmers' incomes came from AAA and other New Deal programs. (The Library of Congress.)

The New Deal programs led to a revolutionary change in how American farmlands were used. In 1935 approximately three million blacks and over five million whites worked as tenants and sharecroppers. By 1940, 30 percent of sharecroppers and 12 percent of tenants had left farming in the thirteen cotton states. Many, however, stayed on the land they had previously farmed because they had no place else to go.

National Perspectives

Considerable disagreement existed even among those in Roosevelt's administration about how to solve the complex agriculture problems. Since the American Civil War (1861–1865), the dramatic growth of U.S. business and industry pushed agriculture into the economic background. The farming tradition of independence clashed with the national trend toward a more centralized economy.

Roosevelt recruited many people with a broad range of backgrounds to help in the nation's recovery. Addressing farm issues were rural traditionalists who believed in farmer independence and maintaining local control of agricultural activities, and urban liberals who believed in a strong government role. In the past agriculture was addressed separately from the rest

of the U.S. economy. Some now argued for a new approach, however, insisting agriculture should be treated as an integrated part of the U.S. economy. They advocated that farming reform go beyond the farm to the companies that purchased farm products and processed them into food.

Because the Agricultural Adjustment Act was proposed in early 1933 included a tax on food processors, the lobbyists for the processors sprang quickly to action to oppose it. After the act's passage, the processors soon challenged it in the courts. Eventually they were successful. The U.S. Supreme Court made a ruling in their favor in early 1936.

Many in Congress thought the AAA offered too little help to farmers as foreclosures continued. The AAA loans proved a massive bailout of large commercial farms, but they offered little for farmers without capital. Sharecroppers and tenant farmers of the South, debt-ridden farmers of the Midwest and Great Plains, and migrant farm workers in the West did not enjoy the prosperity of large landowners.

The plight of the small farmer during the Great Depression was the subject of major literary works of the period. Three novels of famed author John Steinbeck deal with the topic. In *Dubious Battle* (1936) concerns an agricultural strike by laborers. *Of Mice and Men* (1937) is a story of two migrant workers in California dreaming of better days. *Grapes of Wrath* (1939) is about a tenant farmer and his family who migrate from Oklahoma to California. It won the 1939 Pulitzer Prize in fiction and raised widespread sympathy for the plight of migratory farm workers. The following year Hollywood released a movie of the same name. John Ford won the Academy Award for Best Director and Jane Darwell for Best Actress. Henry Fonda was nominated for Best Actor, and the movie was nominated for Best Picture. Steinbeck received the Nobel Prize for Literature in 1962 based largely on his work of the 1930s which endured through the following decades, reflecting on the difficult plight of the laborer in U.S. society. Noted American writer James Agee and photographer Walker Evans produced the 1941 book about Alabama sharecroppers titled *Let Us Now Praise Famous Men*. The book resulted from their experiences living with sharecroppers for about six weeks in 1936. Written originally for *Fortune* magazine, it did not appear in publication until released as a book in 1941. The book is still considered one of the best collaborations between writer and photographer and an excellent record of sharecropper life during the Great Depression.

International Perspectives

Trends in agriculture worldwide were similar to those in the United States. Industrial production following World War I declined with the drop in demand for arms, and unemployment increased. Influenced, however, by increased mechanization and the use of newly developed chemical fertilizers, agricultural production soared. With mechanization and fertilizers, agricultural labor was no longer needed at previous levels. As in the United States, crop overproduction in various western countries led to demands for protection from foreign competition. Germany placed a high protective tariff on imported farm produce, including imports from the United States. These high tariffs continued into the 1930s. Continued overproduction of wheat came at a high cost to taxpayers. They were required to pay price supports to German farmers for storage of surplus wheat. In other words, the consumer was paying artificially high prices.

Many looked to the United States, with its newly gained international prominence following World War I, to provide world leadership. The world in general was dismayed by the United States' turn inward toward isolationism, represented by passage of the Hawley-Smoot Act. The act raised taxes on foreign goods, making it more difficult for other nations to gain much-needed income by selling their products in the United States. Roosevelt's New Deal continued this uncooperative spirit towards the worldwide economic problems. As foreign countries retaliated against the high U.S. tariffs, the Great Depression only deepened.

The rest of the world was not as quickly affected by the stock market crash in the United States. When the economic depression did spread, countries responded in different ways to help farmers. Australia was heavily in debt to British banks. The government instructed wheat farmers to boost production to raise money through exports. It became known as the "Grow More Wheat" program. With the world oversupplied in wheat, however, farmers found themselves selling their new bumper crops at prices below what it cost to grow them. To provide financial support, the Australian government passed the Wheat Advances Act, but banks did not have funds to provide the loans. Devaluation of Australian currency in 1931 bailed out the farmers by increasing farm exports, because Australian products then cost less in foreign countries.

Canada was another nation whose economy heavily depended on the export of grain and raw materials. Canadian exporters and farmers suffered huge losses as the United States and other countries entered into tariff wars, which resulted in fewer goods exported. Canadian unemployment rose from 3 percent in 1929 to 23 percent in 1933.

Impact

The U.S. economic farming crisis began in the early 1920s and became a major factor in the Great Depression of the 1930s. The combination of technological advances, the growth of science applications, and a greater government role in regulating farm production brought dramatic changes to rural America.

During the 1930s farming continued a shift from the earlier labor-intensive but simpler rural life to a capital-intensive major industry. New Deal programs greatly encouraged increased mechanization and the use of newly developed fertilizers, insecticides, and herbicides. By World War II farming had become big business, requiring special skills and sufficient capital to purchase modern equipment. The "horse age" of farming had drawn to a close, replaced by gasoline tractors. New machines, such as the grain combine harvester and the mechanical cotton picker, steadily decreased the need for field laborers. By the 1990s about 500,000 of the total 2.3 million farms in America produced over 80 percent of farm income. The commercial farms required increasing amounts of investment in equipment and supplies. In 1990 about

67 percent of small farm operators gained income from other jobs away from the farm.

As a result of New Deal policies and technological change, the social landscape of rural life also dramatically changed. For the first time, the U.S. census taken in 1920 indicated more people lived in cities than in rural areas. With the New Deal emphasis on larger farm operations, that trend continued. By 1930 some 30 million Americans lived on farms—25 percent of the U.S. population. A half-century later, in the 1980s, that number had further declined to 5.7 million, or less than 3 percent. Yet the amount of farmland remained about the same through that time period at about one billion acres.

The New Deal farm programs greatly altered the fundamental relationship between the federal government and farmers. The programs provided many benefits to farmers that were never before available. The 1938 Agricultural Adjustment Act provided the foundation for future U.S. agricultural policy. A lasting relationship between the government and farmers grew with government aid, available through loans and price supports. Importantly, farmer expectations of assistance during difficult times in the 1930s continued throughout the remainder of the twentieth century. Since the 1930s government has played a major role in agriculture, setting minimum farm prices, deciding on quality standards for farm products, and inspecting food and livestock feed.

The REA program demonstrated that the government could successfully provide cheap electrical power and increase the quality of life in rural areas. This success led to more government-sponsored power programs in the following decades.

Rural poverty of the Great Depression largely came to an end with World War II. The high demand for farm products and increased prices helped those still on the farm. Urban industrial jobs and military service helped those who were no longer needed in the increasingly mechanized farm operations.

Notable People

Mordecai Ezekiel (1899–1974). Holding a graduate degree from the University of Minnesota, Ezekiel began work in the Bureau of Agricultural Economics in the U.S. Department of Agriculture in 1922. He became one of the leading proponents for production control measures, in which farm prices might be increased by limiting the acreage being farmed. In 1932 Ezekiel wrote speeches on agriculture for presidential candidate Franklin Roosevelt. Following Roosevelt's election, Ezekiel became the Secretary of Agriculture Henry Wallace's chief economic advisor. He was one of the lead authors of the 1933 Agricultural Adjustment Act. Through the 1930s Ezekiel became an outspoken supporter of national economic planning programs.

Jerome N. Frank (1889–1957). President Roosevelt selected Jerome Frank to be the lead attorney, general counsel, of the Agricultural Adjustment Association. After graduating from the University of Chicago law school, Frank became a corporate lawyer in New York City and Chicago before joining the Roosevelt administration in 1933. Frank selected a number of young upcoming lawyers as assistants. These included future U.S. Supreme Court justice Abe Fortas, future presidential candidate Adlai Stevenson, and future secretary-general of the United Nations Alger Hiss. Frank and his associates became leading proponents among the New Dealers for liberal reform. Roosevelt, however, dismissed Frank in 1935, to relieve tensions with others who favored more conservative measures. He was later to return in 1937 as commissioner of the Securities and Exchange Commission, eventually becoming its chairman. He was later appointed judge to the U.S. Court of Appeals for the Second Circuit.

Herbert Hoover (1874–1964). Having gained personal wealth as a mining engineer and businessman, Hoover served as U.S. food administer under President Woodrow Wilson and then secretary of commerce under Warren Harding and Calvin Coolidge. Hoover became president of the United States from 1929 to 1933. Unlike President Calvin Coolidge before him, Hoover sought to relieve agricultural economic problems. He called Congress into a special session in early 1929 to pass the Agricultural Marketing Act. The act created the Federal Farm Board to organize a national system of farm cooperatives. Hoover called it a "new day in agriculture." But with no direct financial aid and the onslaught of the Great Depression, the remedy proved unsuccessful. Hoover became a leading critic of the New Deal by the mid-1930s and continued to fight the New Deal's influence into the 1950s.

Harry Leland Mitchell (1906–1989). The operator of a dry cleaning business in northeastern Arkansas, Mitchell helped found and became executive secretary of the Southern Tenant Farmers' Union in the 1930s. Mitchell was a socialist involved in political organizational work in the region. He sympathized with the plight of sharecroppers and tenant farmers. Mitchell gave inspirational leadership to the union, which grew to over 25,000 members in several states.

More About...

Southern Tenant Farmers' Union

A key criticism of the New Deal agricultural economic aid programs is that they favored large landowners. The small farmers, including sharecroppers and tenant farmers, were left to fend for themselves against great odds. Sharecroppers and tenant farmers worked on lands controlled by large landowners and gave a part of their crop to the landowner in exchange for use of the land, shelter, food, tools, and other necessities. They were being let go in large numbers as the landowners cut back crop production to qualify for government benefit checks under the AAA production control program. In 1934, in northeastern Arkansas, the Fairview Farms plantation evicted forty tenant families. They were reducing acreage to receive AAA payments. The Agricultural Adjustment Act, however, prohibited landlords from releasing tenant farmers for purposes of increasing their own share of payments.

Eighteen white and black sharecroppers decided to unite and form the Southern Tenant Farmers' Union. Membership dues were 10 cents a month for those who could pay it, free for others. The union soon expanded into Oklahoma, Texas, and Mississippi, gaining 25,000 members. Led by Harry Leland Mitchell, the union's goal was to gain enough strength through memberships to force reforms, particularly the stopping of tenant evictions. Mitchell and union members suffered years of threats. Opponents of the union physically beat members as government officials stood back doing nothing. Local officials usually sided with the landowner. Federal officials did not want to lose the votes of southern landowners for the 1936 presidential election or set back the successful AAA acreage reduction program. One state even made it illegal to possess more than five copies of the union literature.

Henry A. Wallace, secretary of agriculture, finally agreed to investigate anti-union activities, but did little to intervene in what they called a local matter. The violence decreased later in 1935. The union gained limited success against major odds. After merger into a larger industrial union in 1937, the union declined in strength.

He was subject to many threats, however, and labeled a communist. Boycotts eventually ruined his business. Mitchell fled across the Mississippi River to Memphis, Tennessee, as did other union leaders.

George Peek (1873–1943). President Roosevelt selected George Peek to head the Agricultural Adjustment Administration in 1933. He was of an older generation than most New Dealers. Peek went to work for Deere and Company selling farm equipment in 1893 and became an executive for the company by 1911. He had served as an industrial representative on the War Industries Board during World War I. Following the war, Peek was president of the Moline Plow Company of Illinois and lobbied for agricultural legislation in the 1920s. Peek believed the solution to agriculture's economic problems lay with tariffs, international marketing agreements, and government export programs. Peek was known for his tough and combative personality. He had gained considerable respect in Washington, drawing the attention of Roosevelt's administration. Never comfortable with the AAA's production control measures, Peek resigned after only seven months. He became sharply critical of New Deal farm policies and lobbied against them. He succeeded in raising the visibility of agricultural issues, and his ideas were later adopted in U.S. farm policy after World War II.

Milo Reno (1866–1936). Reno was a noted farm activist fighting for government relief. After joining the National Farmers' Union in 1918, he became president of the militant Iowa branch in 1921. Reno was a popular country preacher who promoted nineteenth-century populist ideals. He urged farmers to organize and take action against the U.S. corporate structure of banks and insurance companies, as well as against law authorities to save their farms. Described as tireless and obsessed, he spoke for government policies that would guarantee farmer incomes to cover production costs and provide a reasonable profit. In May 1932 he was elected leader of the National Farmers' Holiday Association. The association sought to keep produce from reaching markets until favorable government policies were established. The protests caused widespread disruption of farm produce being delivered to markets in five states and led to some violence as well. Frustrated with New Deal programs that did not provide the relief Reno was seeking, he continued to crusade for farmers until his death in 1936.

Franklin D. Roosevelt (1882–1945). Roosevelt was the leading architect of New Deal programs in the 1930s while he was serving as president of the United States. Born into a wealthy New York family, Roosevelt earned a law degree from Columbia University. He won a New York legislature seat in 1911 and became assistant secretary of the navy under Woodrow Wilson from 1913 through 1920. After battling polio in the 1920s, he was elected governor of New York in 1928 and again in 1930. He won the presidential election of 1932 over Herbert Hoover.

To attack the complex economic problems of the Great Depression, he oversaw passage of numerous new laws and programs in 1933, including the Agricultural Adjustment Act. Roosevelt's popularity skyrocketed, but as the Great Depression continued into the mid-1930s, the popularity of his programs slipped. Roosevelt decided to support the everyday worker, including farmers. This new tactic brought him a resounding victory in the 1936 presidential elections. With the beginning of World War II, emphasis switched from domestic to foreign issues. Roosevelt served as president until his death in 1945. He is the only president to be elected to four consecutive terms of office, though not completing the fourth.

Rexford Tugwell (1891–1979). Having earned a Ph.D. in agricultural economics from the University of Pennsylvania, Rexford Tugwell became a professor at Harvard University. He was an advocate for government regulation of private enterprise and national farm programs. In 1933 Roosevelt recruited him to be assistant secretary of agriculture under Henry Wallace, as well as economic adviser to Roosevelt himself. Tugwell was eager to use the New Deal to guide economic and social change in the United States. He played a major role in writing the Agricultural Adjustment Act.

In 1935 Roosevelt appointed Tugwell to be head of the controversial Resettlement Administration to assist poor farmers in relocating to better lands. The agency became part of another agency in 1937, and Tugwell resigned. He was appointed governor of Puerto Rico, serving through World War II, before returning to an academic post at the University of Chicago. He died in 1979.

Primary Sources

Reflections of Oscar Heline

Iowan farmer Oscar Heline later reflected on life during the Great Depression. President Herbert Hoover's approach to aiding the farmer from 1929 to 1932 was a disappointment. Hoover believed in limited government assistance and reliance on voluntary reform. This approach was highly ineffective for such complex problems and disappointed much of the public. Desperate farmers established the Farmers Holiday Association in the Midwest in 1932. They were determined to take action to save their farms and communities. The farmers would ban together and block other farmers from delivering their produce to market. They hoped to decrease the supply of produce. This action would hopefully increase prices paid to farmers for what was sold. In the meantime families had to make do on the farm during the Great Depression. Due to little income, they had to make every scrap of material serve some purpose until it completely wore out. In the end Heline sadly reflected on what brought an end to the Depression in rural America—World War II. The New Deal programs, from the Agricultural Adjustment Act of 1933 to the act of the same name passed in 1938, could not bring full economic recovery to America's farms, though they did buy time and rescue many farmers from bankruptcy. It was finally the increased demands of farm produce brought by World War II that ended the difficult economic times, but at the high cost of pain and suffering that a war brings (quoted in Terkel, *Hard Times: An Oral History of the Great Depression,* 1986, pp. 217–220):

The struggles people had to go through are almost unbelievable. A man lived all his life on a given farm, it was taken away from him. One after the other. After the foreclosure, they got a deficiency judgment. Not only did he lose the farm, but it was impossible for him to get out of debt ... What's the use of having a farm sale? ... It doesn't cover the debts ... He's out of business, and it's still hung over him. First, they'd take your farm, then they took your livestock, then your farm machinery. Even your household goods. And they'd move you off. The farmers were almost united. We had penny auction sales. Some neighbor would bid a penny and give it back to the owner.

We had lots of trouble on the highway. People were determined to withhold produce from the market—livestock, cream, butter, eggs, what not. If they would dump the produce, they would force the market to a higher level. The farmers would man the highways, and cream cans were emptied in ditches and eggs dumped out. They burned the trestle bridge, so the trains wouldn't be able to haul grain ... One group tried to sell so they could live and the other group tried to keep you from selling so they could live ...

We did pass some legislation. The first thing we did was stop the power of the judges to issue deficiency judgments ... The next law we passed provided for committees in every county: adjudication committees. They'd get the person's debts all together and sit down with his creditors. They gave people a chance. People got time ...

Farmers at an auction in Hastings, Nebraska in 1940. Farmers would bid only pennies for the foreclosed farm, equipment, and livestock. Many would then give it back to the owner after the auction. (The Library of Congress.)

Through a federal program we got a farm loan. A committee of twenty-five of us drafted the first farm legislation ... We drew it up with Henry Wallace. New money was put in the farmers' hands. The Federal Government changed the whole marketing program from burning 10-cent corn to 45-cent corn. People could now see daylight and hope. It was a whole transformation of attitude. You can just imagine ... (He weeps.) ... It was Wallace who saved us, put us back on our feet ... he didn't want to write the law. He wanted the farmers themselves to write it.

We had lessons in home economics, how to make underwear out of gunny sacks, out of flour sacks. It was cooperative labor. So some good things came out of this. Sympathy toward one another was manifest ... They even took seat covers out of automobiles and re-used them for clothing or old chairs ... We had our freedom gardens and did much canning. We canned our own meat or cured it in some way. There was work to do and busy people are happy people ...

We had a boy ready to go to service. This neighbor one day told me what we needed was a damn good war, and we'd solve our agricultural problems. And I said, 'Yes, but I'd hate to pay with the price of my son.' Which we did. (He weeps.) It's too much of a price to pay.

My family had always been Republican, and I supported (Herbert Hoover). To my disappointment. I don't think the Depression was all his fault. He tried. But all his plans failed because he didn't have the Government involved. He depended on individual organizations ...

Reflections of Harry Terrell

The following reminiscence was made by Harry Terrell of Des Moines, Iowa, concerning foreclosures, penny sales, and the Farm Holiday. Foreclosure on farms was a terrifying prospect for once-proud farmers. Having few places to go, often the farm family would end up moving to town and living on handouts. Foreclosures were hard felt throughout the community. Terrell also describes the methods used to help save the farms of neighbors in the early 1930s. The process was perfectly legal but did require a level of intimidation to ensure everyone went along with it Terrell is quoted in Terkel's *Hard Times: An Oral History of the Great Depression* (1986, pp. 214–216).

Corn was going for eight cents a bushel. One county insisted on burning corn to heat the courthouse, 'cause it was cheaper than coal ...

Mortgaging farms was getting home to us. So they was having ten cent sales. They'd put up a farmer's property and have a sale and all the neighbors'd come in, and they got the idea of spending twenty-five cents for a horse. They was paying ten cents for a plow. And when it was all over, they'd all give it back to him. It was legal and anybody that bid against that thing, that was trying to get that man's land, they would be dealt with seriously, as it were ...

The Farm Holiday movement was to hold the stuff off the market, to increase the price. It saw its violence, too ...They stopped milk wagons, dumped milk. They stopped farmers hauling their hay to market. They undertook to stop the whole agriculture process. They thought if they could block the highways and access to the packing plants... They'd say: we're gonna meet, just east of Cherokee, at the fork of the road, and so on ... they were gonna stop everything from going through. And believe me, they stopped it. They had whatever was necessary to stop them with. Some of 'em had pitchforks. (Laughs.) You can fix the auto tire good with a pitchfork. There were blockades ... The country was getting up in arms about taking a man's property away from him. It was his livelihood ... The farmers broke the laws, as a last resort. There was nothing else for them to do. To see these neighbors wiped out completely, and they would just drift into towns and they would have to be fed ...

Observations on the Plight of the Farmer

Historian Arthur Schlesinger, Jr., provided a collection of first-hand observations regarding pleas for farm relief and growing farmer rebellion in rural America in *The Coming of the New Deal: The Age of Roosevelt* (1988). In a letter to Roosevelt advisor Harry Hopkins, (p. 376), a Georgia farmer wrote,

> I have Bin [sic] farming all my life. But the man I live with Has turned me loose taking my mule all my feed ...I have 7 in family. I ploud [sic] up cotton last yeare I can rent 9 acres and plant 14 in cotton But I haven't got a mule no feed ... I want to farm I have Bin [sic] on this farm 5 years. I can't get a Job So Some one said Rite [sic] you.

The plight of the small farmer, including tenant farmers and sharecroppers, was a constant issue. The New Deal farm programs were primarily aimed at larger, commercial farms that were already economically competitive. Most effort by the New Dealers was to save the productive farms. They believed helping the small family farms that were no longer competitive in the new age of farm mechanization was too costly to be worthwhile. Obviously, the policy was hard for the farming community to accept as they saw their friends and neighbors lose their farms and live on a day-to-day basis without a home.

Suggested Research Topics

- Identify what programs the local agricultural extension service might offer and how many of the programs result from New Deal policies.

- When and why did the U.S. government begin to pay farmers to not grow certain crops?

- What were the major differences in U.S. farming before 1930 and after 1940?

- What are special crop growing methods to conserve soil, such as plowing techniques and crop rotation strategies?

- What role have migrant farm workers played in the United States and what special problems have they faced?

Bibliography

Sources

Hamilton, David E. *From New Day to New Deal: American Farm Policy from Hoover to Roosevelt, 1928–33.* Chapel Hill: University of North Carolina Press, 1991.

Hurt, Douglas. *American Agriculture: A Brief History.* Ames: Iowa State University Press, 1994.

Perkins, Van L. *Crisis in Agriculture: The Agricultural Adjustment Administration and the New Deal, 1933.* Berkeley: University of California Press, 1969.

Schlesinger, Arthur M., Jr. *The Coming of the New Deal: The Age of Roosevelt.* Boston: Houghton Mifflin Company, 1988.

Terkel, Studs. *Hard Times: An Oral History of the Great Depression.* New York: Pantheon Books, 1986.

Further Reading

Agee, James, and Walker Evans. *Let Us Now Praise Famous Men: Three Tenant Families.* Boston: Houghton Mifflin Co., 2000.

Conrad, David E. *The Forgotten Farmers: The Story of Sharecroppers in the New Deal.* Westport, CN: Greenwood Press, 1982.

Dregni, Michael. ed. *This Old Farm: A Treasury of Family Farm Memories.* Stillwater, MN: Voyageur Press, 1999.

Gorman, Carol. *America's Farm Crisis.* New York: F. Watts, 1987.

Halberstadt, Hans. *The American Family Farm.* Osceola, WI: Motorbooks International, 1996.

Horwitz, Elinor L. *On the Land: American Agriculture From Past to Present.* New York: Atheneum, 1980.

McMillen, Wheeler. *Feeding Multitudes: A History of How Farmers Made America Rich.* Danville: IL: Interstate Printers and Publishers, 1981.

Roth, Charles E., and R.J. Froehlich. *The Farm Book.* New York: Harper & Row, 1975.

Stephen, R. J. *Farm Machinery.* New York: F. Watts, 1986.

See Also

Black Americans, Civilian Conservation Corps, Dust Bowl, Ethnic Relations, Global Effects, Literature, New Deal (First, and Its Critics), Supreme Court, Tennessee Valley Authority, World War II Mobilization

Food

Introduction

Many scenes of parents, children, and others struggling daily to gather enough food to eat played out during the lean years of the Great Depression. After the stock market crash of 1929, the American economy plummeted. Thousands of people lost their jobs. At this point in U.S. society, most families relied on the man to work and provide a source of income, while the mother cared for children and the household. With many men now out of work, it often became difficult for families to support themselves. Parents struggled to cut corners to make ends meet. Men, women, and at times even children, took on what jobs they could find and used all the means available to them to stretch their resources to their limits.

Imagine being the teenage son in a West Virginia coal miner's family. Your dad lost his job more than a year ago. You take turns with your sister eating, meaning you eat every other day. You hunt for dandelions on the hills with your mother. Dandelions, cornmeal cakes, and hog lard can make a feast. You worry about your dad, who has been unable to find another job and seems to have lost hope.

An unemployed factory worker and father during the Depression may have stayed away from home at mealtime so as not to eat the food his children needed. Instead, he may have gone to wait patiently in a breadline with hundreds of other men for a meal of soup, bread, and coffee. He and those waiting with him had no thought of turning the line into a protest

Chronology:

1930–1933: Breadlines and soup kitchens serve millions of meals.

1930: The electric range is created.

1930: General Foods introduces Birds Eye frosted foods to the marketplace.

1930: Jell-O introduces lime flavor to its lineup.

1930: Ruth Wakefield invents the Toll House chocolate chip cookie.

1930: A Hostess plant manager creates the Twinkie.

1931: Scattered food riots occur across the United States.

1931: New York City reports 95 cases of death by starvation.

1931: General Mills develops Bisquick.

1932: Elmer Doolin discovers the fried corn chip, known as the Frito.

1933: Prohibition ends with the repeal of the Eighteenth Amendment.

1933: J. L. Rosefield produces Skippy peanut butter.

May 12, 1933: President Franklin Roosevelt signs an act creating the Federal Emergency Relief Administration.

October 1933: Jerome Frank creates the Federal Surplus Relief Corporation.

1934: Nabisco introduces the Ritz cracker.

1935: Agricultural and relief officials create the Federal Surplus Commodities Corporation (FSCC).

1936: Bobbs-Merrill Publishing Company prints *The Joy of Cooking.*

1936: Betty Crocker's face first appears in public on bags of Gold Medal flour.

1937: Kraft introduces the "instant" macaroni and cheese dinner.

1937: Hormel introduces Spam.

1937: Margaret Rudkins establishes Pepperidge Farms, Inc.

June 1938: President Roosevelt signs the Food, Drug, and Cosmetic Act.

May 16, 1939: The FSCC begins the Food Stamp Plan.

1939: Nestlé introduces the chocolate "morsel."

1939: Vitamin tablets become a national obsession.

---

demonstration. Many men felt that they were responsible for providing for their families, and some may even have felt that they were to blame for the problems that had befallen them.

A middle-class mother whose family income was greatly reduced due to the Depression still needed to find ways to provide her family with satisfying meals that fulfilled basic food needs. She would "make do" using a limited number of foodstuffs kept in the pantry, grown in the garden, or perhaps obtained from the local butcher or even a chain food store. Creative cooks could make a pot roast last as a base for meals for the entire week. Meal portions were stretched with the inclusion of gravy, potatoes, biscuits, and macaroni. Newly famous cooks and their cookbooks, such as Fannie Farmer's *The Boston Cooking School Cookbook* and Irma Rombauer's *The Joy of Cooking,* helped mothers and others struggling to put food on the table plan simple, nutritious meals. It was not

uncommon for families to invite those less fortunate for Sunday dinner.

Imagine that you are a grandfather or grandmother who works diligently growing food in the garden and canning in the kitchen to help out your family. The colorful array of fruit and vegetable jars lined up on the pantry shelves is a constant source of pride for you through the winter months. You are thankful you do not live in the Midwest Dust Bowl, where gardens are drying up.

Stories like these played out across America during the Great Depression of the 1930s. Breadlines, "making do," and subsistence gardens were all part of the Depression food culture. Most families—the 70 to 75 percent that still had income—were able to "make do," but the faces and stories of the desperately hungry made lasting impressions on all Americans. As quickly as it could, the administration of President Franklin Delano Roosevelt (served 1933–1945) created government relief agencies to distribute surplus farm foods to the needy. Food programs stemming from the creation of these relief agencies persist into the twenty-first century. Food Stamps and the protections of the Food and Drug Administration are two examples of programs that sprung from events of the 1930s Depression.

Breadlines, relief agencies, and "making do," however, were not the whole story of the struggle for sustenance during the Depression. A host of new processed foods were introduced during the decade. The American entrepreneur, always ready to try something new in hopes of making more money for a better living, developed inexpensive, quality foods such as meat in a can. Fun, cheap snacks, such as fried corn chips or spongy little cakes with a filling, were also created. Increasing numbers of food chain stores stocked the mass-marketed, processed foods. Food entrepreneurs became millionaires during the Depression, and people searching to get the most out of what money they had were able to purchase inexpensive foods.

The short and long term health implications of those unemployed and eating at soup kitchens, or even for those simply cutting back on some necessities to make budgets stretch, has been little explored or recorded. Larger health concerns came from the poor sanitary conditions in overcrowded city slums and rural shanties. Nutrition actually improved for those who could still afford the new innovations for the kitchen, such as modern refrigerators and the new products available in the markets. Perhaps the most lasting legacy of the 1930s for most Americans was their diligence in eating every last bite on their plate.

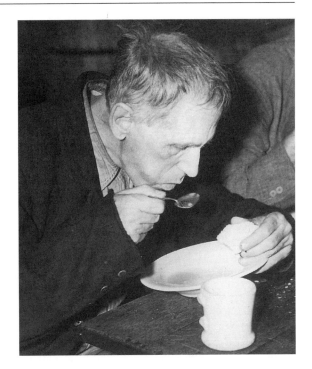

An unemployed man eats a meal in the Volunteers of America Soup Kitchen in Washington, DC. For many Americans impoverished by the Great Depression, the soup kitchen was the only place for them to get a hot, nutritious meal. (FDR Library.)

Issue Summary

The Desperately Hungry

Following the stock market crash of 1929 and the onset of the Great Depression, factories began to close. Many workers lost their jobs. The newly unemployed looked on helplessly as their resources dried up and their families went hungry. Between 1929 and 1933, unemployment steadily grew from only 3.2 percent of the labor force in 1929, to 8.7 percent in 1930, almost 16 percent in 1931, over 23 percent in 1932, and 25 percent in 1933. More than 4.3 million people were unemployed in 1930. At the height of the Depression, about 13 to 15 million individuals were unemployed, many for the first time in their lives. It became difficult for many families to "make do."

As people's diets deteriorated, malnutrition became more common. Thousands lined up at soup kitchens and in breadlines in quiet desperation. The term "soup kitchen" was originally applied to army kitchens in the mid-nineteenth century, but by the later nineteenth century was applied to kitchens of charitable organizations where free soup and bread were served to the poor and unemployed. A common feature of the Great Depression, soup kitchens have continued in the United States into the twenty-first century, but they often are officially known by other names, such as emergency food programs. The term breadline, on the other hand, was not a familiar term in the United States until 1900. Breadlines became more of a unique feature of the Great Depression as people lined up on city sidewalks to receive loaves of bread and other food from charitable organizations.

The prevailing belief of the 1930s, known as the American Creed, was that people were responsible for their own fates. During the Depression there existed a denial or general lack of recognition of the national, social, or economic forces that could be affecting millions of people despite their own individual actions or skills. A strong social stigma was therefore attached to going to soup kitchens or breadlines for assistance. According to the creed, being needy meant that some serious character flaw existed.

Assisting Those in Need

Handouts were simple but filling—stew and bread; soup, bread and coffee; beans, bread and coffee; or sandwiches and coffee. The Red Cross, Salvation Army, Catholic charities, fraternal orders, hospitals, newspapers, and individuals operated the breadlines. One of the most famous soup kitchens opened on South State Street in Chicago in 1930. Run by gangster Al Capone, it served three meals a day. On Thanksgiving Day of 1930 alone, Capone's kitchen served five thousand meals. By early 1931 New York City had 82 breadlines, serving approximately eighty-five thousand meals each day.

Most Americans remained employed, though perhaps at decreased wages, but the increasing visibility of breadlines, soup kitchens, shanty towns, and homeless brought alarm to the nation. Many of those still following more normal daily routines soberly considered that it could soon be them standing in relief lines if the economic conditions deteriorated further. So, although those experiencing various degrees of hunger were less than one-fourth of the work force, their plight was highly visible and unsettling to many of the rest. The upper class still enjoyed fine cuisine, and the broad middle and working classes were able to avoid breadlines, despite the need to make some adjustments to their diets.

As people were unable to find new work and unemployment increased, so did hunger. The social thinking of the time was that private charity should care for the hungry. President Herbert Hoover (served 1929–1933) and state governors urged Americans to donate to the Red Cross and to other charitable organizations. Local county authorities were responsible for any government relief efforts and, during the winter of 1931–1932, some states made grants to local authorities to help handle costs. All of these efforts, however, proved to be inadequate.

One interesting aspect of the unemployment and hunger problems during the Depression was that, as historic photographs show, there were very few women in the cities' breadlines. Standing for hours in long lines for food assistance was more a man's role, while the wife tended to home and children. A strong social stigma also existed regarding women standing in relief lines. Author Meridel Le Sueur's dramatic description in her book *Women on the Breadlines* (1984), highlights this social phenomenon:

> ....[T]oo timid to get in breadlines... they simply faint on the street from privations [deprived of food], without saying a word to anyone. A woman will shut herself up

in a room until it is taken away from her, and eat a cracker a day and be as quiet as a mouse so there are no social statistics concerning her... unless she has dependents, [she] will go for weeks verging on starvation....

Fending Off Starvation

In New York City in 1931, 95 cases of death (men, women, and children) due to starvation were reported. The undernourished also fell victim to diseases more easily than those with access to adequate food supplies. At the time there was no way to calculate the number of people who died from malnutrition-related diseases such as tuberculosis and dysentery.

Sad and desperate stories were reported across the nation. In 1930 a Pennsylvania man caught stealing a loaf of bread for his four hungry children felt so ashamed that he hung himself in his basement. Fathers kept themselves and older children out of their living quarters when younger children were fed to avoid being tempted to literally grab food from the mouths of babies. Children took turns eating from day to day and stayed in bed to conserve calories. The systematic stealing of food was sometimes a family affair, with children and adults assigned certain shoplifting duties for necessary foods. Investigations of city garbage dumps revealed in Chicago and New York City that, when city garbage trucks unloaded, forty to fifty people would begin digging with sticks or hands for morsels of food. Men fought over the garbage in barrels behind city restaurants. People scoured ship docks for any edible scraps.

Food riots erupted in several states. Unemployed Virginia miners smashed shop windows, filled baskets with food, and fought their way back out onto the street. Hundreds of sharecroppers and tenant farmers, who had been put off of the land they had worked but did not own, marched into England, Arkansas. They harassed Red Cross officials until enough food was handed out to satisfy them. A group of Minneapolis working class women broke windows of a store and raided the shelves, but left notes saying they would pay as soon as they could. Similar food riots occurred in Michigan, Oklahoma, and in San Francisco, California.

Some of the most desperate rural areas were the hills of Kentucky and West Virginia, where milk was considered medicine by some. The rural hungry searched for such wild greens as dandelions. Ground corncobs, cornmeal, and hog lard (fat) rounded out their meals. The family with a cow who gave milk had a precious possession.

The Paradox of Food and Hunger

By 1933 statistics revealed that at least 25 percent of the labor force was unemployed—13 to 15 million individuals. It was estimated that those unemployed were responsible for feeding approximately 30 million hungry family members. As the situation worsened, a paradox arose in America. While the destitute ate their meals at garbage cans, American farmers still produced surpluses of crops and livestock.

Farmers, however, were not completely unaffected. They suffered as prices for their goods fell drastically low due to consumers' inability to pay for the goods they demanded. The market for farmers' goods shrank, but farming production did not. Additionally, no efficient structure existed to get surpluses into the hands of charitable organizations and local government agencies.

In California the hungry saw food being destroyed all around them. In 1932, in the Imperial Valley alone, 2.8 million watermelons, 1.4 million crates of cantaloupes, and 700,000 lugs of tomatoes were destroyed because they could not be sold. In Orange County, huge mounds of oranges were covered with thick oil to stop pilfering. The fruit rotted in full view of people who needed them.

The Government Responds

President Franklin D. Roosevelt, who had taken office in March 1933, introduced a broad range of federal programs designed to bring relief and economic recovery to a struggling nation. The term New Deal came from Roosevelt's nomination acceptance speech at the Democratic National Convention in June 1932 and came to represent a whole new way that government responded to the needs of its citizens. The broad range of legislation and federal programs through most of the 1930s would touch just about every aspect of peoples' daily lives.

During the first one hundred days of his administration, from March to June 1933, President Roosevelt pushed through Congress an amazing amount of legislation. This period would mark the beginning of the New Deal. In the third month of that period, on May 12, Roosevelt signed into law the Agricultural Adjustment Act. The law created the Agricultural Adjustment Administration (AAA). The AAA was not directly designed to help feed the needy but rather to help farmers get better prices for their crops and reduce their growing surpluses of produce. Combined with other programs, however, the AAA would provide the foodstuffs that other agencies could distribute to the hungry.

Federal Emergency Relief Administration (FERA)

More directly aimed at hunger relief was another act Roosevelt signed on May 12 creating the Federal Emergency Relief Administration (FERA). FERA was created to provide several avenues of relief, including cash payments directly to city and state work relief programs. FERA also tackled federal work projects such as building hospitals, roads, and bridges, and helped states that had already begun such projects. Presidential support of existing local relief programs would sustain ongoing food relief projects and the works program would put money in the hands of the unemployed to purchase food. Roosevelt appointed Harry L. Hopkins to head FERA. He directed Hopkins to relieve suffering as quickly as possible and to ignore local and state politicians who tried to control the relief process.

Oddly, the AAA and the FERA had almost opposite missions. The AAA was designed to reduce food supplies in order to increase farm prices. FERA was designed to provide immediate relief to the needy including the hungry. A link was needed between the two programs.

Federal Surplus Relief Corporation

In September 1933 President Roosevelt channeled $75 million to FERA to purchase surplus food. Four weeks later, Jerome Frank, a lawyer appointed as counsel for the AAA, established the Federal Surplus Relief Corporation (FSRC). The FSRC's president would be Harry L. Hopkins, who continued to serve as head of FERA.

The FSRC would operate as a subsidiary of FERA, serving as a go-between for FERA and the AAA. The FSRC's purpose was to direct relief for the hungry. It took agricultural surpluses—pork, butter, flour, syrup, and cotton among others—and transported them to state emergency relief officials, who directed them into the hands of the needy. After considerable success in November 1935, the FSRC closed as it had been designed to do in the original legislation. Its success and the continuing need for food distribution led quickly to further action. Agricultural and relief officials arranged to continue the food distribution program by creating the Federal Surplus Commodities Corporation (FSCC). The FSCC would continue the effort of purchasing surplus food from farmers to distribute to the hungry and needy. The FSRC's chief legacy was that it began a pattern of federal food distribution. Its program was a primary example of New Deal humanitarian concern. The FSCC food programs led to the later twentieth century programs of school lunches and food stamps.

Food Stamp Plan

The FSCC established the first Food Stamp Plan on May 16, 1939, to continue to provide surplus agricultural products to the needy. The

Christmas dinner consists of potatoes, cabbage, and pie for these children in Iowa in 1936. Although most Americans could "make do" during the Depression, the poorest had to rely on government relief and whatever they could grow in their gardens. (The Library of Congress.)

Food Stamp Plan's goals were to improve the diets of those in need and create an increased demand for various foods. It was hoped the increased demand for foods would raise the incomes of farmers.

To participate in the plan, individuals had to be enrolled in relief programs, Works Progress Administration (WPA) workers, or other needy people specifically identified by relief agencies. Participants could purchase "orange stamps" in amounts roughly equal to their normal expenditure for food. Many purchased between $1.00 and $1.50 worth of "orange stamps" for each family member for each week. For every $1.00 in orange stamps purchased, they received 50¢ worth of "blue stamps" as a bonus. The blue stamps could only be used to buy agricultural goods declared as surplus by the Secretary of Agriculture.

The plan was established in one hundred cities by 1940. Approximately four million people participated in this experimental program while it existed. Industrial mobilization in preparation for World War II (1939–1945), however, soon brought full employment as well as the elimination of food surpluses. As a result, the food stamp program was cancelled but revived again by 1961. Through the remainder of the twentieth century, the food stamp program remained

the primary means for the government to provide food assistance to the low-income and needy citizens. It continued to lessen farm surplus problems while improving the diets of people in poverty.

Making Do

Although the plight of the desperately poor and hungry made lasting impressions on all Americans, 70 to 75 percent of families still had income and concentrated on "making do." During the Depression years of the 1930s, women worked hard to meet their families' basic food needs. Meals had simple ingredients and were filling. These basic foods are described below.

As food historians and ordinary Americans look back on the Depression years, they frequently use the terms "creative" or "resourceful" to describe the cooking of mothers and grandmothers who found ways to make satisfying fare out of some unusual ingredients. Nothing edible was ever thrown out or wasted. Leftovers always reappeared over the next few days. Sunday's roast would be Monday's stew, or hash, then Tuesday's vegetable beef soup, and so on. Liquid from jars or cans of vegetables became a base for soup, and juice from canned fruit could be thickened and poured over bread and cakes. Indeed, homemakers found many ways to "make do."

Eggs provided an important source of protein for Depression families and were an important item when "making do." Eggs from the hen house were always plentiful. Even when the weather became too hot for crops, the hens continued to scratch for seed and bugs, and they kept laying eggs. Chickens were kept not only on farms but also in suburban back yards. Both rural and urban women learned to use eggs in every imaginable way. Eggs were "dropped" (into boiling water), scrambled, beaten into omelets, used in a variety of breads and cakes, mixed into meat, potato and onion dishes, and used for pasta making.

Another product that remained popular during the Depression was coffee. In the late 1920s and early 1930s coffee overproduction in South America caused coffee prices to slide downward. In the United States the price of coffee fell from 22¢ per pound to 8¢ per pound. Despite the lower costs, many people still could not spend 8¢ on the luxury of coffee or, if they did, they found ways to make it last by mixing it with other ingredients. For example, roasted wheat kernels could be mixed with coffee as a coffee extender or could be substituted entirely and perked as if they were the real thing. An "extender" is any foodstuff added to another to make it last longer.

Tea also maintained its popularity. A popular tea at the time was hot lemon water. Lemon tea also served as a common remedy for a cough and the congestion of a cold. Another favorite treat was an occasional cup of hot chocolate made from cocoa powder, sugar, canned milk, and hot water.

Casseroles proved to be popular and filling fare at Depression tables. A handful of this, plus some leftovers of that, and a family could be fed a nourishing and filling meal. Casseroles were budget stretchers, as more homemade noodles, potatoes, rice, onions, beans, and/or vegetables could be added to stretch the life of the casserole.

Although recipes appeared in cookbooks as early as the late nineteenth century, food historians point to the Depression as the point in time where the popularization of macaroni and cheese casserole occurred. It was filling, easy to make, and cheap. Kraft foods introduced its packaged seven-minute elbow macaroni and cheese dinner in the 1930s. Boxed macaroni and cheese dinners continued to provide economical meals throughout the twentieth century.

Cracklings are the by-product of rendered lard, or fat, and were commonly used in households where meals were feeling the pinch of lean economic times.

At a Glance
Aunt Sammy

Aunt Sammy was a fictional female counterpart to the U.S. government's Uncle Sam. Beginning in 1926 and running until 1944, the U.S. Department of Agriculture broadcast on the radio a daily 15-minute home economics program coast to coast. A female voice, known as Aunt Sammy, anchored the program. In a friendly voice, Aunt Sammy taught women how to stretch their dollars in cooking meals, sewing, and even plumbing. Aunt Sammy's money saving recipes were so popular that they were bound into a cookbook that sold over one million copies during the Depression.

To render lard means to cook lard for a long time. The lard is then put into a press and squeezed. The result is called crackling. As a menu extender, crackling could be mixed with bread or potatoes. Sometimes it was mixed with flour, baked on a cookie sheet, and eaten as a bread substitute.

Buttermilk was considered to be a staple food during the Depression. Women used it for everything from breakfast pancakes to breads and biscuits to buttermilk soup to simply drinking it. Farmers even used it for livestock feed. Butter was often churned at home, and the by-product was buttermilk. The buttermilk was chilled in an icebox, a cellar, or hung in a pail in the well and served as a beverage with meals. If a family couldn't churn it themselves, they took a bucket and purchased it at the local creamery. Creameries, however, often gave buttermilk away for free. In baking, buttermilk made everything lighter, moister, and added a delicious flavor. Buttermilk nutritionally compares with modern low-fat yogurt.

In Depression homes soup was served warm and was often thick and nutritious. Big families could be fed with soups from leftover meats, beans, and homegrown vegetables. Homemakers made many varieties of soup from available foods. The results included split pea, chicken-rice, potato-onion, bean, hamburger, and all vegetable. Dumplings were a filling addition to complement the soup. For some families, soup was the evening meal every night.

Beans—navy, pinto, white, black-eyed—were a good substitute for meat during the Depression and were even an actual lifesaver in the 1930s. Highly nutritious, beans of all varieties were baked, used as fillers for sandwiches, made into bean cakes, and included as chief ingredients in hardy soups. Boston baked beans were navy beans baked with molasses and leftover bacon, ham, or salt pork. Bean sandwiches consisted of bread spread with cooked beans and a slice of tomato and lettuce, if available. Bean cakes were mashed beans mixed with flour and fried in lard.

Bread in the Depression

By 1932 a bag of flour sold for 16¢, down almost 40 percent in the three years since the stock market crash of 1929. A loaf of bread sold for 5 to 10¢, compared to its pre-Depression price of 7¢. Bread was a vital part of keeping a family fed. Everyone tried to keep flour and cornmeal in the pantry. With these two staples a family could always have something to eat. If no butter was available, cooks would spread lard on bread. Bread was frequently served with toppings, including honey, corn syrup, or fruit syrups. Fruit syrups were often intended by the cook to be jelly, but for lack of enough sugar turned out runny and hence were pronounced syrups. A variety of breads were filling items at every meal. Biscuits would be used for breakfast with honey or syrup, as sandwich bread for lunch, or with gravy poured over them for dinner.

Johnny cake and corn bread were standard bread favorites. According to Patricia R. Wagner in *Depression Era Recipes,* Johnny cake, a descendent of recipes from England, got its name from the eastern United States. It tasted like sweet corn bread. United States. Since the cake kept well, men would take it along when traveling. New Englanders don't always pronounce the letter "R" when it falls in the middle of a sentence, so "journey cake" became "jou'ney cake," and eventually "johnny cake."

Midwestern and southwestern cornbread, slightly less rich than Johnny cake, was a direct descendent of Indian ashcake. Ashcake was mixture of cornmeal and water, formed into cakes, and baked in the cinders of prairie camp fires.

Homemakers always tried to have plenty of fresh-baked bread on hand during the Depression. Loaves of white or whole wheat bread were often prepared in batches, with perhaps the last loaf used for cinnamon rolls for children coming home from school. Another favorite variation of bread was the dumpling. Dumplings were made of eggs and flour, then boiled in water.

Finding Meat

Meat was more of a scarcity and was not served at every Depression meal. When used, it was often combined with potatoes, onions, rice, macaroni, biscuits, and other extenders. "Loafs" were popular meat stretchers and remained prevalent on dinner tables into the twenty-first century. Sunday meatloaf was made with ground beef; salmon loaf with cannon salmon; ham loaf, made with ground pork, was popular in southern states; and venison loaf was prepared in areas with abundant deer.

Families living near hunting and fishing sources were able to supplement their Depression era diets with highly desirable meat sources. Game included deer, squirrels, ground hogs, raccoons, and rabbits. Rabbits were eaten by so many people that they were dubbed "Hoover Hogs," after President Herbert Hoover. Fish fries were popular in areas where lakes and rivers could be fished. Fresh fish were seasoned, rolled in a flour-milk batter, and fried in lard.

In areas of the west where cattle and hogs remained plentiful, families felt the effects of the Depression less. The first freeze of the season meant it was time to butcher a cow or hog. Homemakers would can part of the meat, and the rest would be wrapped in paper and frozen outside until needed.

Putting meat into the family diet of the inner city poor called for innovative measures. Too ashamed and self-conscious of their plight, Chicago parents would send their children to the butcher for bones for the make-believe family dog. The butcher would give them large meaty bones that made a filling soup. The meat would be saved for the next day's hash. Of course, the make-believe family cat also got hungry so the kids went back to the butcher for liver. Liver, onions, potatoes, and gravy made for a hearty meal.

Another butcher by-product to be dealt with cleverly was bundles of chicken feet. Boiling chicken feet with greens, which could be obtained even in the city, resulted in a good pot of soup. The feet were discarded before serving, but the leftover broth was good for cooking cereal products such as farina and cracked wheat.

Fried chicken was a Sunday dinner main course for many families during Depression times. If you neither raised chickens nor had any money to buy one, you could substitute with the recipe "City Chickens," shared by Beverly Carman of Broadway, New Jersey, in Karen Thibodeau's book *Dining During the Depression.* City chickens were ground veal and pork, shaped around Popsicle sticks into the form of drumsticks, rolled in cornflakes, and fried and baked until golden brown.

A husband and wife pull beets from their garden in Sheridan County, Kansas. The seed for the garden was provided by a FSA program in the former Dust Bowl. (*The Library of Congress.*)

Growing Vegetables

Many families of the 1930s say their gardens got them through the Depression. Gardens were tended on farms, in suburban backyards, and in vacant lots and parks in the cities. Produce was eaten fresh or "put up," meaning it was canned, pickled, or dried. Much of the same produce found in contemporary gardens was also planted in Depression gardens. The difference between the two is that Depression gardens were most often a means of survival, while contemporary gardens are largely hobbies. Common vegetables planted during the Depression were potatoes, onions, corn, beans, cabbage, beets, peas, cucumbers, green peppers, carrots, turnips, greens such as spinach, turnips, celery, and, in the warmer southern states, black-eyed peas and okra.

When readied for the table, in addition to being eaten raw, vegetables were boiled, baked, fried, stewed, or creamed. A bit of salt pork or bacon was frequently used for flavoring. Vegetables were chief ingredients in soups and casseroles.

Between 1933 and 1937, much of America's heartland suffered drought and severe dust storms. The season of spring, with its nurturing rainfall, could no longer be depended upon. In the event that spring remained a dry season, precious water had to be hauled in from lakes and rivers to grow crops. Many gardens failed. Although wild greens became quite popular in many areas, they became survival food for those in drought areas. Unemployed miners and their families in the hills of Kentucky and West Virginia, for example, ate wild greens to stave off hunger. Dandelions were gathered and cooked with bacon or side pork. Together with eggs and potatoes, if available, a wholesome dinner could be prepared.

Making Do at Breakfast

Breakfast was the meal most likely to be skipped by many in the Depression. Sometimes coffee, tea, or hot milk was breakfast. Cereals were generally cooked, as oatmeal, with raisins added as a special treat. Corn was plentiful and ground into cornmeal. Cornmeal mush was served plain, fried, or with milk and syrup.

Milk toast, another favorite Depression breakfast, included old bread or toast, sugar and cinnamon, and warm milk poured over. If no milk was available, coffee was used. Buttermilk pancakes were also cheap, filling, and very popular.

Dessert

The custom of taking dessert at the end of a meal continued through the Depression for many families. What kind of dessert was served often depended on where you lived. Those on farms not affected by the severe drought in the southern Great Plains region generally had lots of eggs, milk, butter, and cream for custards and puddings. Many city residents, however, found eggs and cream too scarce to use on an everyday basis. Rice, raisins, and milk became the pudding of the city. Many city residents received bags of rice and raisins from government surplus. In regions such as the Northwest, where fruits and berries grew abundantly, desserts such as berry cobblers and baked pears were daily treats. Pies could be made with fruit and other handy items, using substituted ingredients—sour cream for butter; honey or brown sugar for white sugar; even Ritz crackers in place of apples. Sour cream raisin pies were a favorite. Substitutions like these were common. For instance, if there was no sour cream on hand, one tablespoon of vinegar added to milk produced a good substitute.

As more cooks acquired electric mixers, chiffon pies—pumpkin, lemon, chocolate, pineapple—became the rage. All began with a gelatin "custard" and were topped with fluffy, stiffly beaten egg whites.

A delicious pie made from ingredients usually found in the kitchen was chess pie, a southern favorite. There are two reported stories as to how it got its name: (1) when children came home from school they asked their mom what she was baking. "Jess' pie" she replied. "Jess' pie" became chess pie; and (2) the pie's ingredients allowed it to be kept in a pie chest for days, hence chess pie.

Americans' love of cake did not diminish during the Depression. Fueled by the arrival of both the electric range and the mixer, cake baking continued. Perhaps no other type of recipe was more experimented with due to scarcity of ingredients, however, than the cake recipe. Some cakes were for very special occasions, and others were for filling up stomachs. Depression cakes, especially those baked by urban residents, often cut back dramatically on milk, eggs, and butter. An example was the "milkless, eggless, butterless cake," with main ingredients consisting of brown sugar and flour. This cake was likely developed during the shortages of World War I (1914–1918). In fact, other recipe books called it "war cake." Sugar was the cheapest, quickest form of energy, and it was saved for the soldiers. Cooks at home learned to use brown sugar, molasses, corn syrup, or honey for sweeteners. For butter they substituted lard, which generally came from bacon fat or rendered chicken fat. The same basic recipe resurfaced as Depression cake in the 1930s, and again as wartime cake during World War II.

For the chocolate lovers there was the 1937 chocolate mayonnaise cake, invented by the wife of a Hell-mann's mayonnaise company salesman. The recipe substituted Hellmann's mayonnaise for butter and milk. Another interesting twist on ingredients for Depression era cakes was the relatively common cinnamon mystery cake, which included the contents of a can of tomato soup, and the gum drop fruit cake. Applesauce cake was yet another way to use ingredients from the pantry and cut down on eggs, sugar, and butter. At the other end of the spectrum was the decadent Lady Baltimore cake, an old Charleston, South Carolina, recipe full of eggs, butter, sugar, milk, and a nutty filling. It was served in the homes of the wealthy, fine restaurants, and the middle class enjoyed it on very special occasions.

To top off a cake, the simple seven-minute icing appeared in the 1930s, and its popularity coincided with the introduction of the electric mixer. The icing is made with sugar, water, a dash of salt, egg whites beaten about seven minutes until stiff, and vanilla. Seven-minute icing survived well past the Depression.

No discussion of Depression cake could be complete without mention of the Hostess Twinkie. Introduced in 1930, the creme-filled sponge cake cost one nickel and delighted young and old. As of the beginning of the twenty-first century, it remained a popular snack food.

Finally, Depression era children pooled their pennies to buy the 5¢ twin Popsicle that had been introduced earlier in 1924. They pulled it apart to share, then checked the stick to see if it had "free" stamped on it. If so, they got another Popsicle for free. The Popsicle sticks went home for mothers to use or were used in other creative ways by the children.

Gardening

During the 1920s many Americans sought employment opportunities in the central cities, but chose to live in the suburbs. Suburban gardening flourished. Popular garden magazines struggled with such dilemmas as how to garden without stable manure. Newspapers added gardening as a regular feature of their weekend editions. Many affluent and leisured Americans of the 1920s, however, ceased to rely on their gardens for a chief food source. Instead, they drove their Oldsmobile or Model T to the local store for food. Yet the small town and country poor still grew food to preserve their standard of living. Homemakers in rural areas depended on their gardens to supply large amounts of their food. Through preparing fresh dishes and preserving food, everything that grew in their gardens was used.

After 1929 the hard times of the Depression turned many of the newly affluent, the middle class, and the rapidly increasing numbers of unemployed back to their gardens. With country clubs, restaurants, and travel beyond the family budget, Americans in suburbia could still pick up their gardening tools. Whether as a rediscovered simple pastime, or as sustenance for the family, vegetable gardening regained widespread popularity.

"Back to the land" movements, supported by President Roosevelt and his administration, became popular. Roosevelt and others firmly believed the human spirit could best prosper in the country and not in the city. Many middle-class persons who still lived in the central cities of the Northeast, disillusioned seeing the urban breadlines, fled to the country seeking the security of food and shelter. They were determined to try their hand at subsistence farming. In the first three years of the 1930s, more than one million central city residents moved to country homesteads. Some were able to adequately survive with their new rural lifestyle, but most failed and suffered economically along with their city peers.

For those left in the cities, subsistence gardening reemerged to help the unemployed. In Detroit, Michigan, employees made monthly contributions from their salaries to raise $10,000 to finance a free garden program. The city plowed up school property and vacant lots, creating five thousand garden plots. Across America, from California to Maine, welfare garden plots blossomed as a means of supplying food and work for the unemployed. By 1934 seventy thousand subsistence gardens yielded approximately $2.8 million worth of food to persons on relief. New York City, by 1935, had welfare garden plots in every borough except Manhattan, to feed both the bodies and spirits of the poor. At the close of the 1930s, the looming world war continued to fuel the popularity of gardening. With the outbreak of war in Europe during 1939, although food shortages were no longer prevalent in America, gardening continued to offer psychological comfort to Americans.

Preserving the Garden's Harvest Food from the 1930s garden was never wasted. Canning, pickling, and drying were the preserving practices of choice for both rural and suburban residents. Mildred B. relayed her experiences in canning during the Depression in Thacker's *Recipes and Remembrances of the Great Depression* (1993):

> We canned corn and tomatoes. You poured boiling water over the tomatoes and the skins slipped right off. The corn had to be cut off the cobs with the big butcher knife and I hated that part. My hands would ache by the end of the day. But it was worth it. Those half gallon jars of yellow corn and red tomatoes sure looked good setting on the shelves of the fruit cellar.

Green beans—commonly referred to as string beans during the Depression—and cut corn were the commonly canned vegetables. Even greens such as dandelion leaves, spinach, Swiss chard, and collards were regularly canned. Fruit such as peaches, pears, tomatoes, and cherries, and berries including strawberries, blackberries, elderberries, raspberries, gooseberries, and currants, kept summer and fall canners busy.

Thick canning syrups of sugar and water were prepared and poured in jars with the fruit and berries. Especially popular were spicy peaches with brown sugar, cinnamon, and cloves. Proudly placed in the pantry or fruit cellar, spicy peaches appeared on Sunday dinner tables and at holidays. Jellies made from fruit and berries and apple butter filled every extra jar. In colder states vegetables that didn't can well could be stored outside between layers of soil and straw through the winter.

Homemakers in the Depression raised the pickling of cucumbers to an art. Other vegetables that were also pickled were carrots, beans, cauliflower, onions, okra, squash, beets, asparagus, and even brussels sprouts. Relish—mixtures of chopped vegetables—provided spice to dinners through the winters. Pickling is a way to preserve food by fully submerging the food in a strong salt or acidic solution, such as vinegar or lemon juice. Most any kind of spice can be added to enhance the flavor of the pickled food. The solution keeps the normal decaying processes from occurring.

Drying was another basic preserving method. The food is heated inside something with plenty of air circulation to get rid of any moisture. In warm and dry climates, fruits that contain lots of natural sugar to prevent decay can be sun-dried. Successful drying retains much of the original nutrition. Dried foods remain good for long periods of time, even months or years.

Entrepreneurs

Although times were difficult, cleverness and creativity still flowed in the veins of Americans. In the 1930s the inventiveness of American entrepreneurs grew. To be an entrepreneur means to be an individual willing to try new approaches and take the risks of organizing and managing new enterprises. Products introduced by food entrepreneurs of the 1930s are familiar to contemporary families. Some of those products include Fritos, Kool Aid, Skippy peanut butter, Spam, Pepperidge Farm baked goods, Toll House chocolate chip cookies, and Birds' Eye frozen foods.

Fritos Many men took up the occupation of traveling salesmen in the 1920s and 1930s. Elmer Doolin

A Spam advertisement from the late 1930s. Originally called Hormel Spiced Ham, it was a highly popular food during the late-Depression years and beyond. (The Advertising Archive Ltd. Reproduced by permission.)

was an ice cream traveling salesman in 1932. Moving through Texas he stopped for lunch at a San Antonio sandwich shop and happened to purchase a bag of fried corn chips for a nickel. Astounded by their unusual and irresistible flavor, he sought out the maker of the delicious chip. The maker turned out to be a Mexican man eager to go home to Mexico. For $100 he agreed to sell Doolin his corn chip recipe and the Frito name. Frito means "fried" in Spanish. One hundred dollars, however, was a lot of money in the depths of the Depression. Doolin's mother sold her wedding ring to raise the money.

Doolin began selling Fritos from his Model T and gradually expanded his territory. At first, he made about two dollars per day selling the inexpensive treat. Soon it was Doolin's good fortune to connect with potato chip king Herman W. Lay. With Lay's distribution help, Fritos were soon being munched from coast to coast, and the brand Frito-Lay was launched.

Kool Aid Following its introduction in 1927, by 1929 Kool-Aid had become a huge hit and was available across the country. Mothers liked how Kool-Aid fit their Depression-times budget and provided children a treat.

Kool-Aid was cheap, simple to make, and easy to store. Favorite flavors were cherry, grape, lemonade, and tropical punch. Edwin E. Perkins, the inventor of Kool-Aid, abandoned all of his other products to concentrate on keeping up with the demand. Net sales reached close to $4 million by 1936, making Perkins a very wealthy man amid the worst years of the Depression.

Spam and Skippy Inexpensive quality foods were in high demand. Spam and Skippy peanut butter became classic examples of foods that met that demand. In the mid-1930s, a Hormel Company executive acquired several thousand pounds of pork shoulder. He quickly needed a creative way to use the pork and decided to chop it up with ham, add spice, and can it with a gelatin preservative. Hormel realized it had a tasty, inexpensive meat product that was likely to be very popular with consumers. A contraction of "spice and ham," Spam received its name in a 1937, $100 naming contest. The meat in a can was an instant hit. Spam recipes emerged, it became a staple for soldiers during World War II, and millions of cans per year continued to be sold in the beginning of the twenty-first century.

Another product that has endured into contemporary times is Skippy peanut butter. In the 1920s J.L. Rosefield developed a new process that kept peanut butter from separating out into oil and peanut meat. By 1933 Rosefield was producing his own brand of peanut butter in red, white, and blue tins. He called it Skippy peanut butter. Mothers realized they had an affordable, nutritious food that their children loved, and the product retained its popularity long past the Depression's end.

Pepperidge Farm Soft white American bread and peanut butter, or bread and Spam, became basic sandwiches in the 1930s. When the family doctor of Margaret Rudkin, however, advised her to keep processed foods from her allergic son, she set out to improve on the lifeless and additive-filled white bread that had become so popular in the United States. The young Connecticut homemaker began experimenting with stone ground, whole wheat flour, whole milk, honey, molasses, and butter. Her home baking expertise attracted her doctor's other patients and his colleagues. Her commitment to wholesome goodness never wavered, and eventually the company known as Pepperidge Farm emerged. Rudkin assumed some customers would pay up to three times the 1930s going rate for a loaf of bread. She was correct. Enough customers paid 30¢ per loaf that her business thrived and expanded.

Toll House Chocolate Chip Cookies Another famous baker of the time was Ruth Wakefield. Wakefield baked the popular Butter Drop Do cookie at her Toll House Inn near Whitman, Massachusetts, a Boston suburb. In the midst of baking a batch in 1930 she discovered she was out of nuts. Frantically, with guests waiting, she chopped up semisweet chocolate bars and dumped the pieces into the cookies in place of nuts. Amazed that the chocolate morsels did not melt in the oven, she named the cookies Chocolate Crispies before later renaming them Toll House Chocolate Crunch Cookies. Guests loved them, and she included them in her 1930 cookbook, *Ruth Wakefield's Toll House Cook Book.* The recipe called for two bars of Nestlé yellow label chocolate, semi-sweet, cut into pea size pieces. Suddenly, sales of the chocolate bar rose dramatically in the Boston area, and a Nestlé representative visited Wakefield to see what was going on. Nestlé began scoring (making grooves across the surface so it will break into smaller pieces easier) its bars and including a small chopper in the package to break them into pieces. In 1939 Nestlé introduced chocolate morsels, and Wakefield signed a forty-year contract to print her recipe on the back of every package of morsels. The morsels and the cookie recipe, like Pepperidge Farm, remain popular in contemporary times, and Wakefield became yet another American food entrepreneur who became a millionaire during the Depression.

Birds Eye Frozen Food Clarence Birdseye from Brooklyn, New York, is known as the "father of the frozen food industry." He managed to launch this creative new line of food during the Depression. As a young scientist Birdseye traveled to Labrador, a peninsula in Canada, where he observed that fish "frozen before you could get them off a hook" would taste perfectly fresh when cooked weeks later. Birdseye experimented with freezing foods throughout the 1920s. He found that the quicker foods were frozen, and the lower the temperature at which they were frozen the better the quality was when cooked. Quick freezing worked not only for meats, but also for fruits and vegetables. When cooked they tasted far fresher than canned foods.

In search of money to launch a frozen food company, Birdseye cooked frozen food dinners for prospective investors and, along with borrowed money from his life insurance, he successfully raised the money he needed. In 1929 Birdseye merged his company, Frosted Foods, with Postum Company, creating General Foods.

Offering freezer units to stores for about eight dollars a month, General Seafood Corporation introduced Birds Eye frosted foods in 1930. With the country sinking into the Depression, it seemed poor timing to introduce a completely new line of food. Nevertheless, the frozen foods slowly caught on with the public. Homemakers stored the foods in rental freezer lockers, as suitable freezer units were not yet available for homes. Quality, however, was not always dependable. The Birds Eye Division did not turn a profit until the 1940s, when housewives in large numbers decided that frozen foods were the most convenient new product to arrive in their kitchen. By the mid-1940s, frozen foods were in everyday use by a vast number of Americans.

Cooks and Their Cookbooks

Another entrepreneur in the food industry was the cook—the cook who could write the steps of his or her craft in books that people wanted to buy. Between 1896 and 1930, the *Boston Cooking School Cook Book,* written by Fannie Merritt Farmer, was the most influential cookbook in America. Farmer, the most famous cooking instructor and cookbook author of the day, taught the nonwasteful technique of level measuring. Level measuring means keeping a smooth flat surface of the measured ingredient level with the rim of the measuring device, such as a measuring spoon. This simple technique made following recipes easier and resulted in more uniform dishes. Not only did her book contain help for beginning cooks, but for advanced cooks as well. In addition, every page taught homemakers how to put their heart and soul (love and creativity) into cooking. Nonwasteful techniques and heart and soul would all be required of cooks during the Great Depression. Farmer's cookbook was unrivaled until 1931, when Irma Rombauer's *The Joy of Cooking* appeared.

The Joy of Cooking was born out of its author's need to survive in the Great Depression. Mrs. Irma Rombauer's husband, an attorney, committed suicide in February 1930. Having always lived a privileged, genteel life, Irma saw the Depression closing in on her by the summer of 1930. She had placed her shares of American Metals stock in the hands of her nephew. He could only report that dividends were headed down with no change in sight. Rombauer and her daughter Marion moved from their comfortable home into a walk-up apartment in the West End of St. Louis. Faced with the necessity of making a living, the cheery, witty, and congenial Rombauer set out to gather recipes from family and friends to include in a cookbook.

By fall she had a set of loose-leaf notebooks full of typed recipes. She and her daughter called in a printer and paid for three thousand copies to be printed in 1931. Rombauer altered the traditional recipe format of first listing ingredients then giving instructions. Instead, using Farmer's technique of giving specific measurements, she gave specific instructions for each ingredient. For example: Sift 1/2 cup sugar; Beat until soft 1/4 cup butter; Add sugar gradually; Blend these ingredients until creamy; Add grated rind of one lemon, and so forth.

Women found the book, which contained five hundred recipes, very simple to use. It was especially helpful to those middle-class and affluent women whose budgets no longer allowed for hired "help" to do the cooking and cleaning. In 1936 the Bobbs-Merrill Company, a publishing company in St. Louis, began publishing the cookbook. Rombauer's persistence in finding a way to survive the Depression proved highly successful. *The Joy of Cooking* has subsequently undergone decades of reprinting and revision, and remained in print as of the early twenty-first century.

Product Driven Recipes

New mass-marketed processed foods began appearing in the 1920s and continued to be introduced right through the Great Depression years and the World War II years. Processed food refers to the more highly processed foods in which physical or chemical operations are applied to foodstuffs. Through numerous industrial means available, these foods are greatly altered in their appearance, taste, structure, or texture as the result of considerable processing. The nutritional value of the food is often raised or lowered as well. Sometimes certain essential minerals or vitamins are lost during the process. Processing has its benefits, such as converting perishable food into more storable food. The explosion of processed foods paralleled the growth of large food chain stores and the modernization of kitchens with ranges and refrigerators. Many people at the beginning of the twenty-first century remembered the much-loved recipes of their mothers and grandmothers, which often included store bought crackers, canned soup casseroles, molded Jell-O salads, and Bisquick baked breads and desserts. The recipes, known as product-driven recipes because the recipes were offered by companies to encourage use of their products, were easy and inexpensive.

Ritz Crackers
While soda crackers were handed out in breadlines and soup kitchens, and unemployed Wall Street bankers sold apples on the streets of New York City, Nabisco Company introduced a round, richly buttery cracker called the Ritz in 1934. Nabisco hoped people would associate Ritz crackers with the grand Ritz-Carlton Hotel in Manhattan and feel lavish as

they ate it. In 1935 a box of Ritz crackers sold for 19 cents, and unlike the Ritz-Carlton, most people could afford it. It became the world's best selling cracker. The Ritz also became the main ingredient of Ritz mock apple pie. The pie, made with 36 Ritz crackers, tasted remarkably like apple pie, and its recipe became the most requested Nabisco recipe of all time.

Canned Soups
In the 1930s many varieties of canned soups, from companies such as Campbell's and Heinz, were available in stores. Campbell's boasted 21 varieties of canned soup, and by 1939 Heinz listed 46 flavors. These soups offered a shortcut to the traditionally long cooking process of simmering ingredients all day in a soup pot. Companies produced charts for mixing two soups together to create more flavors. For example, on President Roosevelt's inauguration day, a favorite dish served was mongole soup, a combination of pea soup and tomato soup. Homemakers could make an easy mongole soup by mixing together canned pea soup with canned tomato soup.

Canned soups also helped cooks use every scrap of leftovers. Noodle or rice soups, poured over leftover meats, served as inexpensive sauces and created a second and even a third meal. Casseroles got a tremendous boost in 1930s Depression cooking when Campbell's introduced its Cream of Mushroom soup in 1934. No longer did cream sauces have to be prepared from ingredients that cooks did not always have. The Cream of Mushroom soup was used in a multitude of meat and vegetable dishes.

Jell-O
During the 1930s popular comedian Jack Benny advertised the six delicious flavors of Jell-O—orange, cherry, lemon, lime, strawberry, and raspberry—on his radio shows. During the Depression Jell-O served as an affordable yet fancy food. A patent for a "gelatin dessert" was issued as early as 1845, but the Jell-O name originated in 1902. The Postum Cereal Company, known at the beginning of the twenty-first century as General Foods, purchased the rights to Jell-O in 1925. General Foods published a booklet entitled *What You Can Do with Jell-O*. The booklet's recipes instruct a user on how to whip Jell-O, set various fruit within it, or layer it. The inexpensive product delighted Americans, who have at various times referred to it as "shivering Liz," "nervous pudding," and "shimmy treat." Unflavored Knox gelatin was also used in many recipes, such as a popular southern gelatin salad called Coca-Cola salad. Coca-Cola salad contained gelatin, sugar, water, lemon juice, Coca-Cola, and mixed, diced fruits.

More About...
"America Eats"

"America Eats" projects were a part of the Federal Writers' Project department of the Works Project Administration (WPA). As part of President Roosevelt's New Deal push to create employment for all, between 1935 and 1942 the Federal Writers' Project had various job openings. Among the positions advertised were interviewers, writers, editors, researchers, geologists, and map draftsmen. Responsibilities included collecting information on all aspects of American community life—history, settlement, business, art, architecture, social and ethnic studies, folklore, and food. The material was to be edited and published in a series of books, the American Guide Books. One of the major efforts of the Federal Writers' Project was to be a monumental book, *America Eats.*

By the mid-1930s, mass-produced processed foods were prevalent, and homemakers, especially in urban areas, began to spend less time preparing food from scratch. The government believed that many of America's food customs would be lost if not recorded soon. *America Eats* was intended to document the U.S. eating habits as an important American social institution. It would trace the history of U.S. food consumption, describing how immigration, settlements, and customs related and expanded food customs. Five regions for *America Eats* projects were designated—Northeast, South, Midwest, Southwest, and South.

Vast quantities of information were accumulated. The Montana Writers' Project collection alone included 250,000 items that required 57 linear feet of storage space. By the early 1940s, however, workers saw their reports for *America Eats* filed away, as the government turned its attention to World War II, and the project was never fully realized.

Fortunately, project supervisors, editors, and writers had taken time to sift through material, organize the findings, and write manuscripts. Yet the completed volume, *America Eats,* was never published, and manuscripts languished for years in university archives and personal homes. Manuscripts from the Midwest and far West surfaced in the late 1980s and 1990s.

Author and editor of the midwest manuscript, Nelson Algren, held a silent auction of his apartment contents in March 1975. Chef Louis Szathmarz purchased the manuscript, entitled in pencil, "Am Eats Algren." Chef Szathmarz presented the Algren manuscript to the University of Iowa libraries in 1987. The University published *Nelson Algren America Eats* in 1992. Likewise the manuscript "America Eats Far West" was located in Special Collections at Montana State University in Bozeman. It was published as *Whistleberries, Stirabout, and Depression Cake* (Falcon Publishing, Inc., Helena, Montana) in 2000.

A low-cost yet seemingly luxurious dessert also evolved from Jell-O and Knox unflavored gelatin—chiffon pies. Chiffon pies were light and fluffy, containing gelatin, cream, and egg whites beaten stiff. Favorite 1930s chiffon pies were lemon, pumpkin, chocolate, and pineapple.

Bisquick In 1930 on a late night train bound for San Francisco, a Depression-era bread product was discovered. Carl Smith, a weary General Mills traveling salesman, boarded a train in the evening and headed for a diner. He expected only a cold plate for supper ,but to his amazement the chef served him a dinner that included hot fresh biscuits. The clever chef explained to Smith that he premixed the dry ingredients with shortening and kept it in the icebox until needed. Smith reported his finding to General Mills

and, within the year, Bisquick appeared, along with a booklet entitled *101 Delicious Bisquick Creations.* More than 500,000 cases of the mix sold over a few months. Bisquick fans were so loyal to the product that no competitors survived, and the product remained popular into the twenty-first century.

Contributing Forces

Trends Toward Urbanization

Between 1900 and 1930, the character of U.S. cities dramatically changed due to several factors. One trend was the shift of the population from farms to cities. America's farm dwellers declined and, by 1930, 56 percent of the country's population lived in cities.

Factors contributing to this trend included continued low market prices for farm products through the 1920s that caused many farmers to go out of business, farms getting larger because of the greater use of mechanized farm equipment and thus squeezing out the smaller farms, and more jobs available in the ever-expanding industries.

At the same time as rural farmers were moving to the industrial cities another urban trend was occurring. Many of the more prosperous city residents moved to the outskirts of town—to the suburbs. This shift was made possible by the increased prevalence of automobiles which made longer commutes more feasible. This allowed many to escape the increasingly dense inner cities, filled with factory workers, where crime and health conditions were problems. There in the outskirts they had a home with a yard big enough for a garden. By contrast large numbers of the urban working class rented their living spaces in the city. They had no access to plots of land for gardens, so they often had a more difficult time obtaining vegetables and fruits to eat that were easily available to those with gardens. If inner city workers lost their jobs and therefore their wages, they and their families would find themselves in a desperate situation. This is exactly what happened to millions during the Great Depression.

Herbert Hoover's Food Administration

Food use practices during World War I (1914–1918), although no one realized it at the time, were good preparation for the hard times of the Great Depression that was to follow ten years later. Just before World War I scientists discovered vitamins A and B. With these discoveries the general public's interest in nutrition rose. Problems of supplying sufficient quantities of nutritious food appeared on a massive scale during World War I. It became necessary to feed American soldiers overseas, to feed people at home, and to supply food to European countries whose own agricultural production was disrupted by the war. As the government did later in World War II, Hoover encouraged Americans to eat perishables so that such staples as wheat and beef could be sent overseas.

President Woodrow Wilson (served 1913–1921) set up the Food Administration, which was headed by an efficient mining engineer and future U.S. president, Herbert Hoover. Hoover was directed to increase food production and cut waste. Hoover was very successful—some would say too successful. Increases in food production by farmers during World War I and continuing high levels of production after the war led to large farming surpluses in 1920s and 1930s. Those surpluses, however, were not effectively distributed to people in need.

The Food Administration also educated the public about vitamins, proteins, and carbohydrates, as well as about the importance of fruits and vegetables and the best means of canning, preserving, and drying foods. The use of oatmeal, potatoes, and beans, among other foods, were promoted to the public. Hoover's wife, Lou Henry, also participated in the education efforts. She offered a recipe for war pudding, which was included in *Conservation Recipes,* compiled by the Mobilized Women's Organizations of Berkeley, California, in 1918. Herbert Hoover also urged the use of "victory bread," which had a greater whole wheat content but with less butter and sugar per person. People also planted "liberty gardens" in vacant lots or in yards. Overall, Americans learned to use more whole wheat bread, less sugar, and more fresh vegetables that they grew themselves. These would be valuable lessons for surviving the Great Depression.

Chain Stores and the Processed Food Business

Chain stores are two or more retail (sell to the public) stores that have the same ownership and sell the same goods. A specific chain may be only in a certain city or region, or may be national or international. Chain stores may be grocery stores, department stores, hotels, or drugstores. The first chain store, the Great Atlantic and Pacific Tea Company (A&P) had thirty locations in 1869, and sold staple foods at lower prices than the corner grocery. Three years later the Jones Brothers Tea Company of Brooklyn, later called Grand Union, began operating stores. In 1916 the Piggly Wiggly chain started offering low prices and self-service. By 1915 A&P had 1,726 stores, and a total of fourteen thousand by 1925. Chain stores often favored national brands of food, shipped from distant locations, rather than local farmers' products. Because of this, chain stores contributed to the growing business of production, processing, and sale of foods and drinks with labels recognized nationwide.

The advantages chain stores had over local small retailers were several. These advantages became much more evident during the Great Depression when people needed to get the most out of their money. Chain stores had central organizations that purchase the goods for sale. Supplying a whole chain rather than a single store, the purchasers could buy on much more favorable terms since much larger quantities were being obtained. Chain stores had lower operating expenses since costs were shared throughout the chain. Advertising was largely handled by the central organization, therefore less expensive for individual stores. Because of financial support from the complete chain, chain stores could operate on smaller profits. For all these reasons, prices of goods at chain stores would normally be less than at independent local stores.

Perhaps most importantly to consumers, chain stores offered a vast variety of foods including fresh meats, canned and baked goods, and the new frozen foods. Consumers found the chain stores so much more attractive to purchase goods at in the 1930s that small independent retailers began going out of business. Some European nations acted to restrict chains in their countries so as to protect local store owners.

Women found careers as home economists in large food businesses, developing and introducing prepared ready-to-eat products. Entrepreneurs introduced new products for marketing. Sets of recipes were often created for the new products. The mass-produced products were cheap and easy to use. They made the chore of cooking easier for homemakers. New technology in the homemakers' kitchens was also changing the way food was prepared.

Kitchens

Home kitchens became smaller and more efficient. During the 1920s gas stoves replaced the difficult, labor-intensive wood and coal stoves that had to be stoked, prodded, and frequently attended to. The new stove provided clean, easy heat, quick and accurate temperature control, and freedom from excessive kitchen warmth. The electric stove became prevalent in the 1930s.

Iceboxes, which had upgraded the flavor and freshness of the American meal, began to be replaced by refrigerators. The earliest electric refrigerator, which did not include freezer compartments, appeared around 1916. Refrigeration improvements advanced quickly from there. As homes electrified through the 1920s, the number of refrigerators in kitchens increased. The number of refrigerators in homes rose from twenty thousand in 1923 to 3.5 million by 1941. Home freezers did not appear until the late 1930s, and were not in wide use until the 1940s. The two-temperature refrigerator, which included the built-in freezer, came on the market in 1939. Small electric appliances such as toasters, percolators, grills, and waffle irons also began to appear in homes in the 1910s and 1920s.

Technological advances for the kitchen continued through the 1930s despite the economic hard times. The modernization of the kitchen did not reach the poorest Americans or those in rural areas without electricity. Not being able to afford the new technological advances, they maintained cooking traditions of earlier decades and could not stimulate the economy. For the middle class and for affluent Americans in cities, suburban areas, and electrified rural homes, the more dependable methods of food preparation that came with this modernization allowed them to utilize the mass-marketed foods. This utilization created a market for new products introduced in the 1930s. At the same time, purchase of the appliances by more and more households increased the market for new food innovations, thus supporting expansion of the food industry. Sale of these new food and appliance products eventually helped in the nation's recovery from the Great Depression by creating much-needed jobs.

Perspectives

The Poor and a National Response

The economic troubles of the Great Depression made it difficult for many people to make ends meet. Lack of money often meant lack of food, and the poor became desperate. A few scattered food riots took place across the country in 1931. Some of those who took food said that they would pay for it when they could. Others simply said that they refused to starve when food was available on store shelves. This desperation did not spawn mass riots and revolution, however, due to the "American creed."

By 1929 an American creed was ingrained in American culture. That creed was: Success was open to all that were willing to work for it. Those who failed deserved to fail and had done so through their own fault. This creed persisted at most levels of society following the stock market crash and after President Roosevelt had introduced his New Deal programs of relief and recovery. Consequently, many of the lower class felt they were to blame for their economic misfortune and were ashamed to accept government assistance. The strong individualism and striking financial successes of the booming 1920s economy had largely fixed this creed in the American mind.

Being on relief carried with it a great deal of shame. Relief could take various forms of assistance, most commonly in the form of money, food, shelter, and other necessities for the poor and needy. Relief was more commonly known in later decades as welfare or public assistance. Those who lost their jobs felt forced to accept charity to feed themselves and their families.

Beginning in late 1933, the Federal Surplus Relief Corporation (FSRC) distributed surplus food to the poor. FSRC officials reported that, while people were grateful, they did not want to be on relief but had no

Men sort care packages of food for needy families in the central warehouse established by the Emergency Unemployment Relief Committee in an effort to feed those severely affected by the Great Depression. (AP/Wide World Photos. Reproduced by permission.)

other choice. Accepting relief was, to them, similar to begging. What people wanted were jobs. Lorena Hickok, a special assistant to the head of the FSRC, was quoted by Watkins in *The Hungry Years: A Narrative History of the Great Depression in America* (1999, p. 178), as reporting to her superiors, "These people don't want to be on relief. They loath it. The percentage of those who call up and announce that they have jobs and won't want any more food orders is truly impressive."

The U.S. government's attitude towards the deepening economic crisis altered dramatically with a change in the presidential administration. President Hoover (served 1929–33), served at the time of the 1929 stock market crash and in the early years of the economic troubles. He never doubted that the Depression was a psychological, not an economic, problem that would pass in time. At this time no government-backed social safety net existed for people who fell on hard times. You took care of you and yours, and the government left you to your own devices. Hoover felt that charity organizations, not government, should care for the hungry and poor. He strongly urged Americans to contribute to these organizations. He believed that the unfortunate should be cared for within their local communities and that the federal government should let the economic problems run their course without interference.

The change in government attitude came in 1933. When Franklin D. Roosevelt took office, millions of people were out of work and hungry. President Roosevelt and Harry L. Hopkins, head of the new Federal Emergency Relief Agency, believed that a more aggressive, organized approach had to be immediately pursued, and they did just that.

Americans, including the poor, had remarkable affection for President Roosevelt and his wife, Eleanor. Many of the poor believed that the Roosevelts would bring about the necessary changes for them. During his presidential campaign, Franklin Roosevelt promised to help the poor, and the people believed he would do so. Through the many social and work programs that Roosevelt established in his New Deal packages, changes were made. Even as dissatisfaction arose with existing relief programs, Americans still wrote to President and Mrs. Roosevelt for help. The poor saw the president and his wife as individuals who truly cared about their plight and were trying to make it better, so they were willing to wait and trust in the country's leadership.

As the difficult years of the Depression continued, however, many people in the working class found pessimism replacing American optimism. When you were very hungry and had no hope for the future, it was difficult to be optimistic. Fundamental changes in American thinking began to surface.

The Middle Class

Many Americans were opposed to government relief programs, believing it would make "loafers" out of individuals, which would be a detriment to the country and to taxpayers. Thus, according to this opinion, people in need of relief should improve their own situation rather than accept handouts. Over the course of the Great Depression, however, neighbors shared and cared for each other. The self-centered individualism of the 1920s gave way to compassion and humanitarianism in the 1930s. People contributed to private relief organizations. Families and friends helped other families and friends who were out of work. Food was stretched with extenders, and dishes such as casseroles graced the meal tables. Those that had less were often invited to Sunday dinner. This was

an uncommon period in U.S. history in many ways. One was certainly the level of community spirit demonstrated, even between strangers. Many of those who still had a means of support knew they could be the next out of a job and in need. The U.S. would not see such a level of humanitarianism throughout the remainder of the twentieth century.

The faces of the most desperate Americans seen on the streets of their local communities left permanent marks on those who did have enough to eat. The effects of the Depression were so great that, for the rest of their lives, the average American who "made do" during the 1930s remained thrifty. Decades after the Depression, grandparents would save twist ties— just in case—and eat every bite of food on his or her plate at meals.

The Wealthy

Most of the rich remained quite comfortable throughout the Depression. Some of the well-to-do were sensitive to the problems of the hungry, such as was Daniel Willard, president of the Baltimore and Ohio Railroad. In a June 1931 speech at the University of Pennsylvania, Willard noted, "While I do not like to say so, I would be less than candid if I did not say in such circumstances [of no work and no food, that] I would steal before I would starve" (quoted in Watkins, *The Hungry Years: A Narrative History of the Great Depression in America,* 1999, p. 106). Harry A. Mackey, the mayor of Philadelphia, commented on wealthy men and women's failure to contribute significantly to the poor (quoted in Abraham Epstein, "Do the Rich Give to Charity? " *Reader's Digest* June 1931, p. 121):

> Up to the present a great proportion of the relief funds has been contributed by the working class. It is a lamentable fact that many of our wealthy men and women have failed to respond, while many others who are rich have sent contributions for insignificant sums. I say to you it is the poor man who has saved the situation up to this time.

The most arrogant of the wealthy believed that the poor deserved their fate. The upper class, like the middle class, believed that a person's misfortune was strictly the result of a flaw in the person's character, not because of social forces beyond their control such as government policies and bad business management. Many wealthy men and women failed to contribute or sent insignificant sums to charities. Michigan senator James Couzens offered to contribute $1 million to a $10 million relief fund if other millionaires would come up with the remaining $9 million. They refused. Although some wealthy people did contribute significantly to relief efforts, most did not. Most wealthy people were

Shopping during the Depression, 1932-1943

Food	Cost
Sirloin steak, per pound	$0.29
Bacon, per pound	.22
Ham, per pound	.31
Chicken, per pound	.22
Pork chops, per pound	.20
Salmon, per pound	.19
Milk, per quart	.10
Butter, per pound	.28
Margarine, per pound	.13
Eggs, per dozen	.29
Cheese, per pound	.24
Bread, 20-ounce loaf	.05
Coffee, per pound	.26
Sugar, per pound	.05
Rice, per pound	.06
Potatoes, per pound	.02
Tomatoes, 16-ounce can	.09
Oranges, per dozen	.27
Bananas, per pound	.07
Onions, per pound	.03
Cornflakes, 8-ounce package	.08

During the Depression a sirloin steak at 29¢ per pound became a luxury item for many people. (The Gale Group.)

not greatly affected by the economic pressures of the Depression and continued to dine in luxury at such famous restaurants as the Ritz Carlton in New York and the Brown Derby restaurants in Los Angeles.

There were some wealthy, however, who did support New Deal programs and believed President Roosevelt's intentions were indeed designed to save private enterprise, not undermine it. Winthrop Aldrich of Chase National Bank, Thomas Watson of IBM, Walter Gifford of AT&T, Gerard Swope of General Electric, and W. Averell Harriman of Union Pacific Railroad served as advisors to Roosevelt to assist in relief and recovery programs. Otherwise, a primary contribution of the wealthy was keeping millions of workers employed building skyscrapers and manufacturing the new refrigerators and other products coming on the market.

Impact

Diet and Nutrition

Despite the escalating unemployment rate and growth of breadlines on city streets, malnourishment was not considered a major health concern of the early 1930s. Heart disease, cancer, pneumonia, and infec-

tious diseases were the leading causes of death. Though many were hungry, starvation was not a reality. Deaths from hunger and thirst was less than one per 100,000 of the total population.

Diets of ordinary people improved with the new processing and preparation technologies, such as canning and refrigeration, made available through the 1930s. Vegetables were consumed in greater abundance, and improved preservation and storage allowed for consumption longer through the year. In addition, federal food relief programs introduced foods to the South that were foreign to residents there, such as whole-wheat flour, coconuts, and grapefruit juice, as opposed to the customary pork and white flour. Overall, however, the novelty of canned foods led to a decrease in eating fresh foods that offered greater nutrition. Meat consumption during the Depression dropped from 130 to 110 pounds per person per year. Dried beans took their place, with the average American eating almost ten pounds a year, up from six pounds a year in 1920.

World War II

The conservative food usage of the Great Depression turned out to be needed again during World War II, which for the United States began late in 1941. Huge shipments of food shipped to Europe led to shortages and hoarding in America. Industry could not produce enough of certain products to satisfy the demand both overseas and at home. The U.S. government introduced a system for distributing certain scarce products, such as food, among the U.S. population, called rationing. Each household would be given a certain number of coupons by the government for certain products, such as gas. Sugar rationing came early and caused significant adjustments in homemakers' baking. War cakes again were full of raisins and other dried fruit just, as in Depression days. Beef was scarce by the spring of 1942. Just as in Depression times, rural people hunted game, and others depended on chickens, cheese, and eggs. By 1943 butter and canned goods were also rationed.

The establishment of a large government system for supplying food to the most needy during the Depression paved the way for yet another government system for rationing certain food items and other commodities. For many who had to cut back considerably during the Depression, war rationing seemed much less of a burden than it might have otherwise.

In 1943 General Mills published a Betty Crocker booklet, *Your Share,* which showed women, many of whom had been teenagers during the Great Depression, how to prepare appetizing, healthy meals with

More About...
Betty Crocker

In 1924, five years before the stock market crash and the onset of the Great Depression, an program from WCCO radio in Minneapolis, Minnesota, introduced "Betty Crocker's Cooking School of the Air." Though it began as a local radio program, Betty Crocker was soon broadcast nationwide to an audience of homemakers and cooks. It was the first women's service program to be broadcast nationally. "Betty Crocker" was, in fact, Marjorie Child Husted, a home economist with the food company General Mills.

Unbeknownst to her listeners, Betty Crocker was not an actual woman, but simply a name created by advertiser Sam Gale for Washburn Crosby, a milling company that merged with General Mills in 1924. The need for Betty began when, in October 1921, Washburn Crosby's advertising department ran a jigsaw puzzle advertisement in a national magazine offering pincushions resembling a miniature sack of flour to anyone who could put the pieces together. This was a promotional ad campaign for Washburn Crosby's flour, Gold Medal flour. The company received an overwhelming number of answers. Accompanying the puzzle answers were requests for answers to food questions: "Why doesn't my dough rise?" and "How long do you knead?" Sam Gale was put in charge of the responses. Agnes White and Janette Kelley, two of Crosby's home economists, wrote the responses, but Gale signed the letters. Soon they all agreed a woman should be telling women how to shape their rolls and buns, and Betty Crocker was born.

The name "Betty" was chosen because it was a nice, friendly name. Crocker was chosen in honor of a retired director of the company, William G. Crocker. A piece of paper circulated in the office for women of the company to sign the name. The easiest to read was chosen as Betty Crocker's signature. This fictional fantasy quickly became a spokesperson for Crosby's Gold Medal flour. Women wrote letters to Betty and sent her gifts. In the early 1930s, Betty Crocker published a meal planning booklet that advised women on how to maintain an adequate diet on Depression-era wages and relief foods.

Marjorie Child Husted served as Betty's radio voice for many years. Not until 1936 did Betty have a face to show the public. Neysa McMein, an artist-illustrator, created the face as a composite of her perception of women who worked in test kitchens. From 1936 onward, the public saw portraits of Betty on cookbooks, magazines, and General Mills' products. Millions tuned into Betty's cooking school radio program during the Depression and World War II for her advice on low cost menus that would keep their families well fed. When *Betty Crocker's Picture Cookbook* appeared in 1951, it became an instant bestseller.

Betty's face underwent six major changes over the years, including one in 1996. The 1996 change was a computerized composite of 76 American women of varying ages and ethnic backgrounds, intended to give Betty Crocker widespread appeal. Betty aged well, as her face retained its 32-year-old youthful appearance of the first portrait in 1936.

Later versions of *Betty Crocker's Illustrated Cookbook* were entitled simply *Betty Crocker's Cookbook*. The many revisions and additions continued to sell well at the beginning of the twenty-first century, when the book's contents also became available on a floppy computer disk. *Betty Crocker's Cookbook* is acknowledged as America's top selling cookbook, with an estimated 55 million copies sold by the mid-1990s.

foods that were available. The booklet included charts to use corn syrup or honey in place of sugar for cakes. Homemakers turned to the familiar casseroles and food extenders—macaroni, potatoes, beans, rice, and dried peas—of the previous decade.

Located in backyards, vacant lots, or adjacent to war plants, 20 million "victory gardens" grew 40 percent of the country's vegetables. In 1942, all across America, gardeners bought Burpee's victory garden packets, which contained fifteen vegetables for one dollar, the Suburban Garden package of 25 varieties also for one dollar, and the Country Garden package of thirty types for three dollars. Even Eleanor Roosevelt had a victory garden on the White House lawn, and Harry Hopkins and his family tended to it. Home canning of vegetables was prevalent in approximately three-fourths of American homes, and families produced an average of 165 jars a year.

Eleanor Roosevelt helps to serve food to unemployed women at the Grand Central Restaurant kitchen in New York City in 1932. (AP/Wide World Photos. Reproduced by permission.)

Processed Foods

With the social dislocations of the war, homemakers in temporary military housing or wives working for the war effort turned to processed and ready-to-eat foods. Many of these foods had been developed in the 1930s during the Great Depression. Large food companies gained strength as they received massive orders from the armed forces. Hormel's Spam, first made popular in the 1930s, was the soldier's staple. General Foods' sales to the government rose from $1,477,000 in 1941 to $37,840,000 in 1944.

The processed food industry continued to grow throughout the twentieth century. By the later 1950s, cooking habits changed. There existed greater demand for convenience in food preparation and consumption. For example, demand for fresh fruits declined in favor of the less nutritious canned preserved fruit. Also, soft drinks and pizza became popular. Easier to prepare packaged foods became common as did as fast food restaurant chains. The processed food industry was concentrated in the large food producing companies of Beatrice Foods, Borden, Campbell Soup, General Foods, General Mills, Heinz, Kellogg, Nestlé, Kraft, Pillsbury, and other standard brands. New appliances included food processors, blenders, and in the 1980s, microwave ovens.

The agricultural community of farmers consisted of less than 3 percent of the population as of 1980, down from 25 percent in 1930 and 23 percent in 1940. Most people did not grow their own foods, and home gardening was more of a hobby than a supplemental and necessary food source. They instead bought their food in large chain food stores. Frozen and canned foods dominated the shelves, and fast and easy cooking for many meant popping a frozen dinner into the microwave to heat and eat. People did still cook fresh meals, but much less attention was paid to utilizing the most of every food source than it was on putting together a meal with the most ease and convenience.

As the twenty-first century began, the simple cooking of the 1930s persisted among few families. Depression-era recipes and cookbooks gained popularity by the end of the twentieth century, nostalgically harkening back to a different period of food preparation.

One development in the modern kitchen that was far beyond the imaginations of Depression families was the use of genetically modified foods. Though still in the experimental stages in early 2001, some farmers were planting and growing genetically modified crops. Designed to repel threatening insects that could affect plant health and to grow hardier crops, genetically modified foods were not without controversy. Environmental groups in particular renewed promotion of organic foods, so called because they were grown naturally and without the use of pesticides.

In the more than five decades since the Great Depression, Americans have gone from integrating new developments like Birds Eye frozen foods into their meals to having many of those same new Depression food items serve as a natural and daily part of their lives. Foods that were once scarce or utilized to the last scrap were being examined for genetically modified "improvements." The food industry in America had undoubtedly come a long way since the 1930s, and many of the most far-reaching impacts on the industry arose out of the Depression.

Food Stamps

The Federal Surplus Commodities Corporation (FSCC) established the Food Stamp Plan on May 16, 1939, to ensure that surplus agricultural products got to the needy. The FSCC grew out of the New Deal program called the Federal Surplus Relief Corporation (FSRC), created in the fall of 1933 for emergency relief for the hungry. Although the Food Stamp Plan was cancelled during World War II when full employment made it unnecessary, it was reestablished as a pilot program under President John F. Kennedy (served 1961–1963) in 1961. Kennedy directed the Agriculture Department to establish an experimental program based on the original Food Stamp Plan. This experiment later became a full-fledged program under the Food Stamp Act in 1964. By 1971 Congress had established uniform standards of eligibility for food stamps. During the later twentieth century, various changes to regulations and available funding tended to differ under each new administration.

As of 2001 the Food Stamp Program operated under the Agriculture Department's Food and Nutrition Services. The program helped 7.3 million households put food on the table in 2000. Participating individuals used food stamp coupons just as they would cash at most grocery stores. Considered a transitional measure for individuals moving from welfare to work, the food stamp program, which first got its start due to the hard times of the Depression, is a cornerstone of federal food assistance programs.

Federal Food, Drug, and Cosmetic Act of 1938

During the Great Depression, many consumers became convinced that food, drug, and cosmetic businesses were practicing price gouging—charging too much money for products—and were engaged in consumer fraud. Consumer fraud usually took the form of companies claiming their products could perform better or benefit the consumer more than they actually could. The product was basically misrepresented in advertising. The existing Pure Food and Drug Act of 1906 proved ineffective since it did not regulate drug makers' performance claims unless fraud could be proven. Concern also arose as a host of new processed foods came on the market. Their quality and standard of safety was virtually uncontrolled, and the health impact for consumers was unknown. The American Medical Association (AMA) and state and federal drug officials all attempted to strengthen food and drug laws and to expose wrongdoing and misleading claims.

In 1933 Rexford G. Tugwell, assistant secretary of agriculture and advisor to President Franklin Roosevelt, led the drafting of a new food and drug bill. The bill greatly expanded government control over the drug- and food-processing industry. Drug claims contrary to general medical opinion were made illegal, and medical ingredients were now required to be clearly disclosed. Food labels were also required to list all ingredients. The government could establish quality and fill of container standards, and government officials could

Food Stamp Participation, 1970-1995

Year	Number of Recipients in millions	Cost
1970	4.3 million	$577 million
1975	17.1	4.6 billion
1980	21.1	9.2
1985	19.9	11.7
1990	20.1	15.5
1995	26.6	24.6

The number of food stamp recipients has grown markedly since the program was first implemented during the 1930s. (The Gale Group.)

inspect factories to ensure the law was obeyed. The food, cosmetic, and drug industries adamantly opposed the bill and successfully lobbied against it.

Senator Royal Copeland of New York, whose main interest in Congress was food and drug issues, became a major supporter of the bill and continued to fight for its passage. Then, in 1937, 107 people, including many children, died from taking a drug called sulfanilamide, which a small pharmaceutical plant in Bristol, Tennessee, produced. A toxic chemical, diethylene glycol, had been added without the company first checking it for human toxicity. An angered public called for congressional action. Under the leadership of Senator Copeland and Representative Clarence Lea of California, and with the assistance of Walter Campbell, head of the Food and Drug Administration (FDA), the Federal Food, Drug, and Cosmetic Act of 1938 passed through Congress. President Franklin Roosevelt signed it in June 1938 as one of the last major New Deal measures.

The new act greatly expanded consumer protection and increased the minimal penalties of violation set out in the 1906 act. The new provisions extended government oversight and standards control to cosmetics and medical devices, such as the modern day pacemaker, required new drugs to be shown safe before marketing, and eliminated the requirement to prove intent to defraud in drug mislabeling cases. The law authorized factory inspections and allowed food standards of identity, quality, and fill of containers to be set. For example, a product labeled "fruit jam" must contain 45 parts fruit and 55 parts sugar or sweetener; there may not be excessive pits in canned cherries; and minimum weights of solid food must remain after drainable liquid is poured off of canned foods.

At a Glance

A Pinch of This, a Dash of That

Although Fannie Farmer had urged the use of "level measurements" since 1896, many Depression-era cooks still used a pinch and a dash. Emily Thacker, in her book *Recipes & Remembrances of the Great Depression,* translates for the "measurement conscious world."

This	is about
Pinch	1/2 teaspoon
Lump	1/3 cup
Handful	1 cup
Dash	1/8 teaspoon
Glob	1 tablespoon
Some	enough to do the job
Size of a walnut	2 tablespoons
Fingerful	1/2 teaspoon
Palmful	1/2 cup
Saucerful	1/4 cup

Today, some 1,100 investigators and inspectors, plus the agency's 2,100 scientists, assure the enforcement of the law. These employees are located in offices throughout the country. The FDA is an agency within the Public Health Service which is a part of the Department of Health and Human Services.

Notable People

Royal Samuel Copeland (1868–1938). Copeland is in large part responsible for the enactment of the Food, Drug, and Cosmetic Act in 1938, which changed the way the government treated food and other materials, ensuring greater safety for the public. Copeland received a medical degree from the University of Michigan in 1889. He moved to New York in 1908 to serve as the dean of the New York Flower Hospital and Medical School and was a syndicated medical columnist. In 1918 Copeland was appointed commissioner of health for the city.

Although previously a Republican, Copeland, running as a Democrat, won a race for the U.S. Sen-

ate. He was reelected in 1934. Although initially he supported various New Deal programs, he became disillusioned with Franklin Roosevelt. His real interest in the Senate was food and drug legislation. Copeland supported the Food, Drug, and Cosmetic Act from the time Rex Tugwell wrote it in 1933 until its passage in 1938. Under the leadership of Copeland, the measure moved through Congress in 1938, and President Roosevelt signed it into law on June 24, 1938.

Fannie Merritt Farmer (1857–1915). Fannie Farmer, considered the "brainiest" of the four Farmer girls, was headed for college until she contracted a disease—most likely polio—that left her an invalid. She learned to walk again, but had a pronounced limp. With marriage and job prospects poor, she found work as a housekeeper, and in 1888 she enrolled in the Boston Cooking School. A star student, within five years Farmer became principal of the school. In 1896 she struck a deal with Little, Brown Publishing Company to print *The Boston Cooking School Cookbook,* providing she pay the publishing costs herself. The book actually was based on *Mrs. Lincoln's Boston Cook Book* (1883) by Mary J. Lincoln, a teacher who preceded Farmer at the Boston Cooking School.

Farmer's cookbook was extremely popular for decades to come, undergoing many reprints and updates. The success was attributed to Farmer's use of level measurements, which standardized cooking recipes, rather than referring to a pinch of one ingredient or a dash of another. The book's influence and popularity were unrivaled from 1896 until 1931, when Irma Rombauer's *The Joy of Cooking* was first published. Continued printings of Farmer's cookbook prepared Depression cooks to be less wasteful with ingredients and instructed those who lost their kitchen "help" to 1930s budgets in the basics. Farmer died in 1915, leaving an estate of nearly $200,000—a handsome sum for that period.

Jerome Frank (1889–1957). A prominent young lawyer in New York City, Jerome Frank took the post of general counsel to the Agricultural Adjustment Administration (AAA), which was established early in President Franklin D. Roosevelt's administration. Dedicated as he was to liberal reform, one of Frank's major contributions was the development of a plan to distribute surplus farm products to the unemployed and needy. He helped create the Federal Surplus Relief Corporation to carry out the plan. Frank also served as commissioner of the Securities and Exchange Commission beginning in 1937, and later was appointed to the U.S. Court of Appeals for the Second Circuit.

Lorena Hickok (1893–1968). Hickok, a journalist, became close friends with Eleanor Roosevelt while writing a series of articles on her during the 1932 presidential campaign. New Dealers needed to know how the public perceived the legislation moving rapidly through Congress in the early years of the Roosevelt administration. How the legislative programs were affecting people and how well they were being administered around the country was vital knowledge. They selected Hickok to quietly travel around the country to investigate these issues and report back. Her reporting included descriptions of the hungry and how breadlines and soup kitchens were barely keeping them alive. She also included observations of men fighting over Civil Works Administration (CWA) shovels to prove they could work and descriptions of "wicked" politicians manipulating New Deal programs for their own gain. Hickok's often humorous, sad, or angry, but always direct reports conveyed an accurate picture of the public's situation to the Roosevelt administration and influenced further legislation.

Harry Lloyd Hopkins (1890–1946). After graduating from Grinnell College, Hopkins held several social work positions in New York City. In 1931 then-governor Franklin Roosevelt appointed Hopkins deputy director of New York's Temporary Emergency Relief Administration, where he learned about dealing with widespread poverty. When Roosevelt was elected to the presidency, he appointed Hopkins to head the Federal Emergency Relief Administration in May 1933. It became Hopkins' job to feed the hungry. A few months later, Hopkins agreed to also head the Federal Surplus Relief Corporation, charged with distributing surplus agriculture products to the needy.

Hopkins directed the Civil Works Administration (1933–1934) and the Works Progress Administration (1935–1938). He also served as secretary of commerce (1938–1940), and as special advisor and personal emissary to President Roosevelt during World War II.

Irma Louise (von Starkloff) Rombauer (1877–1962). Born in St. Louis, Missouri, to professional parents, Irma von Starkloff was educated in a Swiss boarding school, where she learned to converse in both German and French. In college she majored in fine arts at Washington University, but at age 22 she left her studies to marry Edgar Roderick Rombauer, an attorney. As her husband's political career took off, Irma complemented him by being an efficient and highly entertaining hostess. When Irma was fifty-three, Edgar, who had long suffered with bouts of depression, committed suicide.

With the Great Depression closing in, Irma set about gathering recipes for a cookbook in an effort to provide herself with income and to combat loneliness.

With the help of her daughter Marion, Rombauer located a printer and paid him to print three thousand copies of *The Joy of Cooking* in 1931. Sales were strong, and the Bobbs-Merrill Publishing Company began publishing the cookbook in 1936. The book was more fun and easier to use than Fannie Farmer's cookbook. *The Joy of Cooking* was revised and reprinted throughout the twentieth century. It is regarded as America's most influential cookbook, giving clear instructions that keep even inexperienced cooks from failing.

Rexford Guy Tugwell (1891–1979). In 1931 Rexford Tugwell was an economics professor at Columbia University specializing in agricultural economics. He supported the use of national planning and government regulation of private business to bring about economic and social change. President Roosevelt appointed Tugwell assistant secretary of agriculture; his main function, however, was as a close advisor to the president. Tugwell had served in this capacity as a member of Roosevelt's "Brain Trust" advisory team prior to the 1932 presidential election, so it was a role with which he was familiar. Tugwell played a significant role in drafting the Agricultural Adjustment Act in 1933. Also in 1933, along with Professors Milton Handles of Columbia University and David Cavers of Duke University, he drafted a new food and drug act to replace the Pure Food and Drug Act of 1906. Congress debated the legislation for five years before passing the Food, Drug, and Cosmetic Act in 1938.

Primary Sources

Breadline Day

Breadlines provided sustenance to many who could not afford to buy food. Work was scarce, so the money to buy food was also scarce. Many people who were out of work due to the Great Depression supported families. One unemployed man described to *New Masses* on January 23, 1934, his day in the city after receiving his ration in the breadline (quoted in Winslow, *Brother, Can You Spare a Dime? America from the Wall Street Crash to Pearl Harbor, An Illustrated Documentary*, 1975, p. 19):

> You get shoved out early; you get your coffee and start walking. A couple of hours before noon you get in line. You eat and start walking. At night you flop where you can. You don't talk. You eat what you can. You sleep where you can. You walk. No one talks to you. You walk. It's cold, and you shiver and stand in doorways or sit in railroad stations. You don't see much. You forget. You walk an hour and forget where you started from. It is day, and then it's night, and then it's day again. And you don't remember which was first. You walk. There

A storekeeper fills a Red Cross order of basic foodstuffs for a man and his family of three in rural Kentucky.
(The Library of Congress.)

are men with fat on them and you know it. There are lean men and you know it.

Coal-Miner's Hunger

Widespread suffering came to the coal-mining families of West Virginia and the Cumberland Plateau of Eastern Kentucky. Thousands of people were out of work. Many families lived in tents and had no food for days. A West Virginia miner's recollection of the scramble for food during unemployment is recounted

in Hooker's *Food and Drink in America: A History* (1981, p. 309):

> I can remember carrying Red Cross flour maybe 24 pounds of it six miles over these hills. We didn't dare set it down for fear of getting it wet or a hole in it ... Then mothers and sisters would spend all day on hill-sides picking maybe a bushel of wild greens. We'd have corn meal and hog lard, some greens and generally everyone had a cow and we'd have some milk. In the late fall, maybe I'd go to the garden and find an old frozen cabbage to cook.

Then me and my brother we'd go work all day for some farmer for 50¢ and a meal and take the money up in beans and potatoes and apples a bushel of each and walk 3–4 miles home after 10 hours in the fields.

"Making Do"

Since money during the Depression was tight for many families, and food often scarce, family cooks devised creative means to provide tasty and filling meals. Rita Van Amber of Menomonie, Wisconsin, reports on her memories in her book *Stories and Recipes of the Great Depression of the 1930s, Vol. 2.* (1986–93, p. 48):

Mom always set a good table. We had plenty to eat but not much else. It was often just a large pot of vegetable or potato soup, made with water and served with home made bread. Mom always made 18 or 20 loaves of bread a week and we had plenty of hot biscuits made by Dad for breakfast. We loved it; the soup and bread filled us up ... She always made a lot of what we called cowboy stew. It was simple, very filling and delicious with home made bread. It was just venison roast, diced chopped onion and slices of potatoes, boiled until tender. We always had venison; we lived where deer were plentiful. We picked wild raspberries and choke cherries for Mom to can. She made what she called Sunshine.

Depression Impacts and Changes

Living through the Depression and "making do" for so many years often left impressions on people that were hard to shake. One individual, K.S., recounts in Thacker's *Recipes & Remembrances of the Great Depression* (1993, p. 116) how the memory of a Depression "make do" food item led to disappointment later:

I grew up on "sauces" made of flour or cornstarch mixed with water or milk. Uncooked it was wallpaper paste. Cooked with pan drippings it was gravy, add sugar or honey and it was pudding. One day, years later, I ordered "blanc mange" from a menu at a fancy French restaurant. I felt gypped, it was just old cornstarch pudding!

Another individual, G.A., recalls how scarcity and necessity meant eating habits much different from contemporary ones (ibid, p. 123). "I never saw snacks, and no one would eat between meals like they do now. We ate supper at 6 PM and went to bed a couple of hours after that."

Gardens and Canning

The produce from gardens helped many Depression families eat better. Canning was one of the ways to preserve the garden's bounty past the harvest. Billie Hansberger of Cuba, Illinois, is quoted in Thibideau's *Dining During the Depression* (1993, p. 195) as recounting his family's efforts to use their garden to its maximum potential:

During the Depression, my mother and father grew and raised most of the food for our family.

We always had plenty to eat because Dad was a good gardener who could raise anything. He grew vegetables, raspberries, strawberries and peaches.

Besides the more common vegetables like radishes, beans, tomatoes and cabbage, Dad grew some more unusual items including oyster plants and celery. Of course Mother's job was to preserve the extras for winter eating.

Many nights I can remember her staying up late to take the quarts of green beans out of the boiler and set them on the counter to cool before putting them with the others in our big storage closet.

Vegetables that Mother didn't can were stored outdoors between layers of dirt and straw. They kept well and it was always fun to bring in a fresh head of cabbage, carrots, squash or onions during the cold winter months.

The Entrepreneur

The entrepreneur spirit endured throughout the Great Depression, with many advances made in the kitchen in particular, be it through the advent of the refrigerator or the development of frozen foods. Rita Van Amber writes about an entrepreneur from Minnesota in 1936 in *Stories and Recipes of the Great Depression of the 1930s, Vol. II.* (1986–93):

The first Bridgeman's Ice Cream store to open in Minnesota met ominous forecasts from the public.

"How many people would have a nickel to spare to buy an ice cream cone these days?" "Minnesota was just too cold." "The season was too short for anything like that around here in these times." Comments like this were heard as a daring entrepreneur went right ahead and opened a beautiful, shiny, bright ice cream store.

Somehow people found a spare nickel now and then and thoroughly enjoyed going into this cheerful busy place with all those flavors displayed behind glass. One just didn't know which to choose. You sampled each other's cone to see if your selection measured up. And you came back.

Within eighteen months, six more Bridgeman's Ice Cream stores opened and all were highly successful.

Recipes

Cooks devised numerous recipes that allowed them to use substitute ingredients and provide a variety of meals. Using a new processed food item that evolved during the Depression, Spam Stew was consumed in many households. It contained one can of Spam, one large potato, one medium onion, one stalk of celery, one garlic clove, two cups of water, and salt and pepper.

Breads and soups were common staples. A recipe for Baking Powder Biscuits, as noted in Rita Van Amber's *Stories and Recipes of the Great Depression of the 1930s, Vol. II,* (1986–93, p. 29), includes two cups of flour, one tablespoon of baking powder, 1/2 teaspoon of salt, 1/4 cup of shortening, and 3/4 cup of milk or buttermilk. These ingredients were lightly mixed, dropped by a spoon onto a cookie sheet, then placed in the oven to bake at 350° F until browned. Homemade vegetable soup could contain any variety of vegetables. A common version included tomatoes, potatoes, cabbage, carrots, onions, and celery. To "extend" the meal, the cook could add some hamburger meat patties or a can of Campbell's soup.

For special occasions or for a treat, cakes and pies could be made with substitute ingredients. One example of a cake made with substitute ingredients is the milkless, eggless, butterless cake. It contained two cups of brown sugar, one cup of raisins, one teaspoon of cloves, two cups of hot water, one teaspoon of salt, two teaspoons of lard, and one teaspoon of cinnamon. The ingredients were to be brought to a boil and boiled for five minutes. Once they cooled two cups of flour and one teaspoon of soda (previously dissolved in hot water) were added. This recipe made two loaves of cake that were baked for 45 minutes at 325°F.

Suggested Research Topics

- Take a trip to a grocery store and shop for: 1 lb. of chicken, 1 quart of milk, 1 dozen eggs, 1 lb. of coffee, 1 twenty-ounce loaf of bread, 5 lbs. Sugar, 2 lbs. of potatoes, and 1 lb. of bananas. Compose your total cost with the Depression Shopping List cost. Are products such as Spam, Ritz Crackers, Bisquick, and Pepperidge Farm still available?

- Describe how business practices and a willingness to take risks enabled a real entrepreneur to operate even in difficult economic times.

- Compare the government's role in feeding the hungry in the 1930s with the government's role at the beginning of the twenty-first century. What would happen to people if help was not available?

Bibliography

Sources

Anderson, Jean. *American Century Cookbook: The Most Popular Recipes of the 20th Century.* New York: Clarkson Potter, 1997.

Britten, Loretta, and Sarah Brash, eds. *Hard Times: The 30s.* Alexandria, VA: Time-Life Books, 1998.

Hooker, Richard J. *Food and Drink in America: A History.* New York: The Bobbs-Merrill Company, Inc., 1981.

Le Sueur, Meridel. *Women on the Breadlines.* St. Paul, MN: West End Press, 1984.

McElvaine, Robert S., ed. *Down & Out in the Great Depression: Letters from the "Forgotten Man."* Chapel Hill: The University of North Carolina Press, 1983.

Schwartz-Nobel, Loretta. *Starving in the Shadow of Plenty.* New York: G.P. Putnam's Sons, 1981.

Smallzried, Kathleen Ann. *The Everlasting Pleasure: Influences on America's Kitchens, Cooks and Cookery, from 1565 to the Year 2000.* New York: Appleton-Century-Crofts, Inc., 1956.

"The Story of Betty," [cited October 11, 2001] available from the World Wide Web at http://www.bettycrocker.com/meetbetty/mb_tsob.asp.

"The Story of FritoLay," [cited October 11, 2001] available from the World Wide Web at http://www.fritolay.com/company.html

Tucker, David M. *Kitchen Gardening in America: A History.* Ames: Iowa State University, 1993.

Watkins, T. H. *The Hungry Years: A Narrative History of the Great Depression in America.* New York: Henry Holt and Company, 1999.

Winslow, Susan. *Brother, Can You Spare a Dime? America From the Wall Street Crash to Pearl Harbor, An Illustrated Documentary.* New York: Paddington Press, Ltd., 1976.

Further Reading

Algren, Nelson. *America Eats.* Iowa City: University of Iowa Press, 1992.

DuSablon, Mary Anna. *America's Collectible Cookbooks: The History, the Politics, the Recipes.* Athens, OH: Ohio University Press, 1994.

Food and Drug Administration (FDA), [cited October 11, 2001] available from the World Wide Web at http://www.fda.gov.

The Food Stamp Program, [cited October 11, 2001] available from the World Wide Web at http://www.foodusa.org.

Kraft Foods, [cited October 11, 2001] available from the World Wide Web at http://www.kraftfoods.com.

Mariani, John F. *The Dictionary of American Food and Drink.* New Haven: Ticknor & Fields, 1983.

Mendelson, Anne. *Stand Facing the Stove: The Story of the Women Who Gave America "The Joy of Cooking."* New York: Henry Holt and Company, 1996.

Reynolds, Edward B., and Michael Kennedy. *Whistleberries, Stirabout, & Depression Cake.* Helena, MT: Falcon Publishing, 2000.

United States Department of Agriculture, [cited October 11, 2001] available from the World Wide Web at http://www.usda.gov.

Depression Recipes and Remembrances

Thacker, Emily. *Recipes & Remembrances of the Great Depression.* Canton, OH: Tresco Publishers, 1993.

Thibodeau, Karen, ed. *Dining During the Depression.* Glendale, WI: Reminisce Books, 1996.

Van Amber, Rita. *Stories and Recipes of the Great Depression of the 1930s. Vol. I and II.* Menomonie, WI: Van Amber Publishers, 1986–93.

Wagner, Patricia R. *Depression Era Recipes.* Cambridge, MN: Adventure Publications, Inc., 1989.

See Also

Everyday Life

Global Impact

1929-1939

The crash of the U.S. stock market in October 1929 and the ensuing Great Depression did not immediately sweep the world in a universal wave of economic decline. Rather, the degree, type, and timing of economic events varied greatly among nations. Many believed the Depression was largely "exported" by the United States to Europe and other countries in the 1930s through the various economic policies it adopted.

The U.S. economy was flourishing perhaps more than any other nation in the 1920s. With the onset of the Great Depression, it suffered sharp declines in manufacturing output and general employment. Other industrial countries experienced difficulties. For example, one outcome of the Great Depression was a collapse of world trade. The sharp decline was brought on by a round of tax increases on imported goods (tariffs) instituted by any nations turning inward trying to bolster their own sagging economies. In 1931 German industrial production decreased more than 40 percent; 29 percent in France; and 14 percent in Britain from 1929 levels. It was abundantly clear that the world was heading into a global crisis. As a result, international tensions and labor strife began rising. Events of 1931 began cascading, with one crisis leading to another. Austria's largest bank collapsed in May 1931 and concerns over the possible weak financial condition of other European banks immediately led to European residents rushing to banks where they had their money deposited. The rush of crowds of depositors all at once further weakened banks and even affected banks not

previously in financial trouble. This run on banks led to failure of German banks by mid-June. As a result, Germany announced it could no longer keep paying its debts resulting from World War I (1914–1918). This led to economic problems in other European nations and the United States, reliant in part on those payments to fund their own government operations. The new and struggling German government, called the Weimar Republic, itself raised international concern. The young government was heavily burdened by war debts imposed by other European nations. With its economy struggling, its citizens had little faith in the government. Economic crisis continued to spread to other European nations. Great Britain responded with major budget cuts and finally a change in government. By September 1931 Britain had exhausted its options to stabilize its economy and decided to free its currency from the longstanding gold standard, allowing it to pursue other monetary options and strategies. This meant Britain's money was no longer tied formally to exchange rates of other nations based on a standard value of gold. This change gave it much greater flexibility to alter the value of its money in trying to recover from the Great Depression. Other nations began following the same path.

By 1933 unemployment rates in Europe were soaring. Of the available workforce in each country, unemployment rates were 26.3 percent in Germany, 23.7 percent in Sweden, 14.1 percent in Britain, 20.4 percent in Belgium, and 28.8 percent in Denmark. In France social unrest was escalating with the effects of unemployment in addition to the rise of the Nazi Party in neighboring Germany. Political leaders of the various nations were coming under increased pressure to adopt forceful policies to end the Depression. Seeking solutions to the world crisis, more than 60 nations met at the 1933 World Economic Conference in London. When cooperative international solutions proved futile and the conference collapsed, the world seemed sentenced to a prolonged economic depression. Each nation was largely left to recover on its own.

Of even greater consequence to the world, the economic hardships of the Great Depression led to destabilization of European politics. The nations one by one, led first by the United States and then Britain, turned inward to try to solve their problems apart from other nations. The lack of economic and political cooperation fueled the growth of nationalism. Nationalism is when a nation places its needs significantly over the interests of other nations. This trend had major effects for the world economy and politics. Most notably the National Socialist party grew rapidly in Germany bringing with it a new ruler, Adolf Hitler.

Chronology:

October 1929: The U.S. stock market crash damages Latin America economies, but immediate economic effects in Europe are more limited.

June 17, 1930: President Herbert Hoover signs the Hawley-Smoot Tariff Act dramatically raising import taxes on foreign goods leading to a major disruption of world trade and substantial economic hardships in Europe.

May 1931: Austria's largest commercial bank, the Kreditanstalt, collapses triggering a financial panic throughout Europe.

September 21, 1931: British Parliament drops the gold standard meaning British banks are no longer required to back British currency with gold.

January 1933: Adolf Hitler becomes chancellor, assuming governing leadership of Germany.

April 19, 1933: President Franklin Roosevelt takes the U.S. economy off the gold standard.

June 1933: The World Economic Conference unsuccessfully seeks cooperation among nations to resolve the global economic crisis.

September 25, 1936: France, Britain, and the United States agree on monetary stabilization measures marking the beginning of international economic cooperation.

September 1939: Germany invades Poland leading to the outbreak of World War II and eventual end of the Great Depression.

The global economic crisis and the world's poorly organized response to it in part led to the outbreak of World War II in Europe in 1939.

Many nations believed the Great Depression was exported by the United States. Though the European nations were economically struggling from war debts and recovery, the U.S. economy boomed through the 1920s until the October 1929 stock market crash. Hit with huge financial losses from the crash, U.S. investors pulled out of European investments. In an effort to promote more sales of goods produced in the United States, Congress raised tariffs on foreign produced goods making them less attractive to U.S. consumers. The withdrawal of investments, raising of tariffs, insistence that war debts owed European nations be paid to the Untied States, and retreat from the gold standard all served to further weaken foreign economies. This influence eventually pushed them into the Depression as well due to the loss of foreign capital and markets for their goods.

Issue Summary

International Relations During the Great Depression

Increasing economic prosperity in Europe through the 1920s was largely fueled by the industrial and financial strength of the United States. Following World War I (1914–1918) the United States was the largest producer, lender, and investor in the world. As a result when the U.S. stock market crashed, marking the start of heavy economic decline, other nations looked to the United States to help reinforce the shaky economic prosperity in Western Europe and other parts of the world.

The most immediate foreign effect of the economic crisis occurred in Latin America. The Latin American economy was highly dependent on selling raw materials to U.S. industries. Europe was not as quickly affected as American loans and investments kept coming, though at an even slower pace. By 1931, however, the flow of investment capital from the United States had halted. In fact, the flow of money reversed as Americans began withdrawing investment money out of Europe to pay their own debts.

Perhaps the most significant factor leading to a global economic crisis was not the crash of Wall Street but a dramatic decline in world trade. This decline was largely triggered by "protectionist" legislation passed by the major trading nations. Nations were trying to protect prices of their domestically produced goods from foreign competition. This global trend began when President Herbert Hoover (served 1929–1933), attempting to raise America's farm produce prices, signed the Hawley-Smoot Tariff Act on June 17, 1930. The act raised import taxes (duties) on selected goods from 26 percent to 50 percent. This new level was so high that other nations were no longer able to sell their goods in the United States. In reaction they raised their own import tariffs. These increases made it difficult for U.S. companies to sell their products abroad. As a result world trade declined 40 percent. A dramatic decline of income and widespread unemployment in Europe followed. A few European nations such as

Sweden were able to close their doors to the spreading depression due to what proved to be fortunate economic policy decisions.

The dramatic decline in international trade led to sharp drops in European production, increased unemployment, and finally collapse of some banking systems. With the U.S. economy showing some short-lived signs of recovery, Hoover attempted to blame inadequate European policies for the prolonged Depression. He believed the stock market crash would not have led to a full-blown global depression without Europe's panics as evidenced by a number of bank runs in 1931.

Frustrated with Hoover's perspective and lack of interest in substantially helping Europe, many foreign nations looked forward to the newly elected President Franklin D. Roosevelt (served 1933–1945) taking office in March 1933. But much to their dismay, Roosevelt continued the long trend of his predecessors. He turned his New Deal programs inward to solve U.S. domestic problems. As a result hopes of stabilizing the global economic situation at a World Economic Conference held in London in June 1933 met with resounding failure.

With each nation left to individually recover, the effects of the Great Depression on economic and political events in Germany, Austria, France, Russia, Latin America, the Far East, and Australia differed. Because of their diverse experiences, the European nations and other global regions are listed below in the order of most affected to lesser affected nations and regions.

Germany and Austria

The European countries hardest hit by the Great Depression were Germany and Austria. Collapse of world trade in 1930 had major affects. German production fell over 40 percent. Hard times brought growing labor unrest, and with labor unrest political changes began brewing. In 1930, 107 Nazi and 77 Communist party members were elected to German parliament. Austria's economy, intertwined with Germany's, was also severely impacted. Austria's largest commercial bank, Vienna's Kreditanstalt, collapsed in May 1931, which financed two-thirds of Austrian industrial production and held 70 percent of the country's bank assets. Its collapse triggered a financial panic throughout Europe leading to a stampede on European banks by depositors. In June and July 1931 the German central bank, the Reichsbank, lost $2 billion in gold and foreign currency to withdrawals. To provide some economic relief to a struggling Germany in 1931, U.S. President Herbert Hoover temporarily suspended for one year requirements for war debt (reparation) pay-

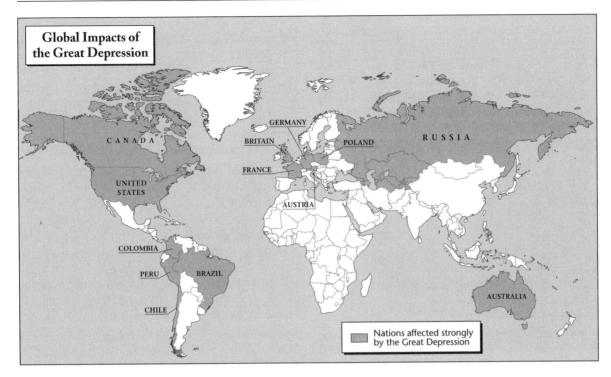

Map of the countries affected strongly by the Great Depression. (The Gale Group.)

ments Germany was making to the United States and other Western European countries. These payments imposed by the victorious nations of Europe and the United States followed Germany's surrender. They were very steep—amounting to $500 million a year. German payments were to be paid to France (52 percent), Britain (22 percent), Italy (10 percent), and Belgium (8 percent). These countries would in turn use this money to pay war debts owed to the United States.

In 1932, as the one-year suspension of Germany's war reparation payments came to an end, European nations tried to convince the United States to cancel the reparations altogether. They believed the payments were undermining the German economy and threatening the stability of its new government. Social unrest that resulted was leading many to political radicalism, supporting the rising communist and Nazi parties. President Hoover refused to permanently relieve Germany of the debts believing Germany should not be let off the hook for its role in World War I and needing the payments to help fight the declining U.S. economy. This disagreement led to further distancing between the United States and European nations and continued economic hardships in Germany. Six million Germans, almost one-third of the workforce, were unemployed. Germany announced it could no longer make war reparation payments and stopped making them. Germany

and central European nations began to adopt additional policies rooted strongly in nationalism that further distanced their economies from the global market.

By January 1933 Adolf Hitler gained the main governing position, known as chancellor, over the struggling German nation. German President Paul von Hindenburg continued serving as the more ceremonial head of state. When a main government building in Berlin, the Reichstag, burned in February 1933, Hitler claimed it was a communist plot and used it as an excuse to assume totalitarian powers. He suspended most civil laws governing Germany.

Throughout the early years of the Depression the National Socialist party led by Hitler's Nazis had steadily gained strength in German elections. By strongly supporting Hitler, the German voters were making a statement against democracy and capitalism in that country. When President von Hindenburg died on August 2, 1934, Hitler replaced him, completing his takeover and gaining full control of the nation.

Ironically Roosevelt's New Deal and Hitler's New Order were launched in the same year. The New Deal was a combination of diverse economic and social programs promoted by Roosevelt's administration beginning in March 1933. They were designed to provide relief to those Americans most affected by the

Adolph Hitler breaks ground on the Autobahn as part of his "New Order" plan to stimulate the German economy in 1933. (© Bettmann/Corbis. Reproduced by permission.)

Great Depression. A key aspect was dramatic growth of the federal government and its increased role in the daily lives of Americans.

The New Order was a grand economic and social scheme promoted by Adolf Hitler built on beliefs such as racial superiority, military expansion, government operation of industry, and strict control of German citizens. The New Order was in response to the post-war economic crisis of Germany worsened by affects of the Great Depression. Americans were fearful of the drastic economic and political change occurring in Germany. Some Americans feared the New Deal could lead to similar changes in the United States and threaten U.S. democracy and capitalism.

A key goal of Hitler's during this period of the early 1930s was the desire to acquire more "breathing room" for Germany. Germany had a large population for a relatively small geographic space. His desire for German expansion would require several years of preparation. To this end he applied major public works programs in the early 1930s to not only aid in economic recovery but achieve his expansion goals. Construction of the famed German autobahn system in the mid-1930s would later support military needs for rapidly transporting military forces long distances.

The actual militarization industrial program itself began in 1935 with building the necessary armament. The German unemployment rate declined to a point that labor shortages existed by 1938. At the time many, even including some prominent Americans such as Henry Ford, hailed Hitler as a hero for his economic recovery achievements. From 1932 to 1938 industrial production rose 75 percent. This recovery, however, came at a great expense to personal freedoms.

The dramatic nature of Germany's economic condition following World War I led to dramatic events that would pull it out of economic strife. The combination of destruction from war, loss of life, collapse of the existing government, and great expense in conducting the war had wrecked the economy. In addition to these factors, the European nations victorious in the war chose harsh financial and other penalties for the war that would almost ensure that Germany would not be able to economically recover. Unemployment skyrocketed and industrial production plummeted. Unrest in the population made it susceptible to radical politics. Into this setting arrived Adolf Hitler preaching a new path to prosperity and power through militaristic means. Hitler gained public support and secured his control over Germany by 1933. Hitler's primary strategy was to disengage Germany from world financial circles, stop war reparation payments, and use wartime industrialization as the path to full employment. The great desire of European nations and the United States to avoid future military conflict opened the door for Hitler to pursue his plan with minimal outside interference. As a result, national pride, economic prosperity, and employment returned by the mid-1930s.

Great Britain

Through the nineteenth century Great Britain was the world's economic leader. But Britain's prominence was distinctly sliding after World War I and was still declining in October 1929 when the U.S. stock market crashed. However, Britain was not immediately affected by the crash.

Several factors contributed to a delayed reaction. First, Britain's stock market had a much smaller proportion of investors than the U.S. stock market. Therefore stock market declines were less an economic factor in Britain. As investors in U.S. stock markets bailed out, British investors, fearful of a broader international economic impact, did as well. In addition U.S. financiers investing in British stocks pulled their money out to cover losses in the United States causing British investors to pull back as well fearing the companies they had been investing in would decline in financial health.

More About...

International Gold Standard

A major factor influencing international economic relations during the Great Depression was the controversy over the gold standard. The gold standard is a monetary system in which a standard unit of currency in any given nation, such as the U.S. dollar and British pound, would be equivalent to a fixed weight of gold. Paper currency, called notes, could be exchanged at home or in another country for a certain amount of gold. In 1929 the United States was required to have enough gold to back 40 percent of its currency. Using the gold standard, exchange rates between nations were fixed. The gold, or a currency that can be converted to gold, provided the means for making international payments. The gold standard was attractive for nations because it created some level of predictability in international trade by fixing currency exchange rates. Briefly, if exchange rates between two nations strayed out of a certain set range, then gold flowed from one nation to the other until the rates returned to the desired level. Predictability of exchanges between currencies came because the gold standard limited the freedom of nations to change the value of their currency.

In the United States the price of gold was $20 per ounce of gold. A $10 coin would have a value of one-half ounce of gold. Viewed in another way, a U.S. dollar equaled 23.22 grains of gold. Since the British pound sterling was 113 grains of pure gold, one British pound equaled almost five U.S. dollars. In the United States the price of gold was held constant from 1791 until 1933.

Yet again nations began returning to the gold standard as the world's economy recovered. The United States introduced a concept known as "pegging" in which a minimum dollar price for gold was set for exchange with foreign nations. This formed a new basis for the gold standard after World War II. The scarcity of gold and mounting foreign debts led the United States to abandon the gold standard in 1971. The role of gold in international financial matters had finally ended as many economists concluded the gold standard offered more disadvantages than advantages. It was an expensive system to operate as nations had to maintain large amounts of gold. It also limited the flexibility of nations in their monetary affairs that at times restricted economic growth and expansion. After 1971 the Federal Reserve controlled the value of U.S. money. Despite no longer basing its currency on gold, in the 1990s the United States still held 8,000 tons of gold at various depositories across the country.

Secondly, Britain's economic troubles came with the general collapse in world trade in 1930, which was triggered by the U.S. Congress passing the Hawley-Smoot Tariff Act. Following the U.S. lead Britain also adopted taxes on goods purchased from other countries (import tariffs). For a century Britain had no tariffs, therefore for a time this action brought additional government revenue. But as a result of tariffs adopted by many nations, worldwide exports fell from $56 billion in 1928 to $22 billion in 1932. By 1935 they had further declined to $20 billion before modestly rebounding to $23 billion by 1938. Britain's pattern of economic trouble generally followed this global trend in trade.

In addition to the 1929 stock market crash and 1930 decline in world trade, the third factor influencing the timing of Britain's economic decline also came from the United States. President Hoover's one-year suspension of German war reparation payments in 1931 further increased economic strife in Great Britain on top of the trade loss. Britain's weakened economy, caused largely by the decline in world trade, had become increasingly dependent on war payments received from Germany. The British continued to argue that German reparation payments were too stiff and endangered the peace and security of Europe. They wished to see the payments suspended permanently while Germany's new Weimar Republic government tried to gain acceptance and stability. Britain's reliance on the payments in the face of its own war debts to the United States, however, also meant it would need those debts reduced or eliminated as well. Neither was to occur, though Germany would soon default on its payments forcing Britain to take major action in salvaging its monetary system, mostly through abandoning the gold standard.

With the loss of war payments, Britain saw no other option but to take dramatic economic action.

An unemployed man stands on a street corner in England in 1939. *(© Hulton-Deutsch Collection/Corbis. Reproduced by permission.)*

Stunning the world, on September 21, 1931, British Parliament suspended the gold standard believing the move would rescue its economy by raising the price of goods through lowering the value of its money. It could not make this move when rigidly tied to economies of other nations through the gold standard. With the British currency no longer backed with gold, however, it was then clear to many other nations that Britain was no longer in position to provide interna-

tional economic leadership. The British pound depreciated (fell in value) 30 percent by that December. Following Britain, twenty other countries abandoned the gold standard by spring of 1932. Each nation would now manipulate their own currencies as they saw fit. Britain's suspension of the gold standard proved a landmark event in disrupting the global monetary system. No longer were international transactions tied to a universal standard such as gold.

Like many others, Britain's economy reached its lowest point in 1932 as unemployment rose. Yet possibly owing to the monetary policies it quickly adopted including getting off the gold standard and raising tariffs, Britain rebounded sooner than most other countries. Amazingly for the next several years Britain actually had one of its economically healthiest periods in British history. The economic impact of the Great Depression on Great Britain actually proved less dramatic than the economic declines it suffered immediately following both world wars. Only Japan and Sweden of the industrially developed countries faced less economic hardship during the 1930s.

Britain's recovery did not mean economic tensions no longer existed with the United States. In fact war debt payments owed by Britain to the United States became a bitter issue between the two nations in 1934. The debts had quickly built up during World War I from both loans and purchasing war supplies on credit. Repayment in annual installments was expected by the United States soon after the war ended. The United States had shown some leniency toward Germany regarding its war reparation payment requirements, even temporarily suspending them at times. But Congress was intent that Britain as well as France pay war debts and Germany eventually as well. Neither Britain nor France could afford to pay the full amounts owed. Trying to avoid default, Britain made token (partial) payments in 1932 and 1933, while France chose not to make any payments. In March 1933 during a special session of Congress called by President Roosevelt to pass domestic emergency bills, a bill was introduced to further press war debt payments. It did not pass during the special session. Not supportive of such legislation, Roosevelt declared in late 1933 that Britain's token payments were sufficient to avoid default. By January 1934, however, Congress passed the war debt bill despite Roosevelt's opposition, known as the Johnson Act. The act prohibited further American loans to foreign governments who were in default of their debt payments.

The Johnson Act essentially declared Britain and France defaulters. This action by Congress became a severe obstacle for relations between the United States and the two European nations for several years. Great Britain defaulted by choice following passage of the act. In the end the Johnson Act brought the opposite result Congress intended. Practically all war debt payments stopped with only Finland continuing to pay.

Following collapse of the 1933 World Economic Conference, Britain established a strong protectionist position keeping aloof of economic developments in other nations. Finally, following 16 months of negotiations at the instigation of President Roosevelt, Britain and the United States signed an Anglo-American Trade Agreement on November 17, 1938. This agreement marked the beginning of a period of increased economic cooperation.

Given the social programs of Britain, as well as other European countries, the specter of breadlines and soup kitchens was less apparent. With decisive actions taken by the British government, such as leaving the gold standard in the early 1930s, conditions would improve. For the middle classes in Britain and other nations the 1930s saw a gradual revival of prosperity following the difficult post-war years of the 1920s. Unlike the United States, Europe had not enjoyed a post-war economic boom. Through the 1930s suburbs grew in Britain outside the main cities. The middle class enjoyed radios, record players, less expensive automobiles, refrigerators, and washing machines. The cheap franc in France enticed vacations to that country. For the working class conditions were far different. Their homes still lacked indoor bathrooms, unemployment was widespread, and for those still working the hours were long and conditions unsafe. Fear of Germany and another war would soon push domestic concerns from the forefront.

France

Based largely on exports, the French economy grew rapidly through the 1920s. About 30 percent of manufacturing was tied to producing goods for selling in other nations (the export business). The French economy was fairly unfazed by the 1929 U.S. stock market crash. The collapse of world trade late in 1930, however, triggered by passage of the Hawley-Smoot Tariff Act brought trouble. Foreign demand for French goods began falling. The value of exports fell from 52 billion francs in 1929 to just 20 billion in 1932. Fortunately for the French economy the domestic demand for French goods rose, somewhat offsetting the effects in declining exports. For this reason unemployment did not peak in France until the mid-1930s. Even at its peak, French unemployment rates were far less than in the United States. It remained, at its height, less than 5 percent of the work force as compared to the

25 percent level the United States had reached in 1933. The fall in production also was gradual, estimated at less than a 20 percent decline, with no recovery by the late 1930s. Whereas employment in Britain began a slow steady improvement trend after 1932, French unemployment stayed up until World War II. In overall production, by 1935 Britain had returned to its 1929 level, but France hit its bottom that year and did not begin recovery until 1938.

A key factor hindering French economic recovery was increased political instability. France experienced a greater decline in social cohesion in the 1930s than most countries. As political instability grew investments in its industry declined. Capital was leaving the country to safer investment opportunities elsewhere. By mid-1936 there was a major drain of gold from the country. French leaders became convinced the only avenue left toward economic recovery was devaluation of the currency, which was accomplished by leaving the gold standard despite substantial French public opposition.

Most likely France's increased economic, as well as, political isolation from world markets kept its economy from falling very far. But it also kept France from rebounding with the other nations as well. Foreign investments in industry declined and stayed down through the remainder of the 1930s. Both the industry's aging equipment and political instability hampered any improvement in production.

Russia

In contrast to most other European nations, Russia was substantially detached from global interaction during the Great Depression. As a fully communist state, Russia removed itself from world markets. Controlling a vast area of the Asian continent and considerable resources enabled it to do so. In 1928 Russian leader Joseph Stalin began a five-year plan for economic development. The plan eliminated private business and focused on production of industrial machinery and farm equipment by state-owned factories. Stalin brought all of Russia's private farms under government control. This policy led to the starvation of millions of people in 1932 and 1933, particularly in the agricultural region of the Ukraine. USSR heavy industry, in contrast to agriculture, expanded rapidly through the 1930s in Russia, Ukraine, Caucasus, and Central Asian regions. The nation was well down the road toward becoming a leading industrial power, but much to the detriment of other domestic economic developments and personal freedoms. Heavy censorship, limitations on individual liberties, and murder of opponents were key elements of Stalin's rule. Due to its extreme detachment from the world's marketplace,

Russia was largely immune to the Great Depression and instead dealt with its own internal political and economic issues.

Latin America

In the Western Hemisphere effects of the Great Depression were felt immediately in Latin America. The flow of U.S. capital fueling industrial development stopped abruptly. In addition Latin American nations saw prices for the region's raw materials drop sharply as the U.S. and European markets greatly declined eliminating their need for the materials. This trade decline led to a substantial decrease in government revenue. To stop the decline in revenues Latin American countries raised their tariffs on imported goods. They also focused more on manufacturing consumer goods for domestic use to replace the more expensive imported goods. Heavy industrial production remained largely centered on Mexico's iron and steel industry.

Naturally some variation among Latin American countries existed as their individual economies responded differently to the economic troubles in the United States and Europe. For example Argentina heavily relied on beef and wheat exports to Great Britain. Being the wealthiest of the Latin American countries, Argentina weathered the Depression relatively well as Britain's recovery came quickly. Other nations felt greater effects. Chile and Peru, which mostly exported ore and oil, were hit harder than Columbia and Brazil who relied more on coffee exports. Chile's exports plummeted by 76 percent. Peru, also experiencing a major political crisis with civil war from 1930 to 1933, saw its cotton exports increase by 1934 making up for the declines in mineral exports. The Columbian textile industry also grew significantly during the 1930s though the coffee industry remained its primary focus.

The Great Depression proved to be a major turning point in Latin American economic development. A strong push toward economic nationalism resulted. Latin American governments, quietly deferring to foreign influence, particularly the United States', became much more involved in economic issues. To protect jobs during the Depression, many Latin American countries adopted measures requiring companies to employ a certain percentage of local citizens rather than workers brought from other countries. Overall, Latin America was able to economically recover relatively quickly from the Great Depression by increasing production of consumer goods rather than relying on imports and by increasing job opportunities for their citizens.

Political impacts of the Great Depression in Latin America were also less severe than in Europe. European political movements during the 1930s of fascism and totalitarian governments developed less in Latin America. Socialist parties in power were largely moderate and not radical. Communist parties did become more active, influenced by developments in Russia, but the ruling elite in Latin American governments largely suppressed them. Exceptions included the rise in Chile of the socialist Popular Front party in 1938 and the briefly successful fascist Integralistas party in Brazil in the mid-1930s.

As Latin American countries increased economic independence, Franklin D. Roosevelt with his Good Neighbor Policy continued decreasing U.S. intervention in Latin American affairs. Instead the United States offered economic, technical, and military aid programs that were warmly received throughout most of Latin America. In 1933 the United States signed a Reciprocal Tariff Agreement with Latin American countries to promote international economic stability in the Western Hemisphere. Otherwise the United States sought to maintain a cordial role in the region. President Roosevelt even quietly accepted Mexico's take over of U.S.- and British-owned petroleum facilities in 1938.

Far East

Just as differences clearly existed among European and Latin American nations regarding their experiences during the Great Depression, China and Japan followed different paths as well.

By the late 1920s Britain, through its colonial policies, still controlled key Chinese ports and the nation's monetary policies. China was largely an agrarian nation primarily producing for its own domestic consumption. Involvement in world trade was limited, therefore China suffered a major recession following World War I. Its currency system, based on a silver rather than gold standard, was in chaos. Some economic gains were made, however, in the 1920s with growth of the textile industry. World demand for Chinese goods remained low essentially until the late 1920s. Impacts on China's economy during the Great Depression largely came when the U.S. Congress passed the Silver Purchase Act in June 1934, which spurred a period of intense silver purchase. China found its silver supply rapidly depleting, which weakened its currency. Finally China was forced off the silver standard and began a currency reform. Prices and the economy in general began recovering but another disruption came when Japan invaded China in 1937.

Japan's economic experiences through the 1930s greatly differed from China's. A major 1923 earthquake upset an already fragile economy. Costs of reconstruction and monetary policies adopted through the 1920s led to ongoing economic problems. Economic growth developed as Japan increased rice exports to U.S. markets by the late 1920s. With the economy growing healthier by 1929 Japan decided to return to the gold standard in January 1930 just before the Great Depression arrived. Consequently the 1930 collapse of world trade greatly affected Japan as the price of rice dropped sharply on international markets. Japan again left the gold standard in December 1931 and charted a dramatic new course.

New internal political developments, primarily involving the Japanese military becoming the nation's principal political force, propelled economic recovery. Growth of heavy industry aimed at a buildup of arms led to a quick Japanese economic recovery. Military expansionism through foreign conquest, begun with an invasion of Manchuria in 1931, grew when Japan invaded China in 1937. Like Germany, Japan's increasing nationalistic direction was made possible by the rest of the world struggling with their own financial crises brought on by the Great Depression. The military took advantage of this economic crisis to seek greater detachment from the international economic relations and pursue military expansion, which would eventually lead to world war.

Australia

Leading up to the Great Depression Australia was heavily in debt to British banks and relied greatly on wheat exports to drive their economy. The collapse of world trade in 1930 led to a major drop in government revenue as well as Australians' income. To address the drop in revenue, the Australian government instructed its wheat farmers to boost production more so as to increase sales abroad. The measure was widely known as the "Grow More Wheat" program. The world was oversupplied in wheat, however, and farmers found themselves selling their bumper crops at prices below what it cost to grow them. To provide financial support to the farmers the Australian government passed the Wheat Advances Act to make loans available to wheat farmers. This proved ineffective because Australia's banks lacked the funds to effectively carry out the program. Australia then turned to other monetary policies to stimulate economic recovery. Devaluation of Australian currency in 1931 finally worked and farm exports increased once again because Australian produce cost less in foreign countries.

World Economic Conference of 1933

In 1933 a key opportunity came for the world's nations, including the United States, Great Britain, and France, to work cooperatively in solving the world economic problems. During the first years of the Great Depression a series of international conferences were held each year focusing on specific issues, such as farm produce prices. By 1931 as the crisis deepened it became evident this piecemeal approach was insufficient. National leaders began pushing for a World Economic Conference to address a range of basic issues. The issues were complicated and varied but generally centered on war debt problems, German war reparation payments, easing international trade restrictions, and stabilizing currencies. Currency stabilization means that each nation's currency would be based on a common standard, such as the gold standard, which in time would greatly benefit world trade by assuring the prices of goods.

Preparation for the conference was itself complicated, as each nation's leaders wanted to address economic situations specific to their country. Britain primarily wanted to solve its war debt problems, while Germany sought to decrease war reparation payments. France wanted to get all countries back on the gold standard and the United States was most interested in reducing trade restrictions. The United States insisted that war debts owed by European nations should not even be discussed. Nor was Roosevelt interested in discussing means for stabilizing currencies. In fact to the shock of many nations, less than two months before the meeting Roosevelt took the United States off the gold standard on April 19, 1933.

Amid this contentious atmosphere the World Economic Conference opened on June 12, 1933, at London's new Geological Museum. Over one thousand delegates from 65 nations crowded into the facility. The opening address by Britain's King George V was broadcast by radio around the world. No conference of this scale had ever been held before. Secretary of State Cordell Hull headed the U.S. delegation.

Despite President Roosevelt's clear disinterest in discussing the topic, the conference immediately focused on the tricky issues involved in stabilizing currencies of the various nations. As a result a complex draft agreement involving the U.S. delegation was completed by June 15. The U.S. delegation promptly journeyed back to the United States to present the draft to President Roosevelt for U.S. approval. The plan called for once again stabilizing the economies in terms of gold. By mid-June, however, prices of goods were rising in the United States and economic recovery seemed to be gaining strength.

A telephone operator in London writes share values on a blackboard two days after the Wall Street stock market crash in New York. (© Hulton-Deutsch Collection/Corbis. Reproduced by permission.)

Roosevelt's advisors warned the new agreement could stall economic progress on the domestic front. President Roosevelt therefore had to weigh domestic recovery based on rising U.S. prices while maintaining international relations and stabilizing international prices of goods. The president deliberated for three weeks during which the delegates at the Conference signed a further declaration on June 28 reaffirming their commitment to the draft agreement. They further stressed the importance of the gold standard for international trade. Expecting word of U.S. approval, nations such as Britain that recently dropped the gold standard planned to once again adopt it.

Finally, on July 3, 1933, Roosevelt announced his momentous decision. He issued a response from his holiday yacht, the *Indianapolis* anchored in Buzzard's Bay along the coast of Massachusetts. He chose to not accept the agreement. The Conference was not only stung by the decision, but also shocked by the harshness of Roosevelt's words in his response. Roosevelt strongly denounced the agreement calling it a distracting "experiment" by international bankers. He did not wish to hold the value of the U.S. dollar to some predetermined level. When the president's harsh note first arrived in London, the U.S. delegates spent several hours debating how to soften its tone. This ultimately proved futile because reaction to Roosevelt's note by other nations was swift. Britain angrily pulled out of the draft agreement to stabilize world currencies.

Some issues were resolved at the World Economic Conference between various participating nations apart from the more general sessions. For instance, Germany was successful in having it's commercial debts to Great Britain lessened. France and the other remaining gold standard countries of Italy, Poland, Holland, Belgium, and Switzerland decided to remain on the standard. They pledged to cooperate closely as a bloc among their central banks to improve trade between them. Ultimately this course charted by France and the other gold bloc countries proved difficult to maintain. It also led to their isolation from the worldwide economic recovery that began later in the 1930s. In contrast Japan had kept a low profile throughout the conference strongly embracing their economic nationalism.

Overall President Roosevelt's stern message left the conference in disarray. The U.S. delegation tried to pursue discussions on tariff reductions to help world trade but these efforts proved unproductive. The conference ended in mid-July ahead of the expected time. Roosevelt's message profoundly affected U.S. economic foreign policy through the remainder of the 1930s.

In the end, the great industrial nations of the western world chose not to seize the opportunity presented at the conference to work together. Protectionism outweighed cooperation as nations sought to protect their economies from influences of other countries. The conference marked a key stepping stone in the transition from internationalism of the 1920s to nationalism of the 1930s. Each nation had its own specific goal. For instance France wanted the gold standard, Britain and the United States did not. The United States wanted European nations to continue payments of war debts and reparation payments whereas most European nations did not. Hitler took advantage of the failure in international cooperation to further isolate German currency. He grew comfortable with the division growing between other nations over currency, trade, and debt issues.

Rise of Global Political Instability

With the collapse of the World Economic Conference in July 1933, it was abundantly clear that each nation was on its own to solve its economic problems. As various nations floundered economically, social unrest escalated. Such were the events in France, Spain, Germany, Italy, and Japan. The left-wing Popular Front rose in prominence in France in 1936 and acted to take France off the gold standard. The Front was then free to independently manipulate France's currency to achieve its economic goals. In May 1936 the Popular Front leader in Spain was elected president. General Francisco Franco led a revolt only two months later leading to the Spanish Civil War that lasted until 1939. In 1933 Hitler had strengthened his hold on the German government, as did Benito Mussolini in Italy. In Japan the military had gained control of the government in the early 1930s.

Concerns over the deteriorating political picture in Europe and Asia stimulated a call for international economic cooperation among some Western industrial nations. On September 25, 1936, France, Britain, and the United States announced agreement on an economic plan. Unlike earlier when Roosevelt dropped the gold standard and avoided international cooperation, by now he was more actively seeking the growth of international cooperation as Hitler and Mussolini had gained firm control of their governments. He had to move cautiously, however, given the strong mood of the nation against forming formal alliances (isolationism). The plan was designed to ensure that monetary exchange rates between nations became more stable. Though not a very sweeping agreement in itself, it represented a start at international cooperation.

Meanwhile Hitler, after forming an alliance with Italy's Mussolini in 1936, began his conquest of

Benito Mussolini, left, and Adolf Hitler, right, took advantage of European nations destabilized by the Great Depression. (National Archives and Records Administration.)

Europe. Germany absorbed Austria in 1938 and occupied Czechoslovakia in 1939. In September 1939 German forces invaded Poland and World War II had begun.

Contributing Forces

A Fragmented Europe

Compared to other continents in the world, Europe is small but highly varied economically and culturally. Temperate climate, fertile soils, and abundant natural resources support high economic potential. Rivers, mountains, and inlets carve up the densely populated region. The diversity of cultural backgrounds has led to centuries of rivalries, conflict, and nationalism. As a result Europe was separated into numerous small nations. These small nations remained continuously at odds with one another over political, social, and economic issues.

World War I took a great toll on European nations leaving them considerably weakened. They were in economic and political disarray. Political efforts were started to guard against such a war ever happening again. The traditional problem of territorial fragmentation posed a major hurdle to overcome. Many believed peace and economic prosperity in Europe was not possible until some formal political structure was created that somehow united these nations.

Several proposals for a political solution were offered. U.S. President Woodrow Wilson (served 1913–1921) promoted a worldwide League of Nations, which gained support and was established in 1920. The organization, however, a loose assembly of nations, lacked much authority to resolve disputes that arose. Ironically, the U.S. Congress with its growing sense of international isolationism voted not to join the League. By refusing to join the League of Nations, the United States stayed distant from European economic issues leaving the European nations to work their own way through post-war recovery.

Other proposals more specifically focused on European unity. French foreign minister Aristide Briand proposed in 1925 the creation of a "United States of Europe" to be called the European Federal Union. A key function of the Union would be to simplify European economics and create a common market. The concept however received hostile reaction from many of the European countries seeking to maintain their nationalistic independence. Little agreement could be reached on how the Union should be structured, or even if there should be one. The crash of Wall Street in October 1929 quickly raised economic concerns above political interests and interrupted such consideration. A still fragmented Europe was ill-equipped to handle the massive economic problems of the 1930s.

Latin American Nationalism

Growing economic wealth in Europe and the United States in the 1920s led to large investments of foreign capital in Latin America. This foreign economic influence coupled with centuries of European colonialism contributed to a growing resentment and nationalistic spirit among Latin Americans. Confrontation became inevitable between nationalists and foreign interests. The Boston-based United Fruit Company, in the banana region of Columbia, was the target of a violent strike in 1928. Conflict over foreign petroleum exploration in Mexico also erupted. In response the United States adopted a policy of less direct intervention in Latin American affairs. the United States, however, remained influential in the region's politics through economic aid and certain ongoing business interests. The nationalistic impulses of Latin America helped buffer to some degree the various economies of the individual nations from the

Great Depression and fuel their own efforts to build their economies with local industries.

The Rise of the Gold Standard

Silver served as the world's principal monetary metal until Great Britain, which dominated international finance through the nineteenth century, introduced the gold standard system in 1821. The Bank of England, a private bank, provided world leadership in maintaining the system. The pound sterling was the premier currency. A "bimetallic" world system based on both gold and silver existed for the next half century with some countries using silver, some gold, and others both metals as standards. In the 1870s most nations joined Britain on a strictly gold standard. The Far East remained on silver. During the peak era of the international gold standard of the 1870s until 1914 there was essentially one world money that directly translated into different national currencies.

The outbreak of World War I in 1914 led to many nations abandoning the gold standard, making the export of gold restricted. Gradually through the 1920s the gold standard had become reestablished. Nations were seeking a return to what they considered an economic golden age prior to World War I. The Great Depression again brought an abandonment of the gold standard. Since the gold standard internationally linked currencies, if an economic depression hit one country it directly affected another. This made it difficult for countries to protect their economies during economically unstable times. By 1937 no nation was on the gold standard.

U.S. Influence on the Global Economy

Through the nineteenth century international economic policies were generally based on the gold standard under Britain's leadership. The economic drain of World War I, however, left Britain and other European nations greatly weakened. The United States became the world's top economic power and they did not actually enter World War I until near the end of the war in 1917. Rather the U.S. role in the war was primarily in financing European war efforts against Germany. By war's end the European nations owed the United States $12 billion.

War debts owed the United States by Britain, France, and other European nations greatly influenced international economics through the 1920s. Congress remained adamant that the allies pay the debts despite persistent requests by the various countries to renegotiate. Great Britain had a 62-year payment schedule at three percent interest amounting to $300 million a year. Debt payments became a key part of the U.S. annual budget.

World Economic Growth

The debt payments posed a major burden on European nations as they struggled toward economic recovery from the war. Britain, having dropped the gold standard at the outbreak of World War I, returned to the standard in 1925, which led directly to monetary problems. Britain set the value of its currency at the same rate compared to the weight of gold as it was prior to World War I. This rate proved too high as they began immediately spending more on imports than it was making on its exports. Money was flowing out of the country and a business recession set in leading to increased unemployment. Declining employment led to labor strikes. Coal miners were locked out for seven months and a national general strike hit the nation for nine days. The war debts could not be met in full leading to tensions with the United States.

As the 1920s progressed Europe began achieving economic growth although much less than the United States. Industrial production still lagged but agricultural production significantly increased. Income in Britain, France, and even Germany was on the rise. By the late 1920s economic production had returned to levels enjoyed prior to World War I. Debt repayment schedules were being met and European currencies seemed to be stabilizing bringing a new optimism in foreign relations

Meanwhile, the United States was, by the late 1920s, the world's largest producer, investor, and lender. The United States accounted for 46 percent of the world's industrial output even though it only had three percent of the world's population. Surplus U.S. money flowed to Europe as the United States invested heavily abroad. As a result European nations were highly reliant on a continuing supply of U.S. money. With the U.S. stock market crash in October 1929 U.S. investment in Europe dwindled, souring European optimism.

German War Penalties

Germany suffered greatly from its role in World War I (1914–1918). Almost 1.8 million German soldiers died from battles and disease comprising 2.6 percent of the population. Approximately 763,000 civilians died of starvation and disease including 150,000 who died from flu alone. Industrial production fell 62 percent and agricultural output fell over 55 percent. With the agreement ending the war, the Treaty of Versailles, Germany lost almost 15 percent of its land including the economically valuable Rhineland region. A new government, the Weimar Republic, was established to govern Germany and replace the previous rule under Emperor Wilhelm II.

Unemployment in Select European Nations, 1900-1940

by percent of workforce population

Year	Britain	Denmark	Germany
1920	2.0%	n/a	3.8%
1925	7.9	n/a	6.7
1930	11.2	13.7	15.3
1931	15.1	17.9	23.3
1932	15.6	31.7	30.1
1933	14.1	28.8	26.3
1934	11.9	22.1	14.9
1935	11.0	19.7	11.6
1936	9.4	19.3	8.3
1937	7.8	21.9	4.6
1938	9.3	21.3	2.1
1939	5.8	18.4	n/a
1940	3.3	23.9	n/a

European nations were also impacted by the Depression, as shown by rising unemployment rates in the 1930s. (The Gale Group.)

In April 1921 the Allied Reparations Committee set Germany's war reparations (financial penalties) bill at 132 billion gold marks ($33 billion). It was to be paid in two billion gold marks a year. The new German government and its citizens were greatly angered by this stiff economic penalty. Deeply in debt, Germany became highly dependent on U.S. investments and short-term loans for incoming cash.

When a period of rapid inflation struck Germany in 1923 economic problems mounted. As a result Germany announced it would cease reparation payments. In reaction France and Belgium seized the Ruhr industrial region of Germany as compensation for lack of payments. Angered, German workers went on strike and the German government printed large amounts of paper money. The German currency essentially became worthless and the national economy sank even lower. A committee of financial experts, headed by American Charles G. Dawes, worked out a plan. The resulting solution was a moratorium (temporary halt) in payments, return of Ruhr to German control, an open door to U.S. loans, and a new schedule of reparation payments extending over 59 years. Different countries had different attitudes toward German reparation payments. Britain wanted to drop them altogether but could not afford to unless the United States would drop the war debt payments owed to the United States. Overall Germany was enraged by international treatment toward them. These events increased their nationalistic feelings leading to the rise of the National Socialist party and its leader, Adolf Hitler.

Perspectives

International Perspectives

The U.S. international monetary and political policies through the 1920s and 1930s disappointed many Europeans. During the 1920s the United States maintained a strong policy of political isolationism. This outlook meant the U.S. government was far more focused on domestic issues and unwilling to participate in international cooperation. The door was still open for American private businesses to invest capital in foreign countries, especially Germany. Requests by other nations for greater political cooperation in solving world problems were consistently turned down. For example the U.S. Congress voted to not join the newly formed League of Nations in 1920. When the Great Depression arrived, the United States added economic isolationism to political isolationism. The new world economic leader, the United States, seemed not ready to assume an active leadership role. Its citizens wanted to turn more inward and avoid commitments to international developments.

Collapse of the 1933 World Economic Conference led to distrust and suspicion between European nations and the United States. Taking the United States off the gold standard just before the conference further decreased economic hope in Europe. Roosevelt had begun to demonstrate that his focus would be on domestic economic reform to the exclusion of cooperation with Europe. On top of the conference failure, the Johnson Act of 1934, labeling Britain and France as defaulters on their war debt, payments marked a low point in international relations. A more hostile environment was created. European nations, viewing President Roosevelt with some disdain, characterized him as a politician who spoke in grand terms but provided little actual world leadership. Not until much later would improved economic cooperation gain momentum—in the late 1930s.

The lack of international cooperation opened the door to radical nationalism in several countries. Germans believed the World Economic Conference collapse affirmed their course toward withdrawing from international monetary systems. Japan was encouraged to further their military expansionism in Asia. Russia was further resolved to continue their anti-capitalist economic course of communism aimed at dismantling the capitalist economy and industrializing the nation.

Impact

World War II

The economic difficulties brought by the Great Depression substantially disrupted international diplomatic relations. The shaken economies of European nations opened the door to German National Socialism, Italian Fascism, and Japanese Imperialism as well as social unrest in other countries. Many believe the devastating effect of the Great Depression on Germany was the key factor breaking up the short-lived German Weimar Republic and bringing Hitler and the Nazis to power. The most destructive war in world history began with the German invasion of Poland in 1939. From 50 to 64 million people were killed including almost 20 million Europeans. Six million died in German extermination camps while sixty million were driven from their homes, including 27 million ousted from their countries. Europe's infrastructure was devastated. Thousands of roads, railways, buildings, bridges, and harbors were destroyed or heavily damaged. No longer was war fought solely at a nation's boundaries. War and its destruction spread throughout the entire nation. The 30-year sequence of war-depression-war had plummeted Europe from world prominence to devastation and disarray. The United States and USSR emerged as the world's two superpowers and Europe became the central stage for Cold War confrontation. European nations were passed economically by the United States and Japan.

Following World War II much closer economic relations between the United States and Western Europe developed and isolationism was no longer a U.S. policy. Some 40,000 American businessmen employed by 3,000 U.S. companies settled in Western Europe. In reaction to the growing American influence, some Europeans decried the Americanization of the region. Nonetheless as a result of economic recovery programs largely funded by the United States, Europe was saved from economic ruin. A foundation for economic growth was created and recovery was well underway by 1950.

Seeking European Unity

Not wanting to repeat past mistakes, eagerness grew around the world for economic and political stability rather than returning to earlier pre-war conditions. New global institutions were created within five years of the end of World War II. These included the United Nations (UN) and the International Monetary Fund (IMF). The UN is an international organization with headquarters in New York City that works for world peace and improvement of living conditions

Left to right, members of the U.S. delegation, Secretary of State Cordell Hull, Senator Key Pittman, Representative S. Reynolds, and Ralph Morrison, arrive in England to attend the World Economic Conference.

(Bettmann/CORBIS. Reproduced by permission.)

around the world. By the early 1990s 159 nations were members. Representatives of each nation attend meetings at the UN to discuss and solve world problems. The IMF, a specialized agency of the UN, focuses on international trade and economics. Composed of 145 nations by 1990 the organization helps its members achieve economic growth, high employment levels, and high standards of living. A key function of the

IMF is to oversee a system of international payments to assist in promoting trade between countries.

Nations also looked for internal change. The British Labor Party defeated Winston Churchill's Conservative party in the late 1940s by promoting national economic planning and an expanded social security system. Such desires were shared elsewhere in Western Europe with an emphasis on central control of the

More About...

European Union

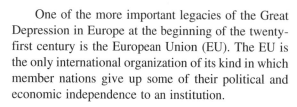

One of the more important legacies of the Great Depression in Europe at the beginning of the twenty-first century is the European Union (EU). The EU is the only international organization of its kind in which member nations give up some of their political and economic independence to an institution.

The Maastricht Treaty, an international agreement created in 1991 among the 12 participating nations of the European Community (EC) organization, created the EU. The agreement became official in late 1993 and the EU became a reality. The original 12 nations were Great Britain, France, Germany, Italy, Ireland, Belgium, Denmark, The Netherlands, Spain, Portugal, Greece, and Luxembourg. By 1998 the number of members grew to 15 and 12 other nations had applied for membership.

The purpose of the EU is to coordinate the member nations' economies and represent those nations with non-member countries in forging trade relations. The EU has power to pass and enforce laws that are binding on member nations. Various governmental institutions compose the EU. The European Parliament is composed of members elected democratically every five years to represent the 374 million citizens of the participating nations. Parliament has power to pass legislation and has budgetary responsibilities. The EU Council is the main decision-making body. It also has legislative power and coordinates the economic policies and other major activities of the various member nations. The European Commission is the EU's executive body, responsible for implementing EU's laws. Importantly, the Commission represents the EU in international relations with non-member countries, particularly in economic trade matters. The EU also has a Court of Justice that resolves disputes involving the member nations, other EU institutions, businesses, or individuals. The European Central Bank guides EU's monetary policies and the European Investment Bank (EIB) finances investment projects among the member nations.

---

economy. Italy created the Institute of Industrial Reconstruction and France proposed a sweeping system of national planning.

The economic hardships of the Great Depression, compounded by the devastation of World War II, led to a renewed search for European unity in the late twentieth century. This time there was full realization that Europe no longer dominated world trade and politics. The new goals were not only to prevent further war but to avoid economic errors made in the 1930s when the European nations acted independently, looking out only for their own self-interests. Such a fragmented response to a worldwide economic crisis only worsened the economic situation and created an environment for dictatorships. Having been economically weakened by 30 years of war and depression, Europe desired to become more economically competitive with the world's new superpowers that emerged after World War II, the United States and USSR. Promotion of shared interests became the focus.

A conference of European nations met in The Hague, Netherlands, in 1948. The 750 attending statesmen from Western Europe called for an economic and political union of European nations. Such a union among the nations would prove a very difficult challenge.

In 1952 a plan was adopted to coordinate coal and steel production in Western Europe. Within a few years this effort more broadly expanded into the European Economic Community (EEC) and in 1958 composed of six nations. The EEC became the European Communities (EC) in 1967 and finally the Economic Community in the 1980s. The EC included a Council of Ministers, a European Parliament, and a European Court of Justice. The EC's authority was limited to economic and social issues with the primary aim to promote European economic unity. More nations joined through the years with the fifteenth member joining in 1995. More possible additions were possible in the future as European politics continued to change in the early twenty-first century.

The EC combined economic resources of Europe into a common market and guarded against the prospects of any economic protectionist measures gaining support as they had in the 1930s. A common agricultural policy was adopted in 1962. Then in 1987 EC members passed the Single European Act, which laid the groundwork for creating a unified, free trade

More About...

The Euro

A major problem in Europe during the Depression was the fragmented economic situation among nations. Various barriers to trade had been created through various taxes on imports by the different nations. No longer on a common monetary standard, such as the gold standard, exchange rates between nations were unpredictable and unstable. The twenty-first century answer to this dilemma is creation of the euro monetary unit. The same international agreement among European nations that created the European Union (EU), the Maastricht Treaty, also called for establishment of an economic and monetary union (EMU) through a common unit of monetary exchange, the euro.

Strict standards were established for individual nations to be able to participate in the EMU and use the euro. The nations must have low annual budget deficits, government debt below a certain level, stability of the present currency, and relatively low inflation rates compared to other nations. Significant benefits are offered by having a common currency within the relatively small continent of Europe. any nations, however, expressed reluctance about losing their individual currencies viewed proudly as a source of identity as well as losing some degree of economic independence. Nevertheless, 11 nations chose to join the EMU in 1998—Austria, Belgium, Finland, France, Germany, Ireland, Italy, Luxembourg, The Netherlands, Portugal, and Spain. Greece joined in January 2001. Britain, Denmark, and Sweden remained outside the union. Also in 1998 the European Central Bank (ECB), based in Frankfurt, Germany, was created to manage the new currency.

The euro was officially launched on January 1, 1999. Euro paper bills and coins were not to be issued until January 1, 2002, but financial markets and certain businesses were making non-cash transactions in euros from 1999 through 2001. Though its value started strong, its value fell by more than 25 percent through 1999 and 2000. Plans remained for all member nations to withdraw their individual currencies from further use by February 28, 2002.

---

market in Western Europe. The act eliminated barriers to Europe-wide banking, stock market investments, and other financial matters.

These successes in improving trade by the EC led to greater integration. The EC became the principal organization within the newly formed European Union (EU) in 1993. The EU established a common banking system and currency, the euro through the economic and monetary union (EMU). The long difficult road to European economic unity is still being traveled into the twenty-first century.

Notable People

Adolf Hitler (1889–1945). Born in Austria, Hitler began his rise to political power in Germany following World War I. With Germany in economic ruin following its defeat, Hitler vowed to rebuild Germany to its past glory. He gained political control of Germany in 1933 as America's New Deal economic programs were just beginning. Through the 1920s he led development of the National Socialist party that gradually gained political strength. The economic hardships brought by the Great Depression and lack of international cooperation gave Hitler the opportunity to chart a bold economic and political course for Germany. Hitler introduced the New Order representing a reordering of German society. The New Order included tight control of all aspects of the national economy including wage and price controls.

Hitler also sought to unite all European territories where German language was spoken. First he regained control of the Rhineland Valley of Western Germany in 1936, a key region lost to France following World War I. The German troops met no resistance from France or any other country. Given the lack of resistance Hitler launched a series of other expansion moves through the next two years that triggered World War II. Until the Allied Forces of the United States, Britain, and others could turn the tide of war, Germany had conquered much of Europe and pushed into Russia. At great expense in life and resources to all nations involved, Germany suffered yet another major military defeat in the twentieth century, leaving its

Congressman Cordell Hull drew up the Reciprocal Trade Agreements Act of 1934, which was central to New Deal economic foreign policy. (U.S. Signal Corp.)

economy once more in shambles. With enemy forces quickly closing in, Hitler committed suicide in 1945.

Cordell Hull (1871–1955). Earning a law degree from Cumberland University Law School, Hull served as a Tennessee state legislator in the 1890s. He was elected to the U.S. House of Representatives in 1907 where he served until 1931 except for two years in the early 1920s. While in Congress, Hull was active in sponsoring domestic monetary legislation. In 1933 President Roosevelt appointed him secretary of state. Hull was a strong advocate of international trade. He drew up the Reciprocal Trade Agreements Act, which was central to New Deal economic foreign policy. Congress passed the act in 1934 Hull pursued agreements with Great Britain and France in 1934 and 1935 to reduce tariffs. Hull also negotiated trade agreements with Latin American countries leading to less friction in the region. Hull became one of the most popular Democrats in America during the 1930s. During World War II Hull was a leading proponent of the formation of the United Nations (UN) for which he received the Nobel Peace Prize in 1945. Hull retired from the state department in 1944.

Benito Mussolini (1883–1945). Mussolini founded fascism and ruled Italy for almost 21 years beginning in 1922. A fascist government is a strong, centralized nationalistic government led by a powerful dictator. Previously a socialist newspaper editor, after serving in World War I he founded the Fascist Party. Promoting a strong nationalistic philosophy the party gained power when Mussolini was named head of government in 1922. He created a dictatorship and seized control of the nation's industries. In 1935 Mussolini led an invasion of Ethiopia in Northern Africa and next invaded France in 1940 following Hitler's successes at expansion of German control in Europe. The Italian army had little success during the early years of World War II in its continued efforts for expansion. Mussolini finally lost favor of Italy's other leaders and was overthrown and imprisoned in 1943.

Joseph Stalin (1879–1953). Stalin was dictator of the Union of Soviet Socialist Republics (USSR) from 1929 to 1953. He ruled through a reign of terror, even executing his own supporters for fear they might challenge him in the future. Promoting a radical economic policy of communism, Stalin placed an emphasis on heavy industry, communications, and transportation. He was responsible also for the deaths of millions of Soviet peasants who opposed his economic measures of government-controlled farms. Though hated and feared by those inside Russia as well as elsewhere, he transformed the USSR from an undeveloped agricultural society to a world leading industrial and military power.

Primary Sources

The Depression Grows Worldwide

Noted British economist John Maynard Keynes spoke the following words in a 1931 lecture in the United States. These comments came during the bleakest of economic times between 1930 and 1933 (from Golby, et al. *Between Two Wars,* pp. 50–51).

> We are today in the middle of the greatest economic catastrophe—the greatest catastrophe due almost entirely to economic causes—of the modern world ... the view is held in Moscow that this is the last, the culminating crisis of capitalism and that our existing order of society will not survive it.

Anticipation of the 1933 World Economic Conference

An insightful editorial, "Yea or Nay?," appeared in *The Economist* (vol. CXVI, June 10, 1933, p. 1229) on the eve of the World Economic Conference. Hopeful anticipation preceded the conference as the impact of the Great Depression had spread throughout the world. Many saw the conference as perhaps the last opportunity for nations to develop international solutions to what had become a worldwide problem. The article proved prophetic as New Deal-era nationalism increased when the conference failed to achieve its primary goals.

> There is one broad question that will underlie every argument put forward, every decision taken by the great Conference of the Nations which will open its session in London on Monday next. It sounds extremely simple and can be shortly put; but its implications are very far-reaching for the future life of nations. It is this. Will the Conference have the necessary courage and imagination to direct the economic life of the world towards revived prosperity by way of co-operation, or will the nations continue to drift towards economic isolation?
>
> France is sceptical; the American delegation, perplexed by an extremely complex situation at home, is new to the international game; while Germany is deeply absorbed in her ideas of national survival at home. England, in her turn, shows signs of a dangerous complacency due perhaps to the happy chance that she has escaped the worst crises of the past year.
>
> But the central issue is not merely a matter of coordinating action. The acid test of next week's meeting is whether the policy adopted is a genuine reversal of recent tendencies and the beginning of a process of reconstructing a world economy. To take one outstanding example: the Peace Treaties split Europe into economic fragments and gave the impulses of nationalism full play. This has proved a profound economic blunder. For years statesmen have talked of rebuilding a sounder and more tolerable economic life in Europe. But almost nothing has been done. Are they now prepared actually to start the process? A similar question faces every one of the delegations that are assembling here as this issue of the Economist goes to press.

Suggested Research Topics

- Which European countries were most and least affected by the Great Depression and why?

- How could the United States have been more helpful on an international basis to help the global economy?

- Why did the breakdown in democratic processes occur in Germany but not in neighboring European countries? If the United States and other European nations had been more helpful in economically aiding Germany, would Hitler have had

a more difficult challenge gathering public support for his initiatives? Explain.

- What key issues are affecting the progress of the European Union? What are the barriers to a unified Europe? What are the latest initiatives to breakdown the barriers?

Bibliography

Sources

Clavin, Patricia. *The Failure of Economic Diplomacy: Britain, Germany, France and the United States, 1931–1936*. New York: St. Martin's Press, Inc., 1996.

Golby, John, Bernard Waites, Geoffrey Warner, Tony Applegate, and Antony Lentin. *Between Two Wars*. Bristol, PA: Open University Press, 1990.

Gregory, R.G., and N.G. Butlin, eds. *Recovery From the Depression: Australia and the World Economy in the 1930s*. New York: Cambridge University Press, 1988.

Hall, Thomas E., and J. David Ferguson. *The Great Depression: An International Disaster of Perverse Economic Policies*. Ann Arbor: The University of Michigan Press, 1998.

Keylor, William R. *The Twentieth-Century World: An International History*. 3rd ed. New York: Oxford University Press, 1996.

Kindleberger, Charles P. *The World in Depression, 1929–1939*. Berkeley: University of California Press, 1986.

"Yea or Nay?" *The Economist*, June 10, 1933.

Further Reading

"Europa—The European Union On-Line," [cited October 31, 2001] available from the World Wide Web at http://europa.eu .int.

Hobsbawm, Eric. *The Age of Extremes: A History of the World, 1914–1991*. New York: Pantheon Books, 1994.

Johnson, Paul. *Modern Times: A History of the World from the 1920s to the Year 2000*. London: Orion Books, Ltd., 1999.

Overy, R. J. *The Inter-War Crisis, 1919–1939*. New York: Longman, 1994.

Rothrmund, Dietmar. *The Global Impact of the Great Depression, 1929–1939*. New York: Routledge, 1996.

See Also

New Deal (First, and Its Critics); World War II Mobilization

Hollywood

1929-1941

Introduction

"Who's afraid of the big bad wolf? Big bad wolf, big bad wolf?" This musical line originates from the *Three Little Pigs* movie, produced by Walt Disney in 1933. The big bad wolf in Walt Disney's animated short film is a metaphor for the Depression of the 1930s. People needed to sing that song through the vehicle of the movie to defend against their fear of what lay ahead. Likewise Americans needed their movies. Movies had become a cultural institution as well as a cultural necessity. No other form of entertainment had come to play as important a role in American's everyday life, not even radio. Sixty million to 75 million people still faithfully attended even if the price of a seat was too much for them to pay.

The great mass of people who were affected in some way by the economic crisis of the Great Depression, not only sought escape into the movies, but they also sought meaning as well. Frequently they sought meaning and escape in the same movie. Movies also depicted things desired or things lost, all of which Depression audiences could relate to. This period was lovingly known as "The Golden Age of Hollywood"

The 1930s were an era that brought about the advancement of film, both technically and with the establishment of specific types of film "genres." Some popular genres explored by Hollywood were gangster films, comedies, musicals, law and order (including federal agent films and westerns), social consciousness films, horror, and thrillers.

Chronology:

1887: Horace Wilcox lays out the city of Hollywood.

1889: George Eastman invents roll film, a critical step for making modern motion pictures.

1893: Thomas A. Edison develops the Kinetoscope, a "peephole machine" with an endless roll of film moved along by means of sprocket wheels, which produce a moving image.

1894: C. Francis Jenkins invents the motion picture projector and shows the first movie in Richmond, Indiana.

1896: Edison's motion picture is shown to an audience at Koster & Bial's Music Hall in New York City on a Vitascope, a projector developed by Thomas Armat who had worked with C. Francis Jenkins.

1903: *The Great Train Robbery* is the first motion picture to tell a story.

1907: Edison wins a lengthy patent conflict and forms a licensing company for production motion pictures.

1908: Filmmakers complete *The Count of Monte Cristo* in Hollywood.

1911: Construction begins for large studios intended for the use of filmmaking.

1920s: Thousands of movie theaters and "palaces" cater to millions of Americans in the era of silent movies.

1927: *The Jazz Singer* is the first successful "talkie."

1930: Motion Picture Producers and Distributors Association of America (MPPDA) headed by Will Hays adopts the Production Code; however, it is not immediately enforced.

1931–1933: Motion picture studio profits plummet as the Great Depression sets in.

1932: Walt Disney adopts a three-color Technicolor process for cartoons.

1933: Walt Disney introduces the *Three Little Pigs* animated feature movie.

1934: The first drive-in movie theater opens in New Jersey.

1934: Three-color Technicolor is used in live action film.

1934: The Production Code of 1930 begins to be enforced.

Devised by the Motion Picture Producers and Distributors of America, the production Code of 1930, enforced in 1934, had a major impact on the content of movies. Various themes important to the Depression populace ran through the films. Americans could find hope while watching a character's success and believe that betterment was still possible. They could laugh irreverently at traditional American institutions or at forces that they could not quite define but that had altered their lives in the 1930s. For two hours each week Americans could enter the dark comfortable movie houses and share in the communal experience of being transported into another reality. In 1939 the quest for better times was confirmed in Judy Garland's hit song, "Somewhere Over the Rainbow," one of the memorable compositions from the popular movie *The Wizard of Oz*. The song was a testimonial to hope that reigned at the end of the decade.

Issue Summary

The Depression Hits Hollywood

Established beneath the San Gabriel Mountains in Southern California was a golden community known as Hollywood. Through the 1920s Hollywood had churned out thousands of silent films captivating the whole nation. Talkies, or movies with sound, premiered in 1927, as more and more Americans flocked to the theaters. Although the stock market crash of 1929 marked the beginning of the Great Depression, 110 million people still went to the movies in 1930. The introduction of sound proved enticing and Hollywood's profits continued. As the economic conditions, however, steadily worsened nationwide Hollywood's apprehension grew. Their fears were legitimate because attendance dropped to roughly 60 to 75 million by 1933 and profits evaporated. The unemployment rate hit 25 percent that

At a Glance

Paramount Studios

Founded in 1913 in a horse barn near Sunset and Vine streets in Los Angeles, Paramount moved to Gower Street in 1926. Today it is the longest continually operated studio in Hollywood. As Paramount Studios grew, it took over the former properties of RKO Studios. In the 1930s major stars acting in films for Paramount included Marlene Dietrich, William Powell, Gary Cooper, Clara Bow, and Claudette Colbert.

---

year and almost everyone's salaries had declined significantly. The public could no longer afford to attend the movies as frequently as before.

The few cents it took to get in the movies was an extravagance for many. Still those 60 to 75 million that faithfully came represented 60 percent of the population. In comparison 10 percent of Americans attended the movies in the 1970s. This figure is a powerful testimonial to movies as a cultural institution. Ultimately the industry would be saved because movies no longer represented simply entertainment but a necessity in the lives of Americans.

In the meantime the movie industry, having expanded wildly in the 1920s, was in trouble. The five major studios were RKO (Radio-Keith-Orpheum), 20th Century Fox, Warner Brothers, Metro-Goldwyn-Mayer (MGM), and Paramount. Loew's, Inc. was a subsidiary of MGM. These Hollywood studios exerted the most influence over actors, writers, directors, and producers. Two smaller studios were Columbia and Universal. As early as 1931 profits were plummeting. A 1930 surplus of $3.3 million at RKO plummeted to a $5.6 million deficit in 1931. After a $9.2 million profit in 1930, Fox posted a $5.5 million loss in 1931. Warner Brother's 1929 profit of $17.2 million declined to $7 million in 1930 and was in red ink by $7.9 million at the end of 1931.

By 1933 the five majors had a combined stock value of $200 million—down from approximately $1 billion in 1930. Paramount, which earned a respectable $25 million profit in 1930, was reduced to filing for

bankruptcy in 1933. MGM was the only major to stay out of the red but its profits of $14.6 million in 1930 fell to $4.3 million in 1933. By summer of 1933 one third of all movie houses had closed. Still the industry hung on; Americans continued saving their pennies to see a weekly movie.

By fall of 1933, Franklin Delano Roosevelt (served 1933–1945) was president and the bank crisis had moderated. The motion picture industry was on the mend as customers began to slowly return. Coincidentally at this same time Walt Disney, who had introduced Mickey Mouse in 1929 in a silent film, had worked out a three-color Technicolor process. He introduced this process in his 1933 film the *Three Little Pigs.* The pigs sung "Who's Afraid of the Big Bad Wolf?" The song cheered Depression audiences and it became a sort of mantra to use as a defense against fear, the "Wolf" representing the Great Depression. All major studios, now less fearful of the "Wolf," hoped for a profit by 1934. Although 60 million attended faithfully, theater managers worked to increase attendance with countless enticements.

Animated (Cartoon) Films

When Walt Disney pioneered the field of animation in the 1930s a totally different form of movie escapism was created. There are two main elements in animation: characters and background. The sketches of the animation are traced, inked and painted on transparent celluloid, also known as cells. In the meantime, the backgrounds are made to fit the various needs of the action. The completed drawings are then placed in frames below a large camera and photographed one cell at a time. Many techniques are used in taking the pictures to create depth, action, and perspective. Dialogue for the film is usually spoken first and the sound effects are then connected with it. This process enables the animator to determine exactly how many frames are needed to cover a particular word or sound.

One of Walt Disney's first creations, Mickey Mouse (1929) was probably more famous and familiar to the public than many politicians of the day. In 1933, when Disney released *The Three Little Pigs,* its theme song, "Who's Afraid of the Big Bad Wolf?" became the national hit. Some of the public thought the movie had as much to do with raising the nation's morale as did the New Deal legislation. Some thought the moral of *The Three Little Pigs* was that the little pig survived because he was conservative, diligent, and hardworking. Others thought that it was the pig who used modern tools and planned ahead who would win out in the end.

More About...

Techniques Developed During the 1930s—Sound and Color

In spite of the Depression experimentation to bring sound and color to the screen, a new era in film began in 1927 with the success of the first "talkie." *The Jazz Singer,* starring Al Jolson, brought a new age for movies as theaters everywhere were wired for sound. At the same time the industry was beginning to experiment further with the medium. Many stars of the silent screen were unable to speak their lines convincingly and so a new type of actor was sought out by the industry. Most of the early "talkies" were successful at the box-office, but many of them were of poor quality. The pictures were often dominated by dialogue with stilted acting and an unmoving camera or microphone. Nonetheless, a variety of films were produced with wit, style, skill, and elegance. The films *Applause* (1929) and *Love Me Tonight* (1932), both directed by Rouben Mamoulian, were revolutionary in many ways. Mamoulian refused to keep the cumbersome sound cameras pinned to the floor, and he demonstrated a graceful, rhythmic, and fluidly choreographed style. *Applause* also introduced a new sound technique with a double-channel soundtrack with overlapping dialogue. After 1932 the development of sound mixing lifted the limitations of recording on sets and locations. Scriptwriters were becoming more advanced with witty dialogue, realistic characters, and plot twists.

The first, feature-length, all-color film was *Toll of the Sea* (1922). Now the director and the designer could use color to add to the effect of the screen story. This became particularly useful in outdoor and costume pictures. In the late 1930s, two films, *The Wizard of Oz* (1939) and *Gone With the Wind* (1939), were expensively produced with Technicolor. Special-effects processes were further developed in the late 1930s, making it possible for more films to be shot on sets rather than on location.

In 1937 Walt Disney Studios premiered the first feature-length animation film, *Snow White and the Seven Dwarfs.* The movie was produced at the unheard-of cost of $1,499,000 during the depths of the Depression. During the next five years Disney completed other full-length animated classics such as *Pinocchio, Fantasia, Dumbo,* and *Bambi.* Disney Studios became known for pioneering sophisticated animation and, most especially, for producing films which delighted generations of children.

Attracting and Holding Audiences

The operators of motion-picture theaters were compelled to resort to many tactics to keep their attendance up. Merely lowering the price was not enough. It was during this period that the double feature was introduced. The double feature consisted of two full-length films as well as short subjects. Usually the fare included a main attraction that was paired with a "B-Movie," a film produced with a low budget and often lesser known actors and actresses. On Saturdays theaters often showed a serial that left the heroine or hero in such a dire situation that viewers had to come back the next week to see the outcome of the story.

Gimmicks known as "Bank Night," "Dish Night," and Bingo Night were very popular with the Depression era populace. Fox Theater first introduced Bank Night in a Colorado movie house. Bank Nights happened on the lowest attendance night of the week and tickets became part of a lottery for prize money. Thankful for even the tiniest windfall, moviegoers showed up for Bank Night, however they were always hopeful that they could win prizes of up to $3,000. One movie official commented that he did not even need to show a movie on Bank Night, just have the lottery and people would come. Bank Nights became common practice throughout the country. Dish Night was another gimmick to draw in people. On Dish Night each moviegoer received a piece of china. A whole set of dishes could be collected over time. Bingo became the most popular gambling game of the decade after a movie house in Colorado first used it as an enticement.

For the first time since 1931 all major movie companies operated in the black during 1936. That same year Columbia Pictures approached the status of a major studio. Despite financial woes throughout the first half of the 1930s, studios never halted production. During those years there were an estimated 23,000 theaters with seating for 11 million people. Those 60 million who managed to attend weekly did so because movies, offered in various disguises,

---

The scene at the premiere of Gone With the Wind *on December 19, 1939. The film was the most expensive film to date at that time, and would go on to win ten academy awards. (AP/Wide World Photos. Reproduced by permission.)*

helped them continue their belief in the possibility of individual success. Movies preserved the traditional American viewpoint that perhaps tomorrow would be a better day. For most Americans movies ranked at the same necessity level as food, shelter, and clothing.

Americans had many types of movies from which to choose and their tastes changed often. The primary genre or types of film in the 1930s included gangsters, shysters, comedies, "fallen" women, musicals, G-Men (federal agents), westerns, and movies with social con-

sciousness. Other types were horror, thrillers, swashbucklers, and literary adaptations (from classical books).

Gangsters

Gangster films did not appear in a cultural and social void. After World War I (1914–1918), and the subsequent increase of immigration, journalistic accounts of gangster stories flourished in local and national newspapers. A large national audience became fascinated with, but also frightened by the evils and deeds of powerful gangsters in the 1920s and early 1930s.

In the early 1930s, however, gangster films enjoyed incredible success among Americans. In the context of social and economic breakdown, dynamic, successful, and flamboyant gangsters contrasted with the hardship and despair experienced by many in the early years of the Great Depression.

Three of the most renowned gangster films, *Little Caesar* (1930), *Public Enemy* (1931), and *Scarface* (1932) are concerned with the social ascension of young men from humble origins in the slums to the luxurious penthouses of High Society. As opposed to paralyzed, inefficient government and ineffective law enforcement agencies, gangster characters appeared competent, modern, and stylish. Gangster films were usually set in an urban environment amid easily recognizable symbols such as neon lights and smoky bars. They provided audiences with fascinating and thrilling stories about the city and the sensuous world of urban pleasures. Gangsters, and the women they caroused with, dressed in fancy clothes. The gangster's charming and stylish appearance reflected the aspirations of a population increasingly attracted by the lights and promise of consumption associated with the city.

Historians and scholars of Depression movies have debated why so many people faithfully went to the gangster movies. According to Andrew Bergman despite their "gangsterism," most of these films implicitly promoted traditional American values. Above all, and despite a moralistic ending depicting the tragic death of the central character, Bergman argues gangster films were stories of individual achievement. *Little Caesar* (Warner Brothers, 1930) was the first great gangster "talkie." The film follows the story of Rico Bandello or "Little Caesar," played by Edward G. Robinson, as he climbs the ladder of the criminal underworld. Rico was a thinly disguised Al Capone, the powerful and captivating mob boss of Chicago. Like Capone, Rico robbed and murdered, but also showed qualities of kindness and generosity. Although Rico's activities blatantly ran outside the law and his life had to end in an early death, Bergman believes Americans connected to Rico's success. They kept up hope in the American ideal of rising up to success and a better life.

Another viewpoint on *Little Caesar* and gangster movies came from historian Robert S. McElvaine in his book, *The Great Depression: America, 1929–1941.* McElvaine believed audiences saw the character of Rico as a representative of the greedy businessman willing to step on anyone who got in his way. Just as

American business fell in 1929, Rico also met a swift end. Nevertheless McElvaine reflects about Rico talking of the "Big Boy," the head of the city's gangsters. The movie implies that Big Boy was still at the top despite Rico's demise just as those men at the highest levels of the business world were still on top despite the Depression.

With the box office success of *Little Caesar,* studios recognized a money maker, money which they were desperately in need. In 1931 some 50 gangster films appeared. Civic groups, religious leaders, and parent-teacher associations denounced glorification of the gangster and the disrespect shown law enforcement. In reality the dismal depiction of law enforcement authorities and politicians accurately reflected the public's opinion of law and politics. They knew corruption ran deep; even if the law and politicians were not corrupt they were highly ineffective in the public's mind. Despite all the clamor people, young and old, packed the movie houses. These people, however, in the throes of the worst part of the Depression did become a bit uneasy about reveling in the gangster exploits. Some feared their attendance added a moral decay to the already existing economic decay. Then Tommy Powers entered their lives in *Public Enemy.* Tommy, played by the irresistible James Cagney, was industrious, classy, a wise guy, a ladies' man, and unfalteringly upheld the code of honor of his fellow thieves. Ordinary men and boys saw themselves in Tommy. Cagney's character was not seen as troubled or vicious but a man who directed his rage against injustice. This rage also dwelt in the hearts of many Americans during those economically bleak days.

The gangster movies' heyday was 1930 and 1931. By 1932, although *Scarface,* a story of Al Capone, came out that year, the moralistic anti-gangster crusade began to take hold and studios produced fewer gangster films.

Shysters

Along with the rise of gangster movies in the early 1930s came shyster movies. Shysters were corrupt, charming, slick individuals who, among other activities, conned, set entrapments, and weaseled their way through life. The shyster's story always was set in the sinful city. Shysters were dishonest lawyers, politicians, and newspapermen who, in the end, sometimes went straight. Shyster movies had the unmistakable mark of an early Depression film because they stamped a laughingstock image on the law. Classic shyster lawyer films were *Lawyer Man* (Warner, 1932) and the *Mouthpiece* (Warner, 1932). In both, flashy lawyers, loved by beautiful women, moved through their cities

From left to right, the Marx Brothers—Groucho, Zeppo, Chico, and Harpo. The films of the Marx Brothers had Depression-era audiences laughing at topics previously held valuable such as government and family.

(The Kobal Collection. Reproduced by permission.)

with confidence and great self-assurance. No crooked politician or gangster seemed to be able to control them. Nevertheless both leading characters eventually renounced their shyster ways to return to upright lives, distancing themselves from the corrupt individuals. In *Lawyer Man* the main character started as a humble honest lawyer, became a shyster in response to an entrapment scheme that he fell into, and, in the end, returns to his original practice to protect others from people who would trample on them. The clear message was that merely returning to righteousness and to work within the traditional American democratic process could put the social order back on a straight course. Shysters always had control over the corrupt individuals and one could never get a hold of them. For Depression audiences, who felt so much out of control, this was a welcome Hollywood fantasy.

Comedies of the Screen Anarchists

An anarchist looks on government authority and established groups with disdain and carries out rebellious acts against them. By the early 1930s the two prominent so-called "screen anarchists" were the Marx Brothers—Chico, Groucho, Harpo, and Zeppo—and W.C. Fields. It is generally agreed that

the Great Depression's worst years were 1930 to 1933. During that approximate time period the screen anarchists entertained a bitter and despairing population that was expecting the worst from everyone. The Marx Brother's and Fields' slapstick and zany words and actions actually had Americans chuckling with irreverence at topics previously held valuable as government and family.

Paramount made five Marx Brothers films between 1929 and 1933: *The Cocoanuts* (1929), *Animal Crackers* (1930), *Monkey Business* (1931), *Horsefeathers* (1932), and *Duck Soup* (1933). Reason and logic were out as the brothers lifted word play to an art; every conversation was a prank. The first two films were early "talkies" and, due to the still-unrefined technology, hard to understand. Nevertheless they became big moneymakers for Paramount. Everyone laughed no matter how silly or nonsensical since the chaotic and absurd language seemed to match the chaotic early years of the Depression. Americans sensed that truths they once held dear were now irrelevant to their lives.

Duck Soup, which historians consider a classic, was perhaps the most interesting of the five because of its subject matter, the timing of its release, and its acceptance by audiences and critics. The film is considered a classic because unlike previous movies this film blatantly attacked the idea that government and national loyalty were important. No previous films had dared adopt such a perspective. The film premiered in 1934 to poor reviews. Audiences who poured into movie houses for the first four and who would enjoy future Marx movies soundly rejected *Duck Soup.* Interestingly, Mussolini, head of the Italian government, banned the film in Italy. The most logical explanation lies in the timing of its release since it was released after President Franklin Roosevelt had been in office long enough for many of his New Deal programs to begin benefiting the public. As a result, Americans found renewed hope and confidence in government and were not as willing to bash the government as they had been only a year earlier.

A W.C. Fields' short film, *The Fatal Glass of Beer,* appeared in 1933. The masterful comedy tore into two American institutions—the family and the Western frontier. America's brilliant funnyman had not had an easy childhood and regarded family as a farce. It was hard to define the exact enemies in Fields' films but man was always susceptible to them. Depression era Americans could relate as they were unsure of who was to blame for the hard times but they had been clearly susceptible. Fields also made the routine of man's daily life into a comic art. In 1933 he made three shorts: *The Pharmacist, The Dentist,* and *The Barbershop.* An example of the humor in *The Barbershop* comes when the barber straps customers into his chair before dropping blazing towels on their faces. The chaotic, edgy, fly in the face humor of the Marx Brothers and Fields produced absurd comedy for a desperate time.

Non-Anarchist Comedy

A comic contemporary of the Marxes and Fields was Charlie Chaplin, but he was not of the anarchist bent. The enemies of his characters were apparent— the wealthy and powerful. His kindly sentimental films contained a great deal of innocence and decency. Chaplin, a master of silent film, continued producing silent movies after talking movies had become mainstay. He produced *City Lights* in 1931, which dealt with unemployment. The hero of Chaplin's 1936 film *Modern Times* depicts man being overwhelmed by the machines that were replacing humans in industry. Chaplin's tramp character represented the "little guy," or underdog, who used wit to win over his adversaries. This theme was highly popular with the Great Depression moviegoers who believed they were fighting for their economic lives against big business and big government.

Greta Garbo was a highly successful actress during the years of the Great Depression. By 1935 she was the highest paid actress in Hollywood, making $500,000 per picture. (The Museum of Modern Art/Film Stills Archive. The Library of Congress.)

Fallen Women

During the early 1930s financial troubles resulted in a dramatic number of prostitutes walking the streets. In Hollywood even megastars such as Greta Garbo, Marlene Dietrich, and Tallulah Bankhead found their only saleable possession was their beautiful bodies. The studios, in their own financial crunch, cast them in roles of sex for sale. In *Faithless* (MGM, 1932) Tallulah Bankhead's business was prostitution. Garbo, in *Susan Lenox, Her Fall and Rise* (MGM, 1931), and Dietrich in *Blonde Venus* (Paramount, 1932) portrayed women forced to be mistresses of rich men. Their characters were allowed redemption only after they submitted to becoming totally dependent on the men they truly love.

Director Ernst Lubitsch, in three sophisticated movies for Paramount—*Design For Living* (1933), *One Hour With You* (1931), and *Trouble in Paradise* (1932)—also played games with adultery and relationships. In *Design For Living* Lubitsch tells the tale of a sort of sexual New Deal. The female lead, Miriam Hopkins, is in love with two men played by Gary Cooper and Fredric March, in the end she decides to live with, or "employ," both men.

It took actress Mae West to demolish the dependent "fallen women" image. Her first words in her first starring role, *She Done Him Wrong* (1933), were in response to a bystander that told her she was a fine woman: "One of the finest women who ever walked the streets" (from Bergman, *We're in the Money: Depression America and Its Films,* p. 51). From the same movie came a line that quickly worked its way into the American common language, "Come up and see me sometime." The line instantly gained popularity because it placed the female in a more assertive character, in control of her destiny, rather than the more passive character traditionally shown in movies and the stereotype behavior expected in U.S. society. Her second starring film, *I'm No Angel* (1933), was the biggest box office attraction of the year. West was witty, tough, strong, and assertive. Her eyes delivered exactly the message she intended. Her refusal to take herself too seriously made women realize they were active partners in sex. She put faith in diamonds—material goods—rationalizing that no women with diamonds would need to walk the streets.

While Depression women did not toy with men or keep diamonds in a safe, they saw the female role on screen as a release from the dependent, subjected role. In the work of the Marxes, Fields, Lubitsch, and West, moral limits and definitions were pushed out and broken apart. It worried much of society that a moral depression was descending on the United States on top of the economic depression as offered in the movies. A line would be drawn by 1934.

Production Codes

During the 1920s a number of films used nudity and immorality and appeared to endorse drinking and smoking. The loose lives of actresses, or "vamps" (sexual vampires) with heavy makeup and scant clothing, led some to demand government control of films and filmmaking. In response to these issues a group was formed to evaluate, comment, and set standards for the film industry.

Once the chairman of the Republican National Committee and President Warren Harding's (served 1921–1923) Postmaster General in 1921 and 1922, Will Hays moved to Hollywood in 1922 to head the Motion Picture Producers and Distributors of America (MPPDA). The MPPDA was a motion picture industry group attempting to institute codes and standards to cleanup the film industry. The West Coast Association of the MPPDA agreed in 1927 to 11 "don'ts" for film production. Ten "don'ts" dealt with sex and nudity and only one with law concerning depicting illegal drug traffic. In response to the first silent gangster films

of the late 1920s, MPPDA created a 1930 Production Code. It established more extensive "don'ts" including showing sympathy to crime, ridiculing law and justice, and showing methods of crime such as theft, robbery, and brutal killings. The 1930 code was not enforced and was basically ignored. Hollywood continued in their pattern of violence and sex for which Americans went right on buying tickets.

In 1933 the Catholic Church in America established the Catholic Bishops' Committee on Motion Pictures. They were to head-up the League of Decency charged with identifying morally offensive films. The powerful Protestant Council of Churches and the Central Conference of Jewish Rabbis joined the campaign. In reaction Hays and the MPPDA began enforcing the 1930 Code by 1934. Movies cleaned up by not showing adultery and violent crime but also nude babies, double beds, long kisses, and four letter curse words. The day of big musicals, law and order, screwball comedies, and socially conscientious movies was ushered in.

Musicals

Not only were the morals of movies transitioning in 1933, but the nation had a new president. President Roosevelt succeeded in quickly reviving a measure of hope and confidence. Nevertheless the Depression was to drag on through the decade and audiences still needed to see that individual success was possible. A cleaned up version of success and hope translated into big splashy musicals. Warner Brothers big three of 1933—*42nd Street, Gold Diggers of 1933,* and *Footlight Parade*—saved the studio from financial disaster. These productions were a "New Deal" in movies and reflected the new, more optimistic spirit under Roosevelt. Busby Berkeley choreographed (producing the dance sequences) the colossal productions. Amid the singing, dancing, beautiful girls, plumes, glitter, and magnificent sets ran Great Depression themes. The main character was broke in *42nd Street,* everyone was broke in *Gold Diggers,* and the star of *Footlight Parade* feared he was headed for the breadline. The song "We're in the Money" originated in *Gold Diggers.* Long-legged girls flipped up flash cards in *Footlight Parade* that displayed a grinning President Roosevelt and another, the Blue Eagle symbol of the National Recovery Administration, a New Deal agency. All three, even in their lavishness, related directly to the 1933 facts of Depression life yet lifted spirits in hopes of a better time. Perhaps if there was enough singing and dancing the Depression would drift away.

The biggest moneymakers in musicals were the enormously popular dance team of Fred Astaire and

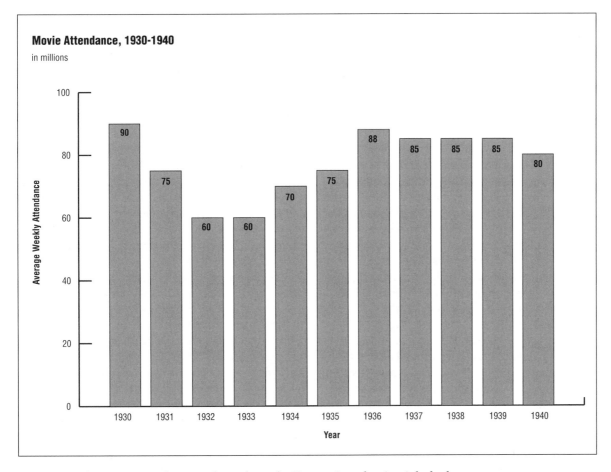

Movie Attendance, 1930-1940

in millions

Movie attendance remained strong throughout the Depression, despite tight budgets. (The Gale Group.)

Ginger Rogers. Perhaps some of the purest escapist fare was offered in their musicals produced by RKO Studios including *Flying Down to Rio* (1933), *Roberta* (1935), *Top Hat* (1935), and *Follow the Fleet* (1936). Also a wonderful escape were the movies of curly headed moppet, Shirley Temple, who seemed to return a lost innocence to the nation.

Shirley Temple Movies

One outcome of the new decency codes was the introduction of Shirley Temple to theater audiences. Adults and children were drawn to the young film star who became the most popular child film star of all time. She was a sophisticated performer who often seemed more mature than the adults around her; she had no problem upstaging her more experienced costars. At the age of six, Temple starred in her first full-length film, entitled *Carolina,* which was made in 1934 for Fox Films Corporation. However it was her next film, *Stand Up and Cheer* (1934), that made her

a star. Some of her other notable films included *Now and Forever* (1934), *The Little Colonel* (1935), *Curley Top* (1935), *The Poor Little Rich Girl* (1936), *Dimples* (1936), *Heidi* (1937), and *The Little Princess* (1939). She appeared in six films in 1934 alone followed by four in 1935 and 1936 each.

By 1938 Temple was the top box office attraction and ended up with 25 movies during the 1930s. A whole industry grew around her including Shirley Temple dolls, clothes, coloring books, and other items. Shirley Temple look-alike contests became popular across the nation as mothers dressed their daughters and curled their hair to resemble Temple.

Return to Law and Order:
The G-Men and Westerns

Ridiculed in gangster and shyster movies, law and order made its movie return in 1935. As so many times before the movies paralleled real life. Just as President Roosevelt took over the reigns of Washington in

1933, MGM Studios released a strange shocking film, *Gabriel Over the White House.* In "Gabriel" fictional U.S. President Hammond assumes complete dictatorial power, putting a quick end to crime by speedy trials and firing squads. Although President Roosevelt chose not to follow such a radical course, the movie illustrates the desperate longing of many for someone to take authority and proceed with immediate action.

When Roosevelt assumed the presidency he appointed Homer S. Cummings as his attorney general in charge of the Department of Justice, which included the Federal Bureau of Investigation (FBI) headed by J. Edgar Hoover. Unknown outside government circles, Hoover had labored to fine-tune his bureau with outstanding agents. Only in 1934, however, were the agents allowed to carry guns and cross state lines in pursuit of criminals. Also at this same time outlaws such as John Dillinger, Charles "Pretty Boy" Floyd, and Bonnie and Clyde were terrorizing the Midwest. In two short years, 1934 and 1935, Hoover's men gun downed or captured all of the infamous outlaws. By 1935 Hoover was America's No. 1 cop largely due to Warner Brothers' 1935 sensational hit, *G-Men.* Hollywood instilled new life and credibility in the law by creating the prototype of a new tough policeman. Jimmy Cagney who portrayed Public Enemy No. 1 in the 1931 film *The Public Enemy,* was the heroic lawman in *G-Men.* The "G" stood for government. Just as New Deal programs were helping the public economically, the government was once again its protector in law enforcement. After a name change, G-men became known to the public as FBI agents. Another bad-guy actor gone straight was Edward G. Robinson who played Rico in the 1930 gangster movie *Little Caesar.* In Warner Brothers' *Bullets or Ballots* (1938), however, Robinson portrayed a plainclothes cop who acts as a double agent. He enters a gang on the bottom level and destroys it on his rise to the top.

Westerns in 1933 had little following left; the public seemed to be bored with the old predictable horse dramas. By 1935, however, the law appeared to be returning to the western landscape. Gene Autry, the singing cowboy, and Hopalong Cassidy rode to fame in 1935. Two Paramount 1936 movies, *The Plainsman* and *The Texas Rangers,* cleansed and civilized the West. There were so many outlaws to be corralled that the westerns endured into the 1960s. By the mid-1930s the federal government again was a benevolent protector and law enforcement quite effective. Just as musicals and law and order films followed the MPPDA Production Code, another type of film— screwball comedy—also toed the line.

Screwball Comedy

Unlike the irreverent and absurd comedy of the Marx Brothers and W.C. Fields, screwball comedy was warm and good humored. It was fast paced, very funny, made use of highly talented actors and actresses, and most importantly, it was healing and unifying. Through its "screwballness" what the Great Depression had divided was pulled back together. Highly fractured social classes and families were united and the wealthy usually abandoned their selfish ways and took on the values of ordinary men. The first screwball comedy, and one of the most popular of all time, was Columbia Pictures' *It Happened One Night* (1934) directed by Frank Capra. The film was produced on a minimal budget and featured the then second-rank star Clark Gable and an actress borrowed from Paramount, Claudette Colbert. Gable portrays a lower middle-class reporter, while Colbert's character is an heiress. The walls of class are broken down as Colbert ends up in Gable's arms. Having made his fortune through hard work, Colbert's wealthy father even appreciates Gable's strength. Capra's film helps dismantle a Depression myth that all wealthy are idle. The wealthy father had put in just as many hours of work as the salaried man or wage earner. *It Happened One Night* ran for months and made fortunes for Columbia. It won all major Academy Awards for 1934. Likewise *You Can't Take It With You* (Columbia, 1938) ends in a kindly feeling toward the wealthy. A popular screwball series of films were *The Thin Man* series begun in 1934, starring the sharp and witty Myrna Loy and William Powell.

By the second half of the 1930s Capra's movies tended to portray the common, ordinary man as the hero, and the wealthy urban businessman as the villain. Capra directed Columbia's *Mr. Dees Goes to Town* (1936) that brings rural values to the city. A screwball tuba-playing small town guy wins $20 million and ends up living in a mansion in New York. Besieged by New York's shysters for money donations, he measured every request by his small town yardstick. Rebuking all the shyster requests he gives his money to the needy in rural communities. Capra manages to reconcile and unite all parties both urban and rural.

In 1939 Capra directed *Mr. Smith Goes to Washington* for Columbia. Jefferson Smith, played by the always affable Jimmy Stewart, is a junior U.S. Senator from this state. In very humorous episodes he attempts to deal with corrupt power wielding senior senators, however, Smith's pure idealism holds out for honest democracy. The underlying meaning that Americans easily read was that dark forces, whether they be at home or looming around the world, could be overcome by faith in democracy.

Some saw the film King Kong *(1933) as purely cinematic escapism, others saw it as a representation of the plight of urban dwellers trapped in the city during the Depression.* *(The Kobal Collection. Reproduced by permission.)*

The Social Conscious Movies

As early as 1932 Warner Brothers began to address social problems. These social conscious, or "topical," films addressed among other issues unemployment, hobo children, and fascism and communism. These films were not major box office attractions but were Hollywood's attempts to dramatize the social and economic upheaval of the time. Warner's *I Am A Fugitive From a Chain Gang* (1932) deals with unemployment, unjustified imprisonment,

and escape. It is a bleak film without hope, a film where a man's life is twisted by forces he can never really explain. The unjust imprisonment according to Robert McElvaine in his book, *The Great Depression,* "becomes an exaggerated vision of society. Innocent people are treated brutally" (p. 212). Further, at the conclusion of the movie, McElvaine observes the main character, "symbolizes all Depression victims, desperately searching for any kind of work, a social outcast ... 'I Am a Fugitive' was the perfect expression of the national mood in 1932: despair, suffering, hopelessness" (p. 213).

Warner produced two topical social films in 1933, *Heroes For Sale* and *Wild Boys of the Road*. *Heroes* was a confused film that was pro-individual work and success but at the same time was anti-capitalist, anti-machines, and anti-communist. On the other hand *Wild Boys* was the simple story of high school kids riding the rails after their parents lose their jobs. At the end one of the boys goes before a judge resembling President Roosevelt. The judge, with a Blue Eagle symbol of the NRA painted behind him on the wall, tells the youth that things all over the country will soon be better. Two more topical films, MGM's *Fury* (1936) and Warner's *They Won't Forget* (1937) were anti-lynching films. Lynching commonly refers to the murder of black Americans by white mobs. These crimes were frequently not investigated by the local white law authorities.

The popularity of films during the 1930s frequently was tied to escaping the brutality of everyday life, at least for a few hours. Few movies realistically portrayed the actual hardships of the Great Depression. One exception was the adaptation of John Steinbeck's novel, *The Grapes of Wrath*. The movie by the same name premiered in 1940 and told the story of refugees of the Dust Bowl who were dubbed "Okies." John Ford directed and Henry Fonda played the leading role.

The last social movie of the Depression era was another John Ford film, *How Green Was My Valley* (1941) adapted from the novel by Richard Llewellyn. The movie was set among the working class culture. Both *The Grapes of Wrath* and *How Green Was My Valley* were clear calls for a spirit of cooperation among people. Ordinary people realized that independence and self-respect could only be had by cooperating and sticking together.

Horror Movies, Thrillers, Swashbucklers, and Literary Adaptations

During the Great Depression Hollywood set the standard for horror films for the rest of the century. Approximately 30 horror films produced by eight of the largest studios appeared between 1931 and 1936. Horror films used dark sets of old castles filled with cobwebs, cemeteries, and deserted city slums. Boris Karloff starred in Universal's *Frankenstein* (1931) and *Bride of Frankenstein* (1935), both directed by James Whale. Bela Lugosi starred in another Universal film, *Dracula* (1931). Universal's *The Invisible Man* (1933) featured Claude Rains. RKO Studios' *King Kong* (1933) had several levels of meaning. It could simply be viewed as an escapist monster movie, but it seemed

to call up a more reflective meaning for many. The people who torment the beast are characters drawn straight out of the lawyer-newspaper-politician shyster films and the setting is New York City, the capital of shysterism for many Americans. King Kong reigned supreme in his natural environment, but his urban captor degraded him. The final scene has him atop the Empire State Building totally entrapped by the city. Many humans during the Great Depression felt senselessly entrapped within cities.

Alfred Hitchcock emerged as a master director of thrillers during the Great Depression. One of his masterpieces was *The 39 Steps* (1935) focusing on murder, a mysterious woman, and an international spy ring. Swashbuckler films involved pirates or knights coupled with swordplay or cannon fire. A typical swashbuckler of the era was *Mutiny on the Bounty* (1935) with Clark Gable. Every decade studios produce literary adaptation or movies from classical books. The 1930s included *Little Women* (1933), *David Copperfield* (1935), and *A Midsummer Night's Dream* (1935).

Hollywood's Golden Year—1939

The period of movies through the 1930s ended the decade with an epic year. Such notable movies as *Gone With the Wind, The Wizard of Oz, Wuthering Heights, Babes in Arms, Stagecoach, Young Mr. Lincoln,* and *Mr. Smith Goes to Washington* entertained massive audiences.

Gone With The Wind (1939) was based on the 1936 novel by Margaret Mitchell which had won the Pulitzer Price. The story dealt romantically with the Civil War (1861–1865) through the life of Scarlett O'Hara, a young woman played by Vivien Leigh. The story included pre-war scenes, the war, reconstruction, and Scarlett's three marriages. The film, made in color, won ten academy awards and was the most expensive movie made at that time. Produced during the Great Depression when racial relations were even more tense than earlier times due to the national economic difficulties and increased competition over jobs. The novel and the film raised disturbing questions about racism and the depiction of the Ku Klux Klan. It secured, however, a wide following. Clark Gable played the role of the dashing Rhett Butler.

Director John Ford's *Young Mr. Lincoln,* starring Henry Fonda, and *Stagecoach,* starring John Wayne, depicted early life in America. Good was pitted against evil on the frontier. In contrast, *Babes in Arms* starring Mickey Rooney and Judy Garland was a sentimental comedy about show business and William Wyler's *Wuthering Heights* was a memorable adaptation of a literary classic.

Paul Robeson, a popular actor of the time, is seen here in a still from the film The Emperor Jones. *Robeson had a successful career as both an actor and a singer. He became an activist for civil rights as well.* (© Underwood & Underwood. Reproduced by permission.)

In the *Wizard of Oz* a young girl played by 16-year-old Judy Garland is carried from the Depression-struck farm country of Kansas by a tornado. She lands in magical Oz where she searches with her make-believe companions for a pot of gold at the end of the rainbow. Garland sings "Somewhere Over the Rainbow," a beautiful uplifting song of hope. Although the end of the Depression was near, Americans would soon find World War II (1939–1945) at the end of that rainbow.

Race Movies

By the late 1910s black American-owned movie production companies began producing movies with strong black characters, in contrast to the way blacks were depicted in the major movie productions. Introduction of the more expensive production methods of sound, however, and the onset of the Great Depression affected black movies. In 1933 white director Dudley Murphy directed black actor Paul Robeson in

The Emperor Jones. Though the movie, produced by United Artists, received poor reviews overall, the acting capabilities of Robeson stood out as he played the lead character Brutus Jones. Jones was a railway porter who lands in prison and escapes to a Caribbean island where he becomes the ruler known as Emperor Jones.

Most of the movies, known popularly as "race movies," were shorts directed by whites and focused on jazz music and the musicians such as Duke Ellington, Cab Calloway, and Louis Armstrong among others. *Barbershop Blues* (1932) was an example of this movie type. New black stars appeared including Hattie McDaniel, Bill Robinson, and others. However their roles still remained largely stereotyped characters such as the servant, Mammy, played by McDaniel in *Gone with the Wind.* McDaniel's exceptional performance earned an Academy Award, the first Academy Award presented to a black American. A notable exception to stereotypic characters was Mae West's *I'm No Angel* (1933) in which the white mistress and black servant both rise from poverty.

Hollywood Provides More Than Entertainment

The Great Depression had a profound influence on the movie industry in various ways. The industry had experienced an economic boon through the 1920s. As attendance sharply declined by 1932, the industry had to make major financial adjustments after having overextended themselves into debt by free spending. Expectations were that the good times would keep coming. Aside from financial concerns, the Great Depression audiences sought much more from the movies they did attend. No longer were movies strictly viewed as a means of entertainment. Most Americans were either directly impacted by the Depression through job loss or income reductions, or simply lived in constant fear they might lose their jobs if economic conditions continued to worsen. Therefore they sought more than entertainment, they sought to escape and they looked for meaning that might apply to their economically stressed lives. They would more than ever place themselves into the characters' roles; characters who faced major obstacles and fought for the good of mankind against "villains," such as the bungling government or greedy business tycoons. Hollywood quickly sensed this desire of its audiences and produced movies to satisfy these demands. Hollywood would again thrive in this new atmosphere. Through the later 1930s attendance at movie theaters broadened and by the end of the Great Depression attending Hollywood movies had become a national pastime.

Contributing Forces

Development of Motion Pictures

The geniuses of the turn of the century, including Thomas A. Edison, contributed to the invention of the gilded screen. The first motion picture was taken in 1872 by a horse. California photographer Eadweard Muybridge set up a row of 24 cameras and from the lens shutter of each he stretched a thread across the track to a fence. The horse, as it ran, broke through each thread in succession and thereby worked the shutter of each camera. By using a white horse and painting the background fence in black, Muybridge was able to obtain clear pictures of the running horse. This photographer, working at the horse farm of Leland Stanford, later to become the site of Stanford University, was one of the pioneers in capturing motion on still film.

Thomas A. Edison invented two devices, the Kinetograph and the Kinetoscope, both of which were important in the history of the motion picture. The Kinetograph was a machine for taking photographs on film and the Kinetoscope was a machine with an eyepiece or "peephole" where an observer looked to see the moving pictures. The problem with the Kinetoscope was that only one person could use it at a time. Both of Edison's inventions used George Eastman's roll film and the sprocket that moved the film along at regular intervals brought each picture into focus for a single moment before moving it on.

On April 23, 1896, the first theatrical showing of a motion picture in the United States was made in New York City. Thomas Alva Edison produced the film, but played it on a projector created and developed by Thomas Armat. Inventors from all over the country, and the world, were rushing to try to improve the film industry. The early days of the motion picture industry were filled with patent disputes, often resulting in producers keeping their cameras under lock and key. They sent out false reports of the places where they intended to take motion pictures in order to defeat spies who were looking to steal ideas and technical advancements.

Attractions of Southern California

Originally, films were produced in or around New York and Chicago. Early in the twentieth century, however, moviemakers discovered California and the bright sunshine that aided in the filming. Located in Southern California, Hollywood in a few years became the movie capital of the world. Lying northwest of downtown Los Angeles, Hollywood is a district at the foot of the Santa Monica Mountains;

More About...

Movies and Movie Stars of the Great Depression

The American Film Institute (AFI) is an internationally prestigious arts organization with the purpose of advancing and preserving film, television, video, and digital moving images. AFI creates and implements programs that train visual storytellers, preserves moving images, and recognizes moving images as an art form.

In 1998 AFI released a list of the one hundred greatest films made between 1915 and 1998. Fifteen hundred distinguished leaders from the American film community compiled this list. Of the one hundred films listed, 22 were released and/or in production during the depression era and four are in the top 10.

Following are those 22 films with their date of release and numbered according to their place on the list (from American Film Institute, 2001). Numbers not included are for movies from other periods.

1. Citizen Kane (1941)
2. Casablanca (1942)
4. Gone With the Wind (1939)
6. The Wizard of Oz (1939)
21. The Grapes of Wrath (1940)
23. The Maltese Falcon (1941)
29. Mr. Smith Goes to Washington (1939)
35. It Happened One Night (1934)
43. King Kong (1933)
49. Snow White and the Seven Dwarfs (1937)
51. The Philadelphia Story (1940)
54. All Quiet on the Western Front (1930)
58. Fantasia (1940)
63. Stagecoach (1939)
73. Wuthering Heights (1939)
76. City Lights (1931)
81. Modern Times (1936)
85. Duck Soup (1933)
86. Mutiny on the Bounty (1935)
87. Frankenstein (1931)
97. Bringing Up Baby (1938)
100. Yankee Doodle Dandy (1942)

In 1999 AFI turned its attention to movie stars. AFI historians nominated 250 actors and 1,800 dis-

tinguished leaders in film were then asked to choose the top 25 male and female "screen legends" from that group. Of the 50, 32 appeared in films during the time of the Depression (17 women and 15 men). The following are the 1930s screen legends with numbers corresponding to their place on the AFI list (American Film Institute, 2001).

Female Screen Legends

1. Katherine Hepburn
2. Bette Davis
4. Ingrid Bergman
5. Greta Garbo
8. Judy Garland
9. Marlene Dietrich
10. Joan Crawford
11. Barbara Stanwyck
12. Claudette Colbert
14. Ginger Rogers
15. Mae West
16. Vivien Leigh
18. Shirley Temple
19. Rita Hayworth
20. Lauren Bacall
22. Jean Harlow
23. Carole Lombard

Male Screen Legends

1. Humphrey Bogart
2. Cary Grant
3. James Stewart
5. Fred Astaire
6. Henry Fonda
7. Clark Gable
8. James Cagney
9. Spencer Tracy
10. Charlie Chaplin
11. Gary Cooper
13. John Wayne
14. Laurence Olivier
16. Orson Welles
20. The Marx Brothers
24. Edward G. Robinson

Beverly Hills is to the west. Horace Wilcox platted Hollywood in 1887; his wife named the community after the home of a friend in Chicago. Because of water shortages, Hollywood in 1910 consolidated with Los Angeles.

Audiences began attending moving picture shows in the 1890s, but not until 1903 with the melodrama *The Great Train Robbery* did moving pictures gain large audiences. The film was not only the first American story film, but was also the first film depicting the cowboy, which influenced movies and "westerns" for years. Five-cent theaters, popularly called "nickelodeons," featured the film. The sudden growth in nickelodeons increased the demand for motion pictures and investors formed companies to produce them.

In 1908 filmmakers completed the movie *The Count of Monte Cristo* in Hollywood. Construction of studios for making films began in 1911 and led to more than 20 companies erecting movie lots and nearby theaters for those who flocked to see their productions. With warm and sunny weather, Hollywood attracted people hoping to be a part of the wonder of the silver screen. Thousands of "extras" found jobs in the cardboard cities behind Hollywood's high wooden fences and sound stages. Early producers often featured nudity and heavily done up females which caused a bit of public outrage. As a result, those involved in the industry were forced to set up their own rigorous code of censorship. Producers had to appeal to the public, for it was their money that would help to propel the industry into the future.

The first World War (1914–1918) helped the motion picture really come into its own, when it was used as an engine of anti-German propaganda. Specially prepared "hang the Kaiser" films aided in selling war bonds and in boosting morale. Those who attended the movies were shown news clips that gave a visual picture of the war in Europe. Viewers were able to see the realities of the war in Europe but were also quickly lost in the fantasy of the movie that they paid to attend.

Another early movie that gained popularity was D.W. Griffith's *The Birth of a Nation* (1915). In spite of its vicious racial intolerance, the movie excited audiences for years. The film cost almost $400,000 to produce, but it was one of the greatest moneymakers in the early industry. The movie followed two families, one in the North and one in the South, through the Civil War (1861–1865) and the following period of social upheaval in the South. Native Americans were portrayed in the movie, *In the Land of the Head Hunters,* produced by Edward S. Curtis in 1914. This film was unique in that it had an all Native American cast and depicted traditional life among the Kwakiutl Indians of Vancouver Island in British Columbia.

By the 1920s movies previously only novelties became big business. Studios produced what they knew would sell. Productions became slick with elaborate costumes and sets. Thousands of theaters and "movie palaces" catered to millions of Americans seeking adventure, romance, and entertainment. Films presented exciting, glamorous views of life.

By 1921 the technology existed to make sound movies, or "talkies." Not knowing how the public might react to the noisy movies, Hollywood continued to make silent films. Toward the end of the decade technology was ready and so was the public. On October 6, 1927, the first talkie, the *Jazz Singer* starring Al Jolson, premiered. Many predicted sound was a passing fad but theaters bought equipment and wired for sound as quickly as they could. The public became all the more enamored with movies.

Perspectives

A Necessity

For most people in the United States movies became a necessity of life during the 1930s. They would save and penny-pinch just as diligently for the price of a weekly admission ticket as for the purchase of food. Hollywood paid careful attention to what genre of movies sold the most tickets and then produced what the public wanted. Early in the 1930s gangster movies were a prime example. After the initial success of *Little Caesar* in 1930, approximately 50 gangster movies appeared in 1931. Why did people flock to gangster movies?

Historians have speculated why so many people spent so many hours watching gangster movies. Many success starved Americans could taste that success in the films. To others the gangsters' self-centered, greedy rise to success must have resembled the rise of the very wealthy Americans whom many now blamed the Depression on. The characters' ultimate failure represented social justice to this group of moviegoers. Yet another group of moviegoers probably simply identified with the characters as men who worked hard but failed just as they had worked but failed.

Morals

Correspondingly in the early 1930s many Americans were becoming more and more alarmed at the glorification of gangsters and the ridiculing of law enforcement agencies. Other threats to the public's

More About...

Movie Palaces

Part of the romance and excitement of going to the movies was to escape grinding realities of everyday life in the 1930s. Theater owners embraced showy architecture and special themes for their "movie palaces." Following the discovery of ancient Egyptian King Tutankhamun's tomb in 1922, a wave of interest swept the United States for Egyptian Revival Architecture. Movie theaters mirrored this interest with sphinxes, pharaohs, hieroglyphics, Phoenix birds, temple facades, and other elements drawn from ancient Egypt into the designs of theater buildings. Moorish dwellings from the Iberian Peninsula, Chinese garden temples, lavish use of terra cotta and glazed ceramic tiles—all became familiar in the nation's "movie palaces" of the 1930s, even in small towns. Most likely the theater in small towns would be the most elaborate building. Ushers saw people to their upholstered seats and lobbies were adorned with breathtaking chandeliers. Construction boomed for large, new movie theaters in the 1920s and slowed with the onset of the Depression, but some new facilities were erected to meet the large markets of movie entertainment. Many theaters were owned by the major studios assuring a ready market for their films.

A movie theater attained an even higher level of wonder if it housed a giant pipe organ. Once the preserve of churches, pipe organs became great crowd pleasers during the Great Depression. Skilled organists played a musical sound track to accompany the older silent films or, when "talkies" arrived, played marches and other compositions during intermission. The "Giant Wurlitzer" and other pipe organs were marvels of modern technology providing sound that poured out of pipes in the walls or lofts of the theater. The pipe organs included drums, train whistles, bells, xylophones, and other unexpected treats which caught the fancy of theatergoers.

Attendance at movie "palaces" provided an escape from drab reality and also coincided with changing moral codes where young couples might go "out" without a chaperone. Movies were a place to take a date or go with friends and family. The snack bar in the lobby of the theater sold popcorn, soft drinks, candy, and sometimes ice-cream.

Movies would be talked about for days and films became the standard for taste, styles, songs, and morals. Young women tried to speak like Greta Garbo or dye their hair like Mae West, while young men tried to emulate Clark Gable or Cary Grant. Movie stars were created, and so was the public interest in the lives of the "stars." Cheap movie magazines unveiled the foibles and adventures of the actors.

Annual Box Office Receipts, 1930-1939

Year	U.S. Box Office Receipts, in millions	Percent of U.S. Personal Spending	Percent of U.S. Recreational Spending
1930	$732	1.05%	18.35%
1931	719	1.19	21.77
1932	527	1.08	21.58
1933	482	1.05	21.89
1934	518	1.01	21.22
1935	566	1.00	21.14
1936	626	1.01	20.73
1937	676	1.05	19.99
1938	663	1.04	20.46
1939	659	0.99	19.09

Though struggling with hard economic times, people sought relief from their worries at the movies.

(The Gale Group.)

moral safely such as scant clothing, vulgarity, suggestive language, reduction, and four letter curse words were decried.

Will Hays and the Motion Picture Producers and Distributors of America (MPPDA) had passed a list of 11 "don'ts" mainly dealing with sexual excesses in 1927. They added violence in the Production Code of 1930. Hollywood, forever producing what they perceived the public wanted, ignored the Code. By 1933 civic groups, parent-teacher groups, the American Catholic Bishops, the powerful Protestant Council of Churches of America, and the Central Conference of Jewish Rabbis all demanded enforcement of the Code. The very edgiest in America were concerned that many people would actually learn techniques of crime and use them against society. By 1934 the Code was tightly enforced.

A Powerful Medium

William Randolph Hearst, a radically conservative newspaperman, had a studio of his own, Cosmopolitan Studios. Cosmopolitan produced *Gabriel Over the White House,* a film about a dictatorial president of the United States. MGM, causing much consternation to many at the studio, distributed the film in 1933 for Cosmopolitan. The film was believed to be Hearst's vision of a more efficient America and it drew considerable attention and publicity. The character obeyed Hearst's fantasy by cutting off the slow moving Congress, using a national police force to eliminate crime, and bullying other countries. Hearst simply recognized what a powerful medium movies were by influencing public opinion. By the late 1930s and with a world war looming studios used the powerful medium to build a strident support of American democracy and America's Armed Forces.

For a time minorities, especially black Americans and Asians in the mid-1930s, were presented in stereotypical roles. Though praised as a great achievement in filmmaking, *Birth of a Nation* has long been criticized for its racist portrayal of black Americans and its sympathetic treatment of the Ku Klux Klan. The brilliant dancing of Bill Robinson and the forceful definition of character portrayed by Hattie McDaniel in *Gone With the Wind,* were overshadowed by the restrictions script writers and directors placed on them because of race.

International Perspective

The American movie industry became much more aggressive in marketing its movies to foreign countries by the late 1920s. European audiences became highly receptive to the new talking American movies. Due to the fact that Britain was an English-speaking country, it became the first major foreign market for Hollywood productions. Britain, however, added important developments to the movie industry, such as new direction techniques introduced by Alfred Hitchcock. Hitchcock made several highly successfully movies, including *The Man Who Knew Too Much* (1934), before moving to Hollywood himself in 1939.

European movie theaters that were slow to technologically adapt to sound and language differences posed problems. The technique of dubbing would not be developed until 1931. The French movie industry went in another direction to compete with the Hollywood domination. Independent movie companies experimented with avant-garde films, characterized as Impressionist films and were met with great success among the French public. From 1928 to 1938 the amount of French film production per year rose from 66 films to 122 films and French audiences were second only to the United States in terms of attendance. By 1938 French movies were the most critically acclaimed movies in the world. With the looming crisis with Adolf Hitler's Germany, however, most French films in the late 1930s were filled with despair.

In Germany, Hitler exacted tight control over the German movie industry. Like Mussolini in Italy, he encouraged filmmakers to produce light entertainment and avoid any themes that might be thought provoking.

Impact

Contributions of the Depression Period in Movies

The "Golden Age of Hollywood" emerged out of the trials of the Great Depression. The Depression audience posed a major influence on Hollywood and the kind of movies it produced. Escapism and movies with meaning replaced movies made for only entertainment value. The impacts of this area were multiple. The growth of the industry almost eliminated vaudeville and minstrel shows. Vaudeville acts were light entertainment on stage involving comedy, dancing, song, and pantomime. The acts traveled around the country entertaining the public. Minstrel shows involved stage performances of black American traditional melodies and jokes performed by white actors impersonating blacks, including having their faces "blacked." Both vaudeville and minstrel shows continued into the new medium of movies, carrying forward those forms of entertainment and racial prejudice.

Filmmakers used new techniques of sound, color, and animation to develop movies that attracted large audiences. Movie production became an important economic activity and generated a flow of income in communities across the nation. Hollywood filmmakers developed important genres of movies in the 1930s. Many of these endured for years and, from time-to-time, have sparked revivals of themes. Hollywood in 1930 adopted a Production Code which set moral standards and self-policing in the film industry, moving away from the use of profanity, nudity, and the role of the "vamp" in films in the 1920s. It was not actually enforced until 1934 but then continued until 1968 when it was replaced with a movie-rating system. "Movie Palaces" built in the 1920s and the 1930s endured for decades becoming important gathering places for promoting popular culture in America. Founded on fantastic architecture, the theaters adapted designs from exotic places to house auditori-

A scene from the 1939 film The Wizard of Oz. *The movie brought hope to moviegoers near the end of the* Depression. *(The Kobal Collection. Reproduced by permission.)*

ums, pipe organs, and snack bars to entertain millions. Actors and actresses emerged as "stars." Most were held by contract to specific studios who selected their roles and managed their images.

The Post-Depression Era

Success of the motion picture industry in the 1930s carried right into the 1940s. During that decade almost five hundred films were made each year. During the early 1940s 80 million people attended the movies each week. The Office of War Information labeled the movie business an essential industry for the war effort. In fact the Bureau of Motion Pictures was created to ensure only positive portrayals of the war effort were shown. Almost four hundred of the over 1,300 movies made between 1942 and 1944 dealt with some aspect of the war. German Nazi and Japanese characters were always represented as evil and the Americans always triumphed. The movies served to reassure the public and keep morale high.

With the high demand for more and more movies in the 1940s, the large movie studios became like factories with assembly production, from shooting, editing, cutting, and distribution. The economic return was definitely worth the effort; in 1946 the studios took in $1.7 billion.

The economic good times were short-lived however. First the movie industry was hit with a major lawsuit claiming the big studios were monopolies, keeping small studios out of the business. The congressional inquiries in the late 1940s into the movie industry regarding possible communist sympathizers ruined the careers of many. In addition television came into common use by the early 1950s causing many to stay away from the movies. Whereas Hollywood was making 550 movies a year during the Great Depression, that figure dropped to 250 a year in the 1950s. Attendance dropped each year until by 1964 it had dropped by 75 percent since 1946. Film companies were facing their greatest financial losses in movie history.

A new generation of filmmakers began appearing by the late 1960s replacing the generation that had become established during the Great Depression. This new group included Francis Ford Coppola, Robert Altman, and Martin Scorsese followed by George Lucas and Steven Spielberg. Movies such as *The Godfather* (1972), *Jaws* (1975), *Star Wars* (1977), and *E.T.—The Extra-Terrestrial* (1982) introduced the era of blockbuster movies. *The Godfather* was the biggest box office success since *Gone With the Wind* of the Depression era. The highly successful *Indiana Jones* series beginning with *Raiders of the Lost Ark* (1981) borrowed from the entertaining action movies of the Depression. These productions greatly revived attendance and interest in the movies. By the 1980s the movie industry became the central focus of media commercial empires. By the 1990s computer-generated imagery had further increased attendance to movies. Computers added greater realism and allowed for more elaborate fantasy. Movies such as *Jurassic Park* (1993), *Twister* (1996), and *Titanic* (1997) highlighted the new special effects and kept the public coming to the movies in substantial numbers.

Later Movies of the Depression

Few movies after the 1941 *The Grapes of Wrath* were centered around the theme of the Great Depression. World War II had captured the attention of Hollywood in the early 1940s ending abruptly much introspection of the period. Of note were *Aunt Mame* (1958) which won six Academy Award nominations including for best picture and was later remade into *Mame* (1974) starring Lucille Ball. The story focused on an eccentric and wealthy woman whose life changes when she becomes guardian of her late brother's young son. The story follows them through the boom years of the 1920s to the Great Depression when they are financially rescued by a wealthy Southern plantation owner.

In the same vein as movies of the 1920s gangsters, particularly Al Capone, came a movie in 1969 focused on the outlaws of the early 1930s. *Bonnie and Clyde* starring Faye Dunaway and Warren Beatty was a romanticized account of the couple on their Midwest crime spree from 1932 to 1934 when finally gunned down by law enforcement authorities. A box office hit, the movie won two Academy Awards and was nominated for seven others.

Places of the Heart (1984) starring Sally Field is the story of a widow during the Great Depression who tries to save her Texas farm and keep her two small children together. She weathers storms and labor problems to make her mortgage payments on time. The movie also explores the racism of the South during the Depression. Field won the Academy Award for best actress and the movie won best screenplay. The movie was also nominated for five other Academy Award including best movie.

Also of particular note was the long running and highly popular television series *The Waltons*. Based on an earlier movie starring Henry Fonda and Maureen O'Hara, *Spencer's Mountain* (1963), the series ran for ten seasons from 1972 to 1981 and remained a popular television rerun into the early twenty-first century. The Walton family lived on a small income earned by running a sawmill in the Ridge Mountains of Virginia. The program followed the family through the Depression and world war.

Another television production in 1997 also explored life during the Great Depression. *Miss Evers' Boys* is set in 1932 in Macon County, Alabama. The story focuses on the federal government's medical study concerning syphilis among black men. Starring Alfie Woodard, the story is from the perspective of Nurse Eunice Evers who is aware that the 412 men in the study are being withheld actual treatment unknown to them. Most eventually died of the disease and the study was not halted until 40 years later when it became the subject of a U.S. Senate investigation. The movie made for television won numerous Emmy Awards including best special and best leading actress. The program also won a Golden Globe Award and numerous international film awards.

Notable People

Fred Astaire (1899–1987). Astaire was known as one of the top professional dancers of the 20th century. Astaire made some 30 movie musicals, including ten highly acclaimed films with co-star Ginger Rogers. Some of Astaire's movies included, *Dancing Lady* (MGM 1933), *Flying Down to Rio* (RKO 1933), *Roberta* (RKO 1935), *Top Hat* (RKO 1935), and *Follow the Fleet* (RKO 1936). Even though Astaire's dance style appeared effortless, it was noted by fellow co-star Bing Crosby that Astaire was a perfectionist. Astaire performed in movies, on the stage, on radio shows, and eventually on TV programs. He also went overseas to Europe during World War II to entertain the troops.

Busby Berkeley (1895–1975). Berkeley was an American film director born in Los Angeles as William Berkeley Enos. He was originally a Broadway choreographer and directed dancing in more than twenty musicals. Samuel Goldwyn brought him to Hollywood in 1930 to direct the dancing in the musical *Whoopee*. In the 1930s Berkeley directed for Warner Bros. and his major works included *Gold Diggers of 1933* (1933) and *Footlight Parade* (1933). He used huge chorus lines, mirrors, special lighting, and a camera mounted on a monorail. His films fostered a sense of freedom and escape.

Frank Capra (1876–1991). Born in Sicily, Italy, Capra's family moved to Los Angeles when he was six years old. After graduating from California Institute of Technology, he became an army engineering instructor. Capra became a director of movie shorts in

More About...

Charlie Chaplin

The onset of difficult times in the nation's economy in the Fall of 1929 set the stage for film makers to find figures with whom Americans might identify and find hope. Charlie Chaplin (1889–1977) was the leader of silent films, often performing, directing, producing, writing, composing music, and editing his own films. Chaplin's genius in acting, dancing, and commenting on contemporary events catapulted him to top billing in the 1930s. Some of Chaplin's most popular films included the two silent films, *City Lights* (1931), *Modern Times* (1936), and his first talking film *The Great Dictator* (1940).

City Lights is regarded by many to be Chaplin's greatest work. The film's theme concerns the suffering of a blind girl, Chaplin's Tramp character, and the effort of a millionaire to persuade them both that life is worth living. *Modern Times,* a story of industry, explores the themes of humanity and crusades in the pursuit of happiness. This film is the classic battle of man and the toil and dehumanization of factory life. Chaplin depicts a hero nearly overcome by the mechanization of the factory. To some *Modern Times* recalled the Chicago World Fair of 1933. While the new machines awed many, others knew these machines meant loss of jobs. The film ends on a happy hopeful note with Chaplin's character, the Tramp, walking into the sunset with his love. Although Chaplin made talking films, including *The Great Dictator,* he was best known for his silent films, which he continued to make despite the increased use of sound. Chaplin had a way with the camera and although no sound was used, viewers were able to relate to the characters through his creative expressions and ridiculous situations in which Chaplin's characters found themselves. Clowning, dancing, and persisting in the face of multiple adversities, Chaplin's character showed that with good spirit and persistence it was possible to survive and even have fun.

1921 and by the late 1920s he had directed some popular comedies. The popularity of Capra's movies grew through the early 1930s. He won the Academy Award for best director for three classic comedies, *It Happened One Night* (1936), *Mr. Deeds Goes to Town* (1936), and *You Can't Take It With You* (1938). During the Great Depression, Capra's movies provided an air of optimism in a humorous setting with the idealistic hero winning over shrewd opponents.

Charlie Chaplin (1889–1977). Chaplin was raised in poverty in the slums of London, England. At a young age he became a music hall performer and while touring the United States in 1913, was persuaded to join Keystone studio. Chaplin's international reputation grew after he released short films for Essanay, Mutual, and First National Studios. In 1919 Chaplin co-founded the organization United Artists and in the early 1920s began independent production of films. Some of his films included, *City Lights* (1931), *Modern Times* (1936), and *The Great Dictator* (1940). The majority of Chaplin's movies were silent films but he did make several talking films in the late 1930s. He was determined, however, to demonstrate the value of the silent medium and continued to produce many silent films after the advent of "talkies." Chaplin was married four times and refused to accept U.S. citizenship. In 1953 he was accused of being a communist while overseas and was unable to reenter the United States. Chaplin had an amazing impact on the early film industry by performing, directing, producing, writing, composing, and editing many of his films.

Cecil B. DeMille (1881–1959). Son of a playwright, DeMille studied at the American Academy of Dramatic Arts. He began an acting career in 1900. In 1913 he joined with Samuel Goldwyn and others to form a play company that eventually became Paramount Pictures in Hollywood. DeMille's first film was one of the first full-length films produced in Hollywood, *The Squaw Men* (1914). DeMille became known for his production and directing of large spectacles including *The Ten Commandments* (1923) and *The King of Kings* (1927). His major films in the 1930s included *The Sign of the Cross* (1932) and *Union Pacific* (1939). His *The Greatest Show on Earth* (1952) won the Academy Award for best picture. DeMille is remembered as the originator of the Hollywood movie epic, a distinctive movie genre.

Walt Disney (1901–1966). Walter Elias Disney was raised on a farm near Marceline, Missouri. He became interested in drawing at an early age. In 1918

Gone With the Wind stars Vivien Leigh and Clark Gable. (The Kobal Collection. Reproduced by permission.)

he tried to enlist for military service but was rejected because he was only sixteen years of age. Instead Walt joined the Red Cross and was sent overseas where he drove an ambulance. Instead of his ambulance being covered with camouflage, Disney painted his with drawings and cartoons. After the war, Walt returned to Kansas City, where he began his career as an advertising cartoonist. In 1923 Walt moved to Hollywood, where his brother Roy was already living, to try and begin his animation career. Pooling their resources, Walt and Roy bought the appropriate equipment and set up their first studio in their uncle's garage. Disney's first screen debut featured Mickey Mouse in *Steamboat Willie,* (1928) and was the world's first fully synchronized sound cartoon. Disney's innovations and techniques continued to grow and so did his business.

Thomas A. Edison (1847–1931). Edison gained recognition as the greatest inventor in history because of the impact of his inventions. Edison's first patented invention was an electrical vote recorder for counting votes in Congress. He also invented the stock ticker at the age of 22 and received $40,000 for its purchase. Edison continued to experiment and invented electric lighting and power, incandescent lamps, electric fixtures, electric railways, electric motors, the carbon

transmitter for telephones, motion pictures, and the phonograph. In the phonograph and motion picture machine, Edison provided a common form of entertainment for all, opening almost unlimited opportunities in the field of recreation and education.

John Ford (1895–1973). Ford was born Sean Aloysius O'Feeney to Irish immigrants in Cape Elizabeth, Maine, in 1895. Following an older brother, Francis Ford, to Hollywood in 1914 Ford found a job with Universal Studios as a property man. Soon he changed his name and became an assistant director for Universal and was assigned work on shorts and westerns. Ford gained recognition for *Iron Horse* (1924), which further opened the door to high-budget westerns. He became director, producer, and writer of over six hundred films. He was noted for use of wide-open expanses and showing depth of his characters. His most acclaimed films dealt with social themes, such as *The Informer* (1935), *The Grapes of Wrath* (1940), and *How Green Was My Valley* (1941). He is remembered most, however, for his westerns including *Stagecoach* (1939). Another popular Depression era film of Ford's was *Young Mr. Lincoln* (1939) starring Henry Fonda. Three of his films including *The Grapes of Wrath* won the Academy Award for best direction.

Clark Gable (1901–1960). Gable was born William Clark Cable in Cadiz, Ohio. After seeing a play he was inspired to become an actor. Gable married Josephine Dillon, twelve years his senior, who was a manager of a theater. She supported him and took him to Hollywood where he met Lionel Barrymore. Barrymore got Gable a screen test with MGM where he launched his career playing a villain in the Western, *The Painted Desert* (1931). Gable soon became one of the hardest working actors of the 1930s. Gable left MGM for the studios of Columbia where he made *It Happened One Night* (1934). The decade ended on a high note for Gable with his role as Rhett Butler in *Gone With the Wind* (1939).

Greta Garbo (1905–1990). Garbo was born as Greta Lovisa Gustafson in Stockholm, Sweden. Garbo's career in front of the camera began with filmed commercials for a department store in Sweden in 1922 and a few European films in subsequent years. At the age of 19 Garbo went to a movie screening where she met Louis B. Mayer (MGM) and signed a movie contract that required that she go to Hollywood. In 1925 Garbo began work on her first American film, *The Torrent* (1926). The film was a success and MGM realized that Garbo might look ordinary in real life but that she could transform herself when on the screen. In 1926 Garbo went on strike to protest the poor quality of scripts being offered to her and her $750 a week salary. After months of negotiating, Garbo signed a five-year contract with MGM for two films a year, with her pay starting at $2,000 a week and escalating to $7,000 by the fifth year. In 1930 Garbo's first speaking film, *Anna Christie,* opened and broke box office records. By 1935 Garbo made $500,000 per film with continued box office success.

Ernst Lubitsch (1892–1947). Lubitsch became known for Hollywood's sophisticated comedies. Born in Berlin, Germany, he studied acting and joined a play company in 1911. He was also known for his elaborate costume features in the early 1920s that were the first German movies shown abroad. In 1923 he was hired to direct actress Mary Pickford in *Rosita.* He remained in Hollywood and produced and directed numerous popular movies through the 1930s. Lubitsch brought a very distinctive style involving graceful wit and implied sexual overtones packaged in sophisticated comedies. His movies included *The Love Parade* 1929), *Monte Carlo* (1930), *Trouble in Paradise* (1932), *The Merry Widow* (1934), *Ninotchka* (1939), and *The Shop Around the Corner* (1940).

Rouben Mamoulian (1897–1987). Born into an Armenian family in the Georgia province of the Russian Empire, Mamoulian became involved in acting, directing, and playwriting at the Moscow Art Theater while attending law school. He moved to London in 1918 where he directed operas and musicals. Mamoulian then immigrated to the United States in 1923 where he became production director for a theater in New York state. His production of the play *Porgy* in 1927 brought him wide acclaim. Mamoulian moved to Hollywood in 1929 where he introduced new concepts in sound and mounting cameras on wheels. His popular films during the Great Depression included the gangster film *City Streets* (1931), *Dr. Jekyll and Mr. Hyde* (1932), *Queen Christina* (1933), the first movie using Technicolor *Becky Sharp* (1935), *Golden Boy* (1939), and *The Mark of Zorro* (1940). Mamoulian also produced musical comedies such as *Love Me Tonight* (1932), *The Gay Desperado* (1936), and *High, Wide and Handsome* (1937).

Hattie McDaniel (1895–1952). McDaniel grew up in Denver, Colorado and, in 1910, left school to join a traveling minstrel show. The Great Depression largely destroyed the vaudeville and minstrel programs, but McDaniel found a job performing at Sam Pick's Club in Milwaukee, Wisconsin, and then a role in a radio show in Los Angeles. McDaniel first appeared in a film in 1932 and secured a major part in *Judge Priest* (1934) where she sang with Will Rogers. Her role as a happy southern servant in *The Little Colonel* (1935) created controversy but McDaniel per-

sisted and played a maid or cook in nearly 40 films. She secured the part of Mammy in *Gone With the Wind* (1939) and became the first African American to win an academy award for that role. After World War II her career was mostly in radio.

Bill Robinson (1878–1949). At the age of eight Robinson began dancing and, in 1908, entered the vaudeville circuit in black musicals and comedies. Eventually Robinson shifted from vaudeville to movies and had roles in 14 films, including *The Little Colonel* (1935), *In Old Kentucky* (1935), *The Littlest Rebel* (1935), *Rebecca of Sunnybrook Farm* (1938), and *Just Around the Corner* (1938). Robinson was an innovative dancer and could run backward almost as fast as others could run forward. Robinson's most memorable movie/dancing roles were with Shirley Temple.

Mickey Rooney (1920–). Rooney grew up in a vaudeville family and made his film debut at age six. Between 1927 and 1933 he starred in over 50 episodes of the Mickey McGuire" series that established his place among Hollywood actors. He began appearing in feature films in 1934. In 1937 he began a 15-film series of "Andy Hardy" that lasted until 1947. He won wide recognition for his performance in *Boys Town* (1938) and was nominated for Best Actor in the Academy Awards for *Babes in Arms* (1939).

Shirley Temple (1928–). Temple was born April 23, 1928 in Santa Monica, California. At two years old she began her dancing and singing lessons. At three years old she began her career and became known as one of the most successful child stars in the history of film. Known for her blond ringlets and her appealing lisp, and recognized for her ability to sing and tap-dance, Temple became a celebrity in 1934 when she starred in four films: *Now and Forever, Little Miss Marker, Baby Take a Bow,* and *Bright Eyes.* At the end of 1934 Temple was given a special Academy Award for her outstanding contribution to film. Shirley Temple retired from acting in 1949 and later became a member of the U.S. delegation to the United Nations (1969–1970), and was U.S. ambassador to Ghana (1974–1976).

Jack Warner (1892–1978). Jack and his three brothers, Harry, Albert, and Samuel, founded the Hollywood motion-picture studio, Warner Brothers. They were sons of a Polish immigrant cobbler. They entered the movie business by acquiring movie theaters beginning in 1903 while they were still inexpensive and then began distributing movies to theaters. In 1913 they began producing their own movies and moved to Hollywood in 1917 where Warner Brothers Pictures was established in 1923. Jack and Sam were in charge

Media Depictions

- The Definitive Collector's Edition of *The Wizard of Oz*, VHS videotape, MGM/UA M904755 (or DVD which includes a behind-the-scenes special, outtakes, and the original film trailer).

- On December 31, 1998, PBS, DANCE IN AMERICA presented *Busby Berkeley: Going Through the Roof*, a documentary about one of the greatest movie showmen ever. Esther Williams and former Berkeley chorus girls Toby Wing Merrill, Pat Wing Gill, and Dorothy Coonan Wellman joined film historians and critics to recall the man whose imagination knew no limits. At a time when film musicals were little more than stage productions on film, Berkeley ignored the conventional limits of the sound stage.

- A&E Biography Series—*Greta Garbo: The Mysterious Lady*. Time: 50 min. Product Code: SOE-14326. Features clips from her performances in silent film, her sound film debut, and her final two comedy films.

- *Jews, Movies, Hollywoodism and the American Dream*. Time: 100 min. Color and b&w documentary by Associated Producers and Ontario Limited, 1997. Cat. No. AAE-17048.

of the Hollywood studio while the other two brothers handled other related business.

The Warner's were responsible for the first sound Hollywood movies in the mid-1920s including *Don Juan* (1926) with only a music soundtrack and then *The Jazz Singer* (1927) with dialogue too. *On with the Show* (1929) was the first sound and color movie. These films brought great profits and established Warner Brothers as a major studio. In the 1930s Warner was producing one hundred motion pictures a year. Its hits included the early 1930s gangster films such as *Little Caesar* (1930) and *Scarface* (1932). During the 1930s they also produced swashbuckling movies with Errol Flynn, musicals, and dramas with Humphrey Bogart, Bette Davis, and many others. Jack Warner retired in 1972 and by 2000 the company had, through mergers, become Time Warner Inc., the largest media and entertainment corporation in the world.

William Wyler (1902–1981). Wyler was born to a Swiss-born merchant in Mulhouse, France. After attending the Paris Conservatory, he joined a New York foreign publicity office of Universal Pictures in 1920. Having moved to Hollywood in 1921, he quickly worked his way up from office boy to director by 1925 and directed over 50 westerns by 1927. By the early 1930s Wyler established his reputation as a serious director and produced a series of popular movies including *These Three* (1936), *Dodsworth* (1936), *Jezebel* (1938), *Wuthering Heights* (1939), and *The Westerner* (1940). He won Academy Awards for *Mrs. Miniver* (1942), *The Best Years of Our Lives* (1946) and *Ben Hur* (1959). Wyler contributed a very technically polished style to the evolving Hollywood movies of the 1930s and focused on human relationships.

Darryl F. Zanuck (1902–1979). Born in Nebraska, Zanuck was abandoned by his parents at age 13. He joined the U.S. Army as a young teenager and fought in Belgium in World War I. Following the war Zanuck pursued a career as a writer though barely literate while working as a steelworker and professional boxer. Having attracted attention in 1923 for a proposed screenplay, he joined Warner Brothers studio in Hollywood in 1924. Zanuck quickly rose to the position of executive producer by 1927 when he produced Hollywood's first sound movie, *The Jazz Singer*. He then began the popular series of gangster films for Warner Brothers including *Little Caesar* (1930) and *Public Enemy* (1931). In 1933 Zanuck founded Twentieth Century Pictures and produced *The Grapes of Wrath* (1940). Zanuck retired in 1971, the last of the major studio leaders of the 1930s. having produced over 165 films including "All About Eve" (1950), which won six Academy Awards including best picture.

Primary Sources

We're In the Money

"We're in the Money" was a song from "Golddiggers" of 1933. The phrase quickly entered everyday language (from Bergman, p. 62, "We're In the Money." Music and lyrics by Harry Warren and Al Dubin. Copyright 1933, Remick Music, Inc.).

We're in the money,

We're in the money.

We've got a lot of what

It takes to get along.

We never see a headline

About a breadline

Today.

Bank Nights

Bank Nights were used as gimmicks to increase attendance at movie houses. The following article by Forbes Parkhill appeared in the *Saturday Evening Post* (December 4, 1937, p. 20).

Of course you've heard about the visiting Englishman.

"At the cinema," he explains, bewildered, "a blindfolded urchin withdraws something from a revolving drum, a blighter standing on the stage calls out a name, a woman shrieks: 'Whoops! I've hit it on the nose!' and everybody else cries out, 'Aw, nuts!' Dashed singular, eh? What is it? A game?

'Yeah,' elucidates his patient American host. 'Everybody plays it. Anew angle on the old sport called Something for Nothing.'

Bank Night has blossomed into an American institution. In the four years since it burst upon an unsuspecting public in a small town in Colorado, at least 100,000,000 persons in motion-picture audiences have participated in Bank-Night drawings. Each week more than 5,000 theaters distribute almost $1,000,000 in prizes, as high as $3,400 each. As many more promote some variation of the Bank-Night idea.

It's got to the point where nobody can schedule a basketball game, a church sociable or a contract party on Tuesday night, because everybody is down at The Gem hoping to cop a cash prize—usually standing in the street beyond the marquee because the theater is much too small.

Bank Night was an oxygen tent for the gasping motion-picture exhibitors, who, during depression depths, had been disastrously dunked in a sea of red ink.

Respect of the Law

Respect of the law in movies and in real life had returned by 1935 as reflected in the following item published in *Time* magazine (June 1, 1936, p. 26).

What makes it [the 1935 Warner Brothers movie *Bullets or Ballots*] a good picture, despite its solemn interest in the obvious, is that it brings Edward G. Robinson (*Little Caesar*) back into the crime fold; this time on the side of the Law. A plain-clothes man exiled to The Bronx, Robinson goes into action when a reform movement attempts to break racketeering from the bottom up.

Suggested Research Topics

- Identify the impact of movies on the public as a means of escape from the economic depression existing in the country during the 1930s. How did

the "movie palaces" create exotic atmospheres for the fantasies of films? What was the role of the Marx Brothers in Hollywood in the 1930s? [Chico Marx (1886–1961), Harpo Marx (1888–1964), Groucho Marx (1890–1977), Gummo Marx (1893–1977), and Zeppo Marx (1901–1979)]

- Discuss the technological developments in photography, animation, sound, and color that enabled the movie industry to develop and grow despite the economic hard times of the Depression.

- Describe the economic impact that the movie industry had in the 1930s when the majority of businesses were struggling to stay afloat.

- Assess the role of movie stars and development of American popular culture shaped by films in the 1930s. Even when most "Westerns" were B-Movies, why were they so popular and sources of stardom for cowboy actors? How were African Americans portrayed in *Gone With the Wind,* the *Little Colonel,* and other popular films of the 1930s? How were Will Hays and the "Production Code" important to the direction Hollywood films took in the 1930s?

Bibliography

Sources

Bergman, Andrew. *We're in the Money: Depression America and Its Films.* New York: New York University Press, 1971.

Bondi, Victor, ed. *American Decades: 1930–1939.* Detroit, MI: Gale Research, Inc., 1995.

Briley, Ron. "The Hollywood Feature Film as Historical Artifact," *Film & History* 26(1–4):82–85.

———. "Reel History: U.S. History, 1932–1972, as Viewed Through the Lens of Hollywood," *History Teacher* 23(3):215–236.

Dobbs, Charles M. "Hollywood Movies from the Golden Age: An Important Resource for the Classroom," *Teaching History: A Journal of Methods* 12(1)[1987]:10–16.

Hyatt, Marshall and Charyl Sanders. "Film as a Medium to Study the Twentieth Century Afro-American Experience," *Journal of Negro Education* 53(2)[1984]:161–172.

Kindem, Gorham B., ed. *The American Movie Industry: The Business of Motion Pictures.* Carbondale, IL: Southern Illinois University Press, 1982.

McDonnell, Janet. *America in the 20th Century, 1920–1929.* North Bellmore, NY: Marshall Cavendish Corp., 1995.

McElvaine, Robert S. *The Great Depression: America, 1929–1941.* New York: Times Books, 1993.

Peduzzi, Kelli. *America in the 20th Century, 1940–1949.* North Bellmore, NY: Marshall Cavendish Corp., 1995.

Powdermaker, Hortense. *Hollywood, the Dream Factory: An Anthropologist Looks at the Movie-Makers.* Boston: Little, Brown, 1950.

Robbins, Peter C., ed. *Hollywood as Historian: American Film in a Cultural Context.* Lexington: University of Kentucky Press, 1983.

Schlesinger, Arthur, Jr. "When the Movies Really Counted." *Show,* April, 1963.

Toplin, Robert Brent. *History by Hollywood: The Use and Abuse of the American Past.* Urbana, IL: University of Illinois Press, 1996.

Washburne, Carolyn Kott. *America in the 20th Century, 1930–1939.* North Bellmore, NY: Marshall Cavendish Corp., 1995.

Watkins, T.H. *The Hungry Years: A Narrative History of the Great Depression in America.* New York: Henry Holt and Company, 1999.

Further Reading

Black, Shirley Temple. *Child Star.* New York: Warner Books, 1989.

Britten, Loretta, and Sarah Brash, eds. *Hard Times: The 30s.* Alexandria, VA: Time-Life Books, 1998.

Britten, Loretta, and Paul Mathless, eds. *The Jazz Age: The 20s.* Alexandria, VA: Time-Life Books, 1998.

Cameron, Kenneth M. *America on Film: Hollywood and American History.* New York: Continuum, 1997.

Dardis, Tom. *Some Time in the Sun.* New York: Scribner, 1976.

Harmetz, Aljean. *The Making of the Wizard of Oz.* New York: Alfred Knopf, 1977.

MacCann, Richard Dyer. *Hollywood in Transition.* Boston: Houghton Mifflin, 1962.

Milton, Joyce. *Tramp: The Life of Charlie Chaplin.* New York: HarperCollins, 1996.

Pechter, William S. *Twenty-Four Times a Second: Films and Film-Makers.* New York: Harper & Row, 1971.

Robinson, David. *Charlie Chaplin: His Life and Art.* New York: Da Capo Press, 1994.

Sklar, Robert. *Movie-Made America: A Social History of American Movies.* New York: Random House, 1976.

Stanley, Robert H. *The Celluloid Empire: A History of the American Movie Industry.* New York: Hastings House, 1978.

Warshow, Robert. *The Immediate Experience: Movies, Comics, Theatre & Other Aspects of Popular Culture.* New York: Atheneum, 1970.

Winslow, Susan. *Brother, Can You Spare a Dime? America From the Wall Street Crash to Pearl Harbor, An Illustrated Documentary.* New York: Paddington Press, LTD, 1976.

See Also

Crime; Escapism and Leisure Time; Everyday Life

Housing

Introduction

"The literally thousands of heart-breaking instances of inability of working people to attain renewal of expiring mortgages on favorable terms, and the consequent loss of their homes, have been one of the tragedies of this depression" (quoted in Glaab and Brown, *A History of Urban America,*1983, p. 299). President Herbert Hoover (served 1929–1933) wrote these words in a letter during his term in office. The problem of foreclosures quickly became critical as the Great Depression began. In 1932, 273,000 people lost their homes. During the next year, a thousand mortgages a day were being foreclosed.

From the time urban settlements first appeared in America during the eighteenth century, selecting, constructing, and purchasing a place to live had been left to the individual. Housing was not considered an appropriate responsibility of government. However, since the mid-nineteenth century, social reformers recognized some housing in cities as inadequate and demanded changes. In 1929, with the onset of the Great Depression, housing problems quickly worsened. The building of new homes came almost to a halt, repairs went unfinished, and slums expanded. The crisis in housing attracted special attention. Many believed an upturn in construction activity was key to stimulating economic recovery.

Another critical housing situation facing Americans in the early years of the Great Depression was foreclosure. Thousands of homeowners were unable

Chronology:

1931–1932: More than 3,600 banks suspend operations.

1931: President Herbert Hoover convenes the National Conference on Home Building and Home Ownership to address the emergency in the construction industry and the rising number of home foreclosures.

July 21, 1932: Congress passes the Emergency Relief and Reconstruction Act to address low-income housing.

July 22, 1932: President Hoover signs the Federal Home Loan Bank Act to establish a monetary reserve for mortgage lenders.

June 13, 1933: Congress passes the Home Owners' Refinancing Act that establishes the Home Owners' Loan Corporation (HOLC) to reduce home foreclosures by refinancing homeowners' loans.

April 28, 1934: Congress passes the Home Owners Loan Act of 1934, further strengthening the HOLC.

June 27, 1934: Congress adopts the National Housing Act which establishes the Federal Housing Administration (FHA).

September 3, 1937: President Franklin D. Roosevelt signs the National Housing Act (Wagner-Steagall Housing Act) of 1937 which creates the United States Housing Authority (USHA).

February 3, 1938: Amendments liberalizing the National Housing Act of 1934 are adopted.

1940: The first comprehensive nationwide housing survey is completed. The housing survey would be conducted every ten years in tandem with the census.

---

to make payments on their home loans, known as mortgages. This situation, called default, led to foreclosure by the holder of the mortgage, generally a bank. In foreclosure the bank seizes and auctions off the borrower's property to pay off the mortgage. By 1933, 40 to 50 percent of all home mortgages in the United States were in default. The home financing sys-

tem was sliding toward complete collapse. The default and subsequent foreclosure of mortgages was a major contributor to the banking crisis of the early 1930s.

Beginning in the 1930s, the U.S. federal government, recognizing the need for government intervention, attacked the housing problems on two broad and distinct fronts. First, in the early 1930s, Congress passed three measures to relieve both distressed homeowners and banks and, as a result, to get new construction restarted. First, during President Herbert Hoover's stay in the White House, the Home Loan Bank Act of 1932 was passed. Then, as part of the broad-ranging New Deal economic policies under President Franklin Delano Roosevelt (served 1933–1945) came the Home Owners' Refinancing Act of 1933 that created the Home Owners' Loan Corporation (HOLC) and the National Housing Act of 1934 that created the Federal Housing Authority (FHA). The HOLC began as an emergency agency to stop the avalanche of homeowner defaults. It accomplished this by refinancing shaky mortgages. The HOLC's lasting legacies were long-term, low-interest, mortgages, and the establishment of uniform national appraisal methods throughout the real estate industry. The FHA's enduring legacies were long-term mortgages insured by the federal government and the establishment of national standards of home construction. The beneficiaries of these programs were typically white, middle-class individuals who could afford to buy houses in the first place. Their houses were generally built on the outskirts of cities, in the suburban areas.

The second major housing front dealt with the inner-city slums. Initiatives in this area involved the federal government using public tax money to build dwellings for the benefit of those who could not pay market rates for shelter. The New Deal's Wagner-Steagall Housing Act of 1937 became the first housing legislation where the federal government recognized housing as a social need. Slowly, the idea to provide temporary housing for those in need evolved to providing permanent housing for the most disadvantaged members of society. The locations of these structures were almost always in the poorest parts of central cities. Unlike obtaining help for private homeowners, getting public support for housing programs for the most needy citizens was much tougher in 1930s America. As a result, public housing initiatives met with very limited success in the late 1930s.

The creation of the Federal National Mortgage Association (Fannie Mae) under the Reconstruction Finance Corporation (RFC) in 1938 completed the New Deal's housing program. Fannie Mae bought mortgages from lenders such as banks, thus increasing the lenders' funds for more mortgages and construction loans. Combined, the New Deal housing policies removed much of the risk from home lending. The FHA and Fannie Mae neither built houses nor loaned money. Their backing, however, provided banks with the assurance that construction and home loans would be repaid with government funds should the loans fall into default. Thus, banks made loans more readily to both builders and homeowners. This stimulated construction and provided a framework for the post-World War II (1939–1945) housing boom. The dream of owning a home came within the reach of all but the nation's poorest.

Issue Summary

The American attitude against government intervention in individuals' lives fundamentally shifted with the onset of the Great Depression. The Depression dealt severe blows to both the construction industry and the homeowner. Between 1929 and 1933, construction of residential property fell 95 percent. Repair expenditures decreased from $50 million to $500,000. In 1932 between 250–275,000 people lost their homes to foreclosure. In comparison, 68,000 homes suffered foreclosure in 1926. By 1933 foreclosures reached the appalling rate of more than a thousand each day. Housing values dropped by approximately 35 percent. A house, worth $6,000 before the Depression, was worth approximately $3,900 in 1932. By the early 1930s, many people owed more money through their existing mortgages than the reduced value of their home. With loss or cut back in employment and the loss of their homes, many middle-class families were experiencing their first taste of impoverishment.

As early as 1930, President Herbert Hoover recognized that the deteriorating real estate and construction industries were dragging down an already embattled economy. The overall unemployment numbers continued to skyrocket, and approximately one-third of those unemployed had worked in construction. Hoover convened the President's National Conference on Home Building and Home Ownership in 1931. The purpose of the conference, attended by over four hundred housing specialists, was to deal with the emergency in the construction industry and with foreclosures.

The conference formulated four recommendations. The recommendations ultimately provided the basis for twentieth-century federal housing policies. They were: (1) the amortization of long-term mortgages; (2) the encouragement of low-interest mortgage rates; (3) low-

A United States Housing Authority poster, created by the WPA, warns against the dangers of slums.
(National Archives and Records Administration.)

ering the cost of home construction; and (4) providing government monetary aid to private efforts to build low-income housing. (Amortization means the payback of a loan by periodic, usually monthly, payments of principle [the amount of the loan owed] and interest [money paid for use of the lender's money]. The monthly payment amount remains the same throughout the payback period. The result is a declining principle balance with eventual repayment of the loan in full.) The conference members also announced that they firmly believed private industry could accomplish these goals with planning and cooperation. Looking to the future, however, they sternly warned that the failure of private industry would lead to government intervention into housing.

Two Unsuccessful Programs

Disagreeing with the ideas promoted by the National Conference, the National Association of Home Builders immediately responded that private contractors alone could not build homes at affordable prices. They demanded prompt government assistance. Taking this perspective and the recommendation from the conference under consideration, the Hoover administration tried two approaches in 1932. On July 22, 1932, the president signed the Federal

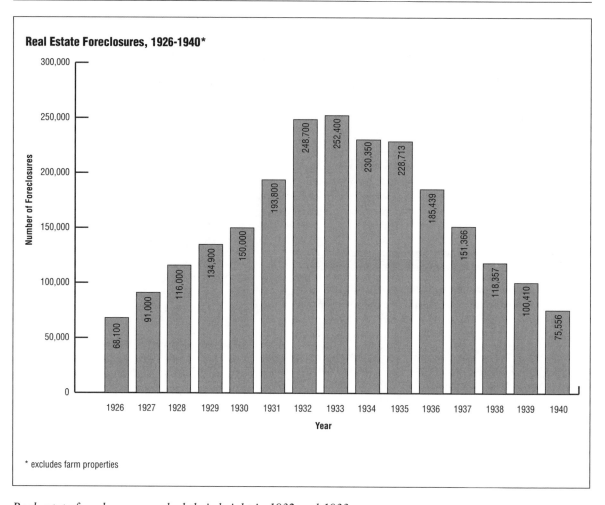

Real Estate Foreclosures, 1926-1940*

Year	Number of Foreclosures
1926	68,100
1927	91,000
1928	116,000
1929	134,900
1930	150,000
1931	193,800
1932	248,700
1933	252,400
1934	230,350
1935	228,713
1936	185,439
1937	151,366
1938	118,357
1939	100,410
1940	75,556

* excludes farm properties

Real estate foreclosures reached their height in 1932 and 1933. (The Gale Group.)

Home Loan Bank Act. The act established a monetary (loan) reserve for mortgage lenders—generally banking institutions. This reserve would increase the supply of money available for housing loans to encourage new housing starts and reduce foreclosures. The program, however, proved ineffective since it was not designed as an emergency measure. Loans could not be made to anyone who owed more than 40 percent of the value of their home. For example, an individual might owe $4,000 on a $10,000 home. Before the Depression in 1929, when their home was worth $10,000, they would have qualified because they did not owe more than 40 percent of the value of their home. If the value of their home had declined by 1932 to $6,000, however, their $4,000 mortgage was considerably more than 40 percent so they could not qualify. Everyone's home value had, in fact, drastically decreased after the onset of the Depression. Within the first two years of the act's operation, 41,000 applica-

tions for direct loans were made to the banks by individual homeowners. Only three were approved.

President Hoover's second effort, the Emergency Relief and Construction Act of 1932, was equally ineffective. This act enabled the RFC to make loans to corporations formed specifically to construct low-income housing and improve housing in slums. The catch here was that the legislation required states to exempt these corporations from all taxes. At that time only the state of New York had legal authority to make such exemptions. Other state legislatures had not had the public support to pass such tax law exemptions. As a result, the only project ever begun under this legislation was Knickerbockers Village in New York City.

Neither of Hoover's approaches halted the slide of the housing industry or the rapidly worsening predicament of homeowners. For the moment the fledgling framework for a realistic home mortgage system and improved housing for all, envisioned in Hoover's 1931 conference, was threatened by a wave of public disappointment with Hoover's ineffective programs. In March 1933 the problems transferred to the incoming Roosevelt administration.

A Man of the Country

Franklin D. Roosevelt, inaugurated as the 32nd president of the United States on March 4, 1933, was in heart and soul a child of the country. He believed the country bred a "better man." In his perfect world, Roosevelt would have solved the housing problem by moving everyone back to the land—out to country spaces. But Roosevelt's utopia sharply contrasted with reality. Despite the general public's widespread dissatisfaction with urban Depression life, the drift of population out of agricultural areas and into cities continued through the 1930s. The agricultural industry had been economically depressed since the early 1920s, and job opportunities seemed greater in the industrial city centers. Roosevelt was a practical man and knew that the Depression-era urban housing problems would have to be solved within the urban setting.

Roosevelt and those creating New Deal policies faced a choice between two different paths in housing issues. They could support proposals from congressional liberals such as Senator Robert F. Wagner for large-scale European-style public housing projects. On the other hand, they could develop measures to stimulate private home construction and individual home ownership, the path Hoover had attempted to take. New Dealers basically adopted Hoover's approach but would carry it much further. Roosevelt believed private home ownership was fundamental to the American way of life. He had the notion of the ideal home as a single detached structure surrounded by a small plot of land. Multifamily dwellings held little interest for him. With nearly 30 percent of the nation's joblessness involving workers in the building trades, Roosevelt decided he must place special emphasis on reviving the housing sector. New Deal help for the home construction industry and homeowners would follow a different path from later New Deal efforts to deal with inner-city housing for the poor.

New Deal Help for Homeowners and the Home Construction Industry

Home Owners' Loan Corporation On June 13, 1933, Congress passed the Home Owners' Refinancing Act that established the Home Owners' Loan Corporation (HOLC). The HOLC's goal was to stop the flood of homeowner foreclosures in urban areas. The foreclosure situation not only devastated homeowners but undermined the holdings of banks and other lending institutions. Normally, when banks foreclosed, they would sell the foreclosed property to a buyer to cover the mortgage loan. Buyers were often investors hoping to resale the property for a profit. Since no market for mortgages existed, however, few buyers were available. Those that were buying mortgages paid extremely low prices that rarely covered the loan amount for the bank.

The HOLC replaced Hoover's unworkable Federal Home Loan Bank Act. It provided loan money to refinance tens of thousands of mortgages in danger of default and foreclosure. Refinancing refers to setting up a loan under new terms of payment of principle and interest that makes it easier for the homeowner to repay the loan. The HOLC even helped persons who lost homes as early as January 1930 to recover their homes. A second act, the Home Owners Loan Act of 1934, passed the following year. This act guaranteed payment of the principle and interest of HOLC loans with government funds should a homeowner fail to make payments on his loan.

By February 1936 the HOLC had refinanced 992,531 loans totaling over $3 billion. The refinanced loans not only halted countless foreclosures but reduced delinquent property taxes. This permitted communities to meet their payrolls for school, police, and other services. Millions were also spent on repair and remodeling of homes. Thousands of men gained employment in the building trade. Thousands more jobs were stimulated in the manufacture, transportation, and sale of construction materials. Conceived as an emergency agency, the HOLC stopped accepting loans in June 1935 and issued its last loans the following June. By then HOLC had refinanced up to one-fifth of all mortgaged urban homes in the nation. The HOLC spent the next fifteen years collecting its payments and in 1951 ended its operations. Although it tackled the most troubled home mortgages, the HOLC concluded operation without a loss to the government and even returned $14 million to the treasury.

To offer similar relief to rural areas, in 1933 Congress passed the Emergency Farm Mortgage Act, which was aimed at farm foreclosure, and the Farm Mortgage Refinancing Act on January 31, 1934, which was patterned after the successful HOLC. Also, to support farmers in their fight to retain their land, Congress passed the Frazier-Lemke Federal Farm Bankruptcy Acts of 1934 and 1935. The Frazier-Lemke Acts provided major financial relief to farmers heavily in debt. The acts changed general bankruptcy laws for farmers whose debts were far more than the value

More About...

Redlining

Redlining, by the last quarter of the twentieth century, was a standard term in the vocabulary of urban affairs. Redlining referred to the fact that property owners in certain areas could not easily obtain credit for purchase or repair of property because lending institutions had written off the areas as high risk.

Redlining originated in the early 1930s as a rating system for the Home Owners Loan Corporation (HOLC). The system undervalued neighborhoods that were densely populated, mixed racially, or aging. The four HOLC categories of quality were first, second, third, and fourth, with corresponding code letters of A, B, C, and D and colors green, blue, yellow, and red. A, or green, areas were new or always in demand, such as professional residential areas. Ethnically mixed areas were never A's. B, or blue, areas were "still desirable;" C areas were "definitely declining." D, or red, areas had physical deterioration and low income prospects. Black neighborhoods were invariably red as were those areas characterized by vandalism.

HOLC appraisers literally ranked every block in every city, drawing red lines around less "desirable" areas, hence the redlining practices. The resulting information was then recorded on secret "Residential Security Maps" in local HOLC offices. The HOLC continued to offer loans in all areas, but the Federal Housing Administration (FHA) adopted the maps a few years later and refused to insure loans in the risky red areas. Likewise, private banking institutions, clearly influenced by the government's maps, did not loan in red and most yellow areas. Redlining contributed greatly to further deterioration of inner cities by discouraging the flow of capital into the areas. This pattern of discrimination continued at least until the early 1970s, contributing to the despair and frustration of the black and racially mixed communities. At that time the practice became illegal.

---

of their farms. Bankruptcy courts could reduce their amount of debt to approximately the same amount as the value of the farm, ensuring that the farmer would not still be hopelessly in debt even after selling his

farm. The farmer also had the opportunity to retain his property if he could pay back his scaled-down debts.

The HOLC refinancing plan is important in history because it introduced and perfected the practical long-term amortizing mortgage. This amortized mortgage revolutionized the home loan and real estate industry-making home mortgages feasible for the common American. With amortized mortgages the loan was completely repaid at the end of the loan period. The HOLC-amortized loans allowed homeowners to pay a set monthly payment of principal and interest at 5 percent for 15 years. At the end of the 15-year loan period, the loan was entirely repaid, and the individual owned his home "free and clear." This approach contrasted to the typical mortgage taken on during the 1920s, a boom period of home building. It was during this earlier period of rising home prices that buyers began using mortgages to finance their home purchases. The typical mortgage was for five or ten years and was not fully paid off at the end of the loan period. The buyer had to either take out another loan for the remainder or pay it off in a large payment. For example, a buyer might have bought a $5,000 home and taken out a $3,000, five-year mortgage at a typical interest rate of six to eight percent. At the end of five years, he might still owe $1,500 that he could pay off or refinance. This practice left the buyer at the mercy of money market forces over which he had no control. If money was easy to come by, he could refinance. If times were difficult and money was tight, as in the 1930s, it could be impossible to refinance. If he could not pay off the loan, foreclosure would result. The HOLC-amortized mortgages ended the need for a large payment at the end of the mortgage period and also lowered monthly payments.

The HOLC made a second lasting contribution by establishing standardized appraisal methods throughout the country. Because HOLC was dealing with problem mortgages, it had to have a way to predict the useful life of the house it was asked to refinance. HOLC appraisers were highly trained in uniform procedures. They put into writing characteristics of the house, such as type of construction; price range of other nearby homes; sales demand; repairs needed; and descriptions of the occupations, income level, and ethnicity of the neighborhood's inhabitants. The ultimate aim was that one appraiser's judgment would have meaning and could be understood by investors in other parts of the nation. Although this practice is credited in raising the level of and standardizing the American real estate appraisal methods, it also had a downside that persisted for decades, called redlining. Redlining originated when appraisers drew red lines on maps outlining neighbor-

---

hoods of mixed race or ethnic background. The redlined districts were considered risky areas for loans. Although the HOLC continued to impartially issue loans in those areas, for decades other lenders would tend to loan only in "good" areas. This practice perpetuated discrimination and the actual decline of certain areas. Significantly, the Federal Housing Administration adopted the HOLC's excellent appraisal methods but also its redlined maps.

The Federal Housing Administration   On June 27, 1934, Congress passed the National Housing Act, establishing the Federal Housing Administration (FHA). Unlike the HOLC, which was established as an emergency agency, the FHA was a permanent New Deal program. The act was designed to meet President Roosevelt's desire to stimulate building without government spending. He wanted a program that relied on private enterprise. The FHA made a powerful impact on American life throughout the rest of the twentieth century. The declared goals of the act were to encourage: (1) sound home financing on reasonable terms; (2) improvement in housing construction standards; and (3) a stable nationwide mortgage market. All of this was to be accomplished through reliance on private enterprise. The government itself would not be making direct loans.

Despite the three long-term goals, the immediate purpose of the act was to stimulate employment in the construction industry which would likely ripple through the entire economy. Not only had new home construction ceased, but the general lack of funds had let homes fall into disrepair. Both new construction and repair and renovation would provide jobs and, at the same time, increase the wealth of Americans by increasing the value of their homes.

The act, through the FHA, essentially accomplished its goals. First, the FHA insured the mortgage lender against default by the borrower. If the borrower defaulted, the FHA would pay the lending institution the amount owed on the defaulted loan. Over 250,000 home mortgages, valued at more than $1 billion, were accepted for FHA insurance between 1934 and December 1, 1937. Bankers freed loan money since they assumed very little risk if the loan turned sour. With the guarantee mortgage interest rates dropped two or three percentage points, making the loans more affordable. Second, the FHA helped guarantee the loans it insured would not go bad by making the loans workable for the average American. Down payments were drastically reduced. No more than 20 percent down was required. This was further reduced to 10 percent in 1938. Next, continuing a trend by the HOLC, the FHA

extended the repayment period for its guaranteed mortgages to 25 or 30 years. This time period greatly reduced the monthly payment, with the loan being paid in full at the end of the loan period. The FHA insisted all loans be amortized. The amortization insured a single stable payment amount for the length of the loan. The FHA also established minimum construction standards to ensure the dwelling would be free of major structural or mechanical deficits. This in turn ensured both the owner's satisfaction with the property and the actual value of the property.

The changes dramatically increased the number of Americans who could afford to purchase homes. According to Kenneth T. Jackson in his book *Crabgrass Frontier,* "Builders went to work and housing starts and sales began to accelerate rapidly in 1936. They rose to 332,000 in 1937, to 399,000 in 1938, to 458,000 in 1939, to 530,000 in 1940, and to 619,000 in 1941" (1985, p. 205). In 1933 housing starts had numbered only 93,000.

Unfortunately, a downside to these achievements also resulted. The FHA actually contributed to inner-city decay by pulling much of the middle class out to the suburbs. First, the FHA favored single-family projects in the suburban areas. It discouraged multifamily dwellings by offering only unfavorable loan terms on multifamily starts. Second, the loan amounts allowed for repair of existing homes were small. A family could just as easily purchase a new home as fix up an old one. Third, in its attempt to set construction standards, the FHA demanded such requirements as minimum lot size, distance from the street, and separation from adjacent structures. These requirements eliminated from FHA loan guarantees whole categories of many dwelling types in the city. Many city residences. were too close to the street. Therefore, existing homes that did not meet this or the other two requirements could not be FHA insured. For example, between 1935 and 1939, statistics from throughout St. Louis, Missouri revealed 92 percent of new homes insured by FHA were in the suburbs.

The FHA strove to meet its goals of stabilization of mortgage markets nationwide in two more ways: (1) the creation of mortgage associations; and (2) establishment of the Federal Savings and Loan Insurance Corporation. The mortgage associations, under FHA regulations, were to be private corporations buying and selling FHA-insured mortgages nationwide. The activities of these corporations were to be limited almost entirely to insured residential mortgages. This process could move funds from areas where mortgage funds were plentiful to areas where local mortgage funds were insufficient. Only one such association was

New York City Mayor Fiorello La Guardia was responsible for the establishment of the New York City Housing Authority, which closed down unsafe tenement homes in slums. (UPI/Corbis-Bettmann. Reproduced by permission.)

formed, on February 10, 1938, actually as a subsidiary of the RFC. It was called the National Mortgage Association of Washington, but changed its name to Federal National Mortgage Association or, as it is known today, Fannie Mae.

The last provision of the 1934 act established the Federal Savings and Loan Insurance Corporation (FSLIC). The FSLIC insured depositors' savings in savings and loan associations up to $5,000. This insurance was similar to that provided to bank depositors by the Federal Deposit Insurance Corporation (FDIC). Savings and loan associations primarily provided mortgage loans.

The National Housing Act of 1934 was amended and further liberalized with passage of the National Housing Act of 1938. Congress passed further amendments in 1939 and 1940. Both programs, HOLC and FHA, assisted Americans who were able with a little help to buy a home. The appraisal standards; long-term, low-interest, amortized, insured mortgages; and construction standards extended the possibility of home ownership to an ever-widening group and resulted in

the development of suburban areas. These policies however, did not reach down to the poor of the inner cities. The New Deal programs, through other avenues, also attempted to improve conditions in the slums and provide the poor with adequate shelter.

Help for Low-Income Inner-City Housing

Until the Great Depression, political and civic leaders expressed little concern for the condition of the cities' inner cores. Only a few social workers and city planners made attempts to deal with the problems of slums, poverty, and poor housing. In an important reversal of policy, the Roosevelt administration involved the federal government directly in construction programs. During the first hundred days of 1933, Congress passed the National Industrial Recovery Act of June 1933. The act's four purposes were to create jobs, improve housing for the poor, remove or renovate slums, and encourage private industry in large-scale community planning efforts. The act established the Public Works Administration (PWA) to provide low-rent housing and slum clearance projects.

The PWA's Housing Division attempted to get private developers involved by encouraging federal loan applications. These private developers, however, seemed more interested in unloading on the federal government undesirable city property at high prices rather than developing low-income housing projects. As a result, the government found only seven applications acceptable out of five hundred submitted by private corporations. Abandoning this approach in February 1934, the Housing Division became directly involved in slum clearance and low-cost housing construction projects, originating projects and supervising the construction.

In four and a half years of operation, it started several projects in such areas as Atlanta, Cleveland, and New York's borough of Brooklyn. Overall, however, the program made little progress in solving the housing problem. The PWA built or started 49 projects containing fewer than 22,000 units. The Housing Division, however, did shed light on the fact that slums and shortage of adequate housing reached across the nation, affecting smaller communities as well as big cities.

On a local level, Mayor Fiorella La Guardia set up the New York City Housing Authority (NYCHA) to deal with the dilapidated tenements of the slums. The NYCHA looked to the Lower East Side where 90 percent of the residential buildings were at least 35 years old, over 50 percent had no central heating or toilets in the apartments, and approximately 17 percent had no hot water. Although the NYCHA meant well, the results of forcing improvements meant more homelessness for the very poor. Forced to make costly improvements in the middle of the Great Depression, many landlords chose to simply board up the buildings. In just two years, 10,000 tenements were closed, eliminating 40,000 living units. Some people affected by the closures became homeless, while others moved in with family elsewhere. Those landlords who did upgrade raised rents above what low-income families could afford, pushing them onto the streets of the Lower East Side.

Between 1934 and 1937, states became increasingly interested in the possibilities of federal housing programs and put pressure on Roosevelt to act. Major support for federal housing projects came from Senator Robert Wagner of New York. He introduced housing bills into Congress in 1935 and 1936, but received no support from President Roosevelt until 1937. The National Housing Act of 1937, better known as the Wagner-Steagall Housing Act, became law on September 1. The United States Housing Authority (USHA), created by the act, took over the PWA projects. The USHA, however, operated very differently than the centralized Washington management of projects of the PWA. Under the Wagner-Steagall Act, all slum clearance and low-rent housing programs had to be initiated in the localities themselves. The act was authorized to make loans to local public agencies—called local housing authorities (LHA)— for the construction of low-rent housing projects. These loans were limited to 90 percent of the development cost of the project. The balance of the cost was raised locally, usually through the sale of LHA bonds. Once the project was completed, the USHA subsidized rents by making annual contributions to each housing project. Payment amounted to the difference between the rent paid by the low-income families occupying the dwellings and the actual cost of providing the housing.

Another important feature of the act was to clear out slums and construct new dwellings. For every new dwelling unit built, one slum dwelling had to be eliminated. This was called the "equivalent elimination."

The fact that the responsibility to form a local housing authority and provide tax exemptions for the projects rested with the community made these projects entirely voluntary. If a community did not want to tarnish their image with public housing, it simply refused to create a housing agency. As a result, the policy, like many other New Deal programs that relied on local administration, invariably reinforced racial discrimination and segregation. In this case if a community wanted to block access to minorities to their

U.S. Housing Authority Operations	
as of December 31, 1940	
Rents, Incomes, and Subsidies	**Status**
Number of projects	140
Number of dwelling units	47,995
Average monthly rent for shelter	$12.71
Average monthly rent for shelter with utilities furnished	$18.08
Average annual family income anticipated in projects	$799.00
Construction Award Data	**Status**
Number of projects under construction or completed	344
Number of dwelling units	118,045
Total estimated over-all cost of new housing	$507,077,000
Estimated wages to be paid at site for projects	$133,843,000

This sample of U.S. Housing Authority operations illustrates the type of resident expected and the costs of construction. (The Gale Group.)

community through low-cost housing, they could choose not to participate in the program. Through such decisions minorities would remain trapped in the declining inner-city areas.

By January 1, 1941, the Wagner-Steagall Housing Act had a very limited impact. Only 118,000 family dwelling units were under construction or completed. Of these units 39,000 were open for occupancy with 36,456 occupied. Although the act's primary function was to provide housing rather than employment, the program did provide thousands of jobs in construction and related industries that supplied building materials. In 1941 President Roosevelt commented in a footnote to the October 1937 executive order establishing the USHA on the success of the agency to provide employment in the building trades and related industries: "While the primary function of the new statute was to provide housing rather than employment, the fact is that the program has provided thousands of men with jobs, not only in actual construction, but in the mines, mills, and factories which supply the materials." (Roosevelt, *The Public Papers and Addresses of Franklin D. Roosevelt: 1928–45,* 1941, p. 470). The act also forged a cooperative relationship between national and city authorities to initiate, plan, build, and operate low-cost housing. Although it underwent many changes, the basic relationship still exists today.

By 1940, a new need for housing surfaced as the nation prepared for war. The problem of providing living quarters for a vast number of defense workers in shipyards, military camps, and clothing and equipment factories became a top priority. In Executive Order No. 8632, President Roosevelt amended the Wagner-Steagall Housing Act to develop, build, and maintain defense housing projects.

1940—The First Housing Census

A related housing issue was the need for accurate statistics on home ownership, types of structures, and home values. This information had long been available only on a local basis. But with federal agencies participating in the housing industry, new nationwide statistics were needed. Before the FHA could wisely guarantee a mortgage or the USHA could fairly loan or grant money for slum clearance, each had to have certain information. They needed reliable figures on the housing market, vacancy rates, credit availability, and housing supply. Senator Wagner introduced a bill in Congress in 1939 to provide for a complete housing survey as part of the regular decennial (every ten years) census. The bill passed easily and resulted in the first national housing census in 1940.

Contributing Forces

Home Sweet Home

As early as the eighteenth century, Americans viewed their zone of private life—their home family space—uniquely. The space was a personal place of refuge from society at large, free from outside control. The early ideal American home included a great deal of land. As cities developed in the 1800s, they were considered centers of progress and culture. Smaller towns patterned themselves after urban models and sought to project an image of growth. Residents of the towns came to define their family home in terms of a house, yard, and neighborhoods with connecting roads.

As towns grew into cities in the mid- and late 1800s, the privileged urban dwellers tended to relocate on the expanding edges and build comfortable homes. Immigrants came to the United States by the thousands and generally settled in the center of cities where jobs were available. All persons, the privileged and the newly immigrated, needed to be within walking distance of their work or of public transportation.

Public transportation included the rail lines and trolleys. Commuter villages sprung up all along the trolley and cable car rail lines serving the cities. The

newly emerging middle-class residents moved to the end of the trolley line where space was available for a house and garden. Between 1888 and 1918, trolley lines radiated out from central business districts, forming large suburban rings. The electric trolleys traveled four times faster than horse-drawn systems and could efficiently take commuters to and from work in the city's core areas.

Cheap land and home prices, good wages, and efficient transportation allowed even the working class to own private homes along the transportation routes. The poor, however, remained clustered in the inner city, unable to afford homes or rents outside the city much less the trolley fares to get to work. The inner-city dwellings were increasingly meager with numerous families crowding into small, unventilated areas. By 1910 the "new American city" was segregated by class and economic function and included a much larger expanse of land than the older walking city. As the trolley suburbs grew, a new invention, the automobile, further revolutionized the American city.

The Automobile and the Bungalow

In 1898 there was only one automobile, a sputtering little offspring of a bicycle, for every 18,000 people. In 1900 Ransom E. Olds began assembling an uncomplicated, inexpensive, and utilitarian model, his "merry Oldsmobile." Sixty-five hundred were on the road in 1905. By 1913 there was one vehicle for every eight people. That same year Henry Ford introduced a moving assembly line to roll out his Model T's. In 1927 Americans drove 26 million cars on a rapidly expanding road system.

Residents in their merry Oldsmobiles and Model T's explored the edges of their cities and the dream of the single family home in the suburbs. In 1920, 46 percent of American families were homeowners, and 51.2 percent of Americans were urban dwellers. In the seven years between 1922 and 1929, 883,000 new homes were built each year. That pace more than doubled the home building rate of any previous seven-year period. Rising wages and the falling price of constructing homes steadily boosted the construction industry, as did real estate tax exemptions that states began to pass. New suburbs dotted the edge of every major city. Automobile access proved critical, and funds for new road construction came from the general taxpayers.

The *Ladies Home Journal*, the most successful magazine of the first quarter of the twentieth century, began publishing plans for houses called bungalows. Costing between $1,500 and $5,000, the bungalow was a humble but attractive one-and-a-half-story home within easy economic reach of the growing middle

An example of the one and a half story, bungalow style home. The bungalow was an affordable and popular style of home for the middle class during the Great Depression. (National Archives—Rocky Mountain Region, Denver. Reproduced by permission.)

class. Suburban neighborhood after neighborhood filled with the American bungalow.

Although the most affluent paid cash for their homes, most middle- and lower-middle-class home-buyers obtained a mortgage from a bank or savings and loan association. During the 1920s first mortgages were limited to one-half to two-thirds of the appraisal value of the home. This meant buyers needed at least one-third of the price of the property for a down payment. First mortgages averaged 58 percent of the estimated property values. This meant the average down payment was actually 42 percent of the home's value. If buyers did not have enough for the down payment, they could take out "second" mortgages to make up the difference. Interest rates in 1923 were generally between six and eight percent. Because buying on credit, or taking out loans, became common in these boom years of the 1920s, many Americans could afford both a home and car. America's poor, however, unable to afford the American dream, remained behind in the aging central sections of cities.

The Slums

As curtains fluttered in the windows of suburban bungalows surrounded by white picket fences, the interior sections of the large cities deteriorated. Dwellings of the inner-city poor became increasingly dilapidated and overcrowded. To accommodate the massive influx of poor immigrants, large rooms of once-fashionable dwellings were subdivided into tiny rooms with no light or ventilation. As the population continued to swell, sanitation facilities became overwhelmed. Such areas grew into what many referred to as slums, which became characterized by poverty, crime, and filth. In some cities slums would consist of large areas of crowded multifamily housing, or multistory tenements, that had low standards of ventilation and plumbing and were in various degrees of deterioration. They were often occupied by impoverished immigrants.

The landowners' interest in profit was much greater than in the welfare of those occupying their tenements. More apartments meant more rent income for the landlord. Housing structures were hastily constructed on every inch of land. Those structures reached higher and higher, shutting out neighbors' sunlight and making rooms gloomy and dust filled.

As early as the 1880s, poverty, crime, disease, ignorance, and alcohol addiction thrived in frightfully overcrowded districts of not only northeastern cities,

The living conditions in many housing projects, like this one Brooklyn, New York, were deplorable. Many housing projects, meant to assist poor families, quickly transformed into slums. (National Archives and Records Administration.)

but in Midwestern cities such as Chicago as well. In 1890 Jacob Riis raised public awareness of the wretched conditions of New York City's Lower East Side by publishing his photographs of the slums in *How the Other Half Lives.* Riis's images showed narrow streets and alleys filled with people; clotheslines strung from one building to another. Families, including the children, were shown laboring in crowded tenements making cigars, sweaters, or other products. The dirty streets were filled with open-air markets selling food and clothing. Riis showed homeless people sleeping on sidewalks and in alleyways, or at tables in restaurants. Over 290,000 individuals per square mile packed the East Side. The crime and health problems of other areas like the East Side—Boston's South End, Pittsburgh's Hill District, Cincinnati's Basin Section—cost their respective cities many more dollars than the tax revenues those areas provided to the local governments.

Although the existence of slums was acknowledged, neither state, local, nor federal governments understood their cause well enough to offer meaningful help. Prior to the 1930s, housing reform in America meant surveying slum conditions and passing codes to improve density, ventilation, and sanitation. New York City passed the first housing codes in 1867, 1879, and 1901. The 1901 codes required "model" ten-

ements to be built with air shafts for ventilation, but the shafts proved only to be a source of foul odors, perpetuating the miserable conditions.

During the prosperous 1920s, as long as they continued to grow with people moving to the outskirts, cities closed their eyes to the problems of the slums. But in actuality conditions were so bad that even entrepreneurs began shunning the low-income housing market, and most private investors lost interest.

First Federal Housing Effort

The first U.S. federal government housing effort was neither a result of a conscious attempt to help the poor nor an increased reform spirit. Rather it was more a war power action. In June 1918, a year after the United States entered World War I (1914–1918), Congress appropriated $110 million for two separate programs to develop housing for workers moving to industrial areas to produce weapons. Since the war ended only five months later, the effort resulted in only a few developments—Yorkship Village in Camden, New Jersey; Atlantic Heights in Portsmouth, New Hampshire; and, Union Park Gardens in Wilmington, Delaware.

After World War I, the U.S. government went back to the business of governing and adopted a hands-off policy concerning housing. The Great Depression and subsequent New Deal legislation, however, ended this hands-off policy. Housing became a central issue in the newly forged federal-local relationships of the 1930s.

Perspectives

A House In The Country

Because Franklin D. Roosevelt believed the rural life bred superior qualities in men and that all people lived a better life in the country, he actually viewed cities as rather hopeless. Roosevelt, like many scholars of the day, believed that urban populations in the future would remain stable or even decline. Much of the early New Deal approach to housing reflected this attitude. Roosevelt refused to endorse public housing as an important part of his recovery drive. He even resisted defending the PWA Housing Division against its enemies in the private sector. Banking, real estate, and construction groups regarded public housing as socialistic.

Roosevelt eagerly endorsed the FHA created in the Housing Act of 1934, since it did not involve the federal government directly in construction or financing, and it allowed many Americans to leave the city and purchase a home in the suburbs. The average American thought a single-family home with a yard was the ideal dwelling. The FHA strongly supported this viewpoint as it routinely insured home mortgages for white middle-class houses in the suburbs. In contrast, after more than 12 years of aiding home construction and repair, not one dwelling unit in Manhattan received FHA coverage.

Public Housing—The Most Controversial Housing Issue

Real estate developers, home buildings, bankers, congressmen from rural districts, fiscal conservatives, and those concerned with public spending leading to public debt, opposed public housing. Campaigns against the ever-worsening slums of the cities fell to liberals, social reformers, and philanthropic organizations. By the mid-1930s, organized labor also identified slum clearance by demolition and building decent low-income housing as legitimate areas for federal action. Senator Robert F. Wagner introduced public housing legislation to Congress in 1935, 1936, and 1937. The 1937 Housing Act, the Wagner-Steagall Housing Act, passed only after Roosevelt, realizing low-income housing needed to be addressed, supported it. The act created the United States Housing Authority (USHA) that immediately began work on projects.

Although a welcome achievement to those who had long fought for Wagner's bill, it was strongly opposed on a wide front. The real estate, banking, and home building interests believed government construction would drive private firms out of the housing business. They worried about rising federal expenditures, taxes, and falling property values. Displeased with the new federal-city housing partnership, they argued for home rule, states rights, and individual initiative. They used their influence in Washington to clamp down on public housing initiatives after 1937.

Congressmen and senators from rural districts also opposed Wagner's bill. They believed public housing would primarily benefit residents of large cities. Conservatives feared the high cost of housing projects cited above. They took every opportunity to reduce the USHA's funds. Together, the opposition led to the demise of public housing programs before the start of World War II.

International Perspectives

While by 1980 public housing still accounted for only 1 percent of the U.S. housing market, extensive European involvement with public housing had become the norm. In industrial nations such as Great Britain and Germany, public housing during the 1930s was a standard part of the welfare state. During the Depression it comprised 46 percent of the market in England and Wales and 37 percent of the French housing market. Following the Depression British and Japanese national governments continued to buy inexpensive land in distant areas, concluding it was the only practical means of acquiring land for public housing projects.

State-constructed housing projects in the Soviet Union housed the majority of Russian citizens and had long been ingrained in the political ideology. Public housing is also an important means to help address massive social problems in third world nations. Whether a necessity or driven by political ideology, public housing is an important institution in most countries of the world.

While government in the United States at the local, state, and national levels remained largely detached from the housing problems during the 1920s, European legislators pursued the matter vigorously, especially after World War I. Great Britain started the European public housing movement with passage of the British Housing Act of 1919. In the 1920s both Britain and Germany built over a million publicly assisted "homes for heroes" for the World War I veterans. The Dutch government housed one-fifth of its population in public housing. In the Soviet Union, all housing rapidly became the responsibility of the government.

A once-ornate Victorian home has become a dilapidated part of the slums of inner-city Chicago in 1941.

(*Corbis-Bettmann. Reproduced by permission.*)

Edith Elmer Wood, a widely traveled American proponent of housing reform, wrote *The Housing of the Unskilled Wage Earner* in 1919. With publication of her book, Wood became an international figure in housing reform. By the early 1930s, Wood would see several groups, including the National Public Housing Conference, lobby for U.S. government involvement in housing construction for people who could not afford adequate housing. Before the New Deal, however, only two states, New York and North Dakota, accepted even

limited responsibility for housing its poorest citizens. A further example of the lack of U.S. government involvement in housing came at the International Congress of Cities in 1932. The meeting promoted expansion of government housing programs for the low income. Only one delegation attending, the U.S. delegation, reported no direct ties between the national government and city governments. International public housing initiatives had only limited effects on resolving housing issues in the United States.

Impact

Private Money Builds Private Suburban Homes

No New Deal agencies had more lasting or powerful impact on Americans and American cities over the last half of the twentieth century than the HOLC and the FHA. Although short lived, the HOLC established standardized appraisal procedures and first introduced the long-term, low-interest, self-amortizing mortgage. The FHA insured mortgages so lenders faced little risk, expanded the favorable terms for the borrower of the amortized mortgage, and set national building standards for home construction. In 1944 the Servicemen's Readjustment Act (the GI Bill) created a mortgage program under the Veteran's Administration (VA). The VA mortgage program largely patterned its policies after FHA procedures and attitudes. Together, the FHA and VA have a remarkable record of accomplishment. The VA helped sixteen million soldiers and sailors returning from World War II to purchase homes. By the end of 1972, the FHA had helped nearly 11 million to improve their homes. Between 1934 and 1972, American families living in owner-occupied dwellings rose from 44 percent to 63 percent. In the 1950s and 1960s, almost half of all housing claimed FHA or VA support.

Following World War II, the uniquely American dream of a private, single-family home surrounded by a yard in a safe suburban neighborhood was possible for all but the poor. Suburbs popped up and grew rapidly. In 1946 families could buy a home for $5,150. The FHA mortgage guarantee meant the buyers only needed approximately $550 for a down payment, and the long-term mortgage produced a payment of only $29.61 monthly for 25 years. Neither the FHA nor the VA directly made loans. Loans came from private banking institutions and went to the individual homeowners, insuring the loans and eliminating the risk for the lenders.

Today, conventional loans are used more frequently than FHA or VA loans. They are not insured by either the FHA or by the VA, but patterns adopted in the 1930s persist in conventional loans. Private banks offer conventional loans that are long-term (usually fifteen or thirty years) amortized mortgages. Conventional loan terms offer a choice of fixed interest rates or adjustable rates, which start very low and move to a predetermined high. They require at least 20 percent down, or less if the borrower takes out private mortgage insurance. In 2000 the American home ownership rate reached a new record high of 67.7 percent. A total of 71.6 million families owned their homes.

At a Glance
Cheaper to Buy Than Rent

In 1939 the Wilmington Construction Company built four hundred six-room houses just north of Wilmington, Delaware. This FHA-backed development was called Edgemoor Terrace. It demonstrated the use of tract production line techniques, including standardized models and lot sizes, construction methods, and model homes. The homes sold for $5,150 with a $550 down payment. The FHA mortgage guarantee meant buyers paid an incredibly low $29.61 monthly payment that included principle, interest, mortgage insurance, and taxes. An apartment of the same size in New York City rented for $50 a month.

Immediately following World War II, tracts using similar techniques sprung up. Levittown, located 25 miles east of Manhattan, eventually included 17,400 separate houses. The dwellings were of Cape Cod style with a living room and fireplace, two bedrooms, and one bath. They were approximately 750 square feet in size. Thousands of young families eager to escape tiny apartments or close quarters with in-laws flocked to Levittown, where it was cheaper to buy than rent.

The Federal National Mortgage Association (Fannie Mae) and the Government National Mortgage Association (Ginnie Mae) completed the New Deal-initiated revolution in the home finance industry. Fannie Mae resulted from the Wagner-Steagall Housing Act of 1937, and by 2000 Fannie Mae was wholly privately owned. Ginnie Mae separated from Fannie Mae in 1968 and today is a government-owned association operating under the Department of Housing and Urban Development (HUD). Through the remainder of the twentieth century, Fannie Mae and Ginnie Mae bought packages of mortgages. This made it possible for funds to travel from regions with historically high amounts of capital to poorer regions. As a result, poor regions had more money to loan than in previous years. Nationally, mortgage funds funneled out of the Northeast to the South and West and out of the cities to the suburbs. In 2000 Fannie Mae and Ginnie Mae were major purchasers of conventional loans, continuing to

This shack is representative of the type of home a sharecropper and his family lived in during the Depression. (AP/Wide World Photos, Inc. Reproduced by permission.)

move money around the nation. Money was moved from where there was ample loan money to poorer areas, equalizing the amount of available loan money around the country.

The New Deal housing legislation put into place the financial structure through which private money built suburbia and the Sunbelt (South and West). The primary beneficiaries were white middle-class families who left racially distressed inner cities by the millions. The U.S. government had adopted policies in accordance with the wishes of most of its citizens. HOLC real estate appraisal methods such as redlining discriminated against racial and ethnic minorities and against older, industrial cities. The HOLC, however, extended aid without regard for its ratings and into all areas of the cities. But, unlike the HOLC, the FHA, acting on HOLC's information, favored homogeneous suburbs over industrial or older mixed sections of the cities. The FHA often denied mortgages solely because of geographical location. In doing so the federal government, for all practical purposes, put its seal of approval on ethnic and racial discrimination. Even more importantly private enterprises, banks, and savings and loans adopted the FHA's practice of denying mortgages due to location. By the mid-1980s, federal housing policies had played a major role in the deterioration of urban centers. The poor had not shared in

America's postwar housing boom. Public housing programs attempted to improve their situation.

Public Housing

Many New Deal public housing projects built under the USHA quickly deteriorated into slums. Whereas housing in the cities before World War II had been inadequate, with wartime reallocation of funds, it became much worse. Even during the war, proposals for public housing, slum clearance, model towns, and regional and city planning were proposed by housing reformers. But the American business community wanted no plan that seemingly interfered with the private real estate market. Cries of "European socialism" and "communist front" abounded. Not until 1949 did another housing act, the National Housing Act of 1949, provide a commitment to federal reconstruction of cities and public housing. The 1949 act tied slum clearance to rebuilding, as had the earlier Wagner-Steagall Housing Act of 1937. This time a new term was coined—urban development. The clearance of slums, however, was generally emphasized over rebuilding. To operate within the private real estate market, private firms would build public housing through local housing authorities. The Housing Act of 1954 was an attempt to speed up slum clearance, and it changed the term "urban development" to "urban renewal." Black

Americans called urban renewal "Negro removal," as new expensive high-rise apartments and shopping centers went up. Over the years many projects were primarily focused on beautification, such as replacing slums with plazas and sports arenas.

Not until 1965 was the federal-city partnership, began in the New Deal era, revived. President John F. Kennedy (served 1961–1963) proposed a cabinet level department for housing. Finally, under President Lyndon B. Johnson's (served 1963–1969) War on Poverty, the Housing and Urban Development Act of 1965 established a cabinet department of Housing and Urban Development (HUD). The War on Poverty was a 1960s comprehensive social and economic program, in the tradition of the New Deal, with the goal to rid the United States of poverty. The war focused largely on racial minorities living in the deteriorating inner cities. The key difference from the New Deal was that the 1960s campaign was pursued during a time of overall economic prosperity.

Unfortunately, the 1965 act called for HUD to pursue a policy of developing new greenbelt towns to move people out to the country. Greenbelt towns are new communities built on the edges of the urban area to relocate the poor from the inner city. The policy proved even less successful than the limited Greenbelt towns of the New Deal and was soon abandoned. Overall, between 1933 and 1970, only 893,500 units of low-income housing were completed, and a substantial number of those—143,000—were for the aged. Dramatically, in 1972 the Pruitt-Igoe public housing project in St. Louis, once hailed for its progressive design, was demolished because it was beyond repair. By 1974 the public housing concept had been severely discredited.

Department of Housing and Urban Development—More Responsibilities

After a difficult beginning, HUD evolved through the 1980s and 1990s to address a broad range of issues. The agency is responsible for national policy and programs that address America's housing needs, improve and develop communities, and enforce federal fair housing laws. Depression "poverty programs" assumed poverty could be eliminated by simply altering the housing of the poor. Having learned from Depression-era attempts, rather than attack the problem of low-income housing on only one front, HUD began operating on many fronts. HUD provides housing assistance for low-income persons through "assisted" housing and public housing. Assisted housing is commonly known as Section 8. It helps low-income households with rental subsidies in private apartment complexes or rental houses. Under the Section 8 certification program, HUD deter-

More About...
Greenbelt Towns

Of all the New Deal experiments, Greenbelt towns were the most daring and innovative. Inspired by the turn of the century "garden city" theories of Englishman Ebenezar Howard, Rexford G. Tugwell, administrator of the Resettlement Administration, set out to build new towns. Tugwell is quoted in Mark Gelfand's book, *A Nation of Cities: The Federal Government and Urban America, 1933–65,* 1975, p. 133):

> My idea is to go just outside centers of population, pick up cheap land, build a whole community, and entice people into it. Then go back into the cities and tear down whole slums and make parks of them.

Surrounded by a belt of open land, Tugwell's communities were to have decent housing, a high level of social and educational services, and be limited to 10,000 residents. Built by the government but leased to local cooperatives made up of residents, the cities would help solve the housing problem of the city. Tugwell hoped to build 3,000 towns. Three were actually built—Greenbelt at Berwyn, Maryland; Greenhills near Cincinnati, Ohio; and Greendale outside Milwaukee, Wisconsin. Building towns from scratch proved very expensive, pushing rents for apartments out of the low-income bracket to the middle-income range. As with most utopian ventures, the towns started out filled with energetic young residents but with excessive rules and meetings the zeal faded. Greenbelt towns never fulfilled their goal of serving as model towns for future developments.

Going against the grain of the American tradition of private property, many denounced the communities as "communist towns." Real estate interests continually fought them. After World War II, they were sold at a great loss by the government. The three communities remained private residential communities into the twenty-first century.

mines the amount of rent a household can afford to pay, then pays the difference up to full market rent rates. This is much like the subsidies under the National Housing Act of 1937. Within a standard rent range, it allows tenants a greater freedom of choice as to where they want to live.

HUD provides job training, encourages local businesses to hire public housing residents, and brings residents into the leadership and management of their developments. It also enforces the Federal Fair Housing laws that prohibit housing discrimination based on race, color, national origin, sex, religion, families with children, and disabilities. HUD programs also help the homeless, individuals with disabilities, and AIDS victims with rental assistance and various shelter care programs.

The Community Development Block Grant helps communities and low- and moderate-income persons by providing grants for renovating housing, improving facilities such as sewers, building neighborhood centers, and assisting private businesses with economic development.

The FHA, the New Deal agency established in 1934, operates under HUD today. FHA activities have greatly expanded. The FHA assists first-time buyers and others who might not be able to meet down payments for conventional loans by providing mortgage insurance.

The FHA also assists in providing affordable rental housing by insuring loans for the construction of multifamily housing developments. This represented new developments in twentieth-century policy. Support of multifamily housing was nonexistent in the FHA's Depression years. As of October 1996, the FHA provided mortgage insurance for 6.5 million single-family homes totaling $401 billion. As of September 1996 FHA provided insurance on 15,935 multifamily developments containing two million units.

Notable People

Catherine Bauer (1905–1964). After graduating from college, Bauer began work in New York's City Housing Corporation in the 1920s. The corporation was in the process of building a model garden community. Bauer spent the early 1930s in Europe, studying solutions to housing problems. On her return in 1934 she published *Modern Housing*. Confident public housing was America's answer to decent housing for all, she became organized labor's top lobbyist for a low-rent housing program. Bauer helped draft the National Housing Act of 1937. After passage of the act, she became a consultant to the U.S. Housing Authority and helped frame its policies. She favored construction of projects on vacant land rather than on slum sites.

Paul V. Betters (1906–1956). Betters served as executive secretary of the American Municipal Association (AMA), a loose federation of municipalities formed to interchange ideas on various phases of city governments. Betters, representing 7,000 members of AMA, repeatedly spoke before Congress, discussing urban problems. In 1933 Betters organized the U.S. Conference of Mayors (USCM). He helped shape the USCM to be an effective lobby for cities with populations over 50,000.

Marriner Eccles (1890–1977). Eccles, a banker from Utah, came to Washington, DC, to serve with Secretary of Treasury Henry Morganthau, Jr. as special assistant in monetary and credit matters. He helped draft the Federal Housing Act of 1934 which created the FHA. Eccles then accepted the position of head of the Federal Reserve Board where he remained until 1951. Eccles believed in government spending to stimulate the economy to preserve the American economic system. During the 1937 economic downturn, he was instrumental in convincing Roosevelt to resume spending which benefited the U.S. Housing Authority.

John H. Fahey (1873–1950). A newspaperman and publisher from New England, Fahey helped establish the United States Chamber of Commerce in 1912 and served as its president from 1914 to 1915. President Roosevelt named Fahey to the board of the HOLC in June 1933, then as chairman in November 1933. Fahey held that position until he retired in 1948.

Cordell Hull (1871–1955). Chairman of the Senate Banking Committee in 1933, Senator Hull masterminded legislation to put the brakes on home foreclosures. As a result, on June 13, 1933, Congress passed the Home Owners' Refinancing Act authorizing the HOLC.

Harold L. Ickes (1874–1952). Ickes, a strong progressive who disliked business domination of municipal government, became known for his honesty and commitment to good government. He became an influential figure in the New Deal. President-elect Roosevelt appointed him secretary of the interior. When the National Industrial Recovery Act (NIRA) of 1933 was passed, Roosevelt also appointed him head of the Public Works Administration (PWA), an agency created under the NIRA. He oversaw the PWA's Housing Authority.

Fiorello La Guardia (1882–1947). Born in New York City, La Guardia served as a Republican in the 65th and 66th Congresses before resigning to join the army air corps during World War I. Elected mayor of New York City in 1933, he proved to be aggressive, energetic, and incorruptible. His election as mayor began a period of close cooperation between the government of New York City and the Roosevelt administration. In 1934 La Guardia set up the New York

City Housing Authority to deal with the city's slums. He believed Roosevelt's relief programs, including the Works Progress Administration (WPA), saved the cities. He served as president of the U.S. Conference of Mayors from 1936 to 1945.

Charles E. Merriam (1874–1953). Merriam, a social scientist from Iowa, helped found the Social Science Research Council, which he headed from 1923 to 1927. He then created what became the Research Committee on Social Trends (1929–1933). The public works administrator appointed Merriam to the advisory committee of the newly formed National Planning Board in 1933. His work through these various groups focused on developing national policies promoting economic and social improvements in U.S. society. He was a champion of urban life and insisted the federal government pay attention to urban problems. He expanded the definition of public works to include broader planning in various areas by both private and public sectors. Merriam worked to forge federal-city partnerships.

Henry B. Steagall (1873–1943). Elected to the U.S. House of Representatives in 1914, Steagall was long a proponent of federal deposit insurance but reluctant to support public housing. He feared public housing programs would only benefit cities and was socialistic. He did not support Senator Wagner's housing bill until President Roosevelt urged him to do so. Nevertheless, the landmark 1937 housing bill partially bears his name, the Wagner-Steagall Housing Act.

Nathan Strauss (?–?). Strauss, an old friend of Senator Robert Wagner, served on New York City's Public Housing Authority. President Roosevelt appointed him head of the newly created U.S. Housing Authority in 1937.

Rexford Tugwell (1891–1979). Tugwell was trained in economics from the Wharton School of Finance and the University of Pennsylvania. He left Columbia University to join Roosevelt's administration as an assistant secretary of agriculture. Informally, his major role was economic advisor to the president. Tugwell was instrumental in creating the Agricultural Adjustment Act. In 1935 Roosevelt appointed Tugwell head of the Resettlement Administration (RA). The chief goal of the RA was to resettle poor farmers into better areas, but another goal was to establish subsistence homestead communities with low-income housing called "Greenbelt towns." The towns were highly controversial, and, in reality, rents were too high for the poor.

Robert F. Wagner (1877–1953). Elected to the U.S. Senate in 1926, Wagner focused on unemployment issues. After the onset of the Great Depression, he concentrated on federal attempts to relieve economic stress, labor issues, and social insurance. In 1935 he continued to press for an expanded welfare state. He had a particular interest in public housing, and he introduced a public housing bill in 1935, 1936, and again in 1937. When President Roosevelt finally supported the bill, it was passed as the Wagner-Steagall Housing Act of 1937 and established the U.S. Housing Authority.

Edith Elmer Wood (1870–1945). An American housing reformer, Wood argued social behavior was conditioned by housing. Having studied housing in European nations, she campaigned for public housing. She lobbied for the U.S. government to replace slums, which would in turn reduce crime and delinquency. Wood wrote *The Housing of the Unskilled Wage Earner,* published in 1919, and became an international figure in housing reform. Joined by Catherine Bauer and others in the 1930s, she worked for public construction of dwellings for people who could not afford adequate housing.

Primary Sources

National Housing Act of 1934

The following words were spoken to Congress by President Roosevelt on May 14, 1934, as he stressed the need to pass the National Housing Act of 1934 to stimulate the construction industry (Roosevelt, 1938, p. 232):

> May I draw your attention to some important suggestions for legislation which should tend to improve conditions for those who live in houses, those who repair and construct houses, and those who invest in houses?
>
> Many of our homes are in decadent (deteriorated) condition and not fit for human habitation. They need repairing and modernizing to bring them up to the standard of the times. Many new homes now are needed to replace those not worth repairing.
>
> The protection of the health and safety of the people demands that this renovating and building be done speedily. The Federal Government should take the initiative immediately to cooperate with private capital and industry in this real-property conservation."

Federal Housing Administration (FHA)

President Roosevelt proclaimed the affordability of homes financed by FHA-insured loans established under the National Housing Act of 1934. As stressed by Roosevelt, many lower-income families were able to now afford homes, and the resulting mortgage payments did not place an unreasonable burden on their monthly expenses. A broad spectrum of the public could now afford homes. The FHA, however, aided mostly white, middle-class homeowners in suburban areas (Roosevelt, *The Public Papers and Addresses of Franklin D. Roosevelt: 1928–45,* 1938, p. 236).

> The records of FHA show that over one-half of the families buying homes under the FHA plan have annual incomes of $2,500 and less; and that most of these are purchasing their homes by payments of $25 a month or less. Nine out of ten of all new home owners under the FHA plan are using less than one-fifth of their incomes to meet their monthly payments on their home.

Neglect of Cities

The National Resources Committee argued in its 1937 landmark report titled "Our Cities: Their Role in the National Economy," that the problems of cities had been largely neglected by the federal government. The Committee had been created by the National Industrial Recovery Act in 1933 to guide national economic planning and advise the president and Congress on needed social and economic policies. Concern for deteriorating inner cities and attempts to plan for the urban environment would be a continuous feature of national policy during the remainder of the twentieth century (quoted in Glaab and Brown, *A History of Urban America,* 1983, p. 298):

> The United States Government cannot properly remain indifferent to the common life of American citizens simply because they happen to be found in what we call "cities." The sanitation, the education, the housing, the working and living conditions, the economic security—in brief, the general welfare of all its citizens—are American concerns, insofar as they are within the range of Federal power and responsibility under the Constitution.

Wagner-Steagall Housing Act of 1937

On March 17, 1938, President Roosevelt, enthusiastic about the start of work on the first five projects under the 1937 Housing Act, wrote these words in a note to Nathan Strauss, chief of the United States Housing Authority (USHA), which was formed under the act (quoted in Jackson, *Crabgrass Frontier: The Suburbanization of the United States,* 1985, p. 224):

> Today marks the beginning of a new era in the economic and social life of America. Today, we are launching an attack on the slums of this country which must go forward until every American family has a decent home.

Suggested Research Topics

- Research the many programs offered by the Department of Housing and Urban Development (HUD) at the beginning of the twenty-first century. Does the FHA still play a role in HUD? How does HUD help low-income persons occupying HUD housing to develop long-term strategies for bettering their lives?

- If you had been part of a family faced with losing their home, how would this possibility affect you, your schoolwork, your family relations. Write a diary entry relating your thoughts.

- Contact and interview a local bank loan officer about the types of mortgages available today. What factors do bankers consider when making a home loan to a family?

- Research the architectural style of the American Bungalow house.

Bibliography

Sources

Davies, Pearl Janet. *Real Estate in American History.* Washington, DC: Public Affairs Press, 1958.

Gelfand, Mark I. *A Nation of Cities: The Federal Government and Urban America, 1933–65.* New York: Oxford University Press, 1975.

Glaab, Charles N., and A. Theodore Brown. *A History of Urban America,* 3rd Ed. New York: Macmillan Publishing Co., Inc., 1983.

Huthmacher, J. Joseph. *Senator Robert F. Wagner and the Rise of Urban Liberalism.* New York: Atheneum, 1968.

Jackson, Kenneth T. *Crabgrass Frontier: The Suburbanization of the United States.* New York: Oxford University Press, 1985.

Roosevelt, Franklin D. *The Public Papers and Addresses of Franklin D. Roosevelt: 1928–45.* New York: Harper & Brothers, 1950.

Further Reading

Duchscherer, Paul. *The Bungalow: America's Arts and Crafts Home.* New York: Penguin Books USA, 1995.

Housing and Urban Development (HUD), [cited November 8, 2001] available from the World Wide Web at http://www.hud.gov.

Kennedy, David M. *Freedom from Fear: The American People in Depression and War, 1929–45.* New York: Oxford University Press, 1999.

Lancaster, Clay. *The American Bungalow, 1880–1930.* New York: Dover Publications, 1995.

Lower East Side Tenement Museum, New York City, [cited November 8, 2001] available from the World Wide Web at http://www.tenement.org.

Riis, Jacob A. *How the Other Half Lives: Studies Among the Tenements of New York.* New York: Dover Publications, Inc., 1971.

See Also

Banking, Everyday Life

The Interwar Era

Introduction

With Europe exhausted from World War I (1914–1918), the United States became the world leader in industrial progress. New energy sources of oil and electricity fueled newly mechanized industrial production systems. As a result, an increasingly mechanized United States greatly influenced developments in Europe and the rest of the world. World modernization arrived Americanized.

The decades of the 1920s and 1930s were separated from the past and the future by two catastrophic world wars. Frequently the two decades are contrasted. The 1920s are known as a period of economic boom. The 1930s are mostly associated with the economic hardships of the Great Depression. They were far more similar to each other, however, than to any other time period before or after. Major trends begun in the 1920s carried through the 1930s, only colored by economic difficulties. For many Americans their daily lives were not drastically different between the two decades. Just as not all people experienced the great prosperity of the 1920s, not all people suffered severely through the 1930s. In terms of overall traits, the two decades shared more in common than often acknowledged. Together they represented a period of dramatic change in U.S. society involving technology, the arts, and general lifestyle.

Assembly line production, first introduced in 1914 by Henry Ford in the Detroit auto industry, was adapted to other industries. Consumers quickly saw a

Chronology:

1925: A new modern style called Art Deco is introduced at a Paris exposition that influences the appearance of many consumer products and architecture through the 1930s.

1931: Construction of the Empire State Building is completed, making it the world's tallest building for the next forty years.

1932: Amelia Earhart is the first woman to fly solo across the Atlantic Ocean.

1932: Babe Didrikson Zaharias wins two gold medals at the Summer Olympics held in Los Angeles, California.

1933: Detroit automobile manufacturers roll out the first models sporting a new modern streamlined look, a departure of the previous square Model T appearance.

1936: Jesse Owens wins four gold medals and sets three world records at the Summer Olympics in Berlin, Germany.

1936: Architect Frank Lloyd Wright builds a Pennsylvania retreat residence known as Fallingwater, reflective of the revolutionary changes to residential and commercial architecture.

1937: San Francisco's Golden Gate Bridge is completed to accommodate the fast-growing automobile traffic.

June 1937: Joe Louis wins the world heavyweight boxing title, becoming a role model for black Americans.

1937: Babe Ruth retires from major league baseball, having created a legend that rose above sports for a Great Depression crowd hungry for heroes.

1938: Lewis Mumford's *The Culture of Cities* is published, providing solutions to improving city livability.

1939: The first television programming appears, but World War II delays further development for the next several years.

broader range of durable goods than ever imagined before. Mass production, and the resulting mass consumption, were born. As it did with the factories, mechanization also greatly affected the home, with various new electrical appliances easing the workload everyday.

The changes on U.S. society proved profound during this era. Farm mechanization allowed fewer farmers to tend larger acreages. Many small farmers who found themselves unable to compete were squeezed out. Displaced farmers and farm laborers replaced by the machines moved to the city looking for work. As a result, the era period marked the major transition of America from a predominately rural society to an urban society. For the first time in U.S. history more people lived in the city than the country.

Of the many products increasingly available, the automobile brought perhaps the biggest change to society. The common availability of the automobile dramatically altered peoples' ability to get from one place to another. They could commute from the suburbs and go just about anywhere they wanted when they wanted.

As the era saw the technology of mass production spread from one industry to another, fueling increased mass consumerism, the mass media also came of age. Movies, recordings, and radio brought entertainment in new forms to more and more people. National sports stars gained mythological stature and a unique American popular culture took a more defined shape. It was during this interwar period of the 1920s and 1930s that modern America emerged, an American culture distinct from its predominately European roots. These new developments affected all other facets of U.S. society and laid the foundation for a post-World War II (1939–1945) economic boom.

Issue Summary

The interwar era of the 1920s and 1930s was filled with an amazing diversity in hopes, achievements, and events. The United States dramatically changed toward an urban, industrial, consumer-oriented society. New scientific and technological advances were steadily appearing on the scene, and recognition of

American arts was growing faster than ever. Despite economic setbacks of the Great Depression lasting from 1929 to 1941, life continued, and Americans made do as best they could. Rapid advances in technology continued, and progress in the arts actually accelerated. A new American culture emerged.

Science, Business, and Technology

As it had throughout its history, U.S. society continued to greatly value science and technological achievement in the early twentieth century. The boom years of the 1920s led to greater investment into scientific research. The stock market crash of 1929 and ensuing Great Depression had only a limited effect on scientific research. Substantial progress was seen in various science applications in industry and business. Skyscrapers, bridges, and airships reflected such new developments in construction in the era.

The era was marked by an incredible number of scientific advancements even throughout the 1930s and despite the decline in available funds to provide support. In fact, whereas three Americans won Nobel prizes in the sciences during the 1920s, nine won Nobel prizes in the 1930s. The building U.S. legacy in scientific achievement would be a key trait of the nation through the next half-century.

Giant corporations continued to dominate business as they had in the previous decades following the Civil War (1861–1865). By the end of the era, in 1939, the top 5 percent of corporations took in almost 85 percent of U.S. corporate income. The growth of mass production during this era also introduced other major new facets of business, the search for maximum production efficiency, and increased attention to the effectiveness of salesmanship and advertising. As a result, many new developments aimed at improving manufacturing efficiency and marketing budgets increased. To the buying public, the era most represented a vastly increased variety of products for sale.

Corporate research programs that expanded greatly in the 1920s established dominance in the technological research field in the 1930s. By 1940 over half the new patents issued were to corporations. As a result, some newly developed materials greatly stimulated the increase in diversity of products. Aluminum, a lightweight rust-free material, came into wider use, ranging from transportation equipment to eating utensils. Airplanes steadily grew larger and safer. Nylon was introduced for ladies' stockings by 1939. Production of plastics, still in its early years, offered great hope for advancements in products. Unlike other materials more commonly used in manufacturing, plastic was resistant to humidity and was sturdy yet flexible. The outlook

appeared bright, though wide use of plastics would not come until the 1950s. Many, however, believed the United States had entered the "plastic age" in the 1930s. The first television programming arrived in 1939, though World War II interrupted further development. In agriculture the introduction of hybrid corn revolutionized a key U.S. crop.

In order to maintain these advances in science and technology, efforts at improving the nation's education system led to significant changes. The increasing technical nature of business and industry required more training than ever before. By 1940 just over half of all youth were graduating from high school, compared to 29 percent in 1930, and less than 17 percent in 1920. The number of students attending college grew even more dramatically. The number of bachelor degrees increased to 186,000 in 1940 from 122,000 in 1930. Improvements in school attendance during the 1930s were due in part to the lack of job opportunities available. This discouraged youth from leaving school early.

Some thought the advances in science and technology would automatically trigger great social progress. Though it was soon discovered this might not be the case despite the ongoing mechanical and scientific advances, still people believed the new technologies could at least cure some problems. For example, the Committee on Technocracy, formed in 1932, called for a larger role of the engineering profession in running the nation. Later, Lewis Mumford in the 1938 book *The Culture of Cities* studied how cities function. He offered technological solutions to the major social problems coming with the increased growth of cities.

Transportation

Clearly the product stimulating most change for the 1920s and 1930s era was the automobile. Factory sales of cars increased from 1.6 million in 1919 to 4.5 million in 1929. By the end of the 1920s, the nation's leading industry had become auto manufacturing. Production and new advances continued into the 1930s. A radical change in auto design came in 1933. The look of the previously popular box-like Ford Model T with its high-perched chassis, exterior trunks, and square engine compartments, gave way to more modern designs. The passenger compartment, trunks, bumpers, and engines were combined into a more unified design with graceful curving lines. As a result, cars became longer, lower, and more powerful. Rides were consequently much smoother. Though production continued through the 1930s, auto manufacturers such as General Motors and Chrysler decreased the

More About...

Mass Production

A key characteristic of the 1920–40 interwar era was the dramatic expansion of mass production thanks to assembly line technology. This development revolutionized industrial production and permanently changed American culture. The primary characteristics of mass production are specialization of labor so that workers focus on only a small part of the production process, the use of machines in making products, and the standardization of parts so that they are interchangeable on the products. In early American history, highly skilled craftsmen produced most goods. The craftsmen spent years in training and held a clear position in society. They would manufacture a product from beginning to end of the process. Mass production in Western society began in earnest in Britain's textile industry of the eighteenth century. A major advance came with steam engines in 1785. This low-cost new energy source replaced the traditional human, water, and animal power. By the mid-1800s, the application of division of labor, use of machines in manufacture, and production of standardized parts was well established. But production processes of going from one step to another still remained largely informal.

Studies in the late 1880s identified how production processes could be more efficiently organized. Modern production planning was born with the "time-and-motion" studies. Specialized work areas were established and motion patterns of workers streamlined. It was Henry Ford who pulled all the new production concepts, involving production lines and conveyor belts, together. The highly analytical production process proved exceptionally successful in dramatically reducing production times for manufacture of cars. The mass-production principles applied by Ford spread quickly to other industries. Ramifications of this new process were major and diverse. The role of the professional manager rose to oversee the synchronized activity of a modern production system. By the 1930s the quantity and variety of material goods were greatly expanding. These methods demanded much more capital, requiring corporate ownership. Smaller businesses became less competitive and were squeezed out of business. In place of the skilled craftsmen of earlier times, the specialization of labor required for production lines required very narrowly defined skills of many specialized employees. The laborer was more detached from the product, and his role in society less clear. These worker issues demanded new approaches by management to maintain high worker efficiency.

These basic improvements in manufacturing productivity lead to exceptional increases in material wealth and living standards in industrialized nations through the rest of the twentieth century.

---

variety of car models produced. The economic austerity of the Depression years also spawned a busy used car market.

The demand for petroleum products similarly shot up, with less than three billion gallons of gasoline sold in 1919 up to 15 billion in 1929. An entire automobile industry grew, involving dealerships, tourism, roadside advertising, repair garages, and other roadside businesses.

As the Depression years dragged on, thousands took to the roads, often looking for work or better times. Despite economic hardships, the number of automobiles purchased actually increased from 26 million to well over 27 million during the 1930s. To accommodate more car travel, new roads and bridges were built. The miles of state-controlled surfaced roads increased from 350,000 in 1919 to 662,000 in 1929. The number of miles of surfaced road almost doubled in the 1930s. Another technological achievement of the era was San Francisco's Golden Gate Bridge, completed in 1937 to accommodate the increasing automobile traffic. The 4,200-foot span was longer than anything previously built and represented a major engineering feat.

To serve this growing number of travelers, campgrounds and motor courts sprung up across the nation. A whole new roadside architecture and industry developed. For example, both Howard Johnson's and Big Boy restaurants started in the 1930s. What was described as a "Roadside Americana" was born.

Truck and bus traffic increased significantly as well. There were 898,000 trucks registered in 1919. By 1939 this number had skyrocketed to 4.7 million. Also, bus registration doubled in just four years, from

A great technological achievement of the era, the Golden Gate bridge was completed in 1937. (Corbis-Bettmann. Reproduced by permission.)

17,800 in 1925 to 34,000 in 1929, and then almost tripled in the 1930s. As highway traffic expanded, the great era of railroad dominance came to a close. The 1920s saw the growth of railroads end, as the size of the U.S. railway system remained about the same as before with a 10 percent increase in freight tonnage. During the 1930s the amount of material hauled by railroads declined by approximately one-third, and the miles of track declined. Inland shipping did increase considerably. There was an approximate 50 percent increase of shipping on the Great Lakes and traffic along the New York state canals doubled.

Another major change in transportation was the growth of aviation. Aviation grew dramatically from just a novelty in 1920 to 38 airline operators in 1929 carrying 162,000 passengers. Although the number of airline operators actually decreased due to the economically troubled times in the 1930s, the number of miles flown by commercial airlines increased substantially from 22.7 million miles in 1929 to almost 83 million in 1939. The number of passengers increased to 1.7 million in 1939.

Style

As technological change influenced consumer products, it also influenced their appearance as well.

In decades prior to the 1920s, busy designs and elaborate adornment were popular. In contrast the linear elegance and geometry of Art Deco was introduced in 1925. The style of Art Deco is simple, clean shapes. The earlier highly decorative and ornate designs became greatly streamlined. This change in style was influenced by the growing ideals of technological efficiency introduced by the new emphasis on mass production.

The new style, also labeled Streamline Moderne, reflected technological progress of the time and symbolized speed. The new sleek aerodynamics of airplanes, trains, and automobiles embodied these streamlined elements. These design elements appeared in many other forms as well, including radio cases, furniture, tableware, and even toasters. Clothing design also became more simplistic and efficient. U.S. fashion styles began diverging from the French and moving toward a more distinctive American style that would fully emerge in the 1940s. The streamlined appearance symbolized sophistication and wealth.

Architecture

Architectural changes were another hallmark of the era. Streamlining associated with automobiles and airliners was also evident in building styles as well.

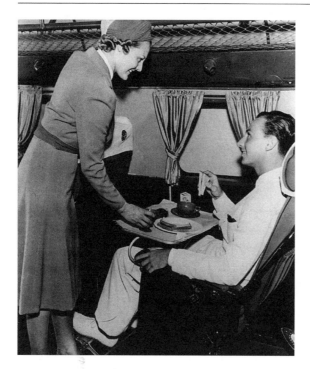

An airline passenger receives his meal from a United Airlines stewardess. The American public took advantage of fast aviation travel as 1.7 million passengers flew on airplanes in 1939. (Corbis-Bettmann. Reproduced by permission.)

The structures built for the Century of Progress International Exposition in Chicago in 1933–1934 clearly reflected this trend. Also, the Rockefeller Center in New York, built between 1931 and 1939, followed this trend of modern sleek design. The center consisted of 14 Art Deco buildings and sculptures celebrating the progress of mankind. Ironically, this celebration of progress came during a time of extreme hardship and doubt in much of the public.

The skyscraper had begun making an American appearance in Chicago in the late nineteenth century. With a number of buildings approaching or exceeding two hundred feet in height, the city passed a restriction limiting buildings to ten stories. As a result, the world of skyscrapers moved east to New York City. Advances in elevators and the use of heavy steel frames made possible much taller buildings. Competition was a key ingredient of the world's skyscraper construction. Shortly after the turn of the century, Frank W. Woolworth requested architect Cass Gilbert to build an office building for him that would exceed the height of the seven hundred foot Metropolitan Life Insurance Tower in New York City. In a Gothic architectural

style, the striking 792-foot Woolworth Building was the world's tallest building from 1913 to 1930. The heavily braced steel frame rose some sixty stories.

A building boom in Manhattan in the late 1920s and early 1930s produced the Chrysler Building in 1930 and the Empire State Building in 1931. The Chrysler Building was designed to be three hundred feet higher than the Woolworth Building. It, too, was built of a heavy steel frame. The top of the 1,046-foot tall building was decorated with distinctive radiating crescents of chrome, nickel, steel, and triangular windows. Quickly, the Art Deco Chrysler Building gave way in height to the Empire State Building, constructed from 1929 to 1931.

Under the guidance of chief designer William Lamb, the building had to conform to city regulations that required a minimum amount of light and air reach the street below. The requirement meant the building would have to be stepped back at certain intervals. The building grew to 85 stories, attaining a height of four feet above the tip of the Chrysler Building's spire. On top of the building, Lamb added a two hundred foot tall tower. The building would remain the tallest building in the world for the next forty years until the 1,100-foot John Hancock Center in Chicago was completed in 1969. Later, taller buildings replaced the heavy masonry (brick and stone) siding of the 1930s with walls of glass covering steel skeletons.

The era saw other major changes in buildings introduced by prominent architects. U.S. architect Frank Lloyd Wright modeled building design after nature and environment. Each building was designed specifically to its surrounding, integrating nature with technology. The Johnson Wax Company Administration Building in Racine, Wisconsin, reflected well Wright's design advances for the era. He was also noted for Taliesin West, his winter residence and school located in Scottsdale, Arizona, and Fallingwater, a residential retreat located in Bear Run, Pennsylvania. Similarly, Walter Gropius arrived from Germany in 1936 to teach architecture students at Harvard University. Gropius emphasized the incorporation of new technology into residential places.

Media

A major driving force in shaping American culture at this time was the rise of mass media. Effects of radio on American society were far reaching. The first commercial radio station, KDKA, began operation in 1920 in Pittsburgh. By 1929 approximately 40 percent of American homes owned radios. The number of radio stations increased to 618 in 1930 and 765 in 1940. The number of families with radios more than doubled, rising from 12 million to 28 million. Programming included adventure stories, soap operas, comedies, sports, and music. Millions listened to World Series baseball broadcasts and championship prizefights.

Popularity of mass publications also increased. Detective, western, movie, and romance magazines attracted more and more readers. Major new publications included *Readers Digest, Look,* and *Life* magazines. Affordable, mass-produced paperback books also became popular in the late 1930s and 1940s. These books reached out to the immense magazine-buying public and could be found on racks in department stores, drugstores, and newsstands. Top-selling books in the 1930s were Pearl S. Buck's *The Good Earth,* Hervey Allen's *Anthony Adverse,* and John Steinbeck's *The Grapes of Wrath.*

The most popular form of entertainment out of the home was clearly the motion picture. Movies with sound became standard by 1930, and Technicolor became common by the end of the decade. Despite the Depression, attendance remained high through the decade. Popular movies of the era tended to reflect the wishes of people to escape the monotony and hardships of the Great Depression. Gangster films such as *Little Ceaser* and *The Public Enemy,* comedies such as *A Night at the Opera* and *Modern Times,* and animated features such as *Three Little Pigs* and *Snow White and the Seven Dwarfs* entertained audiences and offered a respite from everyday life.

As during the nineteenth century, literature remained the most respected element of U.S. culture in the interwar era. Many new authors had become established in the 1920s, such as Sinclair Lewis, Ernest Hemingway, F. Scott Fitzgerald, William Faulkner, and Eugene O'Neill. In the 1930s John Steinbeck, Pearl Buck, John Dos Passos, Erskine Caldwell, James T. Farrell, and Thomas Wolfe were added to this group. Major themes of American literature during the Depression were social protest against the increasing influences of industrialization and modernism, journalistic documentaries taking in-depth looks at the "real" America, anti-Fascism in reaction to the rise of European dictators, and cultural nationalism supporting the U.S. cause against foreign influences.

In art, Modernism of the 1920s changed to Realism in the 1930s. Through substantial support of various federal relief programs, the focus shifted to nationalism (intense loyalty to one's own country) as the most common theme. With the generous infusion of public funds, American art was coming of age by the end of the 1930s.

Reaching Back

Rapid changes almost inevitably led to reactions against these changes by some. With the 1920s and 1930s being an era of rapid technological and social change, attempts were made at preserving and connecting with the past. This reaching back took several forms. For example, American folktales were comprehensively collected and published in *American Humor* (1931) by Constance Rourke. Folk art became increasingly popular. The first major exhibition of U.S. folk art occurred at the Newark Museum in 1930 by Holger Cahill. The public found these links to the past comforting. They reflected a slower paced life with less social isolation than people were experiencing in the expanding industrialized cities.

Some searched even further back than early American folklore and folk art. The thirst for links to the past also was expressed in a growing interest in "primitivism." Spurred by the economic and social problems of modern society, people reached toward what they believed to be the superiority of primal human existence. In this vein the Harlem Renaissance of the 1920s brought forward African heritage into American culture. Jazz, ragtime, blues, and spirituals provided the public access to the "primitive" world throughout the 1930s. Such "jungle music" became popular along with certain black American performers such as Louis Armstrong and Duke Ellington. Jazz also became recognized as the nation's most unique art form, free from European association.

The reach to the primitive also influenced efforts to "salvage" what were considered the vanishing native cultures in the western United States and elsewhere. Franz Boas from Columbia University and others, including Margaret Meade, conducted extensive fieldwork recording the traditions of native cultures around the world. Collections of American Indian artifacts grew, led by such institutions as the Brooklyn Museum and the Museum of the American Indian.

In another attempt to connect to the primitive, by 1930 noted artists, including Georgia O'Keefe and Ansel Adams, were making journeys to remote areas in the West away from the eastern cities. They believed the richness of the native cultures rejuvenated their inspiration and work. As American life was becoming more technologically oriented and mobile, people were searching for these connections to the past.

Another form of reaching back came in some applications of architecture. In contrast to the sleek modern look of residences as introduced by architect Frank Lloyd Wright and others, foreign architectural styles became more desirable for many institutional and business buildings. Gothic Revival style became common for churches and educational buildings, including the Ivy League schools. This heavy, ornamented style symbolized to people medieval society's spiritual inspiration as opposed to the more modern secularization (nonreligious) reflected in the unornamented streamlined modern style. Revivalist furnishings also provided an avenue for people to escape from the more mass-produced commercial culture of the 1920s and 1930s.

Even Henry Ford, who greatly contributed to this era of mass production, had yearnings for the simpler past. As a result Ford created an outdoor museum, Greenfield Village, established in the late 1920s. The museum included replicas of famous American historic buildings, such as Philadelphia's Independence Hall, and some actual historic structures transported from their original locations. Old tool exhibits represented the American pre-industrial craft traditions. Ford considered the museum a link between the early American craft industries and his assembly line form of mass production.

Golden Age of Sports

Another major defining aspect of the era related to the emergence of mass media and technological change was the growth of organized sports. Described by many as the "golden age of sports," it was during this interwar period that professional and organized amateur sports became a prominent part of U.S. society. As has often been the case since, major sports figures reflected social issues in the larger society. Particularly prominent athletes included Babe Ruth, Jack Dempsey, Red Grange, Barney Ross, Babe Didrikson Zaharias, and Joe Louis. Among other things, they each represented the daring and rugged individualism that larger society celebrated during the 1920s and considered a link to the past in the 1930s.

Concurrently, it was an era of talented sportswriters who greatly influenced the public perception of sports and sport figures. Legends were created, such as the Babe (Babe Ruth), the Four Horsemen of Notre Dame, and the Manassa Mauler (Jack Dempsey). Lively stories routinely filled the daily sports pages. In addition, improved transportation during the era enabled sports teams to travel further, opening up new opportunities and exposing more people to the exploits of star athletes. Other new technologies also influenced sports equipment enhancing performance on the field.

The sport of baseball in particular was strongly linked to the modern American ideals of democracy (everyone has a chance to better their position), individualism, and meritocracy (achieving success based on the individual's achievements). There were many heroes at the time in baseball, including Babe Ruth, Lou Gehrig, Ty Cobb, Rogers Hornsby, Jimmie Foxx, Lefty Grove, Dizzy Dean, Carl Hubbell, and Mel Ott. They each had their own unique persona and amassed great followings in the news.

An athlete in another sport who personified the American dream of success while also representing a link back to rugged individualism was football legend Red Grange. Coming from humble origins, Grange was an All-American halfback at University of Illinois from 1923 to 1925. After completing his career at Illinois, Grange signed to play for the Chicago Bears in the newly emerging National Football League (NFL). After an impressive career throughout the 1930s, Grange became a charter member of the pro football Hall of Fame. In contrast to others such as boxer Jack Dempsey and Babe Ruth, Grange maintained a modest, hardworking, and clean living reputation. Like Dempsey, however, he represented a link to the frontier values of rugged individuals in an increasingly industrial and urban nation. This link reaffirmed traditional values in an era of rapid change.

Women in Sports Though sports in America in the 1920s and 1930s were male dominated, changes were occurring in the status of women in sports, just as it was in the greater society. Sonja Henie, a Norwegian figure skater, led the way in gaining recognition for women athletes. Henie won world's figure-skating championships for ten consecutive years from 1927 to 1936 and three Olympic medals in 1928, 1932, and 1936. She then became a movie star.

Remarkable achievements by others came as well. In 1926 Olympic medallist Gertrude Ederle was the first woman to swim the English Channel. In 1928 Amelia Earhart became the first woman to fly across the Atlantic Ocean, doing it again solo in 1932. Earhart, representing daring, courage, and independence, set other aviation records in the 1930s. Helen Wills Moody won 19 Wimbledon, French, and U.S. singles tennis titles from 1923 to 1938. Moody was perhaps the most widely admired female athlete of the period because she more closely represented traditional values of femininity than other sports stars of the era. She was both athletic and attractive, well-behaved, and not overly aggressive on or off the court. These traits more closely conformed to public expectations of women in society at the time.

Recognized as the greatest woman athlete of the era was Mildred "Babe" Didrikson Zaharias. Born in Texas to Norwegian American immigrants, Didrikson broke numerous sports gender barriers while growing up. As a youth she participated in baseball, basketball, football, tennis, volleyball, boxing, skiing, cycling, and swimming. In 1932 Didrikson won the Women's National Amateur Union track championship, competing in all eight of the events held. That same year she won two gold medals in the Los Angeles Summer Olympics. She might have won even more medals, but rules restricted women to a limited number of events. Later in her athletic career, Didrikson became the top female golfer in the world, winning 53 amateur and professional tournaments. She was named Female Athlete of the Year six times and in 1950 was honored as Female Athlete of the Half Century. Didrikson did much during the 1930s to challenge the stereotypes of female physical inferiority.

Race and Ethnicity As with women, some barriers were weakening regarding black Americans and other minorities. Despite rigid racial segregation in public life, some black American athletes became embraced by white society. While the Negro Leagues, founded in 1920, grew separately from baseball's white Major Leagues, two players achieved a high status in U.S. society, pitcher Leroy "Satchel" Paige and catcher Josh Gibson. Paige was a legendary pitcher in the Negro Southern Association and the Negro National League. Gibson became known as the "Babe Ruth" of the Negro Leagues, hitting some eight hundred home runs in a career lasting from 1927 to 1946. Over 40 years of age, Satchel later joined the Cleveland Indians in 1948 and sparked them to the American League championship and into the World Series that year. Paige remained in the Major Leagues until 1953. Paige was elected to the Baseball Hall of Fame in 1971 and Gibson the following year.

Other black athletes gained national recognition. Track star Jesse Owens was the son of an Alabama sharecropper and grandson of a former slave. Raised in Cleveland, Ohio, Owens broke three world records and tied another at the Big Ten track championships in 1935 while a sophomore at Ohio State University. In the 1936 Summer Olympics in Berlin, Germany, Owens set three world records, tied one, and won four gold medals. It was a dramatic performance as German leader Adolf Hitler was presenting the Olympics as a showcase for his Aryan propaganda of white supremacy. Because Owens was humble and patriotic in character, he was embraced by white society as a national celebrity. Despite his fame, the limited economic opportunities for blacks in America left him to financially struggle in later life.

Joe Louis was also born into a southern sharecropper family. Raised in Detroit, Michigan, Louis excelled as an amateur boxer and turned pro in 1934.

Mildred "Babe" Didrikson Zaharias is recognized as the greatest female athlete of the era. Didrikson's participation in sports did much to challenge the stereotypes of female physical inferiority during the 1930s. (AP/Wide World Photos. Reproduced by permission.)

From 1934 to 1937, Louis won 28 of his 29 fights. He won the heavyweight title in June 1937. Louis worked on a public image that would be acceptable to white America. He was quiet, unassuming, read the Bible, and was openly patriotic. Supporters claimed Louis instilled hope in black America. In 1938 Louis defeated former world champion German boxer Max Schmeling. As with Owens, to many Louis' victory represented the triumph of American democracy over Nazi aggression. The "Brown Bomber" at that point became a mythic national hero.

Another boxer won greater acceptance for Jews in America. Barney Ross, a Jewish boxer, held the titles of lightweight, junior welterweight, and welterweight between 1934 and 1935. Ross countered the stereotype of Jews with his masculinity and physical ability. He represented the newer image of Jewish American success and toughness.

Sports reflected various aspects of the new American culture. It reaffirmed for many the new dominant cultural values of the interwar era. In some cases it also provided a link back to old ideals and national perceptions of rugged individualism of the frontier.

A New America

The era was most characterized by urbanism, modernism, mass media, and mass production and consumption. A common and distinctive American culture had emerged, driven by large-scale advertising, radio, motion pictures, increasingly standardized education, and increased movement due to automobiles. By the late 1930s, people were realizing that success and prosperity could be achieved along with the economic security provided by New Deal programs. Despite the Great Depression, a belief in progress still persisted. For many this was best demonstrated by the Century of Progress Exposition in 1933–1934 in Chicago, and the world's fairs in New York and San Francisco in 1939. The era's urban-based attitudes gained greater strength in society. The traditional perspectives toward tobacco, dancing, liquor, and other social activities were being increasingly challenged. Attitudes toward women's role in society did not change as much, however. Women were still subject to inequality with men.

More diverse racial and ethnic groups were increasingly influencing American culture. For example, by the end of the 1930s Jews had gained prominent positions in U.S. society in the fields of law, art, science, literature, education, business, and politics. Two men of Jewish background were elected governors of Illinois and Kansas. However, as with women, attitudes toward racial and ethnic minorities still had a long way to go in recognizing equality under the law.

Contributing Forces

Growth of Industrialization

Following the American Civil War (1861–1865), the numerous small workshops and manufacturers that typified early U.S. industry began giving way to corporations. As part of this industrialization, mechanized factory production grew faster than ever. The resulting rise of commercialism and industrialization in the late nineteenth century presented major new problems to U.S. society. From 1865 to 1900, however, in what has been called the Gilded Age, optimism ran high. American business believed industrialization would eventually lead to unbounded social progress and incredible wealth. The rise of the new wealthy industrial leaders during this period, however, did not correspond to a rise in public well-being. Labor standards were incredibly low in the mills and sweatshops. Hours were long, conditions intolerable, and pay insufficient. Discontent rose regarding what was considered the social irresponsibility of industrial leaders. The newly forming modern mass production industries were not benefiting the growth of a healthy democratic society.

In addition, other factors were disturbing to many in the late nineteenth century. First, the nation's economy became more vulnerable to the whims of fluctuations in business cycles, and hence less stable. Secondly, the economic inequality between citizens increased. Thirdly, many businesses combined into yet bigger businesses. With fewer companies, competition declined and business monopolies grew. The greater economic instability, greater differences in economic classes, and lessened competition did not bode well for the common citizen.

In response to these business trends, government oversight began to grow through regulatory agencies. The Interstate Commerce Commission, the Federal Reserve System, and the Federal Trade Commission were formed. Nonetheless, by 1920, the top 5 percent of U.S. corporations, consisting of about 17,000 businesses, cornered almost 80 percent of the nation's corporate income. While the nation's top business leaders worried about further government regulation, the public feared the ever-increasing power of the industrial giants.

Some still questioned how good these business developments were for the common worker. One response to the social problems brought by industrialization was the growth of the Socialist Party, founded in 1901 by Eugene V. Debs. Debs contended that modern industrial capitalism degraded the worth of the nation's citizens for the sake of industrial efficiency and profit making. Debs' popularity peaked in the presidential elections from 1912 to 1920. The party attracted a broad spectrum of workers, including craft workers, machine operators, farm laborers, and farmers.

Reaction to the products of large-scale industrial production also grew. One expression of distaste was the Arts and Crafts Movement. The movement stressed the use of products relating back to earlier cottage industry days and handmade products. A major focus of the Arts and Crafts Movement was to guard against the artlessness of mass-produced items in interior house décor.

The Gilded Age gave way to the Progressive Era from 1900 to 1917. As a reaction to the Arts and Crafts Movement, progressives accepted industrial progress as inevitable. Architect Frank Lloyd Wright, who first gained national attention in the 1890s, insisted that machine and art could indeed coexist and demonstrated this in his designs.

Labor Activism

Another trend was the increased activism of laborers. A labor movement grew, fueled by the rapidly growing mass-production industries. Workers in the meat packing, textile, and garment industries began taking action to improve their working conditions. Massive garment industry strikes occurred between 1909 and 1915 in Chicago and New York. Though some gains were made in passing regulations on manufacturing, strong resistance by business and adverse rulings by the U.S. Supreme Court largely inhibited such responses to the growth of business. Factory conditions and length of work days largely evaded regulation as most successes in labor law came in the protection of women and child laborers.

The stage was set for large industries to transition into mass production using assembly line techniques introduced by Henry Ford in 1914. As a result large corporations dominated because they were able to use their vast resources to expand and to market and distribute their products of mass production across the nation. Following World War I (1914–1918), the automobile became the central product in the economic boom and the dominant symbol of the new American middle-class success.

Technology Advancements

Technological advances triggered other major changes in industry. As industrialization had increased, management began focusing more on production efficiency. Continued increased mechanization, in addition to expanding assembly line production, brought new approaches to industry. Studies targeted reduction of wasted time and physical motion of the workers. Continued business consolidations eliminated those businesses that could not achieve sufficient efficiency. As a result of industrial advances, new inventions boosted production and expanded the variety of commodities available as well as the choice of colors of many products. New fabrics appeared such as rayon and celanese.

The 1920s saw a substantial increase in electricity available to homes. This led to a much greater demand for products such as radios, electric irons, vacuum cleaners, refrigerators, and washing machines. In an effort to capitalize on this demand, the focus on salesmanship rose to new heights. Numerous newspaper and magazine articles explored the many facets of selling products or services. Along with salesmanship came the further growth of the advertising business. The nature of ads in magazines and newspapers changed dramatically from the pre-World War I years. They were becoming larger and more eye catching.

More About...
An Era of Population Change

A population growth rate that had been slowing in the 1920s slowed even more in the 1930s. Two key factors influencing this decline in population growth were a sharp drop in immigration due to very restrictive immigration laws passed in the early 1920s and a lower birthrate. The population grew from 105.7 million in 1920 to 122.8 million in 1930 to 131.7 million in 1940. Most of the growth was in urban areas. Urban population grew from 54 million in 1920 to 74 million in 1940, while the rural population only grew from 51.5 million to 57.2 million. Despite the difficult years, in which many went undernourished, the life expectancy of Americans actually increased from 59.7 years in 1930 to 62.9 by 1940 due to improved medical care. Death rates from such diseases as whooping cough, measles, diphtheria, and paratyphoid fever also declined dramatically. Longer life expectancy, combined with lower birth rate, led the population to age more with the average age increasing from 25.3 in 1920 to 29.0 in 1940.

Other trends included black Americans migrating at a high rate from the South to the North and West, and women and men becoming almost numerically equal for the first time in the nation. Because of the drop in immigration, the number of foreign-born Americans dropped from 13.7 million in 1920 to 11.4 million in 1940.

These major population changes, including the resettlement of blacks to northern and midwest cities, the relative increase in women, the declining number of immigrants, and a general westward movement of the nation set the stage for major social and economic change following World War II.

Advertisements became a regular feature in movie theaters, on radio programs, and on billboards along the newly improved roadways.

The Roaring Twenties

The dramatic industrial growth since the Civil War led to the 1920s becoming the most prosperous decade in U.S. history up until that time. From 1922 to 1929, industrial workers' wages increased 13 percent. Many factory workers were gaining new fringe benefits. The average workweek in industry declined from 47.4 hours in 1920 to 44.2 hours in 1929. The average unemployment rate between 1923 and 1929 was a low 3.7 percent, down from 6.1 percent the previous decade. Because of these improvements in the workplace, disputes between management and labor declined. Consumer prices remained stable through most of the decade as the quantity of manufacturing production increased a whopping 50 percent between 1922 and 1929. The number of businesses increased from 1.7 million in 1919 to 2.2 million in 1929. With financing easier, more people were starting businesses. The number of patents for new inventions almost doubled in the decade.

Growth of the super-corporation was spurred by this economic boon. Corporations that became familiar household names include Westinghouse, Bell Telephone, Eastman Kodak, Bank of America, Standard Oil, General Motors, and U.S. Steel. The nation's wealth continued to become more concentrated in U.S. society, with the top two hundred corporations controlling approximately 50 percent—$81 billion—of corporate wealth by 1929. This figure represented 22 percent of the national wealth in general

The Arts

Whereas the technological ingenuity of Americans was gaining increased international recognition in the nineteenth century, the arts presented a different picture. The fine arts in the United States grew slowly through the early nineteenth century. Europe would remain the center of art achievements for the Western world entering the twentieth century. Various leading American artists, including sculptors, writers, and painters, would go to Europe for months or years to study and improve their skills. Many would stay in Europe to enjoy the long-established community of artists and the governmental support not present in America. The United States had not supported artists, and few schools in the arts were available until after the Civil War.

After the war industrialization in the United States greatly expanded. A large accumulation of wealth by business and financial leaders provided a new market for American artists. Art collections grew, and fine arts museums began appearing in the 1870s, such as New York's Metropolitan Museum of Art and Boston's Museum of Fine Arts. The rise of the Modernism art style in the 1890s proved a major change in the arts. Suddenly art was much more accessible to the general public as Modernism styles were increasingly being adopted in the production of various goods by 1910. The Armory Show in New York City in 1913 exhibited 1,600 art works. Finally, the massive show brought a major change in how fine arts were viewed, presenting them as no longer the sole domain of the wealthy. Art had become part of the new era of growing mass consumerism and newly growing urban industrial centers. Art institutions became very popular in the United States, and by the later 1920s American artists were being invited to exhibit their works in Europe.

By the mid-1930s, American artists began returning to America as fascism and communism was spreading in other countries. A renewed appreciation of the relative freedom in the United States grew among the arts community. Given the difficulties of the Great Depression, the Realism style in art grew, with depictions of everyday life becoming more common. For example, paintings often focused on rural and small town scenes.

One field of the arts in the United States that gained international recognition early in the nineteenth century was literature. Fiction writers, beginning with Washington Irving in the early 1820s, gained international acclaim. Other notable authors were James Fenimore Cooper, Edgar Allen Poe, Nathaniel Hawthorne, Walt Whitman, and Samuel Clemens. Philosophers included Ralph Waldo Emerson and Henry David Thoreau. The turn to Realism in the fine arts was reflected in books such as John Steinbeck's *The Grapes of Wrath.* By the 1920s writers had begun to react to the narrow and strict values and attitudes of the Victorian period in which society was closely confined. Authors focused more on rootless characters. In the 1930s writers, such as Steinbeck, protested what they felt were unjust social conditions in the nation.

By the late nineteenth century popular music consisted of the highly rhythmic piano music of ragtime, band music such as the "Stars and Stripes Forever" by John Philip Sousa, the comedy music of vaudeville, and church music. Jazz began its spectacular growth in the 1920s as a unique American art form. The Harlem Renaissance played a key role as black American musicians combined ragtime with the blues musical forms of the South into an internationally popular jazz sound. New dances developed along with it. By the 1930s the jazz sound led to the spread of big bands playing swing music. The record industry became well established in the 1910s. By 1914, 500,000 homes had phonographs, and they were becoming a standard piece of furniture in middle-class homes. Record production peaked in 1921 at 100 million records, but then declined to only six million in 1932 at the depths of the Great Depression.

The Depression significantly damaged popular cultural industries producing movies and music, though movie houses actually flourished until 1932. Later in the 1930s, New Deal programs would eventually come to the aid of many artists, including actors, painters, and writers.

Perspectives

The Rise and Fall of Great Expectations

All in all, a new U.S. economic system had emerged in the 1920s. New dominant giant corporations were producing commodities for mass consumption. The oil, automobile, chemical, radio, airline, and advertising industries were booming. They offered a greater variety of standardized goods produced more cheaply. Rugged individualists were making fortunes. On top of that, the financial stock market was producing riches for almost anyone who invested. Wages and salaries were sufficient to allow consumers to purchase goods and services and have a credit standing to take out more and more loans to increase buying power. An urban middle class began to be a major factor in the nation's economy, involving industrial and white-collar work. This segment of society enjoyed rising wages and greater access to installment buying. Purchase of goods not necessary for sustaining life increased, and a revolutionary change in values followed. Individual fulfillment through conforming to a national consumer culture weakened traditional ties to neighborhoods, religion, and family. Many believed this economic prosperity had become a permanent feature of U.S. society.

Not surprisingly, the average U.S. citizen was highly optimistic about the future of America until the stock market crash in October 1929. It was an era of great expectations. The economic downturn during the early years of the Great Depression—from 1929 to 1932—brought a dramatic change in expectations. Many believed the long-lasting economic woes indicated that capitalism was no longer effective, and that the American system of production and distribution formed in the 1920s had broken down. The closure of banks on the eve of President Franklin Roosevelt's inauguration in March 1933 was taken as proof of this failure of the economic systems of mass production and mass consumerism that were the hallmarks of this era.

Backlash to the Industrial Era

Many Americans were skeptical of the new modernism entering into American society during the interwar era. The horrifying scenes of World War I, with

Jazz became recognized as America's most unique art form. Duke Ellington was one of jazz's top purveyors during the Great Depression. (Archive Photos, Inc. Reproduced by permission.)

mass death resulting from armaments and toxic gases, left a disdain in many for the new technologies and industrial processes behind that destruction. These psychological effects of the war carried through the 1920s and 1930s. While exciting to some, the increased presence of the assembly line, a quicker pace of life, continual scientific and artistic developments, and rapid growth of new skyscrapers caused anguish to others. Critics bemoaned that the new machine age had changed the nation's moral and spiritual foundations without offering a substitute. Some foresaw the machines taking jobs away from laborers. Evangelical and fundamentalist Protestants led opposition to the rising consumer culture. They and others feared a spiritual starvation rising in America. Author Walter Lippmann labeled the new developments the "acids of modernity." An Agrarian Society, formed primarily of southern intellectuals, charged the rising consumer society spawned a "rootless individualism."

Critics of the newly emerging industrial society also came from the literary world, including Waldo Frank who wrote *Our America* in 1919 and poet T.S. Eliot who published "The Waste Land" in 1922. A number of the leading literary figures sought refuge

More About...

Mass Consumption

The outgrowth of mass production of goods was mass consumption by the public. The low-cost production by the new manufacturing processes of the 1920s and 1930s led to more and more products available, and hence increased consumption by the public. New social and environmental issues arose. Mass production made greater demands on raw materials. Conservation of natural resources and disposal of the wastes of production and discarded goods became long-term issues.

Mass production of goods also led to concerns over the quality of products across the nation. The growth of consumerism led to government agencies being charged to insure consumer protection and the rise of consumer protection organizations. Food and drugs received the greatest government control. The Federal Trade Commission (FTC) was created in 1914 to guard against deceptive practices and regulate the package labeling of consumer products. The Food and Drug Administration (FDA), first established in 1927, addressed consumer protection in foods, cosmetics, and other substances. Nonfood products were less thoroughly regulated. Standards institutions largely operated by industry addressed their quality. These

institutions set minimum standards and addressed such topics as standardized electrical fittings.

By the 1950s safety standards for consumers gained greater attention. The standards, largely formed by industry, are normally not legally enforceable but are voluntary in nature. Standards regarding the effectiveness of products are not regulated but left for consumers to determine. The biggest inroads for insuring safe products were related to the auto industry in the 1960s, resulting from the work of consumer advocate Ralph Nader. The National Highway Traffic Administration was created in 1970 to deal with all aspects of auto safety.

Greater attention and stronger oversight was focused on advertising. As business competition rose on a national basis with the development of national brands, advertising became more complex, utilizing the powerful media of first radio then television. Enormous amounts of money were involved. Oversight of advertising centered on misleading and untruthful claims. Legislation also focused on minimum standards of accuracy for labeling some products, primarily food and drugs.

---

in foreign countries, including T.S. Eliot, Ernest Hemingway, Ezra Pound, and Gertrude Stein. Artists maintained rustic rural retreats and modernist art colonies grew up in rural New England. The traumas of the Great Depression only intensified these criticisms.

Curing Social Ills

The continued pace of industrialization through the early twentieth century spawned various viewpoints on how to address the social problems resulting from the growth of industrial cities. Starting in the late nineteenth century with the rise of industrialization, a number of people published accounts of how technology could potentially contribute to a perfect society. These people were labeled utopians. They believed the ills of industrialization witnessed during that time period, including terrible working conditions for factory laborers, would be only temporary. As technology further developed, a clean, harmonious world would

evolve. Technology would provide solutions to social problems where religion and political ideologies had failed.

Since these magical solutions seemed unlikely to materialize, private efforts grew to correct the social problems growing out of industrialization. The idea of "settlement houses" first began in London in 1884. The goal of a settlement house was to improve conditions in the neighborhood in which it was located. The facility would provide certain services, including counseling and sponsoring various types of local group activities. Social activist Jane Addams brought the idea to Chicago in the United States, establishing the Hull House in 1889. The facility, which expanded to 12 buildings and covered half a city block, gained international recognition.

As well as working on social reforms and assisting local trade union organizations, the Hull House provided kindergarten and day nursery services and secondary and college-level extension classes. Settlement houses in the United States became very active in assisting the many new immigrants arriving in the country and leading efforts at social reform legislation such as passing child labor regulations, establishing workmen's compensation funds, and establishing juvenile court systems. An international organization of settlement houses was formed in 1926. Whereas President Herbert Hoover relied on such private programs to assist the needy during the early Great Depression years, President Franklin Roosevelt recognized their inability to deal with such a major economic crisis. His administration's New Deal programs provided assistance and relief on a scale that private organizations could not approach.

Reaching Back

Other forms of backlash grew against mass production. An Arts and Crafts Movement grew, promoting handicrafts as morally superior to the dehumanized mass-produced industrial goods. Some promoted pre-industrial handicrafts trying to bring back the idealized American spirit of the colonial period. The Arts and Crafts Movement's primary affects were on household furnishings. By living among such items, one could be transported back to a different era, at least to some degree.

This interest in turning back the clock was also stimulated by the great influx of immigrants to fill the rapidly growing numbers of factory jobs in the late nineteenth and early twentieth century. Many felt the new immigrants threatened the ideal America; that they were "unfit" to be Americans and would destroy the predominant culture and values. In 1921, and again in 1924, Congress passed laws to severely restrict the number of immigrants coming into the country.

Prosperity for Many

Most Americans embraced the new industrial production geared toward mass consumption and the resulting prosperity that rose to unprecedented levels. Many businesses and those workers with jobs prospered from the era of rising mass production. Employers enjoyed major profits, and workers the availability of a broad range of consumer goods. For those who could afford them, the new home appliances made daily life easier and freed more leisure time. The automobile, which had become a status symbol, was central in F. Scott Fitzgerald's novel *The Great Gatsby* (1925).

For many this prosperity carried into the Great Depression, despite high unemployment and many

The Chrysler Building, completed in 1930, was part of a skyscraper building boom that lasted from the late 1920s to the early 1930s. (UPI/Corbis-Bettmann.
Reproduced by permission.)

business failures. For example, with the rise of mass production and mass consumerism came the increased need for advertising on a scale never before seen. Advertising agencies were hired by manufacturers to entice the public to purchase newly available commodities. Many ad companies flourished during the 1930s. For example, the Chicago firm of Benton and Bowles, established in 1929 just before the stock market crash, grew to be one of the largest agencies in the world by 1935. Often owing to the creative work of these advertisers, some manufacturers prospered as well. The sales of Pepsodent toothpaste and Maxwell House coffee soared.

Impact

Rise of American Pop Culture

The era saw a distinctive American culture become much more defined. A national vision of what the "good life" should be like took shape. This rise of mass consumption and production led to a more uniform life throughout the nation. As a result, the long-standing regional variations in economy and society decreased considerably. This increased uniformity in American culture reflected a revolutionary change in American business. One such change was the growth of advertising and marketing expenditures. They became a major part of the U.S. economy. Another major outcome of this growing uniformity was that personal success and people's self-awareness became defined very differently from before. The traditional socializing framework oriented predominantly around God, nation, and family added a new fourth major dimension, pop culture. Radio greatly propelled this profound change to U.S. culture by opening up a whole new way of perceiving the world. These changes in social values, attitudes, and ideas were accompanied with dramatic changes in public health, education, and technology.

A distinction grew throughout the interwar era of the 1920s and 1930s between the elite arts (such as portrait paintings, ballet, and symphony) and the more common ones (handicrafts, folk songs, theater). This distinction steadily became clearer during this era as technological innovations mounted, and the large super-corporations rapidly grew. Film, radio, and musical recordings greatly expanded the range of artistic expression in America. Motion picture studios, radio networks, and record corporations produced a steady stream of entertainment, often for great profit. Hollywood prospered as approximately 90 percent of money spent by the public on amusement went to movie theaters. As a result, the era was the golden age of radio and movies—an age that would be greatly altered by television after World War II.

This process, which led to an increasingly homogenous distinctive national culture, was referred to as "Americanization," as it reflected the departure from past European influences. Of course, Americanization only readily embraced those citizens of north-

ern European, Protestant ancestry. Largely excluded from pop culture were ethnic and racial minorities. Ironically, black Americans, who were denied economic and social opportunity in almost every facet of U.S. society, played a major role in shaping this popular culture. Contributions by black performers such as Louis Armstrong and Billie Holiday made American culture distinctively American. Jewish Americans also began to make their mark in American pop culture. This influence was particularly true in the film industry where eastern European immigrants including Adolph Zukor, Carl Laemmle, the Warner brothers, Marcus Loew, and others became the new movie moguls. Their dominance lasted well past World War II. Popular Jewish performers included Al Jolson, Eddie Cantor, and Fanny Brice, all of whom opened the door for other Jewish entertainers in later years.

The new capitals of the modern consumer society were New York City and Hollywood. New York was the literary, cultural, and financial center. It contained publishing houses, music halls with the new jazz sound, and the big city vitality. Hollywood furnished widely watched films which largely promoted the new American popular culture.

In 1940 the United States stood at the beginning of a new modern world. But World War II greatly disrupted this trend toward modernism. After the war the United States experienced unprecedented prosperity from the late 1940s into the late 1960s; a prosperity built largely on the developments of the 1920s and 1930s.

Notable People

Jack Dempsey (1895–1983). Dempsey was the first major athlete in the interwar era following World War I—an era that became known as the Golden Era of Sports. At 6'1" and 190 pounds, he was not as big as modern day heavyweights, but his rise from humble origins, aggressive boxing style, and rugged persona gained him substantial popularity. Dempsey was born to poor Irish immigrants in Manassa, Colorado. During much of his youth, he rode the rails in the West as a hobo, looking for work and getting into fights. He entered professional boxing in 1917 and quickly rose to the heavyweight championship on July 4, 1919. Dempsey remained champion for over seven years. To the American public, Dempsey represented a link to the nation's rugged past in an era of rapid change. He also complemented the vitality of the new age of jazz and the automobile. Dempsey lost his title to ex-marine Gene Tunney in September 1926 before a

Biography:

Henry Ford

1863, July 30–1947, April 7 Henry Ford was an American industrialist who revolutionized factory production through the use of assembly line methods. This innovation spawned mass production and mass consumerism, a hallmark of the era of the 1920s and 1930s. Ford was born and raised on a farm in Dearborn, Michigan. At age 16 Ford began work in Detroit machine shops where he first became familiar with the internal combustion engine. He moved back to the farm where he built his own machine shop and began working on a small farm tractor using a steam engine. Ford again returned to Detroit where he gained employment as chief engineer for the Detroit Edison Company, which provided electrical service to the city. Pursuing his interests aside from his employment, he completed his first working gasoline powered engine by late 1893 and in 1896 built his first horseless carriage. With help from various backers, Ford formed the Detroit Automobile Company in 1899. After leaving and creating the Ford Motor Company in 1903, Ford marketed his first automobile. Then, in a move that would revolutionize America, in October 1908 Ford introduced the Model T automobile. In an effort to produce cars for the ordinary person rather than only the rich, Ford stressed low prices. The Model T sold for only $290 in 1927. Ford sold over 15 million cars in the United States in the next 19 years, and another one million in Canada. That was half of the automobiles sold in the world.

Because of Ford's goal to reach the common person, the car produced one of the greatest and most rapid changes in world history. The automobile industry became the strongest contributor to the American economy and greatly influenced the growth of cities and the spread of suburbs. It was production of the Model T that revolutionized industrial production by introducing the assembly line concept. Ford first introduced the concept in the new Highland Park, Michi-

gan, auto plant in 1914. A new car was produced every 93 minutes, six times faster than previously possible. It was a giant gain in industrial productivity.

Another major achievement by Ford was attaining complete self-sufficiency with the opening of the River Rouge plant in 1927. With his new assembly line techniques, Ford was producing cars faster than his parts suppliers could keep up in the early 1920s. To fix that problem, Ford gained control of all aspects of the car manufacturing business, including the mining of raw materials, their transport to machine and auto plants, and the production and delivery of the automobiles.

Despite his major early achievements, the new auto industry kept changing rapidly, with many new innovations. By the late 1920s, Ford's company was lagging behind the innovations introduced by other car manufacturers. In December 1927 he introduced the Model A, but General Motor's Chevrolet and Chrysler's Plymouth outsold it. By 1936 Ford Motor Company ranked third in auto sales.

In addition to not keeping up with new innovations, Ford also bitterly opposed the formation of labor unions in the 1930s. He hired company police who incited violence to prevent unionization. This intimidation continued even after Chrysler and General Motors had come to terms with the United Automobile Workers (UAW). Ford workers did not organize until 1941.

Though Ford introduced tremendous technological change to U.S. society, he was still a believer in the rural values of his early life. Yet in an era marked by a major change in America from a rural agricultural to an urban industrial nation, Henry Ford perhaps was the most influential individual. He had triggered a permanent change in the economic and social character of the United States.

---

crowd of 130,000 spectators. The two boxers offered stark contrasts in style and personality which reflected the social conflicts in America during the 1920s. Tunney, coming from a middle-class family, represented a more scientific approach to boxing as opposed to Dempsey's brawler image.

Lewis Mumford (1895–1990). Mumford was an American historian, urban planner, and architectural critic. He studied at the City College of New York and at the New School for Social Research. Mumford wrote on urban issues and architecture for *New Yorker* magazine from 1931 to 1963. After publishing several

Baseball hero Lou Gehrig is honored at Yankee Stadium in 1939. Gehrig's contributions to baseball strongly represented the American ideals of democracy, individualism, and meritocracy in the 1930s. (© Bettmann/Corbis. Reproduced by permission.)

books from 1926 to 1931 on the history of American architecture, Mumford authored another series of four books from 1934 to 1951 criticizing the dehumanizing aspects of modern technological society. He urged that technology should be brought into harmony with more humanistic goals. He offered solutions to achieve this harmony in these books, which were entitled *Technics and Civilization* (1934), *The Culture of Cities* (1938), *The Condition of Man* (1944), and *The Conduct of Life* (1951). A key later work by Mumford was *The City in History* (1961), which assessed the role of the city in the history of human civilization. He received the U.S. Medal of Freedom in 1964 from President Lyndon Johnson. Mumford continued his criticism of the role of technology in a two-volume set titled *The Myth of the Machine* (1967–1970).

George Herman "Babe" Ruth (1895–1948). Baseball legend Babe Ruth dominated the sports world like no other during the 1920s and 1930s. His exuberant personality off the field, and accomplishments on the field, contributed to a mythology. Ruth was born and raised in the slums of Baltimore, Maryland. Largely neglected by his family, Ruth became a very mischievous youth. Lacking the financial means to

raise Ruth, his parents legally committed him to St. Mary's Industrial School for Boys, a reformatory and orphanage, at age seven.

A standout in baseball, the local Baltimore minor league team signed Ruth in 1914. His contract was sold to the Boston Red Sox later that same year. In 1915 his hitting and pitching led the Red Sox to the World Series. He led the Red Sox to two more World Series in 1916 and 1918 before being sold to the New York Yankees in early 1920 because of the Red Sox's financial problems. Ruth's notoriety quickly took off in New York with his penchant for fast cars and women, rich food and drink, and stylish clothes. On the field he set hitting records and led the Yankees to seven World Series between 1921 and 1932. Until his retirement in 1935, he led the American League in home runs twelve times, including sixty in 1927 which stood as a major league record for the next 34 years.

Ruth projected a vibrant cultural image and was admired for both his rambunctious behavior and success. He symbolized the realization of the American dream through his display of power, natural ability, uninhibited lifestyle, and success rising from a rough childhood to fame and fortune. Ruth represented the ultimate spendthrift in the age of rising consumerism. He was the ultimate hero of the era and loved playing that role.

William Carlos Williams (1883–1963). A U.S. poet as well as medical doctor, Williams became a critic of the world's social trends during the Great Depression through such poems as "Proletarian Portrait" and "The Yachts." Later in *Paterson,* a five-volume set published between 1946 and 1958, Williams continued to assess modern man in America. Williams also wrote novels, including *White Mule* (1937), short stories, and an off-Broadway play. He was posthumously awarded the Pulitzer Prize in poetry in 1963.

Frank Lloyd Wright (1867–1959). Wright was one of the most influential architects in U.S. history and greatly contributed to the rise in modernism in America. Through his career Wright designed some eight hundred buildings, of which 380 were built. He briefly attended the University of Wisconsin at Madison from 1885 to 1886 where he took engineering courses because no architectural training was offered. Eager to practice architecture, Wright left college for Chicago, where he found employment in an architectural firm. By 1893 he opened his own firm. His first work, designing a house for W.H. Winslow, attracted considerable national attention. Wright became a key part of the "Prairie School" movement in architecture. The Prairie School became widely recognized for the innovative approach to building modern homes. Contrary to architectural trends of the time, Wright utilized mass-produced materials and equipment, normally used for commercial buildings. Wright also diverged from the more elaborate compartmentalization (dividing into small rooms) and ornamental detailing of homes, opting for plain walls, open space, and roomier living areas. Wright built fifty Prairie houses between 1900 and 1910. He also designed and built apartment houses, churches, company buildings, and recreation centers. In 1909 he built his own residence, named Taliesin, in Spring Green, Wisconsin.

The stock market crash in 1929 stopped almost all architectural activity in the United States. During the early years of the Great Depression, Wright lectured at Princeton, Chicago, and New York City. He also began writing on urban problems in the United States, publishing *The Disappearing City* in 1932. Wright began the Taliesin Fellowship program, a training program for architects and related artists at Taliesin at Green Springs, Wisconsin. During the Depression Wright developed a new system for constructing low-cost homes known as Usonians. Among them were the Jacobs house (1937) in Wisconsin and the Winckler-Goetsch house (1939) in Michigan. When the economy improved, Wright began receiving commissions once again. Perhaps most notable was the weekend retreat, known as "Fallingwater," Wright built in Pittsburgh in 1936 The house extended out over a waterfall. Other work included the campus and buildings at Florida Southern College during the 1940s, the Guggenheim Museum in New York City, and the Marin County government center north of San Francisco.

Wright introduced a whole new style of American architecture. It involved considerable use of open space and "organic architecture" in which buildings harmonize with their setting as well as the inhabitants. To this end Wright published *An Organic Architecture* in 1939.

Primary Sources

The Progress of Science

In assessing the potential psychological costs of the machine age in the interwar era, Lewis Mumford made the following observations in *The Story of Utopias,* first published in 1922 (Peter Smith, 1959, pp. 271–282):

> Science has provided the factual data by means of which the industrialist, the inventor, and engineer have transformed the physical world; and without doubt the physical world has been transformed. Unfortunately, when science has furnished the data its work is at an end: whether one uses the knowledge of chemicals to cure a patient or to poison one's grandmother is, from the standpoint of science, an extraneous and uninteresting question. So it follows that while science has given us the means of making over the world, the ends to which the world has been made over have had, essentially, nothing to do with science .

> Indeed scientific knowledge has not merely heightened the possibilities of life in the modern world: it has lowered the depths. When science is not touched by a sense of values it works—as it fairly consistently has worked during the past century—toward a complete dehumanization of the social order. The plea that each of the sciences must be permitted to go its own way without control should be immediately rebutted by pointing out that they obviously need a little guidance when their applications in war and industry are so plainly disastrous.

> The needed reorientation of science is important; but by itself it is not enough. Knowledge is a tool rather than a motor; and if we know the world without being able to react upon it, we are guilty of that aimless pragmatism which consists of devising all sorts of ingenious machines and being quite incapable of subordinating them to any coherent and attractive pattern.

Future Progress

Walter Lippman was an influential and internationally famous American journalist who often wrote about politics and modern society. He wrote a column for the *New York Herald Tribune* from 1931 to 1967. Lippmann was a critic of the New Deal, opposing big government solutions posed by President Roosevelt. In 1936 he offered observations on the increasing promise of science and technology in America despite the political uncertainty and economic hard times of the period. Lippmann penned the following thoughts as introductions to two sections of a book he co-edited, *The Modern Reader: Essays on Present-Day Life and Culture* (1936, p. 76, 164):

> Even had the World War [World War I] never occurred, the economic structure of the globe and of the United States would doubtless have changed with unparalleled rapidity in the two decades between 1915 and 1935. For a century there had been a steadily accelerating pace in such change. But the war threw the world into confusion. It was responsible for a tremendous stimulation in some economic fields, a powerful retardation in others... In much of the world... the years immediately after the war witnessed an unexpected and illusory revival. This season of 'prosperity' was most exuberant and extravagant in the United States, where it came to an abrupt and calamitous end with the crash of 1929. The result has been, throughout the world but most of all in the United States, a drastic revision of certain economic ideas popular in the flush days of the boom, and a searching reexamination of old concepts of the proper relation between government and industry.
>
> ... [T]hanks to the achievements of science and invention, mankind now possesses the means to furnish ample security, leisure, and comfort to the people of the Western nations. For countless centuries men labored to solve the problem of producing enough food, fuel, and clothing to save them from want; now that problem is more than solved, and the new task is to find means of distributing the wares that technology could easily make superabundant. The contrast between the existing state of society, harassed by war, poverty, and a hundred other ills, and the peaceful and abundant state that ought now to be obtainable, sharpens the pens which castigate [attack] our social order and which present plans for altering it. Social criticism has never been more abundant, social Utopias have never been presented more alluringly... There are... philosophers... who contrast the serenity of Oriental civilization with the sick hurry of Western civilization.... Some men, believers of equality, would trust for movement forward to the masses, while others, believing in inequality, trust for progress to an aristocracy of leaders.

Sports Issues

Sports figures assumed larger-than-life dimensions during the Great Depression. A key factor was the sportswriters who wrote powerful characterizations of the exploits of sports heroes. One key sport-

ing event was the victory of American black boxer Joe Louis over German Max Schmeling in a 1938 world championship bout held in the United States. The International News Service distributed the following article written by Bob Considine, reporting on Louis' victory and reprinted in David Halberstam's *The Best American Sports Writing of the Century* (1999, pp. 138–139):

> Listen to this, buddy, for it comes from a guy whose palms are still wet, whose throat is still dry, and whose jaw is still agape from the utter shock of watching Joe Louis knock out Max Schmeling.
>
> It was a shocking thing, that knockout—short, sharp, merciless, complete. Louis was like this:
>
> He was a big lean copper spring, tightened and retightened through weeks of training until he was one pregnant package of coiled venom.
>
> Schmeling hit that spring. He hit it with a whistling right-hand punch in the first minute of the fight—and the spring, tormented with tension, suddenly burst with ... activity. Hard brown arms, propelling two unerring fists, blurred beneath the hot white candelabra of the ring lights. And Schmeling was in the path of them, a man caught and mangled in the whirring claws of a mad and feverish machine.
>
> The mob, biggest and most prosperous ever to see a fight in a ball yard, knew that there was the end before the thing had really started. It knew, so it stood up and howled one long shriek ...
>
> Schmeling staggered away from the ropes, dazed and sick. He looked drunkenly toward his corner, and before he had turned his head back Louis was on him again, first with a left and then that awe-provoking right that made a crunching sound when it hit the German's jaw. Max fell down, hurt and giddy, for a count of three.
>
> He clawed his way up as if the night air were as thick as black water, and Louis—his nostrils like the mouth of a double-barreled shotgun—took a quiet lead and let him have both barrels ...
>
> The big crowd began to rustle restlessly toward the exits, many only now accepting Louis as champion of the world. There were no eyes for Schmeling, sprawled on his stool in his corner ...
>
> But once he crawled down in the belly of the big stadium, Schmeling realized the implications of his defeat. He ... now said Louis had fouled him. That would read better in Germany, whence earlier in the day had come a cable from Hitler, calling on him to win.

Suggested Research Topics

- Examine Lewis Mumford's series of four books that began being published during the Great Depression in which he assessed the new modern technological society. The books are *The Tech-*

nics and Civilization (1934), *The Culture of Cities* (1938), *The Condition of Man* (1944), and *The Conduct of Life* (1951), all published by Harcourt and Brace of New York. What key problems in modern society did Mumford see? What solutions did he offer to make technology more helpful to cities?

- What were the main industries of the interwar era? How and when were they affected by the assembly line technologies?

- What sports were available to America's women? Did they change through the interwar era? How did they reflect U.S. society in general?

- What factors made baseball America's pastime? How did it represent basic aspects of democracy?

- Identify various architectural buildings best reflecting the interwar era. How do they differ from those of previous eras?

Bibliography

Sources

Baker, Houston A., Jr. *Modernism and the Harlem Renaissance.* Chicago: University of Chicago Press, 1987.

Corn, Wanda M. *The Great American Thing: Modern Art and National Identity, 1915–35.* Berkeley: University of California Press, 1999.

Erenberg, Lewis A. *Steppin' Out: New York Nightlife and the Transformation of American Culture, 1890–1930.* Chicago: University of Chicago Press, 1984.

Evensen, Bruce J. *When Dempsey Fought Tunney: Heroes, Hokum, and Storytelling in the Jazz Age.* Knoxville: University of Tennessee Press, 1996.

Flink, James J. *The Automobile Age.* Cambridge, MA: MIT Press, 1988.

Lears, T. J. Jackson. *No Place of Grace: Antimodernism and the Transformation of American Culture, 1880–1920.* Chicago: University of Chicago Press, 1994.

Marchand, Roland. *Advertising the American Dream: Making Way for Modernity, 1920–40.* Berkeley: University of California Press, 1985.

Miller, Donald L. *Lewis Mumford: A Life.* Pittsburgh: University of Pittsburgh Press, 1992.

Mumford, Lewis. *The Story of Utopias.* Gloucester, MA: Peter Smith, 1959.

Pells, Richard W. *Radical Visions and American Dreams: Culture and Social Thought in the Depression Years.* Urbana: University of Illinois Press, 1998.

Tichi, Cecelia. *Shifting Gears: Technology, Literature, and Culture in Modernist America.* Chapel Hill: University of North Carolina Press, 1987.

Westbrook, Robert B. *John Dewey and American Democracy.* Ithaca, NY: Cornell University Press, 1991.

Wilson, Richard G., Dianne H. Pilgrim, and Dickran Tashjian. *The Machine Age in America, 1918–41.* New York: Brooklyn Museum, 1986.

Further Reading

Bradbury, Malcolm, and James McFarlane, eds. *Modernism, 1890–1930.* New York: Penguin, 1976.

Cooney, Terry A. *Balancing Acts: American Thought and Culture in the 1930s.* New York: Twayne Publishers, 1995.

Fitzgerald, F. Scott. *The Great Gatsby* (1925). New York: Collier Books, 1986.

Gelderman, Carol W. *Henry Ford: The Wayward Capitalist.* New York: Dial Press, 1981.

Haskell, Barbara. *The American Century: Art and Culture, 1900–50.* New York: W.W. Norton, 1999.

Hoyt, Edwin P. *The Tempering Years.* New York: Scribner, 1963.

McCoy, Donald R. *Coming of Age: The United States During the 1920s and 1930s.* Baltimore, MD: Penguin Books, 1973.

Mumford, Lewis. *The Culture of Cities* (1938). New York: Harcourt Brace and World Inc., 1970.

———. *The Condition of Man.* (1944). New York: Harcourt Brace and World Inc., 1973.

———. *The Conduct of Life.* New York: Harcourt Brace and World Inc., 1951.

———. *Sketches from Life: The Autobiography of Lewis Mumford, The Early Years.* Boston: Beacon Press, 1983.

———. *Technics and Civilization* (1934). New York: Harcourt Brace and World Inc., 1963.

Noble, David F. *America by Design: Science, Technology, and the Rise of Corporate Capitalism.* New York: Knopf, 1977.

Twombly, Robert C. *Frank Lloyd Wright: His Life and His Architecture.* New York: Wiley, 1979.

See Also

Escapism and Leisure; Everyday Life; Hollywood; Labor and Industry; Radio; World's Fairs

Isolationism

1930-1941

Introduction

Between World War I (1914–1918) and World War II (1939–1945) the United States was gripped by contradictory urges and interests in foreign relations. Some Americans, called internationalists, were strongly in favor of full participation in world affairs. Other Americans, sickened at the toll of World War I, turned inward. They became ardent isolationists, supporters of keeping the United States uninvolved with foreign affairs and instead focusing only on domestic matters. They opposed economic or political alliances with other nations and wanted to avoid wars abroad. The 1930s was a period of tension between isolationists and internationalists.

The stock market crash in late 1929 and the following Great Depression led President Franklin Delano Roosevelt (served 1933–1945) to introduce a wide range of economic relief and recovery programs collectively known as the New Deal. The Depression and New Deal further deepened this political divide between isolationists and internationalists. Isolationists increasingly viewed international relations as potentially detracting from the United States being able to make economic decisions for the best of the American public. While this battle limited President Franklin Roosevelt's foreign policy, unintentionally it gave Roosevelt's key advisors and administrators, known as the New Dealers, greater freedom in designing unprecedented domestic programs. Isolationist U.S. senators, many of whom were progressive Republicans, supported Roosevelt's New Deal programs at first. Progressive Republicans were those Republicans who believed government had a distinct role in furthering social needs. This perspective was in strong contrast to most Republicans who strongly believed in a very limited role in American daily life. With changes in the direction of New Deal programs, however, by 1935 emphasizing more long-term economic reform and permanent government involvement in private business, the isolationists increasingly opposed New Deal programs as well as Roosevelt's internationalist perspective.

Internationalists sought peace through cooperation between nations. For example internationalists supported the work of the League of Nations. The League was an international organization created in 1920 to resolve world issues before they could lead to war. Although U.S. President Woodrow Wilson (served 1913–1921) championed the organization, the United States was not a member because of the pressure of isolationists within its government. Some internationalists wanted to develop a "Good Neighbor Policy" with Latin America and an "Open Door" for economic trade in Asia. The Good Neighbor Policy attempted to improve relations with Latin American nations by refraining from armed intervention in Latin American political developments and improving economic relations. Internationalists were well aware of the financial benefits of international trade and commerce for the United States from anywhere in the world. They sensed industries' need for raw materials located in foreign nations and also desired overseas markets to sell American manufactured goods. Some internationalists also had concern over the growing government role in private economic matters. They supported unfettered capitalism in which markets for their goods were unhindered by government regulation or oversight. Many believed in a government role in nurturing trade relations with other countries, but not government control over industrial operations.

Isolationists disavowed treaties with foreign nations and argued that events on other continents were not of concern or consequence for the United States. Their opposition largely grew from distrust of East Coast financial leaders who they believed would not develop treaties that would benefit the general public. They believed America could lead the world best by being an example of democracy rather than through involvement in formal economic alliances. They had been successful in keeping the United States out of the League of Nations though the League had been the idea of President Woodrow Wilson. By the late 1930s, as Europe tipped toward warfare, these Americans held to a noninterventionist (do not get involved in conflicts between other nations) position. They sought laws from Congress to

Chronology:

1928: The United States signs the Kellogg-Briand Pact renouncing war as a part of national policy.

1934–1936: The Nye Committee of the U.S. Senate begins investigating the causes for U.S. involvement in World War I.

1935: Congress passes the first of a series of neutrality acts to protect the United States from world problems.

1935: The Roosevelt administration adopts the Moral Embargo to keep faith with neutrality commitments in Congress.

February 24, 1936: The Nye Committee publishes its final report highlighting industry profits made from World War I arms sales but clearing industry of conspiring to lead the United States into war.

1939: Congress passes the last of the series of neutrality acts to further maintain American isolation from world problems.

1941: In a major step away from isolationism, Congress passes the Lend-Lease Act to provide aid to the Allies including support to Great Britain for its war with Germany.

discourage involvement of the United States in assisting the warring countries of Europe. Though opposing formal alliances, isolationists did not oppose foreign commercial and financial activity that could relieve Great Depression economic problems.

Many factors fed the attitudes favoring isolation. These attitudes included a distrust of international agreements, fear of involvement in another war, pride of American accomplishments in business and rapid industrialization, and the distance across the seas from troubled parts of the world. Another powerful force in isolationism was the peace movement. It attracted thousands of newly enfranchised (right to vote) women in the 1920s. Though women sought international cooperation to achieve peace, they too fed isolationist tendencies. Isolationists sought peace by avoiding treaties with other nations and staying out of their business activities.

Many isolationists believed that U.S. munitions makers and bankers, hoping for windfall profits, conspired to lead the country into World War I. As U.S. Senator Gerald Nye's investigations into these matters made front-page news in the mid-1930s, the number of isolationists grew. Peace advocates worked closely with his committee and helped it secure information. Although the committee uncovered immense profits made by banks and companies like DuPont, it could not confirm a conspiracy. The public disgust with bankers and the munitions industry, however, fed the great disillusion with business leaders and financiers at the beginning of the Great Depression.

Isolationism posed a major challenge for both foreign and domestic policy in the New Deal. President Roosevelt was, by conviction, an internationalist and realist. He and his advisers saw the coming fury in Europe. They were constrained, however, by actions in Congress both to assist future allies as well as to prepare the United States for what appeared an inevitable world war. The eventual mobilization of U.S. industry proved the ultimate cure for the Great Depression. The isolationism of Congress and the public, however, had delayed this cure. On the other hand, isolationism kept U.S. ties with foreign nations at a minimum. This detachment from other economies gave the New Dealers a unique opportunity to experiment with the U.S. economic system without complications of complex foreign ties. This likely allowed for a more dramatic and immediate response of New Deal economic relief and recovery programs.

Issue Summary

Despite the growth of industry and international trade through the 1920s, isolationism remained strong in the United States. Most Americans opposed any involvement in foreign wars or establishing alliances with foreign nations. Isolationism came to the fore again by the mid-1930s due to a series of events. These events included investigations by a congressional committee, passage of neutrality laws by Congress, and the rise of popular anti-war organizations.

Isolationists and the New Deal

The crash of the stock market in October 1929 and the following Great Depression only strengthened isolationism in America. By 1932, 25 percent of the workforce was jobless, amounting to over 12 million people. Farmers in the Midwest, where isolationism was strongest, were finding fewer markets for their crops. They were going bankrupt and losing their

farms through foreclosure to banks. In turn banks were increasingly going out of business as they were stuck with many properties for which there was no market. Congressional leaders began to look for ways to help their constituents in distress.

As the Great Depression worsened in its first few years the mood of isolationism was strong among the American public and its elected representatives in Congress. Those senators strongly supporting isolationism included independent progressive Republicans. Their sentiments were in contrast to main Republican support of international trade alliances to expand markets for satisfying the increasing productivity of U.S. industry. With innovations in manufacturing, including adoption of assembly lines and increased electrical service, U.S. factories were producing commodities faster than American consumers could purchase them. The Eastern business establishment sought new markets elsewhere. The isolationist progressive Republicans represented an independent political block, who believed New Deal relief and recovery programs offered better prospects for economic improvement for the common man than international alliances that they believed would only serve to fatten the wallets of East Coast business tycoons. They also provided critical support for many of President Roosevelt's early New Deal initiatives.

Isolationism, with its strong supporters in Congress, served to influence the development of government programs under Roosevelt's New Deal. The president needed support in Congress for his New Deal programs, which he hoped would assist the country out of the Great Depression, and he could not risk alienating the isolationists. The main progressive Republican spokesmen for isolationism in Congress included George W. Norris of Nebraska, William Borah of Idaho, Hiram Johnson of California, Burton Wheeler of Montana, Gerald Nye of North Dakota, and Robert LaFollette, Jr., of Wisconsin. These men largely distrusted the involvement of East Coast business leaders and financiers in European affairs. All were strong supporters of the massive amount of legislation Roosevelt was able to pass through Congress in his first one hundred days of office in 1933. These measures, the first of the New Deal, included work relief, farm relief, industry recovery efforts, and the creation of the Tennessee Valley Authority (TVA).

In general isolationists felt that restoration of economic prosperity in the United States was crucial for maintaining independence from world events. For example Senator Norris was a long time supporter of government economic planning and public electrical power projects. But efforts had failed in establishing

Senator Burton Wheeler of Montana, a leading proponent of isolationism, gives a speech for the America First Committee and Keep America Out of War Congress on February 20, 1941. (AP/Wide World Photos. Reproduced by permission.)

regional power projects until President Roosevelt arrived in office. Norris was instrumental in getting approval for the TVA project through Congress. As a result a major dam and new town in the project were named after him. The TVA was the first major economic reform act of the New Deal.

Most progressive Republican isolationists were from the Midwest farm country, therefore farm relief was particularly of interest to them. The isolationists supported creation of the Agricultural Adjustment Administration (AAA) to tackle problems of long-term farm overproduction, sagging foreign demand for U.S. farm products, and low produce prices paid to farmers. They were more supportive, however, of providing loans to farmers aimed toward helping reduce debts and saving foreclosures rather than setting limits on how much a farmer could grow, which was a key part of the AAA. The isolationists pushed hard to guarantee farmers that their costs of crop production would be covered. Norris added a much-debated amendment to the bill as it was proceeding through Congress to guarantee production costs. The House of Representatives, however, removed it before the bill finally passed. The deletion of Norris' amendment was a major blow to the Midwest pro-

gressives. They reluctantly supported implementation of the AAA but the resulting programs of plowing up crops and killing pigs drew much criticism. They could not see setting acreage controls for crop production when many of the less fortunate in America were going hungry. Few progressives were disappointed when the U.S. Supreme Court ruled the New Deal agricultural program unconstitutional in January 1936.

Senator LaFollete was less interested in government planning programs and farm relief, but he was a big supporter of public works programs. Therefore he was helpful in passing such work relief related measures as the Civilian Conservation Corps (CCC), the Progress Works Administration (PWA), the National Industrial Recovery Act (NIRA), and the Federal Emergency Relief Act (FERA). All of these programs provided various types of jobs to different parts of the population. For example the CCC employed youths of approximately 18 to 25 years of age to perform land conservation work such as planting trees, constructing irrigation systems, and fighting forest fires.

Isolationists, however, did not support all of these programs. For example both Senators Borah and Nye in particular believed the National Recovery Administration (NRA) created by the NIRA was unconstitutional. The NRA setup committees through which competing businesses could set prices and wages. The isolationists feared the increased concentration of economic power in big business would encourage growth of monopolies. They distrusted the business and financial leaders residing on the East Coast. They believed the growth of these cooperative business practices hurt small business in America in addition to workers and farmers. Once the NIRA was passed and the NRA created, most of the isolationists became opponents of the agency. The progressives pressured Roosevelt to set better controls on the cooperation going on between business leaders. In response on March 7, 1934, Roosevelt created the National Recovery Review Board that was initially proposed by Senator Nye. The board was to determine what effects the new NRA business codes had on business competition. Having no real powers, however, to enforce any decisions the board proved largely ineffective but successfully served to establish a more formal split between the progressives and Roosevelt over the NRA. To the relief of the progressives the U.S. Supreme Court in May 1935 ruled the NIRA unconstitutional just as Borah and Nye had originally argued.

When the NIRA was ruled unconstitutional, Roosevelt took the New Deal off into new directions to which the isolationists were even more opposed. Rather than trying to work in partnership with American business, Roosevelt decided to seek economic reform that would regulate business. Even progressive Republicans found this role of government too intrusive in private business matters. In addition Roosevelt came out strongly supporting labor unions that were looked upon with great disdain by the Midwest population. Meanwhile the isolationists were also making headway. In 1934 Congress passed the Johnson Act that prohibited U.S. citizens from lending money to foreign countries who had not paid their war debts from World War I. This would substantially affect the flow of investment capital (monies) to European nations recovering from war and Depression.

In general the isolationists thought the New Deal was an attack on a traditional way of life they cherished. They represented rural, small town, small business interests. Isolationists supported some pieces of legislation in the First New Deal of 1933 to 1935 but opposed other pieces. Their emphasis was on local community, self-government, and individualism with limited influence from big business and big government. It was an interest in holding onto traditional American lifelines that dominated the nation before

the rise of industrialization and big business. They wanted foreign policy to reflect this simpler, earlier period as well.

Investigations of the Nye Committee

In 1934 and 1935 Senator Nye headed a congressional committee investigating an alleged conspiracy by munitions (war materials) makers to involve the United States in World War I. The Women's International League, a peace group, in December 1933 had identified such a study as its primary objective. Dorothy Detzer and Jeanette Rankin of the League and others helped develop materials for the committee. Those serving with Nye included Walter F. George (Georgia), Bennett Champ Clark (Missouri), Homer T. Bone (Washington), James P. Pope (Idaho), Warren Barbour (New Jersey), and Arthur H. Vandenberg (Michigan). Stephen Rausenbush, an economics professor at Dartmouth College, was the committee's chief investigator.

In 1934, as the Nye Committee began its work, the Book-of-the-Month Club promoted H. C. Englebrecht and F. C. Hanighen's *Merchants of Death*. This wide-selling book rejected the idea that arms makers had engaged in a conspiracy to lead America into war. It documented, however, the enormous profits made by the munitions industry and their blindness to the social consequences of their work. The Nye Committee thus looked at World War I through the concerns of peace advocates as well as those who wanted to isolate their country from foreign entanglements.

To assess the lobbying and influence of armaments manufacturers the Nye Committee examined the proceedings of various post-war conferences focused on disarmament (reducing the amount of weapons on hand) including the 1922 Washington Disarmament Conference and the 1925 Geneva Arms Control Conference. In addition they examined any lobbying by industry on various arms embargo efforts of the early 1930s and a neutrality bill proposed in Congress in 1935. It looked into the influence arms sales had on peace, the relations of the munitions companies with the U. S. government, and international agreements between munitions companies in various countries.

On February 24, 1936, the Nye Committee, more formally called the Special Committee on Investigation of the Munitions Industry, issued the "Nye Report." The committee found that none of the companies engaged exclusively in the manufacture of military materials. In fact the largest firms—General Motors, DuPont, General Electric, Babcock & Wilcox, and Westinghouse—primarily manufactured products for civilians. The committee, however, found that many of the American munitions companies used questionable business methods that bordered on bribery in coercing leaders of foreign governments to purchase their war goods instead of another industry's products. The Committee concluded such activities were clearly unethical and reflected poorly on American business. It also reflected poorly on U.S. government agencies that helped them obtain those orders for war goods. While the committee did not conclude that a conspiracy of these firms led to American involvement in World War I, it condemned the actions of the companies in general.

The work of the Nye Committee and its report gave what isolationists considered concrete documentation of inappropriate dealings by certain industries. As a result publicity from the report only hardened opposition by isolationists to New Deal programs that fostered growth of big government and allowed big business to operate freely. Members of the public, however, who were not isolationists were well aware that the members of the Nye Committee were all committed to isolationism. Therefore that segment of the public only saw the findings as firmly establishing the committee's own biased position. Consequently the debate over isolationism still raged.

Neutrality Acts and the Call for Voluntary Actions

By early 1935 while the Nye Committee was hard at work Adolph Hitler, who had established a dictatorship over a war ravaged and economically depressed Germany, was rearming Germany in clear violation of the Treaty of Versailles. The treaty, established in 1920, had concluded World War I by heavily penalizing Germany for its aggression during the war. One treaty provision limited reestablishment of military forces. Hitler's vision, however, was to bring Germany back to a prominent world position including expansion and control over the rest of the European continent. In March Hitler established universal military training that required all German youth to serve their country in the military service for a minimum amount of time. Meanwhile Italy's dictator, Benito Mussolini who had grand visions of expansion for Italy, had launched an attack on Ethiopia to carve out an Italian "colony" in North Africa through military occupation. The response in Congress to these ominous world events was to withdraw from international engagement and, instead, to announce American neutrality.

In 1935 Walter Millis published *The Road to War: America, 1914–1917,* which became a best seller. It promoted the idea that the United States could have

United States Senator Gerald Nye was a proponent of the United States remaining neutral with regard to U.S. involvement with the conflict in Europe that would eventually become World War II. (© Bettmann/ Corbis. Reproduced by permission.)

avoided World War I, but was tricked into participation by other nations. British propaganda, Allied purchases of war materials, and Woodrow Wilson's weak position on neutrality, he said, were all contributing factors. Those who wanted reasons to avoid American involvement in war saw in the Millis book good evidence for remaining neutral.

Congress passed the Neutrality Act in March 1935, which prohibited the export of the implements of war such as airplanes, tanks, and guns to any nation engaged in a conflict. No U.S. ships could transport arms to warring nations. The measure also authorized the president to withhold protection for any Americans traveling on ships of countries at war. The act also created the National Munitions Board placing some federal control over the armament industry.

Being sensitive to growing isolationism in the United States, the Roosevelt administration sought to figure out how to avoid stirring conflict with isolationists while responding to the deteriorating conditions in Europe. Secretary of State Cordell Hull, for example, asked for a voluntary ban by industry on the export of materials that could ultimately be useful for the manufacture of U.S. war materials. The voluntary nature of the plan would raise less alarm among isolationists than a mandatory strategy. Hull's request proved effective largely stopping the international sale of copper, oil, railroad tracks, scrap iron, scrap steel, scrap tin, old locomotives, and other items that might in the future help the nation go to war.

Following Italy's expanded aggression in North Africa, Secretary of Interior Harold Ickes requested American petroleum producers to stop further sales to Italy. The embargo was voluntary. Also in 1935 the Department of Commerce urged American shipping companies to refrain from transporting war materials to any nation preparing for war. These modest steps by the administration were taken in the spirit of the Neutrality Act but at the same time saving materials for U.S. use. As a way to ease economic problems caused by the Great Depression, small communities, schools, and organizations mounted scrap drives to try to raise money for their communities. They sold useful trash to willing buyers and these drives returned useful materials back into use.

In 1936 the Neutrality Act came up for renewal. Following much spirited debate over placing further restrictions on arms sales, Congress simply extended the existing 1935 provisions for another 14 months. Reflecting the influence of the Nye Committee, Congress did add a new provision prohibiting loans to foreign nations at war. This provision essentially adopted the 1934 Johnson Act restrictions into the Neutrality Act context.

When the Neutrality Act came up for renewal again in 1937, some significant changes were made under Roosevelt's influence. A "cash-and-carry" policy was written into the act. Though still limiting U.S. business contacts with warring nations, the policy allowed the sales of arms to foreign nations. The purchasing nations must, however, pay in cash for the war materials and ship them in their own ships. The law permitted President Roosevelt to send 50 old destroyers to Britain in return for eight naval bases. This provision was designed to keep American ships out of war zones. A main problem with this provision from the British and other foreign countries' views was that due to the Great Depression they had little cash on hand to purchase the much needed materials.

The series of neutrality acts passed by Congress between 1935 and 1937 attempted to keep the United States out of conflicts leading toward World War II. The laws limited the sale and shipment of the implements of war.

As time passed tensions over potential American involvement in the troubles in Europe grew steadily.

On February 7, 1938, Senator Hiram Johnson of California, an ardent isolationist, introduced a resolution asking whether the president had entered into or anticipated any agreement or alliance with Britain. Secretary of State Hull responded, no. When in early 1939 it became known that Roosevelt had suggested to some senators that the nation's "first line of defense" was in France, the President had to cover himself quickly. He denied the statement and then on February 3 clarified his foreign policy by affirming a less engaged position in European politics by his administration. Reinforcing this public position Roosevelt proclaimed that the United States would avoid any "entangling alliances"; would maintain world trade with all nations; support efforts to reduce or limit armaments; and respect the political and economic independence of all nations.

America First Committee, 1940–1941

As the European political crisis deepened in the late 1930s, isolationists became more and more determined to keep the United States out of world affairs and world war. Strong leadership for isolation continued to come from Midwest business and political leaders. Robert E. Wood, a former army officer and president of Sears, Roebuck and Co. was adamantly opposed to war preparations the Roosevelt administration was edging towards. Wood became the first head of an organization known as the America First Committee (AFC).

The AFC was created on September 4, 1940, the day after Roosevelt had signed a deal to provide the destroyers to Great Britain. It was also 12 days after the president had signed the Selective Service Act. The act required all males between ages 21 and 36, both citizens and aliens, residing in the United States to register for the draft. Those inducted into the services would serve for 12 months and only in the Western Hemisphere and U.S. territories. With national headquarters in Chicago, the AFC grew out of a student organization at Yale University. During the summer of 1940 it gained increasing attention of the Midwest business leaders and politicians. By November local chapters of AFC were being formed around the nation.

The AFC drew together isolationists with diverse backgrounds including Communists and pro-Nazi sympathizers. It was primarily made up of conservatives, however, who disliked the British and who opposed American intervention in world affairs. Various principles were formally adopted. These included that the United States must build a strong defense for America; that no foreign power can successfully attack a prepared America; that American democracy can be preserved only by keeping out of the European war;

and, that providing aid to other nations just short of waging war weakens national defense at home and threatens American involvement in war abroad.

John T. Flynn, a New York journalist and sharp critic of New Deal programs and deficit spending (government spending more than the revenue it brings in), became one of the primary publicists for the AFC. He opposed war regardless of the prospects for victory or defeat. Flynn helped organize rallies, create new chapters, and build membership that peaked at over 800,000 in late 1941. By the attack on Pearl Harbor 450 chapters and subchapters existed across the nation.

The Writer's Anti-War Bureau also provided publicity for the AFC. The Bureau wrote and distributed a weekly newssheet titled *Uncensored.* Its editor, Sidney Hertzberg, sought to analyze and expose any information he considered propaganda and bias that he believed was encouraging American involvement in the war in Europe. The newssheet was published from October 7, 1939, to December 6, 1941. It was mailed to radio commentators, newspaper editors, and other publicists.

AFC support came from various well-known citizens. From 1939 to 1941 highly popular aviator Charles A. Lindbergh gave a series of speeches on the radio and at public rallies on behalf of isolationism and the AFC. AFC efforts, however, were ultimately wounded by the public remarks of Lindbergh. The public interpreted some of Lindbergh's comments as anti-Semitic, pro-Nazi, and unpatriotic. Lindbergh, who never recanted his speeches, insisted that his isolationism was driven by the realities of what he observed while living in Europe between 1935 and 1939. Public reaction to his comments undercut public support for anti-war groups such as the AFC. Nonetheless the AFC was the leading isolationist organization for the final 15 months leading up to Pearl Harbor. The AFC's agenda was discredited when, on December 7, 1941, Japan attacked the American military bases at Pearl Harbor in Hawaii. Germany and Italy declared war on the United States on December 11.

Responses Against Isolationism

With Charles Lindbergh mounting a series of strong speeches promoting isolationism, the White House arranged for various senators and others to counter Lindbergh's words. These efforts included new organizations. One organization established during this late period of the inter-war years was the Committee to Defend America. William Allen White founded the committee on May 20, 1940 to counter Lindbergh's speeches and the persistent national isolationist mood. The committee, promoting aid-short-of-war, also sought to sway public opinion and influence congressional members to support greater military preparedness for defense. This was the day following a national broadcast by Charles Lindbergh promoting extreme isolationism. It was also a few days before the evacuation of British troops from Europe at Dunkirk, France. Only a month later France would surrender to Germany. With the German advances against British and French forces, many in America were becoming increasingly alarmed.

One other organization formed to attack isolationism was the Fight for Freedom Committee. This organization contended that defeat of Axis powers (Germany and Italy) in Europe was essential to protecting American interests. This group wanted the United States to take aggressive military action rather than what was simply promoted by the Committee to Defend America. This group argued for a more active military role in supporting Britain in defeating Germany rather than waiting to defend American shores. Appealing to the Eastern urban establishment along the Atlantic seaboard, this group was formed in April 1941 by prominent individuals in New York City.

The support of such groups enabled President Roosevelt to take some action in assisting Britain. Congress passed the Lend-Lease Act in March 1941 replacing the earlier cash-and-carry policy of the neutrality acts. The new act authorized President Franklin Roosevelt to spend up to $7 billion to assist the Allies in their war efforts. Constituting one more major step toward war, the law permitted the United States to provide war supplies to shore up Great Britain, following the German invasion of France. American aid included the sale, lending, leasing, exchange, or transfer of materials to any country whose defense was vital to the security of the United States. It did not require immediate payment that the 1939 Neutrality Act did. The act would provide the primary authority for the U.S. government to contribute military assistance to foreign nations throughout World War II. Such diverse countries to receive such aid were Britain, China, Brazil, and the Soviet Union. Importantly for economic recovery from the Great Depression, the Lend-Lease Act spurred increased mobilization of American industry to produce war goods. This, more than any New Deal program, would ultimately pull the United States out of the economic crisis.

Isolationists were not opposed to forming relations with other nations in the Western Hemisphere. As a result the United States was able to take steps in Latin America to fight the Great Depression as well as keeping German influence at bay. Roosevelt adopted policies of his predecessor, President Herbert Hoover, in forming the Good Neighbor Policy. This included helping resolve existing conflicts in South America and signing trade agreements with Latin American countries. Roosevelt also promised non-intervention in internal political affairs of Latin American countries and unity against foreign aggression.

Isolationism in the 1930s significantly affected the relationship of the United States to former World War I allies—Great Britain and France most particularly. Ironically it ultimately also contributed to the nation's entry into World War II as European nations steadily fell to German expansion having received little support from friendly nations. With the Pearl Harbor attack on December 7, 1941, American isolationism was abruptly over. The nation formally entered World War II the following day and the related mobilization of industry to produce war materials would bring an end to the Great Depression.

Contributing Forces

Isolationism in America stretched back to the colonial times of the eighteenth century since many colonists sought to escape European political, economic, and religious influence. Early U.S. leaders such as George Washington and Thomas Jefferson openly warned the nation about the hazards of forming foreign alliances. They reinforced the prevailing public sentiment. Indeed the U.S. wars of the nineteenth century, including the War of 1812 (1812–1814), the Mexican War (1846–1848), and the Spanish–American War (1898) were all fought in the Western Hemisphere and did not involve Europe or any formal alliances. By the early twentieth century, however, improved transportation and communication including cable, radio, and steamships, increased U.S. contacts with foreign nations. Stronger relations through international trade grew with Europe.

American Involvement in World War I

World War I was the first major break from long-standing U.S. isolationist policies. The United States Senate in 1917 responded favorably to the request for a Declaration of War by President Woodrow Wilson. Wilson saw the importance of European political developments for American security. The prospect of "making the world safe for democracy," as Wilson phrased it, seemed a noble goal. The war, however, bogged down in grueling, deadly combat with troops facing each other for months in the wet mud and cold of Western Europe. Tens of thousands of combatants died and thousands more survived with burned lungs and bodies—the results of chemical weapons. Great

psychological damage resulted from the horror of their military service. Leading isolationists in Congress during this period were William Jennings Bryan of Nebraska, Robert LaFollette of Wisconsin, and George Norris of Nebraska. They became determined not to have this happen again to young Americans.

Shortly after the end of the war in 1918, journalists, politicians, and historians began to assess the causes for U.S. entry into the war. Public opinion was shaped in part by Albert J. Nock's *Myth of a Guilty Nation* (1922) and John Kenneth Turner's *Shall It Be Again?* These books contributed to American disgust with the war. Nock alleged that Germany really had not caused the war, rather, he argued, the real cause was a plan of the Allied powers (the combination of France, Britain, and Russia) to make war on the Central Powers (Germany and Austria-Hungary). Turner argued that President Wilson led America to war to protect American bankers and that the "profits of patriotism" created 21,000 new millionaires. These books were founded on little evidence but were widely read.

In *The Genesis of the World War* (1925) historian Harry Elmer Barnes used substantial sources based on thorough research. He stated that starting in 1911 France and Russia began a campaign with two goals. France wanted to recover control from Germany of the Alsace-Lorraine area on its eastside. Russia wanted control of the Bosporus, the connection between the Black Sea and the Mediterranean. Barnes essentially argued that Germany was forced into World War I because of this plot between France and Russia. Barnes followed this study with articles and another book *In Quest of Truth and Justice* (1928). Using interviews with Kaiser Wilhelm, Alfred Zimmerman, and other German leaders, Barnes more forcefully argued that Germany was not guilty of causing the war for it had nothing to gain.

The revelations in the four books—some of them tinged by dubious documentation and biased writing—fueled American disillusionment with World War I and the complex situation of international involvement following it. For example President Wilson was determined the United States should join the proposed international organization, the League of Nations. He outlined Fourteen Points, a series of actions that he said would make the world "fit and safe to live in." Wilson called for arms reductions, free seas, an end to tariffs (taxes on imported goods), and some degree of independence for colonial peoples (a country under control of another nation). Wilson's opponents in the United States were equally determined that the United States would not participate in the post-war world he wanted to create. In the end

Women and military servicemen celebrate on Armistice Day, which marked the end of World War I. (Archive

Photos. Reproduced by permissions.)

Wilson lost and the United States neither ratified (approved) the Treaty of Versailles officially ending World War I nor did it join the League of Nations, even though Wilson had in part orchestrated both.

These events set the stage for the international disillusionment that gripped the United States in the 1920s. The feelings were not uniquely American, for intellectuals and others in Europe were also sickened by the consequences of World War I. In the United States, however, these feelings tended to move in spe-

cial ways in part due to the vast oceans separating the United States from Europe and Asia. One way was an increase in isolationist sentiment. The United States, it was argued, could get along just fine on its own and not involve itself with the rest of the world. The other matter was the embrace of materialism (to be more concerned with material items than spiritual or intellectual values) as the U.S. turned inward and self-centered. For much of the 1920s the United States seemed prosperous, even though signs of economic

More About...

From the League of Nations to the United Nations

At the end of World War I the victorious nations met in France at the Paris Peace Conference, where they established the Treaty of Versailles setting the terms for post war Europe. The United States, Britain, and France largely developed the treaty with very little participation from other allied countries or Germany. The treaty was signed in June 1919 and became effective January 1920. The treaty terms were severe and angered Germany with loss of territory and exorbitant payments (reparations) to be paid to the victorious nations. Germany lost 10 percent of its territory and population. Many believe the treaty directly contributed to the rise of Adolf Hitler and Germany's new militarism in the 1930s. One of the things the treaty did was establish the League of Nations. The League was formed to resolve international disputes as they arise before they could progress toward war. Due to the lack of any real power to enforce decisions, however, the League ran into many difficulties in resolving international issues including those involving Germany's military expansion in Europe in the late 1930s. Many historians consider this ineffectiveness a key factor leading to World War II. Recognizing this failure British Prime Minister Winston Churchill and President Roosevelt signed the Atlantic Charter in August 1941 in which they agreed to create a new global organization to help resolve conflicts following World War II.

The resulting United Nations (UN) is an international organization established in October 1945. The primary goal of the UN is to maintain international peace and security. To do this, nations who are members to the UN attempt to solve economic, political, and humanitarian problems before they escalate to broader problems. In general the UN, composed of a General Assembly and a Security Council, provides a place where nations can coordinate their activities. When the League of Nations disbanded in 1946 the UN inherited much of the League's facilities as well as the organizational structure and ways of doing business the League had forged over the previous 25 years. The UN, however, adopted some processes quite different from the League that would make it much more effective in maintaining international peace.

Cold War politics and tensions occupied much of the UN's time during its first 45 years of operation. The United States, Great Britain, and the Soviet Union led in designing the new organization and determining how decisions were to be made. This process was long and tenuous with much disagreement before resolution finally came. The main issues revolved around voting procedures in the General Assembly and Security Council when deciding specific issues. To design the UN three major conferences were held in Dumbarton Oaks near Washington, DC, in late 1944, at Yalta on the Crimean Sea in February 1945, and in San Francisco in April 1945. Representatives from fifty nations attended the San Francisco meeting where a final charter was adopted.

As many nations in Africa, Asia, and the Middle East gained independence from European colonial domination following World War II, many political, economic, and social issues arose. Similarly the end of the Cold War created more newly independent nations posing additional challenges in resolving resulting conflicts and delivering humanitarian assistance.

---

difficulties were mounting. Americans bought automobiles, vacuum cleaners, iceboxes and refrigerators, installed electric lighting in their homes, and went to movies where they saw an artificial world created by filmmakers.

Some of the most disillusioned in the 1920s removed themselves from American society by rejecting its materialism as well as any future involvement in war. A generation of intellectuals, mostly writers, moved to Europe and wrote bitter, sometimes haunt-

ing poetry and novels about a world gone wrong. T. S. Eliot's *The Waste Land* became one of the most famous of these works. Another group of writers, artists, and photographers settled in the upper Rio Grande Valley of New Mexico to form the Taos Colony. They sought a simpler, more innocent existence removed from the problems of modern times. World War I and the disillusionment of the 1920s were thus powerful factors in shaping American isolationism in the 1930s during the New Deal.

The Peace Movement

The conclusion of World War I in 1918 was followed shortly in 1920 by the ratification of the Nineteenth Amendment and the extension of suffrage (right to vote) to women. For decades women had watched the ravages of war and mounted campaigns to try to eradicate it from human society. Empowered with the right to vote and a keen sense of the power of organizing for a cause, women stepped up their peace efforts in the 1920s. The Women's International League for Peace and Freedom, founded in 1915 in the Netherlands, became a rallying point. The time was right, for in 1921 the Washington Conference, a meeting of the world's powers at the time, addressed disarmament. Several treaties resulted from the meeting. The Five-Power Treaty (United States, Great Britain, Japan, France, and Italy) agreed that for ten years the five nations would build no battleships and would reduce their fleets. The Four-Power Treaty (United States, Great Britain, Japan, and France) agreed to respect each other's interests in the Pacific Ocean and to confer if hostilities erupted in the area. The Nine-Power Treaty agreed to respect the independence of China and keep open trade relations.

While these agreements were essentially toothless, having little power or ability to enforce them, they inspired peace advocates to press harder for disarmament and an end to war. In 1928 a number of nations, including the United States, participated in conferences in Paris that led to the Kellogg-Briand Pact. The U.S. Senate ratified the Pact in 1929 by a vote of 85 to one. Though the agreement renounced war as an instrument of national policy, it would do nothing to stop the drift toward World War II later in the 1930s. It was, however, a high point for the peace movement affirming that the United States might decline to become involved in future wars. The agreement also contributed significantly to the mood of isolationism.

The peace movement thus included both internationalist as well as isolationist tendencies. Workers in the peace movement sought both world peace and international connections. But they disavowed war and, most particularly, American engagement in anything that might again lead the nation into war. Women in the peace movement felt that the best way to achieve peace was to avoid international agreements that would require U.S. participation in defending other nations who had been attacked. This perspective clearly fed the isolationist mood of the nation.

Economic Concerns at Home

The ardent isolationists also had another factor working in their favor through the occurrence of the Great Depression. Many Americans were substantially affected by the economic hard times. By early 1933, 25 percent of the U.S. workforce, or over 12 million people, were out of work. Many more had their incomes reduced or lived in daily fear of losing their jobs. The future was very uncertain and hope was dimming. As a result, interests in foreign issues greatly decreased as domestic economic issues dominated. Concern about what was going on in the United States far surpassed concerns over political developments across the ocean or international trade relations. These issues seemed much more distant and less important to day-to-day life. In this economic climate of the Depression, isolationists gained political strength and worked diligently to sway the less engaged public in foreign affairs toward their perspective.

Perspectives

Local Perspectives

At the local level isolationism was largely a matter of individual choice. Issues of foreign policy were not overwhelmingly important for those 12 million unemployed workers facing breadlines at the height of the Great Depression in 1932 and 1933 and for many others concerned about the economic strife. They wanted to see the government primarily tackle the domestic economic problems. Public polls showed that unemployment was the number one issue in the 1930s up through December 1936. Prospects of being involved in war did not become a leading concern of the public until May 1939. Domestic issues had continued to be dominant right through the decade.

Organizers, however, seeking to gain support for isolationism found fertile ground for pulling together those opposed to U.S. involvements abroad. Founded in 1940, the America First Committee (AFC) grew rapidly to enlist over 800,000 members whose goals all focused around isolationism. The AFC sought to explain to newspaper writers, politicians, policymakers, and the public its determination to keep the United States out of war in Europe. It fielded speakers, such as Charles A. Lindbergh, issued press releases, and published pamphlets. Members were inspired by the committee's insistence that the United States could maintain an insular, isolated detachment from world events. It ignored international trade and banking, concerns over the well-being of families and friends living across the Atlantic Ocean, and the moral responsibilities of a democracy. By 1941 New York City had more than 80 chapters of the America First Committee.

Map of areas where nationalism and its leaders rose in the 1930s. (The Gale Group.)

Various other local and regional organizations with diverse causes shared a common goal—isolation from world events. In some communities peace organizations worked hard to keep citizens informed about the dangers of international alliances, war, and build-up of armaments. Again, these grassroots efforts succeeded wherever a core of motivated advocates existed.

In addition to the AFC there was also the Committee to Defend America by Aiding the Allies. William Allen White, a nationally prominent newspaper editor from Emporia, Kansas, founded this organization. As warfare spread across Europe in the late 1930s, White argued for nonintervention like the AFC but did argue for the granting of aid.

American women increasingly played prominent roles in the Women's International League for Peace and Freedom. Jane Addams and Emily Green Bach, both founding members, were awarded the Nobel Prize for peace in 1932 and later in 1946. Jeanette Rankin, the first woman elected to the House of Representatives, had voted against American entry into World War I in 1917. Her vote probably cost her position in Congress. Rankin, however, became a prominent peace advocate and lobbied in the 1930s for congressional investigations into why the United States became involved in World War I. Rankin was elected a second time to Congress—in November 1941. She cast the only vote against the declaration of war on December 8, 1941.

Isolationists, who preferred to identify themselves as noninterventionists, were supporters of the Neutrality Acts. They generally opposed Lend-Lease and other programs that would authorize the United States to aid nations suffering from the spread of war posed by Germany, Italy, and Japan. Isolationists, right up to the time of the Japanese attack on Pearl Harbor tended, to be sharp critics of the New Deal's growth of big gov-

ernment and especially its foreign policies that would encourage international connections and alliances.

A shift away from isolationism among the public could be detected in certain public polls in mid-1940. Many were forced to reconsider their opinions with continued German aggression in Europe. In March 1940 only 43 percent of Americans polled thought a German victory in the war in Europe would be a threat to the United States. Only three months later in July 1940 following the fall of France to German forces, 69 percent of Americans polled saw a German victory as a threat. Similarly in May 1940 only 35 percent of Americans polled favored aiding Britain in its war efforts. By September 1940, 60 percent of Americans polled favored aid to Britain. In November 1941 only 20 percent of Americans polled favored a declaration of war against Germany. That percentage rose significantly the following month to almost 90 percent as the vast majority favored declaration of war.

National Perspectives

The Nye Committee investigations dominated the national perspective on isolationism. Between 1934 and 1936 Senator Gerald P. Nye of North Dakota launched a series of investigations into why the United States had entered World War I. Nye was convinced that special interests had conspired to bring about American involvement. Therefore his committee, rather than pursuing objective findings, held preconceptions about what it would discover. Using its subpoena powers to obtain records and compel the testimony of witnesses, the Nye Committee examined specific companies, how they had lobbied Congress, and how much they had earned as a consequence of the war. It found, for example, that DuPont Company, a firm manufacturing paint, chemicals, and munitions, had profits of $5 million in 1914 and $82 million in 1916. To those who wanted to find villains, the Nye

Committee provided nominees. The work of the Nye Committee and passage of the Neutrality Acts in 1935 and 1939 were clear cases where the will of isolationists was felt nationally.

Former President Herbert Hoover was another who joined the isolationists camp during the 1930s. Following his election defeat to Roosevelt in November 1932 Hoover became increasingly critical of President Roosevelt's foreign policies. As he had earlier while in office, Hoover frequently blamed the Great Depression on international events and economic policies of foreign nations.

International Perspectives

Isolationism in the United States in the 1930s went right along with Britain's policy of "appeasement" under Prime Minister Neville Chamberlain. Chamberlain was prime minister from May 1937 to May 1940. Like U.S. citizens, British citizens had no desire for another major war in central Europe. Therefore Chamberlain sought to satisfy expansionist demands of Germany and Italy by giving in. He hoped the two aggressive fascist nations would become satisfied and become less active. For example, Chamberlain in April 1938 officially recognized Italy's new domination over Ethiopia hoping that would keep Italy from forming alliances with Germany. Chamberlain also kept Britain out of the Spanish Civil War that lasted from 1936 to 1939 and failed to aggressively respond to Hitler's establishment of armed forces in the Rhineland in opposition to the Treaty of Versailles and his takeover of parts of Czechoslovakia that Chamberlain condoned through a Munich Agreement. In addition Britain put strong reliance on the League of Nations for resolving conflicts before they went much further. Some in Britain challenged appeasement policies. They wanted to be more aggressive with the German and Italian threat, among these was Winston Churchill.

In September 1938 Chamberlain traveled to Germany three times to negotiate an avoidance of war. When Hitler seized all of Czechoslovakia in March 1939 Chamberlain finally dropped his appeasement policy and pledged armed support for Poland, Romania, and Greece in case of future attacks. Britain began a major rearmament program and started a military draft, the first peacetime draft in British history. When Germany attacked Poland on September 1, 1939, Chamberlain declared war on Germany. Fighting, however, did not immediately begin and when it did, Chamberlain and Britain were less than enthusiastic. Chamberlain resigned the day Germany invaded western European nations and was replaced by Churchill.

More About...
Independence for the Philippines

The United States went to war with Spain in 1898 triggered by a Cuban rebellion against Spanish rule. The Spanish response to the Cuban uprising was especially brutal and led public opinion in the United States to support ending Spanish control of its colonies. The United States essentially went to war to gain an empire. The war only lasted four months and was focused primarily in the Philippines and Cuba. The U.S. lost less than four hundred combat deaths, but over five thousand died from disease in the tropical settings. By capturing the Philippines the U.S. had established its first overseas empire. Following victory, however, forces were soon at work to dispose of major parts of it. Isolationism in the United States contributed to the decision to withdraw from the Philippines in the 1930s. A significant part of the pressure came from Philippine leaders who sent "independence missions" to Washington, DC. In 1933 Congress passed the Hare-Hawes-Cutting Act that set a date for American withdrawal. Support for the law also came from American farmers, a key constituent of the isolationist movement, who believed that the importation of sugar, coconut oil, rope, and other commodities without a tariff had unfairly cut their profits. As isolationists the farmers opposed such formal arrangements with other countries, even those acquired as a territory. Also at this time the United States was suffering from the Great Depression and farmers had suffered economically since the early 1920s. Although the Philippine legislature rejected the American plan, it accepted the Tydings-McDuffie Act that provided for 10 years of commonwealth status and then independence. Congress approved the commonwealth status on November 15, 1935. Residents of the Philippines elected a president and vice-president and the U.S. isolationist stance was further strengthened.

In addition French citizens feared another destructive war on its soil. The socialist party, the Popular Front, won national elections in May 1936, their policies leaning toward government control of industry

With the Great Wall in the background, Japanese infantrymen march along China's northern border in November, 1937. Japan's increasing aggression culminated in the attack on Pearl Harbor in 1941.

(AP/Wide World Photos. Reproduced by permission.)

caused fear in foreign investors. This led to much economic strife and made any organized resistance to developments in Germany and Italy difficult at best. Instability had taken hold of Spain as well. The monarchy gave way to a republic in 1931. As the new leaders moved further toward the Left much dissatisfaction grew. Finally by July 1936 the Spanish military led a revolt, which began the Spanish Civil War. The war dragged on through 1938 until the Nationalists won in March 1939. After losing 500,000 during the civil war, Spain maintained neutrality throughout World War II.

For some Americans, the growing world crisis in the 1930s only deepened their commitment to maintain isolation. It contributed to accepting the aggressive actions of Japan, Germany, and Italy, in half-hearted help to former allies, and in U.S. withdrawal from the Philippines where it had earlier maintained an economic and political interest. This anti-war sentiment was also widespread in Europe as Germany, Italy, and Japan took advantage of these sentiments. Ominous events began in 1933 when Germany withdrew from the League of Nations and an arms conference. Each following year

would bring new major events leading away from peace.

In 1935 international crises became more global in scope. Japan withdrew from an international conference held in London and Italy invaded and seized control of Ethiopia. Italy then also withdrew from the League of Nations following Germany's lead. In 1936 Hitler of Germany and Mussolini of Italy formed the Berlin-Rome Axis (alliance) and Civil War broke out in Spain. In 1937 Japan increased its aggression by invading northern China. Then in 1938 Hitler began Germany's massive expansionist campaign gaining control of one European nation after another. By 1939 Germany had taken over all of Czechoslovakia and invaded Poland with a mighty show of force. With the invasion of Poland, Britain and France declared war on Germany on September 3, 1939. This long series of events drove many Americans to think that their best defense was in further isolating their country from world problems. They strongly sought neutrality and non-intervention.

Isolationism shaped American foreign policy through the 1930s. The noble commitment to enter World War I plunged the nation into disengagement from world responsibilities, retreat from enforcing provisions of the Treaty of Versailles regarding Germany's military buildup, and into repeated efforts in Congress to define foreign policy along isolationist principles. As the world moved toward global war after 1935 the United States did little to help stop the events. In the end isolationism turned the country inward and left Americans blinded to worsening world events. Isolationism exacted a high price for shirking world responsibilities in a global community of which the United States was a part. Because of isolationism the United States was poorly prepared to go to war in 1941. The nation lacked stockpiles of strategic supplies, trained troops, and bases to mount a defensive war.

Impact

The threat of Soviet leader Joseph Stalin and communist expansion after World War II kept isolationism from returning to prominence. An international rivalry grew between the United States and the Soviet Union that drew in their various allies. Known as the Cold War (1946–1991), competition was fierce both politically and economically, but with little actual armed conflict. The Cold War began as the Soviet Union began installing communist governments in the various countries of Eastern Europe. The United States and Britain feared a permanent domination of the

Soviet Union in Eastern Europe and a spread to other parts of the continent.

The United States had learned powerful lessons from the isolationism of the 1930s. In response to the post-war Soviet expansion the United States built a system of alliances and agreements aimed at collective security with other nations. The United States assumed a prominent role as an international peace-keeper and arbiter in disputes. While the old controversies about isolationism versus internationalism did not totally go away, they never gained the same power they had possessed during the Great Depression.

For example the Marshall Plan was initiated by the United States in 1948 to economically rebuild Western Europe. This would make it stronger against the rise of Communist Party influence within their democracies. Through the plan United States gave massive amounts of economic aid to the nations of western and southern Europe. In response the nations were required to pursue joint planning to hasten their recovery from the Great Depression and war in the face of Soviet growing influence.

Militarily the United States and its European allies formed the North Atlantic Treaty Organization (NATO) in 1949. Its primary goal was to provide a unified response to growing Soviet influence in Eastern Europe by establishing a centralized leadership and structure. The alliance included 18 nations at the beginning. Other nations joined through the years including the Czech Republic, Hungary, and Poland in March 1999.

The U.S. provided $1 billion in military aid to NATO in 1950 to start operations. A series of U.S. generals beginning with World War II hero and future U.S. President General Dwight D. Eisenhower served as supreme Allied commanders. During its first 20 years $3 billion worth of infrastructure were built including airfields, military bases, and communications networks. A key function of NATO during the Cold War was deploying U.S. nuclear weapons at western European bases beginning in 1957. By the 1980s, 300,000 U.S. troops remained stationed in Western Europe.

The intensity of global political competition grew as Chinese communists took control of China in 1949. The following year in 1950 the communist leaders of North Korea, supported by the Soviet Union, invaded South Korea that was supported by the United States. The Korean War resulted involving American troops until 1953 when it ended in stalemate.

By 1958 an arms race grew with development of intercontinental ballistic missiles by both the United States and the Soviets. This race led to a major confrontation that took the world to the brink of nuclear war between the two superpowers in 1962 when it was discovered the Soviets had begun installing missiles in Cuba within easy reach of U.S. cities. A resulting agreement led to the Soviets removing the missiles. A Nuclear Test Ban Treaty followed in 1963 between the two nations that prohibited above ground testing of nuclear weapons.

A second phase of the arms race then began involving buildup of conventional and strategic forces for the next 25 years. During this period, actual military operations by the United States avoided direct confrontations with the Soviets in Europe. Rather they involved actions in Guatemala in 1954, an unsuccessful invasion of Cuba in 1961, conflict in the Dominican Republic in 1965, the long and bloody Vietnam War (1964–1975), and military action in Grenada in 1983. The Vietnam War involved unsuccessful efforts at keeping communist North Vietnam from gaining control of South Vietnam. Anti-war advocates during the Vietnam War era did not represent general isolationism, but rather non-intervention in specific events. Many still supported foreign alliances, military aid in other regions of the world, and membership in international organizations.

The collapse of eastern European communist regimes in 1989 and 1990 came in advance of the Soviet Union collapse in 1991. Fifteen newly independent nations including Russia resulted from that collapse. The Cold War had come to an end and NATO turned to other missions by the mid-1990s including peacekeeping operations in Eastern Europe in Bosnia and Herzegovina and the launching of air strikes against Bosnian Serb forces. The rise of international finance and the global economy by the 1990s essentially killed any lingering isolationism.

Notable People

William E. Borah (1865–1940). A Republican U.S. Senator from Idaho from 1907 to 1940, Borah was a criminal lawyer and famous orator. Borah was noted for his inconsistencies in Congress, voting against some measures while following his personal prejudices in favor of others. Although erratic he was generally considered a Progressive.

In foreign policy Borah was initially a militant nationalist (favoring one's own nation over others). He supported U.S. intervention in Mexico in 1914 and 1916 and the declaration of war against Germany in 1917. He then became a leader of the opposition

Biography:

Jeanette Rankin

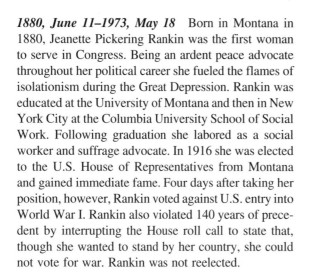

1880, June 11–1973, May 18 Born in Montana in 1880, Jeanette Pickering Rankin was the first woman to serve in Congress. Being an ardent peace advocate throughout her political career she fueled the flames of isolationism during the Great Depression. Rankin was educated at the University of Montana and then in New York City at the Columbia University School of Social Work. Following graduation she labored as a social worker and suffrage advocate. In 1916 she was elected to the U.S. House of Representatives from Montana and gained immediate fame. Four days after taking her position, however, Rankin voted against U.S. entry into World War I. Rankin also violated 140 years of precedent by interrupting the House roll call to state that, though she wanted to stand by her country, she could not vote for war. Rankin was not reelected.

In the 1920s Rankin worked for the Women's International League for Permanent Peace, the National Consumer's League, and the Women's International League for Peace and Freedom. She also worked nine years for the National Council for the Prevention of War. All of these organizations added impetus to the strong isolationist mood of the nation that opposed involvement of the United States in international alliances and foreign wars. In 1941 Rankin was reelected to Congress with isolationism still being a key national issue. Shortly after taking her post, however, she was faced on December 8 with President Roosevelt's request for a declaration of war. Asserting that killing more people would not help the situation, Rankin cast the only "no" vote on the declaration. With the isolationist mood immediately thwarted by the bombing of Pearl Harbor she was widely condemned and again not reelected.

For the next 20 years Rankin traveled widely. In 1968 she led the Jeanette Rankin Brigade, a march of thousands in Washington, DC, to protest the Vietnam War and America's actions in Southeast Asia. Rankin participated in numerous anti-war protests and continued her advocacy for civil rights, child welfare, and women. She died on May 18, 1973.

against American involvement in the international League of Nations. His isolationism hardened when in 1924 he became chairman of the Senate Foreign Relations Committee. He was consistently suspicious of presidents and treaties with foreign nations. He opposed U.S. intervention in Latin America and the Far East and involvement in a World Court. Yet he praised Franklin D. Roosevelt's Good Neighbor Policy toward Latin America and diplomatic recognition of the communist Soviet Union. Borah supported the Neutrality Acts and opposed the sale of arms by "cash and carry" to Britain. Congress finally approved such aid in spite of Borah's opposition.

James Middleton Cox (1870–1957). A newspaper publisher and politician, Cox grew up in Ohio. His career in journalism led to ownership of newspapers and, in turn, entry into politics. Cox gained election as a Democrat to Congress in 1908 and was elected governor of Ohio in 1912 where he served three terms. Cox supported Progressive reforms such as Prohibition, woman suffrage, and a state highway system. In 1920 the Democrat Party on the forty-fourth round of voting by state representatives to the national convention nominated Cox as its candidate for president. He

mounted an active campaign strongly endorsing internationalist positions such as membership in the League of Nations. Cox was soundly defeated in 1920 and never again sought public office. His defeat marked a hardening of public opinion on isolation. Non-interventionist attitudes in the United States would remain a major political factor for the next 20 years.

John T. Flynn (1882–1964). An avid journalist, Flynn was born in Maryland. Though he did not attend college, he earned a law degree from Georgetown University in Washington, DC. He never practiced law though as he devoted much of his energy as a freelance journalist criticizing big business and big government. Initially he supported Franklin D. Roosevelt, however, as the New Deal programs developed he turned against the New Deal. In 1938 Flynn helped organize the Keep America Out of War Committee (KAOWC), serving as its national chairman. The KAOWC was a circle of influential isolationists who tried to coordinate noninterventionist activities.

In 1940 Flynn, enraged with Roosevelt's plan to send 50 destroyers to Britain to assist with their war effort, called for the president's impeachment. He also joined General Robert Wood, head of Sears, Roebuck

Charles Lindbergh delivers a speech at the America First Rally in Manhattan Center on April 25, 1941. The public interpreted some of Lindbergh's comments as anti-Semitic, pro-Nazi, and unpatriotic. (AP/Wide World Photos. *Reproduced by permission.*)

and Company, to form the America First Committee (AFC) that by 1941 engaged an estimated 800,000 members who were isolationists. Flynn headed AFC activities in New York City, delivering radio speeches, writing pamphlets, assembling public rallies, and devising advertisements to support non-intervention in Europe's affairs. Although Flynn supported the U.S. decision to go to war in 1941, he remained convinced that Roosevelt had helped foment the involvement. In 1944 he published *The Truth About Pearl Harbor,* a controversial criticism of the president. In 1945 he expanded it into *The Final Secret About Pearl Harbor.*

Charles Augustus Lindbergh (1902–1974). Lindbergh was born in Detroit, Michigan, to a father who was a progressive Republican and served in the U.S. House of Representatives for 10 years. Young Lindbergh joined the Army Air Service, forerunner to the U.S. Air Force, in 1925. The famed pilot of the "Spirit of St. Louis," Lindbergh made the first solo flight in 1927 between New York and Paris dramatizing the feasibility of flight over the Atlantic Ocean. For this he won the Congressional Medal of Honor and gained tremendous popularity in the United States. In 1938, however, he accepted the Service Cross of the German Eagle, conferred by Herman Goering, head of the German air force.

Upon returning to the United States in 1939 Lindbergh became an ardent advocate of isolationism. Lindbergh had grasped the strength of the German military buildup, sensed the weaknesses in France and Britain, and did not believe that American interests could be served by intervention in European affairs. In the spring of 1941 he joined the America First Committee and became one of its leading public speakers. His speeches drew considerable criticism, especially his comments at Des Moines, Iowa, on September 11, 1941. Many began to believe that Lindbergh was pro-Nazi and anti-Semitic. With Japan's attack on Pearl Harbor in December 1941, Lindbergh threw his energies behind the war effort, but he could not regain his Air Force commission. He fought in the South Pacific as a civilian pilot. In 1954 President Eisenhower restored his commission and appointed him brigadier general. Lindbergh's *The Spirit of St. Louis* (1953) won the Pulitzer Prize for autobiography.

Gerald Prentice Nye (1892–1971). A U.S. Senator from North Dakota, Nye was born in Wisconsin and reared in that state. Following graduation from high school, Nye spent 15 years working as a newspaper writer in Wisconsin, Iowa, and North Dakota. He was actively involved in the Non-Partisan League, a radical agrarian (farmer) organization. In 1925 Nye gained appointment by the governor of North Dakota to the Senate and was later elected in 1926, 1932, and 1938.

Nye was an ardent advocate for farmers. After 1919, he increasingly believed that American involvement overseas met the financial interests of eastern businessmen and bankers but not Midwest farmers. He was a supporter of some parts of Roosevelt's farm relief program. Beginning in 1934 Nye headed a Senate committee investigating the U.S. munitions industry. The committee focused on the profits allegedly made on preparations for and mounting U.S. engagement in World War I. Based on his findings Nye campaigned for neutrality legislation in Congress from 1934 to 1937. His attitudes led him in 1939 to oppose President Roosevelt's efforts to repeal the Neutrality Acts to assist victims of German, Italian, and Japanese aggression. In 1940 and 1941 Nye served as a leading speaker of the America First Committee. When Japan attacked Pearl Harbor in December 1941, Nye supported the war effort but was defeated in his reelection bid in 1944.

Primary Sources

Support for Neutrality

U.S. Senator Bennett Clark of Missouri was one of the Midwest U.S. senators supporting passage of the neutrality acts. The acts would limit the ability of Roosevelt to form ties with foreign nations that might lead to war. Following passage of the first neutrality act, Clark sought to further sell ideas of isolationism to the American public through an article in the December 1935 issue of *Harpers Magazine* (pp. 1–9).

Is there a way to keep America out of war? ...

At present the desire to keep the United States from becoming involved in any war between foreign nations seems practically unanimous among the rank and file of American citizens; but it must be remembered there was an almost equally strong demand to keep us out of the last war ...

Such a policy (isolationism) must be built upon a program to safeguard our neutrality. No lesson of the World War is more clear than that such a policy cannot be improvised after war breaks out. It must be determined in advance, before it is too late to apply reason. I contend with all possible earnestness that if we want to avoid being drawn into this war now forming, or any other future war, we must formulate a definite, workable policy of neutral relations with belligerent nations.

Some of us in the Senate, particularly the members of the Munitions Investigation Committee, have delved rather deeply into the matter of how the United States has been drawn into past wars, and what forces are at

wok to frighten us again into the traps ... As a result of these studies, Senator Nye and I introduced the three proposals for neutrality legislation which were debated so vigorously in the last session of the Congress ...

Senator Nye and I made no claims then, and make none now, that the neutrality proposals will provide an absolute and infallible guarantee against our involvement in war. But we do believe that the United States can stay out of war if it wants to, and if its citizens understand what is necessary to preserve our neutrality. We feel that the temporary legislation already passed and the legislation we shall vigorously push at the coming session of the Congress point the only practical way ...

Some declare we are about to haul down the American flag, and in a future war the belligerents will trample on our rights and treat us with contempt ... The admirals (of the navy), I am told, objected strenuously when the State Department suggested a new policy of neutrality somewhat along these lines.

I deny with every fiber of my being that our national honor demands that we must sacrifice the flower of our youth to safeguard the profits of a privileged few."

Roosevelt Presses for Action

After winning election to an unprecedented third term as president, Franklin Roosevelt delivered a fireside chat in which he dramatically described the foreign dangers he foresaw. The president stressed the need for the United States to take more action to help stop German expansion (from Franklin Roosevelt. *The Public Papers and Addresses of Franklin D. Roosevelt, 1940 Volume.* New York: The Macmillan Company, 1941, pp. 633–644).

This is not a fireside chat on war. It's a talk on national security ...

Never before since Jamestown and Plymouth Rock has our American civilization been in such danger as now ...

The Nazi masters of Germany have made it clear that they intend not only to dominate all life and thought in their own country, but also to enslave the whole of Europe, and then to use the resources of Europe to dominate the rest of the world ...

In view of the nature of this undeniable threat, it can be asserted, properly and categorically, that the United States has no right or reason to encourage talk of peace, until the day shall come when there is a clear intention on the part of the aggressor nations to abandon all thought of dominating or conquering the world ...

Some of our people like to believe that wars in Europe and in Asia are of no concern to us. But it is a matter of most vital concern to us that European and Asiatic warmakers should not gain control of the oceans which lead to this hemisphere ...

If Great Britain goes down, the Axis powers will control the continents of Europe, Asia, Africa, Australasia, and the high seas—and they will be in a position to bring enormous military and naval resources against this hemisphere. It is no exaggeration to say that all of us, in all the Americas, would be living at the point of a gun—a gun loaded with explosive bullets, economic as well as military ...

[D]efinitely there is danger ahead—danger against which we must prepare. But we well know that we cannot escape danger, or the fear of danger, by crawling into bed and pulling the covers over our heads ...

The experience of the past two years has proven beyond doubt that no nation can appease the Nazis. No man can tame a tiger into a kitten by stroking it. There can be no appeasement with ruthlessness ...

Democracy's fight against world conquest is being greatly aided, and must be more greatly aided, by the rearmament of the United States and by sending every ounce and every ton of munitions and supplies that we can possibly spare to help the defenders who are in the front lines ...

We must be the great arsenal of democracy.

Famed Aviator Promotes Isolationism

Charles A. Lindbergh became a featured speaker for the American Freedom Committee (AFC) in promoting isolationism. Lindbergh had spent several years in Europe in the 1930s and was impressed with Germany's armament buildup led by Hitler. Lindbergh returned to the United States and argued for the United States to not get entangled with those superior forces of Hitler. Many believed his racist views mirrored those of Hitler and the Nazi Party, which promoted a pure white race. His speech of October 13, 1939, "Neutrality and War" was broadcast over the Mutual Broadcasting System (from Charles Lindbergh. *The Radio Addresses of Col. Charles A. Lindbergh, 1939–1940.* 1940, pp. 5–8).

> Tonight, I speak again to the people of this country who are opposed to the United States entering the war which is now going on in Europe. We are faced with the need of deciding on a policy of American neutrality. The future of our nation and of our civilization rests upon the wisdom and foresight we use ...
>
> If we repeal the arms embargo with the idea of assisting one of the warring sides to overcome the other, then why mislead ourselves by talk of neutrality? Those who advance this argument should admit openly that repeal is a step toward war. The next step would be the extension of credit, and the next step would be the sending of American troops ...
>
> Our bond with Europe is a bond of race and not of political ideology. We had to fight a European army to establish democracy in this country. It is the European race we must preserve; political progress will follow. Racial strength is vital—politics, a luxury. If the white race is ever seriously threatened, it may then be time for us to take our part in its protection, to fight side by side with the English, French, and Germans, but not with one against the other for our mutual destruction ...

The leaders of the European Axis powers, Benito Mussolini, of Italy, and Adolf Hitler, of Germany, in 1939. (Archive Photos. Reproduced by permission.)

> I do not want to see American bombers dropping bombs which will kill and mutilate European children, even if they are not flown by American pilots. But I am perfectly willing to see American anti-aircraft guns shooting American shells at invading bombers over any European country. And I believe that most of you who are listening tonight will agree with me.

A View from the Media

The editors of the journal *New Republic* noted in the May 20, 1940 issue (pp. 703–704) the struggle between President Franklin Roosevelt in trying to respond in some meaningful way to the crisis in Europe and the prevailing isolationist mood in the nation. His steadily pushing on providing materials to the European nations kept constant tension between the two sides—isolationists and interventionists.

> Prevailing American sentiment during Mr. Roosevelt's eight years in office has been strongly isolationist in the sense of not wishing to be drawn into any foreign conflict. As a result of this struggle, American policy has been less interventionist than the President would have liked and more interventionist than most of the American people have realized or would welcome if they had.
>
> Our neutrality law was an attempt to profit by the lessons of the last war and prevent our being drawn in again ...

The neutrality law of course does not mean that Americans are impartial. About 86 percent of them, according to Dr. Gallup, are pro-Ally and only one percent are pro-German. The neutrality law was intended not to enforce impartiality but to set up as far as possible legal equality of belligerents ...

The technical neutrality but actual unneutrality of the Americans is approaching another great test. Britain and France are now buying war materials in this country on a large scale ... It is said that airplane orders alone will amount to about $1,000,000,000 in the next eighteen months.

Suggested Research Topics

- Following four years of residency in Europe, famed American aviator, Charles A. Lindbergh returned to the United States in the late 1930s and took a strong, public position that the United States should stay out of Europe's war. He became a leading member of the America First Committee. Examine: 1) Lindbergh's advocacy against American involvement in Europe, 2) charges that Lindbergh was pro-Nazi, 3) charges that Lindbergh was anti-Semitic, and 4) the consequences of his isolationism to Lindbergh's reputation.

- One of the founders and chief publicists of the America First Committee, John T. Flynn was a talented and well-published writer. Examine Flynn's writings from 1939 to 1945 in magazine articles and pamphlets to explore the arguments he made against America's involvement in international affairs and, most especially, World War II. Use the Internet and other resources to carry out this research.

- Many of the leading isolationists in Congress in 1933 were also politically progressive, meaning they supported government action in bringing about social change. Therefore they supported much of the early New Deal programs of President Roosevelt. Why specifically did isolationists support Roosevelt's economic relief and recovery programs? What made them change their support by 1935?

- Search the World Wide Web for a copy of the "Nye Report," 74th Congress, 2nd Session, February 24, 1936. What did the committee find out about the various industries it looked at? Do you think based on this report that the isolationists had a strong case that the United States was wrongly led to war?

Bibliography

Sources

Chatfield, Charles. *For Peace and Justice: Pacificism in America, 1914–41.* Knoxville, TN: The University of Tennessee Press.

Cole, Wayne S. *Roosevelt & the Isolationists, 1932–45.* Lincoln: University of Nebraska Press, 1983.

———. *Senator Gerald P. Nye and American Foreign Relations.* Minneapolis: University of Minnesota Press, 1962.

Cull, Nicholas J. *Selling War: The British Propaganda Campaign Against American "Neutrality" in World War II.* New York: Oxford University Press, 1995.

Devlin, Patrick. *Too Proud to Fight: Woodrow Wilson's Neutrality.* New York: Oxford University Press, 1975.

Divine, Robert A. *The Illusion of Neutrality.* Chicago: The University of Chicago Press, 1962.

Jonas, Manfred. *Isolationism in America, 1935–1941.* Ithaca, NY: Cornell University Press, 1966.

Schneider, James C. *Should America Go To War?: The Debate Over Foreign Policy in Chicago, 1939–1941.* Chapel Hill: University of North Carolina Press, 1989.

Further Reading

Buell, Raymond Leslie. *Isolated America.* New York: Alfred A. Knopf, 1940.

Cole, Wayne S. *Charles A. Lindbergh and the Battle Against American Intervention in World War II.* New York: Harcourt Braces Jovanovich, 1974.

Curti, Merle. *Peace or War: The American Struggle, 1636–1936.* New York: W. W. Norton & Company, 1936.

Johnson, Walter. *The Battle Against Isolation.* New York: Da Capo Press, 1973.

Stenehjem, Michele Flynn. *An American First: John T. Flynn and the American First Committee.* New Rochelle, NY: Arlington House Publishers, 1976.

See Also

Global Impact; New Deal (First, and Its Critics); World War II Mobilization

Journalism

Introduction

The increasing concentration of the American population in cities during the late nineteenth and early twentieth centuries led to major cultural developments. More and more children had access to education and the literacy rate skyrocketed. Better education spawned a thirst for knowledge and the American public looked to newspapers, magazines, and books to satisfy it.

Newspaper circulation increased dramatically both in large cities and smaller communities. Giants in the journalism field such as Joseph Pulitzer, William Randolph Hearst, and Edward Wyllis Scripps purchased and merged big city newspapers. Advancing printing techniques, expanded communication, improved newsgathering efficiency, and increased advertising revenues turned huge profits for the newspaper organizations that quickly became big corporate businesses.

The onset of the Great Depression in late 1929 hit the newspaper business hard largely due to a major decline in advertising revenue. Loss of the revenue meant less money for wages for employees and less money for production costs. Between 1929 and 1933 advertising revenue decreased by approximately 40 percent. Most newspapers reduced operating expenses by firing reporters and editors, lowering wages, and increasing workloads of those that stayed. The economic difficulties caused many newspapers to fail or merge with larger, healthier papers or newspaper chains.

Chronology:

February 1930: Henry Luce publishes first issue of *Fortune* magazine.

September 29, 1930: Lowell Thomas begins a nightly radio news broadcast for NBC.

1931: Walter Lippmann begins his syndicate column "Today and Tomorrow" for the *New York Herald Tribune.*

March 12, 1933: President Roosevelt, understanding the power of radio, delivers his first "fireside chat" to the American public.

1933: President Roosevelt begins the first of his informal and informative presidential news conferences.

1933: First Lady Eleanor Roosevelt begins her weekly news conferences open only to women journalists.

1933: The American Society of Newspaper Editors urges all newspaper editors to set aside more space for interpretation and explanation of the news.

December 1933: Heywood Broun founds the American Newspaper Guild.

June 10, 1934: Congress authorizes the Federal Communications Commission (FCC) to oversee the nation's communications industry.

September 1934: Radio stations WGN in Chicago, WOR in Newark, New Jersey, WXYZ in Detroit, and WLW in Cincinnati organize the Mutual Broadcasting System (MBS).

1935: William Randolph Hearst, overseeing the largest publishing empire in the United States, calls the New Deal a "Raw Deal."

1935: Movie houses begin showing the *March of Time,* a series of documentary short films produced for the news publishing group Time, Inc. Originally a radio series beginning in 1931 the short films proceed to be the feature film of the day.

1935: George H. Gallup founds the American Institute of Public Opinion that begins conducting political surveys.

1936: Dorothy Thompson, with the *New York Herald Tribune,* begins writing her syndicated column, "On the Record."

1936: Henry R. Luce, founder in 1923 of the news magazine *Time,* founds the first magazine devoted to photojournalism, *Life.*

1936: The voting public reelects President Roosevelt to the presidency of the United States in a landslide victory even though approximately 80 percent of American newspapers endorse Republican candidate Al Landon.

1938: From CBS studios in New York City reporter Hans von Kaltenborn interprets and broadcasts the "Munich crisis" as events unfolded in Germany for 18 straight days.

August 1939: *Fortune* publishes results of a commissioned Elmo Roper survey comprehensively covering the views of the public toward the press.

For those newspapers that survived the early years of the Great Depression, the 1930s brought major changes to news coverage. President Franklin Delano Roosevelt's (served 1933–1945) policies of reform and relief, also known as the New Deal, gave government far more power to reach into the lives of citizens than in any previous period in United States history. The interest in and coverage of government by journalists expanded accordingly. In an effort to help the public better understand the complex issues of the 1930s, reporting began to include interpretation of the news in addition to presentation of the facts. Published nationwide, syndicated columnists wrote columns that explained the news from their particular point of view

and wrote to the nation as a whole rather than a particular community. Predominately conservative, the columnists could express themselves more freely than local editors on politics and such sensitive topics as government relief efforts and unemployment. Each gathered a faithful following from across the country. As an example of the influence they wielded, when columnist Walter Lippmann turned against the New Deal, many of his readers went with him.

Only in its infancy in 1930, radio increasingly invaded the field of news reporting that had been previously left entirely to newspapers. Wealthy businessmen not heavily affected by the Great Depression bought up local radio stations, creating chains of radio networks. Even in the worst year of the Depression, 1932, early major radio networks such as National Broadcasting Company (NBC) and Columbia Broadcasting System (CBS) turned profits. Many advertisers, realizing they could reach more people at less cost, switched their business to radio. Radio journalists such as Lowell Thomas and Hans von Kaltenborn reported daily events and added their own commentary as radio journalism developed and prospered.

As the political and military crisis in Europe grew, radio commentators found themselves in the spotlight relaying to the American people events as they unfolded. Hitler's Germany was expanding control rapidly throughout much of Europe and Italy had taken over Ethiopia in North Africa. With the entrance of the United States into World War II (1939–1945), the profession of journalism within newspapers, magazines, and radio had matured to the point of keeping Americans informed with up to the minute accounts from both abroad and at home.

Issue Summary

Specialized News Coverage of Government

Following the stock market crash in October 1929 action or lack of action by President Herbert Hoover's (served 1929–1933) administration became a standard topic of news reporting. As President Roosevelt's New Deal programs began to make government a force in the lives of all Americans news coverage increased dramatically and reporters were forced to take new approaches to gathering the news. The New Deal consisted of a combination of diverse federal economic and social programs designed to bring relief to those most affected by the Depression. Rather than a few individuals covering the entire spectrum of government for a newspaper, a full reporting staff developed. Business and economic policies, agriculture, labor, and social work each came to be covered by reporters specializing in each particular area. For example two journalists became the first news specialists in agricultural affairs. Alfred D. Stedman, a reporter from St. Paul, Minnesota, and Theodore C. Alford, reporter for the *Kansas City Star* came to Washington, DC, in 1929 ready to exercise their expertise as correspondents on the agricultural scene. Likewise the rise of labor issues and New Deal labor policies moved labor news coverage to the forefront. Louis Stark, reporter for the *New York Times* became the dean of U.S. labor reporters. John Leary of the *New York World* along with Stark set up their base of operations in Washington, DC, in 1933.

With the increasing complexity of the nation's affairs during the Depression and the pre-World War II years, journalists realized that merely reporting the facts did not adequately cover the issues. The "why" became as important as the "who did what and when." The American Society of Newspaper Editors in 1933 issued statements explaining that in the light of rapidly evolving national and world events men and women were expressing an interest in public affairs to a greater extent than ever before. The society urged newspaper editors to set aside more and more space for interpretation and explanation of the news to better enable the average reader to understand the important events of the time.

Syndicated Columnists

The rise of the syndicated political column was a response by the journalism profession to increasingly interpret national and world news. Syndication of a column means selling a piece or column written by one journalist to many newspapers across the country for publication at the same time. The signed columns were often printed on the editorial pages and became commonplace in most newspapers.

Before the late 1920s syndicated columns tended to be humorous columns or concentrated on reviewing literature. By the end of the 1920s, however, journalists Frank Kent of the *Baltimore Sun,* David Lawrence writing for various Washington, DC, publications, and Mark Sullivan of the *New York Herald Tribune* had established columns commenting on economic and political affairs. Walter Lippmann joined the trio by 1931 as a columnist with the *New York Herald Tribune.* By 1940 Lippmann's column appeared in some 165 larger papers and he was the highest paid columnist in America.

During the 1930s numerous other syndicated columnists caught the public's attention for their interpretation of the politics of the Depression. Raymond Clapper's "In Washington" column, for the *Washington Post* presented a balanced interpretation of the political scene of Washington, DC. Based on his excellent reporting abilities Clapper's opinions on national and foreign problems were highly respected. Conservative Westbrook Pegler delivered a personalized type of political column that seemed to speak directly to the reader. His writing attacked labor unions, New Dealers, who were supporters of New Deal policy, and members of President Roosevelt's family. The affable Heywood Broun began his newspaper days in 1910 as a reporter for the *New York Morning Telegraph.* In 1921 he went to the *New York World* where he began writing his column, "It Seems

Two salesmen man their newspaper stand. Newspapers became an increasingly popular and inexpensive way for Americans to get their news during the Depression. (AP/Wide World Photos. Reproduced by permission.)

to Me." Writing on a wide array of national matters, Broun usually leaned to the liberal side of political issues. His friendly writing style, a departure from the more cold, less friendly styles of previous years, gathered a large reading audience in the 1920s and 1930s.

Dorothy Thompson, a widely syndicated woman columnist, was an expert in international affairs. She served as the European correspondent for the *Philadelphia Public Ledger* and the *New York Post* in the 1920s and early 1930s. Upon her return to the United States

Thompson joined the *New York Herald Tribune* where in 1936 she began her syndicated column, "On the Record." She generally criticized Roosevelt for not going far enough with his social reforms and wealth redistribution. Thompson, however, supported him for a third term as president because in her opinion he would be able to stand up to Adolf Hitler's aggression in Europe.

Meanwhile in 1932, a second type of political column emerged—a personalized or gossip type column.

This type of column was greatly welcomed by readers as they were looking for more ways to escape from the bad news of the Depression whenever possible. A spin off from the best seller *Washington Merry-Go-Round* published in 1931, the column was written by the book's authors, Drew Pearson of the *Baltimore Sun* and Robert S. Allen of the *Christian Science Monitor*. The co-authors developed the column into a political behind the scenes column. Roosevelt's New Deal policies were both increasing government's role in people's daily lives as well as making government more accessible to the public. As a result interest in the day-to-day affairs of government was greatly increasing. Roosevelt's warmth and charm expressed in his speeches and fireside chats on the radio were mirrored by some of their new columns. It gave people a greater sense of security. By 1940 this syndicated column, given the same name as the book, appeared in about 350 papers.

More of a news item itself, George H. Gallup's American Institute of Public Opinion surveys began appearing in many newspapers in the later 1930s. Gallup's Institute, founded in 1935, covered various social and political questions. In the 1936 presidential election Gallup's final poll accurately reflected the popular vote while other polls predicted Republican candidate Alfred Landon to be the victor. Landon carried only two states, overwhelmingly losing to Franklin Roosevelt.

Criticism of the Press

Many journalists, including major syndicated columnists, tended to be for the most part quite conservative and often reflected the big business and management viewpoint. As a result the press came under a great deal of criticism by the American public. Many newspapers were criticized over their reporting of the Great Depression when much of the public perceived that the papers were downplaying the hardships. Especially in the early Depression years of 1929 to 1932 the newspapers responded to calls by politicians not to panic the American public. After the collapse of the stock market in the fall of 1929 President Herbert Hoover pressured journalists to report only the positive side of government relief efforts and to assure Americans the crisis would end quickly. He cautioned reporters to not overdo their coverage of the worsening economic circumstances that he argued would only make the situation more difficult. Complying, many newspapers of the day appeared to divorce themselves from Depression hardships and attempted to maintain a discreet silence until the Depression passed. As a result the public believed the press did little more than issue propaganda that served the special interest of

business. Consequently the press was never more distrusted by the American people.

Those Americans who supported Roosevelt believed his sweeping victories of 1932 and 1936 should signal to journalists that Americans by and large supported Roosevelt's proposed socioeconomic reforms. Those same Americans often viewed the press bitterly, seeing it as undemocratic and stuck in a conservative mode not at all reflective of the general public. In 1936 more than 80 percent of the press had opposed Roosevelt yet he won the reelection to the presidency by a landslide. A group of publishers known as the "press lords" were most heavily criticized. Reading about the "press lords" proved very interesting for many Americans. Those "press lords" included publishers William Randolph Hearst, Colonel Robert R. McCormick, and Roy W. Howard.

Conservatism and the Press Lords

Hearst by 1935 oversaw a publishing empire of 26 dailies (newspapers published every day) and 17 Sunday editions in 19 cities. These newspapers represented 13.6 percent of the total daily circulation and 24.2 percent of Sunday circulation in the United States. Hearst also controlled several news service agencies, 13 magazines, and eight radio stations. He had helped to elect Roosevelt in 1932, but by 1935 Hearst called the New Deal a "Raw Deal." Believing the government was wrongfully intruding into business and American lives, Hearst views turned radically conservative and very anti-government. Anyone who happened to disagree with Hearst, he immediately labeled a "communist." He denounced the new Social Security Act and supported Republican presidential candidate Alfred Landon in 1936. Critics denounced Hearst but his empire was powerful and he weathered public attacks.

Colonel Robert R. McCormick pushed the *Chicago Tribune*, founded in 1847, toward an ultra-conservative stance competing with Hearst's conservative *Chicago Examiner*. On the front page of the *Tribune* he printed daily boxes that called on American voters to save the United States from President Roosevelt. In 1937 Washington correspondents voted the *Tribune* the second least reliable and least fair newspaper. They voted the Hearst papers as having the most unfair reportage of all major newspapers.

The third press lord receiving a great deal of criticism in the 1930s was Roy W. Howard of the Scripps-Howard dailies. The predominately Midwestern dailies established by Edward Wyllis Scripps in the early twentieth century had been known as "people's papers." As Howard came to dominate management of the chain,

		Upper	Lower			
News Source	**Wealthy**	**Middle Class**	**Middle Class**	**Poor**	**Negro**	**Total**
Newspapers	70.7 %	70.0%	63.6%	58.1%	51.6%	63.8%
Radio	17.8	21.0	26.8	31.3	28.3	25.4
Magazines	4.5	2.7	1.9	1.3	3.1	2.3
Friends	1.1	1.2	2.5	4.8	12.2	3.4
All other	1.2	1.1	1.5	1.0	1.6	1.3
Don't know	0.7	0.5	0.6	0.8	1.9	0.7

Where Did They Get Their News? News Resources Used Most Frequently in 1939
by Social Division

Most people, regardless of race or social status, got their news from newspapers and radio in 1939. (The Gale Group.)

however, the papers took a very conservative turn. Although the Scripps-Howard dailies ranked third in circulation behind Hearst and McCormick papers, many Americans became dismayed that their "people's papers" had turned away from the people's president—Roosevelt.

Books abounded in the 1930s that sought to expose the "press lords." Publications included Ferdinand Lundberg's *Imperial Hearst* (1936), *The Changing American Newspaper* (1937) by Herbert Brucker, George Seldes' famous *Lords of the Press* (1938), and *American House of Lords* (1939) by Harold L. Ickes. Ickes was an influential New Dealer, as those who supported Roosevelt's New Deal policies were called, who served in numerous government capacities under President Roosevelt.

The Everyday Reporter of the 1930s

Despite the growing influence of the syndicated columnists and the wealth of the "press lords," the life of the everyday reporter was generally neither particularly adventurous nor glamorous. The profession had become, during the Depression, one of the most crowded and poorly paid of all white-collar occupations. Between 1929 and 1933 newspaper advertising revenue fell 40 percent and radio, offering more exposure for less cost, seized much of advertisers' business. Those newspapers that did not fold reduced operating expenses by firing reporters and editors, lowering pay of those they retained, and increasing workloads. Working hours were very long, six days a week for ten to twelve hours each day, and job insecurity was a constant worry. Being dismissed during the depth of the Depression was frightening since finding another news job would most likely be impossible.

While other workers such as typesetters in newspaper plants were unionized and able to work for improved benefits by the beginning of the 1930s, men and women reporters, columnists, and desk workers remained unorganized and underpaid. This in part was the fault of the reporters themselves who in better days had resisted unionization. They resisted because they feared the loss of the freedom of their unconventional and "romantic" profession. The economic crisis of the Depression in the summer of 1933, however, had many reporters talking of a newspaper writers' union. Then on August 7, 1933, a syndicated columnist for the *New York World-Telegram,* the liberal maverick Heywood Broun, called for the formation of a newspaper writers' union and dedicated himself to the task. The timing was right and newspaper people rallied to the call. Reporters in Cleveland formed the first local in what came to be known as the Newspaper Guild on August 20, 1933. In Washington, DC, on December 15 of that same year, representatives from various cities officially founded the Guild. By the next convention in June 1934, the Guild had eight thousand members. During the next five years the Guild was actively involved in about 20 strikes, the most bitter lasted 508 days and was against the Hearst newspapers in Chicago. The Guild joined the Congress of Industrial Organizations (CIO) in 1937, extended its membership base to office employees and had negotiated 75 newspaper contracts by 1938. By the end of the 1930s newspaper employees within the Guild saw their economic conditions stabilize.

President Roosevelt and the Journalists

Irregardless of a particular journalist's political persuasion, as soon as Franklin D. Roosevelt assumed

More About...

Major News Stories, 1929–1940

The major ongoing story of the 1930s was the political-economic-social events surrounding the Great Depression. Key stories emerging from the Depression era were the Wall Street Stock Market crash of October 24, 1929; the ineffectiveness of President Hoover from 1930 to 1932; the bonus army march, World War I veterans marching on Washington, DC, to demand immediate payment of a promised bonus in 1932; the 1932 landslide election of Franklin D. Roosevelt to the presidency of the United States; the bank holidays of 1933; the various relief and recovery policies, programs, and agencies of the New Deal; President Roosevelt's reelection in 1936; and his failed attempt to enlarge the Supreme Court.

One sensational story stands out above all others: the kidnapping and murder of aviator Charles Lindbergh's son in 1932; the subsequent hunt for and arrest of Bruno Hauptmann in 1934, his trial and ultimate electrocution in 1936. Major trials covered in addition to those of Hauptmann and Capone, were District Attorney Thomas E. Dewey's prosecution of corruption in the government of New York City, and the Scottsboro trials that lasted almost seven years and focused on the civil rights of blacks. Other crime stories included the gang murder in 1930 of Jake Lingle, a reporter for the *Chicago Tribune* who turned out to be a gangster himself; the arrest of Chicago gang leader Al Capone; and the killing of outlaw John Dillinger in 1934. Assassination stories included the attempted shooting of President-elect Roosevelt in

1933 in Miami, Florida, and the murder of Senator Huey Long of Louisiana in Baton Rouge in 1935.

Top on the list of public interest stories of the decade was the birth of the Dionne quintuplets in North Bay, Ontario, Canada. Another story that captivated Americans was the abdication (giving up the throne) of King Edward VIII of England in 1936 to marry his love, an American Mrs. Wallis Simpson.

The great disaster stories of the decade were the Chicago stockyards fire of 1934; the great drought and dust storms throughout the Midwest between 1934 and 1936; the flood of the Ohio Valley in 1936; and the 1938 New England hurricane.

A human tragedy was the death of Will Rogers, a much-loved humorist, in an airplane crash in Alaska in 1935.

Top sports figures covered by the press were, among others, boxers Joe Louis and Jack Dempsey, baseball heroes Babe Ruth and Lou Gehrig, and women athletes, such as figure skater Sonja Henie and all-round athlete Mildred "Babe" Didrikson Zaharias.

As the decade progressed the American press carried more news of foreign conflicts. Major stories were the Spanish Civil War, which began in 1936, the undeclared war between China and Japan, and the Munich Agreement of 1938 whereby Great Britain and France accepted Germany's demand for territory in Czechoslovakia in return for a halt to Germany's aggression.

---

the presidency of the United States in March 1933, it was obvious to all reporters that the new president would pursue a "new deal" relationship with the press. President Roosevelt clearly enjoyed the give and take of a news conference. Against his staff's advice Roosevelt's press conferences were undertaken with no prior written questions. He was lively, serious, happy, or somber, whatever the news of the moment dictated, and his voice was always reassuring and sincere. President Roosevelt's conferences were informal in tone and he often met with reporters in his White House office. This informality and honest informativeness prevailed throughout his 12 years in office.

Meeting the press an average of 83 times a year, Roosevelt held a total of 998 presidential news conferences. This average was twice the number of press conferences President Harry Truman (1945–1953) held, and almost four times the combined number of conferences held by Presidents Eisenhower (1953–1961), Kennedy (1961–1963), and Johnson (1963–1969).

President Roosevelt's news conferences became the regular show in Washington. He knew how to "break" a story as well as any journalist. In longer conferences he would thoroughly answer up to 30 different questions, all the while masterfully managing the group of reporters.

Members of the Milwaukee Newspaper Guild on strike against Hearst newspapers. William Randolph Hearst was notorious for his refusal to recognize the union. (Archive Photos. Reproduced by permission.)

Gradually rising worries over the growth of government brought by New Deal policies and America's involvement in foreign affairs triggered increasingly critical questioning of Roosevelt by journalists. Whether supporting Roosevelt's views or not, journalists considered Roosevelt a newspaperman's President. Not only was he skillful with the traditional newspaper journalists, but he seemed to instinctively understand the potential and power of radio broadcasting. Although in its infancy radio journalism would begin in the early 1930s to impact the perspectives of Americans across the nation.

Radio Journalism

Between 1930 and 1938 radio news broadcasting matured and reached into the everyday lives of most Americans. By 1938 more than 91 percent of urban American households owned radios. Largely because of President Roosevelt's rural electrification program, electricity extended to an increasing number of rural homes allowing approximately 70 percent of rural homes to use radios. A well developed news broadcast system was crucial by the spring of 1938 as Americans were able to follow the disturbing events in Europe which led to the start of World War II in 1939.

Early 1930s By the summer of 1930 only one daily news broadcast reached across the United States to serve an ever increasing national audience. It was under the sponsorship of the weekly newsmagazine *Literal Digest* and was read by the *Chicago Tribune* correspondent, Clyde Gibbons. Wearing a white patch over an eye the flamboyant Gibbons delivered the news at a rapid fire pace, always beginning with a boisterous, "Hello, Everybody." Gibbons commanded a $10,000 per week salary, an astronomical sum in the early days of the Depression. In September of 1930 *Literary Digest's* publisher R. J. Cuddihy had arranged to hear Lowell Thomas, a veteran newsperson, read the news on Columbia Broadcasting Company (CBS) ahead of Gibbons show carried on National Broadcasting Company (NBC). After listening to both, Cuddihy fired Gibbons and hired Thomas. Thomas' program, always captivating, lasted remarkably from his first broadcast on September 29, 1930 to May 14, 1976.

In 1931 Henry R. Luce the magazine journalist who founded *Time* magazine in 1923 began a radio program series, the *March of Time* that did not shy away from stories of the effect of the Depression on Americans. Drawing attentive audiences with dramatic reenactments of the week's news, over 100 stations carried the series. Despite the Depression, increasing numbers of American families found a way to purchase a radio so as not to miss out on the latest news. Radio audiences were also built up by the desire to hear President Roosevelt's "fireside chats" begun in March 1933 explaining, over radio broadcasts, his actions and programs.

As the Depression deepened it affected the radio business much as it did other industries. Small radio manufacturers and broadcasters were forced out of business but larger ones remained. Major networks such as National Broadcasting Corporation (NBC) and Columbia Broadcasting System (CBS) continued to post profits even in the Depression's worst year, 1932. Those wealthy businessmen unaffected by the Depression continued to found local radio stations, then formed chains of networks. Some argued the Depression was actually good for radio since advertisers looking for the most exposure for the least cost increasingly chose radio over newspapers.

By 1934 NBC had 127 affiliated radio stations to which it fed news stories while CBS had 97 affiliates.

Hans von Kaltenborn, broadcasting from CBS studios. Kaltenborn was famous for his 18 day broadcast of the Munich crisis. (UPI/CORBIS-Bettmann. Reproduced by permission.)

Four independent stations established the Mutual Broadcasting System, a cooperative to sell radio time to advertisers and to contract with American Telegraph and Telephone (AT&T) to connect its affiliate stations to phone lines. The Mutual System had 160 affiliated stations by 1939.

Radio Commentators As President Roosevelt took charge of the United States government in 1933 and his administration formulated New Deal legislation radio commentators attempted to assist Americans in understanding the new policies. One of the most famous of the commentators to emerge in the 1930s was Hans von Kaltenborn.

Kaltenborn worked as a reporter for the *Brooklyn Eagle* newspaper from 1910 until he lost his job in 1930 due to the financial crisis of the Depression. As a sideline, beginning in 1922, he broadcast a series of talks on current events for radio station WEAF in New York. CBS hired Kaltenborn in 1930 to do weekly broadcasts. With a perfectly pitched radio voice and an ability to ad lib endlessly, he made sense of the day's news.

Conservative leaning radio commentators with large audiences were Boake Carter, Upton Close, and

Fulton Lewis, Jr. Boake Carter, a close friend of conservative radical Father Charles Coughlin, known as the radio priest of Detroit, broadcast news and commentary each weekday from January 1933 to August 1938. He harshly attacked President Roosevelt's programs and was eventually pulled off the air for increasingly irrational statements. Upton Close analyzed the news over NBC stations from 1934 to 1944. He was sympathetic to right-wing politics, and espoused hatred of Jews and Russians. Fulton Lewis, Jr. began broadcasting commentary over the Mutual Network in 1937 and followed the Republican Party, always opposing Roosevelt.

The more liberal commentators, in addition to Kaltenborn were Dorothy Thompson, Raymond Gram Swing, and Edward R. Murrow. Their commentary generally concerned international issues and whether or not the United States should involve itself in European affairs. Already a respected syndicated newspaper columnist, Dorothy Thompson while living in Europe began radio broadcast commentaries for NBC in 1937. Thompson firmly believed the United States needed to be involved in international affairs and was interested in women's issues. Raymond Gram Swing began regular commentary in 1936 over the Mutual Network and quickly ranked third behind Kaltenborn and Thomas as a top radio journalist in a poll of radio editors. Edward R. Murrow, a CBS program arranger vaulted to fame in 1938 as a European correspondent and thereafter as a radio war reporter. Thompson, Swing, and Murrow hated Hitler, feared for the Jewish people, and were in sympathy with Great Britain believing the United States must indeed become involved in the European conflicts.

One other leading commentator who began his career in the 1930s was Walter Winchell. Although his career was predominantly involved with scandal and gossip about Hollywood and gangsters, he helped educate Americans about German actions and strongly supported President Roosevelt. Winchell built a huge audience and his familiar words were, "Good evening, Mr. and Mrs. North America and all the ships at sea. Let's go to press..." (Emery and Emery, *The Press and America: An Interpretive History of the Mass Media.* p. 328).

Women in Journalism

By the 1930s, hard work, willingness to take on varied and difficult tasks, competitive spirits, plus talented and skillful writing had won women an increasingly prominent role in the field of journalism. Two of the most prominent newswomen, both of whom began their careers in the 1920s, were Dorothy Thompson and

Anne O'Hare McCormick. Thompson became the first American woman head of a European news bureau. McCormick became the first woman on the *New York Times* editorial board. Nevertheless women reporters were generally excluded from the "hard news," that is political and economic news that was covered almost solely by men. When Roosevelt moved into the White House, both the president and first lady developed outstanding relationships with the press. A reformer and women's rights advocate, First Lady Eleanor Roosevelt scheduled press conferences every Monday at 11 o'clock AM for women journalists only. From 1933 to 1945 the first lady opened her "new deal" conferences to women reporters but barred men. This meant that the major newspapers and newsgathering services had to have a newspaperwoman in Washington.

The conferences attracted 20 to 30 reporters each week including regulars May Craig, who wrote a column for the Portland, Maine *Press-Herald;* Bess Furman of the Associated Press (AP); Marie Manning Gasch reporter for the International News Service (INS), who was the original Beatrice Fairfax, advice columnist; Genevieve Forbes Herrick of the *Chicago Tribune;* and journalist Lorena Hickok, reporter for the AP, who would become the first lady's close confidant. Hickok would resign the AP job to take positions in the Roosevelt New Deal programs. Marie Manning Gasch, who had been a news reporter before writing her advice column, had returned to the news world out of economic hardship brought on by the Depression. May Craig would eventually become the best known journalist of the group. She attended presidential press conferences for 30 years from the administrations of Roosevelt to Lyndon Baines Johnson (served 1963–1969). She would also be a regular on the NBC-TV program, "Meet the Press." She served as a correspondent in World War II and was the first woman reporter allowed on a battleship at sea.

Bess Furman, who had come to Washington to cover the presidential political campaign in 1928 for the Omaha, Nebraska *Bee-News* took a job with AP. Although starting at the bottom rung of AP Washington reporters, Furman became a regular at the first lady's conferences. She was still on the job in 1945 when Mrs. Roosevelt gave her last press conference expressing the hope the Roosevelt years had improved the lives of American women.

The first woman news commentator on radio was Kathryn Cravens. She went on the air in February 1934 at KMOX in St. Louis, Missouri with a program entitled, "News Through a Woman's Eyes." CBS brought her to New York in October 1936. Cravens began to fly across the country and became known as the "flying reporter." She enjoyed opening up the world to women often caught in a drab Depression existence.

With the beginning of World War II many men left their newspaper and radio jobs to serve in the military. By 1943 women made up 50 percent of newspaper staffs. Most newswomen stayed at home covering local stories but a few became foreign war correspondents following in the steps of Martha Gillhorn, who had covered the Spanish Civil War in the late 1930s. They included Betty Wason on radio, Helen Kirkpatrick for the *Chicago Daily News,* Tania Long and Sonia Tomara for the *New York Herald Tribune,* and Sigrid Schultz for the *Chicago Tribune.*

Magazine Journalism

During the 1930's Depression hardships, many of America's largest and most popular magazines attempted to avoid sensitive or controversial issues. They stuck to fictional entertainment and discussions to which neither their owners, their readers, or their advertisers would take exception. Owners hoped to please advertisers, provide agreeable entertainment, and make money. A magazine that presented condensed versions of current interest and entertainment news, the *Reader's Digest* saw its circulation numbers mushroom in the 1930s.

Founded in 1922 by DeWitt Wallace and his wife Lila Acheson Wallace the *Reader's Digest* published shorter versions of articles found in other magazines. Readership grew slowly in the 1920s but increased to a circulation of one million by 1935, three million by 1938, and five million in 1942. *Reader's Digest's* staff was skillful in editing articles down to a reader friendly length, producing an inexpensive pocket size magazine that appealed to a cash poor public during the Depression. *Reader's Digest* enjoyed a circulation of over 30 million copies worldwide by the 1950s.

Magazines that proved to be unafraid to address sensitive and controversial topics such as New Deal policies, poverty, and employment were *The New Republic, Time, Life, Look, Literary Digest,* and even the *Saturday Evening Post. The New Republic*— always a stronghold of liberal opinion— had been founded in 1914 and was edited by Herbert Croly between 1914 until his death in 1930. Croly urged social reform as an eight-hour workday, women's suffrage, or voting rights, prison reform, and support for labor unions. The magazine opposed prohibition, the Ku Klux Klan and, following the Wall Street stock market crash of 1929, attacked democracy itself as the culprit in America's economic collapse. During the 1930s *The New Republic* first supported Socialist Norman Thomas for president in 1932 but switched to

More About...

Representation of Women in Journalism

By 1910 there were approximately four thousand women in writing and editing jobs within the journalism field. The number of women in reporting and editing jobs increased in the 1920s for a total of nearly 12,000 or 24 percent of the profession. Although most jobs were still working on women's pages or in book publishing, a new group of talented, serious-minded women with considerable journalistic skills found employment during the progressive twenties. The career option of female journalist matured and the numbers of women continued to rise in the profession. The economic downturn in the 1930s slowed the growth slightly as both women and men lost their jobs and papers folded. The war years of the early 1940s, however, again brought opportunity to women journalists often taking the place of newspapermen who left their jobs to serve in the military. By 1950 women held 32 percent of the total editing and reporting jobs (Statistics taken from Marzolf, *Up From the Footnote: A History of Women Journalists.* pp. 32, 52).

Franklin D. Roosevelt. After pushing for a more radical planned economy, the magazine's ownership decided to moderate and support the reforms of the New Deal. Gradually *The New Republic* accepted as a necessity the United States entry into World War II. Although never commanding a large circulation, *The New Republic* remains influential still today.

Time, founded in 1923 by Henry R. Luce, organized national and foreign news, business, science, education, and religion into a format for reading by the "busy" man. *Time* had a circulation of 200,000 in 1929 and extended its success through the Depression. Copies were inexpensive and the news was clearly presented and interpreted. To compete with *Time,* Thomas J.C. Martyn, a former foreign news editor for *Time,* founded *Newsweek* in 1933. Its format was the same as *Time's* but it injected less opinion into its articles. Luce also founded *Fortune,* a magazine for wealthy businessmen. Although its founding was in the first year of the Depression and it cost one dollar a copy it proved successful with an audience least harmed by the economic crisis.

Another magazine that would be successful even though it was founded in 1929 was *Business Week* from McGraw-Hill Publishing Company.

Literary Digest, established in 1890, had reached a circulation of 1.5 million in the 1920s, second only to the *Saturday Evening Post. Literary Digest* condensed a wide variety of articles from American as well as European newspapers and magazines. It began yet another service in 1916, polling readers to try and predict U.S. presidential elections. In 1924, 1928, and 1932 it accurately forecast the winner in each election. In 1936, however, it sent out 10 million polling ballots and less than a quarter of those were returned. The poll gave a considerable lead to Alfred Landon, the Republican presidential candidate. After Roosevelt won by a landslide, the magazine, which had already dipped in circulation and advertising due to the economic hardships of the Depression, folded in 1937. What was left of the magazine was absorbed by *Time.*

Henry Luce would again mastermind a highly successful magazine *Life* in 1936. Luce was convinced that pictures as well as words could tell a compelling story. Photojournalism, defined as telling a story with photographs, was coming of age largely due to a team of photographers working under the guidance of Roy E. Stryker for the Farm Security Administration, a New Deal agency. The FSA photographers documented the devastation of rural poverty in the 1930s. *Life's* pages carried photographic essays of the later years of the Great Depression and provided extensive photographic coverage during World War II. When *Life* first came out at ten cents a copy in November 1936 people fought over purchase of the copies and its circulation grew rapidly. In 1938 Gardner Cowles created *Look,* a similar but less slick magazine than *Life.* In competition with each other, both magazines provided readers with photographs of harsh Depression scenes and a variety of human interest stories.

The *Saturday Evening Post,* a weekly widely known as the favorite magazine of America, was edited for the average reader and filled with romantic fiction, mysteries, and western tales. Founded in 1821 the *Post* remained a favorite right through the Depression offering escape to Depression weary Americans. It held a circulation of three million despite steadfastly opposing the New Deal programs. Although overall a congenial entertainment magazine, the journalists of the *Post* reflected a decidedly conservative and Republican point of view. They urged immigration restrictions, and remained steadfastly in the isolationist camp opposing America's entry into World War II.

The New Yorker, founded in 1925 by Harold Ross, continued in the 1930s to be a leader in literary journalism while largely steering clear of taking political positions. Journalists looked to *The New Yorker* to publish the kind of thoroughly researched features they longed to write but had no time for when meeting daily deadlines for the newspapers. Famous columns were "The Talk of the Town," and "A Reporter at Large." A review of 1930s journalism would not be complete, however, without a look at the traveling journalists.

Traveling About America

When the nationwide economic crisis of the Depression struck it seemed natural for newspapermen and even novelists who had started out as news reporters to leave their solitary desks and travel about America. Their goal was to see for themselves the condition of all Americans and the impact of the Depression on ordinary individuals and families. With this experience they could more accurately write about the Depression. Their work reflected America's distress nationwide. One of the earlier works came from literary critic Edmund Wilson, *The American Jitters: A Year of the Slump* (1932). In 1933 the brilliant and funny Sherwood Anderson roamed around the United States for two months just observing and listening. He collected his stories in *Puzzled America* (1935). Nathan Ashe similarly took to the road to discover what was happening to his country and digested his findings in *The Road: In Search of America* (1937). One of the most famous accounts came from Louis Adamic in *My America* (1938). Author Erskine Caldwell teamed with *Life* photographer Margaret Bourke-White to document southern rural poverty in *You Have Seen Their Faces* (New York: Viking Press, 1937).

One book stood out above all others, James Agee's *Let Us Now Praise Famous Men* first published in 1939 (New York: Ballantine Books, 1960). Writer Agee partnered with photographer Walker Evans to examine the lives of Alabama sharecropper families in his famous book. Although originally contracted for by *Fortune* magazine in 1936 the daring probe into lives of helpless and damaged people proved unpalatable to *Fortune.* The book was not published until 1941 and then reprinted in 1960 when it became recognized as an American masterpiece of journalism that documented actual conditions of rural poverty in Depression America.

Contributing Forces

Between the end of the Civil War in 1865 and 1900, life in the United States underwent an enormous change. Industrialization, the rise of factories and industries, advanced unceasingly in and around cities bringing with it jobs. More and more mechanization dominated production processes. The age of steel production, major expansion of electricity for light and power, a dazzling array of new inventions, and emergence of new businesses transformed the American economy. The national wealth doubled between 1865 and 1880 then again by 1900. The U.S. population in those 35 years doubled to 76 million by 1900. By 1900, 32.9 percent of the population lived in cities.

Swift and sweeping developments in social and cultural affairs were inevitable. The cities with their concentration of population set the national pace for developing libraries, museums, theaters, retail stores as bookstores, and newspapers. Smaller communities throughout the nation attempted to pattern themselves after the large urban centers that were seen as at the forefront of progress. A general thirst for knowledge, seen as the key to leading a better life, spawned progress in education. The number of children attending public schools in the United States rose from 57 percent in 1870 to 72 percent in 1890 and the literacy rate reached 90 percent. This educational progress was particularly important for the growth of mass media: newspapers, magazines, and books.

Between 1870 and 1900 the number of general circulation daily newspapers rose from 489 to 1,967. Total circulation for all daily publications rose from 2.6 million copies in 1870 to 15 million by 1900. Weekly publications that tended to serve smaller towns and rural areas grew during that same time period from four thousand to over twelve thousand. These weeklies still largely represented personal newspaper ventures owned by local residents and reflecting local happenings. The revolution in newspaper journalism clearly was taking place at the level of the big-city daily. At the forefront of the newspaper business stood the journalism giants such as Joseph Pulitzer, William Randolph Hearst, and Edward Wyllis Scripps.

The Early Journalism Giants

Joseph Pulitzer The leading journalist of the later half of the nineteenth century was the storied Joseph Pulitzer. At his death in 1911 he had accumulated a fortune of nearly $20 million, all through the newspaper business. In the terms of his will, Pulitzer provided $2 million for Columbia University to establish a School of Journalism. A portion of that was set aside for yearly prizes in journalism, literature, drama, and music. These prizes have been awarded annually since 1917 and are called Pulitzer Prizes.

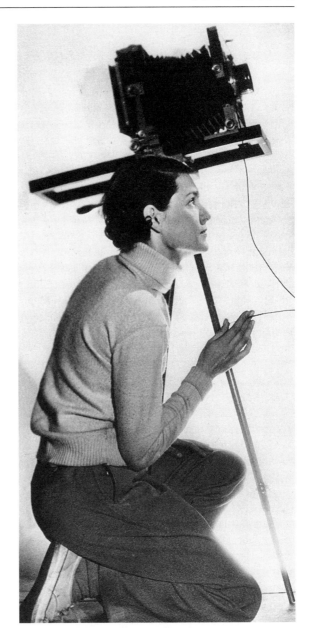

Photographer Margaret Bourke-White at work with her camera in 1934. Bourke-White made history with her photos of southern rural poverty in the book You Have Seen Their Faces. *(AP/Wide World Photos. Reproduced by permission.)*

In 1878 Pulitzer bid $2,500 for the bankrupt St. Louis, Missouri newspaper *Dispatch* and sealed his destiny as a journalist. Within days he combined his *Dispatch* with another St. Louis area newspaper, the *Post* and one of the country's early great newspapers, the *Post-Dispatch* was born. In 1883 Pulitzer purchased the ailing *New York World*. Pulitzer enticed his readers with sensational stories—crime, scandals, disasters—to win a large circulation then also provided strong editorial columns and good news stories about public affairs. Aware that four out of five residents in New York were immigrants or children of immigrants he provided effective coverage of issues most important to the people. Pulitzer developed crusades on behalf of the immigrants, the poor, and the working classes. By 1887 the *World* with 250,000 copies per day had the largest newspaper circulation in the United States. Pulitzer also successfully established the *Sunday World* demonstrating how a Sunday edition could be highly profitable. To the *Sunday World* Pulitzer added pages of entertainment and feature material to the regular addition to attract the whole family. By the early 1890s the Sunday paper grew to 40 to 48 pages as retail advertisers realized the advantage of running ads in a paper that reached all family members. Meanwhile in the far west a wealthy young San Franciscan, William Randolph Hearst, watched with great interest the rise of Pulitzer's *World.*

William Randolph Hearst William Randolph Hearst was born in 1863, the only child of George and Phoebe Hearst. The Hearst family had acquired riches in the silver and copper mines and western ranch lands. In 1880 George Hearst purchased the *San Francisco Examiner* a debt burdened morning paper. Young William Hearst immediately showed interest in the newspaper business but his father sent William off to Harvard University. Although the freewheeling William left Harvard after only a few years his interest in journalism grew stronger. While in the east, William studied both the *Boston Globe* and Pulitzer's *New York World.* He even worked as a cub reporter for the *World* while on one of his vacations.

Returning to San Francisco Hearst, at age 24, assumed the editorship of the *San Francisco Examiner* when his father was named Senator from California in 1887. Senator Hearst died in 1891 but not before he watched his son turn the *Examiner* into the leading San Francisco daily. Always looking for the next challenge the ambitious young Hearst decided to enter the New York journalism field and compete directly with Pulitzer's *World.* In the fall of 1895 Hearst purchased a failing New York newspaper, the *Morning Journal* for a mere $180,000 and, competing directly with the *World,* immediately ushered in the era of yellow journalism.

The Yellow Journalism Battle In 1893 the United States entered into an economic downturn, a crisis that did not ease until the end of the decade. The expanding newspaper business had to find a way to weather the depression of 1893. By 1896 sensationalism carried to extremes became the way to sell newspapers. The drama of real life events were twisted and turned into stories that caught the public's attention. This sensational "yellow journalism" not only exaggerated stories but actually misrepresented facts, faked pictures, and treated editorials with recklessness. While the *World* had used sensationalism in the 1880s to promote sales, it also contained quality news coverage and quality editorials.

When Hearst dove into the New York journalistic scene with his newly purchased *Journal* he openly adopted the sins of yellow journalism while largely ignoring quality news coverage. Hearst hired away much of the *World's* staff with lavish monetary offers which Pulitzer could not counter. He used striking, exaggerated headlines splashed across the papers. The *Journal's* circulation surged and as a result the *World* and the *Journal* battled for readers. Both newspapers not only survived the economic depression of the 1890s but thrived. Their success led papers across the country to use yellow journalism techniques. The use of the term yellow journalism continued through much of the twentieth century.

Edward Wyllis Scripps Unlike Pulitzer and Hearst whose newspapers commanded giant circulations in big cities, Edward Wyllis Scripps looked to the smaller but growing industrial cities of the Midwest. Starting out at the same time as Pulitzer in the late 1870s, Scripps learned the newspaper trade under his brother James at the *Detroit News.* His first papers the *Cincinatti Post* and the *Cleveland Press* were inexpensive afternoon dailies that attracted the common working man. Scripps became known as the people's champion. Scripps' papers consistently reflected an air of protest opposing the rich and intellectuals and supporting laborers. By 1911 Scripps had expanded his newspaper empire to include 18 papers located in Ohio, Indiana, Tennessee, Iowa, Colorado, Oklahoma, and Texas. This empire would grow to over 30 papers by 1926.

Scripps also organized the United Press Association (UP) newsgathering organization in 1907 to compete with the Associated Press Association (AP) founded in 1848. Scripps hired Roy W. Howard as the general manager of UP. Howard left UP to become a partner in the Scripps newspaper chain in 1920. Eventually Howard would dominate the entire Scripps publishing empire that became known as the Scripps-Howard newspaper chain.

Other Early News Leaders

Adolph S. Ochs rescued the *New York Times* from bankruptcy in 1896 and began to build it into one of the world's great newspapers. He refused to match the sensationalism of Pulitzer and Hearst and instead published solid news coverage and editorials for those readers who did not like an overemphasis on features and entertainment. Another effort at clean journalism was Mary Baker Eddy's *Christian Science Monitor* founded in 1908. In 1902 George W. Hinman bought Chicago's *Inter Ocean* and turned it into a paper that obtained the services of talented journalists, many of whom later became leaders in the journalistic field.

Out west Harrison Gray Otis founded the *Los Angeles Times* in 1881 for the then small town of 12,000. The Otis paper would become in the future a giant in the newspaper world. To the north of Los Angeles, Fremont Older was beginning a municipal reform campaign at the *San Francisco Bulletin* in 1885. In Denver, Colorado, Harry H. Tammen, a former bartender, and Fred G. Bonfils joined forces to buy the *Denver Post* in 1895. The undisciplined *Post* used every tactic of yellow journalism available and created fortunes for Bonfils and Tammen—both flamboyant characters.

Women Pioneers in Journalism

Colonial America provided a cornerstone for women in journalism. It was quite common for widows of printers to carry on the family's printing business. By 1696 the earliest colonial woman printer known was Dinah Nuthead of Maryland. By the start of the American Revolution (1775–1783) fourteen women ran printing establishments in the colonies. These women are considered the "foremothers" of generations of women in journalism.

Four more recent pioneers who paved the way for women journalists of the 1930s and beyond were Ida B. Wells-Barnett (1862–1931), Elizabeth Cochrane Seaman known as Nellie Bly (1865–1922), Ida Minerva Tarbell (1857–1936), and Winifred Black Bonfils, known as Annie Laurie (1863–1936). Despite oppressive discrimination, Ida B. Wells-Barnett, a black woman, became a highly influential journalist by the late nineteenth century. Wells crusaded for racial justice and is especially remembered for her fight against lynching. In the 1890s she took a job writing for the respected black journal *New York Age* and before long was one-fourth owner of the journal. At the invitation of the British Anti-Lynching committee, committed to crusading against the brutal treatment of blacks in America, Wells toured England, Scotland, and Wales. The Chicago *Inter Ocean,* a white newspaper carried a weekly column, "Ida B. Wells Abroad." Wells eventually settled in Chicago and continued writing for the Chicago *Defender, World, Broad Ax,* and *Whip.*

Elizabeth Cochrane Seaman, known to her readers as Nellie Bly, was always exploring the globe on adventure after adventure. She was often referred to as a "stunt girl" reporter. Joseph Pulitzer, as a circulation-building stunt for his *New York World* sent Nellie Bly on an around-the-world trip beginning in November 1889. Nellie energetically reported her adventures to a fascinated America. Nellie, however, was not only a stunt reporter but proved to be a solid investigative journalist.

Ida Minerva Tarbell, a soft-spoken middle-aged woman became the only woman to rise to fame alongside male journalists of America journalism's muckraking era, 1902–1912. She candidly revealed the corrupt business practices of powerful executives in John D. Rockefeller's Standard Oil Company. Her crusading articles appeared in *McClure's Magazine* in 1902 and she actively sought out and exposed corruption in government politics. Her sensational pieces appeared in *McClures, Cosmopolitan* and *Munsey's.* Tarbell mellowed somewhat by the late 1910s. President Woodrow Wilson (served 1913–1921) appointed her to the Women's Committee of the Council on National Defense during World War I (1914–1918). After the war, she attended the Paris Peace Conference as a correspondent for *Red Cross Magazine.*

Winifred Black Bonfils, known as Annie Laurie, was a star for William Randolph Hearst during his powerful reign over San Francisco and New York newspapers. Bonfils had a talent for vivid, highly emotionally charged writing that brought tears to the eyes of readers, so much so that she was often referred to as a "sob sister" journalist. In the Hearst organization she occupied various positions as city editor, society editor, drama critic, managing editor, foreign correspondent, and syndicated columnist. She investigated Juvenile Court problems in Chicago, New York charity schemes, and covered organized disaster relief for the victims of the hurricane and flood of Galveston, Texas, in 1900. In San Francisco, she helped reform ambulance service and hospital care, saved the flower street vendors, and protected the Palace of Fine Arts from destruction. Until just before her death she continued to write her column, "Annie Laurie" for the *San Francisco Examiner* and about six weekly articles for the Hearst chain.

Two women who gained enormous readership were Marie Manning, writing as Beatrice Fairfax and Elizabeth Meriwether Gilmer, writing as Dorothy Dix. Manning and Gilmer pioneered the advice column. Both achieved fame by the early 1900s in New York papers.

Along with stunt girls, "sob sisters," and advice columnists, a considerable number of young women

More About...

The Black Press

The interests of black Americans were not represented in mainstream American journalism until the later 1950s and the 1960s. Therefore, as early as the 1820s a separate "black press" developed. Although it had very little economic support the black press survived and flourished. The most famous of early black newspapers, the *North Star,* was founded by former slave, editor, and publisher Frederick Douglass in Rochester, New York, in 1847. Denouncing slavery and advocating emancipation (freedom from slavery) the paper's name was changed in 1951 to *Frederick Douglass' Paper* then to *Douglass' Monthly* from 1860 to 1863. Hundreds of black papers were founded between the end of the Civil War in 1865 and the early 1900s but many had a short life span. The most enduring and influential papers founded during that time were the *Philadelphia Tribune* (1884), the *Age* (1887), the *Afro-American* (1892), the *Boston Guardian* (1901), New York's *Amsterdam News* (1909), Norfolk, Virginia's *Journal and Guide* (1909), and the *Pittsburgh Courier* (1910).

In 1910 W.E.B. DuBois founded and became editor of the NAACP's magazine, *The Crisis,* setting out to demolish the idea of black inferiority, and to attack discrimination of black soldiers in World War I, the lynchings of the 1920s and 1930s, and Ku Klux Klan terrorism. *The Crisis* combined its editorial opinion with news reporting of events concerning blacks and review of black literature. DuBois stepped down as editor in 1934 to become a major leader in the black equal rights movement of the 1960s.

Chris J. Perry, Sr., founded the semi-weekly *Philadelphia Tribune* (1884), continuously keeping it headed by a member of the family. The *Tribune* helped organize charities as well as scholarship programs.

The *New York Age*'s editor T. Thomas Fortune, the son of slave parents, learned to typeset while working as an errand boy for a southern paper. Within a decade of the *Age*'s founding the Fortune's editorials were widely read by political leaders, including Theodore Roosevelt. In 1907 Fortune sold his share of the *Age,* joined the back to Africa movement of

journalist Marcus Garvey and began writing for Garvey's *Negro World.* Meanwhile, under new editor Fred R. Moore the *Age* continued as a major New York paper until it was sold in 1952.

John H. Murphy, Sr., founded *Afro American* (1892) and at his death in 1922, son Dr. Carl J. Murphy continued it as editor. *Afro American* constantly fought to eliminate slums and provide jobs for all. William Monroe Trotter founded the *Boston Guardian* (1901). The *Guardian* took on a militant tone in support of the black cause, winning praise from DuBois.

Although many "white" and "black" papers resorted to sensational stories to promote sales, several black papers refused to follow this pattern. The New York *Amsterdam News,* started by James H. Anderson in 1909, ran sedate news accounts and editorials and remained for decades a leading weekly. Likewise Norfolk, Virginia's *Journal and Guide* had long been a voice of moderation and non-sensationalism among black papers.

The *Pittsburgh Courier* (1910) under the capable direction of Robert L. Vann commanded the largest circulation numbers—300,000 of black newspapers by the late 1940s. Vann, a lawyer, used his paper to fight racial discrimination and also supported black athletes, such as Jackie Robinson's break of the color barrier in baseball. The *Courier* attracted many talented black journalists and developed its circulation on a National basis with a large following in the South.

Although the Depression years did take their toll on circulation of black newspapers, capable management allowed the most influential papers to survive the 1930s. A significant change occurred in black papers in the 1930s with a complete switch from endorsing Republican candidates to backing Democrats. Throughout the Depression black newspaper editorials concentrated on discrimination, black civil rights, and jobs. Despite the economic upheaval several papers even hit circulation records: the *Amsterdam News,* the *Defender,* and the *Courier.*

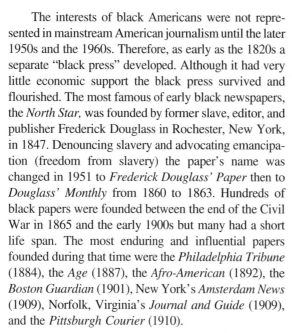

journalists were entering the field as citywide reporters, determined to do serious investigative reporting. Ida M. Tarbell was certainly in that category. One of the first full-time professional women journalists to serve

as a Washington correspondent was Cora Rigby. Appointed Washington correspondent for the *Christian Science Monitor* in 1918, she remained at that post for seven years. Since women were not allowed to be members of the National Press Club, a small group formed their own club, the Women's National Press Club in 1919 and Rigby served as its second president from 1920 to 1928.

In 1919 ten women along with 100 men were accredited to the House and Senate Press Galleries to cover activities within the U.S. House of Representatives and the Senate. Rigby was one of those women as was Elizabeth King of the *New York Evening Post*. King covered the League of Nation debates in 1919.

The Modern American Newspaper

The early large city daily newspapers set the tone for newspaper journalism for the entire twentieth century. Increased communication and newsgathering efficiency, specialization, and growth of newspaper staffs, and advancing printing techniques all led to soaring circulations. The newspaper adopted its recognizable form of banner headlines, feature stories, illustrations, and later—photographs, comic strips, sports news, and advertising. The newspaper business became big corporate business.

Communications networks began to tie the cities together. By 1900 the Bell System of telephone lines reached coast to coast. Railroads had over 193,000 miles of track crisscrossing the United States. The federal postal service greatly expanded its free carrier areas by 1897 providing a low cost delivery system for publications. The Atlantic Cable that had begun operating in 1866 linked London and the United States. The Associated Press (AP) newsgathering agency, founded in 1848, by seven New York City morning papers, began reciprocal exchanges with news services in Britain, France, Germany, and Italy. In 1907 Scripps founded the United Press Association (UP) to compete with the AP. Likewise in 1909 Hearst founded the International News Service (INS). Unlike the AP that only served its member newspapers, both the UP and INS collected and sold news at home and abroad to newspapers who could pay for but did not have the capability to gather news on their own.

Increasing circulations and competitiveness brought increasing specialization. The editorial staff grew from one person to many and there was an emphasis on reporters who traveled about, gathering stories. Leading city dailies had a chief editor, managing editor in charge of news, night editor, city editor directing a staff of dozens of reporters, a telegraph editor, financial editor, drama critics, and editorial writers. Sunday papers became common with human interest features, cartoons, sports, news, and many advertisements.

Better printing techniques of the late nineteenth century included bigger and faster presses. By 1890 presses could run off 48,000 12-page papers in one hour. Color inserts had been printed separately until the early 1890s when the *Chicago Inter Ocean* and *New York World* built full color presses. Improved processes for newsprint paper manufacturing lowered prices for the paper.

Leading papers realized the need for more illustration and by 1891 over one thousand artists were at work producing drawings for five thousand newspapers and magazines. Early reproductions of photographs called half tones began appearing in papers by 1897.

The expansion of staff with its news gathering activities and the ever increasing need to obtain the latest printing equipment led to rapid development of business departments at the dailies. The *New York World,* with its annual profit of one million by the 1890s, was the first to reflect the new corporate nature of modern journalism. Business managers scrambled for advertising to feed their ever-increasing need for revenue to cover large payrolls, escalating mechanical costs, and reams of newsprint paper. By 1910 advertising supplied up to 64 percent of newspaper revenue. Business managers worked tirelessly to keep advertisers like Eastman-Kodak, Kellogg's Cereals, and Wrigley's Gum happy.

Newspaper Chains

Control of two or more newspapers under a single ownership constituted a newspaper chain. The trend for newspapers to combine or consolidate began in the early 1900s. Chain ownership was primarily spurred on by rising costs that smaller papers had trouble keeping up with. Hearst and Scripps were major players in consolidation. By 1922 Hearst owned 20 dailies, six magazines, a Sunday supplement, and two news wire services. One of the most dramatic consolidations occurred in 1931 when the Scripps-Howard chain successfully purchased the *New York World* and merged it with their *New York Evening Telegram.*

Successful New England businessman Frank A. Munsey played a large part in the consolidation of New York City's papers. Frank E. Gannett, another newspaperman with a vision for consolidation, began to build his chain in the 1920s by buying and merging papers in New York State. The Gannett chain would become one of the largest chains in the second half of the twentieth century. Mergers also occurred in Philadelphia, Chicago, Detroit, New Orleans, St. Louis, and Kansas City. Chain owners staunchly maintained each newspaper would be given total editorial independence and that chain ownership greatly improved the efficiency of the newspaper business.

Charles Lindbergh is hounded by reporters and photographers after giving his testimony at the trial of Bruno Richard Hauptmann, the man who was convicted of the kidnapping and murder of Lindbergh's son. It came to be known as "the trial of the century." (AP/Wide World Photos. Reproduced by permission.)

Claims, however, that chain papers could maintain independent perspectives, not influenced by chain owners, came under scrutiny by critics of the press. This remained a controversial point throughout the twentieth century.

One Daily Cities

The number of English language general daily newspapers peaked in 1910 at 2,200 as did the number of cities, 689, with several competing dailies. By 1930 with the consolidation trend firmly established the number of cities with competing dailies had dropped to 288.

Overall newspaper circulation increased dramatically at an even faster pace than the population. The U.S. population increased from 92 million in 1910 to 122 million persons in 1930. During that same time period circulation approximately doubled from 15 million to 30 million copies. Newspaper advertising revenue tripled from World War I lows in 1915 of approximately $275 million to $800 million in 1929.

Twenties Journalism

The atmosphere of the jazzy, fun-loving 1920s was reflected in the newspapers. Papers carried sto-

ries of daily life, comic strips, and pictures—all aimed at entertainment. A majority of Americans were rather self-content, more interested in prosperity and activities on Wall Street than politics or social issues. Political conservation reigned in the White House during the 1920s with three Republican presidents. To attract readers the press again introduced sensationalism as it had in the late 19th century. The experts in sensational journalism were newspaper tabloids. Tabloids filled their pages with crime, sex, contests, comic strips, and headline stories designed to grasp the audience. "Jazz" journalism was the term used to refer to 1920s journalism. Three tabloid leaders were the *New York Daily News* founded in 1919 by Capt. Joseph M. Patterson; the *New York Mirror,* a Hearst paper founded in 1924; and the *New York Evening Graphic,* founded in 1924 and owned by Bermarr Macfadden. The majority of U.S. newspapers followed the New York tabloids' example, rather than try to tackle significant issues as the world situation, racism, or sexism. The papers cried corruption over doings in the Warren Harding (served 1921–1923) administration, especially the Teapot Dome oil-lease scandal. Harding's Secretary of Interior Albert Fall received illegal monetary "gifts" from the oil companies to whom Fall secretly leased naval oil reserve lands. The exposure of graft, or illegally gained money, was entertaining, but little effort at examination or interpretation of news surfaced. The national experiment of banning alcoholic beverages in the United States, Prohibition, made great copy as did the associated stories of speakeasies, rumrunners, and gangsters such as Al Capone. Stories about glamorous socialites and Hollywood stars filled pages. Celebrities such as aviator Charles A. Lindbergh and sports figures such as baseball's home run hitter Babe Ruth made for fascinating reading. Newspaper advertising continued to dramatically increase as Americans had money to spend. The written word was no longer the only journalistic medium in the United States in the 1920s. Early radio programming began to include news and sports reports—radio journalism had begun.

Radio Journalism

Radio journalism began in 1920 with a Detroit experimental station, 8 MK, which broadcast news reports in August under the sponsorship of the *Detroit News.* In November Pittsburgh station KDKA broadcast election returns of the Harding-Cox presidential race. 8 MK in Detroit became WWJ in October 1921, broadcasting music, talk, and news for a part of each day. Many other newspapers followed the *Detroit News* in establishing radio stations.

Communication and electric manufacturing industries established their own stations in the early 1920s. Westinghouse station KDKA broadcast speeches by public figures and major league baseball games enticing the public to buy radio sets. General Electric established WGY in Schenectady, New York, and American Telephone and Telegraph began WEAF (later WNBC) in New York City. The number of radio receiving sets jumped from 50,000 in 1921 to over 600,000 in 1922. News programs more and more were broadcast on a regular basis. Often the programs consisted of an announcer merely reading stories from newspapers or from the wire services.

By 1927 there were 733 stations and they constantly interfered with each other on the broadcast bands. To straighten out the situation Congress passed in February 1927, the Radio Act of 1927 establishing the five-member Federal Radio Commission. The Commission granted licenses for use of certain bands for three-year periods to help eliminate confusion.

The entrance of radio into the news delivery business caused some major conflicts with newspaper publishers. First publishers feared the loss of advertising income to radio. Secondly a controversy erupted between newspapers and radio stations as to whether newsgathering agencies should supply information to newspapers exclusively or if they could also supply radio stations. Soon all news gathering agencies such as AP, UP, and INS supplied information to radio stations. Millions of Americans owned radio sets, and there would be no slowing of radio journalism in the future.

Magazines

Magazines offered yet another journalistic work that would reach large numbers of the general public. Beginning about 1900 and twelve years thereafter an era in journalism known as "muckraking" prevailed in magazine journalism. Muckraking was a term used to refer to a certain type of journalism that exposed misdeeds and corruption in American business and politics.

In 1893 three new magazines, *McClures* (1893), *Cosmopolitan* (1886), and *Munsey's* (1889) charged only a dime per copy and their circulation numbers climbed significantly. Also by the turn of the century *Ladies Home Journal* (1883), *Collier's* (1888), and *Everybody's* (1899) had circulations in the hundreds of thousands. All of these magazines, supporting social justice issues to varying extents, joined in a crusade against corruption in big business and government with muckraking articles.

McClure's, hiring a group of talented journalists, led the way in 1902. Writing for *McClure's*, Ida M. Tarbell exposed the unfair business practices of John D. Rockefeller and his Standard Oil Company. Lincoln Steffens explored government corruption first in St. Louis and then in numerous other large mid-western and northeastern cities. Third, Ray Stannard Baker wrote on labor difficulties including child labor and mistreatment of blacks. In addition to *McClure's* efforts, by 1905 *Colliers* and *Ladies Home Journal* explored fraud in the medical drug trade.

The muckraking era ended with the approach of World War I. Some of the country's magazines became important players in a new trend toward interpretation of the news, increasingly important with the heightened complexity of issues. *The New Republic* (1914) and *The Masses* (1914) expressed the liberal point of view on political issues, siding with the common man and labor as opposed to big business. *The Masses* focused on political and social protest. In the 1920s the *Literary Digest* (1890) condensed a wide selection of material from both American and European newspapers and magazines. It reached a circulation of 1.5 million by 1927 topped only by the ever popular and entertaining *Saturday Evening Post.*

Public Opinion: The Press and the President, 1939
Should the press be allowed to attack President
Roosevelt?

Social Status	Yes	No
Wealthy	66.1%	21.7%
Upper Middle Class	58.2	31.4
Lower Middle Class	49.6	38.6
Poor	39.9	47.3
Negro	27.4	49.3

Public attitudes towards President Roosevelt did not extend towards a lack of criticism, despite his popularity. (The Gale Group.)

In 1923 Henry R. Luce and Briton Hadden, two young graduates of Yale University and reporters for the *Baltimore News* founded *Time,* a weekly news magazine which became highly successful. *Time* displayed informative, to the point news coverage and appealed to the post World War I generation. Two older magazines, *Atlantic Monthly* and *Harper's* both adapted in the 1920s to the same upbeat tempo of *Time* and published articles on current affairs of the day. Two other highly distinctive magazines of the 1920s were Henry Louis Mencken's *American Mercury* and Harold Ross' *New Yorker.*

Mencken was a newspaperman with the Baltimore *Baltimore Sun,* an editor and critic, but most importantly he was a journalistic rebel. Mencken had delighted rebellious minded young adults with his work since 1914 in the *Smart Set,* a magazine published from 1900 to 1930. He could find fault with most anything. Along with George Jean Nathan, Mencken founded the *Mercury* in 1925 and edited it from 1925 to 1933 attacking such widely varying entities as prohibitionists (those favoring a nationwide ban on alcohol), the racial hate group Ku Klux Klan, and the American middle class. He wrote with sophistication and great style and the college generation and younger journalists greatly admired Mencken's writing.

With the Wall Street stock market crash of 1929, and the depression that followed, the mood and attitudes of Americans altered. Mencken's entertaining but caustic *American Mercury,* for example, no longer played well to most Americans and the publication died out by 1933. Overall greater serious coverage of people in trouble and the government trying to find solutions would dominate journalism in the 1930s.

Perspectives

Mouthpieces of Big Business

At the beginning of the Great Depression in 1929, then President Herbert Hoover pressured newspaper journalists to downplay the crisis. Hoover hoped the crisis would soon blow over and did not want newspaper coverage to make the situation seem worse than it was. For example many papers did not tell the American people all the facts of the early 1930s banking failures then accepted praise from bankers' associations for steadying communities by not panicking residents. As the truth emerged, however, public trust of newspapers plummeted. Gradually the public came to identify American newspapers as the mouthpiece of big business. Very wealthy individuals in America owned most large newspaper chains. As would be expected, those individuals concentrated their influence on behalf of big business and of advertisers. Journalists put forth the standard conservative business viewpoints such as arguing against government intervention in business affairs.

The press went on the defensive against the liberal New Deal policies ushered in when Franklin D. Roosevelt became President of the United States in March 1933. The conflict heightened when the Roosevelt New Dealers proposed that the regulatory codes of the National Industrial Recovery Act (NIRA) applied to the publishing industry as to any other industry. The press vehemently resisted, calling the code applications an infringement on freedom of the press.

Out of Step in '36

Taking an anti-big government, hence anti-Roosevelt position, approximately 80 percent of newspapers during the 1936 presidential race endorsed the Republican candidate, Al Landon. Yet Landon carried only two states as Roosevelt swept to victory in a landslide. In no other decade had the American press been so out of step with the American public. When Roosevelt toured Chicago in 1936 during his reelection campaign the massive crowds lining the streets openly raged with banners and signs against the *Chicago Tribune* and the Hearst papers that were bitterly opposing Roosevelt.

On the other hand radio journalism, quickly coming of age, was gaining a positive perspective from the American public. In 1939 *Fortune* magazine commissioned an extensive survey by Elmo Roper, the most accurate pollster of the day, on how the American people viewed the media, both newspapers and radio. The completed survey published in *Fortune* in

August 1939, reflected the true perspectives about the U.S. press as seen by the nation at large.

The Press and the People—A Roper Survey

The Roper Survey of 1939 revealed that while 63.8 percent of Americans got *most* of their news from the newspaper, already 25.4 percent depended most on the radio. When asked, however, which does a better job to get news to the public free of prejudice 49.7 percent answered the radio, while only 17.1 percent answered the newspaper (18.3 percent said they were the same and 14.9 percent did not know). Asked which news interpreters they liked best, 39.3 percent answered radio commentators, 15.9 percent newspaper editorials, and 10.7 percent newspaper columnists. Only the most prosperous Americans rated radio commentators and newspaper editorials equally. The middle and working class man and woman, and the poor, all preferred radio commentators. Next came the telling result of the following question: Given two conflicting versions of the same story which type of media would be more believable? A total of 40.3 percent of respondents voted for radio press while only 26.9 percent voted for a newspaper item. Why did Americans trust radio news more?

Fortune magazine gave the following interpretation. Radio news offered three types of coverage: (1) on-the-spot, immediate coverage of an event as it happened—impossible for a newspaper to do; (2) bulletins, which were shortened versions of news stories obtained from the news gathering wire services—these versions gave fewer facts than newspapers, but got the facts to the public more quickly than newspapers; (3) commentary—unlike newspaper commentary, radio commentaries rarely expressed any opinion on issues that might generate controversy and get the station in trouble with the Federal Communications Commission. In the first two types of coverage the radio confined itself to the "naked" truth and facts and had no time intervals to mold the story to fit a certain mode of journalistic thinking. In commentary radio strived to be totally impartial on the air. For these reasons *Fortune* writers believed that "doing less" with a news item actually kept radio out of trouble and lent it more credibility.

When the poll turned solely to questions about newspapers the survey revealed that between 60.6 percent and 65.8 percent of the public believed newspapers "soft-pedal" bad news or go easy on friends of the publisher and big advertisers. For business in general, 50.1 percent believed the newspapers generally protected business while only 41.5 percent thought they protected labor unions from unfavorable news. In the west coast states of Washington and California the major newspapers—exceptions being the *San Francisco News, Los Angeles Daily News,* and the McClatchy papers of Sacramento, Fresno, and Modesto—were anti-New Deal and supported Republican candidates, attitudes that proved to be hopelessly out of step with their public. The superbly edited *Portland Oregonian,* however, seemed in better alignment with the majority of the states' populace thinking who largely supported Roosevelt and his New Deal policies.

The Roper poll also asked several questions about the press and President Roosevelt. Dividing responses along income lines, the most prosperous, many of who disliked Roosevelt, said it was fine for the press to attack Roosevelt. The poor, who liked him, were much more inclined to have him protected. The overall questions concerning freedom of the press and need of more government control produced the most uniform responses. Even of people who believed there should be brakes on journalism, almost two-thirds said the brakes should only be informal and voluntary, based on the editor's good judgment and public opinion. After analyses of the collective nationwide responses, the overwhelming majority, despite widespread distrust of papers, said to leave newspapers alone.

Impact

By the end of the 1930s the overall pattern for American newspaper journalism that would continue throughout the twentieth century was established. The public's voracious appetite for knowledge about President Roosevelt and the New Deal policies caused expansion of journalism into coverage of government activities. Additionally the complexity of the issues and their importance to all Americans' lives led to the beginning of interpretative reporting. The political columnists and their news analysis became standard fare.

The investigative journalism so prominent in the 1960s and 1970s continuing on into the twenty-first century had its start in the 1920s and 1930s. The 1920s era of "muckraking" journalism, uncovering misdeeds and corruption in business and government, and the 1930s investigations into conditions of poverty in the United States, greatly impacted by the birth of photojournalism, set the stage for investigative reporting. As the century progressed, race riots, civil rights violations, hunger in America, the era of Vietnam (1964–1975), government deception of President Nixon (served 1969–1974) and Watergate, white collar (business) crime, the problems of criminal activities, and drugs, and environmental issues all came under the scrutiny of investigative journalism.

More About...

The Modern American Newspaper Guild

By the last quarter of the twentieth century the Newspaper Guild was a labor union affiliated with the AFL-CIO labor organization. It boasted guilds in over one hundred cities in the United States, Canada, and Puerto Rico. Its over 30,000 members worked in various newspaper departments: advertising, business, circulation, editorial, maintenance, and promotional. The Guild held contracts with most leading newspapers such as those in New York City, Baltimore, Chicago, Washington, Minneapolis, St. Louis, and San Francisco. Contracts were also established with the Gannett newspaper chain, the Knight-Ridder chain, Scripps-Howard chain plus nine news service agencies and 18 news and feature magazines. Magazines under Guild contracts included, among others, *Time, Fortune, Newsweek, Sports Illustrated, Consumer Reports, People,* and *The Nation.* The Guild concentrated on negotiating minimum wages, maximum hours, paid vacations and holidays, sick leave, overtime pay, and severance pay, which is pay provided to employees for a period of time after they are laid off. This union organization for newspaper writers and office workers, however, was non-existent until the early 1930s.

Another trend started in the early twentieth century, that of group owned newspapers—or chains—which continued to the end of the twentieth century. In 1900 there were only eight chains controlling 27 newspapers and ten percent of total circulation. In 1935 63 chains controlled 328 papers and 41 percent of circulation. By 1990 there were 135 chains although this was down from an all-time high in 1978 of 167. Those 135 chains controlled 1,228 papers and 81 percent of total daily circulation. Independent dailies numbered 383 newspapers.

The impact of the growth of news service agencies as Associated Press (AP), United Press (UP) and International News Service (INS) in the 1930s was seen in World War II. Their correspondents gathered the fast breaking stories to send back to the United States. American journalists were given high marks for the achievement during the war years. Often cited for their excellent coverage were the *Chicago Daily News, Chicago Tribune, New York Times, New York Tribune, Christian Science Monitor,* and the Scripps Howard Newspaper chain.

The Dailies Number Shakedown

The Great Depression, wars, and general ups and downs of the U.S. economy from the 1930s into the 1990s impacted the numbers of newspapers and their circulation. In the early 1930s a sharp drop in advertising revenue directly brought on by the economic crisis destroyed many newspapers profit margins even though they cut back salaries, product costs, and laid off workers. Between 1931 and 1933 there were 145 suspensions of dailies and during the recovery years of 1934 to 1936, 77 more closed. The business recession of 1937 caused advertising revenues to drop again after they had rebounded slightly and more newspaper suspensions occurred between 1937 and 1939. By 1945 the number of general circulation daily newspapers had dropped to 1,744 from an all-time high of approximately 2,600 in 1915. The numbers remained steady until the 1970s and 1980s, which brought many consolidations of morning and evening newspapers to enhance cost efficiency. By 1994 a new low of 1,556 dailies was reached. Likewise the percentage of cities with competing dailies continued downward as it had in the 1930s. By 1940 only 12.7 percent of American cities had competing dailies and by 1994 that number was a mere 0.2 percent of U.S. cities.

Circulation did not keep pace with population increases. In 1930 the U.S. population was approximately 122 million and 40 million copies of newspapers were published. In 1990 the U.S. population had doubled to 246 million but the number of newspaper copies published was only 60 million.

Rise of Radio and Television Journalism

The decline in dominance of print journalism coincided with the rise of radio and television. Radio journalism came of age during World War II. Some stations devoted up to 25 percent of their broadcast time to news. Television was still in an experimental stage during this period. The first television broadcasting began in 1939 when President Roosevelt opened the New York World's Fair at a ribbon cutting ceremony. He was therefore the first American president to appear on television. Television advanced from nine stations and 8,000 sets in 1945 to 156 stations and 55 million sets by 1960.

Television broadcast news over the three major networks, American Broadcasting Company (ABC),

Columbia Broadcasting Company (CBS), and National Broadcasting Company (NBC), matured in the 1960s and 1970s during the Vietnam War. Just as with newspaper columnists in the 1930s, television news commentators reported not only the facts but moved into interpretation of those facts. In the 1990s television sets were in virtually every American home and by the late 1990s the majority of those with television had access to cable network television. Cable network stations such as Cable News Network (CNN) and Entertainment and Sports Programming Network (ESPN) were available to American homes for a monthly fee. Not only did CNN and ESPN anchor journalists (those broadcasting regularly for the stations) report facts but "news analysis" was available throughout the day and evening.

Notable People

Robert Sengstackle Abbott (1868–1940). Robert Abbott, known to some as the "Dean of Negro Journalism," founded the *Chicago Defender* in 1905. Starting a newspaper that would serve the black community was a dream Abbott had long held and he accomplished it with little monetary support. It was predominately a one-man operation with volunteer help from Abbott's friends who helped in writing, printing and distributing. The *Defender* related the accomplishments of blacks, social gatherings, and various community activities. The *Defender* encouraged black pride and was the only link for blacks to the larger black community beyond their own local boundaries.

Abbott moved his *Defender* into the modern journalistic world by adopting the sensational makeup and headlines of the Hearst and Joseph Pulitzer papers. He probed political issues on behalf of his race and challenged the Ku Klux Klan, reported on racial rioting, lynching, and any other threat to black security. Within ten years the *Defender* had a circulation of 230,000 and in 1919 Abbott installed his own complete printing shop.

During the Depression the *Defender* lost money for the first time as circulation dropped to 60,000 in 1935 when people could no longer afford to pay for the paper. Yet the *Defender* survived and Abbott's nephew John H. Sengstackle assumed its editorship at Abbott's death in 1940.

Heywood Broun (1888–1939). Born to a successful printing and stationery businessman, a Scottish immigrant, and a mother from a wealthy German American family, Broun grew up in comfortable surroundings in Manhattan. He attended Harvard but found poker, drama circles, and baseball more to his liking and did not graduate. Hired successively by various New York papers Broun flourished as a reporter, drama critic, and sportswriter. Broun, often referred to as having the appearance of an unmade bed was a very large man, 6'4" and 275 pounds but gentle, good natured, and a multi-talented writer. In 1921 Broun moved to the widely circulated *New York World* where he began his column, "It Seems to Me." Broun became increasingly political, even running for Congress in 1930 as a Socialist in New York's 17th District. Broun finished third in the race.

As the Depression closed in Broun's great compassion for his fellow man shown through as he participated in efforts to aid the unemployed. He performed in a 1931 musical revue designed to employ out-of-work show business people in New York.

In December 1933 Broun founded the American Newspaper Guild to organize news journalists, many of whom were in desperate circumstances due to the Depression. He served as its president marching on picket lines and organizing meetings until his death. For decades the Guild stabilized the employment benefits and conditions of American newspaper journalists and office workers. Broun's only child, Heywood Hale Broun, followed in his father's and mother's (Ruth Hale) journalistic career becoming famous himself as a national sports journalist.

Boake Carter (1898–1944). Boake Carter began his career in journalism in English newspapers. Moving to the United States he worked in American newspaper journalism eventually becoming a radio news broadcaster, commentator, and syndicated columnist for the Philadelphia *Public Ledger*. He opposed Prohibition, the New Deal, labor unions, and was in sympathy with the right wing radio priest from Detroit, Father Charles E. Coughlin. Carter also authored several books on current affairs including *"Johnny Q. Public" Speaks! The Nation Appraises the New Deal* (1936) and *I Talk As I Like* (1937), both published by Dodge Publishing Company in New York City.

Raymond Lewis Clapper (1892–1944). Raymond Clapper, reporter, columnist, and radio commentator, was the son of a hardworking but poor family who provided little intellectual stimulation at home. Nevertheless Clapper showed an early strong interest in reading, pouring over the Kansas City *Star,* his local paper, every day. After a determined effort to finish high school while working in a local print shop and taking a few journalism classes at the University of Kansas, Clapper joined the staff at the *Star.*

Quickly recognizing Clapper's skills, United Press (UP), a news service agency owned by the

Scripps-Howard chain, hired Clapper and in 1923 he went to Washington, DC, where he served as Chief UP political writer. Angered by the corruption he found in Washington he authored a book, *Racketeering in Washington,* published in 1933. That same year he joined the *Washington Post* and began his daily column, "Between You and Me." Moving the column to the Scripps-Howard chain in late 1934 it was syndicated to 176 papers with ten million readers. He also wrote for magazines and was a news commentator for the Mutual radio network.

Clapper gained a reputation for being fair and conscientious, able to communicate to the common man. He admired Franklin D. Roosevelt and supported most of his programs. He did not, however, support Roosevelt for a third term as president and never shied away from criticisms when he thought Roosevelt was misguided. Clapper died in 1944 in an air collision during an invasion of the Marshall Islands in World War II.

W.E.B. DuBois (1868–1963). W.E.B. DuBois graduated from Fisk University in Nashville, Tennessee, in 1885 and took a second B.A. degree in 1888 from Harvard University, where he also received his Ph.D. in 1895. DuBois was the first black American to receive a degree from Harvard. DuBois' dissertation, *The Suppression of the African Slave-Trade to the United States of America, 1638–1870* was published in 1896 in the Harvard Historical Studies series. The dissertation forecast Du Bois' lifetime comment to civil, economic, and political equality for blacks.

Du Bois taught economics and history at Atlantic University from 1897 until resigning in 1910 to become Director of Publications and Research for the National Association for the Advancement of Colored People (NAACP). That same year he founded *The Crisis* the official publication of the NAACP and led the magazine for almost 25 years. DuBois left the NAACP over a clash of segregation ideologies. In 1940 he established *Phylon* while back with Atlantic University. *Phylon* was a scholarly journal dedicated to study of race problems throughout the world. DuBois held the position as editor until he retired from the university in 1940.

By the 1950s, DuBois moved further and further to the political left. In 1961 he officially joined the Communist Party and moved to Ghana where he died in 1963. In total DuBois through his life served as editor of five periodicals, authored many books, contributed to newspapers, and wrote many articles for scholarly journals.

Elizabeth Meriwether Gilmer (Dorothy Dix) (1861–1951). Elizabeth Gilmer, writing as Dorothy Dix, authored a common sense advice column from 1896 to 1949. She first wrote the column for the *New Orleans Picayune.* When asked by William Randolph Hearst, Gilmer joined his *New York Journal* in 1901. Eventually her column, renamed "Dorothy Dix Talks," was distributed by the Wheeler news chain and the *Philadelphia Public Ledger* chain to three hundred newspapers around the world. Known as "America's Mother Confessor," Dix reached an estimated 35 million readers.

William Hard (1878–1962). Having written on national affairs in various newspapers and magazines for years, around 1930 Hard began work as a news commentator for the National Broadcasting Company (NBC). He covered several international conferences and political conventions for NBC during the 1930s. By 1936 he made nightly news broadcasts for the Republicans blasting the policies of the New Deal. Hard began writing for *Readers' Digest* in 1939 on politics, labor, and international affairs, and was an editor from 1941 until his death.

William Randolph Hearst (1863–1951). Born to George and Phoebe Hearst in San Francisco, Hearst led a privileged childhood. His father, wealthy from mining strikes, was a rancher, U.S. Senator, and publisher of the *San Francisco Examiner.* Young Hearst entered Harvard University in 1882 only to be expelled in 1885 for practical jokes played on professors. He returned to San Francisco, took over the *Examiner* and built it into a highly sensational and successful Bay area paper. In 1895 Hearst bought the *New York Journal* and went into direct competition with Joseph Pulitzer's *New York World.* Highly successful with huge, splashy headlines, pictures, and flamboyant news coverage, Hearst, by the mid-1930s, operated the largest newspaper chain in the country. His empire, reaching across class and ethnic groups, included 26 daily newspapers in 19 cities, two news services, King Features Syndicate, 13 magazines, eight radio stations, and two film companies.

Hearst supported Franklin Roosevelt for U.S. President in 1932, then supported Roosevelt's New Deal for a time. By 1935, however, he dubbed the New Deal a "raw deal," representing big government, high taxes, and unions. Hearst looked abroad as troubles in Europe escalated. He was adamantly opposed to communism and thought that communists were everywhere on American college campuses and demanded that state legislatures investigate.

The Depression took a monetary toll on the Hearst news empire. By 1937 his empire was $125 million in debt and his personal salary went from $5 million a year to $100,000. Hearst was forced to give up personal control of his enterprises.

Hearst, nevertheless, continued to be outspoken. He pressed Roosevelt to keep the United States out of World War II. By 1940 only 17 newspapers remained but his was still the largest news chain in America. Heart's empire had shaped American newspaper journalism for many decades.

Roy W. Howard (1883–1964). Roy Howard's newspaper career began as a newsboy for the *Indianapolis Star*. After high school he was hired onto the *Indianapolis News* and in 1907 became the New York manager of United Press (UP) newsgathering agency. He advanced in the UP organization and only five years later became president. In 1920 Howard resigned to join Robert P. Scripps, son of the powerful eccentric news magnate Edward W. Scripps, to run the Scripps-McRae League of Newspapers. Howard became part owner and the League was renamed Scripps-Howard and eventually grew into one of the nation's largest journalistic empires with daily newspapers, weekly newspapers, radio stations, and television stations.

In the 1930s, Howard spent much of his time running the *New York World-Telegram* for which many top journalism columnists worked, even Eleanor Roosevelt contributed with her column, "My Day." Howard supported Franklin D. Roosevelt for the U.S. Presidency in 1932 and 1936. By 1940, however, he broke with Roosevelt to support Republican candidate Wendell Wilkie.

Howard bought the *New York Sun* in 1950, which he managed until 1960. He was still active as the chairman of the executive committee of Scripps-Howard Newspapers at his death in 1964.

Hans von Kaltenborn (1878–1965). Hans von (H.V.) Kaltenborn grew up in the small town of Merrill Wisconsin where he published his first articles in the *Merrill Advocate*. Always intrigued with travel, Kaltenborn left Merrill in 1900 to sail to France. Upon his return he became a reporter for the *Brooklyn Eagle* where he remained until 1930 and rose to associate editor. Meanwhile, as a sideline, Kaltenborn began broadcasting a series of current events talks for the fledgling radio station WEAF in New York City.

In 1930 while encountering major financial difficulties the *Eagle* let Kaltenborn go. He went to work for CBS, at the time a new radio network. He broadcast the Republican and Democratic national conventions in 1932, the London Economic Conference in 1933 and from Spain, the Spanish Civil War in 1936. Kaltenborn's most famous broadcast came in 1938 when for 18 consecutive days he broadcast from New York City the Munich, Germany crisis as quickly as the news came in.

During that period catching some sleep on a cot in the studio, Kaltenborn broadcast 102 times ranging from two minutes to two hours. In 1940 he switched to NBC and broadcast news of World War II from all over the world. After the war his broadcast became more opinionated and when he retired in 1955 his listening audience had decreased.

Kaltenborn was a leader of the first generation of journalists to make the transition from the written word to broadcasting.

Frank Kent (1878–1958). Frank Kent, a political syndicated columnist, wrote for the *Baltimore Sun* from 1924 until his death. His column, "The Great Game of Politics," appearing in over 100 daily newspapers, analyzed the American politics and politicians. He was considered one of the "big four" syndicated columnists along with David Lawrence, Walter Lippmann, and Mark Sullivan.

Arthur Krock (1886–1974). Born in Kentucky, Arthur Krock became a noted journalist and foe of the New Deal programs. Krock broke into journalism in 1905 with the Louisville, Kentucky, *Herald.* He moved on to New York in 1923 where he worked for the *World* until 1927 when he joined the editorial staff of the *Times.* Krock was a reporter, conservative columnist, and Washington bureau chief for the New York *Times* from 1927 to 1967. He was one of only a handful of people who could determine the *Times'* policy during the Great Depression and afterward. His reporting won two Pulitzer Prizes in 1935 and 1938. His award in 1938 was for an exclusive interview with President Franklin Roosevelt, Roosevelt's first such interview since taking office in 1933. On the editorial page of the *Times* wrote a column titled "In the Nation" which was frequently highly critical of Roosevelt and the New Dealers.

David Lawrence (1888–1973). David Lawrence, an editor and columnist, received his journalism training at Princeton University where he worked as a campus correspondent for Associated Press. Upon graduation Lawrence began his career with a full-time job at Associated Press. Covering the Washington, DC, scene for over 60 years, in 1926 he founded the *United States Daily* covering daily activities of the U.S. government—factual reporting only with no opinions added. In keeping with the need for more news interpretation in the 1930s, Lawrence reorganized his paper in 1933 into a weekly, *The United States News* with broad offerings of factual content and editorial opinions. Lawrence's own views were conservative. He spoke of the New Dealers as extremists and promoted anti-strike legislation to combat the labor movement. Circulation, which was 30,000 at the end of 1933 reached 85,000 by January 1940, and with still further expanded national news coverage reached 300,000 in 1947. Meanwhile in 1946 Lawrence founded a world affairs weekly *The World Report.* Lawrence merged the two weeklies in 1948 to create *U.S. News and World Report,* which had a circulation of two million by his death in 1973.

Walter Lippmann (1899–1974). An influential political journalist, Walter Lippmann began his career on the left, leaning toward socialism, moderated to a New Deal liberal, and then grew more conservative by 1936. Lippmann, who graduated from Harvard University in 1910, helped his friend Herbert Croly found *The New Republic,* a liberal weekly, in 1914. From 1923 to 1929 Lippmann was editorial staff chief for the *New York World* and its editor from 1929 to 1931. In 1931 the *World* was sold to the Scripps-Howard chain and combined with the chain's *New York Telegram* to become the *World Telegram.* Roy Howard invited Lippmann to remain as the merged paper's editor and William Randolph Hearst offered Lippmann $50,000 a year to write for his papers. Lippmann chose, however, to write a column for the conservative *New York Herald Tribune* when its publisher, Ogden Reid, convinced Lippmann the *Herald Tribune* wanted to win the *World's* Democratic readers. He began his column, "Today and Tomorrow," for the *Herald Tribune* in 1931 and continued to write it until 1962. By 1932 the column was syndicated to one hundred newspapers with a readership of ten million. The syndicated column would eventually appear in two hundred newspapers.

Originally skeptical of Franklin D. Roosevelt's presidential candidacy, Lippmann soon decided Roosevelt was just the enlightened leader the United States needed. He threw all of his support behind Roosevelt and then supported all early New Deal measures. Yet by 1935 Lippmann became convinced that the executive relief powers were no longer needed and joined in opposition to any further New Deal legislation. He actually supported Republican Al Landon for president in 1936.

As World War II drew to a close, Lippmann wrote a column on April 7, 1945, five days before Roosevelt's death, praising Roosevelt as the man who led United States out of World War II to its high point of influence and respect in the world. Following World War II Lippmann went on to become the nation's foremost analyst of foreign affairs.

In 1962 Lippmann joined the *Washington Post* published by Philip Graham. He worked closely with Katherine Graham who succeeded her husband as publisher after his death. Lippmann convinced Katherine

Graham to take an anti-Vietnam stance. Lippmann died in 1974 after a magnificent and prolific journalistic career.

Henry R. Luce (1889–1967). Henry Luce, editor and publisher, founded the first modern magazine, *Time* in 1923 with the help of a friend he met at Yale University, reporter Briton Hadden. Luce and Hadden together also founded *Fortune* in 1930, a magazine devoted to covering the business world. In 1936 Luce then founded the first magazine devoted to photojournalism, *Life,* which reached a circulation in the millions. In 1954 he established another magazine still popular at the beginning of the twenty-first century, *Sports Illustrated.*

Marie Manning (Beatrice Fairfax) (1868–1945). A tough-minded and energetic woman, Marie Manning started her journalism career at Joseph Pulitzer's *New York World* then moved to the *New York Evening Journal* in 1897. After editor Arthur Brisbane brought three letters from women asking for advice into Manning's office, with youthful rashness she proposed an entire column devoted to advice. Manning wrote the column under the name of Beatrice Fairfax and it was a success from the start, receiving thousands of letters from readers with relationship problems. Manning actually left the column in 1905 to raise a family and returned only once briefly during World War I. In 1929 financial reverses brought on at the beginning of the Depression caused Manning to return to writing the column that by then was syndicated to two hundred newspapers. In addition she covered women's news in Washington, DC, for the news gathering agency, International News Service. Manning covered Eleanor Roosevelt's women-only press conferences. In World War II Manning expanded her column to give advice to servicemen and their families.

Robert R. McCormick (1880–1955). Robert R. McCormick was editor and publisher of the *Chicago Tribune.* From 1910 until his death in 1955, McCormick, an ultra conservative, campaigned in the 1930s against President Franklin D. Roosevelt's New Deal, labor unions, and the right to strike. He was a strict isolationist opposed to U.S. involvement abroad. He ignored the Nazis and opposed most all foreign aid.

Edgar Ansel Mowrer (1892–1977). Edgar Ansel Mowrer, a foreign correspondent for the *Chicago Daily News,* won a Pulitzer Price in 1933 for his reporting on the rise of Adolf Hitler in Germany. Mowrer continued to cover events in Europe in the 1930s then after World War II became a syndicated columnist for the *Daily News* for which he worked a total of 55 years.

Paul Scott Mowrer (1888–1971). Paul Scott Mowrer, foreign correspondent and editor, worked with the *Chicago Daily News* from 1905 to 1944. He received a Pulitzer Prize in 1929 for his international affairs coverage. He was responsible for hiring his younger brother Edgar Ansel Mowrer who also received a Pulitzer Prize for his foreign affairs coverage in 1933.

Edward R. Murrow (1908–1965). Edward R. Murrow, radio and television news reporter, joined the Columbia Broadcasting Company (CBS) in 1935. He was assigned to the European bureau from 1937 to 1939 and was a CBS war correspondent from 1939 to 1945. Murrow's nationwide fame came as he reported from London during the air raid bombings.

Eleanor Medill Patterson (1884–1948). Eleanor Medill Patterson, granddaughter of Joseph Medill, owner of the *Chicago Tribune,* started her journalism career in 1930 when she took over as editor and publisher of the ailing *Washington Herald.* She had the gutsy nerve and perseverance of a seasoned reporter as she interviewed such diverse notables as Franklin D. Roosevelt and gangster Al Capone. She also hired excellent women feature writers and a woman photo editor and greatly expanded the paper's appeal to women. Circulation increased dramatically and in 1939 Patterson was able to purchase both the *Washington Herald* and Hearst's other Washington paper the *Washington Times.* Patterson combined the two into the *Times-Herald,* which had the largest circulation in Washington by the mid 1940s.

Westbrook Pegler (1894–1969). Westbrook Pegler, son of a top news reporter for papers in Minnesota, Chicago, and New York, was at work for the United Press (UP) newsgathering agency by the age of 16. After World War I, Pegler wrote sports for the *Chicago Tribune* and UP. He developed the reputation as an unconventional writer who excelled at cleverly attacking famous individuals. In 1933 he was hired by the *New York World-Telegram* as a national affairs columnist for the next 11 years. The ultra conservative Pegler attacked in caustic terms the New Dealers, the Roosevelt, labor unions, and communists. In 1941 he won a Pulitzer Prize for exposing corruption in labor unions.

Mark Sullivan (1874–1952). An accomplished journalist by the early 1920s Sullivan was already published nationwide in the *New York Evening Post* when he joined the *New York Tribune* (later the *Herald-Tribune*). He became one of the "big four" syndicated political columnists along with David Lawrence, Walter Lippmann, and Frank Kent. Sullivan's column appeared in over one hundred newspapers at its peak.

Edward. R Murrow was a European correspondent for CBS during World War II. Murrow set the standard for future radio and news reporters. (Archive Photos. Reproduced by permission.)

After Franklin D. Roosevelt's election, Sullivan cautiously supported the New Deal policies. By the mid-1930s, however, he was afraid Roosevelt's policies were not pulling the nation out of the Depression and by 1937 his columns were critical of Roosevelt.

Between 1926 and 1936 Sullivan authored a six volume set on U.S. history entitled, *Our Times: The United States, 1900–1925.* In 1945 Sullivan retired to his farm in Pennsylvania but continued to author his column until his death in 1952.

Lowell Thomas (1892–1981). Lowell Thomas, a world traveler, author, and radio and television commentator, often said he was not a journalist but an entertainer. He broadcast an account of the days' events in a conversational tone from 1930 to 1976 to the American people. He broadcast those years for either CBS or NBC—only when his location made it impossible to broadcast did he fail to go on air. He always opened with, "Good evening, everybody," and closed with, "So long, until tomorrow." In 1935 Thomas began as editor and narrator of 20th Century Fox's Movietone newsreels, continuing in this position for decades.

More About...

The Newsreel

American newsreels were widely popular in the 1930s. Shown at most movie houses between feature films, the standard American newsreel ran for about ten minutes mixing the latest news with human-interest stories, sports, and a small amount of disaster or crime. In a decade when television did not exist and picture magazines were just making their appearance, the newsreels at the movies were eagerly awaited. Releasing new newsreels twice each week, were five major production companies. Fox Movietone News showed the first sound newsreel in January 1927. Hearst Metrotone News came on the scene in 1929. The other three major producers were Paramount News, Pathé News, and Universal News.

The March of Time productions although made as documentary short-subject films, were shown as newsreels for 16 years, between 1935 and 1951, reaching an estimated 20 million moviegoers. The series was a unique example of motion picture journalism. Produced for the news publishing group Time, Inc. by Louis de Rochemont, a journalist and film maker, the series explored often controversial social issues of the day. Events were reenacted then actual newsreel footage, maps and diagrams were added. *The March of Time* attacked Senator Huey Long of Louisiana, Detroit's radio priest, Father Charles Coughlin, Adolf Hitler, and Benito Mussolini. There were episodes on the misery of the Dust Bowl, the desperate conditions of migratory farm workers, and the build-up of conflicts in Europe. The most famous episodes were *Veterans of Future Wars* (1936), *Rehearsal for War in Spain* (1937), and *Inside Nazi Germany* (1938). The series was narrated by Westbrook Van Voorhis who made famous the phrase, "Time Marches On."

Dorothy Celine Thompson (1893–1961). An avid reader as a child, Dorothy Thompson graduated from Syracuse University in New York and immediately went to work for women's suffrage (right to vote) groups in western New York in 1914. She soon moved to New York City where she befriended intel-

lectuals and political activists and wrote freelance articles for newspapers and magazines. Thompson traveled to Europe in 1920 where she was hired by the International News Service (INS) and then by the *Philadelphia Public Ledger* as its central European correspondent.

Thompson met and married American novelist Sinclair Lewis in 1928. She proceeded to establish her career as a lecturer and freelance writer on international issues for major American magazines. She interviewed Adolf Hitler in 1931 and wrote in 1932 "I Saw Hitler!" In that widely published article she described Hitler as ineffective, an outlook she soon completely reversed. She began her syndicated column "On the Record" in 1936 with the *New York Herald Tribune* and continued writing articles for various newspapers and magazines. Thompson's *Herald Tribune* column, a monthly article for the *Ladies' Home Journal,* an NBC radio contract, and her lecture appearances made Thompson one of the most influential journalists of the 1930s. In 1939 *Time* magazine called Eleanor Roosevelt and Thompson the most influential women in America.

Thompson supported opening the United States borders to refugees from Nazi Germany, and supported Jewish hopes of a Palestine homeland (a position she reversed in the 1940s and 1950s). She was a constant critic of President Roosevelt in the 1930s believing his social reforms and wealth redistribution did not go far enough. She did, however, support him in the 1940 and 1944 presidential elections viewing his foreign policies the best able to stand up to Hitler's aggression.

Walter Winchell (1897–1972). Although predominantly a gossip columnist and radio commentator offering juicy tidbits of the lives of the famous, Walter Winchell reached millions. The public generally thought of him as a journalist and his radio broadcasts were popular from 1930 to 1950. By the early 1930s his material became more political as he backed the policies of Franklin D. Roosevelt, attacked Hitler and all fascists, and fought against radio censorship.

Primary Sources

Interpretive Commentary

Walter Lippmann, outstanding political journalist, wrote these comments about President Roosevelt's first year in office for the New York *Herald Tribune.* This column typifies the interpretive commentary found in newspapers and magazines in the 1930s.

(From Lippmann, *Interpretations: 1933–1935.* pp. 249–250.)

PRESIDENT ROOSEVELT'S LEADERSHIP

1. THE FIRST ROOSEVELT YEAR (February 27, 1934)

The achievements of the past year can be measured statistically. But there is perhaps a better measure. A year ago men were living from hour to hour, in the midst of a crisis of enormous proportions, and all they could think about was how they could survive it. Today they are debating the problems of long term reconstruction.

It is a decisive change. When Mr. Roosevelt was inaugurated, the question in all men's minds was whether the country could "recover." The machinery of government was impotent. The banking system was paralyzed. Panic, misery, rebellion, and despair were convulsing the people and destroying confidence not merely in business enterprise but in the promise of American life. No man can say into what we should have drifted had we drifted another twelve months. But no man can doubt, if he knows the conditions—which responsible observers hardly dared to describe at the time for fear of aggravating the panic—that the dangers were greater than they have been at any time in the experience of this generation of Americans. Today there are still grave problems. But there is no overwhelmingly dangerous crisis. The mass of the people have recovered their courage and their hope. They are no longer hysterically anxious about the immediate present. They have recovered not only some small part of their standard of life but also their self-possession. The very fact that they can take a lively interest in...the bill to regulate the stock exchange and the permanence of NRA is the best kind of evidence that the crisis has been surmounted.... The question then was how to stay out of the bread line, and whether there would be money to supply a bread line, and how to avoid foreclosure or eviction or bankruptcy.

The questions about the future which agitate Mr. Mark Sullivan and Mr. David Lawrence and other critics of the Administration are very important. They should be discussed thoroughly. But we should not be in a position to discuss them thoroughly if the President had not pulled the country out of the pit and brought about a recovery.

Columnist Talks to Readers

John Monte LeNoir, journalist for the small, local West Los Angeles *Independent* wrote a daily column written in a personal conversational style exploring and interpreting his nation and world in the late 1930s. This type of column began to appear regularly in papers across the country in the 1930s.

I AM....

by J.M.L.

FED UP with all the different official proclamations of "buy-used-car week," "send-somebody-posey-day," "national-canned-goods-week," "half-sole-your-shoes-day," etc., etc., etc. The latest insult to the intelligence of Mr. Average American is "Employment Day" next

Sunday. The resolution says that "it is increasingly difficult for persons over 40 to find employment." Gosh, I didn't think age had anything to do with it. Will somebody please tell us where ANYBODY, regardless of age, can get a job! I am sure that we are all grateful for this movement whereby a proclamation and a few Sunday morning sermons will solve the most serious problem ever confronting this country (*West Los Angeles Independent,* May 20, 1938).

Dorothy Thompson, Journalist

On the cover of the June 5, 1939 issue of *Time* magazine was the picture of Dorothy Thompson, one of the most important journalists of the 1930s. The article about Thompson, entitled "Cartwheel Girl," looked at her career and influence.

...although she [Dorothy Thompson] and Eleanor Roosevelt are undoubtedly the most influential women in the U.S....and quoted by millions of women who used to get their political opinions from their husbands, who got them from Walter Lippmann...in March 1936, Mrs. Ogden Reid, super-clubwoman vice president of the New York *Herald Tribune* , hired her to write a column. It was to run on the same page as Lippmann's *Today and Tomorrow* three times a week, and it was expected to present the woman's point of view toward such public matters as women could be expected to grapple with.

Dorothy Thompson surprised everybody, including her employer and herself, by turning out a column that was sensationally informative. To a sound reportorial instinct she added an astonishing capacity to read and absorb vast quantities of printed matter.... She had tremendous energy and insatiable curiosity; she wrote lucidly and was not afraid to pour into her column whatever emotion she felt. Her warmth and sincerity, her hatred of Fascism wherever she saw it (it was usually in Europe in those days) and the passionate indignation with which she wrote of injustice to the defenseless soon gave her a following far beyond the circulation of the *Herald Tribune.* Her column, quickly syndicated, spread through the hinterland. She appealed to women because she wrote like a woman. She appealed to men because, for a woman, she seemed surprisingly intelligent.

Today, after writing nearly a million words for *On the Record,* she has lost some followers and gained more. But to those Americans who live in the smaller cities and towns, and especially to the women, Dorothy Thompson is infallible—not so much because of what she thinks as because of what she is. To these women she is the embodiment of an ideal, the typical modern American woman they think they would like to be: emancipated, articular and successful, living in the thick of one of the most exciting periods of history and interpreting it to millions....

Columnist's Credo. Dorothy Thompson thinks: a) that Roosevelt is headstrong (so is she) but b) has "a real world sense" (and so has she); c) that WPA is unhealthy (it smacks of social work); d) that the democratic ideal is most nearly realized in Vermont ("where the town meeting is still a living, functioning institution," i.e., where democracy functions as in the past); e) that the New Deal is incipient Fascism (she sees dictators in every closet); f) that government should be decentralized (her first seven years in small towns were happy); g) that "the educated female is, in general, dewomanized" (but not Dorothy Thompson)....

For writing her column, speaking over the radio, doing a monthly article for the *Ladies Home Journal* and delivering lectures, Dorothy Thompson was paid $103,000 last year. Her business expenses were $25,000 and she contributed $37,000 in taxes, which left her $41,000 to live on. She gave 20 percent of that away (*Time* June 5, 1939, p. 47, 49, 50).

Suggested Research Topics

- Imagine yourself a writer wanting to write a magazine article. What would be some topics of public interest related to the Great Depression for 1933? Which magazines might want to publish your article and why?

- What opportunities did women and minorities have in the field of journalism? Would they be able to portray the Great Depression-related issues most relevant to women and minorities in national publications? Which publications would be more likely to print their stories and why?

- What kind of relationship did President Roosevelt have with the press? Did it change during different time periods?

Bibliography

Sources

Allen, Frederick L. *Since Yesterday: The Nineteen-Thirties in America, September 3, 1929–September 3, 1939*. New York: Harper & Brothers Publishers, 1940.

"American Society of Journalists (ASJA)," [cited March 1, 2002] available on the World Wide Web at http://asja.org.

Emery, Michael, and Edwin Emery. *The Press and America: An Interpretive History of the Mass Media*. Boston: Allyn and Bacon, 1996.

Hartsock, John C. *A History of American Literary Journalism: The Emergence of a Modern Narrative Form*. Amherst: University of Massachusetts Press, 2000.

Lippmann, Walter. *Interpretations: 1933–1935*. New York: The Macmillan Company, 1936.

Marzolf, Marion. *Up From the Footnote: A History of Women Journalists*. New York: Hastings House Publishers, 1977.

Mott, Frank L. *American Journalism: A History of Newspapers in the United States Through 260 Years, 1690 to 1950*. New York: The Macmillan Company, 1950.

Schilpp, Madelon Golden, and Sharon M. Murphy. *Great Women of the Press*. Carbondale: Southern Illinois University Press, 1983.

Stott, William. *Documentary Expression and Thirties America*. Chicago: The University of Chicago Press, 1986.

Wolseley, Roland E. *The Black Press, U.S.A.* Ames: The Iowa State University Press, 1971.

Further Reading

"American Newspaper Guild," [cited March 1, 2002] available on the World Wide Web at http://www.newsguild.org/mission/history.php.

"American Society of Newspaper Editors," [cited March 1, 2002] available on the World Wide Web at http://www.asne.org.

Emery, Edwin. *History of the American Newspaper Publishers Association*. Minneapolis: The University of Minnesota Press, 1950.

"High School Journalism, American Society of Newspaper Editors," [cited March 1, 2002] available on the World Wide Web at http://www.highschooljournalism.org.

Kent, Frank R. *Without Grease: Political Behavior, 1934–1936, and a Blueprint for America's Most Vital Presidential Election*. New York: William Morrow & Company, 1936.

Peeler, David P. *Hope Among Us Yet: Social Criticism and Social Solace in Depression America*. Athens: The University of Georgia Press, 1987.

Peterson, Theodore. *Magazines in the Twentieth Century*. Urbana: University of Illinois Press, 1964.

Ross, Ishbel. *Ladies of the Press: The Story of Women in Journalism by an Insider*. New York: Harper & Brothers, 1936.

Steel, Ronald. *Walter Lippmann and the American Century*. Boston: Little, Brown and Company, 1980.

Streitmatter, Rodger. *Raising Her Voice: African-American Women Journalists Who Changed History*. Lexington: The University of Kentucky Press, 1994.

Vanden Heuvel. *Untapped Sources: America's Newspaper Archives and Histories*. New York: Gannett Foundation Media Center, 1991.

See Also

Employment; Everyday Life; Interwar Era; Radio

Labor and Industry

1933-1938

When the Great Depression began in 1929, and deepened into 1931, the demand for goods produced in U.S. factories began to plummet. The average citizen did not have the money or job stability to pay the same amount of money as before for goods that were not necessities. In addition the financiers who had lost money in the stock market crash were no longer investing in American businesses as they had before. As a result unemployment and under-employment swept through factories across the United States. It became a vicious cycle as the public had less money to spend on the goods, leading to factories cutting back, meaning the public had even less money to spend. Due to this downward spiral during the Great Depression industrial production in the United States fell 35 percent. Depressions in the 1830s, 1870s, and 1890s had not had nearly as severe an effect on the economy. Workers faced diminished wages, fewer work hours, or loss of jobs altogether. The situation became desperate for millions of laborers; without jobs they could not pay for shelter, clothing, or food. They had little place to turn. The states and federal government offered no unemployment insurance and provided only limited welfare assistance. Most relief had to come from the private sector, especially churches and lodges or clubs that had assistance programs.

The labor sector was ill equipped to deal with an economic crisis of such proportions. By 1932, 16 million were unemployed, which was equivalent to nearly a third of those who were able to work in the U.S. at

Chronology:

June 16, 1933: The National Industrial Recovery Act (NIRA) creates the Works Projects Administration (WPA) and the National Recovery Administration (NRA). Section 7A of NIRA gives employees the right to organize and engage in collective bargaining with their employer through representatives they select and a legal standing for unions to engage in strikes.

1933: The Norris-LaGuardia Anti-Injunction Act makes it impossible to enforce Yellow Dog contracts and limits the power of courts to protect company unions and to stop strikes.

1935: The American Federation of Labor (AFL) established the Committee on Industrial Organization, thus beginning the broad coordination of industrial unions.

May 27, 1935: The U.S. Supreme Court in the *Schechter Poultry Corporation v. United States* rules that parts of NIRA are unconstitutional and removes legal protections for labor union activities; this day becomes known as "Black Monday."

July 5, 1935: Congress passes the National Labor Relations Act, also known as the Wagner Act, prohibiting employers from engaging in certain unfair business practices and defining the actions of a newly established National Labor Relations Board.

1936: The Committee on Industrial Organization becomes the Congress of Industrial Organizations (CIO) and represents more than 30 industrial unions.

June 25, 1938: The Fair Labor Standards Act restores legal protections over child labor, minimum wages, and maximum hours, lost when NIRA was held partially unconstitutional in 1935.

---

that time. During the economic prosperity of World War I (1914–1918) and the early 1920s, activity of the union had steadily declined. Unions are organized groups of workers joined together for a common purpose, such as pushing management for better working conditions. Such conditions include wages, health and

safety, hours required to work, and benefits including retirement. Before the late nineteenth century unions were primarily composed of skilled craftsmen, however, with the rapid growth of industry and factories after the Civil War (1861–1865), semi-skilled and unskilled workers grew in number and began efforts to organize. Having historically received little support from government and strong resistance from management who did not want to share any control of companies with workers, the early labor movement took a more aggressive path to gain recognition from employers. This path discouraged many workers from participating. The main issue of confrontation between these early unions and business management was simply seeking acceptance from the company and an opportunity to negotiate working conditions.

In addition, during good times, workers did not find compelling reasons to work together in unions for better wages and other benefits. Further, the Republican administrations of Warren G. Harding (served 1921–1923), Calvin Coolidge (served 1923–1929), and Herbert Hoover (served 1929–1933) were not friendly towards unions. They refused to adopt any policies that would recognize rights of workers to collectively bargain, or negotiate as a group, over working conditions including wages, hours worked, health and safety, and various benefits. The right to strike, to temporarily walk out of a job until workers' demands of employers such as better pay and hours were met, was not protected by law. The prospect of arbitrating disputes, or resolving a dispute between two other parties by a person chosen by both sides, was problematic.

As the Great Depression deepened in the 1930s, the lure of labor unions grew. Volunteers, especially from such organizations as the Communist Party USA, attempted to pull workers together through various social activities and support programs to form unions. By 1935 it was evident that broad, industrial unions— associations joining workers in steel, rubber, automobiles, or loading ships—had particular appeal. Workers were drawn to unions because of the unions' goal of protecting the interests of workers, whereas most businesses were largely concerned with protecting their own interests, regardless of how the decisions based on their bottom line might affect those working for them. Unions provided workers with a voice and protection against unfair working conditions and pay. The largely craft-oriented American Federation of Labor (AFL) composed of skilled workers could not come to terms with the new industrial unions of unskilled and semi-skilled laborers, and expelled the leaders of those new organizations. The Congress of Industrial Organization (CIO), which had existed within the framework of the AFL under the leadership of John L. Lewis of the United Mine Workers, separated from the AFL. The CIO, which was wildly successful in its membership drives in various industries, especially the automobile and steel industries, emerged from the split as a strong player in expressing the interests of labor in general.

To support this growing labor union activity the New Dealers, politicians who supported President Roosevelt's New Deal, or plan for economic relief and reform, in Congress passed laws encouraging it. Parts of Roosevelt's New Deal that assisted labor were the National Recovery Administration (NRA), which was signed into existence in June 1933 as part of the National Industrial Recovery Act (NIRA), and the National Labor Relations Act (NLRA), which became law in July 1935. While parts of the National Industrial Recovery Act were held unconstitutional in 1935, the NLRA, also known as the Wagner Act, extended legal protection to union activities, including the ability to collectively bargain or negotiate with employers to meet workers' demands for better wages, hours, benefits, and working conditions. Firing an employee for joining a union was also outlawed by the NLRA, therefore the 1930s became a highly important decade in the history of American labor.

Issue Summary

Labor Questions

During the 1920s labor unions declined dramatically in membership due to a number of circumstances surrounding industry at the time: support of the government in keeping "open shops" or denying unions the ability to represent all workers in an industry; companies' offers of pensions or stocks to keep employees from joining unions; and severe suppression of strikes by companies in various industries. As a result, their ability to improve and protect the interests of workers greatly declined. Labor leaders wondered if it was possible, in the face of widespread unemployment in the 1930s, to build a union movement and obtain legal protections for union activities. They wondered if the rapidly increasing unemployment would potentially kill any opportunity to become better organized. Many had lost their jobs. Others feared becoming unemployed and did not want to jeopardize their jobs by joining organizations that management disliked.

The federal government provided little protection for unions and when workers engaged in strikes, they often faced arrest or displacement by scab, or replacement, laborers. Violence frequently broke out because

of labor disputes. Key questions arose regarding the government role in labor relations. Could Congress as part of the New Deal chart a new course in protecting organized labor? Could the federal government have sufficient powers to bring both management and labor together to discuss the resolution of their differences?

Representing the large numbers of unskilled workers, the Congress of Industrial Organizations (CIO) grew rapidly in the late 1930s by developing industrial unions, which are unions that includes members of an entire industry, such as automobile or steel production, join regardless of their position or specialty within that industry. With this growth, several new challenges arose regarding labor activities. With the broader diversity of workers represented, the CIO had to create and maintain solidarity among the working classes and in order to do this, they had to rise above differences in ethnicity, race, and occupational skills. The CIO also had to forge a strategy that could use mass strikes and win concessions from big business without further contributing to the problems of the Great Depression. A major issue was the relationship of the CIO to the American Federation of Labor (AFL), which represented skilled workers. The prospect of having relative labor peace and renewed prosperity seemed more complicated when two massive unions had very different philosophies and strategies for obtaining their objectives. While organizing workers across social and work backgrounds was not without problems, unions did find ways to press their causes despite the trying economic times brought on by the Great Depression.

Rebuilding a Labor Movement

The decline in union membership had continued from the 1920s into the 1930s, from more than four million union members in 1920 to less than three million union members in 1933. Along with the unwillingness of the government and industry to facilitate union membership, the shop closings and layoffs prevalent during the Depression contributed to waning union membership. Those who belonged to unions were, for the most part, miners, construction workers, or skilled craftsmen. To rebuild the labor movement, union advocates had to find issues and means to revive the commitment of working men and women to joint action, otherwise they would continue to face long hours, low wages, job insecurity, and poor working conditions. They also needed federal laws supporting their strikes and collective bargaining. The issues most relevant to workers were long work weeks extending up to 60 or 80 hours a week in some jobs, a drop in incomes, (the national per capita income fell from $705 in 1929 before the crash, steadily down to $374 in 1933) and the prevalence of industrial accidents.

As the Great Depression deepened, it was clear that unemployed workers were caught in difficult circumstances. In 1930 no federal or state unemployment programs existed and fewer than 150,000 workers had private unemployment insurance. As a result, those without jobs were without incomes and those without incomes were unable to pay rent, purchase food, and maintain their families' standard of living. Unemployment during the Depression was thus a vicious circle that was hard to escape.

Though rents and costs for food and clothing dropped during the 1930s, unemployed workers were still unable to pay for many of these basic necessities including housing. As a result evictions became common, creating a growing homeless population. In a number of cities both men and women, sometimes helped by the Communist party, formed Unemployed Councils to protest evictions and participate in rent strikes, which was the refusal to pay rent until rental rates were lowered by landlords to meet declining incomes. Black women also formed Housewives Leagues and protested under the slogan "Don't Buy Where You Can't Work." The boycott, which began in Harlem, was targeted against white-owned businesses in black communities that refused to hire black employees. These boycotts helped thousands of black Americans secure jobs in the 1930s.

The turn around in the labor movement during the 1930s was the product of dedicated, determined leadership, a growing realization of the needs of workers, and a softening of government's anti-union stance. As the Great Depression deepened, the appeal of union membership grew and the zeal of organizers mounted. Women formed auxiliaries to a number of the male-dominated unions and assisted with first aid, food supply, and child care during strikes, and sometimes joined men on the picket line.

Congress gave some stimulus to unionization in 1933 when it passed the National Industrial Recovery Act (NIRA). The NIRA was a complex law, which permitted workers to organize into unions, select representatives, and engage in collective bargaining. Importantly the law gave unions greater legitimacy in the eyes of workers. The law also led to creation of the Public Works Administration (PWA) that provided work for many unemployed laborers, and also established the National Recovery Administration (NRA). The NRA partly suspended antitrust laws and laid out a basis for creating codes for business operation. Section 7A of the NIRA contained a special provision protecting unions, which stated: "Employees shall have the right to organize and to bargain collectively through representatives of their own choosing, and shall be free from interfer-

ence, restraint, or coercion of employers—in the designation of such representatives."

A Struggling Union Movement

Using the prospect of union legitimacy offered in Section 7A of the NIRA, John L. Lewis, a conservative Republican who had headed the United Mine Workers since 1919, began rebuilding membership in the United Mine Workers, organizing workers in one of the most dangerous occupations in the country. Long hours, exposure to coal dust and hazardous conditions far below the earth, accidents, and low wages had long beset miners. Lewis became a powerful force in labor as the United Mine Workers grew in membership and strength. Other unions, however, did not fare as well.

Though Section 7A permitted workers to organize and bargain collectively, early in 1934 the NRA ruled that company unions might legally fulfill this section of the law as an alternative to outside unions. Companies established their own unions to appease workers by allowing them to settle disputes with the company, which, through the company union, was essentially overseeing its own negotiations. Employees benefited somewhat through minor improvements in working conditions and pay. The benefits of a company union, however, primarily went to the company that was trying to avoid losing workers who would quit if a union wasn't formed, or having to bargain with a true union that would be more likely to negotiate terms that might increase a company's costs. When a company started its own union, it significantly undermined or made impossible the work of a national or craft union. In the first half of 1934 nearly 25 percent of industrial workers labored in factories which had established company unions.

The events of the Great Depression in the early 1930s thus brought mixed prospects for unions. Unemployment, low wages, evictions, yellow dog contracts (documents signed by employees who promised not to join labor unions), and company unions, were all good reasons for laborers to consider joining craft or industrial unions. A change in atmosphere, however, was needed before that could occur.

The U.S. Supreme Court in May 1935 ruled that the National Recovery Administration (NRA), a major part of the NIRA law, was unconstitutional. The *Schecter Poultry Corp. v. United States* ruling overturned Section 7A. As a result, the right of workers to organize and engage in collective bargaining ceased to exist. The death of the NRA, however, also meant that company unions were less prevalent. With companies no longer obligated under law to allow their employees the choice of organizing into unions, many companies ceased their union support. Company unions

Police and Teamsters clash during a strike in Minneapolis, Minnesota in 1934. (National Archives and Records Administration.)

lost popularity and membership in industrial, skilled, and other unions began to rise again.

Labor Takes Off

The same month as the Supreme Court decision overturning the NRA, Congress again took the initiative to create a situation favorable to organized labor. In May 1935 President Roosevelt (served 1933–1945) signed the National Labor Relations Act, also known as the Wagner Act after its sponsorship by Senator Robert Wagner of New York. The law prohibited cer-

tain unfair labor practices, such as interference and coercion with regard to employees' right to organization and collective bargaining, and created the National Labor Relations Board (NLRB).

The NLRB was given considerable leeway to administer the law; it could help employees hold elections and select a bargaining agent, such as a union. It could prevent unfair labor practices and might issue "cease and desist" orders—telling an employer to stop what it was doing. It could also insist that employers deal in good faith with workers in their efforts to

More About...

Willard S. Townsend, Jr., and the Redcaps

Hardworking and poorly paid, Redcaps—almost entirely black American laborers—handled baggage and scrambled for nickels and dimes at the nation's railroad depots in the 1920s and the 1930s. Willard Saxby Townsend, Jr. (1895–1957), a determined organizer, helped them form a union and gain some protections for their labor.

Townsend, a black American labor leader, organizer, and educator, was born in Cincinnati, Ohio. He graduated from high school in 1912 and worked for two years as a redcap—a baggage handler—at the Cincinnati railroad depot. He served in the U.S. Army in France during World War I and returned to the United States to gain an education. In 1924 he graduated from the Royal College of Science in Toronto with a degree in chemistry. During his years of study, Townsend supported himself as a redcap and dining car waiter on Canadian railroads.

Townsend moved to Texas and taught school before settling in Chicago in 1929 and marrying. With the onset of the Great Depression he was not able to find work; once again he had to work as a redcap and was expected to survive on tips, not on wages. He then considered organizing a union. Most black Americans at that time had been excluded from unions, had little use or no respect for them, and were desperate for work. Townsend, nevertheless, organized redcaps in five Chicago depots and laid the groundwork in 1937 for the Labor Auxiliary of Redcaps, an affiliate for the American Federation of Labor. In 1938 the union became the International Brotherhood of Red Caps and Townsend served as its first president and continued in the position until his death.

Redcaps faced immense obstacles as a union. For example, white railroad workers opposed them claiming the redcaps were independent contractors, not employees. In 1938 Townsend persuaded the Interstate Commerce Commission to rule that redcaps were employees, which set the stage for negotiations for improved working conditions and pay. Townsend also helped form the United Transport Service Employees, a union for porters and laundry workers serving Pullman cars.

In 1942 Townsend joined the executive council of the CIO and became its vice-president. He was the first black American to hold office in a national labor organization. Townsend continued to be active in labor and black American affairs. His critics charged that he did not act with sufficient militancy; however, Townsend was a realist who became a significant figure in American labor during the 1930s.

---

organize and engage in collective bargaining. The rapid growth of labor unions in the United States followed the birth of the NLRB.

Another factor highly significant in the growth of unions was a decision by eight unions in 1935, at a meeting of the American Federation of Labor (AFL), to create the Committee for Industrial Organization (CIO). John L. Lewis sensed that a new era for industrial unions had arrived but the leadership of the craft-dominated AFL did not necessarily agree. The AFL was a loose federation of independent craft unions, the primary unifying force for American labor from its founding in 1886 to the 1930s. They were not eager to open the door to lesser skilled industrial workers, which led to its division. Tempers flared as debate raged over who the new organization should include. When Bill Hutcheson, president of the Carpenters'

Union, insulted Lewis on the floor of the annual meeting in Atlantic City for pursuing industrial union organization, Lewis punched him in the jaw and sent him sprawling. The encounter made national headlines and showed the public the division between craft unions representing skilled workers and industrial unions representing unskilled and semi-skilled workers.

A few weeks after the Lewis-Hutcheson encounter, the AFL suspended from its organization all the unions that formed the new CIO, but they could not stop the momentum. Leaders of rubber workers, laborers in automobile factories, redcaps handling baggage at railroad stations, longshoremen, teamsters (which were a union of truck drivers), and worker organizations of other industries considered joining the CIO. As the CIO grew, tensions with the AFL and its old-line emphasis on skilled workers mounted. Unions represented by the

An aerial view of the Goodyear Tire and Rubber factory complex in Akron, Ohio as it appeared in 1935. The plant was the site of sit-down strikes by rubber workers that spread to plants around the country.

(AP/Wide World Photos. Reproduced by permission.)

CIO were not organized by shared skills in crafts like the AFL member unions, but rather based on the type of industry or shared workplace. A major split in the nation's union movement resulted in the AFL and the CIO trying to out recruit the other for new members. With its new independent status, the CIO changed its name in November 1938 to the Congress of Industrial Organizations.

The new CIO grew dramatically under the charismatic leadership of John L. Lewis, who abandoned some of his former, conservative principles. Like the AFL, the CIO was a broad unifying organization representing numerous labor unions. By 1938 the CIO represented 38 national unions. In spite of the obvious differences in philosophy and approach between the AFL and CIO, unionization in the United States

Men read papers and refuse to work inside the General Motors plant in Flint, Michigan, during the famous sit-down strike of 1937. (UPI/Corbis-Bettmann. Reproduced by permission.)

continued to grow. Both the AFL and CIO attracted hundreds of thousands of new union members.

Union Action Becomes Bolder

The growth of the CIO was, in part, a product of the success of its member unions in fighting for their wants. Some of the efforts came at the grassroots level and were sparked in the factories by the workers, not by the leaders of their unions. Such a case came in late 1935 in Akron, Ohio, when Goodyear Corporation announced it was returning to an eight-hour workday, but because of the Depression's effect on sales, the company would pay wages only for six hours of work. The automobile industry, including related tire manufacturers, had been the leaders in U.S. industry since the late 1910s. The Depression, however, triggered a major decline in car sales. As a result the demand for car tires also plummeted. Rubber workers at plants owned by Goodyear, Firestone, and Goodrich—all manufacturers of tires—without prompting from their union leaders, staged a "sit-down strike" in January 1936. They remained in the factories but refused to work until their demand for a 30-hour workweek was met. This tactic blocked the employers from replacing them with scab laborers.

With the strike continuing for several weeks Goodyear started firing workers that February. In response the sit-down strikes spread, eventually idling over 14,000 workers. At this point the CIO began assisting the rubber workers, giving advice and financial assistance. Finally in March 1936 Goodyear gave in to a number of the workers' demands, including their demand for a thirty-hour workweek. Local opposition to company practices continued to flare from time to time. Unions representing the workers would then call for "wildcat strikes," in which workmen walked off the job. These actions continued at Goodyear for the next five years.

In 1936 the United Auto Workers (UAW), a CIO affiliate, began a series of actions against General Motors (GM). Despite the collapse of car sales due to the Depression, General Motors had risen to the top of the auto industry controlling 43 percent of the market and still showing a profit. Given its relatively strong financial condition, GM became a target for labor unions seeking to gain increased wages and benefits. Laborers had become bolder with the election of Frank Murphy, a liberal, as governor of Michigan because they realized that Murphy would likely not take action against them if they engaged in strikes. In the fall of 1936 strikes began occurring at the local level first without the support of the UAW. With the UAW support coming strikes spread to plants in Cleveland, Kansas City, Atlanta, and Flint, Michigan. Strikers used "sit-down" tactics thus avoiding confrontation on the street with people opposing a picket line and it also kept employers from bringing in scab laborers.

In January 1937 the strike at the GM plant in Flint erupted into a brawl between strikers and the police on the street outside the factory. While the police fired tear gas and strikers retaliated by throwing rocks and bottles, no one was killed, however, a number of people were injured on both sides. The governor of Michigan, Frank Murphy, sent in the National Guard to keep order but not to break the strike. Murphy chose this tactic not only because of his liberal stance and support of unions, but also because of a desire to keep the situation peaceful. In not allowing the National Guard to physically move into the plant, Murphy believed that he was preventing any further violence, especially toward the unarmed workers inside.

In early February the UAW occupied another plant in Flint and in retaliation General Motors secured a court injunction to evict the strikers. A judge who owned a significant amount of GM stock, however, issued the injunction; thus, the ruling could not truly have been impartial. In light of this news, Governor Murphy was unable to force the injunction, instead, John L. Lewis of the CIO came in to negotiate for the UAW.

The UAW conflict with GM proved once and for all the power of unionization in the United States. Historian Robert S. McElvaine later assessed the event (from McElvaine, Robert. *The Great Depression: America, 1929–1941,* 1993, p. 294):

> The results of the GM strike were monumental. It was the acid test of the CIO. A steel organizer said during the auto strike that the steel workers "hesitate to stick out their necks. Wait till you win the auto strike. Then we'll join." And join they did, in steel and automobiles and other industries. The membership of the UAW itself skyrocketed in the eight months after the GM strike from 88,000 to 400,000. In March, 1937, there were 170 sit-down strikes involving 167,210 workers across the nation.

As a consequence of CIO success in the automotive industry, manufacturers in other sectors began to enter into agreements with other unions but all was not peaceful. Labor disputes at the Republic Mill in Chicago on Memorial Day, 1937, turned violent when the police prohibited picketing at the main gate. As workers marched toward the steel mill, the police blocked them. A demonstrator lobbed a tree branch at the police, who began shooting into the air and the demonstrators then began throwing rocks. The police

opened fire on the workers, then pursued the demonstrators, shooting and beating them. Ten demonstrators died—all shot in the back—twenty-eight others were wounded and hospitalized, while three police officers needed medical treatment. This event became known as the Memorial Day Massacre. Despite the "massacre," nothing was immediately resolved between Republic Steel and the strikers. The strike continued until August 1941 when Republic Steel agreed to end unfair labor practices. A year later, Republic Steel signed a contract with United Steelworkers of America.

More Congressional Support and Court Setbacks Arrive

Members of labor unions and other workers were further heartened when, after considerable debate and opposition from conservatives, Congress in 1938 passed the Fair Labor Standards Act. This law addressed some of the advances in NIRA that had been undone when the Supreme Court overthrew NRA and covered all workers engaged in interstate commerce or manufacture of goods moving between states. The law applied several of the codes from the National Labor Recovery Act that addressed maximum hours, minimum wages, and child labor. More specifically, the new law, signed on June 25, prohibited child labor in interstate commerce. It also fixed a minimum wage of 25¢ an hour and a maximum work week of 44 hours, providing that by 1940 wages would go to 40¢ an hour with a work week of 40 hours. Employers who wanted laborers to exceed the maximum hours allowed had to pay time-and-a-half, still, however, an estimated 12 million workers in 1938 were earning less than 25¢ an hour.

Another unwelcome Supreme Court ruling, however, came in 1939. The outlawing of sit-down strikes was disconcerting to workers, especially to members of the CIO. This technique had served the industrial unions well by bringing factories to a close and compelling management to consider the grievances of workers.

As a result of the Great Depression workers in many occupations organized into unions for the first time. New Deal laws, slow in enactment and sometimes incomplete in enforcement, did help change the condition of laborers. Unions gave millions of workers a voice and a sense of solidarity in demanding fair treatment from employers that they had never before possessed.

Contributing Forces

With the rapid industrialization of the American economy following the Civil War (1861–1865), working conditions in factories were often deplorable. Low

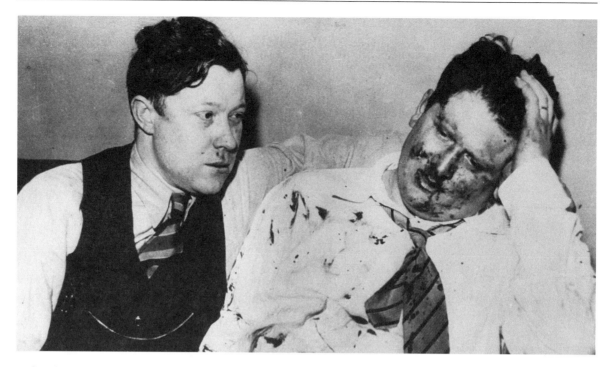

Labor leaders Walter P. Reuther and Richard T. Frankenstein after being beaten by thugs hired by Ford Motor Company. Many labor struggles turned violent during the Great Depression. (UPI/Corbis-Bettmann. Reproduced by permission.)

pay, long hours, no benefits, and unhealthy conditions were far too common for workers as company owners accumulated vast wealth in the growing industrial economy. The railroad industry had led the industrialization efforts of the late nineteenth century by establishing a strong demand for iron, steel, and coal. Efforts to form national unions of unskilled industrial workers in the United States to address these issues began in the 1880s with the Knights of Labor (KOL) and the Federation of Organized Trades. The KOL focused on national political issues and before long lost support of its diverse membership. The Federation, however, focused instead on working conditions such as working hours, safety, wages, and benefits, making its support more stable than KOL's. The Federation became the AFL in 1886, forming a loose federation of craft unions.

Labor activities became more radical with the militant Industrial Workers of the World (IWW), formed in 1906. The IWW attempted to draw into its ranks loggers, sawmill workers, farm hands, and other laborers. The IWW (also mockingly referred to as "I Won't Work") tried to weld together unskilled workingmen and women from all sorts of jobs. To create solidarity, the IWW employed songs, fiery speakers, combative

strikes, and parades, however, the economic boom of World War I and the following decade of the 1920s led workers to back away from the radical group. For various reasons most of these early broad-based industrial unions were not able to fully achieve their objectives and sustain large memberships for any length of time.

The Setting Changes for Unions

During the 1910s unionization swept through many crafts and industries. The craft unions attracted members with commonly held skills, for example, boilermakers, pipe fitters, and carpenters each developed unions specific to their craft.

Unionization did see some growth during World War I, only to decline rapidly afterwards. During the years 1920 and 1923 unions lost almost 1.5 million members; about a 30 percent decrease. A labor surplus, fostered by mechanization, drove workers from jobs as well as from union membership. Mechanization involved major breakthroughs in automating factories. New machines worked faster and were more accurate and consistent for the new mass production strategies that involved interchangeable parts between the individual products. Assembly line production also greatly increased efficiency while reducing the number of workers needed in many industries. Fewer workers meant fewer prospective members of labor unions. The IWW, for example, grew rapidly during the 1910s but, like other unions, declined in the 1920s. The pacifism (opposition to war) of some IWW leaders and general feelings in the public that unions were thwarting the country's efforts to fight World War I by their work stoppages, cost the union support and also raised considerable opposition to them.

The reasons for the general decline in all unions by the 1920s were, in part, founded in the anti-union attitudes and actions of company owners and the administrations of presidents Harding, Coolidge, and Hoover. Some employers, for example, required yellow dog contracts. These contracts required workers to agree not to join a labor union as a condition for their employment, and were so named because workers were essentially required to beg like dogs for jobs from employers. Other businesses formed company unions dominated by the management of the company, which were designed to block the prospects that workers would join a craft or industrial union not controlled by the company. During the 1920s union membership fell sharply from a high of more than 4 million in 1920, to 3.4 million in 1929. This drop in union membership and activity left workers particularly vulnerable to businesses cutting back during the Great Depression, especially among the less organized unskilled laborers.

The lack of any federal or state unemployment insurance programs in the early 1930s, combined with low wages, dangerous working conditions, lack of paid vacation time, and no retirement provisions caused workers to consider what might be gained by combined action. Unions offered the possibility of forcing employers to accommodate the needs of their workers if the workers could stand united before managers and owners.

Perspectives

Worker Gains

After passage of the Wagner Act in 1935, unions grew rapidly. The AFL continued to represent skilled craft workers, controlling access into its skilled labor jobs through programs of apprenticeships, high union fees, and fairly wide discrimination against minorities and women. If a person was not a union member their access to jobs was limited for they could not receive union-sponsored training through the apprenticeships to make them more competitive. Also if they did not pay the high union fees or if they were a woman or

More About...
Factory Work

One of the realities of factory work was its repetitive, monotonous, demanding, and dehumanizing quality. Henry Ford had pioneered in the automobile industry the efficiency of the assembly line. Automobiles moved from chassis to finished product along a great, moving track where workers installed universal joints, transmissions, engines, seats, doors, and windows—each process carried out over and over by the same workers at the same site. The assembly line was paced to force the worker to move as quickly and efficiently as possible. Such work left nothing to the imagination and, to many, appeared a modern form of slavery or imprisonment.

Charlie Chaplin's film *Modern Times* captured the mindless nature of work in industrial plants. The hero of the film, driven by the ever-increasing speed of the assembly line, worked like a maniac to keep up, tightening bolts with two wrenches and, finally, got sucked into the great machine at the end of the belt. Even eating was done with mechanization and, in the film, the owner installed a feeding machine to make lunch breaks more efficient. *Modern Times,* a great satire on the mechanized world of the 1930s, made sense to millions of viewers.

minority, access to the training and other union programs designed to help them gain employment would not be available. The CIO emerged as a new alternative in unionization because it enrolled millions of industrial workers, which the AFL refused to do. The workers were willing to engage in sit-down strikes, or strikes where workers remained in the workplace but refused to work; wildcat strikes, or strikes organized locally rather than through a union in particular; picketing; and strong bargaining to secure gains in wages and benefits.

For female workers, the CIO opened many opportunities. Unlike the AFL, the CIO allowed a number of unions enrolling women to become affiliates. Women's membership in unions grew to 800,000 by 1940. The International Ladies' Garment Workers

Charlie Chaplin gets caught in the gears of the manufacturing industry in his 1936 film Modern Times.
(© Bettmann/Corbis. Reproduced by permission.)

Union (ILGWU) enrolled more than two hundred thousand members, which included Mexican American embroiderers and hand sewers working from their homes, and cutters, fitters, seamstresses, and pressers working in clothing factories. Although having a mixed record on protecting racial minorities, the ILGWU by the mid-1930s included a number of black American women in its ranks from Boston, New York, Philadelphia, and Chicago.

In 1932, 3.1 million workers belonged to unions and this number grew modestly to 3.9 million workers in 1935. By 1939, however, union membership doubled from the 1935 rate to 8 million members.

Unions on the Margins

A number of unions, though remaining small in the 1930s, were critical to voicing workers' demands and meeting workers' needs. The Communist Party helped many small unions with organization and recruitment. The American communists were especially committed to working with minorities, who were often rebuffed or overlooked by the AFL, CIO, and other large unions. This slight by unions was due to the racist attitudes of some union leaders and members and the simple fact that a relatively small percentage of blacks were in the industrial worker population.

Communist party leaders in the United States seized the occasion of growing worker strife to press labor's cause and saw this issue as a key avenue for gaining membership. This association between the communist party and labor scared many Americans who began to associate the labor movement with radical left-wing politics. At the same time the rise of Nazi fascism in Germany reinforced this fear. Though many workers appreciated any support they could muster, few actually joined the Communist Party.

In Alabama, for example, a Sharecroppers Union in the 1930s recruited members for 28 local chapters and a dozen women's auxiliaries. Women played important roles in helping to form this union, which was closely linked to the programs of the Communist Party. They included left-leaning white women, black American women, and working class women. Writing about this organization, historian Nancy Cott noted (in Cott, Nancy, ed. *No Small Courage: A History of Women in the United States,* 2000, p. 470): "The women's auxiliaries met separately from the men in the Sharecroppers Union, both so that one parent could always stay home with the children and to divert the suspicions of local white authorities, who were hostile to this attempt on the part of sharecroppers to drive a better bargain."

In California Dorothy Healey, a member of the Communist Party, worked for most of the late 1930s to organize cannery workers and dock laborers, who faced dangerous conditions with long hours and little pay. Healey served as vice-president of the United Cannery, Agricultural, Packing and Allied Workers of America (UCA-PAWA). In 1939 the UCA-PAWA, representing some 430 workers (mostly women) initiated a strike on the California Sanitary Canning Company, also referred to as Cal San. The workers were seeking recognition of the union by the company in the midst of the peach-canning season. The picket line stood duty 24 hours a day for a duration of two and a half months. Finally the owners of Cal San, reprimanded by the National Labor Relations Board and humiliated by children carrying signs claiming their mothers were underpaid, met with the union representatives. This result gave the union some credibility and standing with the company.

Organized labor gave millions of workers a voice and bargaining power that they had never before possessed during the years of the Great Depression.

(The Granger Collection, New York. Reproduced by permission.)

Impact

Labor and unions charted new ground in America during the Great Depression. Entering the 1930s under desperate circumstances and little legal standing, unions emerged by the late 1930s as a major force in the American economy. Because of congressional protection under the New Deal, labor unions were better able to organize and recruit workers, mount strikes, and engage in collective bargaining.

Although the 1930s were depressed years in the American economy, the advances—many stemming directly from programs and policies formulated to overcome the Great Depression—helped millions of workers rise from lower to middle class in the better economic times during the 1940s and 1950s. Increasingly, the state and federal governments assumed responsibilities for workers, creating employment offices, unemployment insurance, and pension programs, none of which existed at the time of the Depression. The lack of these programs in the 1930s made many workers vulnerable to unemployment and economic despair. Another improvement for workers came with the passage of the Social Security program in 1935, which required the withholding of worker contributions and employer taxes to provide for old-age benefits for workers upon retirement.

Another result coming out of the New Deal's protective policies toward labor was the emergence of broad-based industrial unions. Individual unions found a common voice through the Congress of Industrial Organizations (CIO). The CIO and the AFL both represented different worker interests and often pursued different strategies. By 1940, however, each organization gave laborers a voice in the nation's economy.

The Decline of Organized Labor

After 30 years of considerable strength growing out of New Deal policies the influence of labor unions began to decline in the 1970s. During that decade the percentage of workers in the United States outside of agriculture who were members of labor unions fell from 28 percent to 23 percent, even though the size of the workforce increased. With the Republican administration of President Ronald Reagan (served 1981–1989) being unsupportive of labor unions during the 1980s—much as the Republican administrations of the 1920s had been—the decline in union membership fell further to 17.5 percent of the workforce by 1986.

Also during this time, the technology and service industries were replacing the manufacturing, mining, and construction industries in the U.S. economy. Many manufacturing industries whose workers greatly benefited from New Deal policies shifted operations to foreign nations, often economically undeveloped Third World countries that did not offer its laborers working conditions and benefits that had been gained by workers under New Deal-supported labor negotiation processes in the United States. These growing industries, though largely characterized by low-wage part time jobs, were less susceptible to unionization. With these trends in the 1980s, corporations became much more aggressive towards labor unions. The expanding global economy meant companies could threaten to relocate manufacturing facilities to other countries that had cheaper labor standards. The United States entered a new economic era labeled the postindustrial period. Domestic manufacturing was being increasingly replaced by service industries including communications, commercial banking, and retail sales.

The impact of labor unions and influence of prolabor policies first established by New Deal in the 1930s was further diminished in the 1990s. The development of a global economy was characterized by elimination of tariffs (taxes on imports) and increased international character of corporations. A free-trade movement promoted by the U.S. government under both Democratic and Republican administrations led to major international trade agreements including the General Agreement on Tariffs and Trade (GATT) and the North American Free Trade Agreement (NAFTA) as well as the growth of the World Trade Organization (WTO) to help guide global economic development and trade.

Though the U.S. economy was booming overall through most of the 1990s all of these developments were met with great resistance from unions who saw their influence further erode as corporate earnings were substantially growing. Manufacturing jobs increasingly were shifted to nations where wages were lower, benefits much less, and environmental regulations more limited or non-existent. This shift in turn led to decreased wages and benefits in United States jobs from the resulting job competition. Unions found themselves on the same side as environmental activists protesting the trade agreements and WTO policies encouraging these job shifts. Though the United States remained the world's leading exporter of merchandise in 1999, information technology and communications enjoyed the greatest demand while manufacturing saw a continued decline in importance given the steady shift of industries to other nations with less costs to operate including cheaper labor. In the beginning of the twenty-first century manufacturing industries with the associated labor unions were still on a long-term decline compounded by an economic recession in 2001.

Notable People

John Brophy (1883–1963). John Brophy, son of a coal miner, became a coal miner himself as well as a union organizer and a consistent advocate of education. Raised a Catholic, he attended parochial school until 1892 when his parents emigrated from England to Pennsylvania. The Panic of 1893 brought lean times to the Brophys compelling them to move as his father sought employment in the mines. Six of Brophy's eight brothers and sisters died in infancy or early youth. When Brophy was 12 years old he joined his father in the mines and at age 15, in 1899, he joined a local chapter of the United Mine Workers of America.

Brophy had little opportunity to gain a formal education but displayed keen insight into labor problems. He favored industrial rather than craft unionism, advocated union membership, supported workers' education programs, and was an advocate of social planning. He called for government ownership of coal mining and, though knowledgeable about socialism, shaped much of his philosophy on the principles of "Christian

An auto worker on the assembly line at the Ford River Rouge plant in Detroit smooths the rough spots on a new car. Many auto workers were unemployed because of slumping sales due to the Depression. (AP/Wide World Photos. Reproduced by permission.)

humanism." Throughout the 1920s and 1930s Brophy promoted worker education and was a founder of the Workers' Education Bureau and a member from 1921 to 1938 of the Labor Cooperating Committee of Brookwood Labor College.

Brophy's views on government control of industry and social planning led to conflict with the leadership of the United Mine Workers and the American Federation of Labor. He challenged John L. Lewis in 1926 for the presidency of the United Mine Workers, but was defeated and thrown out of the union. For the next several years Brophy worked as a salesman, but in 1933 he was appointed special representative of the UMW, and in 1934 he served as the national director of the Committee for Industrial Organization (CIO). Brophy was a key player in strikes and union organizing in the later 1930s and he helped found the United Auto Workers, United Rubber Workers, and United

Biography:

John L. Lewis

1880, February 12–1969, June 11   Lewis was born into a coal mining family in Iowa; his parents were from Wales. Lewis entered the mines in 1901 and became a charter member of the local chapter of the United Mine Workers of America. Following various jobs and career shifts, Lewis and family members settled in the coalfields of Illinois where he again became active in union activity. In 1911 he became a field representative for Samuel Gompers, the AFL president. Lewis returned to the UMWA in 1917, rose rapidly in its leadership, and in 1920 became president of the union that then had about 400,000 members.

Although Lewis was a firm and determined leader, the UMWA dropped steadily in membership in the 1920s. Lengthy strikes, deteriorating markets for coal (because of competition from diesel and other oil products), lack of state and federal support for unions, and unemployment hurt the union. The 1925 book *The Miner's Fight for American Standards* discussed the predicament of coal miners and their families. The book carried Lewis' name but was written by his UMWA adviser, W. Jett Lauck. The volume argued that unions were the only means in which workers might rise in living standards and as a result become consumers.

Lewis was a conservative Republican, often at odds with others in the UMWA over politics. He was also an opportunist who used the changing political atmosphere of the 1930s to rebuild his union. Passage of the NIRA encouraged Lewis to rebuild the union and extend its influence. He had almost instant success and began to pressure the AFL to include largely unskilled workers in industry. When the Committee on Industrial Organizations was ousted in 1936 from the AFL, Lewis surpassed John Brophy to head the new CIO. Lewis then became one of the nation's most visible spokesmen for workers and was often personally involved in negotiations on behalf of the CIO with industry.

Lewis left the presidency of the CIO in 1938 and became increasingly alienated from it and finally withdrew the UMWA from it by 1942. Lewis continued for years as a major force in American labor, serving a total of 40 years as head of the UMWA.

Steel Workers. Brophy continued working for the CIO during World War II (1939–1945) and served as a representative on several boards during the 1940s. At his death in 1963 Walter Reuther, president of the United Auto Workers, declared "our industrial unions are living testimonials" to John Brophy's dedicated work.

Henry Ford (1863–1947). Perhaps no other American did more to industry and labor in the United States during the first half of the twentieth century than Henry Ford. Born on a farm in Michigan, Ford received a limited education while attending one-room schools. Rather than farming, he preferred tinkering with machines. In the early 1890s Ford began developing a car driven by an internal-combustion engine.

By 1903 he founded the Ford Motor Company with $28,000 he gained from selling stock. From this modest base, Ford expanded and developed the "Model T" in 1908. This consistently operating, low-cost, efficient vehicle became the nation's first, mass-produced car. In 1910 Ford opened a modern, ventilated, well-lit factory. He and his employees developed the assembly line to improve the efficient production of vehicles.

In 1914 Ford began paying his workers $5.00 a day for an eight-hour day, nearly twice the rate for industrial workers, which was part of his profit-sharing plan. As he became wealthier, Ford became involved in social issues such as education and health.

Ford turned to the Model A in 1927 and, in spite of the Great Depression, kept his plants in operation although production plunged downward as sales slackened. Ford had 170,502 employees in 1929 and only 46,282 in 1932. When his workers formed unions and attempted collective bargaining, Ford became their bitter foe. His company violated the National Labor Relations Act, fired union members, and persisted in tense labor relations into the early 1940s. As a result Ford was one of the latest major car manufacturers to unionize. Henry Ford was a brilliant but erratic industrialist, who made many contributions to the United States, but became increasingly alienated from labor and industry trends.

Frances Perkins (1880–1965). Frances Perkins served as secretary of labor from 1933 to 1945, the first woman to hold this cabinet position. Born in Boston, Massachusetts, Perkins attended Mount Holyoke College where she helped establish a chapter of the National Consumers' League. From her college years, she was a dedicated opponent of sweatshops and child labor.

Perkins was, for a number of years, involved in social work. She worked at Hull House in Chicago, investigated child malnutrition in New York City, campaigned for women's suffrage, and taught sociology. In 1911 following the tragic Triangle Shirtwaist Company fire that killed 146 garment workers, she became involved in worker safety programs. In 1919 Governor Al Smith named her to the Industrial Commission of the State of New York. Governor Franklin D. Roosevelt named her industrial commissioner and head of the state labor department.

Perkins gained attention as a critic of President Hoover's social policies and when Roosevelt was elected president, he named her the first woman Secretary of Labor. She was a leading figure in moving the New Deal toward support of labor, especially with passage of NIRA (1933), the Civilian Conservation Corps (CCC), Social Security Act, and the Fair Labor Standards Act. She tried to heal the rift between skilled and unskilled labor in the troubles between the AFL and CIO but did not succeed and she consistently encouraged good faith negotiations.

Walter Philip Reuther (1907–1970). Reuther was one of the nation's prominent labor leaders of the twentieth century. The Great Depression fired his commitment to leadership of unions.

Reuther was born in West Virginia to German-born parents. His father was an iron mill and brewery worker, who embraced socialism and unionization. Reuther, as a boy, went with his father to visit Eugene Debs, the prominent union organizer and subsequently socialist leader, while he was in jail. These early experiences with unions and socialism helped shape his thinking. In 1927 Reuther found employment with the Ford Motor Company in Detroit, Michigan and due to his good skills, Reuther quickly rose to a high-paying position as a mechanic. He went to school at night and earned his high school diploma when he was 22 years of age.

During the Great Depression, Reuther witnessed Ford's release of more than half of its workers and as a result saw great suffering. He and his brother Victor photographed conditions among the unemployed. When Norman Thomas campaigned in 1932 as socialist candidate for president, Reuther traveled over three thousands miles to rally supporters for him. Between 1932 and 1934 Reuther visited Germany and worked in the Soviet Union as a tool and die maker. He returned a strong advocate for grassroots democracy based on the rights of workers.

In 1936 Reuther became a full-time organizer for the United Auto Workers (UAW), one of the CIO unions. He soon became a paid union official and in late 1936 helped lead a sit-down strike that helped to spur rapid union growth. By 1937 Reuther was in a leadership position in planning strikes. When beaten by hired thugs working for the Ford Motor Company, Reuther's picture appeared in *Time,* and he soon became the most influential leader of the United Auto Workers. Reuther's long career continued to 1970 when he, his wife, and others were killed in a plane crash in Michigan.

Primary Sources

Working in the Auto Industry

Justin McCarthy worked on the Ford assembly line beginning in 1933. He recalled the anti-union tactics of the Ford Motor Company in Studs Terkel's *Hard Times: An Oral History of the Great Depression* (1986, p. 137).

> I sandpapered all the right-hand fenders. I was paid $5 a day. The parts were brought in from the River Rouge plant in Detroit. When I went to work in January, we were turning out 232 cars a day. When I was fired, four months later, we were turning out 535. Without any extra help and no increase in pay. It was the famous Ford Speed-up.

> The gates were locked when you came in at eight o'clock in the morning. They weren't opened again until five o'clock in the evening ... I was aware of men in plain clothes being around the plant, and the constant surveillance. I didn't learn till later these were the men of Ford's service department. Many of them, ex-cons.

> If you wanted to go to the toilet, you had to have permission of the foreman. He had to find a substitute for you on the assembly line, who could sandpaper those two right fenders as they went by. If he couldn't right away, you held it. (Laughs.)

> If you didn't punch that clock at 8:00, if you came in at 8:02, you were docked one hour's pay. There wasn't any excuse. If you did this two or three times, you got fired.

> I made the mistake of telling the foreman I had enrolled at Northwestern University night school. He said, "Mr. Ford isn't paying people to go to college. You're through."

Roosevelt and the NIRA

In 1932 President Franklin D. Roosevelt spoke to the Commonwealth Club of San Francisco about the National Industrial Recovery Act (1933). In his speech Roosevelt commented about labor and industry and the organization of unions (from Rauch, *The History of the New Deal, 1933–1938,* p. 41):

We know, now, that [the great industrial and financial corporations] cannot exist unless prosperity is uniform, that is, unless purchasing power is well distributed throughout every group in the Nation. That is why even the most selfish of corporations for its own interest would be glad to see wages restored and unemployment ended and to bring the Western farmer back to his accustomed level of prosperity and to assure a permanent safety to both groups. That is why some enlightened industries themselves endeavor to limit the freedom of action of each man and business group within the industry in the common interest of all; why business men everywhere are asking a form of organization which will bring the scheme of things into balance, even though it may in some measure qualify the freedom of action of individual units within the business.

Suggested Research Topics

- Search newspapers from late May, 1937 and website databases to examine the causes and consequences of the Memorial Day Massacre at the Republic Steel mill in Chicago, Illinois.

- Compare and contrast the positions of the AFL and CIO in the late 1930s on the matters of permitting communists in union leadership and the inclusion of minorities and women.

- Examine the life and labors of John L. Lewis until 1940 and identify why the 1930s were a turning point in his career as a union leader.

- Identify the important legislation passed during the New Deal that opened the way for the rapid growth of labor unions in the 1930s.

- Explore the career of Frances Perkins, first woman secretary of labor, 1933–1945, and how she helped American workers in the Great Depression.

Bibliography

Sources

Brophy, John. *A Miner's Life.* Madison: University of Wisconsin Press, 1964.

Cohen, Elizabeth. *Making a New Deal: Industrial Workers in Chicago, 1919–1939.* Cambridge: Cambridge University Press, 1990.

Cott, Nancy, ed. *No Small Courage: A History of Women in the United States.* Oxford and New York: Oxford University Press, 2000.

Dubofsky, Melvyn. *Hard Work: The Making of Labor History.* Urbana: University of Illinois Press, 2000.

Fine, Sidney. *Sit-Down: The General Motors Strike of 1936–1937.* Ann Arbor: University of Michigan Press, 1969.

Galenson, Walter. *The CIO Challenge to the AFL: A History of the American Labor Movement, 1935–1941.* Cambridge, MA: Harvard University Press, 1960.

Gall, Gilbert J. *Pursuing Justice: Lee Pressman, the New Deal, and the CIO.* Albany: State University of New York Press, 1999.

Gordon, Colin. *New Deals: Business, Labor, and Politics in America, 1920–1935.* New York: Cambridge University Press, 1994.

Levine, Rhonda F. *Class Struggle and the New Deal: Industrial Labor, Industrial Capital, and the State.* Lawrence: University Press of Kansas, 1988.

Logan, Rayford W., ed. *What the Negro Wants.* Chapel Hill, NC: University of North Carolina Press, 1944.

Morris, James O. *Conflict Within the AFL: A Study of Craft Versus Industrial Unionism, 1901–1935.* Ithaca, NY: Cornell University Press, 1958.

Rauch, Basil. *The History of the New Deal, 1933–1938.* New York: Octagon Books, 1975.

Storrs, Landon R.Y. *Civilizing Capitalism: The National Consumers' League, Women's Activism, and Labor Standards in the New Deal Era.* Chapel Hill: University of North Carolina Press, 2000.

Terkel, Studs. *Hard Times: An Oral History of the Great Depression.* New York: Pantheon Books, 1986.

Vittoz, Stanley. *New Deal Labor Policy and the American Industrial Economy.* Chapel Hill: University of North Carolina Press, 1987.

Watts, Sarah Lyons. *Order Against Chaos: Business Culture and Labor Ideology in America, 1880–1915.* New York: Greenwood Press, 1991.

Zieger, Robert H. *The CIO, 1930–1935.* Chapel Hill: University of North Carolina Press, 1995.

Further Reading

Bernstein, Irving. *The Lean Years: A History of the American Worker, 1920–1933.* Boston: Houghton Mifflin, 1960.

———. *Turbulent Years: A History of the American Worker, 1933–1941.* Boston: Houghton Mifflin, 1960.

Chandler, Lester V. *America's Greatest Depression, 1929–1941.* New York: Harper & Row, 1970.

Dubofsky, Melvyn and Warren Van Tyne. *John L. Lewis: A Biography.* New York: Quadrangle Books/New York Times, 1977.

See Also

Effects of the Great Depression—LBJ's Great Society; Employment; Global Impacts; Interwar Era; National Industrial Recovery Act (NIRA); New Deal (First, and Its Critics); New Deal (Second); Supreme Court

Literature

1929-1941

Introduction

In every period in the history of American literature a diversity of talented writers appear. Likewise readers always exhibit a vast diversity of taste in what they want to read. The Depression years were no different in this regard. Prompted by the economic struggles of the Great Depression many of the 1930s writers authored an array of socially conscious books generally referred to as proletarian (working class) literature. Those writers sought to bring to readers a realistic picture of the hardships endured by their fellow Americans as the economic and social darkness of the Great Depression closed in. Another type of literature that developed in the 1930s was documentary journalism, with titles such as *The Road: In Search of America, Puzzled America,* and *My America.* Documentary journalism also resulted from the Depression as out of work journalists decided they might as well take to the road to discover how the Depression was affecting the country's people as a whole. Other journalists still on the job were sent out to "document" the social changes due to economic difficulties. These works tended to build a national self-awareness, a nationalistic spirit of who the "real" America was. Throughout the troubled times brought on by the Depression there was an undeniable public interest in economic and political subjects. Many writers sat at their typewriters attempting to supply solutions to help put America back on course. Still many other authors went along in their own individualistic ways paying no mind to current issues and topics, providing an

Chronology:

1926: Sinclair Lewis becomes the first American to receive the Nobel Prize for Literature.

1929: William Faulkner published *The Sound and the Fury.*

1930: Pearl S. Buck publishes *The Good Earth,* William Faulkner publishes *As I Lay Dying,* and John Dos Passos publishes three novels that make up his trilogy *USA.*

1932–1936: James T. Farrell publishes three novels that make up his trilogy *Studs Lonigan,* Erskine Caldwell publishes *Tobacco Road,* and William Faulkner publishes *Light in August.*

1933: Jack Conroy publishes *The Disinherited.*

1934: Robert Cantwell publishes *The Land of Plenty.*

1935: Works Progress Administration establishes a branch to support writers called the Federal Writers Project (FWP); John Steinbeck publishes *Tortilla Flat* and Sinclair Lewis publishes *It Can't Happen Here.*

1936: Margaret Mitchell publishes *Gone With the Wind.*

1937: Dale Carnegie publishes *How to Win Friends and Influence People* and author Erskine Caldwell and photographer Margaret Bourke-White publish *You Have Seen Their Faces.*

1938: Louis Adamic publishes *My America* and Pearl S. Buck receives Nobel Prize for Literature.

1939: FWP publishes *These Are Our Lives* and John Steinbeck publishes *The Grapes of Wrath.*

1940: Ernest Hemingway publishes *For Whom the Bell Tolls* and Richard Wright publishes *Native Son.*

1941: Author James Agee and photographer Walker Evans publish *Let Us Now Praise Famous Men.*

escape for their readers' daily lives and problems. Self-help books were also popular as were histories and biographies.

Beginning in 1935 between six and seven thousand writers received support through a branch of a New Deal program, the Works Progress Administration (WPA). That branch, the Federal Writers' Project (FWP), hired many unemployed writers to work on specific publications about the United States. Up to this time federal support for writers was nonexistent. An astounding number of articles, pamphlets, and books on all aspects of life in the United States resulted. Millions of American readers who generally looked no further than the daily newspaper headlines picked up pamphlets and books to try to discover just what was going on in their country.

Literature of the 1930s continued to enlarge the meaning of earlier movements toward realism and modernism. Realism was an attempt to show life as it really was—its cruelties, problems, harsh conditions, sorrows, as well as its joys and successes. Realism was regarded as a revolt against styles of writing that always portrayed life as romantic and idealized. Modernism called for new and different styles and writing techniques to reflect a world order vastly different than the world of the 1800s. Modern fiction stripped away simple descriptions of scenes, characters, and simple plots. Instead complex plots, contradictory viewpoints, and multi-dimensional characters arose.

A wide variety of authors in the 1930s, ranging from John Steinbeck to Richard Wright and Sinclair Lewis, produced books that revealed an America caught in the economic devastation of the Depression. Conversely many wrote without much regard to the situation surrounding them offering escape to their readers. Some passionately wrote of a particular struggle or cause, then fell silent. Others went on to be recognized among the most important and distinguished writers of the twentieth century. This chapter explores the diversified mix of 1930s literature and its authors.

Issue Summary

Moving to the Left

In a country as vast as the United States writers from widely varying backgrounds were bound to go down different pathways. Many writers in the 1930s felt betrayal by the old capitalist society. They looked on the competitive rather than cooperative spirit of capitalism as a chief cause of the Depression. Brilliant business oriented individuals became wealthier and wealthier at the expense of the majority of people who fell further and further behind. Vast wealth was in the hands of a few while the working class remained poor. This feeling of anger and betrayal at the hands of capitalism led many writers to a new vision of American life. That vision was wrapped up in the leftist theory

A man and two children run past a shack in Arkansas in the Dust Bowl. One of the most important works of the time, The Grapes of Wrath, *told the story of a dust bowl family, the Joads, and their struggles.* (AP/Wide World Photos, Inc/FSA. Reproduced by permission.)

of Marxism, which was the sum of the theories of German philosopher, social scientist, and revolutionary Karl Marx. In 2000 the political "left" referred to persons who tended to be liberal, advocating active government intervention in the economy and in daily lives of citizens. In the 1930s literary world "leaning left" referred to those writers who had become disgusted with capitalism and supported Marxist theories of class struggle.

Marx believed societies were strained as a result of the division of people into two classes, the working class or *proletariat* and the *bourgeoisie* or the owners of the means of production, the ruling class. He believed all unfair institutions and customs would disappear when the working class revolted against the ruling class. Marxism teaches that the means for producing of goods must be owned by the community as a whole resulting in general economic and social equality. These ideas of class struggle formed the basis of the communist movement of which Marx is considered the founder. Marx believed free enterprise or capitalism was doomed and that societies must move toward communism.

To many American writers Marxism stood as a rational way to reorder a fairer society. The propor-

tion of writers turning to various degrees of Marxism far out numbered the proportion of the general public turning in that direction. The communist movement in America never took hold in the general public or in the American working class. Nevertheless it appealed to the idealism of many gifted novelists, poets, playwrights, and critics who rejected the greed and materialism they associated with capitalism. They viewed Marxism as a potential solution to the problems of capitalism that had contributed to the Depression.

Support for the brutal communist regime in Russia led by Joseph Stalin, however, was rare. Most all defined Marxism in their own ways, refashioned its ideas, took what they liked and disavowed the rest. What resulted was a theme of the leaning left writers that literature must reveal the suffering of American society during the Depression and actively contribute to social change. Works from this point of view were known as proletarian literature.

Four of the most intense left leaning writers were Michael Gold, Grace Lumpkin, Albert Halper, and Albert Maltz. In 1930 Michael Gold, editor of both left-leaning magazines *Masses* and *New Masses,* was the first American writer to announce the beginning of a proletarian literature in the United States. That same year Gold published *Jews Without Money,* the story of his immigrant parents' struggle to achieve a decent life for themselves and their children amid the squalid slum of New York's Lower East Side. Grace Lumpkin's *To Make My Bread* (1932) was considered the best of several novels concerning the 1929 unsuccessful strike of textile workers protesting their horrible working conditions in Gastonia, North Carolina.

Albert Halper published *Union Square* (1933) that sympathized with the plight of the working class individual whose life was made all the more dismal by the Depression. He followed with two books, *The Foundry* (1934) and *The Chute,* that supported the radical movement reaching toward a more equitable society by embracing left leaning philosophies. Albert Maltz gained fame in literary circles as a playwright, novelist, and writer of short stories. His well-known proletariat story, "The Happiest Man on Earth," first appeared in *Harper's Magazine.* These four revolutionists, although they stirred emotions at the time, slowly sank from sight by the end of the decade as their radical communist-like solutions appealed less and less to the Depression and people took little note of their work. Rather for most Americans the New Deal programs, economic relief and recovery programs introduced by President Franklin Delano Roosevelt (served 1933–1945), represented the best approach to ending the Depression.

Of those authors who produced proletariat literature, those who survived and went on to fame were John Dos Passos, James T. Farrell, Erskine Caldwell, Richard Wright, and John Steinbeck. Dos Passos began his writing career in the 1920s with novels relating his World War I experiences and successfully transitioned into the 1930s with a series of three novels, or trilogy, known as *USA.* Dos Passos experimented and wrote with every innovation developed by writers after World War I. He used slices of life, quick cuts, narrative streams of consciousness, newspaper-like headlines as a literary technique, and sequences of life from real historical figures mixed with his fictional characters. A revolutionary in art and politics, Dos Passos aligned himself staunchly with the left.

In the 1930s Dos Passos believed much of the United States' promise was being destroyed by a small class of wealthy and powerful. This belief was brought home more by the stark distinctions seen during the Depression—the small percentage of the very wealthy in contrast to the large percentage of the population in poverty or barely getting by. In his *USA* trilogy consisting of three books: *The 42nd Parallel* 1930), *1919* (1932), and *The Big Money* (1936) Dos Passos created a historical saga from the growth of American

materialism in the 1890s to the Depression of the early 1930s. Readers eagerly followed each episode of the exciting trilogy. *USA* is considered one of the great fictional works of the twentieth century.

Standing as tall as Dos Passos in the artistry of his literary work was another Marxist, James T. Farrell. Farrell's epic, also a trilogy, was entitled *Studs Lonigan* and consists of *Young Lonigan* (1932), *The Young Manhood of Studs Lonigan* (1934), and *Judgment Day* (1935). The trilogy follows a young Irish American named Studs Lonigan in his attempt to rise from his poor beginnings. Farrell paints a bleak brutal picture of the working class in an Irish Chicago neighborhood as they try to cling to respectability as the Depression closes in. *Studs Lonigan* is proletarian literature that lives on and on.

Erskine Caldwell was a powerful, daring writer who concentrated his work on "poor whites" and the exploitation and brutal treatment of black Americans. His 1932 novel *Tobacco Road,* a study of a poverty stricken Southern tenant family whose life turned desperate in the economic crisis of the Depression, was adapted into a play that ran on Broadway for many years. In 1933 Caldwell published *God's Little Acre* about a poor family who follows only its instinct in digging for gold. It sold twenty million copies in various languages by 1949. Caldwell teamed up with photographer Margaret Bourke-White for *You Have Seen Their Faces* (1937) probably the most engrossing documentary of Southern rural poverty ever published. The book infuriated some Southern city officials, who were trying to keep their towns alive in the Depression, because it showed their communities in a bad light revealing massive poverty. *You Have Seen Their Faces* was banned in several localities.

Although not a Marxist, John Steinbeck wrote several decidedly proletarian novels: *The Pastures of Heaven* (1932) concerns people of a farm community near Salinas, California; *Tortilla Flat* (1935), a story of migrant workers and poor farmers; *In Dubious Battle* (1936) portrays labor strife in California; and, *The Grapes of Wrath* (1939) won the 1940 Pulitzer Prize. *The Grapes of Wrath* chronicled the life of a displaced Oklahoma family, the Joads, who lost their farm in the drought of the Dust Bowl and migrated west to the California promise land. The Dust Bowl was a region in the Southern Plains of the United States especially Oklahoma, Arkansas, Colorado, Kansas, and northern Texas that experienced severe drought and damaging windstorms stirring up massive clouds of dust. By 1935 the farmlands in these areas suffered severe erosion of their topsoil causing a large number of farmers to abandon their land and move to other regions

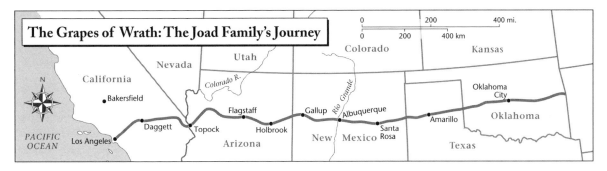

Map of the journey taken by the Joad family from the book, The Grapes of Wrath, *by John Steinbeck.* (The Gale Group.)

of the country. Many sought work as migrant farm laborers in California. In 1937 Steinbeck toured the Dust Bowl and traveled with migrants seeking to find work in California. He wrote of experiences families encountered along the way to California and after arriving there.

Richard Wright, a supporter of the political left, was one of the few black authors recognized for literary excellence in the late 1930s. Wright took on the issue of racial prejudice and the plight of blacks in a collection of four short stories entitled *Uncle Tom's Children* (1938) and his first completed novel, *Native Son* (1940).

Other writers involved during the Depression in the proletariat writers' movement were Jack Conroy with *The Disinherited* (1933), Henry Roth with *Call It Sleep* (1935), and Edward Dalberg with *Bottom Dogs* (1930) and *From Flushing to Calvary* (1932). Conroy, Roth, and Dalberg wrote of their parents' experiences and linked them to the terrible struggles of the Depression. Conroy and Roth fell silent as their faith in leftist politics declined. Only Dalberg would write again in the following decades. Nelson Algren, who would author books into the 1970s, was best known in the 1930s for fiction describing those on the bottom level of the social scale, the *lumpenproletariat,* known as the "social scum" to communists. His "A Place to Lie Down" originally appeared in the January-February issue of *Partisan Review* (1935). He completed *Somebody in Boots* that same year.

Memorable authors and books describing the actual trials of factory workers and immigrants included Ruth McKenney who wrote with emotional communistic conviction about Akron, Ohio, rubber workers in *Industrial Valley* (1939). Louis Adamic wrote a colorful narrative, *Dynamite* (1931), which dealt with labor violence in America. Adamic, a 1913

immigrant from Slovenia, published several books dealing with immigrants. They included *Laughing in the Jungle* (1932), *The Native's Return* (1934), *Grandsons* (1935), and *Cradle of Life* (1937). Robert Cantwell's *The Land of Plenty* (1934) deals with a spontaneous strike in a wood veneer factory in the State of Washington. Mary Heaton Vorse in her book *Strike* (1930) dramatized the struggles of workers for justice as did Clara Weatherwax in the largely forgotten *Marching! Marching!* (1935). Meridel LeSueur became well known for writings about labor in the Depression and the unemployed. Her factual book *Women on the Breadlines* (1932) told of women trying to survive during the Depression. Other writers of proletarian novels included Olive Dargan writing as Fielding Burke in *Call Home the Heart* (1932) and *A Stone Came Rolling* (1935); Josephine Herbst, *Pity Is Not Enough* (1933) and *The Executioner Waits* (1939); William Rollins, *The Shadow Before* (1934); and, Tess Slesinger, *The Unpossessed* (1934).

Every now and then a victim of the Depression rose up to write about his experiences bumming across the United States. One such person was Tom Kromer who wrote *Waiting for Nothing* (1935) about the agonies of bumming across the country. His book was autobiographical and largely written while enrolled in a California branch of Roosevelt's Civilian Conservation Corps (CCC). After being turned down repeatedly by publishers, the manuscript found its way to the publishing house of Alfred A. Knopf who published the book in 1935. His story was hailed as extraordinary, but Kromer wrote no more important works. Suffering from pulmonary tuberculosis by 1935 Kromer rode the rails to the dry climate of Albuquerque, New Mexico. While in a sanitarium where he received treatment he continued to write several articles and short stories. Largely an invalid by the late 1930s Kromer ceased writing.

More About...

League of American Writers

At the first American Writers' Congress held in 1935, those leaning to the left and supporting the ideas of Marxism established the League of American Writers, which was dominated by communist doctrine. Malcolm Cowley, a writer and literary critic long involved with the leftist movement, told those assembled that his interests lay with the proletariat, or working class, and that writers could greatly benefit from this alliance. Those writers adhering to the idea of a rising American proletariat and the "perfect Soviet state" applied moral and psychological pressures on other writers to fall in line. Evidently many complied and when the second national Congress of American Writers convened in 1937 at Carnegie Hall in New York City thousands had to be turned away for lack of room. Even "the most insignificant scribblers" as reported by Harvey Swados, in his book, *The American Writer and the Great Depression* had been persuaded to give up any lingering concerns about the communist approach to social order.

The discussions, though intense, were becoming more and more academic. For all the emotion surrounding proletariat literature, some intellectuals and writers began turning away. The proletarian tone promoting class struggle and a revolution at the time when the United States needed a united front against Hitler and Mussolini seemed less and less appropriate. By the beginning of the 1940s, following the signing of the Stalin-Hitler pact in 1939 and with Russia's invasion of Finland, there was little idealistic illusion remaining about communism. Granville Hicks long involved with literary leftist thinking, had announced his resignation from the Communist Party in 1939. By the fall of 1942 the League of American Writers, the so-called "first child" of the literary left was abandoned by most of its members and disbanded.

Despite all the literary fervor surrounding social issues during the Depression the idealization of the communist way of ordering society began to evaporate at the end of the 1930s. The signing of the Stalin/Hitler pact of 1939 was highly dismaying, and various eyewitness accounts of a less than perfect state by individuals who traveled to Russia dramatically changed perceptions. Promoting class struggle and revolution seemed divisive when, more and more, the United States needed to present a united front against Hitler and Mussolini.

By 1939 most writers had distanced themselves from Marxism's class struggle and the communist state. What remained was an interesting sort of social literature, a sort of made-in-America proletarianism. Writers in the United States would continue to write about people of all class levels and tackle difficult political issues fearlessly from all points of view. By 2000 Steinbeck's *The Grapes of Wrath* continued to rank as the most successful proletarian novel ever written. The proletarian literature of the 1930s had spoken to fundamental concerns of the American society. Depression writers had seen their fellow Americans suffering under an unequal social and economic order and had exposed what they saw to the public.

Anti-Fascism

Although 1930s writers produced proletarian literature, much of it with Marxist underpinnings, writers never extended support to fascism nor suggested it as a remedy for the Depression. Fascism embraces a strong centralized nationalistic government led by a powerful dictator. Increasingly writers showed concern for the rise of Fascist dictators Adolph Hitler of Germany and Benito Mussolini of Italy. The first American novel concerning Hitler's Nazi regime was Edward Dahlberg's *Those Who Perish* (1934). Sinclair Lewis wrote a book with more political purpose than any he had previously authored. Lewis' *It Can't Happen Here* (1935) showed how fascism might come to the United States. Reflecting the public's mood of social consciousness *It Can't Happen Here* reached into the top ten of the bestseller list for 1936. It was one of the few such books to reach the *New York Times* bestseller list.

Supporting the anti-fascist Loyalists, Ernest Hemingway was deeply involved in Spain's fight against Fascism. He told the 1937 American Writers Congress that, "There is only one form of government that cannot produce good writers and that system is fascism. For fascism is a lie told by bullies" (Salzman, *Years of Protest: A Collection of American Writings of the 1930s.* p. 191). A year after Spain's Loyalist defeat he wrote an anti-fascist novel, *For Whom the Bell Tolls* (1940). John Dos Passos also wrote an anti-fascist book, *Adventures of a Young Man* (1939). Thomas Wolfe, who had traveled to the 1936 Olympic Games in Berlin, Germany, returned as an ardent anti-Fascist appalled at Hitler's oppression. He incorporated his experiences in the novel *You Can't Go Home Again,* which was gathered and published after his death in 1940.

Searching for the "Real" America

American writers often came from the ranks of newspapermen rather than being highly educated "men of letters" in the European tradition. It seemed perfectly natural for them to earn a living in between more scholarly efforts with investigative reporting. When the economic disaster of the Depression struck some novelists decoded to leave their solitary desks and travel about the country to better understand their fellow Americans and the impact of the Depression on the ordinary individuals and families. Their works are often referred to as nationalistic, not the patriotic nationalism spurred by wars, but a new awareness that America's distress was nationwide. Solutions to the pain and misery would need to be national solutions. For the first time, writers rather than focusing on local and regional difficulties would write to the nation as a whole. The word "America" or "American" appeared in virtually all the titles. One early work came from literary critic Edmund Wilson, *The American Jitters: A Year of the Slump* (1932). In 1933 the brilliantly intense and witty Sherwood Anderson began a two-month trip around the United States "looking and listening." He collected his stories in a 1935 book entitled *Puzzled America.* James Rorty, in *Where Life Is Better: An Unsentimental American Journey* (1936) showed his dismay that Americans continued to resist radical societal change as a solution. Nathan Ashe also took to the road to discover what was happening to his country and reported in *The Road: In Search of America* (1937). Louis Adamic wrote in the preface to *My America* (1938), "Since 1931 I have traveled perhaps 100,000 miles here in America, by train, by automobile, by plane, as well as afoot, pausing here and there to look and listen, to ask questions to get the feel of things; and I have developed, I think, a fairly steady feeling about this vast place..." (Adamic, p. xiii).

One book stands tall above all others; James Agee's *Let Us Now Praise Famous Men* (1941). Although it was not published until 1941 it was formed in the summer of 1936. The book stands as a symbol of the creative and daring bravery of a few writers of the 1930s to "pry intimately into the lives of an undefended and appallingly damaged group of human beings, an ignorant and helpless rural family..." (Swados, p. xxxii). Coupled with poetic photographs by Walker Evans the book meaningfully examines the life of an Alabama sharecropper's family. Agee found

James Agee wrote the text for Let Us Now Praise Famous Men, *which was partially funded by the Federal Writers Project (FWP).* (The Library of Congress.)

unity and strength of character in those people and above all he found hope in American culture. This effort to look at the "real" America, at the lives of unexceptional people was in part made possible by the Federal Writer's Project.

The Federal Writers' Project

Beginning in 1935 the Federal Writers' Project (FWP), a program of the Works Projects' Administration (WPA), supported over six thousand novelists, journalists, poets, and other professionals such as lawyers, ministers, newspapermen, teachers, and anyone else willing to work in the publication field. The FWP, under direction of Henry Alsberg, hired these unemployed individuals to produce a series of state and city guides, to write ethnic histories of immigrant groups, and to record folklore and foods of the entire nation. The project completed 378 books and pamphlets published commercially between 1935 and 1939. The FWP's publications contributed greatly to the New Deal's focus on documenting the cultural heritage of geographic regions in the United States. The most famous series published under the FWP was the American Guide Series, which included a separate guidebook for each state. The books not only described principle cities and towns but the history, geography, and culture of each state.

Several writers supported by the FWP went on to fame. The FWP helped support Richard Wright so he could complete *Native Son* (1940). John Steinbeck also received FWP support as did Zora Neale Hurston who wrote a relatively apolitical novel, *Their Eyes Were Watching God,* a classic work of black literature which portrays a young black woman's discovery of her identity as a woman in society.

In 1939 the FWP came under state control as directors were appointed by governors. After the Pearl Harbor bombing in 1941, the FWP was renamed the Writers' Unit of the War Services Division of WPA. Its last publication was a series called "Serviceman's Recreational Guides." When the WPA expired in June 1943, the FWP ceased operation.

The FWP writers pioneered techniques of researching peoples' traditions and life histories. They employed interviews to collect oral histories. One of FWP's most critically acclaimed products was *These Are Our Lives* (1939). Members of the FWP in North Carolina, Tennessee, and Georgia recorded the stories of the people from all ordinary walks of life, 35 were published in *These Are Our Lives*. A sampling of the stories includes: "You're Gonna Have Lace Curtains" about white farm laborers; "Grease Monkey to Knitter" about a young man who wandered about looking for work; "Tore Up and A-Movin'" about black sharecroppers; "Till the River Rises" about people of a shanty town in the river bottom; and, "Weary Willie," about a CCC boy.

Going Their Own Way

The 1930s are remembered in American literary history as a decade of literature dominated by social issues. A large group of left leaning intellectuals and writers claimed to speak for American writers as a whole. Few of the proletarian novels, however, ever got very high on the bestseller lists. One exception was Steinbeck's *The Grapes of Wrath*, a proletarian novel that topped the list in 1939 and was still at number eight in 1940. Two other novels that ascended to the top ten were the anti-Fascist works, Sinclair Lewis *It Can't Happen Here* (1935) and Ernest Hemingway's *For Whom the Bell Tolls* in 1940.

Many 1930s writers, however, simply continued on their individualistic pathways writing books unrelated to sociological Depression topics. Most Americans, as always, continued to read what appealed to them not what someone told them they ought to read. Many sought out literature that removed them from their daily struggles with Great Depression hardships.

Authors such as Hemingway, Pearl S. Buck, Thomas Wolfe, William Faulkner, and Hervey Allen all wrote popular books that allowed readers to momentarily escape from the Depression.

With the exception of *For Whom the Bell Tolls* Hemingway, one of America's most celebrated authors, showed little interest in depicting concerns and difficulties brought by the Depression. *Death in the Afternoon* (1932) dealt with bull fighting, *Green Hills of Africa* (1935) with experiences on an African safari, and *To Have and Have Not* (1937) was based on Key West, Florida.

Many other exceptional writers of the decade showed the same detachment. Pearl S. Buck's *The Good Earth* (1930) took readers to China. *The Good Earth* remained at the top of the best seller list in 1931 and 1932. Buck was awarded the 1938 Nobel Prize for literature for this novel. Thomas Wolfe's two classics, *Look Homeward, Angel* (1929) and *Of Time and the River* (1935) were modeled on his own life as a young man. William Faulkner, considered one of America's greatest writers, was known for his carefully shaped novels, his artistic use of language, and the vividness of his characterizations. His novels published during the Depression include *The Sound and the Fury* (1929), *Light In August* (1932), *As I Lay Dying* (1930), and *Sanctuary* (1931). F. Scott Fitzgerald, a popular author of the 1920s, wrote *Tender Is The Night* (1934) but it did not become well known until much later. This finely written story of the decline of a few glamorous Americans living in Europe proved to be of little interest to readers during the Depression. All of Nathanael West's books were published in the 1930s but only after his death in 1940 did his reputation grow. His books offered a harsh, surrealistic picture of contemporary life. *Miss Lonely Hearts* (1933) and *The Day of the Locust* (1939) became minor classics.

Editors of Laura Ingalls Wilder, Harper and Brothers, believed her first book, *Little House in the Big Woods* (1932) had so much appeal that even the Depression would not hinder its sales. They were not disappointed as it was a Junior Literary Guild selection and sold well. Wilder then put out a steady stream of popular books relating her childhood memories of frontier life. *Farmer Boy* (1933), *Little House on the Prairie* (1935), *On the Banks of Plum Creek* (1937), *By the Shores of Silver Lake* (1939), *The Long Winter* (1940), *Little Town On the Prairie* (1941) and *These Happy Golden Years* (1943) all became best sellers. Five received Newberry Honor awards. Depression families related to Wilder's tales of survival in the face of grasshopper plagues, blizzards, ill-

Margaret Mitchell, the author of Gone With the Wind, *in 1937.* Gone With the Wind *was a bestseller in both 1936 and 1937. (AP/Wide World Photos. Reproduced by permission.)*

ness, and debt. Her novels, which always ended in hope, transferred that hope to the weary nation.

Two of the biggest sellers of the decade were long historical fiction novels that were far removed from the 1930's Depression. Hervey Allen's *Anthony Adverse* topped bestseller lists in 1933 and 1934. The romantic historical story took place in the late 1700s and early 1800s. It follows a young man on his travels and adventures through Italy, Africa, and finally to New Orleans in the United States. The wildly popular *Gone with the Wind* by Margaret Mitchell topped bestseller lists in 1936 and 1937.

Other Prominent Literature

Many other popular books enabled readers to escape the Great Depression woes. Dashiell Hammett's *The Maltese Falcon* (1930) was a hard-boiled detective novel. James M. Cain published *The Postman Always Rings Twice* (1934). A selection of titles from the 1930s fiction best seller lists includes: James Hilton's *Goodbye Mr. Chips* (1934) and *Lost Horizon* (1935); John O'Hara's *Butterfield 8* (1935); Walter D. Edmond's *Drums Along the Mohawk* (1936); A.J. Cronin's *The Citadel*; Virginia Woolf's *The Years* (1937); W. Somerset Maugham's *Theatre* (1937);

Daphne du Maurier's *Rebecca* (1938); Rachel Fields *All This and Heaven Too* (1938); and, Richard Llewellyn's *How Green Was My Valley* (1940).

Some non-fiction titles of interest were *Believe It Or Not* (1929) by Robert L. Ripley; Ely Culbertson's *Contract Bridge Blue Book of 1933*; Anne Morrow Lindbergh's *North to the Orient* (1935); T.E. Lawrence's *Seven Pillars of Wisdom* (1935); and, Clarence Day's *Life With Father* (1936).

Self-Improvement Books

Self-improvement books remained popular in the 1930s. At the top of the 1933 *New York Times* nonfiction bestsellers list was Walter B. Pitkin's *Life Begins at Forty*. Edmund Jacobson's *You Must Relax* was in ninth place in 1934. *Live Alone and Like It* by Marjorie Hills sold 100,000 copies in 1936 and she followed with *Orchids on Your Budget* in 1937.

Proving not all Americans subscribed to replacing individual aspirations with a collective, cooperative Marxist spirit, Dale Carnegie's *How to Win Friends and Influence People,* which outlined the keys to success in business, a strictly capitalist pursuit, bolted to the number one non-fiction bestseller in 1937. It is still available in bookstores today.

Langston Hughes, one of the writers whose works are part of the Harlem Renaissance, was known as the "Negro Poet Laureate." (The Estate of Carl Van Vechten. Reproduced by permission.)

Histories, Biographies, Other Countries

A marked revival of interest in histories and biographies took place in the 1930s. *The Rise of American Civilization* by Charles and Mary Beard made its way to the non-fiction best seller list of 1930. Likewise H.G. Wells' *The Outline of History* made the same 1930 list. Biographies of historical figures included Emil Ludwig's *Lincoln* (1930), Douglas Southall Freeman's *R.E. Lee* (1935), Carl Van Doren's *Benjamin Franklin* (1938) and Carl Sandburg's *Abraham Lincoln: The War Years* (1939).

In the second half of the 1930s, with the war looming in Europe and unrest in much of the world, there was great interest in foreign affairs. John Gunther published *Inside Europe* in 1936 and *Inside Asia* in 1939. Winston S. Churchill published *Blood, Sweat and Tears* in 1940. Nora Waln's *Reaching For The Stars* described the tragedy of life in Germany under Hitler. In a class all its own *Mein Kampf* by Adolf Hitler was published in its full text in America for the first time in 1939. Few Americans could understand it as written, therefore it was largely ignored in the United States. Its importance in Germany, however, was undeniable; *Mein Kampf* was the "bible" of Nazi Germany.

Poets

Poets, with styles ranging from iconoclastic (not following the traditional forms) to conservative, made their own marks in the literary world of the 1930s. Nonconformist E.E. Cummings, conservative Robert Frost, black Poet Laureate Langston Hughes, multitalented Archibald MacLeish, bohemian Edna St. Vincent Millay, and the beloved Carl Sandburg all wrote and published during the Great Depression.

E.E. Cummings, son of a Harvard professor, received two degrees from there himself, but never displayed the air of a Harvard man. He was a congenial nonconformist who mocked the established system and was iconoclastic to the end. An aristocratic individualist at heart, he never took up the communist ideology.

In 1931 Cummings visited the Soviet Union briefly. Those who thought he was sympathetic to communism, however, were quickly set straight with the 1933 publication of *Eimi,* Cumming's diary of his trip to Russia. It was a scathing attack of the Soviet system. Again attacking communism, he published *No Thanks* (1935), a volume of poems whose name came from its many rejections by publishers. Cummings, however, also criticized the capitalistic system for destroying the individual. Two of his most profound anti-capitalist speeches were "Speech From a Forthcoming Play: I" that first appeared in the *New American Caravan* and "Speech from a Forthcoming Play: II" which appeared in *Partisan Review.*

Cummings' style of poetry, written unlike any ever seen before, generally disregarded grammar and punctuation rules. He often ran words and sentences together and made up his own words. Illustrated by the use of all lower case letters in his name, "e.e. cummings," he generally did not use capitals.

The 1930s proved to be professionally successful but personally tragic for Robert Frost. His daughter Marjorie died in 1934, his wife Elinor died in 1938, and his son Carol committed suicide in 1940. Professionally he won Pulitzer Prizes for *Collected Poems of Robert Frost* (1930) and *A Further Range* (1936). *A Further Range* was published in the middle of the Great Depression when war was also about to engulf the world. Frost took criticism for his casual, conservative politics revealed in *A Further Range.*

Langston Hughes, often referred to as the Negro Poet Laureate, was a prolific writer from 1926 until his death in 1967. Through his writing he spoke for the poor and homeless black Americans who suffered during the Depression. He wrote of their daily lives, anger, and love. He called Harlem home and enjoyed sitting in its clubs listening to blues and jazz and writing poetry. Black Americans loved his works and hearing him read his poems at public presentations all over the country. His long and distinguished list of works included many published during the Depression: *Not Without Laughter* (1930), *The Negro Mother and Other Dramatic Recitations* (1931), *The Dream Keeper and Other Poems* (1932), *Scottsboro Limited: Four Poems and a Play in Verse* (1932), *A Negro Looks at Soviet Central Asia* (1934), and *The Ways of White Folks* (1934).

Archibald MacLeish led a long and varied life as a poet, scholar, gentleman, librarian of Congress, and friend of President Roosevelt. He went on to be an Assistant Secretary of State and later a professor at Harvard.

Perhaps more than any other writer MacLeish came under fire by the left leaning writers. MacLeish believed a poet must remain true to his art. To do this he must be apolitical and antisocial. If MacLeish remained supportive of capitalism it was because such a system was more favorable than either fascism or communism to the writers' artistic and intellectual freedom. In 1935 MacLeish published a verse play, "Panic." The play had a three-day run in New York's Phoenix Theater. Editors of the *New Masses* including Michael Gold and his Marxist friends criticized the play on stage at the theater at the end of the third performance. They proclaimed the familiar communist charge that the downfall of capitalism was historically inevitable. MacLeish's play reflected his own belief that man's loss of vision, courage, and love had caused the Great Depression and man could make it right again. Some of the poems in MacLeish's *Public Speech* (1936) also attacked Marxists.

Edna St. Vincent Millay's concern with social issues was life long. She lived a bohemian lifestyle in Greenwich Village, New York, after graduating from Vassar College. Penning verse in simple traditional forms, Millay wrote of personal experiences. In 1931 she released her most acclaimed works *Fatal Interview,* with its 52 sonnets it was compared favorably to Shakespeare. Through the 1930s Millay went on many poetry-reading tours and also took advantage of the new radio medium for readings. Her book sales strong, she lived comfortably through the Depression.

Not until 1939 did her work enter the social commentary arena. Although opposed to war, the crisis in Europe concerned her and convinced her that sometimes war was indeed necessary. Her 1939 sonnet, "Czechoslovakia," expressed concern for Czechoslovakia after Germany invaded the country. That same year she appeared with First Lady Eleanor Roosevelt and black American leader George Washington Carver at a

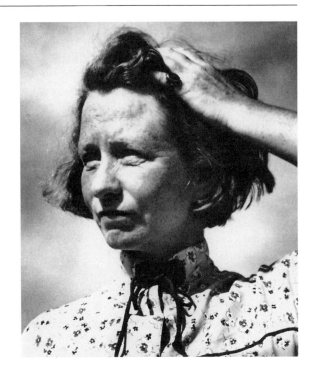

Edna St. Vincent Millay, a poet and playwright, was the first woman to win the Pulitzer Prize. (AP/Wide World Photos. Reproduced by permission.)

New York *Herald Tribune* sponsored forum. Millay spoke, urging repeal of the Embargo Act of 1937 that stopped the United States from selling arms to Britain and France. She encouraged Americans to rethink their isolationist approach and held defend cultures closely akin to the United States from fascist leaders.

Through Carl Sandburg's work ran two major themes, his support for the common man and democracy and a search for meaning in American history. Sandburg worked as a newspaper journalist in Chicago from 1912 to the late 1920s part of a community of important American writers called the *Chicago School* which included among others Sherwood Anderson and Theodore Dreisen. Sandburg won fame for his poetry during that period. One famous poem, "Chicago," published in 1914 both portrayed the harshness of the cities at the same time the power and energy of industry. In the 1920s Sandburg completed the first part of an excellent biography on Abraham Lincoln. The sales enabled him to leave newspaper employment and concentrate fully on his literary works.

In the early 1930s Carl Sandburg, known as the Poet of the People, established a life long friendship with Archibald MacLeish. The two carried on long discussions about the obligations of the poet to issues of the day. Sandburg believed the economic inequality, so striking in the Depression, was the root of all social injustice. He responded to the 1930s economic and social strife with *The People, Yes.* In it he praised the struggling people who were immigrants just as his own parents had been. By 1939 he finished his six volume biography of Abraham Lincoln that won a 1940s Pulitzer Prize for history.

The Publishing Industry

The 1920s were a prosperous time for publishers. Many publishing companies still in business in the twenty-first century were established in the decade before the Depression. Some of those formed in the 1920s were Harcourt, Brace and Company, 1919; Simon and Schuster, 1924; Viking Press, 1925; and, Random House, 1927.

When the stock market crashed in the fall of 1929, publishers were just as confused as the rest of the business world about how severe it would be. Publishers began trimming lists of titles for publication declining from 10,027 titles in 1930, to 8,766 by 1935. Overall publishing suffered less than many other businesses and no major publisher failed due to the Depression. Several new publishing companies even managed to start up including Julian Messner, 1933; Reynal and Hitchcock, 1933; Basic Books, 1935; New Directions, 1936; Crown, 1936; and, Duell, Sloan and Pearce, 1939.

Publishing houses fared better during the Depression for two reasons. Publishers showed creativity in marketing and pricing their books. Book jackets became irresistibility colorful drawing readers to pick up the attractive books. Also nearly 200 books were made into movies. Often a special movie edition was published as the movie premiered. Publishers were also aggressive in cutting prices of their books. Secondly people during the Depression had more time on their hands and reading was one way to fill it.

The publishing industry faced increasing difficulties during World War II (1939–1945) that spelled recovery for most businesses. The problem was a paper shortage. The number of titles published in 1941—11,112—declined to 6,548 by the war's end in 1945.

The Paperback Revolution

Although paperback books had appeared and disappeared in the United States many times before, their production had always been short lived. In the 1930s the low-priced paperback was especially appealing. A distribution network had developed over the years for books to be in drug stores, food stores, and railroad and airline terminals. Also the public's attitude that books were objects to be preserved forever had changed.

Penguin paperback books appeared in 1935 in England. Penguin was so successful it opened a branch in the United States in 1939 with 100 titles and Sam Ballantine as manager. As hostilities increased in Europe with World War II, Penguin began printing more and more titles at facilities in the United States. Even with the shortage of paper during World War II American branches of Penguin continued to produce the popular paperback.

Another paperback publisher also emerged in 1939, Pocket Books. Pocket Books actually began in the United States a few months before Penguin arrived. Started by Robert Fair de Graff along with Richard Simon, Max Schuster and Leon Shimkin, Pocket Books first test marketed Pearl Buck's *The Good Earth.* It quickly followed with ten more titles. Macy's Department Store ordered 10,000 books, which was ten percent of Pocket's first press run. Wire rack book holders appeared in store after store. The little kangaroo logo adorned the cover of each Pocket Book. The paperback industry got another positive nod when the Armed Services Editions for those serving their country were published. Additionally Sam Ballantine formed his own paperback company thereby spreading paperbacks even farther.

Book Clubs

Book-of-the-Month Club (BOMC) and Literary Club both began in 1926 and flourished during the 1930s. Most all homes nationwide had mail service, but many did not have access to bookstores or libraries. In addition to the ease of obtaining a book, the clubs pre-selected a book each month. A panel of literary experts selected books, both fiction and non-fiction, of broad appeal. Members could reject a selection but could only order books the club stocked. Book clubs ran special printings of their selected titles but almost never published original works.

At first publishers and booksellers feared the competition, but it soon became apparent that a selection of a title by a club actually increased sales overall. A greater volume of printings to keep up with sales allowed lower retail prices that in turn spurred more sales.

Contributing Forces

American fiction in 1919 just after World War I took on a rebellious new energy. Writing in the genteel tradition that politely guarded high culture with stylized and romantic characters and plots faded rapidly. Authors who burst to the forefront were Sinclair Lewis, F. Scott Fitzgerald, Ernest Hemingway, Sherwood Anderson, critic Henry Louis (H.L.) Mencken, and John Dos Passos. They urged freer patterns of behavior, thought, and forms of writing to express their feelings and lambasted American society as boring and full of hypocrisy. They expressed disillusionment and contempt for both traditional and contemporary society. They scoffed at the promises that bureaucrats had made about World War I being a war to end all wars. They dealt frankly with sexuality and called the Victorian ideas of decency hypocritical. Despite innovative writing few successfully made the transition to the Depression decade of the 1930s.

Sinclair Lewis criticized the narrow life of the small town in *Main Street* (1920), the middle class businessman and middle sized city in *Babbit* (1922), the medical profession in *Arrowsmith* (1925), the clergy in *Elmer Gantry* (1927), and the big business man in *Dodsworth* (1929). Lewis received the Nobel Prize for fiction in 1926, the first American to do so. In the 1930s his only notable work was *It Can't Happen Here* (1935). F. Scott Fitzgerald became the prophet of rebellious youth and stayed obsessed with World War I's "lost generation," young adults who had lost their way. In *This Side of Paradise* (1920), *The Beautiful and the Damned* (1922), and *The Great Gatsby* (1925), Fitzgerald portrayed the lost generation as living a fast, materialistic life to make up for the meaninglessness of their lives. He remained fixed on this theme in the 1930s and produced no notable works.

Hemingway's first popular success was *The Sun Also Rises* (1926) about a disillusioned group of Americans in Europe. Hemingway, until late in the 1930s, continued use of European settings for his novels rather than dealing with issues in America. Sherwood Anderson, even though he was active in the 1930s leftist movement, produced his two final novels in 1932 and 1936, both considered inferior works to his previous works. H.L. Mencken was the most widely read and listened to social critic, essayist, reporter, and editor of the 1920s. He was known as the man who hated everything. Mencken ridiculed with gusto ministers, doctors, lawyers, Southern leaders, educators, and opponents of birth control. He delighted in getting a rise out of his readers. The rebellious writers of the 1920s felt a kinship with Mencken. In the troubled years of the Depression his influence declined and popularity faded.

One writer who made the jump from the 1920s to 1930s was John Dos Passos who was willing to experiment with every new writing style developed since World War I. He successfully extended the 1920 innovation of portraying life more realistically including all life's oddities and cruelties. Dos Passos widened his focus from the 1920s to the people in the sad society of the Depression.

The center of the literary world in the 1920s was Greenwich Village in New York City, a virtual stronghold of artists and radicals. Many writers translated their boredom with America into a move to Paris where Gertrude Stein, author of *The Autobiography of Alice B. Toklas* (1933) held court. Fitzgerald and Hemingway also lived in Paris during the 1920s.

Other post-World War I writers were William Faulkner, E.E. Cummings, and poet Edna St. Vincent Millay. Faulkner would become an important author with stories set in the South. His first highly successful novel, *The Sound and the Fury* (1929), took a dark look at the demise of a Southern family. He would skyrocket to fame in the 1930s with his carefully structured novels and characters. E.E. Cummings experimented with language in poems, plays, and novels. Millay perfectly expressed the defiant desires of the 1920s with clear, direct poetry that was widely published.

The rebellious literature of the 1920s made for exciting times. 1920s literature constituted a broadening and flowering of writing styles resulting in a new image of American literature. It offered no constructive ideology, however, for building a new America with a fairer social order, an important aspect of 1930s literature.

Proletarian Literature

The proletarian novel in America is generally accepted as a Great Depression decade phenomenon. Men and women of considerable energies and talent wrote proletarian literature. In the 1930s it touched at places that a majority of Americans could relate to, nevertheless it failed to gain wide acceptance.

The first American proletarian novel actually appeared before the American Communist Party and predated the years 1929–1940 by decades. *Fata Morgana* by Adolf Douais was published in 1858 in St. Louis, Missouri. This work, written in German, was the beginning of the proletarian novel in the United States. Its development paralleled the development of the socialist movement in the United States. Socialism refers to political and economic theories calling for common ownership of the means of production and distribution of goods under a strong central government. It is sometimes thought of as an in-between step between capitalism and communism. American socialism emerged between the Civil War and World

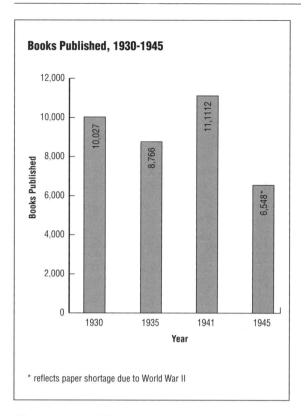

Books Published, 1930-1945

10,027   8,766   11,1112   6,548*

* reflects paper shortage due to World War II

The American Library Association estimated libraries attracted three to four million new patrons between 1929 and 1933. (The Gale Group.)

War I with the struggles of American labor in an industrializing era. Many Americans hoped social experimentation would lead to a utopian (perfect) American society. Socialist oriented novels appeared between 1890 and 1915, but no one writer became well known. The first decades of the twentieth century saw experimentation with poetry and fiction and attempts to link the world of social progress to literature. Authors and journalists such as Van Wyck Brooks, Waldo Frank, and Walter Lippmanall envisioned a sort of socialism to make a perfect country with everyone equal. World War I shattered this spirit and after the war, Americans understood the Industrial Revolution was about power. In the 1920s people got down to the business of getting their share of prosperity often disregarding civil rights along the way. There was a large proletariat, a working class, but no proletarian literature. Instead *bourgeois* (ruling class) literature looked at the American worker as stumbling into the city from rural life or just off a boat from across the Atlantic. By far the majority of the 1920s writers were not intent on changing society or social justice. They were politi-

cally disenfranchised, just not interested in politics or social ills.

Although the old socialist utopian ideas seemed lost, there was some evidence that a Marxist perspective based on programs of international socialism and class struggle was growing in America. Marxist philosophy was the basis of communism. Young writers such as Michael Gold, Joseph Freeman, and Waldo Frank envisioned a brotherhood of workers where the common ownership of all means of production would stamp out inequalities. This American Marxism was closely tied to the growing international Marxist or communist movement. In the late 1920s the American Communist Party formed.

If not in Europe, members of the American literary community lived in New York City, with a few in Los Angeles and Chicago. Few had made much money at their craft so they enclosed their lives and value systems within a brotherhood of writers, separated from the rest of society. Identifying this group as one that might be moved to revolutionary ideas, the Communist Party focused on these poets, novelists, and playwrights to build a propaganda base. John Reed Clubs, branches of the Communist Party, formed for this purpose. So by 1929 the old American socialist impulse was being replaced by a communist influenced leftist movement among the intellectuals and writers of the New York City bohemian community.

The American economic collapse in 1929 and 1930 created many angry disillusioned Americans. Writers were determined to move this disillusioned society to a new equal and classless order through their writings. From ongoing discussions carried on in literary left leaning magazines, the proletarian novel emerged.

Perspectives

New York City's Intellectual Elite

Cocktail parties in the 1920s were popular gatherings for New York City's sophisticated, talented writers, critics, artists, musicians, and professional men and women. These were individuals setting the pace with the newest ideas and tendencies. At 1925 cocktail parties, with martinis poured, lively conversation always turned to the issues of the day. Individuals unleashed their beliefs for all to hear. The discussions ran along the following lines: America was considered a boring machine-dominated culture. More personal freedom such as sexual freedom would generate a more exciting society. Businessmen and their organizations such as Rotarians or the Chambers

More About...

Literary Magazines—Literary Wars

In the 1930s at the center of many heated discussions over socialism and communism were the liberal, leftist, literary magazines. These magazines included *New Masses, The New Republic, Partisan Review, Anvil, Modern Quarterly, Science and Society, Criterion, Common Sense, Dynamo, Dialectics, Symposium,* and *Miscellany*. Literary critics, intellectuals, and writers battling it out with pen and paper included among others, Michael Gold, Malcolm Cowley, Edmund Wilson, Philip Raho, Lewis Mumford, Sidney Hook, Max Eastman, and Robert Lynd. Mumford, speaking for all, was appalled at how the American marketplace and its associated greed of the 1920s had developed a society of selfish people interested in getting and spending at the expense of social responsibilities toward their fellow man. These men wanted to blend their particular Marxist values with American liberalism and socialistic ideas. They did not advocate for the individual to be totally lost in the masses as did communism. Instead they hoped for a redistribution of the United States' wealth and income so that all Americans would have economic security and hence the freedom to express their individuality. These ideas were actually not too far off from President Franklin Roosevelt's (served 1933–1945) and the New Deal's class oriented rhetoric.

How to incorporate these ideas in a new form of proletarian literature was at the heart of discussions in the magazines. Proletarian literature was to be a clear-cut reflection of the struggles of the working class. Michael Gold called for writers to employ "proletarian realism," that is, to focus on working class characters, have social themes, call for political activism, and offer hope through revolution. Gold was considered the "outstanding proletarian." Gold in both *New Masses* and *The New Republic* fiercely attacked popular author Thornton Wilder for continuing to be a genteel writer (writing from only an upper class viewpoint). Edmund Wilson concurred with Gold. The Gold-Wilder controversy thrust the eruption of Marxist issues into general literary discussions.

Each magazine had outspoken free thinking editors who often disagreed over Marxist thought and how to write proletarian literature to further the cause of a better social order in America. For example the *Partisan Review* had long had its differences with *New Masses*. Malcolm Crowley in *The New Republic* expressed his displeasure with the editors of the *Partisan*, a magazine he helped save in 1935. He accused *Partisan* editors of letting politics interfere with their duties to literature, exactly what *Partisan* had itself always accused *New Masses* of. Out of this ferment proletarian literature evolved through the 1930s. All of these highbrow intellectual discussions were sometimes referred to as the "Red Ivory Tower" (Salzman, *Years of Protest: A Collection of American Writings of the 1930s.* p. 195).

---

of Commerce were hopelessly dull and conservative. America had too many laws but reformers amazingly lobbied for more. The writers who clung to Victorian or Puritan themes of the 1800s needed to open their minds. Any really creative person headed for the artistic freedom of Europe.

Only ten years later in 1935 conversation at a cocktail party for the community of writers and artists in New York City would hardly be recognizable. No longer did discussions of more sexual freedom dominate. Instead the chief topics of interest concerned a drastic need for reform of social and economic conditions. Some members raised in capitalist America were calling for a communist revolution to benefit the masses. These masses of poor Americans in the working classes were considered the proper focus for writers and artists. Careful attention to the conversations revealed numerous writers labeling themselves as proletarian (focusing on the working class). This talented group of Americans now saw the Untied States as the most fascinating country in the world and it needed to be studied at every level of society. Writers needed to expose problems and push for correction.

Over the last ten years, a 180° shift had occurred in the beliefs of the literary world. The literary world had been deeply moved by the Depression and the suffering it had caused. The writing community had awakened to social consciousness, acutely aware of those millions in trouble in their own country. Both writers and patrons (supporters of the arts) questioned what good art for art's sake was when people were starving. No longer was there any point to write pretty novels of ladies and gentlemen. Writing of factory workers and sharecroppers got at issues that mattered and would help expose and correct situations. Among the intellectual elite a mood of social evangelism prevailed. Some felt if it took a communist revolution in America to correct social inequality then so be it. This new mood was most widespread in New York, long the center of intellectualism. It was more widespread among the young, rising and frequently unemployed rather than older more established intellectuals. Some writers refused to be restricted to the immediacy of the class struggles in America or refused to be identified with any one cause. Nevertheless the proportion of writers moving to the revolutionary left far outdistanced the number of the general public that did so. The best and most talented American writers had discovered that America was a fascinating subject for exploration and dissection.

Outside New York Intellectualism

Many successful individuals across the United States were quite untouched by the revolutionary spirit of New York. This was strikingly apparent among the affluent people who had always surrounded themselves with books and socially correct magazines. Also academics remote from the new creative efforts in arts would have hardly subscribed to leftist ideas. As for businessmen and bankers who considered themselves sustainers of the arts in their communities by helping to make up the annual deficits of symphonies and local colleges they likely were angered by it all. Likewise club women in book groups, who attended literary lectures, subscribed to concerts and the Book of the Month Club were suspicious, bewildered, and frightened of leftist talk.

Every now and then through the 1930s a few decidedly proletarian or leftist pieces did achieve wide popularity. Erskine Caldwell's *Tobacco Road* was rewritten as a play by Jack Kirkland and opened in New York on December 4, 1935. After almost failing, it ended up running year after year. Only two proletarian books made it to the best seller's lists, Sinclair Lewis' anti-fascist novel *It Can't Happen Here* and John Steinbeck's *The Grapes of Wrath*. Otherwise bestseller lists reflected that only a limited number of people cared to read the socially conscious books. For many it seemed the Depression was too painful and disturbing to read about. They needed escape, often to other parts of the world or into history. For example Pearl S. Buck's *The Good Earth*, set in China, topped bestseller lists in 1931 and 1932. *Anthony Adverse* by Hervey Allen sat atop lists in 1933 and 1934. Then Margaret Mitchell's *Gone With The Wind* was at the same position in 1936 and 1937.

Impact

The 1920s and 1930s were a period of innovation in American literature. Incorporation of realism in writing and the varied array of techniques of modernism made the period a time of energized experimentation. Rather than new stylistic approaches or changes the 1940s proved to be largely a refinement of the techniques. The war did provide a new sort of book—the reporting novel or war novel. War novels commanding a wide audience crowded the bestseller lists throughout the decade. Among the best were John Hersey's *A Bell for Adano* (1944) and *Hiroshima* (1946), Irwin Shaw's *The Young Lions* (1948) and Norman Mailer's *The Naked and the Dead* (1948). Nonfiction titles often were eyewitness accounts of war experiences as William Shirer's *Berlin Diary* (1941), and *The Rise and Fall of the Third Reich* (1950), Ted Lawson's *Thirty Seconds Over Tokyo* (1943), and Richard Tregaskis' *Guadalcanal Diary* (1943).

Novels describing the South proved very successful. Influenced by William Faulkner, Carson McCullers wrote *The Heart Is a Lonely Hunter* (1940), *The Member of the Wedding* (1946), and *The Ballad of the Sad Café* (1951). Robert Penn Warren published *All the King's Men* (1946), Truman Capote's *Other Voices, Other Rooms* (1948), and Eudora Welty's *Delta Wedding* (1946). Continuing a Depression theme of examination of rural poverty, Richard Wright followed *Native Son* (1940) with his autobiography *Black Boy* (1945) about his childhood amid poverty in the South. Written in the same vein but set in a small town in California was *The Human Comedy* (1943) by William Saroyan.

John Steinbeck in his 1962 book *Travels with Charley* comments on the Federal Writers Project publications. He describes the 1930s FWP pamphlets and books about the United States as the most thorough accounting of the culture of the United States ever recorded and published. A fictional book published in the late 1960s, *They Shoot Horses, Don't They* (1969), continued a Depression theme of the hopelessness of some individuals during the miserable economic time. A tersely written story, *They Shoot Horses, Don't They?* by Horace McCoy, captured the hard economic circumstances people found themselves in during the Depression. McCoy's book dealt with contestants in a dance marathon and at the end of the story the main exhausted female character is shot dead by her dance partner. She was exhausted after so much dancing that at her request he shot her. As the police lead him away he says with a shrug, "They shoot horses, don't they?" His comment suggested human life was worth little in the marathon of living through the Great Depression.

Notable People

Erskine Caldwell (1903–1987). Erskine Caldwell ranks with Hemingway and Fitzgerald as a powerful and influential American writer. He contributed over fifty volumes of both fiction and nonfiction over his lifetime. Born in Moreland, Georgia, Caldwell lived throughout the South as a child and teen. During his high school years in tiny Wrens, Georgia, Caldwell decided writing would be his life's work. In the 1920s Caldwell would write as much as 18 hours a day but it was 1929 before he received his first acceptance letter. During the 1930s Caldwell published four significant novels, *Tobacco Road* (1932), *God's Little Acre* (1933) *Journeyman* (1935) and *Trouble in July* (1940). He also had more than 100 short stories published in five collections.

Caldwell would often run into censorship difficulties. Also many southerners were furious at his attack on rural Georgia poverty, especially with *Tobacco Road* and *You Have Seen Their Faces* (1937). He collaborated with photographer Margaret Bourke-White, whom he later married, on *You Have Seen Their Faces*. The photographs and narrative together captured the misery of black and white poor southern farmers. Caldwell's efforts brought attention to the farmers' plight and helped provide intellectual reasoning for government agencies as the Resettlement Administration and the Farm Security Administration. Caldwell continued writing for the next four decades, publishing approximately 150 short stories and 25 volumes of fiction.

John Dos Passos (1896–1970). Dos Passos, born in Chicago, Illinois, the son of a wealthy lawyer of Portuguese heritage, graduated from Harvard University in 1916. He volunteered as an ambulance driver in World War I. Praise and popular recognition came to Dos Passos with his bitter antiwar novel *Three Soldiers* (1921), which portrays the artist sickened at the brutality around him. Traveling in Spain and other countries as a newspaper correspondent, Dos Passos developed his social and cultural perceptions and he confirmed his radical political sympathies.

By the mid-1920s Dos Passos unhesitatingly identified with the extreme left and it nourished his best work, the trilogy, *USA* published as a series of three books in the 1930s. He saw the United States as two nations, one of the wealthy and privileged, the other of the powerless and poverty-stricken. The USA trilogy consists of: *The 42nd Parallel* (1930), *Nineteen Nineteen* (1932) and, *The Big Money* (1936). *The 42nd Parallel* covers the period from 1900 until world War I. *Nineteen Nineteen* covers the war period and *The Big Money* moves through the booming 1920s to the 1930s.

Sometime after the publication of *USA,* Dos Passos underwent a change of philosophy, moving from the left across the political spectrum to the conservative right. He often said that he didn't change, but the world around him changed. When he was young industrial capitalism was the villain according to Dos Passos, but in later years he viewed communism, big government, and labor unions as controlling and dangerous. He continued to write until his death but never again reached the creative highs he had with *USA*.

James T. Farrell (1904–1979). Born into an Irish-American working class family in Chicago, Illinois, Farrell's family was so poor that as a tiny child he was sent to live with relatives for a time. As a young man he worked at odd jobs to finance tuition for the University of Chicago, but after a few years he dropped out to become a writer. Profoundly influenced by his boyhood on the South Side of Chicago, Farrell saw his role as an artist to preserve the memory and dignity of the everyday lives and experiences of the ordinary man. He probed the human condition and the social basis of human experiences. During the 1930s his politics tended to Marxist thought, but he fervently remained true to his own viewpoints and feelings shaped by his childhood.

The *Studs Lonigan* trilogy consisting of *Young Lonigan* (1932), *The Young Manhood of Studs Lonigan* (1934), and *Judgment Day* (1935) achieved high praise from critics and readers alike. Farrell was a famous writer by 30 years of age. Through the trilogy, he revealed how American culture prevented humans from achieving full potential. He believed the only solution was to establish a classless society.

Farrell published 52 books during his career and wrote until his death. But nothing he wrote rivaled *Studs Lonigan* in humanity or despair. The *Studs Lonigan* trilogy is ranked high among the top one hundred novels of the twentieth century.

John Steinbeck (1902–1968). John Steinbeck was born and grew up in Salinas Valley, California, a rural agricultural area near Monterey Bay. As a boy he explored the valley and the towns along Monterey Bay—Carmel, Seaside, Pacific Grove and Monterey. Big Sur, with its cliffs and forests above the ocean, awed Steinbeck and in these areas he found a great deal of the material for his stories. He graduated from Salinas High School in 1919. He entered Stanford University where he attended intermittently through 1925

John Steinbeck, author of The Grapes of Wrath *(1939), for which he won a Pulitzer Prize for Fiction in 1940. The work was also the cornerstone of his 1962 Nobel Prize.* (National Archives and Records Administration.)

taking time off to earn money to pay his way. Steinbeck wrote fiction stories at Stanford and they were published in the *Stanford Spectator*. He took a Marine biology class the summer of 1923 at Hopkins Marine Station in Pacific Grove where he became acquainted with Edward F. Ricketts. Ricketts' views on the interrelationship of all life profoundly affected Steinbeck.

Steinbeck's novels of the 1930s revealed his extraordinary sense of the spirit of ordinary men and women. His best stories were decidedly proletariat. Although Steinbeck was not a Marxist, they are about simple people doing battle with dehumanizing social forces and with their own inner souls to build lives of meaning and worth. The *Pastures of Heaven* (1932) is a collection of stories of people in the agricultural communities close to his birthplace in Salinas Valley. *Tortilla Flat* (1935) is a tale of poverty stricken farmers and migrant workers. *In Dubious Battle* (1936) concerns labor struggles in California. *Of Mice and Men* (1937) deals with a mentally retarded farm worker and his friend. In 1939 Steinbeck published his most famous novel and one of the top literary works of the twentieth century, *The Grapes of Wrath*. The novel tells of a poor Oklahoma farm family, the

Joads, displaced by the Dust Bowl, who migrate to California seeking a better life.

Other major works by Steinbeck are *The Red Pony* (1933), *The Sea of Cortez* (1941), *Cannery Row* (1945), *East of Eden* (1952), *The Winter of Our Discontent* (1961), and *Travels with Charley* (1962). Steinbeck received the Nobel Prize for literature in 1962.

Richard Nathaniel Wright (1908–1960). Richard Wright was born on a plantation near Natchez, Mississippi. His grandparents had been slaves. Wright's father, Nathan, was a sharecropper who left the family when Wright was five years old. His mother Ella, a schoolteacher, became paralyzed when he was nine. Afterwards Wright spent a brief period in an orphanage before shifting between relatives. At one point Wright witnessed the lynching of a step-uncle and a friend.

Through his childhood Wright moved from town to town in the South. Wright completed the sixth and seventh grade in Jackson, Mississippi, where he delivered newspapers and ran errands to earn money. He also became an avid reader.

After briefly attending high school he left and joined the general migration of blacks northward, moving to Memphis then to Chicago in 1927 where he found a job in the postal service. In 1930 he lost his job as the Great Depression began. In Chicago he joined the John Reed Club in 1933 and the Communist Party in 1934. He began submitting revolutionary poetry to leftist magazines. On the strength of a few published poems, he joined the WPA's Federal Writers Project in Chicago and was assigned to research the history of blacks in Illinois. Moving to New York in 1937 he wrote the WPA guide to Harlem. He also served as editor of the Communist *Daily Worker* while continuing his own writing.

Wright first rose to the public's attention with *Uncle Tom's Children: Four Novellas* (1938) which explores the struggles of a black man living in a racist country. The publication of *Native Son* (1940) gained Wright international recognition as a powerful writer of his generation. The best-selling book was transformed into a Broadway play in 1941 by Orson Welles. The following year he published *12 Million Black Voices*. The volume was illustrated with approximately one hundred photographs taken from the Farm Security Administration collection. In 1944 Wright broke his connections with the Communist Party realizing his association with it hurt his acceptance as a writer.

In 1945 Wright published his autobiography, *Black Boy,* which explores the poverty of his childhood, the daily prejudice he endured, and his emerging love of literature. Increasingly subjected to harassment by the government over his former Communist Party affiliation, Wright moved to Paris after World War II where he remained in self-imposed exile until his death.

All of Wright's works had presented an angry black voice against the prejudices of America. During his time he was perhaps the most famous black American author and among the first black American writers to protest white treatment of black Americans.

Primary Sources

Louis Adamic on America in the 1930s

Louis Adamic traveled across the United States in the 1930s studying everyday Americans and trying to understand how the Great Depression affected their lives. Adamic, writing in *My America* (1938, p. 340), compares the vastly different moods of the 1920s with that of the 1930s.

For five or six years this laughing went on. America was a fantastic, preposterous scene. A circus. Let us laugh! Those lacking a sense of humor exiled themselves to Paris.

Then the Crash of 1929; the end of Prosperity. Less laughter. Then the tragic year of 1931. Still less laughter. Now we are facing "the worst winter." Europe is in chaos. America is tied into a knot. Racketeering is the only booming industry. Millions are hungry. In Detroit a person dies of starvation every seven and a half hours. And now there is no laughter, unless it is hysterical. What was amusing in 1923 is no longer funny in 1931 ...

Everybody, it appears to me, is getting serious. Young novelists are no longer thinking of writing smart, witty novels. They are working on labor novels.

Adamic in *My America* (p. 283) comments on the effects of the Depression on family life.

The Depression's effects upon the home or family life in the United States were as varied as they were profound; but they can be put into two general categories: On the one hand, thousands of families were broken up, some permanently, others temporarily, or were seriously disorganized. On the other hand, thousands of other families became more closely integrated than they had been before the Depression.

The reason for these different effects due to the same cause was that the economic crisis, which came upon many families in all sections of the country with the force and suddenness of a cyclone, in most cases intensified the various antagonistic and affectional attitudes or reactions of one to the other among the individuals within the family groups ... In some cases, the so-called "hostility reactions" among the members of the family became more explosive, more damaging to the stability and harmony of the group. In other cases, conversely, the bonds of mutual affection, cooperation, and sacri-

fice were greatly strengthened, or even brought into full play for the first time.

These general statements apply, in greater or lesser degree, to all classes of society, except, of course, the uppermost class, in which the Depression was not felt acutely, at least not so far as family life was concerned. They apply most of all to the classes hit by unemployment.

Federal Writers' Project

Following is an explanation from the members of the Federal Writers' Project of the purpose of their work and how they approached writing *These Are Our Lives* (1939, pp. ix, xiv).

Several months ago the writing of life histories of tenant farmers, farm owners, textile and other factory workers, persons in service occupations in towns and cities (such as bell hops, waitresses, messenger boys, clerks in five and ten cent stores, soda jerks), and persons in miscellaneous occupations such as lumbering, mining, turpentining, and fishing was begun by the Federal Writers' Project in North Carolina. This work has recently been extended to six other states, and a large number of stories have already been written.

The idea is to get life histories which are readable and faithful representations of living persons, and which, taken together, will give a fair picture of the structure and working of society. So far as I know, this method of portraying the quality of life of a people, of revealing the real workings of institutions, customs, habits, has never before been used for the people of any region or country. It seems to me that the method here used has certain possibilities and advantages which should no longer be ignored ...

Here, then, are real, living people. Here are their own stories, their origins, their more important experiences, their most significant thoughts and feelings, told by themselves from their own point of view.

"Grease Monkey to Knitters," one of the 35 stories in *These Are Our Lives,* contains a recounting of riding the rails from city to city looking for work (pp. 169–171).

... in January, 1930, the café where I worked went busted. I was out of a job and I couldn't find a single thing to work at. I was young and had no training, and lots of people were out of work. I had nothing to do all the balance of that winter, and when spring came I was down to $30.

There was another young fellow there in Fort Worth, Sam Haines. He had an old Ford car and we decided to hit the road in search of a job. Sam was a waiter, too, and we got three other fellows to go along with us. Sam was to furnish the car and we were to furnish gas and oil.

We set out in April, 1930. We traveled around over Texas—Dallas, Waco, San Antonio, Houston—but we didn't find any jobs. We left Houston heading for New Orleans. In Monroe, Louisiana, 'old Lizzie' gave out. Something went wrong with her 'innards.' She knocked a few loud whacks, then threw off a connecting rod and busted the block. It's a good thing that happened in a town instead of out on the road. Sam sold her to a junk dealer for $5. That was a good thing, too, because we needed that $5 before we found a job.

We all caught a freight train in Monroe and rode it to New Orleans. There the gang split up. One of the boys got a job on a banana boat bound for South America. The other two struck out for Florida.

Me and Sam stuck together. We made it to Mobile but there was nothing doing there. We rambled on up to Birmingham and there Sam found a job as waiter. We had just sixty cents between us when we got there.

Sam got his room and meals and $5 a week. The proprietor agreed for me to occupy the room with Sam for awhile until I could find something to do. I stayed around Birmingham for a week, but couldn't find any kind of job. Sam wanted me to stay on but I wouldn't. He was only making $5 a week, and was giving me a part of that to eat on.

We had both kept our clothes nice. I had two good suits and plenty of shirts. I left all my clothes with Sam and hit the road light. I only had fifty cents that Sam had give me. I made it to Atlanta in one night on a freight train, but things seemed duller there than they were in Birmingham.

I bummed around in Georgia and South Carolina for three or four weeks. Everywhere I went it was the same old story—'No help wanted.' My clothes got pretty dirty and soiled from sleeping out. I could wash my shirt and underwear, but I had no money to have my suit cleaned and pressed.

But there were lots of people on the road worse off than me. I was young, in good health, and had only myself to look out for. That summer I met whole families wandering around homeless and broke, even women with babies in their arms.

The Desperate Movement West

Author John Steinbeck, in the *The Grapes of Wrath* (1939, p. 207), vividly describes the movement west of displaced families during the Great Depression.

And then the dispossessed were drawn west—from Kansas, Oklahoma, Texas, New Mexico; from Nevada and Arkansas families, tribes, dusted out, tractored out. Carloads, caravans, homeless and hungry; twenty thousand and fifty thousand and a hundred thousand and two hundred thousand. They streamed over the mountains, hungry and restless—restless as ants, scurrying to find work to do—to lift, to push, to pull, to pick, to cut—anything, any burden to bear, for food. The kids are hungry. We got no place to live. Like ants scurrying for work, for food, and most of all for land.

We ain't foreign. Seven generations back Americans, and beyond that Irish, Scotch, English, German. One of our folks in the Revolution, an' they was lots of our folks in the Civil War—both sides. Americans.

They were hungry, and they were fierce. And they had hoped to find a home, and they found only hatred. Okies—

Richard Wright

Richard Wright describes the plight of black Americans in *12 Million Black Voices* (from Wright, 1941, pp. 142–143).

We are the children of the black sharecroppers, the first-born of the city tenements.

We have tramped down a road three hundred years long. We have been shunted to and fro by cataclysmic social changes.

We are a folk born of cultural devastation, slavery, physical suffering, unrequited longing, abrupt emancipation, migration, disillusionment, bewilderment, joblessness, and insecurity—all enacted within a *short* space of historical time!

There are millions of us and we are moving in all directions ... A sense of constant change has stolen silently into our lives and has become operative in our personalities as a law of living.

In his book *Uncle Tom's Children* Wright describes how an activity as simple as checking out books from the public library could be an ordeal for a black American (Wright, 1938, pp. 20–21).

... it was almost impossible to get a book to read. It was assumed that after a Negro had imbibed what scanty schooling the state furnished he had no further need for books. I was always borrowing books from men on the job. One day I mustered enough courage to ask one of the men to let me get books from the library in his name. Surprisingly, he consented. I cannot help but think that he consented because he was a Roman Catholic and felt a vague sympathy for Negroes, being himself an object of hatred. Armed with library card, I obtained books in the following manner: I would write a note to the librarian, saying: 'Please let this nigger boy have the following books.' I would then sign it with the white man's name.

When I went to the library, I would stand at the desk, hat in hand, looking as unbookish as possible. When I received the books desired I would take them home. If the books listed in the note happened to be out, I would sneak into the lobby and forge a new one. I never took any chances guessing with the white librarian about what the fictitious white man would want to read. No doubt if any of the white patrons had suspected that some of the volumes they enjoyed had been in the home of a Negro, they would not have tolerated it for an instant.

Suggested Research Topics

- What were the benefits of government support for writers enrolled in the Federal Writers' Project (FWP)?

- Have groups of students read Steinbeck's *The Grapes of Wrath*, Wright's *Native Son*, Farrell's *Studs Lonigan* or Agree's *Let Us Now Praise*

Famous Men. Have each group engage in discussion of their book to prepare for oral presentation. Present round table discussion to class.

- Discuss the two major points of view depicted in work of the 1930: proletarianism and the new nationalism. Give examples of each.

Bibliography

Sources

Adamic, Louis. *My America, 1928–1938.* New York: Harper & Brothers Publishers, 1938.

Allen, Frederick L. *Since Yesterday: The Nineteen-Thirties in America.* New York: Harper & Brothers Publishers, 1940.

Federal Writers Project. *These Are Our Lives.* New York: W.W. Norton & Company, Inc., 1939.

Hackett, Alice P., and James H. Burke. *80 Years of Best Sellers, 1895–1975.* New York: R.R. Bowker Co., 1977.

Kazin, Alfred. *On Native Grounds: An Interpretation of Modern American Prose Literature.* New York: Harcourt Brace Jovanovich, 1970.

Passos, John Dos. *U.S.A.* New York: Literary Classics of the United States, Inc., 1996.

Phillips, Cabell. *1929–1939: From the Crash to the Blitz.* New York: The Macmillan Company, 1969.

Salzman, Jack, ed. *Years of Protest: A Collection of American Writings of the 1930s.* New York: Pegasus, 1967.

Swados, Harvey, ed. *The American Writer and the Great Depression.* New York: The Bobbs-Merrill Company, Inc., 1966.

Wright, Richard. *Uncle Tom's Children* New York: The World Publishing Company, 1938.

Further Reading

Agee, James, and Walker Evans. *Let Us Now Praise Famous Men.* New York: Ballantine Books, Inc., 1960.

Farrell, James T. *Studs Lonigan: A Trilogy.* New York: The Modern Library, 1938.

Kromer, Tom. *Waiting for Nothing and Other Writings.* Athens, GA: The University of Georgia Press, 1986.

Steinbeck, John. *The Grapes of Wrath.* New York: The Viking Press, 1939.

Wright, Richard. *Native Son.* New York: Harper & Row, 1940.

———. *12 Million Black Voices.* New York: Thunder Mouth Press, 1941.

See Also

Dust Bowl; Education; Everyday Life; Political Ideology—Leaning Left

National Industrial Recovery Act

1933-1935

Introduction

In his first inaugural address on March 4, 1933, President Franklin D. Roosevelt (served 1933–1945) denounced the "rulers of the exchange of mankind's goods," the "unscrupulous money changers," for failing to preserve the prosperity of the nation. As a result of the Great Depression, the boom years of the 1920s now became commonly viewed as the result of greedy excess. The business elites, whose aims focused on unregulated financial markets, had neglected the greater economic good, serving only to precipitate the economic collapse. But the moneychangers, Roosevelt went on to proclaim, had "fled from their high seats in the temple of civilization." No longer esteemed as the oracles of economic faith, the economic depression attested to the failure of the old economic order.

The possibility of piecemeal improvements of the old economic structure was rejected. The language in Roosevelt's first inaugural address clearly alluded to a mandate for sweeping reform. In fact nothing short of a new economic order would suffice. In 1932 campaign speeches, Roosevelt called for a new role of government to assist business in the development of a new economic system. Defenders of the old economic structure, Roosevelt declared in his first inaugural address, had tried, but failed in their efforts to maintain an outdated economic tradition.

Many early supporters of Roosevelt's agenda as president, called New Dealers, believed it was archaic to think of the modern corporation as purely an inde-

pendent actor in the nation's economic system. Just as the national government relies on corporations for economic prosperity, so do corporations rely on the national government for fair regulation of markets, for political stability and sometimes for subsidies of capital (money) and land. Corporations are equally dependent on an adequate supply of labor and good relations with workers. Thus to the New Dealers what was needed to transform American industrial relations was a new public philosophy. This philosophy would recognize the interdependence of large forces in the U.S. economy affected by government, labor, and industry. Large corporations should be viewed in terms of holding a public trust, then the role of government, it was envisioned, would be to coordinate these competing forces and guide the long-term interests of industry.

On a practical level, this meant that industrial relations should be organized in such a manner that the various economic interests would be represented by some associations such as committees that could both advance the interests of and discipline its members, with the help of government, along lines of a greater collective good. This philosophy came to be known as "corporatism." Though many different varieties of it have developed in the twentieth century, such as in post-war Japan and Western Europe, it was not entirely clear what form it would take in America during the 1930s.

Following his inauguration in March 1933, President Roosevelt and his advisors moved quickly in devising a grand strategy of national economic planning. In June Congress passed the National Industrial Recovery Act. The National Recovery Administration (NRA), created by the act, soon tackled the task of developing hundreds of business codes that would attempt to control prices of goods and workers' wages in numerous industries.

To accomplish this massive effort, scores of committees were created composed of business leaders and labor and consumer representatives, each group seeking to develop for codes for a particular industry. The sheer size of the effort, however, made the process unwieldy. In addition the voluntary nature of industry actually adopting the codes proved a major weakness. Numerous problems in use of the codes quickly developed. Just as Congress was engaged in heated debates over what to do about the NRA system, the U.S. Supreme Court issued a ruling in May 1935 that held the NIRA was unconstitutional. A major attempt at national economic planning ended abruptly. The New Deal would quickly chart a wholly different course from 1935 onward.

Chronology:

June 16, 1933: Congress passes the National Industrial Recovery Act (NIRA) and members are appointed to the Consumer's Advisory Board.

July 27, 1933: President Roosevelt signs Executive Order No. 6225 creating the Central Statistical Board.

June 30, 1933: The National Planning Board is established.

August 5, 1933: The National Labor Board is established.

August 10, 1933: Roosevelt signs Executive Order No. 6246 requiring all government purchases to be made from suppliers cooperating with NRA codes.

December 16, 1933: Executive Order No. 6514 authorizes the National Labor Board to investigate and resolve labor-management disputes.

March 7, 1934: Executive Order No. 6632 establishes the National Recovery Review Board.

June 19, 1934: The National Labor Relations Board (the first board) is established.

June 30, 1934: Executive Order creates the Industrial Emergency Committee and Executive Order No. 6777 establishes the National Resources Board.

October 15, 1934: General Hugh S. Johnson resigns as Administrator of the NRA.

May 27, 1935: The Supreme Court strikes down the NRA in *Schecter Poultry Company v. United States* (295 U.S. 495).

Issue Summary

Problems With Early Economic Theories

Initially, the new administration did not have a detailed program for reform. It was guided by a set of general principles shaped by the failure of the nation's economic system and the old intellectual framework that had supported it. Many New Dealers rejected as "outworn" certain basic elements of classical economics developed in the late nineteenth century, which had guided both business thinking and national economic policy. For example one belief was that pure, uninhibited competition in the marketplace was sufficient to channel individual greed for profit into beneficial paths for the market as a whole. This fundamental principle of *laissez-faire* economics, according to early New Deal theorists, was clearly a fallacy. What happens in the case of massive over-production and underconsumption? What happens when manufacturers in a given industry begin losing profits because consumers cannot afford to buy, as was widely perceived to be a root cause of the Depression? The old solutions no longer seemed to work.

According to the old, competitive *laissez-faire* model, manufacturers ought to become more competitive with each other. They should reduce the cost of production and ultimately the price for the consumer. Some manufacturers will lose out and fail in the process. In the end, however, the invisible hand of the market would adjust production and consumption in an economically efficient equilibrium.

Clearly several problems existed with this theory as economists in the early 1930s began to point out. First, nobody really knew how long it would take for a market to reestablish equilibrium under such circumstances. For all anybody knew, it could take years. Second, costly price wars clearly hurt many businesses and the resulting wage cuts limited the ability of consumers to buy the products produced by the firms. Such price wars, it seemed, could go on indefinitely. A third observation was that certain choices were now available to large scale manufacturers that might be highly beneficial to the individual company but ultimately counterproductive to the economy as a whole. If, for example, the output of a manufacturer was so great that its share of the market became large enough to influence the industry price, then it would essentially operate as a monopoly (a company or group of companies who control the supply of a product) and push smaller firms out of the market. Many large corporations in the 1930s, such as those in automobiles, steel, and consumer electronics, were so large that they did, in fact, control the market.

Laissez-faire theories of perfect competition did not appear to fit the facts of industry relations in the 1930s. Rather, it seemed to only apply to conditions where manufacturers were small enough that no one firm controlled the market. But in the case of vast concentrations of production that now characterized the American economy in the 1930s, many markets were no longer competitive. To treat the economy as if it were made up of firms in perfectly equal competition would ignore this fundamental reality. The damaging result to firms competing in imperfect markets came to be recognized as the result of "destructive competition."

Rise of Corporate Influence

There was also a more basic philosophical barrier that hindered legal reform of the economic system, which could be found in the traditional view of the corporation as an independent entity free from either the government or the economy. The antitrust tradition of the Progressives—those who believe in using the powers of government to solve social and economic problems—in the early part of the century began to question this concept. Corporations had grown larger and more dominant both over the lives of workers and over the economic destiny of the nation.

Evidence of the end result of this process was published in 1932 in a study titled *The Modern Corporation and Private Property*. The book was by two Columbia University economists, Adolph Berle and Gardiner Means, who would soon become influential advisors in the Roosevelt administration. The book itself had a far-reaching impact in the new administration. Berle and Means demonstrated in statistical and economic terms that modern enterprise was made up of greater and greater concentrations of economic power.

Creating a Cooperative Movement

It was certain that the new economic order Roosevelt envisioned would rely on "a great cooperative movement throughout all of industry," as Roosevelt himself stated on May 17, 1933 in a recommendation to Congress, rather than simply a variation of the U.S. economic structure of the past. If a few manufacturers in various industries could control that industry's market, as in fact was the case, then the best interests of the economy would be served by promoting regulation of the industry by itself. This would be through agreements assuring fair competition within a particular industry. This strategy would become the core of the new industrial program. As if to illustrate his willingness to abandon the old approach to fair trade regulation, Roosevelt rejected too much reliance on the old antitrust (opposing large combinations of business that act to restrict competition) laws designed to combat monopolistic price-fixing. While necessary to safeguard against the most flagrantly improper business practices, the antitrust laws, designed to split up monopolies into smaller firms, were seen as clumsy if not obsolete tools to correct market abuses. Instead, divisions of economic interests would be formally incorporated into cooperative associations of industries that would agree on their own fair practices based on general guidelines provided by the federal government. The agency responsible for instituting this new form of industrial organization, the National Recovery Administration (NRA), was established under the administrative organ of the executive branch and would become the centerpiece of Roosevelt's recovery program.

This new economic program was not, however, entirely new. In fact the War Industries Board (WIB) had developed a similar scheme during World War I (1914–1918). Many New Dealers looked to that experience as an appropriate model. The WIB was a very flexible board of voluntary committees made up of representatives from industry. Based upon a philosophy of industrial self-government, it agreed upon production and prices grounded in a shared commitment to winning the war. Voluntarism alone did not always assure compliance, however, and occasionally the government did use coercive power primarily by threatening to divert future government contracts to other companies or appealing to public pressure to force adherence to agreed direction. But on the whole, noncompliance was rare and the pressure of public opinion and sense of duty among industrial leaders was enough to insure that the board functioned effectively.

The conditions that were necessary to inspire industrial cooperation with the government during the time of the WIB, however, were not entirely the same as the conditions that existed during the 1930s. The desire for cooperation under the WIB during the war was driven by national security concerns and was widely understood to be a short-term emergency measure. The New Dealers were convinced that the Great Depression posed an equally dangerous threat to the national welfare. Any recovery program would have to be presented as a national emergency akin to war. Unlike the temporary WIB, however, they envisioned the creation of a permanent corporatist economic system.

Roosevelt was initially cautious about introducing a legislative proposal, presumably because of the sweeping scale of the reforms being contemplated. Legislative drafting began early in the new administration. Roosevelt appointed "brain trust" member Raymond Moley to gather and consider various proposals. Moley, in turn, appointed several advisors, including Hugh Johnson, a former WIB official; Donald Richberg, a labor lawyer; and Rexford Tugwell, an economist from Columbia University. At the same time, the President encouraged Senator Robert Wagner of New York to work on his own draft.

The administration would not be able to control the tempo of recovery proposals for long. On April 6, 1933, an impatient Senate passed a bill introduced by Senator Hugo Black of Alabama. The bill would ban from inter-

Nancy Cook, left, and Eleanor Roosevelt show their support by hanging an NRA sign at the furniture shop they owned in the 1920s and 1930s. (AP/Wide World Photos. Reproduced by permission.)

state commerce all goods produced in factories that employed workers for more than six hours a day or more than five days a week. Senator Black's "Thirty hour" Bill professed to reduce unemployment and appealed broadly to organized labor. But the bill made no provision for establishing minimum wages or maximum hours, partly because the American Federation of Labor (AFL) labor union organization was hostile to minimum wage legislation. Black believed that a shorter workweek would reduce the supply of labor and thereby push wages up. Roosevelt, however, was not convinced that this would actually help wages rise. He believed that the program his administration was developing would ultimately prove more flexible. But the introduction of the Black Bill created a problem of political urgency for the administration that ultimately forced Roosevelt's hand. Organized labor was hinting at a general strike if the Black Bill did not pass. A veto was therefore out of the question if it passed Congress. Instead, Roosevelt was able to use his influence in the U.S. House of Representatives to postpone action on the bill until he could introduce his own legislation. When Roosevelt did finally introduce the National Industrial Recovery Act on May 17,1933, it effectively scuttled further consideration of the Black Bill.

The NIRA

On May 17 Roosevelt introduced the National Industrial Recovery Act (NIRA) to Congress. The House, firmly controlled by Democrats, approved the bill within nine days, while the Senate took a little longer. In a foreshadowing of the eventual fate of the NIRA, a number of Senators questioned the bill's constitutionality on the grounds that it gave too much power to the president. The U.S. Constitution gave such authority over business to Congress, not the Executive Branch of government. Concern also existed that the NIRA would blur the lines of interstate commerce and as a result infringe upon states' rights. Under the U.S. Constitution the federal government only has power to regulate interstate commerce, meaning economic trade crossing state lines. States are responsible to regulate all other businesses.

Senator Borah of Idaho also argued that the bill would foster control by large business. When it came time to draft and administer codes of fair trade competition, the larger companies, Borah argued, would surely dominate the process. The protection against such abuse did not appear to be included in the legislation. How, Borah asked, could the President oversee so many codes for every industry? Senator Wagner attempted to persuade Borah that the safeguards to protect small business and labor were in the bill and that the proposed legislation did not nullify the antitrust laws. But Borah, an avid antitruster, insisted that the Senate add an amendment prohibiting company combinations from restraining trade, fixing prices, or any other type of practice that may have results like a monopoly. Borah's amendment was in fact so sweeping that it would have undermined cooperation among industries needed to agree upon minimum wages or prices and would undermine the very purpose of the NIRA. Fortunately, the merge committee to reconcile the House and Senate versions eventually convinced him to water down his amendment to include only language prohibiting monopolistic practices.

The greatest opposition to the bill came from conservatives, who opposed the minimum wage provision and the right of collective bargaining guaranteed to labor. But conservatives could not exert enough pressure to stop the bill. It had been designed to satisfy nearly everybody else—labor, public works advocates, trustbusters, and economic planners. The AFL as well as the Chamber of Commerce and the National Association of Manufacturers supported it. Labor liked it because it guaranteed collective bargaining, and business liked it because it permitted price-fixing. It was, in short, a measure that had something for everyone. The momentum for its passage simply could not be restrained. On June 9 the Senate passed the measure by a vote of 58 to 24 and on June 16, 1933, Roosevelt signed the NIRA into law.

There were three titles, or main parts, to the NIRA: Title I outlining the general framework of industrial self-regulation; Title II establishing an emergency Public Works Administration (PWA) to construct highways, dams, federal buildings, naval construction, and other projects; and, Title III providing for taxes to help finance the PWA.

The substance of economic reform, however, lay in the ten sections of Title I.

- Section 1 was a broad description of policy, which was, in fact, a common feature of legislation passed by Congress during the period. The section defined the intent of the NIRA, which was to promote cooperative agreements in industry, eliminate unfair trade practices, increase workers' purchasing power, and reduce unemployment while expanding production.

- Section 2 gave considerable authority to the president to create administrative agencies, appoint employees without regard to civil service laws, and delegate power to his appointees. This expanded power was not indefinite but imposed a time limit of two years on the act.

- Section 3 gave the president authority to approve codes for various trades and industries. He could add or delete parts of proposed codes or even establish entirely new codes.

- Section 4 granted the President authority to assist businesses in entering into voluntary agreements.

- Section 5 exempted all businesses operating under an approved code from the antitrust laws.

- Section 6 gave the president authority to determine whether a particular organization as truly representative of a particular trade or industry it claimed to represent.

- Section 7 was the most controversial part of the NIRA. It established basic labor standards, and minimum wage provisions. Under Section 7(a), a phrase would become famous in its own right—employees were given the right to organize and bargain collectively.

- Section 8 excluded agriculture from the reach of the NIRA. It also guaranteed that none of the codes could conflict with the Agricultural Adjustment Act, another New Deal law designed to financially assist farmers.

- Section 9 gave the president authority to regulate the shipment of petroleum across state lines.

- Section 10 authorized the president to re-write any of the codes at any time during the life of the NIRA.

To administer the NIRA, the act provided for the creation of the National Recovery Administration (NRA), an administrative agency directly under the authority of the President.

Selling the NIRA

Initially business welcomed the NIRA, but underlying the positive reception of the act was a wait and see attitude. Success of the NRA would ultimately depend on how it was administered. Therefore it remained to be seen how much influence a particular group would have on the code drafting process.

Despite the heavy bureaucratic oversight and enforcement of the codes, the actual spirit of the NRA, like its predecessor the WIB, was very much voluntary. Coercion did not feature prominently in the scheme. It was therefore imperative that public support and enthusiasm be behind it. To do this, the administration launched a major campaign nothing short of a national crusade.

Roosevelt appointed General Hugh Johnson, who had designed and administered the selective service system during World War I, to head the agency. Johnson was a tough, action-oriented military man, whose occasional flair for colorful language only contributed to a sense of wartime crisis that he seemed to enjoy promoting. Johnson had also been an administrator for the Bureau of Purchase and Supply during the war and had served as a member of the WIB. Because of his unique experience, Johnson was in many ways the perfect man for the job. In other respects, however, he was not. For example, Johnson was not the most politically effective negotiator, often appearing to browbeat industry representatives into quickly drafting a code. This political insensitivity, as well as a quick temper, tended to make him very unpopular.

Johnson proceeded to launch the greatest outpouring of patriotic fervor since the war. From the radio and the press the General exhorted everyone to do his part. Johnson demanded that individual firms pledge themselves to eliminate child labor, pay a minimum wage of twelve or thirteen dollars a week for 40 hours work, and work together to set floors for minimum prices. Those businesses that complied with the NRA could display a Blue Eagle emblem, a symbol designed by Johnson that became the national symbol of the NRA. The sign would indicate their willingness to participate in the recovery program. The legend under the symbol of the Blue Eagle, "We Do Our Part," summarized the sentiment of national emergency. Blue Eagles began to appear in store and factory windows across America as part of a great patriotic drive to defeat the depression.

The Codes of the NIRA

By the summer of 1933 the NRA was drafting codes by the dozen. Before July only the cotton textile industry had created codes. As the campaign gained strength, codes for the shipbuilding and the wool textile industries soon followed. Then came steel, petroleum, and lumber. Throughout the summer, Johnson flew across the country on an army plane in order to convince major industries to adopt the Blue Eagle. Late in August, the automobile industry joined with the noted exception of Ford Motor Company. On September 18th, the coal industry, the last of the major industries, accepted the Blue Eagle. Many more months of code writing for smaller industries lay ahead but in the end, some 546 industrial codes and 185 supplemental codes were written and approved.

The administrative challenge of the NRA was enormous. The codes themselves eventually filled 18 volumes, including 685 amendments and modifications, 11,000 administrative orders interpreting the provisions of individual codes, 139 administrative orders bearing upon the procedures of the NRA, and some 70 executive orders signed by the president. This activity created a complex body of administrative law and an even greater body of administrative interpretations and decisions. Despite this enormous bureaucratic growth, the structure of the NRA was fundamentally decentralized in a key respect. The industries recognized under the various codes became self-governing. As a means of implementing the codes, the NRA approved 585 code authorities under which there were several thousand regional and divisional subordinate agencies. Most of the approved code agencies were also granted the authority to levy fines. Not surprisingly, the staff of the NRA grew as administrative activities of the code authorities expanded. In August 1933 the staff numbered nearly four hundred. By February 1935 it had risen to a high of 4,500 in Washington and the various field agencies. The scope of the authority of the NRA was staggering. It covered industries in many fields ranging from banking and insurance to transportation to public health. As Roosevelt anticipated, it was possibly the most far-reaching legislation ever passed by Congress.

Drafting the codes was essentially a process of negotiation. Government officials and business representatives hammered out agreements based on general principles of industrial organization. There was, however, a disadvantage for the government. Most

More About...

The Ford Motor Company and the NRA

Perhaps no other company during the two years of the NRA received as much attention as the Ford Motor Company. This stemmed from the refusal of Henry Ford to sign the auto industry code and his unwillingness to supply the federal government with assurance that it would comply with the NRA. Although others in the auto industry were initially persuaded that the NRA would aid recovery, Henry Ford did not view it that way. Ford was temperamentally opposed to putting himself under the authority of any type of organization over which he had little control. He had refused to join the National Automobile Chamber of Commerce with the other automobile manufacturers, and he absolutely opposed labor unions, though he had attained recognition for his wage and hour policies—the most progressive in the industry. At first Ford had considered joining the NRA. General Johnson secretly flew to Dearborn, Michigan, on July 15, 1933, to persuade Ford of the advantages to economic recovery by reducing working hours and setting minimum wages. Ford agreed, since he had been advocating such a system for years and Johnson left the meeting with the impression that the Ford Motor Company was on board. Once Ford became aware of the implications of section 7(a), however, recognizing labor's right to collective union representation, Ford had second thoughts and refused to sign the code.

When the auto code went into effect on September 5, 1933, the Ford Motor Company was conspicuously absent. Henry Ford, however, had no intention of upsetting the industry's price structure and he did not cut wages. For all practical purposes he was complying with the automobile code. Soon, however, some of the other automobile manufacturers, notably Chrysler, were accusing Ford of violating the provisions of the code, and Johnson began to turn on the heat. A series of exchanges between the NRA administrator and the president of Ford Motor Company led to Ford's refusal becoming well publicized. Several intermediaries attempted to arrange a meeting between

Ford and Roosevelt but with no success. Henry Ford still refused to join the NRA.

By late 1933 labor organizers in the Ford plants were demanding a seven-hour day, a five-day week, and a minimum wage of $5.00 a day. These demands were presented at the Chester, Pennsylvania plant on September 26, where approximately 2,500 workers were employed. The demands were in response to a wage reduction to $4.00/day for a four-day week. The plant superintendent said he would send the demands to company headquarters in Dearborn but to be back at work at 7:30 AM the next morning. The superintendent called Dearborn and was instructed to post a sign closing the plant indefinitely. The company decided to reopen on October 16, but terminated the jobs of the former employees and told them to re-apply if they wanted their jobs back. The workers' case was eventually turned over to the compliance division of the NRA. A hearing was held on March 3, 1934, but representatives from the Ford Motor Company refused to attend the meeting. The Compliance Board found that the company practiced discrimination against those who had walked out, in violation of section 7(a) of the NIRA, and several hundred had been denied re-employment.

The matter was eventually turned over to the Attorney General in order to compel Ford to abide by the law. The Justice Department was prepared to move ahead but Johnson was concerned that if they lost, the damage to the NRA would be immeasurable. Scrutiny of the evidence pointed out its weaknesses. The behavior of workers at both plants could be interpreted as a refusal on the part of the workers to bargain with the company representatives and could therefore be difficult to prove discrimination by the company. Despite the urgings of the Compliance Division Attorney, J.C. Randall, the Justice Department decided the case was too weak to prosecute and Ford triumphed. He demonstrated that he could resist joining the NRA and that any attempts to unionize his plants would be fiercely resisted.

---

government representatives were not as familiar with the industry as business representatives and no real policy guidelines existed to follow. Policy assumptions involved in drafting the codes very much came

down to the individual deputy administrators involved in the code writing process. Personal desires and the manner in which issues were presented and negotiated naturally varied for each deputy administrator. The code authorities would formally adopt the codes through a voting process among the members. Members would also vote on enforcement issues when a company might not be properly complying with the codes. The members would decide how to respond to the situation.

Political pressure in certain industries, such as potential labor strife, could also be a factor in the sense of urgency in drafting codes. As a result the codes varied considerably from one industry to the next, however, business usually had the upper hand. Given the information at their disposal, experience, and political clout, it was almost inevitable that business would dominate the code writing process. Moreover many deputy administrators were themselves almost entirely drawn from the ranks of business. Most of Johnson's immediate subordinates came from either industry or the military and shared his views and background.

Nevertheless business did have to make concessions and in a few industries, such as textiles where unions were strong, business representatives were not able to dominate the drafting process. Overall, however, the wage and hour provisions were full of exceptions not originally contemplated by the legislation and labor representation on the code authorities was also limited wherever possible. In fact only 51 code authorities, less than 10 percent, contained labor representatives, moreover only 10 had consumer representatives. Business leaders in several industries succeeded in including a number of provisions designed to establish business cartels. A cartel is a combination of businesses formed to regulate prices and production in some industry.

The NRA and the Rubber Tire Industry

In the 1920s and 1930s, the rubber tire industry saw tremendous change, which resulted from changes in the sale of rubber tires to the public. The emergence of mass distributors intensified competition and erratic materials prices within the industry led to terrible price wars. In 1928 the rubber tire manufacturing industry employed over 83,000 workers, and by 1932 that number had fallen by half. Nearly everyone in the industry welcomed the National Recovery Administration (NRA), hoping that it would prevent fluctuating rubber prices and bring order to industry.

By 1920 the rubber tire market was dominated by the "Big Four" tire rubber firms: Goodyear, B.F. Goodrich, U.S. Rubber, and Firestone. These companies produced tires that were sold to automobile manufacturers as "original equipment." There were also a number of smaller and medium size firms that dealt with the "replacement" market, selling to individuals

Ford employees engaged in a physical confrontation during a strike. Henry Ford was one of the only industrialists who refused to join the NRA. (FDR Library.)

and bus and taxi companies. The smaller firms served local markets and generally sold at the lowest possible price while the "Big Four," aimed for the highest prices.

Throughout the 1920s, however, the industry structure began to change. Rubber costs were unstable, and toward the end of the decade automobile sales declined, which affected the Big Four. As a result the larger firms began moving into the replacement market and began producing cheaper lines of tires. Some of the smaller firms shifted to producing specialty tires, but most could not compete. In 1923 there were 166 tire manufacturing firms and by 1933 there were only 35.

Unlike other prominent industries, such as automobile or cotton textile manufacturers that negotiated primarily over labor issues when drafting NRA codes, the rubber tire industry fought almost exclusively over distribution practices. At first the code looked promising; tire manufacturers unanimously agreed not to sell tires below cost. There was little agreement, however, on the matter of production controls. Three of the Big Four favored a production and sales quota plan. Firestone was the maverick and instead proposed a flexible plan where prices would be set according to the size of the company. The smallest firms would be able to charge the lowest price. Goodrich, Goodyear, and U.S. Rubber remained supporters of production quotas. Five of the smaller companies represented on the industry's eight-member Code Committee favored the Firestone plan. It was this plan that was approved in the final draft of October 1933. This decision was met with an uproar as many considered the plan to be blatant price-fixing. When the NRA finally approved a code at the end of October, the Firestone plan was conspicuously absent as was the production quota plan. The NRA administrators hoped that several months might bring a consensus on controlling the stability of prices. The stalemates never dissolved and the adopted code was completely ineffective.

It took five months of bitter negotiations before a code was approved in May 1934. Immediately afterwards accusations of noncompliance began flying. The tire industry condition was recognized as dire and if ever a situation required the declaration of an emergency, the tire industry was it. The emergency provisions classified tires into four price levels based on their quality of manufacture. A flexible price system was used but not between companies like the earlier Firestone plan but between products. This code was, critics objected, price-fixing and soon proved a failure.

Next manufacturers pushed for a long-term cost control plan. The industry presented a cost report to the NRA in June 1934 based on the current cost of raw materials. The NRA, however, refused to consider the plan because it would raise prices for the consumer. It would only accept the plan if it changed the value of raw materials. Neither side would budge. The last resort of the industry was to petition the NRA to modify its emergency price provisions by raising the minimum prices. The NRA agreed but the eventual changes, effective on August 27, 1934, were still too low and too late to help the industry. Thereafter tire manufacturers so widely ignored the NRA that by September's end, the NRA had given up on the tire industry. The NRA tire manufacturing and retail codes were not only a major failure but also likely contributed to even greater industry strife and price wars.

Controlling Prices

A major feature of the NRA was controlling prices of goods. Most of the codes, approximately four hundred, prohibited sales of goods below cost of production. In practice, many businesses did not always follow the plain meaning of this term and tended to substitute "price" for "cost." This allowed them to set minimum prices sufficiently high for all of their mem-

bers to make a profit. A few codes, such as in lumber, cleaning and dyeing, and coal, actually contained language that allowed for direct price-fixing. These industries had traditionally engaged in price wars that threatened the existence of smaller firms within the industry.

Deputy administrators pursued several strategies for controlling prices set by the codes. One path was through what were known as price-filing plans. These were placed into 444 codes and called for the filing of current and future prices, required the identification of sellers, and prohibited deviation from filed prices without notifying the code authority. Penalties could be meted out to those who failed to comply. "Waiting periods" were established before a filed price became effective.

Other methods to control minimum prices were placed in codes. Some attempted to place into their codes existing geographical relationships so as to preserve existing avenues for distributing goods. Others tried to regulate bidding practices for winning new orders. Generally, the approach to standardize costs and sales practices in the codes presented an incredibly diverse collection of restrictions on economic competition.

Over 60 industries approached the control of prices by controlling production. Limitations were set on machine use or plant hours, production quotas, and even, in four codes, provisions for limitations on inventory control. These all restricted the productive capacity of industries. General Johnson tried to discourage production controls but admitted there were cases where they might be useful such as in natural resource industries like oil or timber.

Provisions were also set up for enforcing the codes. This provided the punishment approach for not falling into line. The amount of requirements differed from code to code and business was often reluctant to punish its own members. Many code authorities preferred instead to use their power to make exemptions for industries not willing to comply with the codes and interpret the code language in a favorable light for those industries. While every code authority did include government members appointed by the NRA, usually they were part-time, unpaid, and given little or no power to vote. When NRA administrators did not have duties elsewhere and were able to attend code authority meetings, their presence was usually negligible. The drift of the code authorities toward favoring the larger more economically powerful companies or groups of companies gradually became apparent. In practical terms, the larger and securely established trade associations (businesses having a common interest in a particular industry) controlled the process. Though some allowance was made for legally required labor clauses, what began to emerge was a system of business cartels.

Conflict Over the NIRA

Critics of the NRA argued the codes were being misused. To substantiate this claim, they pointed to the gradual rise in prices for many goods and services. But Johnson was not concerned about rising prices. Since prices had collapsed as a result of the Great Depression and the new costs imposed on industry by the codes for wage increases and work hour reductions made price raises inevitable in many cases. In fact prices needed to rise according to Johnson and the NRA staff. Otherwise numerous shaky businesses trying to recover from the Depression would be driven into bankruptcy. What did alarm Johnson and the NRA staff was that prices of goods were rising faster than wages paid to workers. According to the overall NRA recovery plan, wages would rise with prices. The increased income would give more purchasing power to consumers. What was essential to the program was balance between price changes and wage changes. If business cartels increased prices beyond those justified by the new costs of production, then the usefulness of any increase in wages would be negated. By January 1934 growing evidence was suggesting that this is exactly what was happening. Business self-restraint was failing and many businesses were cooperating to produce cartels. Suspiciously large price increases in certain commodities (goods) were eating away at any benefit of increased wages. Thus the drive to create increase purchasing power of the public was working in reverse. The public was quickly becoming disenchanted with an economic recovery program that brought higher prices instead of better jobs.

In October Johnson decided it was time to counterattack. He started a "Buy Now" program in an attempt to encourage a consumer buying spree. This, it was thought, would stimulate enough spending to offset a drop in business confidence. With business confidence restored, there would be proof that the NRA was working and that businesses should follow the codes and cooperate with the code authorities. General Johnson envisioned the campaign to be a reenactment of the Liberty Bond drive he had undertaken during World War I. He soon discovered, however, that the same level of moral enthusiasm was not present. The campaign proved a dismal failure because consumers had very little to spend as the public grew exasperated with the Blue Eagle. If there were fears about the failure of the recovery program before, there was little doubt by the end of October.

Businesses that registered with the NRA could display the Blue Eagle symbol to publicly demonstrate their support of the program. (FDR Library.)

By the fall of 1934 it had become clear that noncompliance with the codes was widespread. The temptation to violate the provisions of the codes was just too great. The competitive advantages over rivals who followed the codes were enormous. Wage slashing and "chiseling," the dumping of goods on the market at below the code cost, became common. Once it became evident that certain businesses in a given industry were violating the codes, economic self-interest reasserted itself. Even those businesses committed to the NRA were ultimately compelled to violate the codes in order to compete with those businesses that had no qualms about ignoring the NRA. A few non-complying businesses in an industry could force the rest to abandon the codes in a vicious circle. Gradually the traditional competitiveness found its way back into the economic system.

During this period code-abiding businesses demanded that the NRA take steps to curb violations. By late 1933 the NRA put greater emphasis on compliance and created an independent Compliance Division, a National Compliance Board, and regional compliance offices in every state. The credibility of the NRA was at stake and a new emphasis on punishing violators ran through the agency. But if voluntary cooperation proved difficult, the problems posed by enforcing compliance would prove insurmountable. The codes were often very detailed and overly ambitious in many cases. Sometimes they included the smallest details of sales transactions in less organized industries like the service industry. Therefore violations were often difficult to detect. Businesses monitoring compliance in the industry was one thing, but the extent of highly detailed management that would have been required for government to oversee business compliance with the codes was never contemplated.

A few well-publicized prosecutions might have delayed the breakdown in compliance, but the most frequent violators were small businesses on the verge of bankruptcy. Attempts to penalize these businesses, which usually had nothing to lose, would only bring worse publicity for the program. Many within the agency now began to fear that the NRA was embarking down a dangerous path toward regulating industries. Compliance with the codes could only be assured by a much larger bureaucracy, and business would never be sympathetic to a development such as this. The NRA was stuck in a quandary. Without more enforcement, it would lose the support of those willing to comply, with more enforcement, opposition to the NRA would only increase.

Although both consumers and labor were increasingly vocal in their objections to the NRA, the majority of the complaints actually came from the increasing disharmony within industry. The inevitable conflicts between manufacturers and distributors, large firms versus smaller firms and chain stores versus independents could no longer be resolved in the marketplace. Resolving conflicts would have to come through political negotiations and the decisions of code authorities. Frequently businesses were put in the position of judging their competitors. The losers of NRA decisions were quick to conclude that their rivals were simply making a business maneuver by using the code and that the code authorities were discriminating to put them out of business. Inevitably the Roosevelt administration would be caught in the middle of such confrontation.

The old antitrusters in Congress, such as Senator Borah, were now convinced that the NRA was creating monopolies everywhere. Other departments within the administration became critical as well. The Department of Labor voiced concern about the accuracy of statistical reporting turned over to the code authorities. The Department of Agriculture was anxious about rising industrial prices. The Federal Trade Commission thought the objectives of the NRA were a complete corruption of the purpose of government

regulated competition. Secretary of the Interior Harold Ickes was almost continually in disagreement with General Johnson. The General thought that Ickes was slow to get the PWA off the ground. Ickes accused the NRA of promoting monopoly as evidenced by the fact that he was receiving identical secret bids on public works contracts in terms of the dollar amounts proposed. Such marked similarities strongly suggested the companies were overly cooperating and essentially forming a cartel to corner the new government projects among themselves. Johnson and Ickes would spar at meetings of the Special Industrial Recovery Board, an interdepartmental agency designed to coordinate the activities of the NRA with the rest of the economic recovery program. The board had other critics sitting on it as well. Johnson would usually get an earful from Secretary of Agriculture Henry Wallace and assistant Secretary of Agriculture Rexford Tugwell about the futility of price controls unless they were accompanied by government regulation. Johnson vehemently disagreed, arguing that the price controls in the codes did much to limit destructive price wars. He was also aware that opposition by key players in the Department of Agriculture was actually part of a broader political break between the Department of Agriculture and the administrator of the Agricultural Adjustment Administration George Peek who generally supported the NRA. Partly due to his awareness of competing views within the Department of Agriculture, Johnson increasingly ignored the board, refused to provide it much information, and finally asked Roosevelt to abolish it. In December 1933 Roosevelt agreed with Johnson and the board's functions were transferred to a coordinating agency, the National Recovery Council. The council was unlikely to give Johnson much difficulty.

Through 1933 attempts to reorient the focus of the NRA had been thwarted by conflict within the agency that was now growing. The increasingly vocal presence of the Consumer Advisory Board and the Research and Planning Division within the NRA was gaining notice by Congress. These sections were primarily staffed with economists and sociologists who had little faith in industrial self-government. Johnson generally ignored their policy proposals but they were assertively challenging existing policy. After much pressure in December 1933 he agreed to schedule public hearings on the so-called "price question" in January.

The complaints centered around areas where there was suspiciously too much similarity in price bids for government contracts and unjustified price increases, mostly in lumber, textiles, printing, steel, cement, coal and scientific instruments. In all only 34 codes were questioned. Days later Johnson would state publicly that the people complaining were mostly "chiselers," and knew very little about industry. Nevertheless Johnson did concede to use labor and consumer advisors for the government representatives on each code authority. This policy, however, strongly opposed by industrial leaders, was never really implemented.

The biggest problem, critics charged, was that small firms were at a disadvantage because they could not challenge larger firms by lowering prices. In many industries, large firms had advantages that smaller firms did not. These included access to credit, advertising, research funds, control of patents, and managerial talent. The only advantage many small firms had was that they could offer lower prices, either by cutting wages or relocating, to undercut the larger firm's brands. It was therefore to the advantage of larger firms to make sure that prices and wages could not be used to undercut them. The majority of codes seemed like efforts to eliminate any special advantages that made it possible for smaller firms to cut prices. There were exceptions, which Johnson pointed out, in retail, cotton textiles, and coal where reduction of competition did possibly maintain higher labor standards. Overall, however, it seemed to many that the codes were an effort to force small companies out of business. Small business protested that it was unable to pay the same wages and charge the same prices as the larger firms. Also many small businesses could not continually afford legal and accounting fees to work through the code authority directives and reports. To an administration dedicated to helping the "little man," such complaints were politically devastating. On January 18, 1934, Senators Borah and Senator Gerald Nye of Wisconsin opened a Senate debate on the NRA. They charged the agency with breeding monopoly.

Fixing the NIRA

Roosevelt moved quickly to please these current champions of small business in the Senate. The President issued an executive order creating a formal way that small businessmen could appeal directly to the Federal Trade Commission if they were dissatisfied with the NRA's decision in a case. On March 7, 1934, Roosevelt issued another executive order creating a National Recovery Review Board that would investigate the effect of codes on small business and recommend any changes. Johnson had considered the idea for such a board much earlier. Johnson had actually recommended that the great criminal defense attorney Clarence Darrow chair it. Darrow agreed, but instead of reporting to Johnson as Johnson had instructed him, Darrow decided he would report directly to the president. It was perhaps an indication

that Darrow intended for the commission to make his findings public.

However much the general's tough-minded persistence had induced him to dismiss critics in the past, it was becoming clear the NRA was reaching a crossroads. Johnson would have to face the two significant policy choices with which he was confronted. The first was how to eliminate or reduce price and production controls. The second was how to develop more responsible code authorities through closer supervision. Johnson wavered on what to do. He recognized that there were price increases that gave some firms, mostly smaller ones, an advantage. But price increases allowed average producers some profits and this was needed, in theory, if employment was to increase. Johnson also defended the NRA for its successes—wages had risen, child labor had been abolished, bankruptcies were down, and the right to join a union was being protected. There were enough successes, Johnson pointed out, to merit reform of the NRA rather than dismantling it.

As for eliminating price controls, one useful innovation came out of the January hearings. It was called the "emergency minimum price" concept. The approach was designed to simplify administration and get around complex accounting systems. Under this procedure, a code authority could determine when destructive price-cutting was so severe that it threatened an "emergency" for the industry. The code authority could then determine the industry's "lowest reasonable cost" and submit this figure to the NRA administrator. If approval was given, the administrator would then declare an emergency and it would become an unfair practice to sell below what was found to be the "lowest reasonable cost." The problem, as Johnson soon discovered, occurred when the NRA Administrator had to evaluate the basis for determining the "lowest reasonable cost" and make a determination. This was not always easy given the complexity of a company's operations and the nuances of their bookkeeping in determining their overhead costs of doing business and outstanding debts as well as closely guarded details of various sales contracts.

In developing greater supervision over abuse by code authorities, the NRA began to shift in the direction of greater government control. At the end of January 1934, code authorities were stripped of much power and were prohibited from modifying code provisions, exempting members, and engaging in enforcement. These functions were taken over by state compliance officers, while code authorities were to stick to investigation, education, and arbitration. In March the Bureau of Labor Statistics took over the duty of collecting data directly from the code authorities.

A street in New York City during the NRA Day parade, September 13, 1933. (AP/Wide World Photos. Reproduced by permission.)

Johnson reasserted his power to review, suspend, or veto code provisions. Policy in the NRA was definitely changing, although gradually. As for the idea of "industrial self-government," it was the beginning of the end.

By executive order on June 30, 1934, President Roosevelt created two new organizations to assist the NRA: the Industrial Emergency Committee and the National Planning Board. The Industrial Emergency Committee was to coordinate government relief and employment programs under the NRA. Donald Richberg was named as its director. Other committee members were Secretary of Labor Francis Perkins, Secretary of the Interior Harold Ickes, Harry Hopkins, and NRA Administrator Hugh Johnson. The committee was established as part of the National Emergency Council, which Roosevelt had established a year earlier. It was an attempt to put the Committee in charge of the NRA and assert more control over General Johnson. The Committee was short-lived, however, in October the president merged the Industrial Emergency Committee into a new National Emergency Council headed by Donald Richberg.

The National Planning Board enjoyed a longer lifespan. Title II of the National Industrial Recovery Act established the National Planning Board under the Public Works Administration. An earlier model for the board existed in the War Industries Board during World War I and in some of the ideas of Herbert Hoover while he was Secretary of Commerce. The Planning Board became the first experiment in peacetime national planning. The National Planning Board changed names several times: National Planning Board (1933–1934), National Resources Board (1932–1935), National Resources Committee (1935–1939), and the National Resources Planning Board (1939–1943). But its personnel remained remarkably continuous. Over the course of the board's existence, planning committees were set up to study a broad range of social and economic projects. Committees studied land use planning, mineral policy, transportation, energy, and the impact of science and technology. Regional planning agencies were also established in the Pacific Northwest and New England. Many of the studies remained unique for the remainder of the twentieth century.

Another key policy decision that gave hope to small businesses and others was the creation of an advisory council on May 21, 1935, to coordinate the various advisory boards within the NRA. It was anticipated that internal disputes within individual industries could be settled more peacefully. A new Policy Group was also created, which was made up of a single administrator and three deputy administrators, one each for trade practices, labor provisions, and code authority administration. Leverett S. Lyon of the Brookings Institution, a former critic of the price production policies of the NRA, was appointed to head the Trade Practices Division. Lyon's recommendations furnished the NRA's most controversial declaration of policy. In a famous office memorandum of June 7, 1934, which came to be known as "Memorandum 228," a new approach to price policy was outlined, essentially recognizing that the goal of the NRA was to create a free market. Code provisions, therefore, should strengthen, rather than limit, competition. Strict safeguards were to be provided against price fixing, and price cutting would be considered unfair practice where it imperiled small business, labor standards, or tended to promote a monopoly. Lastly the fixing of minimum prices was to take place only in emergencies after full study by NRA economists.

Memorandum 228 was hailed as an abandonment of all price-fixing. This perception brought an immediate wave of resistance from the business community who liked the ability to fix prices whenever they wanted. Johnson was forced to make a public state-

ment to stifle the clamor. When he spoke he announced the new policy would not affect already approved codes. It would neither create changes nor be applied to codes near completion at the time the memo was issued. As a result of the confusion, the NRA found it difficult to take any action at all. The great policy shift, like so many other attempts at reform within the agency, amounted to little more than organizational change. Critics now attacked the agency for the inconsistency between its policy and practice. Matters were made worse by the release of the Darrow Board reports that found exactly what it had been looking for: the NRA promoted monopoly and discriminated against small business. In reaction an Industrial Appeals Board was established to handle small business complaints. It, however, dealt only with individual complaints of misconduct, not general reform of the program.

Organized labor felt especially out of the picture by the summer of 1934. Johnson was not highly receptive to union representation and generally refused to get involved in labor disputes created by section 7(a). As time went on small businesses and antitrusters continued to claim the NRA assisted big business to the detriment of the "little man." Even leaders of large industry were increasingly disillusioned by shifting policy changes and the seeming lack of stability within the agency. Frustration and disappointment was now so great that Johnson could not keep a lid on bickering within the organization. As pressured mounted, he had become increasingly emotional and would occasionally explode in an angry tirade and also took refuge in alcohol. It became clear to Roosevelt that Johnson would have to go, and on August 21, 1934, the President summoned Johnson to the White House to discuss having him chair a commission to study recovery programs of several European nations. Johnson refused and immediately submitted his resignation.

The National Industrial Recovery Board

Instead of one-man rule, the President would now try using an administrative board to run the NRA. On September 27 Roosevelt announced the appointment of a five-man National Industrial Recovery Board under the chairmanship of S. Clay Williams, former chief executive of R. J. Reynolds Tobacco Company. Sidney Hillman of the Amalgamated Clothing Workers would represent labor. Two economics professors, Leon C. Marshall and Walton Hamilton, and a former Division administrator, Arthur D. Whiteside, would also serve on the Board. Policy, however, would be at the direction of Donald Richberg who would manage and formulate the broad policy of all recovery agencies from the Industrial Emergency Committee. The press praised the new reorganization as a victory for the liberal economic men who advocated maintaining the price controls and protection from the antitrust laws while introducing policies that strengthened competition.

Free markets were not feasible under such dire economic conditions, although it was believed that stronger institutions and controls could be created to accomplish the same ends that a free market would achieve. Planners, as well as business, continued to be hopeful of a fair, recovering economy. In the end, however, the board only proved effective in balancing opposing interests, and it was never able to take effective action. Advocates of change scored minor gains, but the complexity of the problems and potential political fall-out from moving too far in one direction prevented any significant revision in the program. Many industrial leaders still supported the idea of industrial self-government in a corporatist state, but only to the point at which concessions had to be made to labor. In the end, the Board's only real accomplishment was that it more skillfully presided over stalemates between parties.

Renewing the NIRA

By January 1935, the timeframe set for the NRA by Congress was reaching its end. Congress was beginning to discuss whether to extend the agency. But it was increasingly apparent that divisions within the NRA were well established along rigid battle lines. Official policy had strayed from the original provisions of the business codes, agency officials were exhausted, and the future of the program was uncertain. There was little inclination to take action since Congress would decide the very existence of the program in a short period of time, with new hearings scheduled for January 1935. Once again economists within the NRA argued that price and production controls were economically harmful. The majority of business, however, made it clear that they opposed Memorandum 228 and that industry still needed price protection. Some way had to be found to stop destructive price wars and establish a minimum "price floor" below which prices could not fall. The hearing was followed by two other major hearings in early 1935, but little was gained in changes of policy. Lines of conflict within the agency went unchanged. Officials were left feeling that they were doing little more than biding their time until the program would be ended.

With few friends for the agency as it shuffled toward the end of its two-year authorization by Congress, critics began to look toward a potential replacement. Nobody supported an extension of the agency in

its original form but the diversity of proposals were broad reflecting the different perceptions of the NRA's success or failure. Business was generally unhappy about its perceived lack of control, while labor believed business had too much control. There was little agreement regarding an alternative. Some industry leaders proposed adopting purely voluntary codes, while a few in Labor were advocating continuing wage and hours standards but eliminating the price controls.

Roosevelt's task was to arrive at a compromise between conflicting groups if the NRA was to be renewed. Donald Richberg advised the President that this could be done if sharper distinctions were drawn between restraining destructive competition and promoting monopoly. Roosevelt realized antitrust laws had to be revived, and in a message to Congress on February 20, 1935, the President recommended a two-year extension of the NRA in a revised form. The new program would keep the labor provisions but limit price and production controls only to those industries who needed to protect small business, conserve natural resources, or prevent monopolies. The address was not as well-received as hoped, and considerable resistance to renewal was gathering in the Senate as the Senate Finance Committee was preparing to begin an investigation.

The Senate hearings were devastating. Much publicity was given to the NRA's enemies who insisted the agency was dominated by big business. There was conflicting evidence on the different effects of the code system in different industries. In the end the Senate approved a much watered-down measure. The NRA would only be extended a year, applying only to businesses engaged in interstate commerce and barring all price-fixing. Existing codes had to comply with the new provisions within 30 days.

The President's hopes lay in the House of Representatives where he had much greater support. The House Ways and Means Committee recommended a two-year extension. By the end of May, however, it became clear the Senate would not agree to such an extension. In fact it looked as if a deadlock between the two chambers would block any resolution at all. The Ways and Means Committee pressed forward and scheduled a vote in the House for May 28, 1935, but the vote was never to be cast. A day before the House vote was scheduled, the Supreme Court handed down a decision that held the NRA and the entire system of codes unconstitutional. The case that brought the NRA to its knees involved an attempt by the NRA to prosecute several violations of the "Live Poultry Code." The press would facetiously refer to it as the "Sick Chicken Case."

The U.S. Supreme Court Strikes Down the NIRA

ALA Schecter Poultry Corporation and its affiliate Schecter Live Poultry Market operated wholesale slaughterhouse markets in Brooklyn. They would purchase live poultry in New York and Philadelphia, slaughtered the poultry according to Jewish law, and sold the poultry within the state of New York. In June 1934 the Justice Department began investigating a number of alleged violations of the NRA live poultry code. Enough evidence was gathered to obtain indictments against the corporation and its affiliate, as well as the four Schecter brothers who operated them. The Schecters were indicted for conspiracy to violate the codes and 18 specific violations of the code. They were accused of filing false reports, violating the hours-and-wage provision, ignoring the health inspection requirements in the code, and selling "unfit chickens." In October the Schecter brothers were found guilty in district court of all 19 counts. The brothers appealed and in April 1935 the Circuit Court upheld the conviction on 17 counts. Two counts charging violation of the maximum hours and minimum wage provisions were ruled to be beyond the regulatory powers of Congress and therefore unconstitutional. Having faced criticism in the past that the NRA was afraid to face a judicial test, the administration decided to make Schecter a test case. The case was argued before the United States Supreme Court on May 2 and 3 and decided on May 27, 1935, a relatively short time later.

The Schecter Brothers claimed that the provisions in the code under section 3 of the NRA were an unconstitutional delegation of legislative power by Congress. The government responded by arguing that the national crisis justified extraordinary measures. Writing for a unanimous majority, Chief Justice Charles Evans Hughes rejected the government's argument. Extraordinary conditions, he stated, do not create or enlarge constitutional power. The adoption of codes by industries and their administration by the president were acts of legislative not executive authority. Only Congress had the authority to legislate matters effecting commerce. This authority could not be delegated to another branch of government. But Congress, Hughes held, only has the authority to regulate interstate commerce. It cannot regulate commerce exclusively within a state. Because the Schechter Brothers were not involved in interstate commerce—they sold poultry only within the state of New York—their business was outside the range of congressional commerce power. In fact all the NRA codes exercised this power beyond the scope and authority of Congress. On the basis of these conclusions, the Court reversed the con-

viction of the Schechter Corporation. The code provisions of the NRA were found unconstitutional and the National Industrial Recovery Act was invalidated.

The decision produced both dread and relief. While some businesses praised the decision as a necessary check on presidential power, others feared tremendous uncertainty as to the potential for industrial chaos now that the codes were suddenly dead. At the White House the President conferred with his advisors for over two hours and, in the end, all accepted the conclusion that the codes were now unenforceable. Ironically the Supreme Court's decision gave the appearance of bringing America's great experiment with corporatism to an abrupt and untimely end. In actuality, the NRA had long been disinherited of its popularity and support. Congress had become increasingly hesitant about renewing the program and the agency's chances of survival had grown slim. Frozen in deadlock, the numerous and contradictory policies of the NRA had effectively brought the agency to a standstill. Even though several advisors suggested ways around the Schecter decision, Roosevelt decided against an effort to restore the NRA. Privately the president breathed a sigh of relief as the agency had created the most perplexing administrative problems imaginable.

Contributing Forces

The Antitrust Acts

Antitrust laws are designed to curb the growth of monopolies and monopoly practices. A monopoly is where a company or group of companies, called a cartel, that have total control over the production and price of a certain good, or commodity. Antitrust laws were based on belief that the public could be protected from the power of business monopolies by breaking up complex monopolistic companies into smaller companies. The federal government through its constitutional power to regulate interstate commerce (trade that crosses state boundaries) could best accomplish this. The Sherman Anti-Trust Act of 1890 was the first of three laws passed during the so-called "Progressive" era that sought grater government regulation of economic activity. The two other acts were the Clayton Act and the Federal Trade Commission Act, both passed in 1914. The Sherman Act provided that every business contract, business combination in the form of a trust or otherwise, or conspiracy to restrain trade was illegal. Penalties included a $5,000 fine, a year in prison, or both. The Anti-Trust Division of the Department of Justice administers the act. Much of the teeth

Workers at the Ford River Rouge plant elect union representatives in June 1941. After years of struggle Ford workers were finally allowed to negotiate a labor contract after a successful strike in April of that year. (The Library of Congress.)

of the Sherman Act, however, were removed by a Supreme Court decision, *United States v. E.C. Knight Company* (1895). The ruling severely limited the definition of what was considered an act of trade. Thereafter government attorneys made few attempts to enforce the law and only 18 lawsuits were brought between 1890 and 1900. Some of these were designed to restrain labor unions rather than industries.

The Democratic administration of Woodrow Wilson (served 1913–1921) brought a renewed vigor to expand government regulation of business and a revival of interest in strengthening the Sherman Act. Both the Clayton Act and the Federal Trade Commission Act were proposed to Congress by the Wilson administration. The Clayton Act, a supplement to the Sherman Act, specifically excluded organized labor from the provisions of the Sherman Act. Among other things the Clayton Act prohibited corporations from purchasing the stocks and bonds of other corporations for the purpose of eliminating competition. It also provided that individual corporate officers could be held personally liable for violating the antitrust laws. The Federal Trade Commission Act established the Federal Trade Commission (FTC). The FTC was

authorized to prevent persons, partnerships, or corporations from using unfair methods of competition. The FTC was also given power to gather information, require corporations to file annual or special reports concerning their business practices, investigate trade conditions, and reorganize businesses convicted of violating the antitrust laws.

A Working Relationship Is Formed

After World War I, there developed in the United States a growing acceptance of cooperation between business and government to achieve social and economic stability. The experience of the War Industries Board (WIB) had shown, however briefly, that this cooperation could be successful under certain conditions. Governments in Western Europe were also embracing the social philosophy of "corporatism." Corporatism envisioned an economic system in which business, labor, and agriculture could be organized and guided by government to pursue the common good. In America corporatists sketched a picture of society in which industry was organized by trade associations that could formulate plans for achieving stability and progress. The chief proponent of this cooperative scheme in America was, ironically, Herbert Hoover (served 1929–1933). Hoover had been head of the wartime Food Administration and Secretary of Commerce during the Harding and Coolidge administrations. Bernard Baruch, chair of the WIB and a wealthy Wall Street financier during the 1920s, also advanced a corporatist model for American industry. Both men favored a voluntary corporatist system of "associations." In an "Associative State," as the term became known, business would subordinate their immediate interests to the long-term welfare of the nation. In turn laws that hindered cooperation, such as the antitrust laws, would be abandoned.

As Secretary of Commerce from 1921 to 1928, Herbert Hoover did much to establish relations between industry and the government. Throughout the period he was a zealous advocate of voluntary association to solve the problems of a modern industrial nation. By the mid-1920s an array of trade associations and professional societies had taken shape and were working with the Department of Commerce. Hoover had transformed the Department of Commerce from a collection of small technical bureaus into a unified and expanding agency with a genuine spirit to guide development and serve business groups. The dream of such an economic order was symbolized by the new Department of Commerce building approved for construction in 1926. This new "temple of commerce" would be the largest building in Washington apart from the Capitol.

After the Stock Market Crash

Tragically, the events that followed the stock market crash ultimately proved too unmanageable for a voluntary system. "Associationalism" came to be viewed as a mere front behind which businesses earnestly pursued monopolies in obscurity. The leaders of the new industrial order were less cooperative than Hoover had hoped. They were unable to solve the social problems wrought by the depression or to stop the great economic decline. Demands were made for more effective coordination between business and government. Hoover was confronted with establishing programs and agencies he had never contemplated. The way had to be paved for greater government involvement in industry. The government's use of antitrust prosecution, however, was increasingly viewed as an obstacle to more extensive business-government cooperation. Attacks on the antitrust laws intensified from groups as diverse as the American Bar Association and the American Mining Congress. A system of antitrust exemptions, it was proposed, could be replaced by greater cooperation between business and government developed according to a

national plan. In fact many "national plans" began appearing in 1931 and 1932. They called for a revival of the WIB system of World War I, the creation of trade associations or syndicates that represented various interests in industry. A national board could coordinate these associations.

In October 1931 a long series of Senate hearings considered a variety of planning schemes. Disagreement existed about the degree of autonomy (freedom) businesses would have. A general consensus, however, emerged for a system that offered more power for labor and consumer groups and a central planning and regulatory structure run by experts. A general concurrence developed for a "superorganization" of industry that would be strong enough to both contain and guide the range of interests in a far-reaching business commonwealth.

Various proposals appeared. Former chairman of the WIB and economic advisor to President Woodrow Wilson (served 1923–1929) at the Paris Peace Conference, Bernard Baruch, proposed the creation of a Peace Industries Board modeled on the industrial cooperation of the WIB. Others offered similar proposals that were variations on the same theme. Henry Harriman, the chairman of the Chamber of Commerce Committee on Continuity of Business and Employment, released a report in October 1932. The report called for coordination of trade associations. The coordinating agency would be a "national economic council" chosen by leaders of various interest groups. The plan that eventually would become the blueprint for the National Recovery Administration, however, came from General Electric's president Gerard Swope. Long revered as an "industrial statesman," Swope proposed a system that would operate through trade associations made up of major industries empowered to regulate production, prices, and trade practices. Labor would benefit from unemployment insurance administered by committees in each industry. Coordination would come through a supervisory agency that would act in the public interest. Critics of the plan charged that it would be an administrative horror. Swope, however, argued that administrative matters would be problematic in the beginning, but eventually an efficient system of cooperation would develop.

From the onset of the Roosevelt administration, Swope was recruited to serve as chairman of the new Business Advisory Council, which would eventually supply expertise for the NRA. The National Industrial Recovery Act was essentially the end result of these schemes, particularly the Swope plan. Roosevelt relied heavily on the "corporate liberals" to guide the NRA.

Perspectives

National Views of Business and Government

The federal government and U.S. business leaders brought very different desires for applying the NRA to economic recovery. The NRA was inspired by a utopian (socially perfect) vision of a new economic order involving close working relations between government and business. This dream, however, collapsed as economic self-interest undermined the lofty ideal of a business commonwealth. The corporatist framework of the NRA was intended to provide not only recovery but also the foundation of a new cooperative relationship between business and government. It unintentionally, however, created more industrial strife. The demand that business recognize labor as an equal partner in the industrial system led to much conflict. The decline in enthusiasm for the NRA created a crisis of compliance in the agency. Also contrary to the intentions of the framers of the NIRA, the codes became a vehicle for business creating cartels. This was a very much unintended, if widespread, consequence. Despite attempts to distinguish legitimate from illegitimate cartels, cartels flourished under the NRA. In actuality such theoretical distinctions proved meaningless. Johnson believed the development of cartels could have its advantages, so long as the abuses, such as price-fixing and squeezing out other firms, could be eliminated, and in the end this proved an impossibility.

Many believed the NRA was a poorly administered agency and that Johnson was a poor choice for administrator. He was continually unable to assess the agency's resources and abilities. To his credit, he was a visionary, believing that the NRA would usher in a new, cooperative stage of capitalism, but he underestimated how much government supervision of the codes would be necessary. Johnson also frustrated many of his subordinates by his apparent unfamiliarity of the problems of assessing cost—a key component in the NRA's attempt to promote fair competition. Critics charged there was no easy, objective way to determine costs over an entire industry, and Johnson naively dismissed this concern by pointing out that anybody could hire an accountant to figure it out. But all the blame could not be directed toward Johnson. Given the enormity of the endeavor, it is difficult to imagine anyone succeeding as NRA administrator. The failure of the NRA was ultimately due to the impossibility of the task. Attempts to bring prices in line with costs and to establish fair competition assumed that it was possible to arrive at a political agreement as to what these costs and provisions should

be. The sheer variety of industries, types of products produced, accounting practices used, and channels of distribution, as well as variation in the practicality and authority of code authorities, combined to form insurmountable administrative difficulties. A more modest program, confined to only a few key industries, might have fared better. But Johnson rejected this plan and the viability of such an approach is purely speculative.

Importantly the NRA had never been designed to function as a regulatory agency, since it was conceived as an experiment in corporatism. The very structure of the code authorities made it extremely difficult to detect abuses, let alone regulate them. As various business interests refused to accept the sacrifices the NRA demanded of them, administrators relied less and less on industries to regulate themselves. The agency moved toward a more regulatory posture, and the responsibilities of the code authorities were pared down, while the authority of the central administration grew. Business watched this development with a distrustful eye, and in time, business elites would come to loathe Roosevelt and the New Deal as a radical threat to their interests. Through time the NRA functioned less and less as a vehicle for big business to form cartels to control prices and wages. Big business had been willing to come under the Blue Eagle, to give the program a chance, especially since it would relax the antitrust laws. The NRA experience, however, demonstrated that any attempt to formalize a cooperative relationship between business and government would fail because of fundamental conflicts between business elites and New Dealers. There were many corporate liberals like Bernard Baruch and Gerard Swope who envisioned a new type of industrial state, but these men were ultimately the exception and not the rule. In general, business attitudes were in opposition to the proposed changes. Much hostility toward the New Deal derived from a strong belief in a *laissez-faire* capitalist system whose roots lay in the nineteenth century. The belief that only a free market could maximize economic growth and that government intervention only obstructed this process was too strong a faith in the 1930s to be undermined, even by an event as devastating as the Great Depression.

Impact

The end of the NRA in May 1935 marked a significant shift in the political direction of the New Deal. Ambitious designs to restructure American industrial relations and society through cooperative schemes between business and government were shown to be fundamentally flawed. It proved impossible for a central coordinating agency to administer such a comprehensive national plan with so many contradictory aims and interests. Separate agencies and boards would instead pursue these various objectives. Their sole function was to pursue reform on a piecemeal basis for a particular interest. The grandiose ideal of redirecting American society through central economic planning was reduced to a more limited but more realistic approach. The NRA experiment had with little doubt proven a failure, perhaps the greatest failure of the New Deal. But the shattering of the agency scattered many of its functions across a broad range of newly created boards and committees.

Some of the functions of the NRA were quickly recreated by executive order after the *Schechter* decision. On June 7 the president established the National Resources Committee, and the Labor Relations Board was reestablished by executive order a week later. Several divisions and their employees were transferred to the Department of Commerce on June 15 and the Consumer Division was transferred to the Department of Labor on June 30. For the rest of the summer Roosevelt forced Congress to remain in session through a hot Washington July and August. On July 5 Congress passed the National Labor Relations Act, which made the board a permanent agency. Roosevelt further extended the power of the board through a later executive order.

At the end of August Congress passed the Public Utility Holding Company Act and a Bituminous Coal Stabilization Act. Both were plainly the result of disillusion with the NRA's attempts to coordinate each industry. The Public Utilities Holding Company Act gave the Federal Power Commission authority to regulate interstate shipments of electrical power. It also gave the same authority to the Federal Trade Commission over natural gas shipments. The act also eliminated some holding companies (companies whose sole function is the ownership of other companies). All utility companies also had to register with the Security Trade Commission, which could supervise their financial transactions. The Guffey-Snyder Bituminous Coal Stabilization Act was the immediate outcome of the demise of the NRA. Both the United Mineworkers and northern mine operators wanted more rigid controls on production, prices, and wages in order to loosen competition from western and southern mines. The Guffey Act went well beyond the NRA's code provisions for the industry. A Bituminous Coal Labor Board was revived to oversee administration of the act. Instead of a central agency, however, the jurisdictional authority of the act was divided into districts that would determine prices for each region. The U.S. Supreme Court struck down parts of the Guffey-Snyder Act in 1936 but other parts were reenacted in 1937.

After 1935 Roosevelt abandoned attempts at working closely with business, which represented a major shift in the administration. The NRA had shown, above all else, that voluntary cooperative arrangements between government and business did not work. The New Deal became more aggressively anti-business and pro-labor after 1935. Business could not be expected to act beyond its own self-interest. Nowhere had this been more apparent than the refusal of most industries to recognize labor's collective bargaining rights or abide by the wage and hour provisions set out in the NRA codes. These would never be recognized, the administration concluded, without the coercive power of government. The National Labor Relations Act, or Wagner Act, guaranteed labor rights that had been essentially ignored under the NRA codes. Majority rule within unions was ensured, the right of collective bargaining was secured, and the act specified unfair labor practices. The Wagner Act thus enacted industrial relations procedures that the administration had attempted to impose through the NRA but in a more sweeping manner.

On a broader scale, the philosophy of central planning had been permanently disgraced. Certainly some still dreamed of a business commonwealth and the idea of national planning was not totally erased. But the concept of cooperative self-regulation was dead. The demise of the NRA also signified the end of a decade-long attempt by industry to repeal the antitrust laws. Attacks on monopolistic business practices would now find renewed support through old-fashioned trust-busting. Increasingly New Dealers came to recognize the function of government in industrial relations not so much as one of coordinating and planning, but more as a regulator, or "broker," of opposing interests. In hindsight, one can discern in this development the emergence of the modern American state.

Notable People

Adolph Augustus Berle (1895–1971). Adolph Berle was one of the original "brain trust" advisors of Franklin Roosevelt during the 1932 presidential campaign and has been acknowledged as one of the most brilliant of the New Dealers. Born the son of a Congregational minister, Berle came from an intellectually gifted family and was pushed to succeed academically at an early age. This did not seem to be difficult for Adolph who was a child prodigy. He graduated from Harvard at the age of 18 and from Harvard Law School at 21. During World War I he did intelligence work for the army Signal Corps. Also during the war a request by the South Puerto Rico Sugar Company in the Dominican Republic went to the army. They needed legal help in disentangling a confusing web of land-holding laws that inhibited sugar production, considered an "essential" commodity in time of war. The army sent Berle to Puerto Rico as the United States occupied the Dominican Republic. This became a turning point in Berle's life. He witnessed firsthand the effects of American imperialism (extending rule over a foreign nation) and it introduced him to the sugar trade as well as the Caribbean and Latin America, a region for which he developed a life-long passion. When Berle left the Dominican Republic in 1918, he was a firm believer in self-determination of colonial peoples. Berle was next sent to Europe and at the age of 23 he became the U.S. advisor to Russia at the Paris Peace Conference.

Upon returning to the United States, Berle practiced corporate law for a brief time in New York before becoming a professor at Columbia Law School. Together with the economist Gardiner Means, he published one of the most influential books of the next two decades. *The Modern Corporation and Private Property* (1932), documented a trend toward greater concentrations of corporate power, increasingly separated from stockholder or public control. The book eventually became somewhat of an ideological blueprint for the NRA. Berle's views on corporate power, and the means necessary to regulate it through planning and corporate control, put him in conflict with many established old-line Progressives. These included Felix Frankfurter and Louis Brandeis who continued to advocate an antitrust approach.

After the 1932 presidential election Berle served only for a brief period in the Roosevelt administration in the Reconstruction Finance Corporation. In 1934 he had returned to New York to work with Mayor Fiorello LaGuardia where he was instrumental in saving the city from bankruptcy. While in New York he remained one of Roosevelt's closest advisors through frequent meetings and letters. In 1938 Roosevelt asked Berle to become assistant Secretary of State. Berle remained assistant Secretary of State until 1944 before becoming Ambassador to Brazil for two years. A generation later, he would again develop policy with Latin America when he served as chairman of President Kennedy's Latin American task force in 1961. The task force originated the Alliance for Progress. During the 1960s Berle became increasingly disenchanted with the New Left's criticism of American society, and he had a growing realization that a middle ground in politics and economics would not overcome the political extremes in American society. His final work

was an analysis of political power based on his long experience in government.

Hugh S. Johnson (1882–1942). Hugh Samuel Johnson was born in Ft. Scott, Kansas, on August 5, 1982, but was raised in the Cherokee Strip of Oklahoma. He graduated from Northwest Teachers College before attending the U.S. Military Academy at West Point. Johnson quickly rose from second lieutenant to brigadier general in 1918 after receiving a law degree at the University of California in 1916. During World War I Johnson served as chief of the Bureau of Purchase and Supply for the War Industries Board. He retired from the military in 1919 to become vice-president and general counsel to the Moline Plow Company, and by 1925 he was chairman of the board. Because of his extraordinary business and administrative experience, Hugh Johnson was Roosevelt's choice to head the National Recovery Administration.

Johnson's political skills were not as highly developed as his business skills. He was never as tactful or diplomatic as politics often required, having been used to giving orders in the army or as a corporate executive. He never quite came to grips with the necessity of unifying fragile coalitions within a public agency, and as a result he quickly alienated many people. This situation was not helped by Johnson's increasing anger toward business for refusing to cooperate with the NRA, especially to pledge to maintain the wages and hours standards.

Throughout the summer of 1933 Johnson traveled across the country in an army plane to persuade businesses to join the NRA. By September Johnson had brought nearly every major industry on board, including the automobile industry with the noted exception of Ford. He had reached the height of his popularity. While extremely able at completing the code writing campaigns, Johnson quickly became the symbol of controversy as the NRA began to be assaulted. Southern Democrats in Congress attacked the NRA for the bureaucratic power it represented. Progressive Republicans saw it as a vehicle for monopoly. Labor attacked the NRA for failing to enforce section 7(a). Economists argued that the production controls actually slowed down the economy and inhibited recovery. Once the National Recovery Review Board, headed by famed lawyer Clarence Darrow, accused the NRA of exploiting labor and small business, public discontent with the NRA hardened. This criticism combined with Johnson's political insensitivity and drinking problem made him expendable. Johnson was urged to resign and left the NRA on October 15, 1934. He went to New York where he worked briefly as an administrator for the WPA but then left the New Deal altogether. Johnson became a newspaper columnist and, by the late 1930s, his relationship with Roosevelt and the New Deal had further deteriorated. He attacked the dictatorial ambitions of Roosevelt and spent the last years of his life viewing the New Deal as anti-business.

Donald R. Richberg (1881–1960). Donald Randall Richberg was born on July 1881, in Knoxville, Tennessee, to John Richberg, later a prosperous attorney in Chicago, and Eloise Randall, who would become a physician. Donald Richberg graduated from the University of Chicago in 1901 and Harvard Law School in 1904. Upon graduating Donald joined the family firm of Richberg and Richberg in Chicago. Seeing the city government corruption in the city firsthand, the young attorney supported the municipal reforms urged by the progressive movement. Consequently he endorsed Theodore Roosevelt and the "Bull Moose" campaign of 1912 representing a break of the progressive wing of the Republican Party from the main party. This led to his appointment to a position in the Progressive Party in 1913 and 1914. But when the Progressive Party backed Charles Evans Hughes for President in 1916, Richberg turned to the Democrats and campaigned for Woodrow Wilson. During the 1920s, Richberg served as special counsel for the city of Chicago and continued in private practice of law. He was instrumental in drafting the Railway Labor Act of 1926 and continued to stay active in party politics. He supported Democratic candidate Al Smith in 1928 and worked with Senator George Norris of Nebraska in forming the National Progressive League that endorsed Franklin Roosevelt in 1932.

Richberg wrote speeches for Roosevelt during the 1932 campaign and then went to work for General Hugh Johnson as a deputy administrator of the NRA. Johnson quickly appointed him chief counsel where Richberg served until Johnson was forced to resign in 1934. Roosevelt then appointed Richberg to a five-member board that would administer the NRA. Richberg strongly believed in the potential for industrial cooperation and the establishment of a business commonwealth based on government cooperation with industry. He believed that this industrial framework should be self-regulatory and felt uneasy about too much government regulatory authority. When the Supreme Court struck down the NRA, Richberg returned to private practice in Chicago. Although he remained a steadfast supporter of Roosevelt, Richberg viewed the New Deal's leftward drift with increasing alarm after 1935. He felt that labor exerted too much control over the administration and by the time Harry Truman (served 1945–1953) took office, was convinced the country was on the road to becoming a wel-

C.T. Coiner was the creator of the NRA's Blue Eagle, which showed customers that the business displaying it was "doing its part" to help the nation recover. (AP/Wide World Photos. Reproduced by permission.)

fare state. A man who was renowned for his ironic sense of humor, Richberg eventually became a celebrated figure among conservatives by the 1950s.

Gerard Swope (1872–1957). Gerard Swope was born in St. Louis, Missouri, on December 1, 1872. He attended the Massachusetts Institute of Technology from which he graduated in 1895 with a degree in electrical engineering. He then went to work for the Western Electric Company, where he rose quickly up the corporate ladder. He became general sales manager of the New York office in 1908 and then vice-president of the company in 1913. In 1919 he was elected president of the company and three years later, chairman of the board.

Swope was an early architect of business and government cooperation. A so-called "corporate liberal," he saw the benefits of a corporatist or business association with government form of industrial order. As the first president of the National Electrical Manufacturers Association, Swope strongly supported business self-regulation. He quickly rose to become a prominent spokesman for the business community during the 1920s. But he was very different than many of his conservative colleagues. He worked for years in Greenwich

House in New York and was sympathetic to the needs of the poor and unemployed. He was also a close associate of Herbert Hoover in the Department of Commerce and worked hard to encourage trade associations as a means of stabilizing the industrial economy.

Once the Great Depression hit, Swope urged the federal government to adopt a plan of industrial self-regulation through trade associations, codes of fair competition, long-term economic planning, and a suspension of the antitrust laws. His proposal was, in short, the blueprint for the National Industrial Recovery Act. During the New Deal, Swope became the most influential business policy advisor in the country. He was appointed to be the first Chairman of the Business Advisory Council in the Department of Commerce and Chairman of the Coal Arbitration Board in 1933. He later became a member of the National Labor Board, the Committee on Economic Security, and the Advisory Council on Social Security. Swope eventually concluded that the NRA should be scrapped and turned over to the Chamber of Commerce, but he always remained an active and effective business participant in the New Deal.

Primary Sources

The Rising Influence of Corporations in America

In their 1932 book *The Modern Corporation and Private Property,* Adolf Berle, Jr., and Gardiner Means proposed that the modern corporation's economic power was such that it could compete on equal terms with the state and its political power. The growing power and influence of corporations through the 1920s into the 1930s had a profound impact on the ordinary lives of Americans. No longer a nation of predominately small shopkeepers or farmers, most people worked for a large corporation of some kind and nearly all purchased goods produced by them. Given such influence, it was argued that large corporations should function in greater measure for the common good. This argument took new strength with the economic decline during the Great Depression. Much of the public lost confidence in business leaders during the early years of the Depression and Roosevelt sought to restore that faith. The following statements demonstrates the faith many in business had for the rise of large corporations in the United States (from Berle and Means, 1932, pp. 1–2, 357).

Corporations have ceased to be merely legal devices through which the private business transactions of individuals may be carried on. Though still much used for

this purpose, the corporate form has acquired a larger significance. The corporation has, in fact, become both a method of property tenure and a means of organizing economic life. Grown to tremendous proportions, there may be said t have evolved a "corporate system"—as there was once a feudal system—which has attracted to itself a combination of attributes and powers, and has attained a degree of prominence entitling it to be dealt with as a major social institution.

We are examining this institution probably before it has attained its zenith. Spectacular as its rise has been, every indication seems to be that the system will move forward to proportions which would stagger imagination today ...

In its new aspect the corporation is a means whereby the wealth of innumerable individuals has been concentrated into huge aggregates and whereby control over this wealth has been surrendered to a unified direction. The power attendant upon such concentration has brought forth princes of industry, whose position in the community is yet to be defined.

The rise of the modern corporation has brought a concentration of economic power which can compete on equal terms with the modern state—economic power versus political power, each strong in its own field. The state seeks in some aspects to regulate the corporation, while the corporation, steadily becoming more powerful, makes every effort to avoid such regulation. Where its own interests are concerned, it even attempts to dominate the states. The future may see the economic organism, now typified by the corporation, not only on an equal plane with the state, but possibly even superseding it as the dominate form of social organization. The law of corporations, accordingly, might well be considered as a potential constitutional law for the new economic state, while business practice is increasingly assuming the aspect of economic statesmanship.

The President Charts a New Course for Business

To provide quick economic relief to the nation, President Roosevelt was poised in his first hundred days of office to take bold actions never attempted before by the U.S. government. On May 17, 1933, the president addressed Congress and argued strongly for a new approach in business, by proposing the creation of industry agreements. Rejecting a strong reliance on antitrust (opposing large combinations of business that act to restrict competition) laws he envisioned cooperative associations of industries that establish their own fair practices with general guidance from the federal government. To accomplish this change in direction Roosevelt proposed passage of the National Industrial Recovery Act (NIRA) (reprinted in Franklin Roosevelt's *The Public Papers and Addresses of Franklin D. Roosevelt, Volume Two, 1933,* pp. 202–204).

Before the Special Session of the Congress adjourns, I recommend two further steps in our national campaign to put people to work.

My first request is that the Congress provide for the machinery necessary for a great cooperative movement throughout all industry in order to obtain wide reemployment, to shorten the working week, to pay a decent wage for the shorter week and to prevent unfair competition and disastrous overproduction.

Employers cannot do this singly or even in organized groups, because such action increases costs and thus permits cut-throat underselling by selfish competitors unwilling to join in such a public-spirited endeavor. One of the great restrictions upon such cooperative efforts up to this time has been our anti-trust laws. They were properly designed as the means to cure the great evils of monopolistic price fixing. They should certainly be retained as a permanent assurance that the old evils of unfair competition shall never return. But the public interest will be served if, with the authority and under the guidance of Government, private industries are permitted to make agreements and codes insuring fair competition ...

The other proposal gives the Executive full power to start a large program of direct employment. A careful survey convinces me that approximately $3,300,000,000 can be invested in useful and necessary public construction, and at the same time put the largest possible number of people to work.

Provision should be made to permit States, counties, and municipalities to undertake useful public works ...

Finally, I stress the fact that all of these proposals are based on the gravity of the emergency and that therefore it is urgently necessary immediately to initiate a reemployment campaign if we are to avoid further hardships, to sustain business improvement and to pass on to better things.

For this reason I urge prompt action on this legislation.

Suggested Research Topics

- Imagine trying to convince business leaders of a particular industry, labor representatives, and consumers to sit in the same room to develop strict price and wage control codes. What would be the most likely perspectives of each category of person?

- Volunteerism by businesses was a key ingredient of the National Recovery Administration codes. List and describe the various factors that would influence a business to voluntarily comply with the codes. Next list and describe the various factors that would influence a business to not comply with the codes.

- The U.S. Supreme Court ruled that the National Industrial Recovery Act was unconstitutional. Research the reasons the Court gave in justifying their ruling.

- If you were a consumer in the United States in 1934, what would be your reaction to seeing a Blue Eagle sign in a store's window? Would you more likely purchase goods from that store rather than one who did not have a Blue Eagle sign?

Bibliography

Sources

Bellush, Bernard. *The Failure of the NRA*. New York: Norton, 1975.

Berle, Adolph and Gardiner Means. *The Modern Corporation and Private Property*. New York: Columbia University Press, 1932.

Brand, Donald R. *Corporatism and the Rule of Law: A Study of the National Recovery Administration*. Ithaca: Cornell University Press, 1988.

Fine, Sydney. *The Automobile Under the Blue Eagle: Labor, Management, and the Automobile Manufacturing Code*. Ann Arbor: University of Michigan Press, 1963.

Hawley, Ellis W. *The New Deal and the Problem of Monopoly: A Study in Economic Ambivalence*. New York: Fordham University Press, 1995.

Himmelberg, Robert F. *The Origins of the National Recovery Administration: Business, Government and the Trade Association Issue, 1921–1933*. New York: Fordham University Press, 1976.

Himmelberg, Robert F., ed. *Survival of Corporatism During the New Deal Era, 1933-1945*. New York: Garland, 1994.

Pearce, Charles A. *NRA Trade Practice Programs*. New York: Columbia University Press, 1939.

Further Reading

Bernstein, Irving. *The Lean Years: A History of the American Worker, 1920–1933*. Boston: Houghton Mifflin, 1960.

———. *Turbulent Years: A History of the American Worker, 1933–1941*. Boston: Houghton Mifflin, 1960.

Chandler, Lester V. *America's Greatest Depression, 1929–1941*. New York: Harper & Row, 1970.

Conkin, Paul Keith *The New Deal*. Arlington Heights, IL: Harlan Davidson, 1992.

Freidel, Frank. *Franklin D. Roosevelt: Launching the New Deal*. Boston: Little, Brown, 1973.

Leuchtenberg, William E. *Franklin D. Roosevelt and the New Deal, 1932–1940*. New York: Harper & Row, 1963.

See Also

Labor and Industry; New Deal (First, and Its Critics); Supreme Court

The First New Deal and Its Critics

1933-1934

Introduction

"The capital is experiencing more government in less time than it has ever known before ... it is now as tense, excited, and sleepless and driven as a little while ago it was heavy and inactive." These words by Anne O'Hare McCormick, published in the *New York Times* and reprinted in Ronald Edsforth's *The New Deal: America's Response to the Great Depression* (2000, p. 143) describe the atmosphere in Washington, DC, after Franklin Roosevelt was elected to the presidency.

President Herbert Hoover (served 1929–1933), though known as politically progressive and as a humanitarian, was unable to meet the public outcry for economic relief through the first years of the Great Depression. His terse behavior did not connect well with the public and only added to the growing public resentment. The considerable public disfavor toward Hoover opened the door to victory for Franklin D. Roosevelt, then governor of New York and the Democratic Party candidate in the 1932 presidential election.

The victorious Roosevelt exuded charm and optimism, offering fresh hope to millions of Americans that someone in the White House truly cared about the average citizen. Roosevelt had to deliver more than hope, however, because the economic problems before him caused by the Great Depression were monumental. He and his trusted group of advisors brought an entirely new perspective on how to bring relief to the struggling public.

Unlike Hoover's administration, the nation's new leaders did not trust that a private marketplace, free from government oversight, would be able to successfully control production and prices to the nation's benefit and thus lead the country to economic recovery. Roosevelt's administration, operating under the belief that government involvement could actually help the economy chose a path of major structural reform of the U.S. economy. To Roosevelt's good fortune, business leaders were in no position in early 1933 to oppose the very popular new president. The public was desperate to see a change in tackling the economic problems, which included high unemployment, numerous businesses in distress, and a growing poor population. They clearly were attracted to Roosevelt's warmth and charm, and gave him great leeway to act during his first few months of office. Any criticism or efforts to hinder the new programs during this period, including by business leaders, would be met with great public wrath.

Roosevelt and his key advisors quickly got to work, even before he was officially inaugurated as president. They designed relief programs they hoped could buy time until long-term recovery measures could begin stimulating production and employment. At President Roosevelt's request, Congress met in a special session from March 9 until June 16, 1933. Banking and agricultural crises drew President Roosevelt's attention first, but other issues soon followed. With nearly 15 million people unemployed across the nation, federal relief for workers was a critical need. The intense legislative activity during this Hundred Days period is some of the most dramatic in U.S. history. More legislation developing public policy was passed at this time than in any period in the nation's history.

The numerous relief and recovery measures passed during the 18-month period from March 1933 to June 1934 became collectively known as the First New Deal. President Roosevelt received greatly expanded power, changing the nature of the U.S. presidency forever. The president, through the new agencies he would create, more closely controlled business activities through the National Industrial Recovery Act. Also, the federal government became a regular player in the private business world for the first time. The United States had long operated with the belief that government had a very limited role in American daily life and that business activity was considered personal property, protected by the U.S. Constitution from government regulation. The Republican administrations of the 1920s preceding Roosevelt's term held to this traditional perception of limited government with great zeal. The relief programs of the First New Deal included the Civilian Conservation Corps, Civil Works Administration, and the Federal Emergency Relief Administration. Recovery programs included the National Recovery Administration, the Agricultural Adjustment Administration, and the Tennessee Valley Authority.

Chronology:

July 2, 1932: Franklin Delano Roosevelt delivers a speech accepting the Democratic nomination for president pledging "a new deal for the American people."

November 1932: Roosevelt handily wins the presidential election over incumbent Republican Herbert Hoover.

March 4, 1933: Roosevelt is inaugurated as president, declaring that there is "nothing to fear but fear itself;" two days later he closes the nation's banks for one week, proclaiming a "bank holiday."

March 9, 1933: Congress begins a special session to approve legislation aimed at economic relief and recovery.

June 16, 1933: Congress finishes the special session, having passed 15 major laws; the intensive period of lawmaking becomes known as the First Hundred Days.

November 9, 1933: Roosevelt establishes the Civil Works Administration to assist unemployed workers through the winter months.

June 6, 1934: Congress passes the Securities Exchange Act, establishing the Securities Exchange Commission.

June 28, 1934: Passage of the Farm Bankruptcy Act and the National Housing Act marks the end of the First New Deal as political opposition to New Deal programs gains strength.

Issue Summary

The New Deal is Born

The term "New Deal" came from a speech by then-New York Governor Franklin Delano Roosevelt delivered to the Democratic National Convention in

Columbia professor Adolph A. Berle, Jr., was an important member of Franklin Roosevelt's "Brain Trust." (AP/Wide World Photos. Reproduced by permission.)

July of 1932. He was accepting the Democratic Party's nomination as their candidate for U.S. president and referring to a fresh new approach in trying to address the severe economic hardships caused by the Great Depression. Roosevelt had been a two-term governor for New York. He was also a distant cousin of former U.S. president Theodore Roosevelt. Roosevelt spoke, "I pledge you, I pledge myself, to a new deal for the American people. Let us all here assembled constitute ourselves prophets of a new order of competence and courage."

Samuel Rosenman, political advisor and speechwriter for Roosevelt, wrote the speech. Just previously, the journal *New Republic* had published a series of articles by Stuart Chase entitled, "A New Deal for America." Perhaps these influenced Rosenman and Roosevelt. Following Roosevelt's speech a political cartoonist used the phrase, fixing it in the public's mind. From then onward the "New Deal" became the adopted label of Roosevelt's political and economic policies for the next six years in his fight against the Depression. The phrase "New Deal" is now one of the most familiar phrases in American politics and government.

To address the complex economic and social problems posed by the Great Depression Roosevelt gathered a "Brain Trust" to assist in his 1932 presidential campaign. They attracted the label of Brain Trust because these were the actual people to analyze all the options available to the president on specific issues and then to draft policies he might wish to pursue. The group included young lawyers, social workers, and economics professors. They were considered the brightest minds of the day in dealing with complex economic and social issues. They were also known to be fearless about pursuing actions never tried before. Three of the members were Raymond Moley, Rexford Tugwell, and Adolf Berle, Jr., all Columbia University professors. Basil O'Connor, Roosevelt's law partner prior to his presidential terms, and Samuel Rosenman, Roosevelt's general counsel in New York, were also part of the elite group, in addition to William Woodon, a New York businessman and former director of the New York Federal Reserve Bank. The six men played major roles in the New Deal. Their mission was to advise Roosevelt on how to end the Depression and to write his campaign speeches.

Franklin D. Roosevelt Wins Franklin D. Roosevelt sounded a hopeful note in 1932 to a public desperate for a new approach to solve the nation's economic woes brought by the Great Depression. President Hoover, embracing a belief that people should be self-reliant and should not rely on government, took a very conservative approach to solving the problems. He primarily asked for voluntary cooperation from industry to not increase unemployment and called for private charities to help those in need. Both approaches were woefully inadequate to deal with the magnitude of the problem at hand. Roosevelt, on the other hand, promised to help the unemployed, poor, and aged, something Hoover had not been able to do during his four years in the White House. Certainly problems of poverty and financial security had been increasing issues since the rise of urban industrial centers, but they were greatly magnified by the Depression and the general public became much more sensitive to their needs.

As a result of the public's mood Roosevelt won the 1932 November presidential election by a wide margin, receiving 23 million votes to Hoover's 16 million. In addition, the Democrats also gained two-thirds of the Senate seats and three-fourths of the House of Representatives. It would be four months, however, between the November election victory and Roosevelt's inauguration in March 1933. The Twentieth Amendment to the U.S. Constitution, changing the inauguration date to January, was still going through the state ratification process and would not take effect until the next presidential election in 1936.

During the weeks following the November election the economy continued to fall steeply. Industrial production was declining, more businesses and banks were closing, and more people were losing their jobs, homes, and farms. Roosevelt decided he must start working on solutions to the Great Depression right away, rather than waiting until March when he would be sworn into office. This early action was largely unheard of in previous U.S. history, especially to the extent that Roosevelt pursued it.

The New Deal Takes Shape

President-elect Roosevelt prepared for his presidency during the winter of 1932–1933. Rather than seeking a single major solution to the economic problems, Roosevelt and his advisors chose to treat the Depression as a number of individual crises. Each of these crises could be treated separately by emergency actions. The focus would be on the "Three R's"—Relief for the needy, economic Recovery, and financial Reform. The First New Deal was to focus on the first "R"—Relief.

Adolf Berle believed that the most immediate needs to be addressed were farm relief, stabilizing industrial prices and employment, and relief for the poor. He also believed banking problems would have to be solved soon.

The Brain Trust members each received their assignments. Woodon was to develop monetary and banking policy. Tugwell took the lead for agricultural policy. Berle tackled farm foreclosures, business bankruptcies, and railroad problems.

Roosevelt believed that they needed to build a broad coalition of support for any of his measures to be successful against the Depression. Therefore he recruited dozens of men from universities, business and finance, and agriculture to work in small task groups with Brain Trust members. Each group was assigned to draw up specific legislation for a special session of Congress. As the groups worked Roosevelt, accompanied by Raymond Moley, who served as his personal advisor, spent his days meeting with each of the task groups to review their progress.

Despite the large majority of Democrats in both the House and Senate, Roosevelt and his Brain Trust knew the road to passing legislation would not be smooth. Democrats in Congress were divided between Southern conservatives who believed in a limited federal government and liberals wanting extensive federal aid. In business matters the more conservative legislators wanted to focus on antitrust action. That path

would mean the main government role would be breaking up big corporations that hindered fair competition. Moderate and liberal legislators believed business reform should focus on broad national planning and a regulatory role for government. Predictably Roosevelt's task groups also had conflicts over what kinds of solutions to the Depression were appropriate.

The "First Hundred Days"

On March 4, 1933, Franklin D. Roosevelt was sworn in as U.S. president. On the evening of March 5 Roosevelt called Congress into a special session, beginning March 9. Congress was to act on an emergency banking bill and the proposed legislation his task groups had developed. Congress was to remain in special session until June 16, or one hundred days. At 1:00 AM March 6 President Roosevelt declared a closure of all banks for one week, calling it a "bank holiday," and ending the runs on banks by a nervous public wanting its money, which frequently put banks at a loss for funds. He essentially put the U.S. economy on hold in an attempt to calm panic among the public and give business and the economy a chance to regroup.

The month of March brought a flurry of action by President Roosevelt and Congress, with Congress passing the Emergency Banking Act, the Economy Act, the Beer Tax Act, and the Civilian Conservation Corps Reforestation Act. President Roosevelt also created the Farm Credit Administration in the same month. All were intended to provide relief to different parts of society: work relief for young adults, mortgage relief to homeowners, and a stable banking system for depositors.

April was a time of preparing more legislation for another lawmaking flurry to follow in May and June. No New Deal acts were passed in April and the only executive order created the Civil Conservation Corps, authorized under the Civilian Conservation Corps Reforestation Act. On May 12 Congress passed three key bills to address the Depression. Two of them dealt with the critical farm situation. Congress passed the Agricultural Adjustment Act, the Emergency Farm Mortgage Act, and the Federal Emergency Relief Act. A few days later the Tennessee Valley Authority was created on May 17, and Congress passed the Federal Securities Act on May 27.

The special session of Congress wound down through the first half of June. The National Employment Act (Wagner-Peyser bill) and Home Owners' Refinancing Act were passed on June 6 and June 13, respectively. Then on the final day of the "Hundred Days," four acts were passed and a key executive order issued. The acts were the Farm Credit Act, the Banking Act (also known as the Glass-Steagall Act), the National Industrial Recovery Act, and the Emergency Railroad Transportation Act. That same day President Roosevelt created the Public Works Administration through an executive order.

A Bank Holiday—Emergency Banking Relief Act

President Roosevelt's first order of business was to restore public faith in the nation's banking system. The nation was experiencing widespread bank failures. People were unable to repay loans made for their homes and farms and the number of depositors was declining as unemployment mounted. People needed to withdraw their savings to live on and could no longer afford to deposit money into the bank. Banks could not keep up with the demands for withdrawal. Added to that, bank runs, in which depositors would suddenly show up en masse to withdraw their funds when a rumor would surface that the bank was in financial trouble, plagued banks. Even if the bank was not actually in trouble, it would be after the bank run since it would normally not have sufficient funds on hand to satisfy everyone's request for withdrawal.

Some six hundred banks failed in late 1929; more than 1,300 closed in 1930; some 2,200 banks failed in 1931; and another 1,400 closed in 1932. More were adding to the list in early 1933. These numbers were in addition to the many rural banks closed during the 1920s as the farm economy struggled. The number of banks declined from 25,000 in late 1929 to only 14,000 in early 1933. Almost 40 percent of the nation's banks had either closed or merged with other banks. With no government system to guarantee the financial health of individual banks, people had lost confidence in the national banking system. Therefore on March 6 President Roosevelt declared a "bank holiday," which closed all banks for eight days to prevent the public from withdrawing more money.

President Roosevelt then sought a banking bill to safely reopen the banks he had closed on March 6. An emergency banking bill was introduced in Congress at noon on March 9. It was debated in the House for 38 minutes and in the Senate for three hours before being passed. President Roosevelt signed it into the resulting new law, the Emergency Banking Relief Act, later that night at 9:00 PM. The act authorized the U.S. Treasury Department to inspect the nation's banks and was the first pieces of legislation passed as part of the New Deal.

With the passing of the act, federal and state officials hurriedly examined bank records across the nation. Their goal was to determine if the individual banks had sufficient funds to conduct normal business and those banks in good shape could reopen. Those that could not pay debts could not reopen right away, but they would qualify for loans under the act to correct their financial problems. The examiners issued new licenses to the healthy banks so they could reopen March 13. On Sunday March 12, the day before banks were to reopen, President Roosevelt gave his first radio broadcast Fireside Chat in his friendly manner. The chat was a relaxed and informal discourse explaining why he had taken this action.

When the newly relicensed banks reopened the following day calm returned. Many people re-deposited the savings they had earlier withdrawn in fear of losing it. Public confidence in banks was restored with greater reassurance of the banks' financial conditions. The financial panic had ended and over half of the banks that held 90 percent of all bank deposits reopened on March 13. Others reopened later with federal assistance.

To Economize Government—Economy Act

The second bill passed by the special session of Congress was the Economy Act. President Roosevelt personally believed in balanced government budgets—not spending any more than the revenue, or income, taken in. During his presidential campaign he sharply criticized Herbert Hoover for expanding the federal budget too fast. President Roosevelt was convinced that he could cut some federal spending and perhaps raise the morale of the public somewhat in doing it. Congress passed the Economy Act on March 20, with President Roosevelt's goal in mind to cut $500 million by decreasing federal worker salaries, reducing certain disability payments to veterans, and combining some federal programs. He was, in the end, only able to save $243 million by economizing.

Many criticized Roosevelt for supposedly trimming back government expenses on one hand while signing massive emergency relief bills to address the Great Depression on the other. President Roosevelt tried to distinguish between the two by claiming relief funds were an investment in the nation's future. Almost exactly a year later Congress passed a bill over President Roosevelt's veto, increasing once again the salaries of government employees.

Ending Prohibition—Beer Tax Act

Fundamentalist religious movements were quite active in the early twentieth century, but their legislative successes were few following World War I (1914–1918). One major accomplishment for social reformers was adoption of the Eighteenth Amendment to the U.S. Constitution, the Prohibition Amendment.

More About...

The First Hundred Days

The first one hundred days of President Franklin Roosevelt's first term of office is regarded as one of the most active periods in U.S. legislative history. The economic crisis was at its height and the American people were desperate for action after the ineffectiveness of the Hoover administration. Democrats controlled both houses of Congress and the new Democratic president was too popular for opponents to attempt to block. As a result fifteen major bills were introduced and passed within the short three-month period of time from March 9th to June 16th of 1933.

- Emergency Banking Relief Act: introduced and enacted on March 9.

- Economy Act: introduced on March 10; enacted on March 15.

- Beer Tax Act: introduced on March 13; enacted on March 22.

- Agricultural Adjustment Act: introduced on March 16; enacted on May 12.

- Civilian Conservation Corps Act: introduced on March 21; enacted on March 31.

- Federal Emergency Relief Act: introduced on March 21; enacted on May 12.

- National Employment Act: introduced on March 21; enacted on June 6.

- Federal Securities Act: introduced on March 29; enacted on May 27.

- Emergency Farm Mortgage Act: introduced on April 3; enacted on May 12.

- Tennessee Valley Authority: introduced on April 10; enacted on May 18.

- Home Owners' Refinancing Act: introduced on April 13; enacted on June 13.

- Emergency Railroad Transportation Act: introduced on May 4; enacted on June 16.

- Farm Credit Act: introduced on May 10; enacted on June 16.

- National Industrial Recovery Act: introduced on May 17; enacted on June 16.

- Glass-Steagall Banking Act: introduced on March 9; enacted on June 16.

The amendment prohibited the manufacture, sale, or transportation of alcoholic beverages. Liquor consumption in the nation dropped dramatically, but gangsters became millionaires smuggling liquor into the United States. By the end of the 1920s people were weary of the ineffective ban and public pressure mounted to end Prohibition.

In early 1933 the Twenty-first Amendment repealing liquor prohibition was going through the time-consuming process of state ratification. President Roosevelt decided to give the public a morale boost by having Congress pass the Beer Tax Act on March 22. The act allowed the manufacture and sale of beer and light wines with no more than 3.2 percent alcohol. It also applied a tax on the beer to raise government revenues. The public, long weary of Prohibition's ban on alcohol consumption, greeted the act with much relief as a first step in legalizing alcoholic beverages of all kinds.

Farm Loans—Farm Credit Administration

A growing number of federal agencies provided loans to farmers during an agricultural economic crisis that began in the early 1920s and continued into the 1930s. The matter of farm loans had become very complex with numerous agencies involved. Because of income loss due to the Great Depression many farmers could not afford to make their payments on their farm mortgages.

To improve service to farmers, President Roosevelt signed an executive order on March 27 creating the Farm Credit Administration (FCA). The agency was to coordinate loan activities of all these other agencies. Within only 18 months the FCA had refinanced 20 percent of all farm mortgages in the nation. Millions of farms facing foreclosure and thousands of small rural banks were saved. By 1941 the FCA had loaned almost $7 billion and had become part of the Department of Agriculture.

Unemployed men wait in line to receive food from a federal agency in Cleveland, Ohio, in 1933.

(AP/Wide World Photos. Reproduced by permission.)

Youth Employment—CCC Reforestation Act

After stabilizing the banks, Roosevelt wanted to pass a land conservation work bill. He wanted to employ 250,000 young men in reforestation, flood control, and soil conservation projects. Such a bill would not only perform valuable conservation work, but would also provide work relief for youth who were particularly hard hit by unemployment brought on by the Depression.

In response Congress passed the Civilian Conservation Corps Reforestation Act on March 31. The act gave authority to the president to create the Civilian Conservation Corps (CCC), which he did by executive order on April 7. The CCC was aimed at young men between 18 and 25 years of age whose families were already on relief. It was operated by the U.S. Army. By August of 1933 275,000 men were placed in 1,300 camps and were assigned for six to 12 month tours to restore historic buildings, build roads, develop parks, fight forest fires, plant trees, and help in soil erosion and flood control projects. They received $30 a month plus uniforms, room, and board. Out of their monthly pay, $25 was automatically sent home to the workers' families. The program grew to one million

men by 1935 and by its end in 1942 the CCC had employed three million young men.

Farmer Relief—AAA and Emergency Farm Mortgage Act

Relief for farmers was also a pressing matter. At the time 30 percent of the U.S. population lived on farms and President Roosevelt wanted to boost their purchasing power. A key victory of the First Hundred Days was passage of the Agricultural Adjustment Act on May 12. Farmers had been suffering from low farm prices throughout the 1920s, following the end of World War I. Already economically struggling, the Great Depression hit farmers especially hard. Farmer production remained high, even increasing with new innovations being steadily introduced during this period, but as production rose prices declined further. Debt built up in the 1920s resulting from purchasing newly available farm equipment that could not be repaid as the economy worsened.

The act sought to raise farm prices by encouraging farmers to lower their production. It created the Agricultural Adjustment Administration (AAA), which was designed to pay farmers not to plant a certain amount of their land. They were paid to grow less corn, cotton, pork, and other products. To solve immediate surpluses of cotton and hogs, the government paid cotton farmers a total of $200 million to plow up ten million acres of cotton and it also paid hog farmers to slaughter six million pigs. These actions drew considerable criticism by the public for destroying food at a time when many people were going hungry. In time, however, the program pushed farm prices up 50 percent to the benefit of many farmers.

Another major farm issue of the Depression besides low prices for farm products was high farmer debt. In addition to the Farm Credit Administration Congress passed the Emergency Farm Mortgage Act, also on May 12. To help with the debt problem the act provided new mortgages to farmers at lower interest rates.

A major criticism soon arose from advocates for farmers and the poor that neither of the AAA programs of crop reduction payments nor mortgage debt relief helped the small farmer. Those small farmers who owned their own land did not commonly have enough to set aside to qualify for government payments. The tenant farmers and sharecroppers who rented the land they worked were even more disadvantaged. The landowner would cut back acreage farmed and get rid of the tenants and sharecroppers, who were then left with little or no recourse. Small farm operators would have to wait for assistance under later programs. Many went broke in the meantime, and the later programs would only partially help those still farming.

Relief for the Unemployed—Federal Emergency Relief Act

Another key issue of the Depression addressed in the New Deal was relief for needy families. In July 1932 under President Herbert Hoover, Congress passed the Emergency Relief and Construction Act. Under this act the federal government loaned money to state and local governments to provide relief programs to the unemployed and needy. Federal funding was limited because of Hoover's continued emphasis that relief should primarily come from private organizations and local governments. By March of 1933, when President Roosevelt took office, funding for the program was depleted. Public pressure was great to pass another relief bill and Roosevelt and other relief advocates sought to shift the welfare burden from private charities and local governments to the national government.

One of several bills passed by Congress on May 12 was the Federal Emergency Relief Act, which created the Federal Emergency Relief Administration (FERA). The agency provided $500 million in direct aid to states for them to provide food and clothing to the unemployed, aged, and ill. President Roosevelt named one of his closest advisors, Harry Hopkins, to be its director. By the end of 1934 FERA had spent over $2 billion in relief. The program proved critical for providing immediate relief until other programs could become effective. President Roosevelt, however, did not want to simply give people money. Therefore he replaced FERA with works programs later.

Tennessee Valley Authority—TVA

The most ambitious government planning initiative created in the First New Deal was the Tennessee Valley Authority (TVA). The TVA was established on May 17, 1933. This ambitious program focused on broad economic development of the Southeast, a badly depressed region even before the Great Depression had arrived. Unemployment was high and many lived without access to electricity. President Roosevelt had a personal interest in developing federal hydroelectric power. The TVA, a government-owned corporation, gave him the opportunity to put his ideas into action.

Opponents called it a "Russian idea," since government ownership was perceived as closely linked to communism, and private utility companies opposed government competition. (A key aspect of communism is the ownership of industry by government.) The program went forward, however, and over the course

of its existence renovated five dams and built twenty new ones. Improvements to the region were many, including flood control, improved navigation, cheap hydroelectric power, and new industrial development throughout the southeastern United States.

The program created thousands of jobs and the TVA became an international model for rejuvenating poor regions. It did, however, remain controversial—opposed by private power companies, disrupted landowners, and advocates for the most impoverished, who received relatively few TVA benefits.

Stock Market Reform—Federal Securities Act

More financial reform was the next challenge for Congress. The government needed to stabilize the stock market and protect private investors from the fraud that pervaded the market and largely led to its crash in 1929. Congress passed the Federal Securities Act on May 27th in the face of intense Wall Street opposition. The act required companies and stockbrokers to provide full information about new stocks to potential investors, including the financial condition of the company. False statements, which were abundant at the time of the 1929 stock market crash, would be subject to criminal prosecution. The Federal Trade Commission (FTC) was given oversight responsibilities and considerable legal powers to enforce the act.

The FTC had been created in 1914 to oversee business and avoid unfair practices. Under the Securities Act, companies filing false information were subject to criminal prosecution and civil suits by investors. The FTC received new powers to take legal action in gathering information about a company. This act was the first effort by the federal government to directly regulate the U.S. securities markets.

It met considerable opposition by business following its passage. They argued that it was too broad and vague in its prohibitions, which greatly hindered all future stock transactions. Congress would fix this problem in 1934 with passage of the Securities Exchange Act, which would protect investors through the establishment of the independent Securities and Exchange Commission.

Help to Find a Job—National Employment Act

For many years various proposals had been made to create a network for assisting people in finding jobs. None of the proposals, however, made it into law. With the onset of the Great Depression public interest in a job assistance network increased. A bill toward that end passed Congress in early 1931, only to be vetoed by President Herbert Hoover. The bill was reintroduced again in 1932 and once more as part of the New Deal in 1933.

Finally, the National Employment Act, also known as the Wagner-Peyser Act, was readily passed by Congress and signed into law on June 6, 1933. The act created the U.S. Employment Service within the Department of Labor and established the first nationwide employment service that matched jobs to workers. The act provided matching grants to states to establish local Employment Service offices. Many saw this bill as a necessary step before creating unemployment programs in later bills.

Homeowner Debt—Home Owners' Refinancing Act

Another immediate concern of President Roosevelt's was the number of people losing their homes through foreclosure due to the economic pressures of the Great Depression. Many homeowners were losing their jobs or facing reduced incomes. After overspending on credit during the boom years of the 1920s, many people were suddenly caught in a major financial bind. By early 1933 Americans had $20 billion in home mortgages, while more than 40 percent of that amount was in default, placing the banks and other businesses holding the mortgages in dire trouble.

The Home Owners' Refinancing Act, passed on June 13, and provided $2 billion to refinance home mortgages for owners facing foreclosures. The act created the Home Owners Loan Corporation (HOLC) to provide the loans. The amount of assistance available was increased to almost $5 billion in 1935. The HOLC could also take properties foreclosed after January 1, 1930, and give them back to their owners under a finance plan. The homeowner would then pay back the money to HOLC over 15 years at low interest.

By 1936 the HOLC had made over 992,000 loans for more than $3 billion and had financed almost 20 percent of home mortgages in the United States. It stopped making loans after June 1936, when its funds for making loans as provided by Congress was depleted.

Farm Credit—Farm Credit Act

Because crop prices and farm income had dropped due to reduced consumer demand brought on by the hard times of the Depression many farmers were having trouble obtaining loans to help pay for production costs. After the president created, through executive order, the Farm Credit Administration on March 27, 1933, Congress passed the Agricultural Adjustment Act and the Emergency Farm Mortgage Act on May 12.

On June 16 Congress acted to formalize the Farm Credit Administration through the passage of the Farm Credit Act, which created a system of credit institutions for farmers. These included a central bank and twelve regional banks to support the work of local farm cooperatives. The banks would make money more available and help with the marketing of farm produce. The system replaced the Federal Farm Board, which was created earlier under the Hoover administration.

Banking Act of 1933 (Glass-Steagall)

President Roosevelt and Congress wanted to provide long-term assurance to the public that banks would remain strong. The Depression had greatly shaken public confidence in banks. People were hesitant to deposit their funds into a bank where they had little assurance of its actual financial health. Congress passed the Banking Act, commonly known as the Glass-Steagall Act, on June 16, 1933, creating the Federal Deposit Insurance Corporation (FDIC). This agency provided federal insurance for individual bank accounts up to $2,500.

The FDIC insurance program provided considerably more comfort to depositors and greater confidence in banks. The government would pay depositors up to the $2,500 to any person who lost their money because a bank went out business. This amount would cover most depositors at that time, particularly those who could least afford to lose their money.

The bill restructured how banks operated by separating commercial banking activities from investment activities. Investment banking activities primarily referred to buying and selling stocks and bonds. Assets could not be so readily lost during economic downturns. The existing Federal Reserve Board also gained much greater control over bank loan procedures. The bill faced opposition from the banking community, but public demand was too great. The act brought about a significant increase in federal involvement in business activities previously left to bankers and the states to manage. All national banks had to join the FDIC, as well as state banks participating in the Federal Reserve System.

Industry—National Industrial Recovery Act

The First New Deal focused primarily on economic relief and recovery in response to the Depression. By the 1930s it was clear that industry was the driving force of the U.S. economy rather than agriculture as it had been throughout U.S. history up to the 1920s. Therefore President Roosevelt and the New Dealers decided to stimulate industrial production and employment through national planning.

FDR also wanted to tackle the Great Depression, which caused problems of worker wage cuts, falling prices of manufactured products, and employee lay-offs. Congress passed the National Industrial Recovery Act (NIRA) on June 16, 1933. President Roosevelt was not originally supportive of giving labor (unions) power, rather he preferred providing relief through benefits. When it became apparent that the NIRA was going to pass, however, he quickly shifted his support behind the bill.

A very complicated act, the NIRA created a process to establish codes of fair practice. The act sought to limit competition by developing agreements on prices, wages, and production among competing industries. The goal was to increase profits, expand production, and rehire laid-off workers. This type of activity is called "price-fixing" agreements. Congress suspended anti-trust laws that made such agreements illegal. The bill created the National Recovery Administration (NRA), which set prices for many products, established work hour standards, and banned child labor. The NIRA also prohibited adoption of new technologies that would lead to employee layoffs.

More than 740 codes of fair competition were established through meetings between business leaders, workers, and consumers. The NIRA also guaranteed workers the right to form unions and to conduct collective bargaining, which means employees, as a group, could negotiate for better pay and working conditions with an employer. Critics of the NIRA claimed that the act favored big business and that many code violations occurred. Many businesses who participated had to restructure their business operations in order to be in compliance.

The act also created a jobs program. The Projects Works Administration (PWA) was created by executive order on the same day as passage of the NIRA—June 16—in order to operate the jobs program. A sum of $3.3 billion was set aside to stimulate the economy and increase employment. Workers were to build public projects such as parks, schools, and airports. The agency, however, saw only limited success.

Railroad Recovery—Emergency Railroad Transportation Act

The railroad industry was economically struggling by the early 1930s. Two factors were responsible for the significant decline in income—the stock market crash and competition from the growing trucking industry. Many railroad companies had previously established considerable debt and intense competition of the late nineteenth century led to overbuilding of duplicate lines and sizable capital investments. The nation's railroad system was in desperate need of reorganization to make it profitable once again.

The Emergency Railroad Transportation Act, passed on the final day of the First Hundred Days on June 16, pushed for recovery measures. The act allowed bankrupt railroads to reorganize. The act also divided the nation's railroad system into regions and each region was assigned to eliminate duplication of service and begin sharing the use of tracks and terminals. The act also exempted railroads from anti-trust laws.

The Emergency Railroad Transportation Act met with great resistance, however, from railroad companies, railroad employees, and local communities that were afraid of losing their jobs and service. Large users of the railroad system for the transport of goods also feared losing cheap competitive fares for shipping their freight. By 1936 the effort to reorganize the railroad system had lost momentum.

Government Grows

Once Congress completed its special session on June 16, President Roosevelt was left to establish a means to carry out the laws. Through the remainder of 1933 he created various boards and councils by executive order to carry out the various relief and recovery programs. These boards and councils included the Consumers' Advisory Board (June 26), the Cotton Textile National Industrial Relations Board (July 9), the Emergency Council (July 11), the Central Statistical Board (July 27), the National Planning Board (July 30), the Coal Arbitration Board (August 4), the National Labor Board (August 5), the Petroleum Administrative Board (August 28), the National Emergency Council which replaced the Emergency Council (November 17), and the Petroleum Labor Policy Board (December 19). Three new agencies were also created.

More Farm Reform—Commodity Credit Corporation
Despite the AAA and FCA programs begun earlier during the First Hundred Days, farmers were still having problems late in 1933 with wide price fluctuations through the year for their produce. To stabilize prices President Roosevelt created the Commodity Credit Corporation on October 18. The agency was to assist farmers in marketing their produce by providing them loans so they could hold their produce off the market until better prices came along. The Corporation made it easier for farmers to get loans through private banks by guaranteeing payment of their loans. By 1936 the Corporation had helped with $628 million in loans to farmers and by 1940 loans made to farmers totaled nearly $900 million.

Winter Work—Civil Works Administration Though economic conditions had improved during 1933 companies were producing more goods than consumers could afford to buy. The growing inventories of unsold goods led to more layoffs that winter. Under authority of NIRA, President Roosevelt created the Civil Works Administration (CWA) on November 17 to help unemployed workers through the 1933–1934 winter. The CWA funded a massive employment program to perform public work. By the following February over 4.2 million workers were employed and public work became a basic key part of the New Deal. The CWA constructed 255,000 miles of streets, 40,000 schools, and 469 airports and provided salaries for 50,000 rural schoolteachers. The program ended in mid-1934 as the funding allocated by Congress had been spent.

As part of the CWA, the Public Works of Art Project was established on December 10, 1933, to bring work relief to artists. Within a few months over 3,600 artists and assistants were employed in art production projects costing about $1.3 million. The artists created murals and sculptures for public buildings, receiving between $35 and $45 a week. This was the first federally funded nationwide art program, an idea that would return in the Second New Deal as part of the Works Progress Administration.

Bringing Electricity to the Farm—Electric Home and Farm Authority With the earlier development of the TVA program, cheap electricity was available in a large portion of the Southeast. But few rural homes had electrical appliances because of their limited need. To boost electrification in rural areas, Congress created the Electric Home and Farm Authority (EHFA) on December 19. The agency set up a system of credit through local appliance companies so that farmers could afford to buy refrigerators, stoves, and other electric appliances. The program was effective and remained quite active through the remainder of the 1930s.

More Legislation in 1934

In 1934 Congress once again passed a number of acts, including the Gold Reserve Act, Farm Mortgage Refinancing Act, Federal Farm Bankruptcy Act (Frazier-Lemke bill), Securities Exchange Act, Corporate Bankruptcy Act, and the National Housing Act. Also established were the National Recovery Review Board (March 7) and National Labor Relations Board (June 19).

The Price of Gold—Gold Reserve Act With the prices of goods and services decreasing well below desired levels during the Depression, President Roosevelt was determined to use various methods to raise them back up. One strategy controversial among conservatives was Roosevelt's decision to abandon the gold standard on April 19, 1933. The gold standard represented an international system in which every nation on the standard had the value of its money rigidly tied to a certain amount of gold. For instance one dollar in U.S. currency would equal a certain amount of ounces of gold. By removing the U.S. economic system from the gold standard the value of the U.S. money was no longer rigidly set. The federal government could, as a result, manipulate its money supply, printing more money would decease its value and raise prices.

To further spur price increases, in late 1933 President Roosevelt also decided the federal government should start buying gold at steadily increasing prices. This scheme failed, however, as farm and commodity prices continued to fall. The government stopped buying gold in January 1934 and Congress passed the Gold Reserve Act on January 30. The act gave authority to the federal government to set the price of gold in the United States.

Farmer Bankruptcy—Farm Mortgage Refinancing Act and Federal Farm Bankruptcy Act As reflected in the First Hundred Days priorities, the plight of farmers was extreme. Farmers, suffering from low prices for their crops, could not keep up with their monthly payments on their farm mortgages. Given the success of the HOLC for relieving homeowner debt, Congress passed the Farm Mortgage Refinancing Act on January 31, 1934. The act created the Federal Farm Mortgage Corporation to issue $2 billion in loans to refinance farms. Many, however, were hopelessly in debt far beyond the value of their farms. To provide relief and hope, Congress passed the Federal Farm Bankruptcy Act on June 28, which allowed federal courts to reduce a farmer's debt to near his farm value. The farmer could then keep farming and then repurchase their farms with small payments on loans with very low interest rates.

The Federal Farm Bankruptcy Act was clearly not popular among some creditors who would not be repaid the amount originally owed by the farmers. Therefore loan organization challenged the act in the courts and the Supreme Court declared the act unconstitutional the following year. The Court's ruling provided a boost to New Deal critics, who strongly argued that the president was expanding the powers of government well beyond the limits provided in the Constitution. Roosevelt and his supporters, however, strongly disagreed with the ruling, believing the Court was reading the Constitution far too narrowly, particularly in times of national economic crisis.

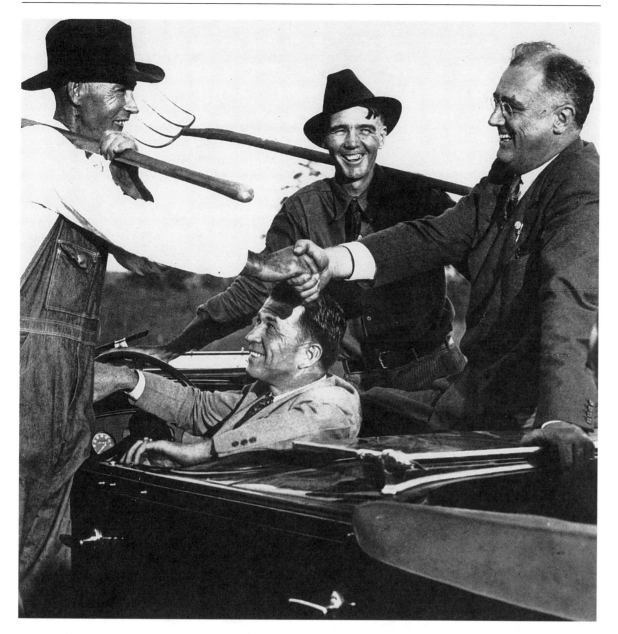

Franklin D. Roosevelt visits with two Georgia farmers during the presidential campaign of 1932. Roosevelt's farm-related legislation did little to help those who operated small farms. (Hulton Archive/Getty Images. Reproduced by permission.)

In response to the Court's decision Congress provided a new, revised process to help farmers. Congress also passed the Farm Mortgage Moratorium Act in 1935, which allowed foreclosed farmers to rent their land from the creditor, usually a bank, for up to three years. In this way the creditor got his money, while at the same time the farmer was given a chance to pay off his debts.

More Stock Market Reform The Securities Act passed in the First Hundred Days had not revitalized stock market investing and companies became fearful of the vaguely described prohibited activities and associated penalties. To address these major concerns and rejuvenate stock trading, Congress passed the Securities Exchange Act on June 6. The new act more narrowly defined the prohibited actions and the penalties.

It also transferred responsibility of stock market oversight from the FTC to the newly established Securities and Exchange Commission (SEC). The commission, under leadership of Joseph P. Kennedy, father of future president John F. Kennedy, was charged to regulate the stock market and control the sharing of stock information. The act was successful in reviving trade and private capital investment. Changes in stock trading were cautiously introduced through the next following years.

Corporate Bankruptcy President Roosevelt and Congress wanted to extend the same relief to corporations that they had provided to homeowners, farmers, and others facing bankruptcy. They hoped to save companies so that they could begin hiring more workers and increase the nation's production of manufactured goods. With widespread support, President Roosevelt signed the Corporate Bankruptcy Act into law on June 7. The act made it easier for a corporation to seek reorganization and not be blocked by a small number of shareholders or creditors. A corporation needed approval of only 25 percent of stockholders to apply for restructuring its debt. A resulting reorganization plan required approval of 67 percent of stockholders to go into effect. All of a company's creditors were required to honor the new organization.

Home Construction To further assist homeowners struggling to afford new houses during the Depression Congress passed the National Housing Act on June 28, 1934. The act established the Federal Housing Administration (FHA). Almost one third of those who were unemployed had previous experience in the construction trades. The FHA was designed to revive the housing industry by providing jobs in home construction and repair of existing homes. The FHA also helped new homebuyers get low interest mortgages. It encouraged lower interest rates by banks by guaranteeing repayment of home mortgage loans.

Amendments to the act in 1938 expanded its ability to promote construction of new houses. From 1934 to 1940 the FHA assisted homeowners in repairing over 1,544,200 houses and building over 494,000 new houses. It also provided over $4 billion in loans. Homes became affordable for many people who were previously unable to buy a home.

The First New Deal and Its Critics

President Roosevelt's perception of government's role in society went against the popular political culture of the day. Roosevelt's and the New Dealers' activism was challenged from many directions—conservative and liberal politicians, business leaders, trade groups

such as realtors, Congress, and even the U.S. Supreme Court. They each had their reasons—unique to their own interests—for concern over the radical new approach of the president.

Conservatives believed that the First New Deal went beyond limits on power given by the Constitution to government, particularly to the president. Liberals believed much more radical change was called for, including government ownership of banks and industry, while business leaders believed government had no role in the private marketplace. Trade groups resisted government regulation of their activities. Some members of Congress did not want to delegate such sweeping authority to the president for setting industry regulations and other actions. Eventually the Supreme Court would deliver setbacks by ruling several key First New Deal programs unconstitutional.

Despite the many critics of his bold new approach, President Roosevelt was able to accomplish a great deal. His successes were in large part owing to the desperation of the public due to the severe hardships brought on by the Great Depression and by Roosevelt's own personal skills in reaching the public through speeches and Fireside Chats.

Contributing Forces

President Hoover and His Response to the Great Depression

Herbert Hoover entered the presidency in 1929 with a reputation uniquely different from his predecessors. Previous administrations believed in a very limited government role in people's lives. Hoover had gained a strong reputation as a humanitarian, by serving major roles in food relief for Europeans during World War I and assistance for the downtrodden at home. This humanitarian perspective, however, was balanced with the ideal of individual self-reliance. Therefore the government role in Hoover's thinking should be to encourage cooperation within U.S. society to solve problems and any financial government assistance should still be quite limited. Hoover believed handouts would undermine character and individualism.

With the economy beginning its decline in late 1929 following the stock market crash, Hoover clung to his belief in a balanced federal budget and was unwilling to create massive government debt through direct relief programs. He believed it was primarily the role of private organizations and churches to tend to the needy. Also, Hoover's demeanor was very reserved and he did not connect well with the public desperate for a sympathetic leader during difficult times.

"Hoovervilles," like this one in Seattle, Washington, became prevalent during the Great Depression.

(© Bettmann/Corbis. Reproduced by permission.)

Hoover refused to acknowledge that a long-term problem existed. Meanwhile citizens lost confidence in the banks that were failing due to lost investments in the stock market and loans not being repaid by its customers. People no longer could tell how financially healthy their own banks were. If a rumor started about a specific bank, depositors would rush to withdraw their funds, causing a financial problem if none previously existed. They also decreased their buying of consumer goods. They were hoarding their money for necessities, especially if the Depression would keep getting worse. This led to a faster decline as employers laid off workers and homeowners lost their homes and people increasingly resented Hoover's unwillingness to help.

By 1931 local relief funds in many areas were running out and private donations were decreasing. New homeless shantytowns became known as "Hoovervilles," an uncomplimentary reference to the president. Responding to the worsening economy,

More About...

The Alphabet Soup of Organizations

To carry out programs created by Congress through the numerous bills passed during the "First New Deal" from 1933 to 1934, President Franklin Roosevelt and the legislature established a host of new agencies. Given their long names these agencies were often known by the first letters of their names. The multitude of organizations made up an entire alphabet of recovery measures referred to as the "Alphabet Soup" of agencies. The actual derivation of that phrase is not well documented.

There was the Agricultural Adjustment Administration (AAA), the National Recovery Administration (NRA), Federal Emergency Relief Administration (FERA), Public Works Administration (PWA), Tennessee Valley Authority (TVA), Home Owners' Loan Corporation (HOLC), Farm Credit Administration (FCA), Federal Deposit Insurance Corporation (FDIC), Civilian Conservation Corps (CCC), Civil Works Administration, and Electric Home and Farm Authority (EHFA). These agencies reached into just about every area of peoples' lives. More were to be added in the next several years as part of the Second New Deal.

Hoover started taking some action. Some jobs were created through federal public works projects such as Hoover Dam and Grand Coulee Dam construction. To help homeowners who were unable to make their payments and falling into foreclosure, Hoover created the Federal Home Loan Bank in 1932. In 1932 the Reconstruction Finance Corporation (RFC), which also offered loans, was created. But these sources of assistance went directly to the mortgage companies. They offered little real assistance to the actual homeowners in making their payments. Housing values were dropping, and the financial health of the lending institutions was failing.

In regard to job losses and wage cuts in businesses, Hoover took the course of trying to persuade business leaders to not lay off workers and to not lower wages. He also encouraged state and local governments to join with private charities in helping the needy.

Similarly, Hoover created the Federal Farm Board in 1929, prior to the stock market crash, to help the already struggling farmers market their produce. The goal of the Board was to raise produce prices without forcing a decrease in production. The Board relied on voluntary efforts of farmers to reduce their production. This approach proved inadequate to help agriculture out of its economic problems.

Hoover's approach of limited government involvement and encouragement of voluntary actions proved inadequate for the severity of the economic problems. The financial problems were far bigger and more widespread than he gave credit for. Private charities were overwhelmed by the demand of those in need. By 1932 one out of every four workers was unemployed. Millions of workers took pay cuts by having their hours decreased or working for lower pay rates for the same number of hours. In one instance, 25,000 women attempted to apply for six vacant jobs cleaning offices. Many former businessmen sold apples or other items on sidewalks or shined shoes on street corners. Wholesale prices had dropped 32 percent, one third of banks had closed, over 40 percent of home mortgages were technically in default, and industrial production had declined by half.

By the summer of 1932 Hoover was convinced that the low point of the depression had been reached and recovery on its own would occur. But the nation's banking system began unraveling that autumn as the 1932 presidential elections were approaching in November. His opponent in the race, New York Governor Franklin Roosevelt, offered the public a new direction. Roosevelt believed the situation was not about to improve without more aggressive government action. In New York Roosevelt had shown a willingness to take bold actions and experiment with the economy. Clearly under Hoover, private enterprise had been unable to recover on its own.

Perspectives

Critics of the New Deal Increase

Opposition to President Roosevelt's new government measures began surfacing from various directions in early 1934. When proposals to regulate the stock market began to surface, the business community had enough. Business conservatives called President Roosevelt's key advisors communists and power-hungry bureaucrats. Private power companies opposed the TVA program claiming government interference with private business. State and local governments were uneasy with the growing federal presence.

The New Deal programs attracted critics from the Left also. Socialists claimed President Roosevelt and Congress did not go far enough in changing the structure of capitalism through economic reform. They also charged the program was following the path to a dictatorship as in Germany and Italy. Roosevelt during this early period of the New Deal, however, clearly had the strong support of the general public. He could afford to largely ignore these criticisms though some bothered him personally. Roosevelt shifted his focus away from trying to work with big business to regulating business and emphasizing assistance for the middle class, workers, and the poor to strengthen his support.

Conservative Critics Unite

Conservatives were alarmed by President Roosevelt's boldness. In addition to issuing hundreds of proclamations and executive orders, the President had even expanded his presidential staff beyond legal limits by appointing some of his staff advisors to high government positions. Sometimes executive orders would create important government policy, something normally left to Congress. Conservatives were especially upset with President Roosevelt issuing executive orders to establish new monetary policies.

They were also dismayed with the broad powers Congress itself was delegating to Roosevelt and his Cabinet regarding control over various economic activities. Congress granted Roosevelt powers to close and open banks, provide relief to the poor, raise farm produce prices, and provide relief to industry. Conservatives believed too much government funding was provided for direct relief and the government went too far to control business, particularly agriculture and industry through the AAA and NIRA. Like President Hoover, they believed the free market economy of the United States would revive itself. They were convinced government interference through attempts to regulate the production and supply of goods and to control prices was hindering revival.

The strongest conservative critics, largely wealthy business owners, banded together in 1934 to form the American Liberty League. Two former Democratic presidential candidates, Al Smith and John W. Davis, were included in the organization, which believed the New Deal measures violated personal property rights. Jovett Shouse, a corporate lawyer, was named chairman of the organization. Many of its members had opposed Roosevelt in the 1932 presidential election. They claimed AAA was "fascist control of agriculture," the NIRA "unconstitutional" and relief programs as the "end of democracy." Not all businesses joined but some prominent leaders remained firmly behind President Roosevelt. The president believed business opposition was ironic since he was trying to save the very economic system that made the businessmen wealthy to begin with.

Liberal Critics Attack

Political liberals were also tough First New Deal critics. Three of particular note were advocates for the poor and needy. They were Charles Coughlin, Francis Townsend, and Huey Long. Coughlin was a Roman Catholic priest from the Detroit, Michigan, area who originally supported President Roosevelt and the New Deal programs but soon became disappointed. He believed they were not adequately reaching the most needy. Coughlin, having extensive influences, advocated for guaranteed annual incomes and nationalization of banks. He had a weekly national radio program that broadcast his views across the nation to some forty million listeners.

Dr. Francis Townsend, a doctor in Long Beach, California, believed the aged were being ignored. Townsend proposed a national pension plan that would provide monthly payments to the elderly. Townsend Clubs sprung up throughout the nation in support of his plan.

Senator Huey Long of Louisiana was an outspoken advocate for the poor. Interested in future presidential prospects, Long proposed a social program called Share Our Wealth, proclaiming "Every Man a King." The proposal gained strong support up until Long's assassination in 1935. Pressure from supporters of Townsend and Long pushed Roosevelt to create expansive social insurance programs in the Second New Deal.

Support in the Center

Despite the high profile attacks on President Roosevelt and his First New Deal programs, the general public was highly supportive. Business leaders and Congress found it highly unpopular among the public to openly criticize or block the New Deal's proposals. This support was reflected in the large volume of mail received by Roosevelt from the public and the exceptionally high number of people listening to his Fireside Chats. Roosevelt drew a friendly crowd wherever he went and the public believed President Roosevelt truly cared and was trying hard to help the difficult situation.

March of 1933 would end up being the bottom of the Great Depression. Widespread popularity of the programs led to further Democratic political gains in the 1934 mid-term elections in both houses of Congress. Desperation in early 1933 was a strong motivation to support new, creative programs, perhaps less acceptable in better times. President Roosevelt would find it difficult to gain such a broad based support again as the early public desperation faded. Momentum for the First New Deal slowed by late 1934 and was essentially lost in 1935.

National Court Rulings

Besides big business, conservative, and liberal opposition to the federal measures, the U.S. Supreme Court provided some severe blows as well. Business interests challenged the Agricultural Adjustment Act (AAA) and National Industrial Recovery Act (NIRA). Here, the Supreme Court delivered two stunning decisions setting back President Roosevelt's New Deal reform efforts.

First, in 1935, the Court struck down the NIRA in *Schecter Poultry v. United States,* when the Court ruled that Congress unconstitutionally gave its own legislative powers to the executive branch. Only Congress could regulate interstate commerce, yet Roosevelt through the NIRA largely had a free hand to set policy for specific industries without the need for congressional approval. It also claimed the industry codes violated the interstate commerce clause of the Constitution because many of the businesses participating only conducted business in a single state. Those businesses operating within states, it concluded, were the responsibility of states to regulate, not the federal government.

For similar reasons the Court in 1936 struck down the AAA, asserting that the federal government could not tax food-processing companies. Again, these were businesses operating within single states and according to the U.S. Constitution could only be regulated by state governments.

International Disillusionment

Economic prosperity in Europe in the 1920s was largely fueled by the industrial and financial strength of the United States. Following World War I the United States had become the world's leading producer, lender, and investor. Most dramatic was the impact on Germany. Germany, facing stiff international fines following its defeat in World War I, was particularly dependent on U.S. investments in the 1920s. After the stock market crash U.S. investments declined sharply, causing German production to decrease dramatically. The decline of the U.S. economy after the stock market crash of 1929 affected other nations as well.

Great Britain, once the financial leader of the world, was steadily losing ground. Stunning the world on September 21, 1931, British Parliament suspended the gold standard. This meant British currency, once the world's most dependable currency, would no longer be backed with gold. Britain's action proved a world landmark event in disrupting the international monetary system. Following Britain, 20 other countries left the gold standard by spring of 1932. No longer were fixed exchange rates between nations tied to gold and each nation could now manipulate their own currencies as they saw fit.

A major part of the declining world economy was also due to the sharp drop in world trade, triggered by new policies by the United States and other nations. World trade declined 40 percent. As a result a sharp decline of income and widespread unemployment hit Europe. By 1933 U.S. foreign investments in Europe dropped by 68 percent. Many of the world's leaders looked to President Roosevelt and his New Deal in early 1933 to help stabilize the global economic situation. A special world economic conference was called for by June in London to seek solutions.

But Roosevelt, continuing the trend of his predecessors, chose to focus his New Deal programs on domestic economic reform to the exclusion of cooperation with Europe. To the shock of many countries, Roosevelt took the United States off the gold standard on April 19, 1933, just weeks before the world conference began. This action caused further decline of economic hope in Europe. Europeans were bitter that the United States would not fulfill its new world leadership role in working cooperatively to solve the economic problems. European and other foreign nations were not to be part of the New Deal.

More significantly, with major financial problems mounting in Germany and little help coming from the New Deal, Adolf Hitler's National Socialist party—proclaiming a New Order—gained strength. Later in 1933 Adolf Hitler firmly held the ruling position over the struggling nation. Ironically Roosevelt's New Deal and Hitler's New Order were beginning at the same time. The New Order denounced democracy and capitalism and in only a few years led to the very costly World War II.

Impact

A key goal of the first three months, called the First Hundred Days, was to build a broad base of political support. FDR tried to provide something for everyone—bankers, farmers, corporations, unemployed, railroads, stock investors, and homeowners. Congress passed more than fifteen major laws in the First Hundred Days of President Roosevelt's first term

NEW DEAL PROGRAMS

Year Instituted	Program	Description
1933	Agricultural Adjustment Administration (AAA)	Farmers were paid to stop growing specific crops. Consequently, the demand for and the value of the crops rose.
1933	Civilian Conservation Corps (CCC)	Provided jobs for urban youth in work such as planting trees, maintaining fire lines, and improving hiking trails.
1933	Federal Deposit Insurance Corporation (FDIC)	Insured individual savings held in banks and other institutions across the country. Monitored and defined standards for the banking industry.
1933	Federal Emergency Relief Administration (FERA)	Provided food and shelter to those most affected by the Great Depression. Distributed cash grants to the states for disbursements to individuals and families on the "dole."
1933	National Recovery Administration (NRA)	Set standards for wages, prices and production to encourage business recovery and investment.
1933	Public Works Administration (PWA)	To stimulate demand in the construction industry, the PWA initiated large building projects such as dams, aircraft carriers, schools, and government buildings.
1933	Tennessee Valley Authority (TVA)	Constructed a series of dams on the Tennessee River to provide electricity and flood control for seven southern states. The program also established health centers and schools.
1935	Rural Electrification Administration (REA)	Encouraged the growth of rural electrification cooperatives, spreading electricity throughout the country's rural areas.
1935	Social Security Act (SSA)	A government-run pension program, designed to provide financial assistance to the elderly, the disabled, and the unemployed.
1935	Works Progress Administration (WPA)	Created urban work projects, such as repairing streetcar tracks and cleaning streets.
1937	Farm Security Administration (FSA)	Loaned money to struggling sharecroppers. Helped relocate farmers to more productive land and provided shelter for migrant workers.
1938	Fair Labor Standards Act (FLSA)	Established a minimum wage and set a maximum of work hours for unskilled laborers employed by business associated with interstate commerce.

President Roosevelt initiated many New Deal programs from 1933–1938. (The Gale Group.)

of office. A whirlwind of change in the U.S. government resulted. The government's role in society greatly increased and many new faces entered Washington's political circles. President Roosevelt and Congress had greatly expanded government's role in the nation's economy. The NIRA was the first direct government involvement in private business activities. Most importantly at the time, public confidence in the nation's future significantly rebounded. After the first 18 months five million unemployed workers had found jobs. Some business leaders even found a few of the programs—the NRA, Emergency Banking Act, and Economy Act—to their liking.

A Second New Deal

Many were unhappy with the First New Deal's reform changes of the national economic system and did not like new taxes. Many feared a dictatorship was growing as in Europe at the time. Business hostility, damaging Supreme Court decisions, and opposition from Townsend, Coughlin, and Long were critical factors influencing President Roosevelt in late 1934. With legislative momentum lost and his popularity in decline, Roosevelt shifted to a new approach. As he began preparing to run for a second presidential term he observed that mass unemployment and widespread poverty persisted in America. He decided to place greater emphasis on social reform, anti-trust action, and more aggressive government spending. The foundation was laid for the "Second New Deal," which would begin in 1935.

The Second New Deal in responding to some criticism, loss of business support, and declining public enthusiasm would chart a new course aimed at long-term reform of the U.S. economic system. This reform would include greater regulation of U.S. business activities and social programs offering greater long-term financial security for the citizens. The numerous acts of the Second New Deal included would be the Social Security Act, the National Labor Relations Act, the Emergency Relief Appropriations Act creating the Works Progress Administration, a Wealth Tax Act, the Rural Electrification Act, the Bankhead-Jones Farm Tenancy Act, the Wagner-Steagall Housing Act, and a new Agricultural Adjustment Act.

Roosevelt and the Court

Another outcome of the First New Deal was a resulting war between President Roosevelt and the U.S. Supreme Court. With adverse decisions such as *Schechter Poultry Corp. v. United States* (1935) striking down the NIRA and AAA, President Roosevelt was greatly angered by the Court. Following his reelection in 1936, the president decided on aggressive action. In February of 1937 he went to Congress, this time to persuade Congress to pass reform legislation for the Court. The president wanted the size of the Court expanded from nine to fifteen so that he could appoint six new justices who would be more receptive of New Deal programs.

Critics referred to the proposal as the "court-packing bill," and brought substantial protest from members of Congress and the press. They believed President Roosevelt was interfering with the constitutional balance of powers between the three branches of government. The president, perhaps over-estimating his popularity, suffered damage to his public image. Public opinion, however, was against the Court as well in striking down key First New Deal programs. Fortunately for President Roosevelt some justices changed their views on the government role in business while other justices retired. President Roosevelt made seven appointments through the next four years and the Court, as a result, made more favorable rulings to the new government programs. Because of Roosevelt's overly bold move, much support was lost for new programs.

Lasting Achievements

Economic results of the First New Deal programs were modest. Unemployment fell from 13 million in 1933 to 11.4 million in 1934. Farm income rose fifty percent, but still remained below 1929 levels, while industrial production and wages increased somewhat. On the other hand, four million homeowners had their property saved by the HOLC and many millions had their bank savings protected by the FDIC.

Most importantly the First New Deal began a major transition in American life. A whole new relationship grew between Americans and their govern-

ment. Before the First New Deal only the U.S. Postal Service played a daily role in citizens' lives, but this changed dramatically in 1933. By the beginning of the twenty-first century, farmers still planted according to federal allotments, the FDIC still insured bank deposits, and the SEC still oversaw stock exchange activity. The HOLC introduced long-term, even payment mortgages, and provided uniform house appraisal methods. The FHA established home construction national standards. Overall the First New Deal legislation introduced a great level of standardization on which the U.S. citizens could rely. The Second New Deal would build on these changes.

Another lasting achievement of the First New Deal was advances in natural resource use and conservation. The Tennessee Valley Authority was possibly the brightest accomplishment of all. The TVA greatly benefited the Tennessee Valley area and the Southeast in general, by building dams, providing inexpensive electricity, making rivers more navigable for shipping, producing fertilizers, and planting new forests. The TVA also provided low interest loans to homeowners and businesses. In the 1990s residents in the region still paid only about one-third the cost for electricity than the rest of the nation. Similarly the Civilian Conservation Corps left a lasting mark on National Forests and Western public rangeland, in addition to major contributions to Midwest farmland conservation.

Notable People

Raymond Moley (1886–1975). Moley earned a Ph.D. from Columbia University in 1918 and became a professor of public law there in 1928. Moley was also research director for the New York State Crime Commission in 1926 and 1927. Roosevelt selected Moley as a key advisor during his 1932 election campaign. Moley assembled the Brain Trust and was its unofficial leader helping Roosevelt with his campaign speeches and development of future policy.

Though the Brain Trust largely disbanded following the successful presidential campaign, Moley remained a close Roosevelt adviser helping select officials for his administration. Moley was a key person behind the First Hundred Days surge of new laws in early 1933. He also wrote most of Roosevelt's speeches and Fireside Chats from 1933 until 1935. As Roosevelt's philosophies began to change Moley became more uncomfortable, particularly with Roosevelt's attack on the Supreme Court in 1937. Moley continued on the staff of Columbia University after the 1930s.

Rexford Tugwell (1891–1979). Having earned a Ph.D. in agricultural economics from the University of Pennsylvania, Rexford Tugwell became a professor at Harvard University. He was an advocate for government regulation of private enterprise and national farm programs. Tugwell was a key member of the Brain Trust assisting Roosevelt's 1932 presidential campaign. In 1933 Roosevelt recruited him to be Assistant Secretary of Agriculture under Henry Wallace as well as economic adviser to Roosevelt. Tugwell was eager to use the New Deal to guide economic and social change in the United States. He played a major role in writing the Agricultural Adjustment Act.

In 1935 Roosevelt appointed Tugwell to head the Resettlement Administration, which was to assist poor farmers in relocating to better lands as well as many other controversial goals. The agency became part of another agency in 1937 and Tugwell resigned. He later was appointed governor of Puerto Rico through World War II (1939–1945) before returning to an academic post at the University of Chicago.

Adolf Berle (1895–1971). Berle was one of the three original Brain Trust members along with Moley and Tugwell. An exceptional student, Berle graduated from Harvard at eighteen years of age and Harvard Law School at twenty-one. He worked in army intelligence during World War I. Berle became a corporate lawyer and law school professor at Columbia University and he authored a highly influential economics book in 1932, *The Modern Corporation and Private Property,* discussing the trend of concentrated wealth and power in 200 corporations.

Being an advocate of government regulation of business, Berle became an influential advisor to Roosevelt during the 1932 presidential election campaign. Not wanting a position in Washington, Berle remained in New York where he assisted in the city's financial recovery. Berle finally did come to Washington as assistant secretary of state for FDR from 1938 until 1944. He later advised President John F. Kennedy on Latin American issues in the early 1960s.

Hugh Johnson (1882–1942). Johnson became the key figure carrying out industrial reform in the National Recovery Administration (NRA). A graduate of the U.S. Military Academy at West Point, Johnson was a member of the War Industries Board in World War I. Following the war he became vice-president and lawyer for the Moline Plow Company later becoming chairman of the board. With his business and industry background, FDR nominated him to head the NRA in 1933.

Johnson's responsibility was to create industrial codes and he personally designed the familiar "blue eagle" symbol of the NRA. An unpopular program

Rexford Tugwell, a member of President Roosevelt's "Brain Trust," continued his service to Roosevelt beyond the 1932 election. He served as assistant secretary of Agriculture and then head of the Resettlement Administration from 1935 to 1937.

with most major industries, he had the difficult job of convincing businesses to join. He successfully gained momentum up to September of 1933, but he soon became the center of controversy with the unpopular program. Johnson left the NRA in October of 1934 and worked as a WPA administrator in New York. He left President Roosevelt's administration in 1935 and became an outspoken critic of the president and the New Deal.

Robert F. Wagner (1877–1953). Wagner was born in Hesse-Nassau, Germany, and immigrated to New York City when he was eight years old. He first won election to the New York legislature in 1904 where he was politically progressive toward domestic reform issues. Wagner was responsible for the successful passage of over fifty New York industrial and labor reform bills in 1914. He believed in government oversight and the rights of organized labor.

Elected to the U.S. Senate in 1926 Wagner focused on unemployment issues. He favored public works programs and brought this interest to reality in New Deal programs, such as the National Industrial Recovery Act.

During the First Hundred Days of the New Deal Wagner was central in developing codes for industrial conduct. While still Senator, he became head of the National Labor Board in August of 1933. It was rare for an elected Congressman to serve as an administrative head as well. The Board was charged with resolving labor disputes.

Wagner continued as a key figure after the First New Deal with his brightest moment coming as sponsor of the National Labor Relations Act, more commonly known as the Wagner Act. Congress passed the bill in July 1935. He also was a key sponsor of the Social Security Act that same year. Two years later he saw passage of the Wagner-Steagall Housing Act, a public housing bill. He was unsuccessful, however, in seeking anti-lynching legislation. Wagner went on to become known as the major architect of the U.S. welfare state.

Primary Sources

Expectations of the Roosevelt Era

Many citizens were exceptionally anxious as Franklin D. Roosevelt prepared to move into the White House. An article from *The Nation*, entitled "Do We Need a Dictator?" (March 1, 1933, Vol. 136, p. 220), published three days before Roosevelt's inauguration clearly reflects the conflicting desire of wanting something dramatic done about the nation's problems, but nothing too dramatic. People had clearly given up on President Herbert Hoover, but they were also fearful of Europe's rise of dictators, particularly Adolf Hitler and the German Nazis. In answering the article's title question of "Do we need a dictator?" the author states,

> Emphatically not! Nothing in the existing situation, grave, critical, and menacing as it is, warrants the overthrow of our system of government or the concentration in the hands of the incoming President of powers which are not already his under the Constitution. Congressional government has not broken down. The time has not come to abandon our faith in our democratic institutions, or to proclaim to the world that they cannot stand the stress and strain of the present economic crisis. There is no inherent virtue or wisdom in a dictator not to be found in a President.

> What we are suffering from is far less the weaknesses of the Congress than the total absence of clear-cut, wise, and constructive leadership in the White House ... The truth is that we have had no White House guidance of a progressive kind, none to challenge the imagination or to sketch out far-reaching policies ... We have had from Mr. Hoover the weakest kind of effort to provide a program for the country ... He misconceived the crisis from the beginning, misrepresented it to the public, announced that it was rapidly passing by and was nothing to be worried about. When he was forced to admit the gravity of the situation he was unable to make any worth-while recommendations. It is not possible to know at this date

whether Mr. Roosevelt will be able to prove to the country that he has sufficient knowledge and wisdom to guide us in this emergency ... If the President-elect sounds the keynote and takes the aggressive in well-reasoned suggestions, Congress will follow him willingly or will be compelled to by public opinion.

Making His Mark Quickly

In his inauguration speech delivered at noon on Saturday, March 4, 1933, Franklin Roosevelt immediately addressed the difficult challenge ahead typically in a spirit of optimism. At the time the U.S. banking system was collapsing, farmers in the Midwest were nearing open rebellion, residents in the southern Great Plains were suffering from massive dust storms, 25 percent of the workforce or over 12 million people were out of work, and millions of others lived in daily fear that they might be the next to lose their jobs. After being greatly disappointed with the little response by President Hoover and his administration, the nation listened intently to see what Roosevelt had to offer to relieve their suffering and despair (from Roosevelt, *The Public Papers and Addresses of Franklin D. Roosevelt,* pp. 11—16).

> I am certain that my fellow Americans expect that on my induction into the Presidency I will address them with a candor and a decision which the present situation of the nation impels. This is pre-eminently a time to speak the truth, frankly and boldly. Nor need we shrink from honestly facing conditions in our country today. This great nation will endure as it has endured, will revive and will prosper. So, first of all, let me assert my firm belief that the only thing we have to fear is fear itself—nameless, unreasoning, unjustified terror which paralyzes needed efforts to convert retreat into advance....

> Values have shrunken to fantastic levels; taxes have risen; our ability to pay has fallen; government of all kinds is faced by serious curtailment of income; the means of exchange are frozen in the currents of trade; the withered leaves of industrial enterprise lie on every side; farmers find no markets for their produce; the savings of many years in thousands of families are gone.

> More important, a host of unemployed citizens face the grim problem of existence, and an equally great number toil with little return. Only a foolish optimist can deny the dark realities of the moment....

> Our greatest primary task is to put people to work....

An Assessment of the New Congress

The following editorial, "A War Congress," was published in *The Business Week* on June 17, 1933 (p. 32). It was the day after the First Hundred Days of the special session of Congress had drawn to a close. In just three months Congress had passed fifteen major bills and forever changed the face of government. The powers of the president were dramatically increased. Clearly the policies of Hoover to provide limited help and wait for recovery to come on its own had been dismissed.

> Many Congresses have come and gone almost unremarked; there is no likelihood that the briefest history of the United States ever will omit to mention the special session of 1933. In three months, it enacted more and broader legislation than any previous session, save perhaps in wartime.
>
> Indeed, it behaved like a war Congress. It came into office on the wave of a great popular upheaval, deeply impressed with the fact that the people wanted things done and no mistake about it. On the day it was sworn into office, it was sobered and stunned by the national banking disaster. It faced an emergency comparable in gravity to war...
>
> With minimum of partisanship and of haggling, with a maximum of expedition, it proceeded to cope with the situation. As in wartime, it placed in the hands of the executive, for the period of the emergency, vast powers which ordinarily it guards jealously from encroachment.
>
> It refused to be turned from this course by taunts of "abdication" or cries of "dictatorship." To delegate is not to relinquish; great powers have been delegated to the executive before, and always recovered when the emergency was passed. Nor is this a dictatorship. Dictators are not named by the normal procedure of strong constitutional governments; they seize power from weak governments, overthrowing constitutions ...
>
> The wolves of depression have to be shot, and without the delay ... It is essentially a one-man job ... [T]he whole money, credit, and price system on which business depends is the most completely artificial thing in the world, and there is no such thing as "natural" recovery, and never was. ... The major part of the task of rebuilding economic health remains to be done.

Suggested Research Topics

- What were the major goals of the First New Deal programs and who helped form the First New Deal's policies? Was this an appropriate government response to the economic crisis?

- Why were some people and organizations not supportive of the First New Deal programs? How could the First New Deal have been expanded to include other nations?

- How were U.S. relations with other nations affected by the Great Depression and the First New Deal?

- Research the various relief and recovery programs offered by the First New Deal. What would have happened if Hoover had been reelected President?

- How did President Roosevelt's proclamation of a nationwide "bank holiday" help end the banking crisis that occurred in 1932–1933?

Bibliography

Sources

Andersen, Kristi. *The Creation of a Democratic Majority, 1928–1936.* Chicago: University of Chicago Press, 1979.

"Do We Need a Dictator." *The Nation,* March 1, 1933.

Fusfeld, Daniel R. *The Economic Thought of Franklin D. Roosevelt and the Origins of the New Deal.* New York: Columbia University Press, 1956.

McJimsey, George. *The Presidency of Franklin Delano Roosevelt.* Lawrence: University of Kansas Press, 2000.

Olson, James S., ed. *Historical Dictionary of the New Deal: From Inauguration to Preparation for War.* Westport: Greenwood, 1985.

Reagan, Patrick D. *Designing a New America: The Origins of New Deal Planning, 1890–1943.* Amherst: University of Massachusetts Press, 1999.

Roosevelt, Franklin D. *The Public Papers and Addresses of Franklin D. Roosevelt, Volume Two, 1933.* New York: Random House, Inc., 1938.

Schlesinger, Arthur M., Jr. *The Coming of the New Deal: The Age of Roosevelt.* Boston: Houghton Mifflin Company, 1988.

"A War Congress." *The Business Week,* June 17, 1933.

Further Reading

Conkin, Paul Keith *The New Deal.* Arlington Heights, IL: Harlan Davidson, 1992.

Edsforth, Ronald. *The New Deal: America's Response to the Great Depression.* Malden, MA: Blackwell Publishers, 2000.

Freidel, Frank. *Franklin D. Roosevelt: Launching the New Deal.* Boston: Little, Brown, 1973.

Hosen, Frederick E. *The Great Depression and the New Deal: Legislative Acts in Their Entirety (1932–1933) and Statistical Economic Data (1926–1946).* Jefferson, NC: McFarland & Company, 1992.

Leuchtenberg, William E. *Franklin D. Roosevelt and the New Deal, 1932–1940.* New York: Harper & Row, 1963.

Moley, Raymond, and Eliot A. Rosen. *The First New Deal.* New York: Harcourt, Brace & World, Inc., 1966.

"New Deal Network: A Guide to the Great Depression of the 1930s." available from the World Wide Web at http://newdeal .feri.org.

"Roosevelt University, Center for New Deal Studies." available from the World Wide Web at http://www.roosevelt.edu .

Sternsher, Bernard. *Hope Restored: How the New Deal Worked in Town and Country.* Chicago: Ivan R. Dee, 1999.

See Also

Causes of the Crash; New Deal (Second)

The Second New Deal

1935-1938

Introduction

"When a man is getting over an illness, wisdom dictates not only cure of the symptoms but removal of their cause." President Franklin Delano Roosevelt (served 1933–1945) spoke these words before Congress in January 1935. The president was beginning his renewed push for reform legislation to supplement the earlier relief and recovery programs of the First New Deal from the previous two years.

As the Great Depression continued through the 1930s President Roosevelt was increasingly sensitive to outspoken critics claiming that the New Deal ignored the common man, the needy, and the aged—all of whom were affected by the economic downturn brought home by the stock market crash of 1929. Millions were unemployed, low on money, and in need of help and President Roosevelt was elected on promises that he would help. The charges leveled by critics—that the New Deal did not help—followed the continuing themes of Dr. Francis Townsend, Father Charles Coughlin, and U.S. Senator Huey Long, who were all vocal opponents of the First New Deal. By late 1934 Roosevelt came to the conclusion that trying to get something for everyone in the nation was only leading to everyone being dissatisfied to some degree. His political popularity was declining.

Under President Roosevelt's guidance Congress passed an impressive amount of legislation between 1933 and 1934, creating a number of relief and recovery programs, which sought to offer employment and

social assistance to those in need due to the harsh economic times of the Great Depression. In early 1935 Roosevelt sent to Congress a new list of legislation to revive his economic recovery efforts. Hoping to soothe the growing discontent of workers before the 1936 presidential election, when he was up for reelection, the legislative package represented a major political shift by Roosevelt. No longer able to take a middle path in order to satisfy both big business and the common worker because of growing strife between the two groups, Roosevelt chose to take the side of the workers.

What became known as the Second New Deal essentially began in April 1935, with passage of the Emergency Relief Appropriation Act (ERAA). The act provided $4.8 billion in relief money, to be distributed by various agencies mostly created by the ERAA. These included the Works Progress Administration (WPA), the National Youth Administration (NYA), the Resettlement Administration (RA), and the Rural Electrification Administration (REA).

The WPA created public projects jobs; the NYA provided work for college and high school age youth; the RA resettled poor families to better lands; and the REA provided inexpensive electricity to rural areas for the first time. The ERAA not only put people to work, but its many programs substantially improved the quality of life for millions of citizens. Whereas the First New Deal was focused on national economic recovery largely through aid to businesses and large farm operators, the Second New Deal shifted to the economic needs of individuals, families, and minorities.

Other programs were established as well under the Second New Deal. These included the Soil Conservation Service (SCS) for the farmer, Social Security for the aged and infirm, and the National Labor Relations Act for laborers. The Second New Deal enjoyed strong momentum in 1935 and 1936. Controversy, however, over President Roosevelt's plan to reorganize the Supreme Court in early 1937 and the occurrence of a major economic recession later that year greatly distracted from further Second New Deal legislation.

Though economic recovery was not complete, the American economy was fundamentally changed by the First and the Second New Deal programs, yet many programs were highly scattered in their goals and actions. At times they were even contradictory with each other in what they sought to achieve. The key factor that held it all together, however, was Roosevelt's confident personality, which gave hope and courage to millions.

Chronology:

April 8, 1935: Congress passes the Emergency Relief Appropriation Act, marking the beginning of Second New Deal.

April 27, 1935: Congress passes the Soil Conservation Act to promote protection of the nation's farmlands from erosion and other impacts.

April 30, 1935: Roosevelt creates the Resettlement Administration.

May 1935: The Works Progress Administration and Rural Electrification Administration are formed.

May 27, 1935: The U.S. Supreme Court issues the *Schecter Poultry Corporation* decision, striking down the National Industrial Recovery Act.

June 26, 1935: Roosevelt establishes the National Youth Administration.

July 5, 1935: Congress passes the National Labor Relations Act.

August 2, 1935: The Federal Art Project, Federal Music Project, Federal Theatre Project, and Federal Writers' Project are established.

August 14, 1935: The Social Security Act is passed by Congress.

August 23, 1935: Congress passes the Banking Act.

August 28, 1935: The Public Utilities Holding Company Act is accepted by Congress.

August 30, 1935: The Wealth Tax Act is enacted.

February 5, 1937: Roosevelt introduces a bill to Congress promoting reform of the U.S. Supreme Court, known as the "court-packing" bill.

February 16, 1938: Congress passes the new Agricultural Adjustment Act.

June 25, 1938: Congress passes the Fair Labor Standards Act, the last piece of New Deal legislation.

The major surge of legislation lasted just over three years. Combined with the First New Deal of 1933–1934, the total amount of legislation was staggering, more bills were passed than in any other period. It was clearly a unique period in the history of Congress. By 1939 the New Deal programs had run their course and attention shifted to events in Europe and the looming world war. Various programs of the Second New Deal expanded considerable influence for decades.

Issue Summary

A Change in Goals

By mid-1934 momentum was lost from the First New Deal's surge of economic relief and recovery programs established since early 1933. The Roosevelt administration began thinking of ways to regain its dynamic leadership role. Although the economy had improved through 1934, it was less than what was hoped for. Employment and industrial production continued to register below 1920s levels.

In addition Roosevelt was angered by the lack of business support for the First New Deal. Frustrated by the growing opposition of big business to his programs and aware of the continued fragility of the U.S. economy, he commented in November 1934 that, "One of my principle tasks is to prevent bankers and businessmen from committing suicide." Seeing the need for more government action and recognizing that he could not satisfy everyone, Roosevelt shifted to the left in regard to political philosophy. This meant he adopted a more politically liberal position by focusing on the needs of the common man, small businesses, laborers, and small farmers rather than primarily seeking to satisfy big business. In a sense, he was a politician trying to keep up with the constituency that still supported him.

To reach these new goals, Roosevelt dropped the First New Deal's idea of national planning best represented by the 1933 National Industrial Recovery Act (NIRA) and its industry codes. In its place he focused on social reform, anti-trust activity, and Keynesian finance, involving high government spending to stimulate the economy. Social reform would include such things as old-age pensions and labor union rights, which were represented in the Social Security Act and the National Labor Relations Act. Anti-trust efforts would seek to make business more competitive where small businesses could compete better with the giant corporations. The Public Utility Holding Company Act of 1935 was key in that regard. The push towards Keynesian economics meant that the federal government would increase spending to boost the economy even if it meant spending beyond its revenue, or income.

With gains by Democrats in the fall of 1934 midterm congressional elections, President Roosevelt was ready to make the charge to fix the economy. The resulting Second New Deal lasted from April 1935 to June 1938, though most activity occurred in 1935 and 1936. New people came forward bringing new ideas to the administration. Instead of the First New Deal's Raymond Moley and Hugh Johnson, there were advisors Felix Frankfurter, Thomas Corcoran, and Benjamin Cohen. They believed in a highly competitive economy not dominated by large corporations. They looked to small companies and labor to play an active role in reshaping U.S. economic policy. The Second New Deal also sought to help small farmers, including sharecroppers, tenant farmers, and migrant workers. Some of Roosevelt's harshest critics had maintained that the New Dealers had overlooked these groups.

Given his focus on favoring the working man and woman rather than protecting business interests, Roosevelt and the New Dealers faced intense business opposition to their programs. They would also suffer setbacks by the U.S. Supreme Court who issued rulings blocking New Deal programs and would continue to see economic problems plague the nation.

Worker Relief

The first item of business in the Second New Deal was worker relief. Roosevelt sought temporary employment for the 3.5 million employable people who were still on unemployment relief. In response the Democratic Congress passed a $4.8 billion relief bill called the Emergency Relief Appropriation Act, which became law on April 8, 1935.

Under authority of the act, the biggest relief program of the Second New Deal became the Works Progress Administration (WPA). Roosevelt created the agency by executive order on May 6, 1935. He selected his trusted friend and adviser Harry Hopkins, who previously headed the First New Deal's Federal Emergency Relief Administration (FERA), to head the program. Through the new jobs it created, the WPA was dedicated to modernizing U.S. rural areas. The agency received $1.4 billion to build or renovate public buildings, water systems, recreational facilities, and rural roads. By its end in 1943 WPA workers had built 850 airports and 110,000 schools, hospitals, and libraries, and constructed or repaired 651,000 miles of roads and streets. Sewing groups that employed most of the female workers in the program made 300 million garments for the needy.

In addition to construction and garment production, in August 1935 the WPA was expanded to include programs for writers, artists, actors, and musicians. A wide variety of projects were tackled. For example while some writers in the Federal Writers Project wrote city guides others collected oral histories of former slaves. Artists in the Federal Arts Project painted murals on walls of public buildings, taught art classes, and made sculptures. Directors and actors in the Federal Theater Project (FTP) worked in organized theater groups producing plays, dance performances, and variety shows. By April 1936 six theaters in Los Angeles showed various FTP performances. In March 1936 the Federal Dance Project was added. The WPA not only helped the performing and fine arts survive the Great Depression but to grow in sophistication and become more distinctly American in character.

Although its name was changed in 1939 to the Work Projects Administration, the WPA lasted until 1943 and employed a total of eight million people. Recruiting workers from local relief rolls, the programs made special efforts at including youth, women, and minorities. The work not only greatly improved rural living standards for decades, but also gave many a sense of hope about the present and the future.

Relief for Youth

As the Civilian Conservation Corps (CCC), created in 1933, and other works programs continued to employ young adults, Roosevelt sought to also assist other youth, many of whom were still in school. In early 1935 estimates were that five million youth were unemployed. Roosevelt wanted to provide them with hope and faith in the U.S. economic system so they would be less likely to join radical political movements as was occurring in Europe. On June 26, 1935, Roosevelt created the National Youth Administration (NYA).

The NYA proved to be one of the more successful agencies of the New Deal. It employed more than two million high school and college students in part-time jobs at their schools, often in clerical positions. Unlike the CCC that was specifically created to employ young men between the ages of 18 and 25, the NYA reached both male and female students. These part-time jobs gave students just enough money so they could afford to stay in school. The NYA also provided jobs for almost three million youths out of school. In 1936 alone the NYA provided aid and assistance to over two hundred thousand students. Most of these out-of-school youth were males being taught vocational skills. By the beginning of World War II, with the young men entering military duty, the NYA primarily benefited young women until it ended in 1943.

Besides clerical positions, some programs taught vocational skills. NYA workers paved 1,500 miles of road, built six thousand public buildings and 1,400 schools and libraries, and constructed two thousand bridges. Also unlike the CCC and other works pro-

The WPA created public works jobs such as eradicating the white fringed beetle, which destroyed crops in Louisiana. (AP/Wide World Photos. Reproduced by permission.)

grams, the NYA made a much stronger effort at recruiting black American youth. President Roosevelt had selected Aubrey Williams as executive director of the NYA, who was noted for his concern about minorities in America. Williams in turn hired Mary McLeod Bethune to establish the Division of Negro Affairs.

Farmer Relief

Just as with the First New Deal, the agricultural situation in the United States drew immediate attention once again. Not only was the agricultural economy continuing to struggle but farmers in the Dust Bowl region of the Southern Plains were experiencing episodes of massive soil erosion. The Dust Bowl was a region of five states that began experiencing a prolonged drought in 1932. The heart of the Dust Bowl was western Kansas, eastern Colorado, northeastern New Mexico, and the Oklahoma and Texas panhandles. The drought persisted for much of the 1930s, with crops withering and soils dried, windstorms swept across the Plains stirred up massive, dense clouds of dust burying fields and even homes in sand dunes. Farmers went broke and thousands migrated out of the region seeking new opportunities elsewhere, but finding few due to the Great Depression.

Young people fell on hard times because of the Depression as well. The National Youth Administration of the Second New Deal attempted to reach out to youth by providing employment for young people. (AP/Wide World Photos. Reproduced by permission.)

To provide assistance to this region and others Congress passed the Soil Conservation Act on April 27, 1935, which permanently established the Soil Conservation Service (SCS). The agency sought to establish soil conservation districts throughout the country to promote a wide range of conservation practices. Chief among its responsibilities was to guard against wind and soil erosion and conserve the nutrients in soils. Later the Flood Control Act of 1936 added more responsibilities to the SCS.

Next Roosevelt turned to the issue of providing electrical power to farmers because in early 1935 nearly 90 percent of farms had no electricity. Roosevelt had earlier gone to the private power companies urging them to supply power to farmers, however, the companies balked at such an idea. They claimed they would lose money since farmers had little need for electrical power and, besides, there were too few of them to make any rural project profitable. In response, under authority of the Emergency Relief Appropriation Act, President Roosevelt established the Rural Electrification Administration (REA), with Morris Cooke as the head, on May 11, 1935, to bring electricity to the rural areas.

With private power companies unwilling to participate, the REA was set up to use farmer-owned non-profit electric cooperatives. Many new lines were built over the next fifteen years bringing inexpensive and much needed power to farmers. By 1945, 45 percent of farms and rural residences had electricity and 90 percent had it by 1951. Access to electrical power posed a major improvement on rural life in America and the REA was a major success.

In January 1936 the U.S. Supreme Court ruled in *United States v. Butler* that the Agricultural Adjustment Act of 1933, one of the hallmarks of the First New Deal, was unconstitutional. Under the act the Agricultural Adjustment Administration (AAA) raised money to pay farmers for reducing crops by taxing food processors. The Court held that federal government had no legal authority to impose such a tax. In reaction Congress passed the Soil Conservation and Domestic Allotment Act on February 29, 1936.

Rather than paying farmers to simply not plant crops as the earlier act did, this act focused on providing payments to farmers to voluntarily replace crops that were soil depleting, such as wheat and cotton, with crops that conserve the soil, as well as encouraging other good soil conservation practices. The act, however, proved a failure as not enough farmers volunteered to replace crops. Production for crops such as cotton actually soared because farmers were trying to sell as much as possible, although it only served to drive down prices by the increased oversupply.

Debate in Congress ran through 1937 on how to improve the agricultural situation. Finally on February 16, 1938, President Roosevelt signed the new Agricultural Adjustment Act. The act not only made permanent the conservation provisions of the 1936 act, but also provided for price supports and reduced crop production when two-thirds of the farmers in a struggling area voted to implement such measures. Price supports usually take the form of a government guaranteed minimum price for crops so that farmers can be protected from major financial losses due to plummeting produce prices. Despite broad farmer participation the 1938 act proved no more effective in curing the agricultural economic ills than its predecessors and crop surpluses continued to grow. It was not until the

arrival of World War II and its demand for food that the agriculture problem would be finally resolved.

To help the small farmer and sharecroppers, President Roosevelt created the Resettlement Administration (RA) on April 30, 1935, under authority of the Emergency Relief Appropriation Act. He placed his long time advisor Rexford Tugwell in charge to administer the funds. The primary goal of RA was to help poor farmers either improve the use of their lands or purchase better lands and get a new start. More and more farmers in the Depression were becoming tenant farmers working on lands leased from others and by late 1936 the problem of tenant farming became the subject of a congressional study.

On July 22, 1937, Congress passed the Bankhead-Jones Farm Tenancy Act, which made low-interest loans available to tenant farmers, farm laborers, and small landowners to purchase or expand their own lands. The RA also made loans available under a Rural Rehabilitation Program for operating expenses, educational programs, and conservation practices. Under authority of the act Roosevelt created the Farm Security Administration (FSA) on September 1, 1937, to issue the loans and to supervise the Resettlement Administration programs. The FSA loaned almost $300 million to help over 47,000 small farmers become landowners as well as improve the living conditions of migrant workers and by 1946 the FSA had provided almost 900,000 rehabilitation loans. The RA's Resettlement Program also built 164 resettlement projects for 15,000 poor families. The FSA would purchase land and subdivide it among the families; it also established 95 camps for 75,000 migrant workers. Both the Resettlement Administration and the Farm Security Administration attempted to address Roosevelt's critics who claimed the First New Deal policies had overlooked the poor farmers. The programs had only limited success as the problem of rural poverty stubbornly lingered.

Labor Reform

Besides immediate relief for the unemployed and farmers suffering from the struggling economy, President Roosevelt sought to establish long-term reforms for the laborer. On May 27, 1935, the Supreme Court struck down the National Industrial Recovery Act (NIRA) as unconstitutional. With the court ruling, the law giving workers the right to collective bargaining, providing for a minimum wage, and restricting certain forms of employer intimidation had ended. Collective bargaining refers to the right of workers to ban together, often through formation of labor unions, to negotiate better working conditions with the employer.

To restore the right of unions to organize and to collectively bargain, Congress passed the National Labor Relations Act that Roosevelt signed into law on July 5, 1935. The act was also known as the Wagner Act after one of its key sponsors, Senator Robert Wagner of New York. Like the NIRA, the Wagner Act recognized collective bargaining and supported the right of workers to join unions and also listed unfair business practices that were prohibited. These practices included interference with union organizing, and threats or firing of workers simply because they were union members. This act differed from the earlier NIRA by giving much stronger powers to the government to enforce its regulations. It created the National Labor Relations Board (NLRB) with extensive powers to hear charges of unfair practices and assist workers in organizing unions.

The combined effects of the NIRA and Wagner Act were large. From 1933 to 1941 union membership more than doubled growing from three to over eight million laborers. The growth and activity were particularly strong in the coal and various mass-production industries.

Still seeking a guarantee of minimum wages and maximum hours for workers, Roosevelt continued to push Congress through 1937 for passage of legislation. After much debate and opposition by business leaders, Congress finally passed the Fair Labor Standards Act that Roosevelt signed into law on June 25, 1938. The act replaced standards that set earlier and were no longer valid in the NIRA, plus added new ones. For example, a minimum hourly wage was set for the first time, starting at 25 cents an hour but increasing to forty cents by 1945. The national maximum workweek was initially set at 44 hours a week to be reduced to 40-hour workweeks by 1940. The act also prohibited youth less than 16 years of age from working in factories.

Social Security

Besides labor, reform legislation also tackled broader social issues. Creation of the social security system was one of the major accomplishments of the Second New Deal. Critics from the Left that had contributed to the lost momentum of the First New Deal had spoken out for the average citizen and the elderly. With a social security system, President Roosevelt largely thwarted their criticism of his actions. Congress passed the Social Security Act on August 14, 1935, under the guidance of the Secretary of Labor, Frances Perkins. The act provided old-age insurance for workers retiring at 65 years of age or older. Payments depended on the amount paid into the system

by the worker, and originally it was only intended as a supplement to their regular pensions.

Contributions into the program came half from workers and the rest was matched by their employers. Excluded from the program at first were farm workers, domestic servants, and many hospital and restaurant workers. The Social Security Act also provided for unemployment compensation to be funded by a federal tax on employers. The states operated the unemployment program and provided between $15 and $18 a week to those who qualified. Federal funds were also provided to states to aid families with dependent children, including the blind, disabled, elderly, and mothers with dependent children.

Ironically, the newly created social security system was actually counterproductive to economic recovery. The social security tax that went into effect in 1937 took money out of the pockets of working citizens, decreasing their purchasing power to buy goods. The relief also excluded the most needy who did not have jobs. Regardless of these adverse aspects, the new system greatly helped Roosevelt politically. The general public's perception was that the government at last had responded to cries for old-age income assistance and income help during times of unemployment.

Banking and Business Reform

The New Dealers turned once again to banking reform. Banking laws in the First New Deal had stabilized the banking system and separated commercial from investment banking and created the Federal Deposit Insurance Corporation (FDIC) to guarantee bank deposits for depositors. Congress passed the Banking Act on August 23, 1935, as one of the most important laws dealing with banking in the United States. The act centralized control of the U.S. banking system into the Federal Reserve Board located in Washington, DC, rather than with the various regional Federal Reserve Banks. The act established a money management system capable of stabilizing the U.S. economy in difficult times, both in prices for goods and in employment.

To carry forward antitrust actions, in early 1935 President Roosevelt chose the highly unpopular power and utility companies to attack first. Companies called holding companies were buying up utility companies and managing them, some would even own several competing utility companies. By 1932 only 13 holding companies controlled 75 percent of private power utilities. Seeking to ban these kind of holding companies and to address financial corruption in the utilities industries, Congress passed the Public Utilities Holding Company Act in August 28, 1935. The act restricted ownership of

More About...

Keynesian Economics

A major breakthrough in the field of economics was introduced by British economist John Maynard Keynes. Keynes was interested in the dynamics of supply and demand at the national level, including a nation's capacity to produce to meet demands. When demand for goods falls below the industrial capacity to produce, then unemployment and economic depression occur. When demand exceeds production capacity, then inflation occurs as the price of goods rise. Few had considered economics at such a large level before. Keynes highlighted that demand for goods can come from consumer spending, investments, and government spending.

Perhaps most notable in his economic models was that no automatic built-in tendencies exist for a national economy to maintain a stable full-employment economy on its own. This was shocking to many who considered national economies cyclical and almost organic in nature, with built in tendencies to remain healthy. Consequently, Keynes argued that if consumer spend-ing or investments dramatically decline causing the national economy to slump, then government spending must increase to fill the void, even if it means deficit spending until the economy normalizes once again.

Keynes's ideas posed a significant influence on New Dealers trying to solve the nation's economic woes. Economists Marriner Eccles, Lauchlin Currie, and Alvin Hansen embraced Keynesian economic models. To improve the economy, they encouraged President Franklin Roosevelt to increase government deficit spending rather than seeking a balanced budget as Roosevelt had personally favored. This spending approach distinguished the Second New Deal from the First New Deal. Adopting this approach, President Roosevelt chose massive new funding, and all deficit spending, for work relief to get the Second New Deal underway. The Emergency Relief Appropriations Act, passed on April 8, 1935, was the largest funded Congressional bill in U.S. history at that time.

---

utilities by holding companies. The companies, however, intensively fought its enforcement and the law was never fully successful. As other industries came forward to support the utilities resistance, this fight strengthened the break between President Roosevelt and the business community.

Tax Reform

President Roosevelt sought to counter Senator Huey Long's growing support to tax the rich and give to the poor. On June 19, 1935, Roosevelt gave a strong speech unveiling his tax scheme and decrying the "unjust concentration of wealth and economic power." Roosevelt had decided to push for a tax plan that would redistribute the nation's wealth on the same day the House passed the Wagner Act and the Senate passed the Social Security bill. Roosevelt called for federal inheritance and gift taxes, higher income taxes for the wealthy, and a corporate income tax, labeling the proposal a "wealth tax issue." The proposal brought much acclaim as well as criticism. Roosevelt, however, did little to actually push the proposals through Congress.

The resulting Wealth Tax Act passed on August 30, 1935, was much simplified, doing little of what the president originally wanted. The bill included a small corporate tax and a small inheritance tax, however, it did serve to dramatically change how taxes were applied. Taxes would be applied in a progressive manner in which the wealthy were taxed at higher rates than those with lower incomes. This is known as a graduated tax system. The speech and passage of a tax bill clearly established President Roosevelt as a representative of the working class.

Opportunities Lost

The Second New Deal programs created in 1935 and 1936 brought the desired political results President Roosevelt was seeking and his popularity rose once again. In the 1936 presidential election 83 percent of registered voters voted and 60 percent of them voted for Roosevelt. Roosevelt received 27.7 million votes to Republican candidate Alfred Landon's 16.6 million. The landslide victory was a major show of public support for Roosevelt's programs and still remains the largest victory in U.S. history. Democrats won a 76 to 16 margin in the U.S. Senate and 331 to 89 in the House.

Labor unions and miners played a huge role in the victory. It was also the first presidential election that

---

most black Americans voted for a Democrat candidate. In fact 70 percent of black voters voted for Roosevelt. Other support came from big city political machines, ethnic groups, Catholics, and Jews. The South also remained Democratic. These various groups formed the core of the new Democratic majority, a coalition that would continue to support Democratic candidates for the next few decades.

The great public expectations of President Roosevelt and the Democratic controlled Congress of providing more relief did not last long. Roosevelt had great disgust for the Supreme Court justices over their rulings, which struck down key New Deal programs, particularly the AAA and NIRA. With a major election victory under his belt in the fall of 1936, Roosevelt boldly introduced a Supreme Court reform bill on February 5, 1937 that he had secretly developed with U.S. Attorney General Homer Cummings. Among its various provisions, the bill proposed to increase the number of justices on the Court from nine to fifteen. President Roosevelt could then appoint additional justices friendly to his programs and end the series of rulings against New Deal programs. The surprised legislators were greatly alarmed and debate over the controversial proposal dominated Congress for the next six months. Despite urging by his supporters, Roosevelt refused to back down. As a result momentum on New Deal programs was almost completely lost.

In addition to Congress losing focus, in early 1937 many believed the Great Depression was drawing to a close. The public and Congress became less supportive of further new government programs, industrial production levels were finally back to 1929 levels, and unemployment was down to 14 percent, well below early 1930s levels. As a result the president came under pressure to scale back programs.

In addition many of the Democrats elected to Congress in 1936 were actually not very supportive of the president's programs, proving to be much more conservative politically. With the controversial Supreme Court proposal being forced on Congress, many of these conservatives decided they had enough of liberal New Deal reforms. Massive government borrowing to fund relief programs, a compulsory, or required national social security program, an income tax system that taxed the rich at progressively higher rates than others, and labor collective bargaining was all they could handle. Congressional members began to organize in opposition to further New Deal programs.

One Last Push

To try to generate enthusiasm for his programs once again, Roosevelt toured across the northern por-

tion of the country in September 1937. His primary goal was to promote the accomplishments of the WPA and other New Deal works programs. He highlighted the construction of hydroelectric dams, irrigation projects, airports, rural roads, urban infrastructure, and conservation work in national forests. With enthusiastic crowds greeting him through the tour, he returned to Washington, DC eager to do more.

Roosevelt called for a special session of Congress as he did when he first took office in 1933. He wanted a new agricultural act, a bill for minimum wage and maximum hours, reorganization of government to give the executive branch more power, and creation of the seven regional planning boards patterned after the First New Deal's Tennessee Valley Authority (TVA).

The timing was not good, however, and by the time Congress gathered in special session to consider the proposals a new economic downturn had struck. The economic growth that began increasing steadily in 1934 was not as evenly spread as hoped in the various industries. By late in 1937 the demand for goods and services slowed to a stop and farm surpluses grew once again. Farm prices and industrial production fell and unemployment rose making economic recovery come to a stop. Trying to keep public morale up, President Roosevelt introduced a new term to the world of economics. He referred to the economic downturn as a "recession," trying hard to avoid the term "depression." The number of unemployed workers increased from seven million in early 1937 to 11 million by early 1938.

In addition to Roosevelt's unpopular Supreme Court proposal and the new economic recession, labor, one of the New Deal's biggest allies, was embroiled in major issues. Organized labor become badly split in a political battle between the main two labor organizations, the American Federation of Labor (AFL) and Congress of Industrial Organizations (CIO). Union membership had been growing quickly with CIO's industrial unions growing the most. In unpopular moves, the CIO was electing some socialists and communists to leadership positions as well as aggressively supporting racial integration. Also organized labor strikes became numerous, with most aimed at obtaining union recognition from their employers under the Wagner Act. More than 4,700 strikes occurred in 1937 alone and these various union activities alarmed conservative members of Congress and much of the public.

Housing

The late 1937 special session of Congress lasted five weeks, but the legislators resisted passing any

First Lady Eleanor Roosevelt visits a coal mine in Ohio. She was there to gain first hand knowledge of work conditions. *(Bettmann/CORBIS. Reproduced by permission.)*

major bills. What did see passage at this time was the Wagner-Steagall Housing Act on September 1, 1937. This bill which provided public housing for the needy had been debated in Congress for several years. Proponents claimed it would also revive the construction industry. Construction interests, however, opposed the bills because they believed it would be unfair competition against the private housing industry. Those congressmen representing rural areas also opposed the bills because they saw them as only benefiting cities.

With final passage of the bill into law, the newly created U.S. Housing Authority was to provide $500 million in loans for low-cost housing. By 1941 over five hundred projects had been funded totaling over $690 million. During World War II the Housing Authority became involved in defense housing projects. Congress addressed housing once again a few months later. A federal housing construction program begun under the First New Deal's Progress Works Administration (PWA) became permanent under the Housing Act passed on February 3, 1938.

The Last New Deal Legislation

When Congress began their next regular session in January 1938 proposed anti-lynching legislation dominated debate. Though the legislation was ultimately defeated, the anti-lynching debates pushed New Deal programs to the back burner once again as the Supreme Court reorganization debates did earlier. Some new legislation did pass, however, the last of the New Deal era. These included the new Agricultural Adjustment Act, signed on February 16, 1938, and another $250 million for ongoing WPA projects.

An important consumer protection bill was also passed. President Roosevelt signed the Food, Drug, and Cosmetic Act into law on June 24, 1938. The act greatly expanded government control over the processing of food and drugs in the United States. The law required all ingredients in drugs be listed and food labels be complete when they are provided on a product. It also brought cosmetics under federal control for the first time. The Fair Labor Standards Act, passed on June 25, 1938, proved to be the last New Deal measure. Roosevelt's bill to set up the regional planning projects was eventually killed by congressional conservatives.

The New Deal Ends

Congressional elections in the fall of 1938 marked the close of the New Deal era. Conservative Democrats and Republicans, enjoying election victories, took even stronger control of Congress. This meant that in 1939 Roosevelt would have to compromise much more in getting new bills through the legislature. Bills that did pass usually provided for cuts in New Deal relief programs and termination of others long unpopular with conservatives such as the Federal Theater Project. More pro-business legislation began passing as well.

Major concerns of Congress and the president shifted from domestic economic problems to developing problems overseas. Fear was growing of political developments elsewhere in the world involving the spread of fascist and communist dictatorships. Conservatives charged that the liberal programs of the New Deal might have political infiltration by people sympathetic to these world developments. This fear finally led to investigations of New Dealers, New Deal agencies, and even the CIO labor unions. Seeing the clear shift in the public mood, Roosevelt finally dropped his domestic economic proposals as they were increasingly dividing the nation. He shifted his focus to the foreign threats, becoming committed to inspiring national unity once again as well as reviving his own political popularity.

Economic Recovery Arrives

By late 1938 economic growth resumed with renewed government spending programs and by 1940 expansion of the military industry triggered a more substantial improvement. World War II's (1939–1945) massive government borrowing, investment, and spending brought real economic recovery. Spending greatly escalated for tanks, guns, airplanes, ships, and other warfare materials.

As with the First New Deal of 1933 and 1934, effects of the Second New Deal programs were broad. The National Labor Relations Act supported workers and labor unions, a host of acts including the Soil Conservation Act and the new AAA helped farmers, the Banking Act helped depositors, the Housing Act helped homeowners, the Food, Drugs, and Cosmetic Act helped consumers, and the WPA helped workers just about everywhere. For those who were desperately poor the TVA, Farm Credit Administration, and several relief programs such as the WPA lessened discontent.

The New Deal programs had given many people hope and a sense of dignity by providing jobs, while the provision of jobs, food, and money reduced suffering for thousands. Important for the national psyche, throughout this period of economic strife, President Roosevelt had projected a fatherly image that led to greater public comfort. In the end, however, the New Deal legislation could not by itself resolve mass unemployment and low prices. It would take the massive spending in preparation for World War II to finally end the economic crisis.

Contributing Forces

Lost Momentum in the First New Deal

The First New Deal under the guidance of a confident President Roosevelt produced an impressive array of relief and recovery programs. A very receptive Congress passed an amazing amount of legislation. However, by early 1934 business leaders were increasingly turning against the First New Deal programs. They felt the programs interfered with their business activities through increasing federal regulations and government control of economic activity.

The NIRA codes and regulations were of particular concern and they believed the works programs competed with private business. Business leaders were also displeased with the devaluing of the U.S. dollar, which meant the dollar would have less value. In turn this would mean goods would cost consumers more and it

The Works Progress Administration was the biggest relief program of the Second New Deal. The WPA program, known as the Work Projects Administration beginning in 1939, employed a total of eight million people between 1935 and 1943. (The Library of Congress.)

would also decrease the value of savings accounts and business investments. During this period the value of U.S. currency had decreased by 40 percent. The devaluation had helped increase the prices of products but it also decreased the value of savings accounts and business investments.

As congressional elections approached for that fall, some business leaders decided to politically organize to defeat candidates who supported the president's programs, calling themselves the Liberty League. President Roosevelt was dismayed by the intensity of business opposition, which came after he believed he had acted to help save them from economic ruin. Roosevelt was much irritated by business' seemingly short collective memory of what business conditions had been like when he had first taken office.

Many in the public as well as business were also concerned with the increasing federal debt driven by the growth of New Deal programs. Congress was spending millions of dollars on public works and relief programs. The occurrence of federal deficits was new to many because balanced federal budgets had always been the guiding principle in the past.

On the other hand, liberals were also expressing increased disappointment over First New Deal results. The NRA also had proven not very effective and they wanted Roosevelt to bring banks under stricter control. Pushing even further, the socialists, communists, and other radicals wanted an entirely new economic system in place of free-market capitalism. They pushed for nationalizing banks and industries, meaning the government would own and operate those industries for the benefit of the general population. Minnesota's radical governor, Floyd B. Olson commented that what was needed was "not just a new deal, but also a new deck."

With the economy still lagging, President Roosevelt had to chart a new course. He had found that cooperation with big business did not produce results. In early 1935 Roosevelt was gradually losing public support. The public was also losing confidence in the First New Deal programs as many remained unemployed and the economy continued to suffer. President Roosevelt decided it was time to try something new.

Perspectives

Lasting Impressions

Public perspectives over Second New Deal programs ranged from high praise to bitter criticism but by late 1935 business and President Roosevelt had clearly parted ways. Industry fiercely opposed his public utilities holding company bill that Congress had passed in August. Business also celebrated the NRA ruling by the Supreme Court in *Schecter v. United States* on May 27, 1935. The Court ruled that Congress had unconstitutionally delegated its powers to regulate interstate business to the executive branch of government.

The president had been given responsibility to oversee the development of operating codes by cooperative industry groups. The codes essentially represented regulations guiding business activity of the industries. In addition, much of the business was not actually interstate in character, therefore not even subject to congressional authority. Business was pleased to see both Congress's and the president's authority to regulate business greatly limited. The codes were also proving not to be effective in providing relief to business.

The Conservative View Conservatives of both political parties, the Republicans and Democrats, believed government had grown far too large and become too involved in the nation's economic activities in agriculture, industry, and housing. Government regulation suppressed free enterprise they claimed. Bankers argued that the business of lending money should be left to private enterprise and not the government through its low-interest loan programs. They contended true prosperity could only come through private business activity, not government action.

The Liberal Position Unlike the conservatives, the politically liberal felt President Roosevelt could have gone much farther in aiding the poor who had little political voice in the United States. He also could have promoted civil rights issues by seeking racial integration and greater protection under the law for minorities. Liberal critics claimed the New Deal never truly raised the poor out of poverty, closed the gap in wealth, or came close to establishing economic equality. Some even believed that by not working harder specifically for the poor and minorities, the New Deal actually strengthened the inequality that already existed by simply letting social injustice exist relatively unchallenged for yet another decade. Many charged the reform programs stopped way short of providing financial security by not including some form of national healthcare system, an issue that rose again in controversy in the mid-1990s. Overall a great disparity between the few wealthy and the many poor persisted at the end of the 1930s.

American Liberty League

One of President Franklin Roosevelt's chief opposing organizations during the waning days of the First New Deal and the growth of the Second New Deal was the American Liberty League (ALL). ALL was composed of leaders from American industry, business, finance, law, and other professions. Their numbers were actually relatively few but they had considerable wealth and prestige. Jouett Shouse, a leader of the Democratic Party from 1920 to 1932, was president of ALL. Its membership included Democratic Party candidates for 1924 and 1928 and was funded by the industrially prosperous Du Pont family. ALL's membership peaked at almost 125,000 people in the summer of 1936.

ALL members were conservatives who vehemently opposed New Deal policies and worked hard to end the First New Deal and defeat Roosevelt in the 1936 president election. The same group of leaders who formed the Association Against the Prohibition Amendment, which helped successfully bring Prohibition to an end, formed ALL in August 1934. In fact

Shouse had been president of that organization as well. Their goal was to defend "the rights of persons and property." They charged that Roosevelt and the New Deal were socialistic and endangering the U.S. Constitution. ALL claimed New Deal economic policies were slowing recovery from the Great Depression and hindering free enterprise. Leading up to the 1936 elections ALL raised as much money as either major political party. It spent much of its funds on massive publicity campaigns. From August 1934 to November 1936 ALL produced and distributed 135 pamphlets and used the radio extensively.

Following Roosevelt's landslide victory in November 1936, ALL, which had never gained much support from the general public, declined significantly. It was officially disbanded in 1940, as New Deal policies had ended and foreign issues were outweighing domestic concerns.

Public Perspectives

Public perspectives on the New Deal, like those in government, were mixed. One example was found regarding the Works Progress Administration. The WPA programs supporting the arts were typically targets of varying public perspectives. Many were critical of spending public monies on art and writing projects claiming it was not "real" work. Many young artists and actors, however, got their start in these New Deal programs and became widely recognized later in their careers. For example, painter Jackson Pollock received $7,800 from the WPA to produce paintings and by the mid-1990s those paintings he produced had an estimated value of over $500,000.

Despite these criticisms coming from all directions, many people felt that President Roosevelt struck a satisfactory middle road that eased the nation's economic problems through the 1930s. The New Deal showed that practical national solutions were possible to solve national problems. Government had forever assumed a greater responsibility for the economic prosperity of its citizens.

Impact

Economic production of goods and services significantly grew from 1934 to 1937. During this period the United States had one of the highest economic growth rates of the world's industrialized nations. Only Germany and Japan, who were arming for war, had a higher rate. Eight million more workers had been added to the payrolls since 1933, wage and hour standards were established, including 40-hour workweeks,

At a Glance
Key Bills of the Second New Deal

- Emergency Relief Appropriation Act, April 8, 1935
- Soil Conservation Act, April 27, 1935
- National Labor Relations Act, July 5, 1935
- Social Security Act, August 14, 1935
- Banking Act, August 23, 1935
- Wealth Tax Act, August 30, 1935
- Soil Conservation and Allotment Act, February 29, 1936
- Rural Electrification Act, April 20, 1936
- Bankhead-Jones Farm Tenancy Act, July 22, 1937
- Wagner-Steagall Housing Act, September 1, 1937
- Housing Act, February 3, 1938
- Agricultural Adjustment Act, February 16, 1938
- Fair Labor Standards Act, June 25, 1938
- Food, Drug, and Cosmetic Act, June 25, 1938

and labor unions were rapidly expanding. By the spring of 1937 the economy was better than before the October 1929 stock market crash.

Changing Government Role

The New Deal was the most significant liberal reform era of the federal government in U.S. history. Public faith in a private enterprise system that had previously operated largely free from government restraints was badly shaken. The First New Deal stopped the downward spiral of the economy in 1933 and 1934 through relief and recovery. The Second New Deal sought to establish greater economic security for the future through reform. The New Dealers promoted economic security as a political right of the nation's population.

Both the First and Second New Deal programs marked the beginning of big government in the United States. The active role of government in the nation's economy increased in several ways. The federal government (1) placed millions of dollars into the economy; (2) created federally funded jobs;

(3) orchestrated the supply and demand for certain products; (4) directed business and labor relations; and, (5) regulated banking and stock market activities. The New Deal represented the largest increase in government involvement in the nation's private economy. Supporters proclaimed that a more centralized government with greater powers was created to stabilize a large complex economy while still preserving a free democratic society.

Washington's relation to its citizens also dramatically changed, now the federal government took responsibility for the unemployed, infirm, and aged. Liberals praised the New Deal programs for bringing relief to millions, while conservatives and other opponents claimed New Deal policies allowed large inefficient government bureaucracies to take away from personal property rights and individual rights.

Regardless of the debate over New Deal policies that would continue well after the 1930s, the New Dealers did create a much greater sense of compassion and caring by the government toward its citizens. Selfish attitudes of the past gave way to a period of greater cooperative action. For the first time, many people realized that a completely unrestrained economic marketplace did not always act for the common good of the nation or its citizens.

A New Political Coalition

In addition to the increased role of government in everyday life in America, the politics of America also significantly changed. Throughout President Roosevelt's fight to gain public support for proposed Second New Deal programs, he sought to build diverse support. The diverse categories of people who supported and benefited from New Deal programs essentially represented a loose political coalition in future elections. The coalition was indeed broad and had a dramatic long-term benefit to the Democratic Party. Roosevelt had gained support from racial and ethnic minorities, workers, intellectuals, urban groups, and Southern whites. Groups included labor unions, government relief recipients, and religious organizations. The combined political clout of this coalition dominated politics throughout much of the remainder of the twentieth century.

Labor union members saw their work conditions improve through the late 1930s as their bargaining power increased. Labor unions considered Roosevelt a "friend of labor" and they in turn became a major financial supporter in his reelection campaigns.

By appealing to a broad public support, the New Deal brought a broad recognition to cultural differences in the nation's population for the first time and the idea of cultural pluralism was born in the United States. Pluralism means people of different ethnic backgrounds were recognized and included in government and labor. Roosevelt appointed many people of diverse backgrounds into government posts, Including black Americans, Irish, Italians, and eastern Europeans. White supremacy, which had ruled American politics up through the 1920s, was no longer nationally acceptable. The 1930s became a more purely democratic era, more than any previously in the nation. Racial equality was beginning to rise more prominently as a national goal. In addition to minorities, religious organizations including Roman Catholics and Jews supported Democrats.

Culturally diverse voters in northern urban centers such as New York City, Chicago, Boston, and Philadelphia strongly supported work relief programs and labor reform. In the 1936 election Roosevelt carried the nation's twelve largest cities. As a result of this increased pluralism, the New Deal and its coalition not only posed obvious economic influences but also greatly influenced American society and culture for years to come.

A Changed American Landscape

Twenty million people participated in federal work relief programs in the 1930s. The FERA, CWA, WPA, and NYA construction programs left a physical as well as social legacy. The federal government had become the nation's master builder. The programs left evidence everywhere—streets, sidewalks, sewers, parks, schools, and numerous public buildings.

Not only were the projects occurring in the populous East, but out West as well. To expand the geographic focus, the government took some monies from the East and spent them on the West. As a result of these New Deal programs the rural West saw spectacular changes benefiting those who lived in the Rocky Mountain and Pacific Coast states. Until the New Deal projects, the West had been sparsely populated and economically underdeveloped. New Deal programs built hydroelectric dams, many water projects, and irrigation canals and agricultural potential greatly expanded. New roads also opened up new areas for settlement. Making use of these new facilities the population greatly expanded during World War II and afterwards. The TVA and other New Deal projects posed similar effects in the rural Southeast as well.

Economic Protection

Many of the programs established by the New Deal served to soften the impacts of later economic downturns. These programs included unemployment compensation, Social Security, welfare payments, and bank deposit insurance. Welfare programs provided a safety net for those unable to benefit from the highly centralized capitalist system. In addition, the economic notion of increasing government spending to revive the economy in slow times, known as Keynesian economics, had gained more acceptance.

The WPA was a highly popular program for many because it actually provided jobs, not just money, helping to maintain the individual's self-respect. A well-established work ethic made such an approach much more appealing to the public. By 1943 WPA workers had built 5,900 new schools and 13,000 playgrounds.

Despite their opposition to the New Deal, big business gained greatly by having more secure investments and profits than ever before. They also had more government subsidies in addition to more federal regulation.

Johnson's Great Society

The New Deal's influence extended well beyond the 1930s. The Second New Deal in particular, laid the foundation for civil rights and social services initiatives promoted by later Democratic presidents. John F. Kennedy (served 1961–1963) proposed the New Frontier in his 1960 campaign, with a focus on economic reforms to assist those who did not benefit from the prosperous years of the President Dwight Eisenhower (served 1953–1961) administration. He also proposed Medicare to assist the elderly, redevelopment of inner cities, and more funding for education. Most of Kennedy's proposals, however, were blocked by a coalition of Republicans and conservative Southern Democrats.

Following Kennedy's assassination in November 1963 President Lyndon B Johnson (served 1963–1969) pursued Kennedy's earlier proposals in his "war on poverty." From 1965 to 1968 Congress passed many of the proposals as part of Johnson's Great Society program. Legislation and programs included Medicare (providing medical care for the very poor), Head Start (education for very young underprivileged children), Job Corps (employment for youth), and several major civil rights laws. This period represented the most significant expansion of the government role in U.S. society since the New Deal. Like the New Deal programs, however, success in addressing poverty was modest at best. By the 1970s a broad system of welfare services was established that became the focus of legislative action in the late 1990s as Congress passed major reforms.

Notable People

Benjamin V. Cohen (1894–1983). Son of Polish Jewish immigrants, Cohen excelled at the University of Chicago law school and had a distinguished private and public career from 1916 to 1933. He was recruited into New Deal activities by Felix Frankfurter to serve as a legal and legislative advisor to President Roosevelt. During the First New Deal Cohen had a key hand in crafting the Securities Exchange Act of 1934 and the Tennessee Valley Authority.

In the Second New Deal he authored the Public Utility Holding Company Act in 1935. He and Thomas Corcoran worked tirelessly behind the scenes in the New Deal authoring legislation and working with Congress in passage of numerous bills. To many Cohen was considered the top adviser to Roosevelt during the Second New Deal. Following various advisory roles during World War II, he served as delegate to the United Nations for President Harry Truman (served 1945–1953).

Thomas Corcoran (1900–1981). An Irish Catholic born in Pawtucket, Rhode Island, Corcoran graduated with honors from Brown University and from Harvard Law School where he was a favorite student of Felix Frankfurter. After serving for one year as secretary to Supreme Court Justice Oliver Wendell Holmes, Corcoran had a private practice in New York from 1927 to 1932. Though a Democrat, Corcoran was appointed by President Herbert Hoover (served 1929–1933), a Republican, as legal counsel to the Reconstruction Finance Corporation in 1932 with whom he remained off and on until 1941.

Corcoran had influence on New Deal legislation and programs well beyond the RFC. He teamed with Benjamin Cohen on considerable legislative activity including the Securities Exchange Act in the First New Deal and the Public Utility Holding Company Act in the Second New Deal. While Cohen served as chief author of New Deal legislation, Corcoran was chief lobbyist. Very outgoing, Corcoran would work to get the bills through Congress. Corcoran also played a major role in placing young lawyers in New Deal roles for Roosevelt. He returned to private practice in 1941 for the rest of his career.

Lauchlin Currie (1902–1993). Born in West Dublin, Nova Scotia, Currie received a degree from the London School of Economics in 1925 and a doctorate in economics from Harvard in 1936. Currie got a job with the Department of Treasury in 1934 where he met Marriner Eccles. Eccles gave him a job with the National Labor Relations Board later that year. Currie helped author the Banking Act of 1935 that reorganized the Federal Reserve System. He was also instrumental in providing monthly monetary calculations that guided New Deal policymaking. Currie, through Eccles, played a key role in influencing Roosevelt's adoption of Keynesian economics. He assumed increasingly important economic advisory roles to Roosevelt through the Second New Deal and World War II. Following the war Currie headed the International Bank of Reconstruction and Development.

Marriner Eccles (1890–1977). Eccles was born to a wealthy family in Logan, Utah. Following his Mormon missionary work in Scotland, he built the family's Eccles Investment Company into a multimillion dollar empire. As a highly respected banker, Eccles was called to testify in Congress in early 1933 about possible solutions to the Great Depression. Unlike many business leaders at the time, Eccles urged greater government spending on work relief and loan programs to stimulate the economy. Eccles joined the New Dealers in Washington in 1934 and helped draft the Banking Act of 1935 that reorganized the Federal Reserve System. He became head of the Federal Reserve Board and served on it until 1951.

Felix Frankfurter (1882–1965). Born to Jewish parents in Vienna, at age 12 Frankfurter immigrated to the United States with his family in 1894. He received a degree from Harvard Law School. After private practice and working in the U.S. attorney's office in New York, Frankfurter was appointed to a law position in the President William Taft (served 1909–1913) administration. He had become a friend of Franklin Roosevelt in the early 1920s, who shared ideas on politics and the economy with Roosevelt when Roosevelt became governor of New York in 1928.

While teaching at Oxford in England in the early 1930s he became friends with economist John Maynard Keynes and introduced him to Roosevelt. Frankfurter and Keynes would play influential roles in convincing Roosevelt to adopt major spending programs in 1935 as part of the Second New Deal. A strong shaper of the Second New Deal in general, he was appointed to the U.S. Supreme Court by President Roosevelt in 1939 and helped write the Wealth Tax Act. Frankfurter served on the Court until 1962 when he retired due to ill health.

Alvin Hansen (1887–1975). Born to Danish immigrants in Viborg, South Dakota, Hansen earned his doctorate in economics from the University of Wisconsin. During the Great Depression Hansen began preaching Keynesian economic proposals on government deficit spending to spur economic growth. In 1937 he moved to Harvard University from Minnesota University. Hansen never became part of President

Roosevelt's administration, rather his influence was more through publication, advising various policy groups, and mentoring of various economics students who went on to become economic policy advisers. Hansen became known as the "American Keynes."

Harry L. Hopkins (1890–1946). Born in Sioux City, Iowa, Hopkins became a close friend and adviser to President Franklin Roosevelt and long-time leader of New Deal programs. He was the top relief and public works administrator during the Great Depression and during the First New Deal he was chief administrator of the Federal Emergency Relief Administration beginning in May 1933. While leading FERA he also directed the Civil Works Administration from 1933 to 1934 and the Works Progress Administration from 1935 to 1938. In 1938 he became secretary of commerce and served until 1940. Hopkins and the programs he led were known for honesty and efficiency. During World War II Hopkins consulted with Roosevelt on domestic and foreign matters and traveled extensively meeting with key foreign leaders.

John Maynard Keynes (1883–1946). Keynes was an influential British economist who promoted the idea of government deficit spending to stimulate economic recovery. During the boom years of the 1920s Keynes made a fortune speculating in international stocks. He was also an author on economics issues and professor at Cambridge University, who believed that to recover from a depression a government should increase its spending by placing money in the hands of consumers. The public could then buy goods and services from businesses and lead to economic recovery. His ideas were published in the 1936 book *The General Theory of Employment, Interest, and Money.* President Herbert Hoover did not agree with this approach.

In a visit to Washington, DC, in 1934, Keynes stressed the need for greater government spending on relief programs. Though somewhat receptive to Keynes' ideas, President Franklin Roosevelt greatly believed in balanced government budgets. Keynes ideas greatly influenced the Second New Deal and the expensive programs that were created. The massive government spending of World War II finally proved Keynes correct in his assessment to revive the economy and his belief that the economy could not recover on its own.

Primary Sources

An Assessment of the Second New Deal

New Republic magazine published a lengthy editorial in the May 20, 1940, issue titled "The New Deal in Review, 1936–1940." The editorial took an in depth

Unlike most other programs under the New Deal, the National Youth Administration made more of an effort to recruit black American youth. These young men are working on automobiles as part of a vocational training program. (The Library of Congress.)

look at the Second New Deal. The following excerpts look at the WPA, one of the largest New Deal programs (p. 692).

> Unemployment relief has brought the New Deal more intimately into the lives of Americans than any other of its activities ... The administration officials in charge of relief have had wide influence on general New Deal policy ...
>
> The shortcomings of the WPA have been greatly overstressed, but they are insignificant beside the gigantic fact that it has given jobs an sustenance to a minimum of 1,400,000 and a maximum of 3,300,000 persons for five years. Its work projects have added immeasurably to the nation wealth; in some regions the school, health and recreation facilities it has called into existence have fairly revolutionized communal life. It must also be remembered that, as its permanent technique for dealing with the relief problem, the New Deal has been simultaneously developing its programs for unemployment insurance, old-age pensions, assistance to mothers, dependent children and the handicapped.
>
> No doubt because the unemployed are politically the weakest members of the community, they have suffered most from the resurgent conservatism first manifested in the 1938 election ...
>
> The New Deal, even in its second term, has clearly done far more for the general welfare of the country and its

citizens than any administration in the previous history of the nation. Its relief for underprivileged producers in city and country, though inadequate to the need, has been indispensable. Without this relief an appalling amount of misery would have resulted, and a dangerous political upheaval might have occurred.

Workers Complain

Worker dissatisfaction with President Roosevelt in 1935 was mounting as the Depression dragged on. Many began to believe Roosevelt's actions the previous two years had only helped business not the common person. A Columbus, Ohio, worker who decided to switch his support to Huey Long expressed such disappointment. He wrote a letter to the president explaining his decision to change loyalty (quoted in McElvaine's *The Great Depression: America, 1929–1941,* p. 254).

> We the people voted for you, we had a world of faith in you, we loved you, we stood by you, it was a common thing to hear a man or woman say they would gladly die for you, but it is a different story now. Yes you have faded out on the masses of hungry, idle people ... the very rich is the only one who has benefited from your new deal. Why didn't you turn a deaf ear to the United States Chamber of Commers, and turn to the left, and saved millions of starving people, who believed in you ... but it is so diferent to day the people are disappointed,

More About...
The Recession of 1937

By September 1937 the nation's economy had begun another major decline. Through June 1938 industrial production declined 33 percent, profits by 78 percent, national income by 13 percent, and employment in manufacturing by 23 percent. The recession triggered much debate about New Deal policies and whether or not they had failed.

Changes in government policies, influenced by the increasingly conservative Congress, led away from earlier New Deal strategies by early 1937. A shift in national economic policy away from massive government spending programs likely contributed to the national economic decline. President Roosevelt personally did not embrace deficit spending and believed in balanced budgets.

During 1936 the federal government had poured more than $4 billion into the national income. Most of the government spending had been bonus payments for World War I veterans, which did not continue in 1937. In addition, during 1937 Social Security taxes began withholding money from paychecks and out of circulation. The federal government's contribution to national income in 1937 dropped to $800 million. In addition to changes in veterans' bonus payments and Social Security taxes, the Federal Reserve Board in late 1936 changed its monetary policies. The Board tightened up the money supply and decreased availability of loans. These factors and others likely had a combined effect in contributing to the economic downturn.

With the decline in the national economy, business leaders saw a key opportunity to once again step up their attacks on New Deal policies. They claimed that Second New Deal economic reform efforts had interfered with private industry therefore causing major problems. They wanted government to return to balanced budgets and let industry regulate itself once again. Secretary of Treasury Henry Morgenthau, Jr., sided with this philosophy.

Others claimed business was to blame for the economic downturn, and that monopolies had decreased competition. They argued the government should pursue more anti-trust prosecutions and once again increase federal spending to increase national income and consumers' purchasing power. Proponents for this approach included Benjamin Cohen, Marriner Eccles, Thomas Corcoran, and Secretary of Interior Harold Ickes.

Influential economist Alvin Hansen blamed the recession on declining investment opportunities in American business, tight loan availability, and declining government spending. The loss of investment opportunities was resulting from a declining population growth, decreasing availability of land and resources, and a slowing of technological innovation during the Depression years. He and the others called their policies "compensatory government spending" based on Keynesian economics. The government infusion of money temporarily takes the place of private monies not being spent. They believed this would lead to increased national production, consumption, and higher employment levels. Debate raged among the New Dealers through the winter of 1937–38 over exactly what should be done.

In April 1938 President Roosevelt decided to follow the advice of Eccles and others and press for increased government spending. Congress, however, decided to take control of policy making. They established the Temporary National Economic Committee (TNEC) to help guide recovery efforts. The committee held 15 hearings between December 1938 and March 1941. The nation's economy began to improve in June 1938 causing fears of continued economic slump to decline. Real recovery, however, did not actually arrive until after the spring of 1940 when government spending for war preparations greatly escalated. Very little came from the TNEC's numerous hearings and resulting reports. The 1937 recession and its related debates did much to sidetrack Second New Deal momentum.

---

it is common now to her the people, every where you go say President Roosevelt, has proven to be no diferent from any other President, there all for big business after they get in office ... Today the way people are thinking and talking, if you were to get the nomination in 1936 you will be beation by a great land slide.

Roosevelt Leads the Charge

At his January 1937 inauguration President Franklin Roosevelt, newly reelected despite criticism from some quarters, was feeling strong and set the tone for the next four years by appealing for more liberal reform measures. Roosevelt claimed Social Security, the Wagner Act, and WPA were only a start. He highlighted the need to help impoverished farmers, create fair labor standards, take anti-trust actions, and establish public housing programs to replace the growing slums. The public in turn expected much from the Democratic control in the presidency and Congress (January 20, 1937).

> Four years ago we met to inaugurate a President, the Republic, single-minded in anxiety, stood in spirit here. We dedicated ourselves to the fulfillment of a vision— to speed the time when there would be for all the people that security and peace essential to the pursuit of happiness .... We would not admit that we could not find a way to master economic epidemics just as, after centuries of fatalistic suffering, we had found a way to master epidemics of disease. We refused to leave the problems of our common welfare to be solved by the winds of chance and the hurricanes of disaster ....
>
> A century and a half ago they established the Federal Government in order to promote the general welfare and secure the blessings of liberty to the American people.
>
> Today we invoke those same powers of government to achieve the same objectives ...
>
> In fact, in these last four years, we have made the exercise of all power more democratic; for we have begun to bring private autocratic powers into their proper subordination to the public's government. The legend that they were invincible—above and beyond the processes of a democracy—has been shattered. They have been challenged and beaten ...
>
> By using the new materials of social justice we have undertaken to erect on the old foundations a more enduring structure for the better use of future generations ....
>
> With ... our rediscovered ability to improve our economic order, we have set our feet upon the road of enduring progress ...
>
> But here is the challenge to our democracy: In this nation I see tens of millions of its citizens—a substantial part of its whole population—who at this very moment are denied the greater part of what the very lowest standards of today call the necessities of life.
>
> I see millions of families trying to live on incomes so meager that the pall of family disaster hangs over them day by day.
>
> I see millions whose daily lives in city and on farm continue under conditions labeled indecent by a so-called polite society half a century ago.
>
> I see millions denied education, recreation, and the opportunity to better their lot and the lot of their children.
>
> I see millions lacking the means to buy the products of farm and factory and by their poverty denying work and productiveness to many other millions.
>
> I see one-third of a nation ill-housed, ill-clad, ill-nourished.
>
> It is not in despair that I paint you that picture. I paint it for you in hope—because the Nation, seeing and understanding the injustice in it, proposes to paint it out. We are determined to make every American citizen the subject of his country's interest and concern; and we will never regard any faithful, law-abiding group within or borders as superfluous. The test of our progress is not whether we add more to the abundance of those who have much; it is whether we provide enough for those who have too little ...

Suggested Research Topics

- What were the major goals of the Second New Deal programs? How did they differ from First New Deal objectives? What new people helped form the Second New Deal policies? Did this approach bring greater success to solving the economic crisis?

- What people and organizations supported the Second New Deal programs? How did this political coalition influence later presidential elections in the United States?

- Research the various relief and recovery programs offered by the Second New Deal. What would have happened if Roosevelt had taken the advice of some of his key advisers and kept pushing his plan to reorganize the U.S. Supreme Court, which greatly distracted Congress from New Deal initiatives?

Bibliography

Sources

Andersen, Kristi. *The Creation of a Democratic Majority, 1928–1936.* Chicago: University of Chicago Press, 1979.

Fusfeld, Daniel R. *The Economic Thought of Franklin D. Roosevelt and the Origins of the New Deal.* New York: Columbia University Press, 1956.

McElvaine, Robert S. *The Great Depression: America, 1929–1941.* New York: Time Books, 1993.

McJimsey, George. *The Presidency of Franklin Delano Roosevelt.* Lawrence, KS: University of Kansas Press, 2000.

Olson, James S., ed. *Historical Dictionary of the New Deal: From Inauguration to Preparation for War.* Westport, CT: Greenwood, 1985.

Schlesinger, Arthur M., Jr. *The Coming of the New Deal: The Age of Roosevelt.* Boston: Houghton Mifflin Company, 1988.

Further Reading

Conkin, Paul Keith. *The New Deal.* Arlington Heights, IL: Harlan Davidson, 1992.

Edsforth, Ronald. *The New Deal: America's Response to the Great Depression.* Malden, MA: Blackwell Publishers, 2000.

Leuchtenberg, William E. *Franklin D. Roosevelt and the New Deal, 1932–1940.* New York: Harper & Row, 1963.

"New Deal Network: A Guide to the Great Depression of the 1930s." available from the World Wide Web at http://newdeal .feri.org [cited November 27, 2001].

"Roosevelt University, Center for New Deal Studies." available from the World Wide Web at http://www.roosevelt.edu/newdeal/ index.html [cited February 26, 2002].

Sternsher, Bernard. *Hope Restored: How the New Deal Worked in Town and Country.* Chicago: Ivan R. Dee, 1999.

See Also

Banking; Food; Housing; New Deal (First, and Its Critics)

Photography

1935-1944

From its humble origins in France in the 1830s photography became one of the most compelling means of illustrating the impacts of the Great Depression on the United States. Documentary photography reached a high point in the United States in the 1930s during the Great Depression. No longer working in the studio, photographers went into the field to capture images of common people. The work of federal agency photographers coincided with growing interest in photojournalism and publication of popular magazines such as *Life* and *Look*.

A few pioneers—Matthew Brady, John Hilliers, Adam Clark Vroman, Jacob Riis, Lewis Hine, and Paul Strand—had engaged in photo-documentary projects between 1860 and 1920. What was special about the 1930s was that the federal government funded the photography of the Resettlement Administration (RA), Farm Security Administration (FSA), and the Office of War Information. These projects produced tens of thousands of images of everyday American life and, as never before, illustrated the homes, labor, dress, and conditions faced by millions suffering through the Great Depression.

The federal photos of the 1930s were often simple, stark, and powerful. Taken in black and white and by photographers with superb abilities to frame and compose images, the photographs spoke louder than words. The photos, appearing in newspapers, magazines, and special exhibits, became a trove of images

Chronology:

1935: Congress creates the Resettlement Administration (RA), whose Historical Section mounted a major documentary still photograph project of the Great Depression and the Dust Bowl.

1936: Henry Luce founds *Life,* soon the nation's leading photojournalism magazine.

1937: Congress creates the Farm Security Administration (FSA), successor to the RA. The FSA's Historical Section continues the major documentary still photograph project.

1942: Because of World War II the FSA documentary photograph mission stops and its staff merges into the Office of War Information.

1944: RA and FSA photographic files are transferred to the Library of Congress.

that helped a nation try to make sense out of the new social welfare programs. With the passage of time, they became a national database about this time in history and brought vivid visual documentation to later generations.

Issue Summary

President Franklin Roosevelt introduced the New Deal, a collection of diverse economic and social programs designed to bring relief from the Great Depression, to the American public in the spring of 1933. A key part of the New Deal was to provide economic aid to farmers. Two agencies created to help them were the Resettlement Administration (RA) and the Farm Security Administration (FSA). The photography sponsored by these two New Deal federal organizations and taken during the 1930s would ultimately become a national treasure. Tens of thousands of images documented, for the first time in 140 years of the nation's history, the life, labor, and sorrows of everyday citizens. The federal photographers took photographs that made the sad situation of the rural poor visible to urban dwellers.

Few, if any, photographers had ever focused their lenses on black American cotton pickers, poor white sharecroppers, coal miners in Appalachia, flood victims along the Mississippi and Ohio rivers, Okies and Arkies harvesting agricultural crops in California, or historic houses, grist mills, factories, bridges, and tunnels. From Maine to Washington and even to Puerto Rico and the Virgin Islands, the federal project photographers of the 1930s captured America close-up. Their photographs showed everyday American life in sorrow, achievement, and despair. They documented county fairs, ditch diggers, multi-generational families, and the frightening scenes of the Dust Bowl. They captured images of the ravages of floods and the devastation of the Dust Bowl. These images, when publicized, helped justify New Deal projects such as the Tennessee Valley Authority, the Bureau of Reclamation, and the U.S. Grazing Service.

The RA and FSA projects also became an important nurturing ground for a generation of remarkable photojournalists and photo artists. Some photographers, like Walker Evans and Minor White, with preferences for the arts, stayed only briefly with the federal appointments. Others, like Arthur Rothstein, Dorothea Lange, and Russell Lee, established their careers and went on to other documentary projects. For many Americans the documentary projects of these talented federal photographers lifted photography to the status of an art form.

The photo documentary projects of 1935–1942 were only part of a major commitment of the federal government to the cultural resources of the United States during the Great Depression. Photography was also part of the Historic American Buildings Survey, Historic American Engineering Record, and the Works Progress Administration's Federal Arts and Federal Writers' projects. Never before had the federal government committed so much energy and resources to the arts, and, in this instance, to photography.

The photographs of the RA and FSA fed the rise of photojournalism and contributed to the success of magazines such as *Life* and *Look.* Americans gained a fuller picture of themselves because of the documentary photography of the 1930s. They also became acquainted with simple, direct, even cold and austere photographs that communicated as powerfully and effectively as any written account.

New Deal Agencies and Documentary Photography

In 1935 Congress created the Resettlement Administration (RA) with Rexford Guy Tugwell, a professor of economics at Columbia University and a member of President Franklin D. Roosevelt's (served 1933–1945) "brain trust," (a close advisory group) as the head of the new office. The RA was originally established to help the rural poor who were overlooked by the major New Deal farm agency, the Agricultural Adjustment Administration (AAA). The RA was to grant low-cost loans and assistance to sharecroppers and impoverished farmers, construct model communities for resettlement of migrant laborers and displaced farmers, assist in clean up of polluted rivers and flood control, reclaim eroded land, and build temporary camps for displaced farmers and farm workers. The RA was the major New Deal agency to move farmers off sub-marginal land and convert that land to non-agricultural uses. Displaced farmers were to be relocated on productive soil and have arrangements available where they could eventually buy the land.

Tugwell realized that to carry out its charges in the face of conservative public criticism the RA would have to rally public support for its projects. Tugwell knew the general public held little awareness for the problems of America's neediest, for example the tenant farmers. So Tugwell established the Historical Section in the RA's Division of Information. He charged it with photographing then publishing a portrayal of the crisis of poverty, despair, and conditions of the land itself. At the heart of his original goal was a propaganda effort to sensitize the public to the needs of numerous portions of the American population. At the time information made available to the public was most often collected and distributed in reports full of facts and figures. Instead Tugwell wanted faces and places pictured for all to see, without the distraction of other data.

The role of the Historical Section was to secure documentation of social and land conditions through photographs, hence the term "photodocumentary." Much of the effort of the Historical Section thus focused on rural, impoverished parts of the country. Tugwell named Roy E. Stryker, his former student and teaching colleague at Columbia University, to administer the Historical Section.

Although not a photographer, Roy Stryker grasped the value of documentary still photographs, both to illustrate to Americans the conditions that confronted the RA as well as to show how the projects of the New Deal responded to wretched conditions and human need. Stryker was ideally qualified for his pioneering assignment due to his temperament, editorial experience with photographs as sociological tools, and deeply sympathetic knowledge and understanding of the rural life. Possessing almost a missionary zeal, Stryker set out to capture all aspects of American life.

The visual history Stryker's photographers captured portrayed fear, sadness, and desperation, but also determination that not even the Great Depression could kill. Because of the quality of photographers hired and because Stryker sent them to regions such as the Great Plains, West, and South—areas not yet covered by the major news organizations—the photographs were widely published. The photos were published in newspapers nationally as well as influential magazines including *Life, Look,* and *Survey Graphic.* During the first two years of their work the photographers felt almost an emergency-like need to tell the tale of the nation's rural problems and to make the rest of the nation understand. By 1937 and thereafter they would be able to tell more positive sides of the story of American life.

Although hard to gauge, perhaps partly because of the early photographs taken by Stryker's people, the Bankhead-Jones Farm Tenancy Act became law on July 22, 1937. After President Roosevelt signed the measure, he established the Farm Security Administration (FSA) to carry out its provisions of aiding tenant farmers with rehabilitation loans and conservation programs on sub-marginal lands. The FSA was within the large and impersonal U.S. Department of Agriculture. The previously autonomous Resettlement Administration was absorbed into the FSA and underwent a major change. Rexford Tugwell, always a protector of Stryker's program, resigned as administrator but Stryker's watchdog nature prevailed, although his photographers had to come and go depending on available funds.

Field Assignment

Roy Stryker, between the years of 1935 and 1941, had at any one time, two to six photographers to send into the field on assignment. Before sending anyone out Stryker meticulously reviewed his or her assignment. He required each photographer to read about and research his or her assigned area. For example, Carl Mydans reported before an assignment of photographing cotton fields in the South that, not only did he research the area, but Stryker also followed with instruction on the history of cotton production. Stryker had an encyclopedic knowledge of socioeconomic forces at work in various regions and he also loved to teach and did so with great enthusiasm.

For each assignment Stryker always outlined the types of pictures to be taken. For example, on a small town assignment the outline might read: General notes for pictures needed for files: Small towns: Stores—outside views; inside views; goods on shelves; people buying; displays; people coming out of stores; cars, horses, buggies.

A photograph taken by Arthur Rothstein in 1935. Rothstein and others in the Historical Section photographed anything interesting and vital during the Great Depression: from people and road signs to the weather and barber shops. (The Library of Congress.)

He called the outlines "shooting scripts." Sometimes they were more detailed, sometimes more vague and the photographer could then elaborate in his or her own unique way. Stryker asked his people to capture the "significant detail." A charismatic, persuasive, energetic man, Stryker would always review the entire scope of the goals of the assignment immediately before a photographer's departure. Reportedly, both Stryker and his photographers enjoyed the enthusiastic sessions, which more resembled locker room pep talks.

Assignments were frequently for extended time periods generally six to nine months. Photographers sent film back to Stryker in Washington, DC, where it was developed. He took the prints home at night, studied them, and continuously gave feedback through phone calls or mail. At the end of the assignment, Stryker and the photographer would assess the experience during lengthy sessions.

Stryker was an "enabler," that is, he not only provided educational and psychological support but the cameras and money to travel. He cleared bureaucratic red tape and guarded his artistic photographers from Congress who constantly tried to cut or curtail the program.

Although Stryker specified the type of pictures he needed from an area, he also established in the early days the idea that there was no such thing as wasted film or time. Not only did photographers shoot specific types of photos, but they also had freedom to photograph anything and to shoot anywhere in the United States. They photographed anything that seemed interesting and vital: people, road signs, the weather, barber shops. John Collier, Jr., an FSA photographer, once said that his assignment was to photograph the smell of burning leaves and apple pie in New England in the fall. The dedicated, talented photographers of Stryker's Historical Section seemed to understand the character of life and record it well. The photographs from the field produced a visual record unique in its breadth and quality.

The RA/FSA Photographers

The First Wave. Roy Stryker in the spring and summer of 1935, carefully considered the type of photographers he would need for these special photographic assignments. Stryker looked more for idealism wrapped up in talent than persons with established reputations—reputations that he feared would get in the way of the project. He recruited a remarkable pool of photographers for his Historical Section. The first person hired by Stryker was Arthur Rothstein, a former student of Stryker's at Columbia University. At approximately that same time, July 1935, Stryker hired Dorothea Lange although he had never met her. Likewise Ben Shahn came to Stryker's attention.

Rothstein progressed quickly as a photographer and was in the field within months. In the spring of 1936 he headed to Cimarron County in the Oklahoma Panhandle to one of the most wind-eroded areas in the country. Here he took a photograph that came to represent the devastation of the land within the Dust Bowl. The photograph, *Dust Storm, Cimarron County, 1936,* caught a farmer and his two small sons pressing against the wind to reach shelter in a shed, half buried in sand.

Rothstein headed north to Pennington County in the South Dakota Badlands, where he took another famous photograph, *The Skull,* which showed a cow's skull on parched land, strongly hinting that the desert soon would claim the overgrazed land. Both photographs were widely published in newspapers. Within weeks a congressional committee went to the Badlands to investigate. Rothstein spent much of his assignment time in the Midwest. Like the others who joined him, he had a respect and understanding of situations he encountered.

Dorothea Lange, eventually the best known FSA photographer of all, had been documenting the condition of migrant workers in California for the California Division of Rural Rehabilitation when hired by Stryker. Being on the West Coast she did not meet Stryker personally for nine months. Lange worked primarily in the West, Southwest, and South and became known as the supreme humanist among the FSA photographers. Her photographs were moving visual statements full of compassion. In March 1936 she happened on a pea pickers camp in California's Nipomo Valley were she photographed a desperate mother and her children. The photograph became known as the *Migrant Mother,* perhaps the most famous FSA photograph. The *San Francisco News* ran a story accompanied by two other Lange photographs about the camp on March 10, 1936. Relief authorities immediately sent supplies and food to the camp.

Ben Shahn was not technically part of the Historical Section, instead was with the Special Skills Division of the RA. An artist whose abilities in painting were widely recognized, Shahn had been introduced to photography in the early 1930s by photographer Walker Evans, with whom he shared a studio apartment in Greenwich Village. Although lacking technical ability, Shahn possessed an uncanny awareness of social jus-

tice that his photographs reflected. Shahn's photographs made their way to the Historic Section. In that first year it was Shahn who convinced Stryker that the photographs could be used as propaganda to inspire social action. In the summer of 1938, the only time Shahn was actually on Stryker's payroll, he traveled to central Ohio and took a wealth of documentary photographs all composed as if in a painting.

The Ranks Increase. Those joining with the Historical Section in the fall and winter of 1935 were Theo Jung, Walker Evans, and Carl Mydans. Paul Carter also joined the staff in late 1935, bringing with him an expansive technical knowledge of photographic equipment. He did not, however, possess the "eye" for photographing subjects. Stryker was saved from the embarrassment of firing him when he left to open a camera store. Jung had begun his photographic career strictly as an amateur but on the strength of his portfolio detailing conditions of the slums in Washington, DC, he was hired in September 1935.

Jung traveled to Garrett County, Maryland, Brown County, Indiana, and Jackson County, Ohio, on assignment. His main interest was people rather than their living conditions and his best work was with the elderly and children. Stryker criticized Jung for not taking enough photographs, for not knowing enough about his subject matter, and for not being totally proficient with his camera. Jung was let go in May 1936.

Carl Mydans, who had already been working on a book about suburban resettlement for the RA, was reassigned to the Historical Section when the book project folded. Mydans was a skilled and understanding photojournalist. His photographs of Washington, DC, Cincinnati, New Jersey, and Maryland were taken before he joined Stryker's group, but were used to fill in gaps in those areas of the RA's archives. Mydans took a long assignment throughout the South, learning of the struggles of the rural poor. He stayed with the Historical Section for less than a year before joining the staff of the new magazine *Life* in October 1936.

Walker Evans, a true artist with the camera, set the standard for perfection. Evans went directly from private practice into the RA and then into Stryker's section. From the start friction existed between Stryker and Evans. Evans was totally unconcerned with telling stories with his camera or producing photographs for a particular purpose. He was completely unwilling to compromise his standards on any level. Evans took most of his photographs with an 8 by 10 view camera.

When Evans went out on assignment he would often disappear for months at a time and have no

Major Writings

Let Us Now Praise Famous Men

In the summer of 1936 James Agee, a writer for *Fortune,* gained the assignment to write about an Alabama sharecropper and his family, a portrait of impoverished life in the rural south. Agee secured the services of Walker Evans, who took a leave as a federal photographer from the FSA to travel with Agee and take documentary still photographs for the article. Although the editors of *Fortune* rejected Agee's article, Agee and Evans continued their collaboration and, in 1941, Houghton-Mifflin company published, in five hundred pages, *Let Us Now Praise Famous Men.* The book explored the wretched lives of three families. Thirty-one photographs were inserted before the text so that they might not be construed as illustrations. Evans used close-up photos to capture the features of the people, grain in the wood walls of their dwellings, and wrinkles in their clothing.

All but the most perceptive critics ignored or found fault with the book. It sold fewer than six hundred copies the first year and sales dropped to less than 50 copies a year. The book was not forgotten, however, and rare copies passed from hand to hand.

In 1960 Houghton-Mifflin issued a new edition, in which Evans increased the portfolio to 62 images. With this edition the book became recognized as an American classic and became one of the most famous visual and documentary accounts of the Great Depression.

---

contact with Stryker, who preferred keeping in close contact with his photographers. Evans proved unmanageable for Stryker, who had to answer to the government bureaucracy. Nevertheless when he did send photographs back they were flawless and intellectually amazing.

Evans took a leave of absence from the Historical Section in 1936 to work on a project with author James Agee for *Fortune.* They settled into the life in Hale County, Alabama, where eventually Evans photographs and Agee's words became an American classic of the Great Depression—*Let Us Now Praise Famous Men* (see sidebar).

Evans and Stryker permanently parted ways in mid-1937. Evans, along with Ben Shahn, were the two most artistically influential photographers of the FSA photographers.

When Carl Mydans decided to move on from the government project to *Life* magazine in 1936, Russell Lee took his place. Lee was the perfect FSA photographer. Dedicated to publicizing the rough conditions faced by many Americans, he headed to Michigan, Wisconsin, and Minnesota. He considered some of his best work a series of photographs on the problems faced by "cut-over" farmers. Where once there were lush pine forests, logging companies had cut everything in sight destroying the usability of the land. The land was then sold to unsuspecting farmers who could barely scratch out an existence.

Lee's best-known work was in Pie Town, New Mexico, a town along U.S. 60, which he stumbled onto. The photographs of Pie Town documented a community of people working together to pull themselves out of the Depression. The Pie Town series appeared in the October 1941 issue of *U.S. Camera,* the first series of photographs by one FSA photographer to appear in a serious journal of photography. Lee would later moved with Stryker to the Office of War Information (OWI) in 1942.

John Vachon, an unemployed graduate student in Washington, DC, in 1936, was delighted to be hired by Stryker as an "assistant messenger" to deliver papers between government buildings. Vachon advanced to junior file clerk and, inspired by the staff photographers, began to take an interest in photography. He progressed to junior file clerk "with a camera."

Vachon explored the faces of Lange's photographs, the perfection of Evans, and the insightfulness of Shahn. He began to photograph around Washington, DC, then made his way to the Midwest and, by 1940, he was an official junior photographer. Dorothea Lange described his uniqueness as sensitivity and the ability to get to the place where it "hurts a little."

Wolcott, Delano, and Collier. The last three photographers to join the Historical Section were Marion Post Wolcott, Jack Delano, and John Collier, Jr. All joined the group when Stryker's program was well along and he knew just what directions to move in. Wolcott's first assignment was in mining areas of West Virginia, and she later worked throughout the South. Her work covered a wide range of living conditions, contrasting the rich with the poor. She produced some of the finest photography of children in the FSA file.

Jack Delano joined the FSA photographers in 1940, when Arthur Rothstein left to work at *Look* magazine. Delano had worked for the Federal Arts Project documenting the living conditions of miners in Schuylkill County, Pennsylvania. With the Historical Section, Delano did an in-depth study of life in Greene County, Georgia. When he left Georgia he traveled up the coast covering migrant worker camps all the way to Maine. This trip produced some of his best work. In 1941 Stryker sent Delano on a short trip to the Virgin Islands and Puerto Rico. Delano, however, remained in Puerto Rico, all the while sending back photographs to Stryker.

John Collier, Jr., began his association with Stryker in the summer of 1941 and he would move with Stryker to the OWI in 1942, and later to Standard Oil. While with the Historical Section Collier contributed coverage of the Amish, Portuguese fishermen in Rhode Island, and Mexican Americans in Taos, New Mexico.

An Intimate Vision

From the start of the photography projects Stryker placed high value on the power of visual images. The photographs enlightened the American people and raised its social consciousness. Rather than intruders the photographers became friends and were able to interpret the lives of the unemployed, dispossessed, migrants, tenant farmers, and sharecroppers. The faces of the people and the nature and problems of the land wove together to tell the country a story. The photographs avoided the sensational and sentimental but presented a reality and feeling of truth. It became easier to understand the upheavals caused by economic and climatic disasters.

The FSA photographs became powerful tools in the passage of New Deal legislation. They successfully raised America's empathy and the U.S. Congress funded programs at President Roosevelt's request to help people who had lost the ability to help themselves. For example, the FSA loans to farmers under the Bankhead-Jones Farm Tenancy Act, between 1937 and 1947, totaled $293 million and went to 47,104 farmers. In the photographs the nation saw an expressive and realistic portrayal of America's needy. Lange's poverty stricken "migrant mother," Rothstein's Dust Bowl farmer with his sons fleeing for cover in an Oklahoma dust storm, and Evan's photographs of Alabama sharecroppers all spoke volumes. The FSA photographs came to symbolize a tenacity and courage of people attempting to survive in the harsh years of the Great Depression.

The New Small Cameras

The young idealistic and highly talented FSA photographers adapted quickly to the use of new small

Dorothea Lange's most famous photograph, "Migrant Mother." Photographs like this one were instrumental in educating politicians and the public of the needs of impoverished Americans. (The Library of Congress.)

camera techniques. Documentary photography was revolutionized with the introduction of small film cameras from Germany, such as the 35mm Leica and Contax plus the slightly larger Rolleiflex that Dorothea Lange used. The FSA was one of the first major projects to use the 35mm camera extensively.

Before these cameras the primary camera for documentary or press photography, was a large camera, the Speed Graphic. It required adjustments to be made after each exposure, resulting in considerable time for each photograph. The subject was almost always aware that a photograph was being taken and as a result photos with this camera often tended to be static and unnatural.

The new cameras could easily be fit into a pocket and carried most anywhere. They had faster lenses and larger film capacity that allowed a more natural and an unobtrusive progression of pictures to be taken. The 1930s faces of people finding their way through the Depression were candid and real, not posed, thanks to the new camera technology.

A Farm Security Administration photograph of a Hungarian miner and his wife on their porch, taken by Ben Shahn, a painter turned photographer. (The Library of Congress.)

First International Photographic Exposition

In 1938 the American public first glimpsed Ron E. Stryker's three-year-old project with the Historical Section. The most meaningful and moving part of the First International Photographic Exposition was a series of photographs of the faces and places of 1930s America. Held in New York City's Grand Central Palace, approximately five hundred visitors were so moved by the images as to leave comments in the suggestion box. All but a few were positive and thought provoking.

The public response to the exhibit was overwhelmingly positive. They believed it was time that people in America saw this side of life in their nation. Grace M. Mayer, writing in a pamphlet *The Bitter Years: 1935–1941* for the Museum of Modern Art, New York, recounts the following suggestion box notes: "These show that photography with a purpose may not necessarily be lacking in art or interest." "It's about time these conditions were eradicated—show more and people will understand more." "The Awful Truth (Real Awful)." "Why the hell isn't something done about it?" "Wonderful Pictures, but Am I My Brother's Keeper?" (quoted in Edward Steichen's *The Bitter Years: 1935–1941*, 1963, p. vi).

Works Progress Administration Photographic Projects

Other New Deal agencies also employed photographers and produced an important visual legacy from the 1930s. The Historic American Buildings Survey (HABS) and the Historic American Engineering Record (HAER) were divisions of the Works Progress Administration (WPA). Both were concerned with documenting nationally important buildings and engineering projects. In addition to measured drawings and textual research, each feature was carefully photographed. These images, most of them taken between 1935 and 1942 with large format cameras, are preserved in the Library of Congress. A number of the photographs are now digitized and available on the World Wide Web through the American Memory Project (http://memory.loc.gov/ammem/amhome.html).

The Works Progress Administration also employed photographers to work in other divisions. Photographers took thousands of images for the state guidebook series of the Federal Writer's Project. In the WPA Art Division, photographers taught photography, mounted exhibits, and expanded understanding about photos as works of art. Additionally, the photographs of HABS, HAER, and the WPA proved highly useful in historic preservation programs to stabilize, restore, and interpret the nation's cultural history following World War II (1939–1945).

Set Apart

In all, up to 70 percent of all federal agencies used pictures in one way or another during the 1930s. The work of the FSA Historical Section was set apart from the others by three factors. First, the FSA photographers were highly professional and talented, able to capture remarkable qualities. Secondly, even though their work was frequently used for propaganda for the agency, it was propaganda only in the most truthful way. It focused on real problems and hinted at real solutions. The photographers were also given artistic license to capture anything that seemed vital. Often those pictures had nothing to do with the agency. Third, the staff understood their work was to have a wide scope, a sense of history, for instance not just focusing on poor farmers but showing the relationship between rural poverty and improper use of the land. Other agencies had thousands of photographs of their agency in action, but the FSA's photographs became a national historic treasure because of their sense of history.

Success of Photojournalism Magazines

Illustrated newspapers became popular in the mid-1800s, but printers had no way to reproduce photographs until development of the half-tone process in the 1880s. The etching of a photograph on a metal plate contributed rapidly to use of photographs in newspapers and magazines, both for stories and for advertising. The first important American photo magazine was *Life,* a publication conceived and financed by Henry Luce, founder of *Time.* By the mid-1930s Luce was convinced that pictures, as well as words, could tell a compelling story. He printed the first issue of *Life* in 1936, to enthusiastic acceptance.

The FSA photographers understood their role as stimulators of social reform. The photo magazines, however, were more interested in finding drama in everyday life than to plead any cause. The photographers for *Life* were young, aggressive, had news coverage experience, and prided themselves on the versatility to cover anything. Four photographers made up *Life's* staff when it began publication: Margaret Bourke-White, Thomas McAvoy, Alfred Eisenstaedt, and Peter Stackpole. Carl Mydans, FSA photographer, later joined the staff in 1936.

Margaret Bourke-White, while on the staff of *Fortune,* created some of the first photographic essays ever done in the United States. She completed a pho-

More About...
New Deal Agencies and Photography

The following agencies played a crucial role in promoting photography during the Great Depression.

- The Resettlement Administration (RA) was created in 1935 in the Department of Agriculture. The Farm Security Administration (FSA) succeeded it in 1937. The two agencies by 1945 created 77,000 black-and-white documentary still photographs and 644 color documentary still photographs.

- The Historic American Buildings Survey (HABS) was part of the Works Progress Administration, 1935 to 1942. HABS employed architects to produce measured drawings of significant buildings and hired photographers to take documentary photographs of the structures and their details.

- The Historic American Engineering Record (HAER) was part of the Works Progress Administration, 1935 to 1942. HAER's employees produced measured drawings and photographs of nationally significant engineering features.

- The Office of War Information (OWI) was created in 1942 to document mobilization and events related to World War II. The photographers of the Farm Security Administration were transferred to the OWI because of their skills and success in producing documentary still photographs.

tographic story on life in Montana boomtowns that appeared in *Life's* first issue. That issue's cover showcased one of the Montana photographs.

Bourke-White collaborated with author Erskine Caldwell for a book about the Depression-weary South entitled *You Have Seen their Faces* (1937). Together they traveled across nine southern states explaining with word and photographs what they found. *You Have Seen their Faces* received prominent attention in the magazine. In her 20 years with *Life* Bourke-White published over one hundred photographic essays on wide ranging topics from the praying mantis' life cycle to the Korean conflict.

Thomas McAvoy had spent 10 years as a newspaper photographer, then as a freelance photographer before coming to *Life*. Before joining *Life* Alfred Eisenstaedt, a German immigrant, produced dramatic photographs of Italian dictator Benito Mussolini, and Peter Stackpole had established himself as a freelance news photographer for *Time* magazine.

The term "photojournalism" was coined in 1938 to describe a story told primarily with pictures. The photojournalism magazines were considered editor-dominated because a photographer had to take many photographs on each assignment, then let an editor and an art director decide how those photographs would be used.

In 1938 Gardner Cowles created *Look,* a similar although less glamorous magazine than *Life*. Both magazines, in competition with each other, excelled at offering readers harsh scenes of the Great Depression as well as common interest stories. By the late 1930s the United States had several competing photojournalism magazines. These included *Life, Look, Focus, Click,* and *Pic.*

Much of the popularity of photojournalism was due to the growing interest of Americans in keeping current with news events. The rapid spread of radio stations in the 1920s, the advent of newsreels, and the emergence of photojournalism, especially in magazine format, were all evidence of the literacy and interests of Americans. Many of the stories of the 1930s were about big events: construction of the Grand Coulee and Bonneville dams in the Pacific Northwest, the projects of the Tennessee Valley authority, Dust Bowl conditions on the High Plains, poverty in the South, and military build-up in Germany and events leading to war by 1939 were all subjects that captured the public interest. The photojournalist was well positioned to meet this need.

Contributing Forces

Rise of Documentary Photography

In the 1880s Peter Henry Emerson, an English medical student and amateur photographer, began making images and writing about a revolutionary approach to producing photos. Emerson advised taking pictures outdoors, not in a studio. He proposed sharp focus on an object, subjects, or event and letting the rest of the background remain vague, even out of focus. He pressed for capturing people and scenes on film in their natural condition, not with props, artificial backdrops, or studio lighting.

Emerson became an advocate of pictorial photography and summed many of his views in *Naturalistic Photography for Students of the Art* (1889). Many of Emerson's followers attempted to paint pictures with a camera, using a lens, film, and work in the darkroom to craft a work of art not unlike a watercolor or painting. Darkroom work on negatives was a hallmark of pictorial photography.

In 1899 Alfred Stieglitz, an American photographer and founder of the Camera Club of New York, described scenic photography from an artist's point of view. Some of his favorite pictures were of night scenes actually captured at low light conditions, sunsets, and approaching storms. In 1903 Stieglitz launched with a few friends what he called the Photo-Secession Movement. He believed in high aesthetic standards and the value of pictorial photography, but rejected manual manipulation of negatives or trying to turn a photo into a painting.

Pictorial photography was neither documentary nor motivated by social concern. Documentary photography refers to black-and-white or color photographic images that are realistic, factual, and useful as a historic document. Social reform through documentary photography used elements of both Emerson's pictorial techniques and Stieglitz's Photo-Secession ideas. Like the pictorialists, most social reform documentation work was carried on outside of a studio but, like the Photo-Secessionists, the documentary picture-taker did not manipulate the negative. The goal was to capture life realistically. Edward Sheriff Curtis, taking documentary photographs of American Indians between 1899 and 1930 for his 20 volume work, *The North American Indian,* leaned toward the pictorialist style.

Early practitioners of documentary photography included Matthew Brady, who took vivid scenes during the Civil War, and John Hilliers who photographed the Powell expedition's 1871 voyage down the Colorado River and through the Grand Canyon. Further evidence of this activity appeared in the 1890s in the photographic projects of Adam Clark Vroman. Owner of a California bookstore and camera store, Vroman mounted several field-based expeditions. In 1896 he photographed all of the Spanish missions in California; many were in ruins but that did not deter his activity. For five years he annually photographed the "Snake Dance," "Flute Ceremony," and other religious activities of the Hopi.

In 1899, as a member of an expedition funded by the Smithsonian Institution, Vroman photographed the Rio Grand pueblos. Vroman also took hundreds of photographs of Native Americans engaged in daily activi-

Alfred Stieglitz poses in an art gallery in December 1936. Stieglitz was the founder of the Camera Club of New York and was part of a movement to approach photography as art that can be taken outside of the studio, known as the Photo-Secession movement. (*UPI/Corbis-Bettmann. Reproduced by permission.*)

ties. Few of Vroman's photographs were published before his death in 1916; most of his work was to fulfill his own interests, but he had anticipated the power of the camera in documenting the human experience.

Jacob Riis (1848–1914), a Danish immigrant who arrived in the United States in 1870, became the best-known documentary photographer by the end of the nineteenth century. Riis had several difficult years in the Northeast, working as a peddler, farm laborer, miner, and carpenter. He saw life from the bottom; he was often unemployed, hungry, and homeless.

Due to the fact that he was bright and learned English rapidly Riis, in 1877, found a job as a police reporter for the New York *Tribune*. He soon gained a reputation for his coverage of human disasters and slums. So moved was he by conditions in the urban tenements that he wrote *How the Other Half Lives* (1890), *Children of the Poor* (1892), and *The Battle With the Slum* (1902).

Riis carried his camera into the alleys, tenements, basements, and air shafts of New York's slums. He ignited chemicals to produce flash pictures and published images of the horrible living conditions endured by tens of thousands in the United States. Riis also wrote vivid captions for his photographs. For example, one picture of a man sleeping in a basement on boards resting on top of two barrels was entitled "A Cave Dweller-Slept in this Cellar Four Years." Riis used his writing and photography to press for social reforms.

Lewis Wickes Hine (1874–1940) began in 1901 to use photographs to aid his teaching at the Ethical Culture School in New York City. He took pictures of impoverished immigrants, child laborers in cotton mills in New England and North Carolina. Hine set a style for documentary photography until to his death in 1940. He had wanted to show both the things that needed correcting and the things that should be appreciated.

Paul Strand (1890–1976), one of Hine's students, and a photographer who took his work to Alfred Stieglitz for criticism, worked with what some termed "brutally direct" subjects. Strand served as a cinematographer for director Paul Lorentz's 1936 documentary about the Dust Bowl, "The Plow that Broke the Plains."

Another photographer who gained international attention for his documentary photography was Eugene Atget (1857–1927), a Frenchman. Atget photographed Paris's monuments, old churches, the rag pickers' quarters, the fairs, shop windows, boulevard scenes, the farthest streets, the humblest homes, and the interiors of all types of houses. Atget also photographed carts, wagons, coaches, omnibuses, and automobiles as well as intricate features of architecture.

Once photographers got out of the studio and into society, they had the means to make their work socially relevant. Riis, Atget, and other photographers with a journalistic eye helped pave the way in the early twentieth century for the major photographic projects of the Great Depression.

Perspectives

Should the Government Be in the Business of Taking Photographs?

Public opinion concerning the FSA photography program ranged widely as public opinion in the United States commonly does. One segment, first glimpsing the conditions of their fellow Americans in 1936

through FSA photographs published nationally in newspapers, responded with shock. Some called for poverty to be eliminated immediately. They believed the government should act quickly just as it had in 1933 to save a banking system in crisis. The public grappled with trying to understand the wretched conditions and called for more photographs to be published. Others looked through an artistic eye and realized these photographs were art with a purpose. While some appreciated the quality of the photographs, however, they questioned if the government was responsible for taking care of everyone.

Some individuals showed hostility toward the government complaining that the government was wasting their tax dollars on photography. A relatively sizeable portion of the population believed the subjects of the FSA photographs were hopelessly poor because they did little for themselves to pull themselves out of poverty. These people thought the photographs most likely exaggerated the situations and the government should not bail out everyone who was in economic difficulty. Yet others resented attention being called to problems of dreary conditions in their locality.

The photographs did serve a useful purpose despite the various viewpoints. By 1936 the plight of tenant farmers, farmers who pay a landowner for use of the land to farm, weighed heavy on some of the country's leaders. The photographs only tended to affirm what they saw as a desperate need and called them to action. That year President Franklin Roosevelt appointed a Special Committee on Farm Tenancy. Senator John Bankhead of Alabama and Representative Marvin Jones of Texas drafted tenancy legislation. Numerous congressmen debated ways to improve the rural poor situation. On the other hand, congressmen often considered the photographs from their own district as hostile publicity and a threat to their reelection. These congressmen did not want to see problems revealed in their own backyard.

Views of the FSA Photographers and Roy Stryker

Generally the FSA photographers operated with a zeal and conviction believing their photographs could prompt social change. They reflected the enthusiasm and energy of their administrative leader, Roy Stryker. For the most part photographers felt Stryker was a gifted teacher and had the ability to understand aspects of the photographs both seen and unseen sent back to him. Most viewed him as an enabler, providing guidance, field money, and protection from politicians and officials who attempted to cut the budget of the Historical Section.

Most importantly, as Arthur Rothstein noted, Stryker never restricted what pictures the photographers could take—he believed there was no such thing as wasted film or time. John Vachon, who stayed with Stryker longer than any other photographer, interpreted Stryker's intent as allowing his people to photograph anything they really "saw," and to gather photographs covering many aspects of American life, not just of those people in miserable conditions.

On the other hand Walker Evans saw Stryker as a person who did not understand the artistic approach to photography. He often referred to Stryker as just trying to fill a file. Evans, however, admitted he himself was uncompromisingly independent and almost felt sorry for Stryker trying to put up with him. Ben Shahn also criticized Stryker for punching holes in countless negatives that he did not think would ever be needed. Dorothea Lange recognized weaknesses in the organization but believed these weaknesses just made it a human organization. She and Jack Delano viewed their time with the section as a tremendous learning experience and a chance to help less fortunate individuals in society.

At a Glance
Photographs Online

Photographs made by the Office of War Information Collection of the Farm Security Administration (FSA) are available on the Library of Congress website. The collection is part of the library's American Memory program. The main part of the collection includes 164,000 black-and-white negatives and 1,600 color negatives taken during the last days of the project. Color photography became generally widespread after 1935 with the development of Kodachrome and other color films. The RA and FSA photographers secured a limited number of color images near the end of the Great Depression. In 2001 over 112,000 of the images were available online at http://memory.loc.gov/ammem/fsowhome.html.

Impact

Films and Books Spawned by FSA Photographers

The philosophy behind the FSA photographic project, to educate then stimulate reform, was the spearhead of several classic documentary films. Congress abolished the United States Film Service, headed by Pare Lorentz, in 1941, but not before the production of famed Depression era films. They included *The Plow that Broke the Plains* (1936),*The River* (1937), and *Fight for Life* (1940), all Pare Lorentz epics; Jori's Ivens *Power and the Land* (1940), and Raymond Evans' *The Home Place* (1941). While working on the film adaptation of John Steinbeck's novel *The Grapes of Wrath* John Ford sought out Dorothea Lange's photographs as primary source material.

Lange and her husband Paul Schuster Taylor made artistic use of her FSA photographs in an *American Exodus: A Record of Human Erosion* (1939). The book was a study on migrant labor. *Walker Evans: American Photographs* (1938) and Evans' work with James Agee to produce the masterpiece, *Let Us Now Praise Famous Men* (1941) were related to the FSA web.

Other related books illustrated with and inspired by FSA photographs were Archibald MacLeish's *Land of the Tree* (1938), Herman Clarence Nixon's *Forty Acres and Steel Mules* (1938); Sherwood Anderson's *Home Town* (1940); *12 Million Black Voices* (1941) by Richard Wright and Edwin Rosskam; and, Arthur Paper's *Tenants of the Almighty* (1943).

The War Years and Beyond

The documentary photography of the Great Depression created a remarkable visual history of the United States. Government photographers captured on film sources of everyday life, especially of minorities, poor people, and dwellers of rural areas. By 1941 the nation was gearing up for war and the government's photography needs turned to showing off the wartime buildup. The Office of War Information (OWI), created in 1942, served essentially as a propaganda agency during World War II.

During 1942 and 1943 the OWI had two photographic units. Roy Stryker's FSA Historical Section was absorbed into OWI. Stryker still headed the department and a few of his FSA photographers followed him: Russell Lee, John Vachon, and John Collier, Jr. The second division was the New Bureau, but the two were merged in 1943. The OWI photographers were sent out on missions for the purpose of illustrating the best of American know how. The photographers in both units captured America's war mobilization, focusing on such topics as aircraft factories and women in the labor force.

In 1943 Stryker prepared to leave the OWI to become director of photography for Standard Oil of New Jersey. Paul Vanderbilt, a curator of collections, was responsible for organizing Stryker's FSA negatives and prints. They were then boxed up with their ultimate destination unknown, perhaps even the government dump in Virginia. Only direct intervention at the last minute saved the collection. Poet Archibald MacLeish, an old friend of Stryker's and serving as Librarian of Congress, saw that the boxes came to the Library of Congress where they found a permanent home. In 1944 the Library of Congress received 277,000 negatives and 77,000 prints, the work of the Historical Section of RA, FSA, and OWI, collectively known as the FSA/OWI Collection.

In addition to the collections finding a permanent home and lasting use, a number of photographers involved in the federal projects went on to distinguished careers as teachers, writers, photojournalists, and artists. The RA and FSA were fertile ground for nurturing talent. Dorothea Lange and Walker Evans were among 19 masters who were selected by Beaumont and Nancy Newhall and presented in their book *Masters of Photography.* Arthur Rothstein was the Technical Director of Photography for *Look* magazine and John Vachon was also with that publication. Carl Mydans joined *Life* magazine at its inception in 1936 and was still with the magazine in the 1960s. Ben Shahn became a major figure in American art, often including people from his FSA photographs in his paintings and murals. Jack Delano became the general manager of the radio and television service of the Department of Education of the Commonwealth of Puerto Rico. He composed music that was regularly performed by the Puerto Rico Symphony Orchestra. Russell Lee continued to make important contributions to documentary photography. He joined the faculty of the Department of Fine Arts at the University of Texas where he remained until retirement in 1974.

Art and Photojournalism

The FSA project produced powerful artistic statements amid an accurate photographic record. Although artistic expression was not the original goal of FSA photographers, their work introduced the general public to the modern notion that photography could be an art form. During the 1940s and 1950s the idea grew that photography itself was an artistic medium to be seriously studied. Galleries began selling photography and art museums took photographs into their permanent collections. Photograph collecting, publishing, and exhibiting increased across the nation.

In 1962 the Museum of Modern Art in New York City organized a showing of FSA photography titled "The Bitter Years: 1935–1941." Reportedly when Stryker first saw the exhibit, although only the finest photographs were hung, he was dismayed that none of the later, more upbeat, everyday life photographs were exhibited.

The power of images taken by documentary photographers during the Great Depression contributed significantly to the rise of photojournalism, seen in popular magazines such as *Life* and *Look,* and weekly releases of black-and-white newsreel footage of current events that played at motion picture theaters across the nation. Americans became accustomed to seeing current events. A byproduct of the documentary work of the New Deal was the rise of photojournalism as a profession.

The use of documentary photojournalism to illustrate social concerns was prevalent during the tumultuous 1960s and 1970s. The socially concerned of those decades found support in the private sector rather than government agencies. Unlike in the 1930s, photodocumentaries of civil rights and anti-war movements were often charges against the government and the American culture itself.

The interest in photographs as artistic expression and a form of journalism continued throughout the twentieth century. Photography education opportunities abounded in universities, high schools, technical schools, and recreation programs. Commercial photography interests surged, especially in large cultural centers in the 1980s and 1990s with gallery exhibitions, books, catalogues, and photodocumentary projects. One example was a 1987–1988 large-scale documentary photography project entitled "Changing Chicago." The project involved 33 photographers and was in part inspired by the FSA photographers' work in Chicago.

No other nation secured a documentation of everyday life like that developed during the Great Depression in the United States. The work of Stryker and his staff can be examined in the Prints and Photographs Division of the Library of Congress. There are approximately 80,000 captioned prints and 170,000 unprinted negatives. Books organized by topics, such as transportation, medicine, and by specific states have expanded the public's awareness of the FSA photographers' legacy and the range and diversity of the collection. Also, at the beginning of the twenty-first century, the photographs were available as digitized images in the American Memory Project (see http://memory.loc.gov/ammem/fsowhome.html). The photographs of the 1930s provide a unique historical record of the United States available to people all over the world.

Notable People

John Collier, Jr. (1913–1992). Focused on painting when he was a young man, Collier attended the California School of Fine Arts. Since childhood, he had known Dorothea Lange and that friendship eventually shifted his interest to photography. Collier was the last photographer hired for the Historical Section in the summer of 1941. Collier, however, moved with Roy Stryker to the OWI in 1942 and later to Standard Oil.

His first assignment for the Historical Section was to go to New England to capture the "smell" of burning leaves. He traveled to the South to photograph shipbuilding and to the coal mining areas of Pennsylvania to photograph the now "happy" miners as they helped by providing materials for the war effort. Collier also documented the Amish of Lancaster County, Pennsylvania.

At OWI Collier was assigned to document the lives of minority groups working toward the war effort. Fearing his photographs had little to say he convinced Stryker to allow him to go to Taos, New Mexico, where he covered an FSA project and did a fine, in-depth study of Mexican American culture. Collier combined his photography with the field of anthropology completing books on Alaskan Eskimos and the Navajo Indians. He played a prominent role in the development of federal Indian policy in the mid-twentieth century.

Jack Delano (1914–1997). A student at the Pennsylvania Academy of Fine Arts (PAFA), where he focused on drawing and painting, Jack Delano received financial assistance available to students of PAFA to study in Europe in 1936. Off to Europe, Delano bought a small camera to document his trip. By the time he returned to the United States, he had become quite proficient with his camera and joined the Federal Arts Project to do a study of mining conditions in Schuylkill County, Pennsylvania.

Presenting the two small portfolio albums he had developed to Roy Stryker, Delano next applied for a job at the Historical Section. When, in 1940, Arthur Rothstein was planning to leave the section, Stryker hired Delano. For the Historical Section Delano traveled to New England, Greene County, Georgia, then up the entire east coast from Georgia to Maine documenting migrant agricultural workers.

In 1941 Stryker sent Delano on an assignment to the Virgin Islands and to Puerto Rico. The onset of World War II at the end of that year prevented his return to the United States. His work in Puerto Rico was the first done outside of the country by any member of the Historical Section.

Delano made his home in Puerto Rico and managed the government's Television and Radio Service for many years. He also composed music performed by the Puerto Rico Symphony Orchestra. All the while, Delano continued his interest in photography.

Walker Evans (1903–1975). A native of St. Louis, Missouri, Walker Evans grew up in Chicago, Toledo, and New York City. He attended Andover and Williams College but did not take a degree. Following a year in Paris, Evans returned to the United States in 1927 and turned to photography. He read widely and studied particularly the street photographs of Eugene Atget, a French realist.

Evans's work in documentary photography commenced in 1932 on a yacht trip to Tahiti, and the following year he had developed a photo portfolio for a book about Cuba. Evans began using a large format camera to emphasize what he called his "documentary style." He went to work for the Resettlement Administration in 1935 but had conflicts with Roy Stryker, administrator of the Historical Section. Evans was fiercely individualistic and generally refused to check in with Stryker when he was out on assignment, yet the photographs he did complete for the Historical Section were flawless.

Evans took a leave of absence in 1936 to take photos of tenant farmers in Alabama, which were used in *Let Us Now Praise Famous Men* (1942). In 1937 Stryker terminated Evans due to the difficulty Stryker had in justifying to government officials his keeping of Evans, with his uncooperative practices, on the program. Evans subsequently went on to have a distinguished career as a photographer for *Time* and *Fortune*.

Theo Jung (1906–?). A native of Austria, Jung arrived in Chicago by 1912 and took up an amateur interest in photography. In 1934 he joined the Federal Relief Administration in Washington, DC, to prepare pictorial statistics and develop charts on unemployment. Continuing to take photos in his spare time he prepared a portfolio dramatically illustrating the slums of Washington.

In September 1935 he presented the portfolio to Roy Stryker and was immediately hired for the Historical Section. On assignment Jung journeyed to Garrett County, Maryland, Brown County, Indiana, and Jackson County, Ohio, to focus on people and interiors. A photograph of an old couple in their doorway and another of a woman reflected in her dresser mirror, both taken in Brown County in October 1935, were among his most famous photographs.

By 1936 Stryker had become dismayed at Jung for his lack of background preparation before an

Dorothea Lange, one of the most famous Farm Security Administration (FSA) photographers. (The Library of Congress.)

assignment and also believed his proficiency with a camera was lacking. In May 1936 Stryker let Jung go. Theo Jung went on to pursue an interest in book design and calligraphy, winning many awards in book and publication design.

Dorothea Lange (1895–1965). Dorothea Lange's early life was marked with difficulties. Born Dorothea Margaretta Nutzhorn, she contracted polio at age seven and was left with a damaged right leg; at twelve her father abandoned the family. Dorothea grew up in New Jersey and New York City. At age eighteen she decided to become a photographer. She saw the profession as a trade, not as an art. She took her mother's name, Lange, and, in 1918, moved to California, where she found work in a photo-finishing shop.

Lange established many ties with other photographers and, in 1919, opened her own studio. She was married in 1920 to Maynard Dixon, an artist and illustrator of Western scenes. The Dixons separated in 1931 and, shortly thereafter, Lange began taking documentary photographs, not of the elite in her studio but of common folk on the streets of San Francisco.

In 1935 Lange found employment photographing migrant agricultural laborers in California; she also married Paul S. Taylor, director of California's State

Emergency Relief Administration (SERA). Taylor grasped the value of Lange's haunting photographs and used them extensively in his reports. Intermittently between 1935 and 1942, Lange worked as a photographer for the RA and the FSA, both in California and in the South.

Lange became famous for a number of her photographs, especially "The Migrant Mother" and "Ma Burnham." With the onset of World War II she photographed the relocation of Japanese-Americans, Okies and Arkies who had moved to California, and Mormon families in Utah. Lange became one of the most famous American woman photographers of the twentieth century.

Russell Lee (1903–1986). Lee had a troubled and lonely childhood. He earned a degree in chemical engineering in 1925, but, in 1929, used an inheritance to become an artist. In time Lee turned to photography and, in 1936, went to work for the RA and then the FSA. He was a skilled documentary photographer who captured poverty through realistic images of families and individuals beset by the Great Depression. Lee's work for the federal government continued until 1942. Some of his most compelling images were of life in St. Augustine, Texas, and Pie Town, New Mexico.

Henry Luce (1898–1967). Born in China to American missionary parents, Henry Luce attended Yale University and enlisted for service in World War I. He finished college in 1920, studied at Oxford University, and entered journalism. In 1923 Luce and a business partner, Briton Hadden, founded *Time,* a magazine with thumbnail news stories. In 1929 he launched *Fortune,* a magazine covering business and economic affairs. Luce's company, Time, Inc., purchased *Architectural Forum* in 1932 and in 1935 began the documentary film series, "The March of Time." The films were high quality, documentary photojournalism released in theaters around the world.

In 1936 Luce began publication of *Life,* a magazine devoted to photojournalism. *Life* attracted millions of subscribers, reaching a high of 7 million in 1971. The magazine featured the photographs of hundreds of photographers whose images, it was estimated, were viewed by as many as 20 million a week. *Life* had a wide coverage of subjects: poverty, construction, farming, nature, war, accidents, tragedies, politics, and manufacturing. The magazine became a pivotal element of Luce's prosperous company, Time, Inc., later known as Time-Life.

As war threatened to engulf the United States by 1941, Henry Luce became greatly concerned about the nation's isolationism and the predicament of Great Britain fighting virtually alone against Germany.

Luce's essay, "The American Century," published in *Life* during the winter of 1941, argued for American involvement and construction of a new world order.

Carl Mydans (1907–). Graduating from the School of Journalism at Boston University in 1930, Carl Mydans began his career as a writer but in 1931 purchased his first 35mm camera, a Contax, and began freelancing. Displaying an early talent, a few of his first photographs were sold to *Time* magazine.

It was *Time* editor Daniel Lonwell that recommended Mydans to Robert Thorpe of the Resettlement Administration. Thorpe hired Mydans to work on his Thorpe project, a book of suburban resettlement. Later in 1935 Mydans was reassigned to Stryker's Historical Section. Stryker was delighted to incorporate Mydans's previous work into the section's files.

Finding himself among skilled photographers, Mydans's gift for photography developed rapidly. Mydans traveled through Tennessee, Missouri, Louisiana, Alabama, Arkansas, Georgia, and South Carolina, witnessing the struggle of the rural poor and focusing on the people of the cotton fields.

Mydans stayed with the Historical Section less than a full year but gained a broadened awareness of his country and the conditions that influenced its people. He joined the newly formed *Life* magazine in late 1936 where he became an honored photojournalist. He covered World War II in all theaters, Europe and the Far East, and was even a prisoner of war for a time in both Japan and China. In 1950 Mydans again was at the front in the Korean conflict. He was awarded the Gold Achievement Award by U.S. Camera magazine for his photographs of the Korean conflict.

Arthur Rothstein (1915–1985). Rothstein was born in New York City. When he was about five years old he got his first camera and began his lifelong interest in photography. As a student at Columbia, where he earned a degree in 1935, Rothstein worked as an assistant to Roy Stryker, head of the Historical Section of the RA and FSA. Much of Rothstein's work concerned Dust Bowl conditions in the Midwest. He left federal employment in 1940 and had a long career as a documentary photographer and photo editor for *Look*. Rothstein helped found the American Society of Magazine Photographers and wrote nine books, including the textbook *Photojournalism* (1956).

Ben Shahn (1898–1969). Born in Russia, Shahn and his family escaped Jewish persecution in 1906 and settled in Brooklyn. Shahn dropped out of school to become a lithographer and graphic artist. He eventually completed his high school diploma and studied at New York University and City College of New York

and between 1922 and 1935 Shahn worked primarily as an artist. His works included tempera murals and watercolor paintings.

He began work in 1935 for the RA as an artist and photographer. He had mastered photography while sharing a studio with Walker Evans. During the later 1930s Shahn took more than six thousand photographs, mostly in the rural South and Midwest. He then resumed his work as a muralist. He said that his work as a New Deal photographer shifted his focus from "social realism" to "personal realism."

Roy E. Stryker (1893–1975). Born in Kansas, Stryker grew up in Colorado. He served in World War I, graduated in 1924 with a degree in economics from Columbia University, and joined his mentor, Rexford Tugwell, to teach economics. Stryker and Tugwell collaborated to produce and illustrate *American Economic Life* (1925).

Stryker grasped the value of using photographs in publications and teaching. When Tugwell became a member of President Roosevelt's "brain trust," he gained responsibility for organizing the Resettlement Administration, later the Farm Security Administration. Stryker moved to Washington, DC, in 1935 to serve as head of the Historical Section of the FSA and direct its photo documentation projects.

Stryker recruited some of the nation's finest photographers to work between 1935 and 1945 for the RA, FSA, and the Office of War Information. Stryker was not a photographer, but he saw the value of enhancing public understanding of Great Depression conditions and New Deal projects through still photography. Stryker publicized and made available the work of his photographic staff for newspapers and *Life* and *Look,* photojournalism magazines of the 1930s. Stryker was the highly skilled and insightful administrator of one of the nation's most significant documentary projects.

John Vachon (1915–1975). An unemployed graduate student in Washington, DC, specializing in Elizabethan poetry, John Vachon's job prospects were not good in the Great Depression year of 1936. With the help of a friendly hometown congressman, Vachon became eligible to interview for low-level government jobs. Vachon landed a job in Stryker's Historical Section as an assistant messenger carrying papers between government buildings. Most of Vachon's work, however, would be copying captions onto the back of 8 by 10 glossy prints.

Gradually Vachon, promoted to junior file clerk, grew to know the section's files better than anyone but Stryker. He knew all the photographers' individual styles and memorized the file numbers of the most popular photographs. Vachon became caught up in the photographers' enthusiasm for the New Deal and he would ultimately stay with Stryker longer than any other of the photographers.

As Vachon cruised through the files he noticed there were many scenes in Washington, DC, that needed to be added to the files. With Stryker's permission and under the tutelage of Ben Shahn, Walker Evans, and Arthur Rothstein, Vachon began his photography career. A few of Vachon's photographs found their way into the files.

Vachon, still a junior file clerk but now armed with a camera, was sent to the Great Plains of Kansas and Nebraska in October 1938 for a full month assignment. In 1940, for the first time as a full-fledged FSA photographer, he went on assignment to North and South Dakota. In 1942 Vachon traveled on assignment to Maryland, West Virginia, and throughout the upper Midwest.

Vachon went with Stryker to the OWI, then to active military duty. Upon discharge he spent the better part of his career at *Look* magazine. He exhibited prints at the Museum of Modern Art and taught master classes in photography.

Minor White (1908–1976). Born in Minneapolis, White studied at the University of Minnesota where he earned a degree in 1934. In 1937 White moved to Portland, Oregon, where he became a documentary photographer. He was employed by the Works Progress Administration's Art Program to take photographs of the city's waterfront buildings being razed as part of an urban improvement project. White began exhibiting his photographs and teaching photography. Most of White's career as a teacher, writer, and photographer fell after his service in World War II. He held several academic appointments. He helped found and edited *Aperture,* an important periodical concerned with photography, from 1952 to 1975.

Marion Post Wolcott (1910–1990). Studying at the University of Vienna in Austria, Wolcott became friends with several professional photographers. She was given a Rolleiflex camera just prior to her return to the United States and she took an active interest in photography as a profession.

Post Wolcott landed a job as staff photographer for the *Philadelphia Evening Bulletin* in 1937 and was the only woman on the staff. Rapidly acquiring confidence, experience, and a skill handling all types of people, she presented her portfolio to Roy Stryker in 1938 and immediately found herself in the field with Arthur Rothstein and Russell Lee.

Being a woman, Post Wolcott found she could interact with people without seeming intrusive. She photographed in almost every Southern state. Post Wolcott took some of the best photographs of children in the FSA file. Another of her famed series is of day laborers gambling, dancing, and enjoying their moments away from the fields. Post Wolcott retired from active photography in 1942 to raise her family.

Primary Sources

FSA: The Photographs Talked

Edward Steichen, author of *The Bitter Years: 1935–1941* (1962, p. vi), reflects on the photography that grew out of the Great Depression,

> Have a look into the faces of the men and women in these pages. Listen to the story they tell and they will leave with you a feeling of a living experience you won't forget; and the babies here, and the children; weird, hungry, dirty, loveable, heart-breaking images; and then there are the fierce stories of strong, gaunt men and women in time of flood and drought.... It is not the individual photographers that make these pictures so important, but it is the job as a whole as it has been produced by the photographers as a group that makes it such a unique and outstanding achievement.

"It can never happen again—now we have reminders"

Rexford Guy Tugwell, head of the Resettlement Agency, is quoted in *The Bitter Years: 1935–1941* (Steichen, 1962, p. iii) as he explains why there was a need to visually record the miseries of the Depression.

> It was clear to those of us who had responsibility for the relief of distress among farmers during the Great Depression and during the following years of drought, that we were passing through an experience of American life that was unique.
>
> At least we hoped it would be unique; and we intended not only to bring the resources of government to the assistance of those who were distressed or starved but to make certain that never again should Americans be exposed to such cruelties.
>
> It seemed important to record the incredible events of those years; and the best way was to photograph them. Roy Stryker was asked to organize the work and the superb job he and his collaborators did speaks for itself. It is not only a technical triumph but a record of neglect and a warning.
>
> It can never happen again to so many in the same ways—partly because we have these reminders of what happened when we turned our backs on follow citizens and allowed them to be ravaged.

A Photographer Must Have a Feeling

John Vachon explains in Robert Reid and Larry Vickochil's *Chicago and Downstate: Illinois as Seen by the Farm Security Administration Photographers, 1936–1943* (1989, p. xii) the role of an FSA photographer as he understood it:

> To photograph any American people, phenomenon, or locality, the FSA photographer should have a thorough knowledge of his subject, both information acquired beforehand, and knowledge gained through actual contact. Then he must have *feeling*. Despite the fact that he is going to use an impersonal instrument to record what he sees, he must be intelligent enough to place what he sees in true perspective in the American scene, to feel the humor, the pity, the beauty of the situation he photographs. And lastly, the photographer must have a compelling desire to record what he sees and feels. He will want to freeze instantaneously the reality before him that it may be seen and felt by others.

The Freedom of Photographs

Arthur Rothstein and John Vachon discussed how the photographers greatly expanded the original vision of FSA by photographing anything and everything. Some of Rothstein's comments on the purpose of the FSA and on its photographers are reproduced in Thomas Garver's *Just Before the War: Urban America From 1935 to 1941 As Seen By Photographers of the Farm Security Administration* (1968).

> It is true that the original purpose of the Farm Security photographer was to document rural scenes, especially those that related to the efforts of the Government to improve the conditions of people engaged in agriculture, but all of these photographers were curious, inquisitive people and they could not, by their very personality and nature, confine themselves merely to rural conditions. They were exposed to cities as they went through them and they saw things that they felt should be reported and document[ed] ...

> Naturally, at the same time, I looked at all the other parts of the city and took many photographs that really had nothing to do with my assignment, because one of the great things about being a photographer in that organization was that you were never restricted. You were allowed to photograph anything that seemed of interest and this is the way a photographer should be treated. A principal was established in the early days that there was no such thing as wasted film or wasted time. I like to think that each picture we made was being shot with a great deal of thought and not just to expose film, but the Farm Security file would never have been created if we hadn't the freedom to photograph anything, anywhere in the United States—anything that we came across that seemed interesting, and vital.

> There are probably thousands of negatives that have never been printed in those files and you could create several exhibitions of different sorts if you wanted to. This was a very prolific group of photographers and we

were dedicated to the idea of recording what was happening in the United States in this critical period of our history. It is a period that is just now beginning to acquire some perspective and I'm glad to have been part of it.

Friendly Suggestions—Typical Instructions From Roy Stryker:

Roy Stryker sent the following directions to Dorothea Lange on November 19, 1936 as she prepared for her first major trip for the RA (quoted in Jack Hurley's *Portrait of a Decade: Roy Stryker and the Development of Documentary Photography in the Thirties,* 1966, p.70.). These, and other communications, are preserved in the Roy Stryker Collection at the University of Louisville Photographic Archive.

> Would you, in the next few days, take for us some good slum pictures in the San Francisco area. (Of course, no California city has slums, but I'll bet you can find them.) We need to vary the diet in some of our exhibits here by showing some western poverty instead of all south and east ... When you get to Los Angeles, I think it might be worthwhile to see if you can pick up some good slum pictures there also. Do not forget that we need some of the rural slum type of thing, as well as the urban ...

> As you are driving along through the agricultural areas and if you can do it without too much extra effort, would you take a few shots of various types of farm activities such as your picture showing the lettuce workers. I think Dr. Tugwell would be very appreciative of photographs of this sort to be used as illustrative material for some things which the Department of Agriculture is working on.

Suggested Research Topics

- Using published collections of photographs or images available from the American Memory Project, Library of Congress, on the World Wide Web, assess the importance of buildings and architectural details in the documentary photos of Walker Evans. Or, assess the camera position and distance Evans used when taking portraits. How did his use of the "built environment" or of portraits capture life in the 1930s?

- Using the on-line RA and FSA photographs in the American Memory Project, identify the portrayal of younger Americans in the work of federal photographers. How were the children dressed? What activities were they doing? What can be implied of the children's lives from the photographs?

- Was it possible for government agencies during the New Deal to produce objective, documentary still photographs about the Great Depression,

Dust Bowl, and government relief projects? Was there a danger that such projects would become propaganda?

- Could art-oriented photographers like Walker Evans and Minor White work comfortably within the rules and assignments laid down by a federal agency? Or was the employment of artist-photographers likely to produce tensions and controversy?

Bibliography

Sources

Garver, Thomas H. *Just Before the War: Urban America From 1935 to 1941 As Seen By Photographers of the Farm Security Administration.* New York: October House, Inc., 1968.

Hall, James Baker. *Minor White: Rites & Passages; His Photographs Accompanied by Excerpts from His Diaries and Letters.* Millerton, NY: Aperture, Inc., 1978.

Hambourg, Maria Morris, Jeff AL. Rosenheim, Douglas Eklund, and Mia Fineman. *Walker Evans.* New York: The Metropolitan Museum of Art, 2000.

Hurley, F. Jack. *Portrait of a Decade: Roy Stryker and the Development of Documentary Photography in the Thirties.* Baton Rouge, LA: Louisiana State University Press, 1966.

Mulligan, Therese, ed. *The Photography of Alfred Stieglitz: Georgia O'Keeffe's Enduring Legacy.* Rochester, NY: George Eastman House International Museum of Photography and Film, 2000.

O'Neal, Hank. *A Vision Shared: A Classic Portrait of America and Its People, 1935–1943.* New York: St. Martin's Press, 1976.

Reid, Robert L., ed. *Back Home Again: Indiana in the Farm Security Administration Photographs, 1935–1943.* Bloomington, IN: Indiana University Press, 1987.

Reid, Robert L., and Larry A. Vickochil, eds. *Chicago and Downstate: Illinois as Seen by the Farm Security Administration Photographers, 1936–1943.* Urbana, IL: University of Illinois Press, 1989.

Steichen, Edward, ed. *The Bitter Years: 1935–1941.* New York: The Museum of Modern Art, 1962.

Stieglitz, Alfred. "Pictorial Photography," *Scribner's Magazine,* 26 (November, 1899), 528–37.

Wood, Nancy. *Heartland New Mexico: Photographs from the Farm Security Administration, 1935–1943.* Albuquerque, NM: University of New Mexico Press, n.d.

Further Reading

Agee, James, and Walker Evans. *Let Us Now Praise Famous Men.* New York: Ballantine Books, 1960.

"America from the Great Depression to World War II: Photographs from the FSA-OWI, 1935–1945," [cited July 15, 2001] available from the World Wide Web at http:www.memory.loc.gov/ammem/.

Elliott, George P. *Dorothea Lange.* Garden City, NY: Doubleday & Company, Inc., 1966.

Ganzel, Bill. *Dust Bowl Descent.* Lincoln, NE: University of Nebraska Press, 1984.

Goldberg, Vicki. "Picture This: Magazine Photography, in Just a Few Decades, Has Changed the Way Life Itself is Regarded," *Life,* 22:i5, April 15, 1999, p. 12.

Kirstein, Lincoln. *Walker Evans American Photographs.* New York: The Museum of Modern Art, 1988. [Reprint of 1938 edition.]

Meltzer, Milton. *Dorothea Lange: A Photographer's Life.* New York: Farrar Straus Giroux, 1978.

Newhall, Beaumont. *Photography: Essays & Images Illustrated Readings in the History of Photography.* New York: The Museum of Modern Art, 1980.

Ohrn, Karin B. *Dorothea Lange and the Documentary Tradition.* Baton Rouge, LA: Louisiana State University Press, 1980.

Peterson, Christian A. *After the Photo-Secession: American Pictorial Photography, 1910–1935.* New York: W.W. Norton & Company, 1997.

Rothstein, Arthur. *The Depression Years.* New York: Dover Publications, Inc., 1978.

———. *Documentary Photography.* Boston, MA: Focal Press, 1986.

See Also

Arts Programs

Political Ideologies: Leaning Left

Introduction

"I did what I believed in. I believe Socialism is inevitable. Life cannot go on forever without that step, and setbacks don't change it." These words were spoken by Gus Hall, longtime head of the Communist Party, USA (cited May 30, 2001. Available online at http://www.bookzen.com/obits/o_hall_gus.html).

A variety of political forces influenced responses to the Great Depression. Pressures mounted from the right and left of the political spectrum. Generally forces from the "left" in the United States tended to be liberal. These advocates not only believed in "big government," they advocated the active intervention of government in the economy and daily lives of citizens. To the "right" were the conservatives who sought to preserve the status quo and generally fought against radical changes. Those on the "right" wanted limited taxes and a limited role for government. Generally they supported each citizen helping himself or herself, rather than intervention of the government.

Between 1900 and 1930 the United States was a fertile setting for left-leaning views. Many of these sentiments were imported from Europe by immigrants unhappy with conditions in their countries of birth. They brought with them commitments to socialism, communism, anarchism, and unionism. Socialism is the belief in collective ownership in industry and shared wealth; communism relates to government ownership and control of the economy; anarchism is a belief that government is unnecessary and society is

Chronology:

1932: The Liberty Party, a minor political movement, nominates William Hope Harvey and Andre Nordskog for president and vice-president, respectively, on a ticket committed to the free and unlimited coinage of silver.

1932: The Communist Party, USA nominates William Z. Foster for president; Foster receives 102,785 votes, the largest ever secured by a CPUSA nominee.

1933: Huey Long, once a supporter of President Franklin Roosevelt, breaks with the New Deal administration and begins advocating the Share-Our-Wealth-Plan, a system of redistributing wealth through government action.

1933–1935: Townsend Plan advocates grow rapidly in number to become a nationwide force lobbying for old-age assistance from the federal government.

1935–1939: The Communist Party USA follows the Popular Front, a program of opposition to fascism, and mounts numerous efforts in union organization and cooperation with the Congress of Industrial Organizations (CIO).

1937–1939: The Communist Party USA generally endorses the New Deal and President Franklin D. Roosevelt.

---

based on individual cooperation; and unionism promotes the ability of people to form organizations to improve their working conditions. They came from a background where these ideals were commonplace and government was expected by many to work for the interests of all citizens. As a result they envisioned legalized labor unions, controls on great wealth, regulation of the economy, and social welfare systems, underwritten and administered by the government. Some, impatient with the lack of change in the United States, advocated the violent overthrow of the government through revolution.

The views from the left fell on fertile ground in many parts of the United States. Even though the early twentieth century period, particularly the 1920s, was considered an economic boon time, never had the gap in wealth between the wealthy and workers been greater. With the rapid growth of industrialization, the United States was becoming a nation of mass consumerism. With easy access to credit from banks, the average worker was going deeper into debt to keep up with the modernizing trends. In addition, workers were frequently left to toil in crowded and unhealthy workplace conditions while government was largely unwilling to intervene and impose higher standards on employers.

In the 1890s the People's Party had campaigned for government intervention in the economy. It wanted more money in circulation through the coinage, as it was phrased, of "free silver." It also wanted to check the power of corporations and for the government to own key utilities. Between 1900 and 1920—the era of "progressive" reform—local, state, and federal government activities increased significantly. New laws regulated railroads, set maximum hours for workers, and clearly changed the role of government in the affairs of citizens.

On the left were those who thought the nation had not done enough to help the poor. The pressure to shove the country in new directions arose during the campaign of 1932 and persisted throughout the 1930s. This pressure included the Communist Party, USA (CPUSA), Liberty Party, Socialist Party, and followers of vocal critics of the New Deal, the series of government programs promoted by President Franklin D. Roosevelt in an effort to help the country out of the Great Depression. Among the more notable critics were Dr. Francis E. Townsend, Huey Long, and Father Charles Coughlin. A number of writers, some of them with communist sympathies and many more with disillusionment about conditions during the Great Depression, used their literary talents to raise issue and push from the "left" of the political spectrum.

The occurrence of the stock market crash in 1929 and following Great Depression only worsened the social and economic conditions of many. With unemployment steadily rising to 25 percent of the workforce by 1933 and millions of others fearing reductions in pay, many who had earlier accumulated debt could no longer pay it off. President Herbert Hoover (served 1929–1933), who largely took a hands-off government approach, advocated personal responsibility of individuals for their welfare and reliance on private charities and local government relief organizations. This proved not only highly ineffective in addressing the severe economic woes, but made the federal government appear cold and aloof from people's lives. In addition many blamed the crisis on the greediness of U.S. business leaders and began to question the validity of free market capitalism in general. Confidence was slipping in both the United States' political and economic systems.

Issue Summary

Liberty Party and William Hope Harvey

With faith in traditional U.S. political and economic systems declining due to the Great Depression and President Hoover's ineffective response to it, many were looking for someone to lead them out of the crisis. Hoover was highly unpopular and Roosevelt was seen by some as just another representative of the U.S. system that was failing. A sense of urgency was quickly escalating as breadlines and shantytowns were growing. During the presidential campaign of 1932 a number of candidates espoused unique causes. William Hope Harvey, who had gained national recognition in the 1890s for his advocacy of the "free and unlimited coinage of silver," surfaced as a candidate who had a program to solve the Great Depression. Harvey wrote *Coin's Financial School* (1894) in which he advocated an expansion of the amount of money in circulation through the federal purchase of silver bullion and minting it into coins.

In 1932 Harvey brought out a new volume, *The Book,* in which he presented the same formula. Harvey's faithful followers of the Liberty Party gathered at Monte Ne, Arkansas, to nominate him and his running mate, Andre Nordskog, to carry the banner of free silver. Harvey and Nordskog secured only 54,000 votes in the 1932 presidential election. Although the Liberty Party suffered a crushing defeat, the idea of an inflated (decreasing the value of money so that items cost more) currency attracted attention and was a modest legacy of old "Professor Coin."

End Poverty in California (EPIC) and Upton Sinclair

Franklin D. Roosevelt (served 1933–1945), of the Democratic Party, won the 1932 presidential election. Pressure on Roosevelt's New Deal—his plan to revive the economy and help the people—came from a variety of movements promising basic solutions to the problems of poverty and unemployment. Many believed Roosevelt would not take such radical actions as they believed necessary to end the crisis, such as nationalizing the banking system (having the government assume control) and some industries. They saw the New Deal as offering only simple solutions to much deeper problems. The governor of Minnesota, Floyd Olson, accused capitalism of causing the Great Depression and

stated, "I hope the present system of government goes right down to hell." Olson's sentiments were echoed by Upton Sinclair, the socialist and author of *The Jungle* (1906). Olson and Sinclair both thought the solution was a greatly increased government role in business activities and people's daily lives. They believed government could provide much greater economic security through various types of social programs and that business should be much more beneficial to society. In 1934 Governor Olson even went so far as to propose abolishing capitalism and establishing state ownership of all means of production in Minnesota. This did not, however, come to pass.

In 1934 Upton Sinclair ran for governor of California on the platform "End Poverty in California" (EPIC). The nation had no social safety net in place prior to the 1930s for providing financial assistance to those in need, including the aged who were no longer able to work. He promised a pension of $50 every month to anyone over the age of 60—one of the first proposals of social security. Sinclair sought to finance the program by raising income and inheritance taxes. Sinclair's EPIC proposal asserted that the unemployed would be put to work at productive labor, thus making everything that they consume. Exchanging goods among themselves would be through a method of barter. The unemployed, he argued, should be given access to good land and machinery so that they could work to support themselves thus taking the burden off taxpayers.

Sinclair truly believed that no harm would be done to the private industry because the unemployed were of no use to industry. Furthermore, he believed that if prosperity were to come back, workers would drift back into the private industry. The unemployed would produce something in the meantime, thus relieving the state from providing for the jobless.

Sinclair won in the primary but lost the election, and his EPIC program collapsed. It did, however, generate considerable interest in government circles. Sinclair had argued for welfare, distribution of surplus goods, active government interference in the economy, and stiff taxes on property assessed at more than $100,000. EPIC fostered new ideas that would soon appear in new New Deal programs such as Social Security and the work relief projects of the Works Progress Administration (WPA), as Roosevelt attempted to defuse the popularity of these movements and incorporate them into his own administration.

Social Security and Dr. Francis E. Townsend

Like Sinclair, Dr. Francis W. Townsend, another Californian, developed a plan in 1933 to help the

Dr. Francis E. Townsend was an advocate for old-age pensions. His plan proposed providing $200 a month to all people over the age of 60 who were unemployed, regardless of prior earnings. (The Library of Congress.)

elderly and poor. The plan was originally published in a Long Beach, California, newspaper as an extended "Letter to the Editor." The response to Townsend's plan was swift and massive because the retired doctor had tapped into a major social problem in the United States: the helplessness of the impoverished senior citizens. The plan was then published as a pamphlet and distributed throughout the United States. Plans such as Sinclair's and Townsend's were a challenge to the existing social and political order. Under President Hoover, the government had little to do with people's daily lives. People were expected to take care of themselves. The Depression exacerbated an already existing need for support of the poor and elderly and prompted proposals that, ultimately, gained momentum and found inclusion in Roosevelt's New Deal.

The Townsend Plan went further than Sinclair's proposal and promised $200 a month to all unemployed citizens over 60, regardless of past earnings. The only condition was that they spend the money in the same month they received it. The funds were to be raised principally by a two percent federal sales tax. Despite much criticism from economists, thousands of Townsendites organized Townsend Pension

Clubs across the country. In the early stages of the campaign, supporters saw President Roosevelt as an ally, and Townsend expected Roosevelt to endorse the plan. Roosevelt, like many politicians at this time, however, saw the plan as irresponsible and unworkable since it would be very costly to the government by creating more bureaucracy to run the program and to ensure that people complied with its provisions of spending money.

Through Townsend's zeal for the plan, its simplicity, and the organization of "Townsendites," support for the plan increased despite much condemnation from politicians. Congress, however, continually defeated bills to establish the Townsend Plan. The strength of the movement declined after the economy began to recover and the future effects of new Social Security system were beginning to be anticipated in the United States.

Townsend and his remaining supporters, however, were disappointed with Social Security because it did not promise immediate payments in 1935, and people had to work in order to earn a payment. In fact payments would not begin until 1937, and then would be far less than the $200 Townsend proposed. Although Townsend's plan was never implemented, he inspired plans for social security and helped spark the concept of providing financial aid for the elderly. Like Sinclair's movement, Townsend's movement challenged Roosevelt's New Deal policies, leading the president to shift more to the left politically as he began crafting his Second New Deal strategies in 1935.

Social Justice and Father Charles Coughlin

Although Townsend and Sinclair pressed the New Deal to the left, the protest movements led by Father Charles E. Coughlin and Senator Huey P. Long of Louisiana were of another order. Father Coughlin, a Catholic priest from Detroit, attracted audiences of 30 to 45 million to his national radio show. He supported the New Deal in its early days, but then attacked the plan as excessively pro-business. Increasingly controversial with his speeches, Coughlin mixed his religious commentary with proposed images of a country operating without bankers and businessmen. He also roused his audiences with anti-Semitic (anti-Jewish) comments and further propelled the fury against Jews, who were becoming more commonplace in the United States in the 1930s. Coughlin's message was appealing, especially to the urban lower-middle class who disdained the banking industry and leaders of big business. To many others, his rhetoric, particularly against Jews, was offensive and troubling.

Reverend Charles E. Coughlin, Detroit's "Radio Priest," was widely known for his extreme views against bankers and big business, who he largely blamed for the problems of the Depression. (AP/Wide World Photos, Inc. Reproduced by permission.)

Coughlin railed against "rapacious capitalists" for not living up to their social responsibility. Like William Hope Harvey, he called for the return to a silver standard, issuing more greenbacks, or paper money, and federal control of the banking system. These, he believed, would achieve his agenda of social justice and prosperity. In 1935 Coughlin established the National Union for Social Justice (NUSJ) and launched a strong campaign to influence Congress with his views through this organization's members letters and telegrams.

"Share-Our-Wealth" Plan and Huey Long

Politician Huey Long, like Father Coughlin, had charisma and personality that won him support from millions who were trying to overcome the Great Depression. Long came from further to the left than Father Coughlin and had greater socialist tendencies. In 1924 Long ran unsuccessfully for governor of Louisiana on a platform that included road construction, increased support for public schools, free textbooks for all children, improvements in the court system, and state warehouses for storage of farm crops. Defeated, Long continued to be concerned with the fact that the wealth of the land was tied up in the hands of only a few. He was concerned that wealth

would never trickle down to the poor. In response he launched his "Share-Our-Wealth" campaign after his successful election bid for governor of Louisiana in 1928.

Huey Long's radical ideas were unthinkable to some since they ran counter to basic capitalist ideals of economic markets operating relatively free of government regulation or oversight. He managed, however, to draw many who supported his ideologies. In order to gain support Long developed a successful campaign style. He used mailed circulars, radio speeches, and the warm response of the general public. Long appealed to the populace because, though he was blessed with a phenomenal memory, razor-sharp wit, and work ethic, he was nonetheless a product of his upbringing in Winnfield, Louisiana. Winnfield was a town where some stores and shops were located in tents and where there were no sidewalks, no paved streets, and free roaming livestock.

In 1928 he embarked upon a series of changes that went beyond rebellion against the ruling class. As governor Long raised severance taxes on natural resource industries to pay for schoolbooks for every child, regardless of whether the student went to public or private school. During his term Louisiana built more than 2,300 miles of paved roads, 111 bridges, and several hospitals and new schools. Long sought dental care at mental institutions and to abolish the straitjacketing and chaining of patients. He also instituted the state's first rehabilitation program for prisoners. Additionally Long implemented an adult literacy program that largely served black Americans.

Elected to the U.S. Senate in 1930, Long was impatient to get his views before the American people but refused to resign as governor until 1932. It was only until then that he went to Washington, DC, and took his oath of office. Only because of this strong local popularity and penchant for flamboyance was he able to take this unorthodox path. In 1933 Long published *Every Man a King: The Autobiography of Huey P. Long.*

Although a supporter of President Roosevelt and the New Deal, Long broke with the new president by the fall of 1933 and began advocating his "Share-Our-Wealth" plan. Long talked about a guaranteed income of $2,000–$3,000 for all American families at a time when 18.3 million families earned less than $1,000 per year in 1936. Long also promised pensions for the elderly and college educations for the young. He planned to pay for these programs by taxing the rich and liquidating their fortunes, or changing property into cash by selling it.

Long's plan called upon the federal government to provide families with income so they could afford the necessities of life. Long believed that every family should have a home, job, radio and an automobile. He also proposed limiting fortunes and annual incomes. His ideas were quickly rejected by Roosevelt in 1933 and, though popular with many, had difficulty gaining political momentum outside Louisiana. His promotion of redistributing the wealth in the United States clearly attracted much controversy as it directly conflicted with the basic principles of individualism and capitalism, which was traditionally embraced in America.

In 1935 Long formed the "Share-Our-Wealth" Society to promote his views. Increasingly it appeared he had aspirations to run for president, either as a Democrat or on a third-party ticket. His "Share the Wealth" Society rose from nothing in early 1934, to 27,431 chapters in every state, with a total membership of more than 4.5 million in less than two years.

Many argued that Long abused his position as governor of Louisiana, though he was undoubtedly not the first. Long's public appeal was strong. Even though he was actually in Washington, DC, Long was a virtual dictator of Louisiana, personally controlling the police and the state courts. He appointed members of his family and supporters of his program to gov-

ernment jobs and rewarded key political supporters with state contracts. He used his position to live a fine life and to dress well.

What set Long apart from the fascist dictators of the time in Europe was his belief in the democratic process. Long would do just about anything to get peoples' votes, except lie to them about what he would do once elected. It was that directness and honesty which set him apart from his predecessors. The bottom line was that Long worked hard to represent what he felt were the best interests of the people of Louisiana.

Long was assassinated on the steps of the capital building in Baton Rouge, Louisiana, in September 1935, by Dr. Carl Weiss, son-in-law of a ruined political opponent of Long's. If he had lived Long might have mounted a strong third-party challenge to Roosevelt in the 1936 presidential election. His death curtailed his dreams and the "Share-Our-Wealth" movement.

Revolution and the Communist Party USA (CPUSA)

With the continuation of the Great Depression, the Communist Party of the United States of America (CPUSA) broadened its appeal by downplaying its commitment to immediate revolution. Its magnetism was based on many factors. First, the seeming success of the Soviet Union's planned economy in the face of the worldwide economic depression gave some hope for the Marxist political formula. Second, the Soviet Union's position against fascism and its support of the Loyalists in the Spanish Civil War, appealed to others. Third, the international communist leadership promoted the "Popular Front," an anti-fascist and pro-New Deal organization growing by 1935. Fourth, the CPUSA skillfully out-organized its competitors, especially the socialists, and recruited many new members through the American Youth Congress, the League of American Workers, and the American League Against Wars and Fascism.

The most striking success of the CPUSA was its close association with the Congress of Industrial Organizations (CIO), which formed in the late 1930s. Though not a communist, CIO leader John L. Lewis, permitted members of the CPUSA to hold important positions in his organization in exchange for their recruiting union members and building a bigger and more powerful CIO.

In 1930 the CPUSA had been a small organization with probably no more than 7,500 members. A decade later it had grown to more than 100,000 members. The dramatic growth caused some to refer to the

1930s as America's "Red Decade." A key factor in this growth was the Great Depression that had caused many to question the validity of America's political and economic systems, particularly free market capitalist enterprises.

In spite of membership successes, however, CPUSA failed to draw actual voters. In 1932 William Z. Foster, the CPUSA nominee for president, drew only 103,000 votes compared to nearly 900,000 for Norman Thomas, the candidate of the Socialist Party. In contrast Roosevelt received almost 23 million votes and that rose to near 28 million in 1936. The rise of Earl Browder to leadership of the CPUSA played a critical role in the organization's growth. Browder was a less "pure" Marxist than those holding strictly to the philosophies of German Karl Marx. He embraced the Popular Front and cooperation with the New Deal and President Roosevelt.

While Foster had touted "Towards Soviet America," Browder promoted the slogan "Communism is Twentieth Century Americanism." Marxism, a social and economic concept in which the workers own all means of production, became a theoretical cornerstone for communism. Foster's Soviet America would involve a communist system of government ownership of industries and strong control of the economic system. In contrast Browder was more socialistic in character, adapted more to American traditions of private property. Both perspectives were foreign and frightening to the average American citizen.

By 1939 the CPUSA reached a high point with an estimated 50,000 to 75,000 members. An additional 20,000 were involved in the Young Communist League. The primary strength of the movement lay in its involvement in other organizations, particularly labor unions, and in the literary voice of disenchanted intellectuals who published articles in the *New Masses* or in sympathy with the communist cause.

More "Lefties"

Communist politicians were not the only leftist voices arguing that the New Deal was not going far enough to protect the poor, elderly, and the common people of the United States. Author Meridel Le Sueur, playwright Clifford Odets, labor organizers Gus Hall and Dorothy Healey, actor Paul Robeson, and author Richard Wright were other voices for those who were suffering during the Great Depression.

Meridel Le Sueur became well known for her writings about labor unions, downtrodden women, and the plight of the jobless. She was concerned that unions did not have a recognized voice, lacked negotiating power, and were often unable to recruit new

At a Glance

- In 1932 William Z. Foster, nominee of the Communist Party, USA, received 103,000 votes

- In 1936, 18.3 million families earned less than $1,000 per year

- The "Share the Wealth Society" rose from nothing in early 1934 to 27,431 chapters located in every state and a total membership of more than 4.5 million by 1936

members into the workplace. Le Sueur's books, *I Was Marching,* an account about the 1934 Minneapolis truckers' strike, and *Annunciation,* a tale about a young wife living in a one-room flat with a husband who opposed her pregnancy, were two popular accounts depicting life during the Great Depression.

Gus Hall, born Arvo Kusta Halberg to radical Finnish immigrant parents in Minnesota, became a member of the CPUSA in 1926. Hall was schooled in revolutionary communism at the Lenin School in Moscow in 1931–1932. He returned to the United States to promote communism, especially by organizing workers into union activity and strikes against the capitalists.

Dorothy (Rosenblum) Healey emerged as an energetic organizer in California. Joining the CPUSA in 1928, Healey was an ambitious member of the party in California for the next 45 years. She became active in the Young Communist League (YCL) and recalled in Dorothy Ray Healey and Maurice Isserman's *California Red: A Life in the American Communist Party* (1993, p 28):

> Joining the YCL made a big difference in my life in all kinds of ways. I quickly lost interest in the friends I had made in junior high school. The parties I had started being invited to up in the hills had never really been fun for me . . . In any case the YCL provided a kind of ready-made alternative gang for me. Most of my YCL comrades were older, in their late teens and early twenties, and that also had a great appeal to me."

In the mid-1930s Healey, like many other American communists, became involved in labor organizing. Communists sensed the unrest in American workers and believed taking up their cause against the

More About...

Mother Jones

Mary Harris "Mother" Jones became a nationally known labor organizer in the United States. Born in 1830 in Ireland, she came with her parents to the America, but grew up in Toronto, Ontario. "I'm not a humanitarian; I'm a hell-raiser," she said.

Tragedy beset her life, taking her husband and four children all within one week. Four years later, in 1871, the Great Chicago Fire destroyed everything she owned.

From the 1870s until her death in 1930, "Mother Jones" was an organizer for labor unions in the railway and mining industries. She was a founding member of the Industrial Workers of the World (IWW) and a lively participant in strikes. In 1913 in West Virginia she was arrested, tried, and convicted in a military court and at age 83 sentenced to 20 years in jail. A new governor freed her.

"Mother Jones" inspired strikes and unionization. She last spoke in public in 1926, a "fiery speech for the motion-picture camera," at the age of 96 years old.

"Mother" Jones. (The Bettmann Archive. Reproduced by permission.)

business leaders would be the best path for increasing membership rolls. In addition many workers were immigrants or immediate immigrant descendents who were more comfortable with more radical politics than found in the United States. In 1933 she went to the Imperial Valley, a highly productive agricultural region, to work with the Mexican Mutual Aid Association to build up the Cannery and Agricultural Workers Industrial Union (CAWIU). In 1933 the CAWIU mounted 25 strikes in California that involved thousands of workers. Healey then moved on to organize mariners and dock workers in San Pedro.

Similar to Healey, Harry Bridges, a fiery labor organizer in San Francisco, welded together the International Longshoremen's and Warehousemen's Union (ILWU). Bridges was "close" to the CPUSA and was repeatedly investigated by the FBI but kept a public posture of non-membership in the party. With establishment of communism in Russia and the rise of fascism in Germany and Italy, Roosevelt was increasingly sensitive to the prospects of radical political movements taking hold in the United States. Under Roosevelt's commands the FBI began shifting its focus away from American gangsters and outlaws to activities of political activists.

Playwright Clifford Odets, another voice for labor unions, believed that through union solidarity the little man might find a way out of the despair of America's economic and social ills. Odets's play, "Waiting for Lefty" (1935) reflected his political interests in the Communist Party, USA, which he joined in 1934. The play was a call to arms for labor unions. The play is set in a union hall where workers are discussing the need to organize. The importance of Odets's and Le Sueur's writings was that they pushed the public to go beyond the basic ideas of the New Deal. They were a voice for the people and used specific stories as examples of the plight of all during the Great Depression.

Richard Wright was a writer and supporter of the political left as well as an advocate for equality for African Americans. Wright spent his youth in the South where he was confronted with racial tension. His uncle was killed by whites, but no arrest was ever made. Wright excelled at school and was valedictorian of his high school class. He was appalled with the illiteracy of black Americans and the strife they had to endure in the South. When Wright was a young man, he moved to Chicago where he found a job working at the post office. In 1930, however, with the start of the Great Depression, Wright's hours at the post office were cut dramatically.

Wright began to write stories and poetry for various magazines and organizations and eventually moved to New York. While in New York, Wright joined the Communist Party and expressed his political beliefs through leftist publications. His writing appeared in such magazines as *Left Front, Anvil,* and *New Masses.* As Wright grew as a writer, he continued to explore the ideas of the communist left but was also concerned with the racial strife of the South and the inequality that black Americans had to endure. Some of Wright's most influential works—*Lawd Today! Uncle Tom's Children, Native Son,* and *Black Boy*—propelled him to international fame.

Black American women laundry workers on strike. Strikes were often organized by left-wing political organizations such as the Communist Party. (The Library of Congress.)

Wright's publications about the communist left and the strife of black Americans in the South had an influence not only in the United States but all over the world. He was well received by intellectuals in France, Spain, Italy, England, and Argentina. Wright, however, was unable to return to the United States for fear of being subpoenaed by an anti-communist congressional investigative committee.

The United States, built on principles of individualism, personal freedom, and free enterprise, held a strong distrust of radical politics and group movements. This distrust even included labor unions. By the 1930s the rise of communism and fascism in Europe and increased communist party activity in the United States caused alarm in many. Public pressure would force Congress to investigate communist activities and influences in the United States. Wright eventually settled permanently in France where he died in 1960.

Whether directly involved in politics or simply a voice for the common working class, members of the political left had a great influence on Roosevelt's New Deal, leading to the Social Security Act, creating a formal national retirement financial assistance system and the Wagner Act creating the National Labor Relations Board and recognizing the role of labor unions. A common concern among those with communist leanings was that a system of financial security needed

to be created by the federal government to provide for the elderly. Members of the political left were also involved in fighting high unemployment and worked toward expanding the rights of labor unions. Those who were politically leaning to the left expressed their views and ideologies with much conviction. They in turn gained such support from the public that the New Deal was deeply influenced and affected by their convictions.

Contributing Forces

Populism and Progressivism

The tilt of some Americans to the "left" of the political spectrum during the 1930s was a legacy of trends in politics over the previous 50 years. In the 1890s the People's Party, whose members were known as populists, advocated government-ownership of railroads, telephone companies, and the telegraph. The populists also supported government-price support of farm products through a sub-treasury system, free and unlimited coinage of silver (to cause inflation), and abolition of the Pinkerton Detective Agency, a company of hired security guards used by industrialists to break up strikes and protect their properties. Farmers were a major element of the populist movement who wanted inflation to drive up the prices of their produce. Although the platform of the People's Party seemed radical at the time and did not attract sufficient support to elect major candidates, the ideas drew considerable attention. Eventually a number of the demands were enacted.

Between 1900 and 1920 "progressivism" arose, a reform period where city, state, and federal governments took on increased roles in meeting the needs of society. Supporters of the movement anticipated more and more government intervention in everyday life and labor of Americans. The progressive reformers set maximum hours of work, minimum wages, safety inspections in factories, and limits on railroad rates. Progressives supported conservation and "wise use" of resources, public health campaigns, and "good government." Their sense of what was "good" was founded on the general health and happiness of all citizens.

The legacy of "populism" and "progressivism" was creating an atmosphere where some Americans were receptive to the government regulating and shaping the economy and improving the conditions of all Americans. Socialists tapped these attitudes and, during the 1910s, built a political party that elected a number to public office. The Industrial Workers of the World (IWW), a vocal and militant labor union, also grew as it called for all sorts of government intervention on behalf of laborers. The general prosperity of the early 1920s, however, checked the growth of "isms" in America. Many were horrified with the rise of communism in Russia and pulled back from the socialists and anarchists who had attracted their attention prior to the entry of the United States into World War I (1914–1918).

The onset of the Great Depression in 1929, however, unleashed new forces that built upon old ideas. Advocates from the left seized the opportunity to chart their solutions to the problems of the United States.

Revolution and Marxist Philosophy

The rise of communism with the success of the Bolshevik Revolution in Russia in 1919 led immediately to the formation of the Communist Party of the United States. The CPUSA slowly drew disenchanted laborers, immigrants, intellectuals, and others in the 1920s. The onset of the Great Depression brought a drop in faith in the U.S. capitalist system.

Leaders of big business were seen as greedy and the U.S. government as ineffective, thus leading to the worsening economic crisis creating more fertile ground for the party's growth. The party, in general, endorsed the concepts of revolution and the triumph of the proletariat (working classes) in the overthrow of the bourgeoisie, or middle and upper class capitalists. These concepts helped shape the party's development in the 1920s and its nomination of William Z. Foster for president in 1924, 1928, and 1932.

With the economic strife beginning with the 1929 stock market crash, the Communist Party USA, found new opportunities for attracting members and threw its energies into organizing strikes and labor unions. Unemployment steadily climbed through the first few years peaking at 25 percent, or over 12 million workers, by 1933. With an ineffective response of President Hoover's administration that believed government should largely stay out of the nation's economic affairs, the unemployed workers began looking for other political alternatives.

The party pushed the New Deal of the Roosevelt administration to adopt its ideas but also cooperated with New Dealers by the late 1930s. The CPUSA in combination with advocates of social insurance for the aged, an inflated currency through coinage of silver, and massive government make-work and welfare programs contributed to shoving the New Deal to the "left" of the political spectrum.

Perspectives

Although President Roosevelt clearly rejected the radical politics of many of those on the left, he clearly felt a pressure to respond to some degree to diffuse their attractiveness to the public. Particularly as he became aware that he could not please both business and the average citizen with his New Deal programs, in 1935 he began to focus more on the common citizen. This major shift in focus by Roosevelt and the New Dealers was also clearly in response to some of Roosevelt's main critics, such as Father Coughlin, Sinclair, and Long. Many of the New Deal programs reflected some emphasis of the left, including Social Security and the National Labor Relations Act. As a result much of the support for the more radical groups gradually shifted toward Roosevelt by the 1936 presidential election campaign, giving the president several million more votes.

Roosevelt remained very concerned over radical politics because of the events in Europe with the rise of communism in Russia and fascism in Germany and Italy. Eventually he would instruct the FBI to place more emphasis on keeping track of individuals in the United States who were advocating such political concepts. The much more conservative Congress by 1938 would go further in opening hearings on the subject to investigate communism in America.

Wealth Distribution

Millions of Americans were "have-nots" by the 1930s. They did not have jobs, incomes, or homes. Many had lost their savings in bank failures or foreclosures on mortgages on properties they owned. Yet others, a small majority, continued the good life of wealth and extravagance. Many believed the stock market crash and Depression resulted from the great concentration of the nation's wealth in only a few and the wider gap in wealth between them and the mass public. Therefore some manner of redistributing the wealth among the population was seen as a solution to the economic crisis and a means of avoiding future economic depressions.

A number of proponents raised the prospect of redistributing the nation's wealth through government action. Huey Long, a Democrat and U.S. Senator of Louisiana, proposed his "Share-Our-Wealth Plan" by using taxation to take from the rich and give to the poor. Dr. Francis E. Townsend, a retired doctor living in Long Beach, California, wanted a tax that would enable the government to give old-age pensions to citizens if they agreed to spend the money within the month. Author Upton Sinclair wanted to tax the wealth to create state-owned communal farms and agricultural price supports in California, fostering jobs and what he said would be new prosperity.

Communist Party USA

For the Communist Party USA, the 1930s were initially a time to promote revolutionary communism. The communists believed the Great Depression was a confirmation that capitalism was a corrupt and ineffective economic system allowing only a few to concentrate the wealth and subjugate the remainder to low paying jobs in miserable working conditions. The Depression indicated such a system would eventually collapse. The party thus worked hard to offer a different political and economic option built on government ownership or control of industry. By 1935, however, the international leaders of communism felt that opposition to fascism was more important to the party and thus they promoted the "Popular Front." For the CPUSA this meant shifting support to the New Deal and President Roosevelt and largely abandoning, for a time, the commitment to the ideology of Karl Marx and inevitable revolution. This shift in direction was largely managed by Earl Browder, head of CPUSA after 1932.

Limited or Large Federal Government

Until the New Deal the federal government had played a relatively limited role in the life of the United States. Although the government held vast tracts of

A Communist Party Demonstration in 1930. The Communist Party was heavily involved in the labor movement, organizing unions and strikes against companies. (The Library of Congress.)

land, it had primarily sought to dispose of those holdings by transfer from public to private ownership. The federal government also had, to a large degree, embraced a *laissez-faire* (leave it alone) attitude towards the economy and the conflicts between labor and capitalists.

The advent of the Great Depression provoked a spirited debate about the enlargement of government

Striking mill workers parade through the streets of Patterson, New Jersey in 1931. The right of workers to strike was continually questioned during the years of the Depression. (AP/Wide World Photos. Reproduced by permission.)

activity in the economy and everyday lives of Americans. Debates about centralized planning, legal identity for labor unions, the rights of workers to strike, stiff inheritance taxes, federal make-work projects, income distributions to the elderly, national health insurance, federal management of the public rangelands, as well as range within the national forests, and other matters sharpened the issues between limited and expanded government. Political conservatives generally opted for limited government and a *laissez-faire* philosophy; liberals commonly supported the rapid expansion of government action on behalf of Americans during the Great Depression.

Labor Unions and the Rights to Collective Bargaining

Workers had for decades since the rapid growth of industrialization following the Civil War (1861–1865) often worked in deplorable conditions with low pay, poor sanitation, long hours, few benefits, and little safety. With the Great Depression, many lost their jobs but many others had their pay cut.

The desire to organize, which had declined through the boom years of the 1920s, rose again. At the onset of the Great Depression, however, labor unions had unclear legality. Their right to organize and strike was frequently challenged by owners of com-

panies. During the 1930s, tens of thousands of Americans joined unions in response to the organizing efforts of the Congress of Industrial Organizations (CIO) and the American Federation of Labor (AFL). Although few in number, members of the Communist Party, USA were active labor organizers. They promoted strikes, enlisted workers in unions, and, most particularly, built up the CIO.

Impact

In the long term a number of major changes happened in the United States as a consequence of the "left" tilt of the New Deal. As a result the New Deal brought a major growth in government that would influence almost every aspect of American's daily lives. Many of the New Deal programs and organizations such as Social Security, Works Progress Administration, and National Labor Relations Board felt various tugs from the left in their formulation to help the working class.

In order to enact welfare and "make-work" programs, the federal government engaged in deficit spending. That is, it spent money it did not have by borrowing from future generations. This was viewed as "priming the pump." The argument was to pour

Media Depictions

The following films can be found relating to the subject of the Left during the Depression.

All the King's Men. A black and white feature film based on Robert Penn Warren's novel, founded on the life of Huey P. Long. Starring Broderick Crawford, the 1949 Hollywood movie won Academy Awards for best movie and best actor and actress. It was nominated for several other Academy Awards as well. The fictional story was about politician Willie Stark and his rise from rural roots into the political world involving corruption by those he meets along the way.

The American Experience: Huey Long. Directed by Ken Burns (PBS special) Black and White/Color. Time: 88min. This program, exploring the radical politics and life of Huey Long, is part of the acclaimed Ken Burns' series about people and events in American history produced for the Public Broadcast System.

A&E Biography Series—Huey Long. Time: 50 min. This insight into the life of Long is part of the highly popular biography series produced by the Arts and Entertainment cable television network.

Dorothy Healey: An American Red. Videocassette, 50 min., color, 1984. San Francisco State University, San Francisco, CA. The documentary program provides a portrait of one of the United States' most outspoken advocates for radical social change. It follows her life from her first arrest at age 14 for subversive activity to her later activities following resignation from the Communist Party.

Richard Wright—Black Boy. A 86-minute film by Madison D. Lacy, Jr., produced for the Pubic Broadcasting System (PBS), focusing on the life and work of black American author Richard Wright. Born in Mississippi, Wright highlighted the oppression of minorities during the Great Depression. He joined the Communist Party in 1934 and wrote revolutionary poetry for leftist magazines. He also served as editor of the Communist *Daily Worker*. *Black Boy* was from the title of his 1945 autobiography.

Seeing Red. This 100-minute long, 1983 documentary film interviews 15 former CPUSA members of the Communist Party of the United States (CPUSA). The film was nominated for an Academy Award for best documentary of the year.

---

investment into a dead or sluggish economy in order to stimulate its recovery and in the future to recover the monies borrowed to do it. The concept of deficit spending was highly controversial but was widely adopted. The national debt grew dramatically during the last half of the twentieth century.

The pressure of Huey Long, Upton Sinclair, and Dr. Francis Townsend marked the beginning of increasing assumption by the government for the responsibility of all citizens. As part of President Roosevelt's New Deal programs, Social Security benefits commenced in 1940. Prior to 1940 there was no program in place to assist retired people. In time the benefits were extended to dependent children, surviving spouses, and the disabled.

Incorporating Leftist Ideas into the New Deal

As governor of Louisiana, Huey Long promoted massive construction projects of roads, bridges, highways, and educational facilities. He believed in creating a modern infrastructure for his state. The New Deal picked upon on many of these same ideas and through the Civilian Conservation Corps (CCC), Works Progress Administration (WPA), and Tennessee Valley Authority (TVA) invested in the future of the country.

All three agencies—the CCC, WPA, and TVA—employed the unemployed, giving them jobs when no one else was hiring. Building roads, dams, bridges, and other public improvements, the federal government

Earl Browder, head of the Communist Party, USA, crosses a hammer with a sickle during a rally in New York City on November 2, 1936. Browder sought to move the Communist Party into the mainstream of American politics. (AP/Wide World Photos. Reproduced by permission.)

aimed to keep people employed and productive, and keep the nation moving, through the difficult years of the Great Depression. The extent of government involvement in public life under Roosevelt's administration, as illustrated through these programs, was in stark contrast to the hands off approach favored by Roosevelt's predecessor, Herbert Hoover, and those who went before him. With the New Deal, Roosevelt began a trend of government involvement that, while still debated, has not been reversed.

Continued Government Involvement

The nation recovered from the Great Depression as the 1930s closed and the country prepared for World War II (1939–1945). Following the war the federal government made a commitment to the Interstate Freeway system, which would connect the country by vast interstate roads and make travel easier. Between 1954 and 1990 the nation was linked with a modern, efficient road network, most of it paid for through federal appropriations.

Additionally, government efforts to improve standards for the people endured beyond the New Deal.

In the 1960s President Lyndon Johnson (1963–1969) launched the Great Society program. It was based on social and economic freedom and opportunity for all and was founded on massive federal expenditures to achieve its goals. Of singular importance to the Great Society were the Medical Care Act, which proposed federally funded health insurance for the elderly, and federal revenue sharing with the states to provide medical care to the poor through Medicaid. These programs remained in effect into the twenty-first century.

Johnson's Great Society also established a Head Start program for young children from families of little means. Head Start was designed to better prepare children for public school by providing them with the socialization and other skills they needed.

The political left established a clear base for itself during the years of the Great Depression. Since then it has continued to make its presence felt in American politics and society. The Communist Party, among others, continued to support labor unions. The National Labor Relations Act made unions legal when it was passed in 1935, a result partly owing to the pressures on Roosevelt from the left including the Communist Party.

Unions grew rapidly in mid-twentieth century America and continued to fight for improved wages, working conditions, and retirement programs for workers. Unions remained strongly involved in U.S. business and labor until they began to wane in the latter part of the twentieth century in face of competition by overseas workers in manufacturing products and by the anti-union sentiments of a number of public officials.

Notable People

William Z. Foster (1881–1961). Foster was born in Taunton, Massachusetts, to parents who had emigrated from England and Ireland. The family moved to Philadelphia where Foster, at age ten, left school to work in unskilled jobs. He joined the Socialist Party in 1901, and the Industrial Workers of the World (IWW) in 1909. Foster was involved in free speech fights and even jailed in Spokane, Washington.

Foster eventually broke with the IWW and in 1919 helped form the Communist Party, USA. He was nominated for president by the CPUSA in 1924, 1928, and 1932. In the election, where he campaigned against Franklin D. Roosevelt and Herbert Hoover, he secured 102,785 votes, the largest number ever cast for a CPUSA candidate.

Biography:

Huey Long

1893–1935, "I'm a small fish here in Washington. But I'm the Kingfish to the folks down in Louisiana." Huey Long describing why he gave himself the nickname "Kingfish."

Long was born in Winnfield, Winn Parish, Louisiana, the eighth of nine children of a farmer. Winn Parish was a stronghold of the Populist movement in the 1890s, and Socialist sentiments were strong in the area prior to World War I. As a boy, Long absorbed many of the ideas that circulated around him. He attended high school but quarreled with school authorities and left before graduation. Long then began to study law and after taking only a year of classes was admitted to the bar. He used his law degree only as a starting point for his goal of a career in politics.

Long was governor of Louisiana from 1928 to 1932 and was elected to the U.S. Senate in 1930. As governor he sponsored many reforms that endeared him to the rural poor. He was an ardent enemy of corporate interests, was colorful, charismatic, controversial, and always just skating on the edge. Long desired to be the President of the United States and even wrote a book entitled, *My First Days in the White House*

(1935), in which he named his cabinet. Long's "Share-Our-Wealth" program called upon the government to guarantee every family an annual income so it could have the necessities of life. His program, however, also brought him a lot of enemies. In September 1935 Dr. Carl A. Weiss assassinated Long in Baton Rouge, Louisiana.

Huey Long wrote the book *Every Man a King* which was published in 1935. The following are two excerpts from the book, describing his political philosophy (pp. 291, 298).

> There is no rule so sure as the one that the same mill grinds out fortunes above a certain size at the top, grinds out paupers at the bottom. The same machine makes them both; and how are they made? There is so much in the world, just so much land, so many houses, so much to eat and so much to wear. There is enough—yea, there is more—than the entire human race can consume, if they are reasonable....
>
> We may build more factories, but the fact remains that we have enough now to supply all our domestic needs and more, if they are used. No, our basic trouble was not an insufficiency of capital; it was an insufficient distribution of buying power coupled with an over-sufficient speculation (investment) in production.

Foster suffered health problems in 1932 and was replaced by Earl Browder as party leader. In 1945, however, Foster regained the chairmanship of CPUSA. He was an ardent supporter of Joseph Stalin and declined to acknowledge Stalin's brutality. Foster died in a hospital in 1961, near Moscow.

Gus Hall (1910–2000). Hall was born Arvo Kusta Halberg in Iron, Minnesota, a small town in the Mesabi Range. His parents were Finnish immigrants and active members of the Industrial Workers of the World (IWW). Hall left school after the eighth grade to work in a logging camp and in 1927 joined the Young Communist League. In 1931 the CPUSA selected Hall to go to Moscow to attend the Lenin School to study revolutionary theory and tactics.

In 1933 Hall settled in Minneapolis where he helped organize protests and strikes; he was jailed in 1934 for six months for inciting a riot during a strike. Hall moved in 1935 to Pennsylvania and worked with the Congress of Industrial Organizations (CIO) as an

organizer for the Steel Workers Organizing Committee (SWOC). He was involved in the Little Steel Strike in 1937 against Republic Steel in Warren, Ohio. He was charged with plotting to dynamite company property and homes of scabs. Hall pled guilty and was fined.

During World War II Hall served in the U.S. Navy on Guam. In 1948 he was tried, found guilty, and sentenced to five years in prison for conspiring to promote the violent overthrow of the government of the United States. During appeal of his conviction, Hall jumped bail and fled to Mexico. He was captured, returned to the United States, and served his jail sentence at Leavenworth Penitentiary until 1957.

Upon his release, Hall became general secretary of CPUSA in 1959 and, starting in 1962, was nominated by his party four times for president of the United States. Hall's last years were marked with bitter disputes within CPUSA and he resigned as national chairman shortly before his death in 2000.

Hall was author of several books: *Fighting Racism: The Nation's Most Dangerous Pollutant* (1971); *Ecology: Can We Survive Capitalism* (1972); and *The Crisis of U.S. Capitalism and the Fight Back* (1975). The CPUSA published many of his speeches and pamphlets. Hall received the Order of Lenin, the highest medal in the Soviet Union, following his release from prison in the United States in 1959. During the 1960s Hall became a familiar figure on college campuses, drawing large crowds and animated opposition to his right to speak.

William Hope Harvey (1851–1936). William Hope Harvey was born in Buffalo, West Virginia. He studied at Marshall College after which he taught, practiced law, and was a real estate developer. He became interested in the monetary problems facing the United States during the Great Depression. Harvey was a proponent of bi-metallism at the time the argument over coinage of silver was at its height. He spread his beliefs by distributing pamphlets, which had a great influence on the Populist Party.

In the early 1900s Harvey was convinced that civilization was on the verge of collapse. He began to build a pyramid at Monte Ne, Arkansas, containing a history of the rise and fall of civilization. Included in the structure were instructions for rebuilding society, as well as scale models of important machinery.

Harvey is best noted, however, for his support of the "free and unlimited coinage of silver" as the best solution to the Great Depression. He became the Liberty Party's presidential candidate in 1932, but failed to find a national following and, of course, lost to Franklin D. Roosevelt.

Dorothy Healey (1914–). Dorothy Healey was born in Denver, Colorado, to Joe and Barbara Rosenblum. Her parents were Hungarian immigrants who came with their parents to the United States in the 1880s. Healey became active in the Young Communist League in 1928 and, through the 1930s, worked as a labor organizer and promoter of strikes for improved wages and working conditions in California. Her particular interests were farm and cannery workers.

In the 1940s she was a leader of the CPUSA in Los Angeles, one of the largest organizations of the party in the United States. Healey was indicted under the Smith Act in the 1960s as she plunged into civil rights and anti-Vietnam War advocacy. In 1973 she resigned from the CPUSA and, with Maurice Isserman, published her autobiography, *California Red: A Life in the American Communist Party* (1990).

Meridel Le Sueur (1900–1996). Le Sueur was born in Murray, Iowa, to socialist parents. She became

an author and poet and was known for books about the plight of workers. She wrote about many of the issues during the Great Depression based on her firsthand knowledge of working in garment sweatshops and restaurants. Le Sueur was blacklisted during the McCarthy era during the 1950s for her radical beliefs. From the 1970s to the end of her life, however, Le Sueur became a respected writer and lecturer who continued to support the common working class.

Clifford Odets (1906–1963). Born in Philadelphia, Pennsylvania, Clifford Odets left school at the age of 17 to become an actor. After a series of small parts on the stage and on radio, he formed the Group Theater in New York. Members of this group held leftist political views and sought to produce plays about important social issues. In 1934 Odets joined the American Communist Party.

In 1953 he was investigated by Joseph McCarthy and the House Un-American Activities Committee. Odets argued that he was never under the influence of the Communist Party and that his work was based on his sympathy for the working classes. Odets is regarded as one of the most gifted of the American social-protest playwrights of the 1930s and is best known for his plays, "Waiting for Lefty" (1935) and "Awake and Sing" (1935).

Upton Sinclair (1878–1968). Sinclair was born in Baltimore and moved to New York City in 1888. With his family poor and his father an alcoholic, Sinclair lived with his wealthy grandparents. He excelled at school and entered New York City College at only 14 years of age. He was able to pay for his college education by writing stories for newspapers and magazines.

In the early 1900s Sinclair became an active socialist, and in 1904 he was commissioned by a socialist journal to write a novel about immigrant workers in the Chicago meatpacking houses. Sinclair wrote the novel, *The Jungle,* which was originally rejected by six publishers. Many initially thought the book was too negative and felt that Sinclair did not desire to help the poor but rather hated the rich. *The Jungle* was eventually published by Doubleday in 1906 and was an immediate success.

Although President Roosevelt read *The Jungle* and ordered an investigation into the meatpacking industry, he felt that Sinclair's novel preached socialism— and it did. In 1926 and 1934 Sinclair ran as the Socialist Party candidate for governor of California, but he was defeated in both elections. His EPIC (End Poverty In California) campaign, however, gained considerable support and helped to launch the national movement toward Social Security. In the 1920s Sinclair was a founder of the American Civil Liberties Union (ACLU).

Dr. Francis E. Townsend (1867–1960). Born in Fairbury, Illinois, Francis Townsend graduated from the University of Nebraska medical school in 1903. He practiced medicine in several Western states and in 1919 settled at Long Beach, California.

In 1933, at the height of the Depression, he produced the Townsend Plan, which called for a pension of $200 per month for citizens over 60 years of age, on the condition that the money be spent in the month received. The funds were to be raised by a two percent federal sales tax. Although Townsend's plan created a following of supporters, the plan was not supported by President Roosevelt and was defeated in Congress on a number of occasions. Townsend did, however, publicized the concern of providing for the elderly, which eventually led to the Social Security Act.

Richard Wright (1908–1960). Born in Roxie, Mississippi, Wright spent his youth in the South, where he was confronted with racial tension. White men killed his uncle, a crime for which no arrest was ever made. Wright excelled at school and was valedictorian of his class. He was appalled with the illiteracy of black Americans and the strife they endured in the South.

When Wright was a young man, he moved to Chicago where he secured a job working at the post office. In 1930, however, with the start of the Great Depression, Wright's hours at the post office were cut. He began to write stories and poetry for various magazines and organizations and eventually moved to New York. While in New York, he joined the Communist Party and expressed his political beliefs through leftist publications.

As Wright grew as a writer he continued to explore the ideas of the communist left, but remained also concerned with the racial strife of the South and the inequality between whites and blacks in general. Wright eventually moved to Paris, France, because of the continued racism he experienced in the United States. His most well-known works included, *Lawd Today!, Uncle Tom's Children, Native Son,* and *Black Boy.*

Primary Sources

"Every Man a King"

In 1935 Huey Long teamed up with Louisiana State University band director Castro Carrazo to write a song about sharing the nation's wealth. Long

Major Writings
All the King's Men

Set in the 1930s, this Pulitzer Prize-winning novel authored by Robert Penn Warren is loosely based on the political life of Louisiana Governor Huey Long. The book relays the story of Willie Stark, an ambitious Southern politician who has great appeal with the public due to his policies to help the poor. Stark's initial idealism, however, is eventually overcome by his own ego and lust for power.

Stark's rise from a young, idealistic lawyer to the heights of political power and corruption are recounted by Jack Burden, a reporter who later becomes Stark's right-hand man. Jack soon finds himself embroiled in the governor's political intrigue and is there to witness his fall from power.

announced that if he ran for president "Every Man a King" would be one of his campaign songs. He arranged to have it recorded for presentation on a national newsreel service. The lyrics to the song were as follows:

> Why weep or slumber America
> Land of the brave and true
> With castles and clothing and food for all
> All belongs to you
> Ev'ry man a King, ev'ry man a King

Upton Sinclair's Crusade

The California League Against Sinclairism ran ads in 1934 in newspapers to oppose EPIC and Upton Sinclair's candidacy for governor. Many were in response to a series of books that Sinclair authored describing what he would do as California governor. They include *I, Candidate for Governor of California, and How I Got Licked* (1935, 1994), *I Governor of California: And How I Ended Poverty, A True Story of the Future* (1933), and *We, People of America: And How We Ended Poverty, A True Story of the Future* (1936). The advertisement and further information are recounted in an online display by the Museum of the City of San Francisco. Available from the World Wide

Web at http://www.sfmuseum.org/hist2/sinclair.html (cited February 20, 2002).

> A Challenge to Action! A Call to Arms!! In Defense of California! Sinclairism—the program of Upton Sinclair and his radical associates—is Communism, cleverly disguised, but deliberately designed to Russianize California state government.
>
> It's rooted in class hatred, fostered and fomented by radicals who boast of their hatred of American ideals and American principles of government. If it is successful, it will destroy California's business structure, bankrupt our families, overthrow our organized labor, confiscate our homes, wreck our industries, and rob our employed workers of their employment.
>
> Your personal security is at issue—the welfare of your home and family; your American citizenship, your rights of self-rule and freedom of worship—your job and your independence. At Tuesday's election . . . stay American!"

Recollecting the Communist Movement

Dorothy Healey, an organizer of the Young Communist League, recalled her active work in the Young Communist League which started in Oakland, California, when she was a teenager and led her to San Pedro, California, in 1934 and 1935. Her memories are recounted in Dorothy Ray Healey and Maurice Isserman's *California Red: A Life in the American Communist Party* (1993, pp. 35, 63).

> In my last few years in high school I was involved in a whole range of Party-organized activities including the Young Pioneers. The Young Pioneers was our children's group. The group I was put in charge of was composed of fifteen or twenty Black kids from Oakland. They came each Saturday morning for the activities we sponsored, games and parties and singing and storytelling, always with a political moral ...
>
> I was enchanted with the sailors I met in San Pedro. They were already veterans of great labor struggles, very courageous, militant, and politically sophisticated. I can remember sitting in the headquarters listening spellbound to the yarns they would spin of life aboard ship and in the ports they visited. The YCL also helped organize the Cannery Workers Industrial Union in the fish canneries on Terminal Island in San Pedro harbor. We got a federal charter from the AFL for the cannery union, which was what they gave you when they didn't have a union with jurisdiction over an industry. That allowed us to take all the workers of all the different crafts within the cannery into one industrial union ...
>
> While I was in San Pedro I shared a house with a group of young Communists. I suppose it was what would later be called a 'commune,' but we didn't think in those terms. It was just a question of getting by with little or no money. As the local YCL organizer I was supposed to get paid five dollars a week, but it was part of my job to get that five dollars donated by sympathizers in San Pedro, which meant I often didn't get paid. Every night I'd go eat with a different family. It was like being a

schoolteacher or a minister in the nineteenth century village, it was considered part of your upkeep. For the first time in my life I started to gain weight because I always ate a lot of bread so that I wouldn't have to eat the meat— I didn't want to take the more expensive food out of the mouths of the people I was sharing with.

The President Issues a Challenge

President Franklin D. Roosevelt challenged communism at the American Youth Congress in February 1940. In response to his remarks he was booed and hissed by the delegates on the south lawn of the White House. Roosevelt said:

> More than twenty years ago, while most of you were very young children, I had the utmost sympathy for the Russian people. In the early days of Communism, I recognized that many leaders in Russia were bringing education and better health and, above all, better opportunity to millions who had been kept in ignorance and serfdom under the imperial regime. I disliked the regimentation under Communism. I abhorred the indiscriminate killings of thousands of innocent victims. I heartily deprecated the banishment of religion-though I knew that some day Russia would return to religion for the simple reason that four or five thousand years of recorded history have proven that mankind has always believed in God in spite of many abortive attempts to exile God.
>
> I, with many of you, hoped that Russia would work out its own problems, and that its government would eventually become a peace-loving, popular government with a free ballot, which would not interfere with the integrity of its neighbors.
>
> That hope is today either shattered or put away in storage against some better day. The Soviet Union, as everybody who has the courage to face the fact knows, is run by a dictatorship as absolute as any other dictatorship in the world. It has allied itself with another dictatorship, and it has invaded a neighbor [Finland] so infinitesimally small that it could do no conceivable harm to the Soviet Union, a neighbor which seeks only to live at peace as a democracy, and a liberal, forward-looking democracy at that.
>
> It has been said that some of you are Communists. That is a very unpopular term these days. As Americans, you have a legal and constitutional right to call yourselves Communists, those of you who do. You have a right peacefully and openly to advocate certain ideals of theoretical Communism; but as Americans you have not only a right but a sacred duty to confine your advocacy of changes in law to the methods prescribed by the Constitution of the United States—and you have no American right, by act or deed of any kind, to subvert the Government and the Constitution of this Nation.

Suggested Research Topics

- Identify at least three pressures from the political left which helped shape the New Deal.

- Identify at least two of the following individuals and their solutions to the Great Depression: Upton Sinclair, William Hope Harvey, Francis Townsend.

- Explain why Huey Long's "Share-the-Wealth" campaign gained major popular support by 1935.

- How were American labor unions strengthened as a consequence of events in the 1930s?

Bibliography

Sources

Barrett, James. *William Z. Foster and the Tragedy of American Radicalism.* Urbana, IL: University of Illinois Press, 1999.

Dyson, Lowell K. *Red Harvest: The Communist Party and American Farmers.* Lincoln, NE: University of Nebraska Press, 1982.

Harvey, William Hope. *The Book.* Rogers, AR: The Mundus Publishing Co., 1930.

Healey, Dorothy Ray and Maurice Isserman. *California Red: A Life in the American Communist Party.* Urbana, IL: University of Illinois Press, 1993.

Isserman, Maurice. *Which Side Were You On? The American Communist Party During the Second World War.* Urbana, IL: University of Illinois Press, 1993.

Johanningsmeier, Edward P. *Forging American Communism: The Life of William Z. Foster.* Princeton University Press, 1994.

Kazin, Michael. "The Agony and Romance of the American Left," *American Historical Review,* December 1995.

Scott, Ivan. *Upton Sinclair, the Forgotten Socialist.* Lanham, MD: University Press of America, 1995.

Further Reading

Dennis, Peggy. *The Autobiography of an American Communist: A Personal View of a Political Life, 1925–1975.* Westport, CT: Lawrence Hill & Co., 1977.

Fineran, John Kingston. *The Career of a Tinpot Napoleon: A Political Biography of Huey P. Long.* New Orleans, LA: J.K. Fineran, 1932.

Harris, Leon A. *Upton Sinclair, American Rebel.* New York: Crowell, 1975.

Howe, Irving and Lewis Coser. *The American Communist Party: A Critical History.* New York: Da Capo Press, 1974.

Long, Huey P. *Every Man A King: The Autobiography of Huey P. Long.* New Orleans, LA: National Book Co., 1933.

———. *My First Days in the White House.* Harrisburg, PA: The Telegraph Press, 1935.

Warren, Robert Penn. *All the King's Men.* New York: Harcourt Brace, 1946.

Williams, T. Harry. *Huey Long.* New York: Knopf, 1969.

See Also

New Deal (First, and Its Critics); Social Security

Glossary, Bibliography, & Master Index

Glossary

A

abstinence: a deliberate self denial of alcoholic beverages; an individual who does not drink any liquor is abstaining from liquor.

abstract expressionism: art that seeks to portray emotions, responses, and feelings rather than objects in their actual likeness.

absurd: something ridiculous or unreasonable.

academic freedom: freedom to teach without interference or unwanted influence by another group or government.

Academy Awards: annual awards granted by the Academy of Motion Pictures for outstanding acting, directing, script writing, musical scoring, service, and creative contributions to the film industry.

adaptation: something that is remade into a new form, as in a play being an adaptation of a short story.

administration: the art or science of managing public affairs. Public administration is the function of the executive branch of government and is the procedure by which laws are carried out and enforced. In the United States, the president is the head of the executive branch, which includes an advisory staff and many agencies and departments.

affiliate: a firm closely connected to another.

agribusiness: an industry involved in farming operations on a large scale. May include producing, processing, storing, and distributing crops as well as manufacturing and distributing farm equipment.

alien: foreign-born person who has not been naturalized to become a U.S. citizen. Federal immigration laws determine if a person is an alien.

Allies: nations or states that form an association to further their common interests. The United States' partners against Germany during World War II (1939–1945) are often known collectively as "The Allies" and include Great Britain and Russia. (*See also* Axis powers)

allottee: the legal owner of a specific parcel of land, held in trust by the federal government for a minimum of 25 years under the provisions of the General Allotment Act of 1887. An allottee has an allotment, a specific portion of a reservation that was held apart from other tribal lands for that person's use or the benefit of his or her descendents.

allotment: the parcel of land granted to an individual that was taken out of a tribe's communal land base known as a reservation. While allotments dated to colonial times, they became a major part of national Indian policy in the General Allotment Act of 1887.

AM: amplitude modulation, the first type of radio transmission, characterized by considerable static interference.

amendment: changes or additions to an official document. In the United States government, constitutional amendments refer to changes in the Constitution. Such amendments are rare and may be proposed only by a two-thirds vote of both houses of Congress or by a convention called by

Congress at the request of two-thirds of the state legislators.

American Federation of Labor (AFL): a national organization of craft unions that sought to give voice to the concerns primarily of skilled workers.

amortized: the payment of a loan by stable monthly payments which include both principle and interest over a period of time, resulting in a declining principle balance and repayment in full by the end of the loan period.

anarchism: a belief that no forms of government authority are necessary and that society should be based on the cooperative and free association of individuals and groups.

animated cartoon: a motion picture made from a series of drawings simulating motion by means of slight progressive changes in the drawings.

anti-Semitism: hateful sentiment or hostile activities towards Jews; racial or religious intolerance.

antitrust: opposing large combinations of businesses that may limit economic competition.

Anti-Trust Acts: federal and state laws to protect economic trade and combat discrimination between companies, price fixing, and monopolies.

appraisal: to set a value of a property by the estimate of an authorized person.

appropriations: Funds for specific government and public purposes as determined by legislation.

Aquacade: a program of lights, music, and synchronized swimming developed by Billy Rose for the 1939 New York World's Fair.

area coverage: a system of electrical service designed to serve all possible customers in a given area rather than only those customers pre-selected on the basis of their projected consumption or ability to pay.

assets: total value of everything owned by, and owed to, a business. A bank's assets include its physical building and equipment, the loans it has made on which interest is owed, stock owned in the Federal Reserve System, government bonds it owns, money in the bank's vaults, and money deposited in other banks.

assimilation: a minority group's adoption of the beliefs and ways of life of the dominant culture.

Axis powers: The countries aligned against the Allied nations in World War II (1939–1945). The term originally applied to Nazi Germany and Fascist Italy (Rome-Berlin Axis), and later extended to include Japan. (*See also* Allies)

B

B-Movie (B-Picture, B-Film): cheaply produced movies usually following a simple formula and intended to serve as the second film in a "double bill," the showing of two movies for one theater admission.

bank holiday: a day or series of days in which banks are legally closed to correct financial problems.

bank runs: occurred when worried depositors, fearing about the stability of a bank, rushed to the bank to withdraw their deposits.

benefits: financial aid in time of sickness, old age, or unemployment.

bill: a proposed law. In the United States bills may be drawn up by anyone, including the president or citizen groups, but they must be introduced in Congress by a senator or representative.

bipartisan: cooperation between the two major political parties; for example, Republican and Democratic.

bond: a type of loan, such as savings bonds, issued by the government to finance public needs that cost more than existing funds can pay for. The government agrees to pay lenders back the initial cost of the bond, plus interest.

budget deficit: occurs when money spent by the government or other organization is more than money coming in.

bureau: a working unit of a department or agency with specific functions.

bureaucracy: an administrative system, especially of government agencies, that handles day-to-day business and carries out policies.

Burlesque: a type of variety show that focuses on musical acts and skits with sexual overtones.

business cycle: an economic cycle usually comprised of recession, recovery, growth, and decline.

buying on margin: a fairly common practice in the 1920s when investors purchased stock on credit, speculating on its increase in value. They planned to pay their loans back with the money they anticipated making. Such risks sometimes proved disastrous.

bootlegger: a person who illegally transports liquor; an individual who produces or distributes liquor illegally; smuggler.

bootlegging: the illegal manufacture or distribution of alcoholic products.

boycott: refusal of a group of persons to buy goods or services from a business until the business meets their demands.

bribery: giving gifts of money or property in return for specific favors.

broker: a person who brings a buyer and a seller together and charges a fee for assisting in the exchange of goods or services. A stockbroker brings together sellers and buyers of stocks and bonds.

budget deficit: refers to a government spending more than it receives through revenues and other means; it must rely on borrowing of money thus creating a debt.

C

cabinet: a group of advisors. In the federal government the cabinet is made up of advisors who offer assistance to the president. Each president determines the make up and role of their cabinets, although most include the heads of major departments such as State, Treasury, and Justice, and the vice president.

capital: money invested in a business; capital in banking terms includes the bank's stockholders' investments; additional money invested by the bank owners; any earnings still in the bank that have not been divided up; funds for taxes, expansion, and interest on accounts. Capital is the amount banks owe its owners.

capitalism: an economic system where goods are owned by private businesses and price, production, and distribution is decided privately, based on competition in a free market.

cartel: a combination of producers of any product joined together to control its production, sale, and price so as to obtain monopoly and restrict competition in any particular industry or commodity.

CCC: the Civilian Conservation Corps, a make-work agency for men aged 18 to 25 which operated between 1933 and 1942 and worked on numerous projects on public lands across the U.S. and its territories.

CCC-LEM: the Civilian Conservation Corps, Local Experienced Men, consisting initially of older, local laborers with special skills in carpentry, blacksmithing, auto mechanics, and other trades who came in to teach CCC enrollees.

CCC-ID: units of the Civilian Conservation Corps-Indian Division, staffed with American Indian recruits working on reservation projects.

cells: transparent celluloid on which sketches of animation are traced, inked, and painted.

charter: legal authorization from a federal or state agency to carry out business. To be chartered, a bank must have sufficient capital, competent management, deposit insurance, and a commitment to the local community.

child-centered: hands-on learning with children actively participating in an activity such as counting with blocks or piecing together a puzzle of the United States. This type of learning is a departure from traditional highly structured learning where a teacher tells children information or children read information from a book and repeat it.

cinematographer: the person in charge of camera work during the production of a movie.

civil liberties: freedom of speech, freedom of the press, freedom from discrimination, and other right guaranteed by the U.S. Constitution that place limits on governmental powers.

civil rights: civil liberties that belong to an individual.

civil service: a term describing the system employing people in non-military government jobs. The system is based on merit classifications.

clause: a section or paragraph of a legal document, such as a specific part of the U.S. Constitution.

clergy: ordained as religious priests, pastors, or ministers.

coalition: an alliance between political or special interest groups forged to pursue shared interests and agendas.

collateral: something of value that a borrower agrees to hand over to the lender if the borrower fails to repay the loan. The pledged item protects the lender from loss.

collective bargaining: the negotiations between workers who are members of a union and their employer for the purpose of deciding upon such issues as fair wages and work-day hours.

collectivism: shared ownership of goods by all members of a group; a political or economic system where production and distribution are decided collectively.

colonialism: a foreign policy in which a nation exercises its control over residents of foreign countries.

commerce: exchanging, selling, or trading goods on a large scale involving transporting goods from one place to another.

Commerce Clause: a provision of the U.S. Constitution that gives Congress the exclusive power to regulate economic trade between states and with foreign countries.

commercial bank: national or state bank, owned by stockholders whose activities include demand deposits, savings deposits, and personal and business loans. Many commercial banks also provide trust services, foreign money exchange, and international banking.

commercialism: to manage a business for profit; sometimes used in referring to excessive emphasis on profit.

committee: a group of individuals charged by a higher authority with a specific purpose such as investigation, review, reporting, or determining action.

commodities: any moveable item of commerce subject to sale.

communism: a theory calling for the elimination of private property so that goods are owned in common and, in theory, available to all; a system of government where a single party controls all aspects of society such as the official ideology of United Soviet Social Republic (USSR) from 1917 until 1990.

Communist Party, U.S.A. (CPUSA): a U.S. political party promoting the political and economic teaching of German political philosopher Karl Marx that grew rapidly in membership during the 1930s.

company union: a worker organization formed by a company commonly requiring membership of all employees to prevent their joining a national labor union.

compulsory: something that is required.

"conchies": an abbreviation identifying conscientious objectors who declined to serve in the military when drafted but who took alternative duty at Public Service Camps (former CCC camps) from 1941 to 1947.

congregation: an assembly of persons gathered as a religious community.

Congress: the term used to describe the combined Senate and House of Representatives.

Congress of Industrial Organizations (CIO): a labor organization formed in 1935 initially as the Committee on Industrial Organization within the AFL. The CIO was founded on broad-based industrial unionization rather than specialized crafts or skills like the AFL.

conscientious objector: a person who refuses to serve in the military because of personal beliefs. In the United States a person cannot refuse to serve, but Congress has allowed conscientious objectors to participate in non-combat duty or complete an exemption process on religious grounds. This exemption does not include objection for political, sociological, philosophical, or personal reasons, although the Supreme Court has upheld some requests for exemption based on these grounds if they are held with the fervor of religious beliefs.

conservation: the planned management of natural resources, such as soil and forests.

conservative: politically referring to one who normally believes in a limited government role in social and economic matters and maintenance of long-standing social traditions; conservative thought in education often stresses traditional basic subject matter and methods of teaching.

consumer: a person who buys or uses economic goods.

contour plowing: to till a sloping hillside following the same elevation back and forth, rather than up and down the hill, to prevent water erosion from rains.

cooperative: a private, nonprofit enterprise, locally owned and managed by the members it serves, and incorporated (established as a legal entity that can hold property or be subject to law suits) under State law.

corporatism: a system in which companies are organized into a cooperative arrangement that is recognized by the government and granted exemptions from antitrust laws in exchange for observing certain controls.

correspondent: an individual who communicates news or commentary to a newspaper, magazine, radio, or television station for publication or broadcast.

counterculture: a culture with values that run counter to those of established society.

credit: loan; agreement by which something of value is given in exchange for a promise to repay something of equal value; an advance of cash or a product, such as a car, in exchange for a promise to pay a specific sum in the future.

cultural democracy: the concept of cultural democracy comprises a set of related commitments: protecting and promoting cultural diversity, and the right to culture for everyone in our society and around the world; encouraging active participation in community cultural life; enabling people to participate in policy decisions that affect the quality of our cultural lives; and assuring fair and equitable access to cultural resources and support.

curator: an individual in charge of the care and supervision of a museum.

curriculum: courses of study offered by educational institutions such as English, social studies, and mathematics.

D

dailies: newspapers published everyday.

débutante ball: extravagant parties thrown by the very wealthy to introduce their daughters to high society and advertise their eligibility for marriage.

default: failure to meet the payment terms of a legal contract such as failure to make loan payments in repayment of a home loan; the lender may then begin foreclosure proceedings to recoup his loses.

deficit: the amount by which spending exceeds income over a given period.

deficit spending: a government spending more money than it receives in through taxes and other sources by borrowing.

demand deposits: checking accounts.

democracy: a form of government in which the power lies in the hands of the people, who can govern directly, or indirectly by electing representatives.

democratic: relating to the broad masses of people and promoting social equality and rule by majority.

Democratic Party: one of the two major political parties in the United States that evolved from the Democratic-Republican group that supported Thomas Jefferson. In the twentieth century, the Democratic Party has generally stood for freer trade, more international commitments, greater government regulations, and social programs. Traditionally considered more liberal than the Republican Party.

denomination: a religious organization with local congregations united together under a name and set of specific beliefs under one legal and administrative body.

department: an administrative unit with responsibility for a broad area of an organization's operations. Federal departments include Labor, Interior, Health and Human Services, and Defense.

dependent: persons who must rely on another for their livelihood. Generally applied to children 18 years and younger. The term can also refer to a person 62 years old or older.

deportation: expulsion of an alien from the United States.

deposit insurance: government-regulated protection for interest-bearing deposits, such as savings accounts, to protect the depositor from failure of the banking institution.

depression: a period of economic decline usually marked by an increase in unemployment.

desegregation: to end the legally enforced separation of races.

devaluation: to reduce the value of a nation's currency relative to other nations' currencies; often by lowering its gold equivalency.

disarmament: to reduce the amount of military arms a nation controls that can be used to attack or for defense.

divest: something of value that a person must give up. For example, the Banking Act of 1933 required officers of banks to divest themselves of any loans granted to them by their own banks to avoid a conflict of interest. Bankers could no longer be accused of using their depositors' money for their own, sometimes risky, investments.

Dixiecrat: southern Democrats who bolted from the party during the 1948 presidential campaign because of President Harry Truman's support of civil rights issues, as well as their opposition to a growing federal government by supporting strong state governments.

doctrine: a principle of law established in past decisions.

documentary still photograph: a photographic image in black-and-white or color that is realistic, factual, and useful as a historic document.

dole: when a needy person or family receives a hand-out from the government in the form of money, food, or vouchers from the government for support, it is referred to as "going on the dole." Though rarely used in the United States anymore, it is still commonly used in Britain.

double bill: showing two movies for one admission to a theater, usually with a main feature and a B-Movie.

dramatization: acting out events that actually happened, as in the events surrounding the negotiations were dramatized for television.

drug trafficking: buying or selling illegal drugs, the drug racket.

drys: people who supported Prohibition.

dual banking: the system of banking in the United States that consists of national banks and state banks. National banks are chartered and supervised by the Office of Comptroller of the Currency in the Treasury Department. State banks are chartered and supervised by state banking authorities.

due process of law: a basic constitutional guarantee that laws are reasonable and not arbitrary and their affects are well considered when developed; also guarantees that all legal proceedings will be fair and that a person will be given notice and an opportunity to speak before government acts to take their life, liberties, or property.

durable goods: goods that are not consumed or destroyed when used, often repeatedly for a number of years. Examples include armored tanks, ships, airplanes, and machinery.

E

electric power grid: a system for distributing electricity, interconnecting electric power plants and end users and comprising such equipment as power lines, poles, transformers, and substations.

electrification: the process or event in which a house, farm, industry, or locality is connected to an electric power source.

embezzle: for a person legally entrusted with funds to steal some for his or her own benefit. Embezzlers typically work in banks or other business institutions where they have access to funds.

End Poverty In California (EPIC): Upton Sinclair's proposal to pay everyone over the age of 60 a pension of $50 a month. He also urged that unemployed be put to work to produce necessities of life.

entrepreneur: an individual willing to try new approaches, who takes the risks of organizing and managing new enterprises.

EPIC Tax: Upton Sinclair's proposal in 1934 in California to charge a tax on property assessed at greater than $100,000 in value and use the income to fund the Central Valley Project of irrigation and agriculture to combat the Great Depression.

epidemiology: the branch of medicine dealing with the incidence and prevalence of disease in large populations and with detection of the source and cause of epidemics.

equal protection: a constitutional guarantee that no person or class of persons will be denied the same protection of the laws in their lives, liberty, property, or pursuit of happiness as other people in similar circumstances.

ethnic group: a large number of people considered a group based on shared racial, tribal, national, linguistic, religious, or cultural background.

exchange rate: a key part of international trade in which a rate guides how much one kind of currency can purchase another currency; can be either set by free international market or fixed by governments.

executive order: a rule or regulation issued by the president or a governor that has the effect of law. Executive orders are limited to those that implement provisions of the Constitution, treaties, and regulations governing administrative agencies.

ex-officio: members of a committee determined solely because of the office they hold.

exports: goods shipped to another nation for trade.

extender: foodstuffs to be added to dishes to stretch the meal, make the meal portions seem bigger, and feed more people. Common depression extenders were potatoes, onions, macaroni and spaghetti, rice, breads, and garden vegetables.

extortion: gaining another's property, money, or favors by use of threats of violence, disruption, or disclosure. For example, a crime group visits a shopkeeper and demands protection money. If the shopkeeper does not pay, the group may strike at him or his property until the shopkeeper does pay or is forced out of business.

extras: people hired to act in a group scene in a motion picture; background actors.

F

fascism: an ideology that focuses on nationalism or race as a uniting factor. Fascism first arose in Italy and Germany in the 1920s and 1930s, where it was characterized by government dictatorship, militarism, and racism.

federal: relating to the central government of a nation rather than to individual states.

federal aid: funds collected by the federal government (generally through taxes) and distributed to states for a variety of reasons including education and disaster relief.

federal budget: The annual financial plan of the United States government including all sources and amounts of income and items and amounts of expenditure. The federal budget must be approved by Congress and the president.

federalist: one who supports a strong central government as opposed to those favoring most governmental powers residing with the states and a weak federal government. It was the name of an early political party in the United States.

Federal Reserve System: a system of 12 Federal Reserve banks, a board of governors appointed by the president and state banks that apply for membership that hold money reserves for the banks in their region.

feminism: organized activity seeking political, social, and economic equality of the sexes.

filibuster: a means of obstructing progress in a legislative assembly by a legislator or group of legislators holding the floor for a prolonged period of time to prevent action on a proposed bill.

FM: frequency modulation, a type of radio transmission discovered in the 1930s but not routinely used until later, characterized by a clear, precise transmission.

forced leisure: due to unemployment during the Great Depression a person had lots of time and little choice but to pursue activities traditionally considered as leisure pursuits.

foreclosure: the process in which a bank that loaned money to a customer to purchase property takes over the property when customer fails to make payments. For example, farmers who failed to keep up with payments would have their farm loan foreclosed, thereby losing their property.

Fourteenth Amendment: one of three amendments to the Constitution passed shortly after the Civil War; this amendment guarantees the same legal rights and privileges of the Constitution to all citizens by guaranteeing that state laws cannot deprive any person of life, liberty, or property without due process of law and equal protection of the laws.

fraud: illegal misrepresentation or hiding the truth to obtain property, money, business, or political advantage.

free silver: rallying cry of the People's Party in the 1890s and the Liberty Party in 1932, promoting the increase in silver coinage and the greater amount in circulation per capita.

G

genre: refers to a type or classification. For example, "thrillers" as a movie genre; science fiction as a literary genre.

gold standard: a monetary system in which a nation's unit of money is set as equal to a given weight of gold. For example, one ounce of gold equals $300.

Grange: a rural social and educational organization through which farmers combated the power of railroads and utility companies in the early twentieth century.

grant: money provided by a government or organization to an individual or group for a specific purpose. For example, the federal government makes education grants to students for college expenses and to states to improve schools.

grassroots: political organizing at the most fundamental level of society—among the people.

Grazing Service: a federal agency established after passage of the Taylor Grazing Act (June 28, 1934) to bring federal management to more than 150 million acres of public lands, located mostly in the West. This agency supervised CCC activities in many areas. The Grazing Service merged with the U.S. General Land Office (GLO) in 1946 to become the Bureau of Land Management (BLM).

Great Depression: period in U.S. history from 1929 until the early 1940s when the economy was so poor that many banks and businesses failed and millions of people lost their jobs and their homes. Business problems were combined with a severe drought that ruined many farms and contributed to the economic disaster.

Great Society: term used by Lyndon Johnson during his presidential administration (1963–1969) to describe his vision of the United States as a land without prejudice or poverty, that would be possible by implementing his series of social programs.

Gross Domestic Product (GDP): a measure of the market value of all goods and services produced within the boundaries of a nation, regardless of asset ownership. Unlike gross national product, GDP excludes receipts from that nation's business operations in foreign countries, as well as the share of reinvested earnings in foreign affiliates of domestic corporations.

Gross National Product: total value of all goods and services produced by the nation's economy.

grounds: there exist reasons sufficient to justify some form of legal relief.

H

hierarchy: leadership or ruling structure of clergy organized into rank.

hooch: alcoholic beverages that are made or acquired illegally and are frequently of inferior quality.

holding company: a company or corporation whose only purpose or function is to own another company or corporation.

Hollywood: a section of Los Angles, California, at the base of the Santa Monica Mountains where several film producers established studios to make movies in the first half of the twentieth century.

House of Representatives: one of the two bodies with specific functions that make up the legislative branch of the United States government. Each state is allocated representatives based on population. (*See also* Congress; Senate)

housing starts: the number of residential building construction projects begun during a specific period of time, usually a month.

humanitarian: a person who works for social reform and is concerned about the welfare of people.

hydroelectric power: to generate electricity from the energy of swift flowing streams or waterfalls.

I

icon: an image, picture, or logo that becomes closely associated with a particular event, belief, or organization.

immigration: the legal or illegal entry of foreigners into a country intending to remain permanently and become citizens.

income distribution: the portion of annual earnings or accumulated wealth held by members of a society. The poor have low incomes, while the wealthy usually have high incomes and a resultant growing accumulation of assets.

independent: a voter who does not belong to any political party and votes for individual candidates regardless of their party affiliation.

indoctrinate: to instruct so as to instill a particular point of view.

indolent: a person not working because of laziness.

industrialism: to change an area or economy from agricultural to industrial production.

infrastructure: permanent developments to support a community's economy such as roads, buildings, and bridges.

inflation: a sharp increase in prices for goods and services decreasing the value of currency.

injunction: a judicial order that requires someone to stop or avoid certain actions that might harm the legal rights of another.

inoculate: to inject or implant a vaccine, microorganism, antibody, or antigen into the body in order to protect against, treat, or study a disease.

installment buying: purchasing commodities on credit and, having taken possession of the item, paying for it with a fairly high rate of interest over months or even years. The system encouraged those without savings to buy unwisely.

integration: to unite different races together into equal participation in society.

internationalism: a government policy of cooperation with other nations.

interest: money paid to a lender for use of his money.

interest rate: a percentage of money borrowed that must be paid back in addition to the sum of the original loan for the privilege of being able to borrow.

interventionism: a governmental policy of becoming involved in political matters of another nation.

invalidate: to determine that a law does not have sufficient legal justification to be enforceable; therefore it is no longer valid.

isolationism: opposition to economic or political alliances with other nations.

J

Jim Crow laws: state laws and ordinances primarily created in the South, requiring the separation of races in almost every aspect of public life. Jim Crow laws lasted from the late nineteenth century to the middle of the twentieth century. The laws were powerful barriers to legal and social equality.

journalism: written description of newsworthy events or presentation of facts designed to be published in a newspaper, magazine, or delivered vocally over radio or television.

judicial restraint: for courts not to interfere with what would more properly be the role of a legislature or the executive branch to decide the wisdom of a particular law.

judiciary: relating to the courts and legal system.

jurisdiction: the geographic area over which legal authority extends, such as the legal jurisdiction of a city police force.

juvenile delinquency: criminal behavior of children or young teens.

K

Keynesian economics: the theory of economist John Keynes that advocates government spending and economic recovery programs to promote spending and increase employment.

L

labor market: the people available for employment.

labor racketeering: corrupt activities between labor unions and organized crime. Members of criminal groups position themselves in places of authority within a labor union. Once inside they use funds such as pension and health funds to their own advantage.

labor union: a group of organized workers who negotiate with management to secure or improve their rights, benefits, and working conditions as employees.

laissez faire: a political doctrine that opposed governmental interference in economic affairs except for the minimum necessary to protect property rights and for safety.

lard: hog fat obtained by rendering down the fat deposits that exist between the flesh and the skin and around internal organs of the pig.

laundered money: transferring huge sums of illegally obtained money through banks or businesses with large cash flows until the original source of the money is untraceable.

lay people: membership of a religious faith who are not clergy; the general membership; also referred to as laity.

League of Nations: the forerunner of the United Nations, envisioned by its originator, Woodrow Wilson, as a forum where countries could resolve their differences without resorting to war and promoted economic and social cooperation.

leftist: a term used to describe individuals whose beliefs are on the "left" side of the political spectrum, constituting more liberal views. Often used derogatorily.

legislation: measures that are intended to become law after approval by legislative bodies.

liabilities: what a person owes to others. A bank's liabilities include checking and savings account deposits, investment of stockholders, funds for taxes and expansion, interest to be paid to depositors on their accounts, and earnings not yet divided among the stock holders.

liberal: politically referring to one who commonly emphasizes government protection of individual liberties and supports government social and economic reforms and regulation of business to encourage competition; liberal thought in education is often associated with new methods of teaching or nontraditional subject matter.

liquidate: to convert property into cash by selling it.

liquidity: being able to meet the demands of depositors to withdraw funds and to meet the needs of borrowers for credit (loans) or cash. Liquid assets include cash on hand and securities that can be sold quickly for cash.

loan sharking: loaning money at exorbitantly high interest rates and using threats to receive repayment.

lump-sum payment: one time only payment.

lumpenproletariat: those on the very bottom of the social scale described in the *Communist Manifesto* as "social scum."

M

Mafia: organized crime syndicate concerned with power and profit. The term originated in Italy some six centuries ago from the slogan: *Morte Alla Francia Italia anela!* ("Death to the French is Italy's cry.")

mafioso: member or members of the Mafia. Plural form is mafiosi.

"making do": creating filling and tasty meals with limited ingredients, with foods at hand or those readily available. Typical "making do" foods were flour, cornmeal, lard, eggs, potatoes, and onions.

maldistribution: a substantially uneven distribution of income or wealth to such an extent that it can cause general economic problems.

mandate: an authorization to act given by a political electorate to its representative.

margin call: when a creditor, who has loaned money, calls for immediate payment of the amount due.

Marxism: the theories—political, economic, and social—of Karl Marx, calling for class struggle to establish the proletariat (work class) as the ruling class, with the goal of eventually establishing a classless society.

means test: a battery of questions about a person's financial, employment, and residential history used to determine eligibility for charity or financial assistance.

mechanization: the increasing use of gas or diesel powered machinery such as tractors, harvesters, and combines; often replacing human or animal labor and introducing greater efficiency in growing and harvesting farm crops.

mediation: the intervention of an unbiased party to settle differences between two other disputing parties; any attempt to act as a go-between in order to reconcile a problem.

Mobilization: to assemble war materials and manpower and make ready for war.

melodrama: movies, sometimes referred to as "weepies," focused on characters living through a series of adverse and tragic circumstances. A character with a terminal illness is a frequently used plot.

Memorial Day Massacre: a 1937 Steel Workers' Organizing Committee strike in Chicago at the Republic steel mill of U.S. Steel that led to the deaths of ten workers and 30 others wounded by police.

minimum wage: the wage established by law as the lowest amount to be paid to workers in particular jobs.

minstrel shows: stage performances of black American traditional melodies and jokes performed by white actors impersonating blacks, including having their faces blacked.

moderation: acting in a responsible, restrained manner, avoiding excessive behaviors.

modernism: the cultural expression of Western society including the United States since the late nineteenth century, primarily as expressed in literature and visual designs.

modernist art: modernist art may be defined by its self-conscious interest in experimentation with the materials and creative processes of each individual art medium. Freed from representing objects as they actually exist, Modernist artists have tended to stress the subjective uniqueness of their own particular visions.

monopoly: when only one seller of a product, or a combination of sellers, exists who can set his own price.

moonshiner: maker or seller of illegal liquor.

moratorium: a legally authorized period of delay in performing some legal obligation; a waiting period set by an authority; a suspension of activity.

mortgage: normally involves a long-term real estate loan; the borrower gives the bank a mortgage in return for the right to use the property. The borrower agrees to make regular payments to the lender until the mortgage is paid up.

movie star: an actor or actress groomed for celebrity status by a movie production studio.

muckraking: a type of journalism that exposes the misdeeds and corruption in American business and politics of a prominent individual.

munitions: war supplies, particularly ammunition and weapons.

mutual fund: an investment company that invests the money of its shareholders in a diversified group of securities.

N

National Labor Relations Board: a board created in 1935 by the National Labor Relations Act to assist employees in the free selection of representative organizations (unions) to deal with employers, to prevent unfair labor practices, and to see that employers bargained in good faith.

National Union for Social Justice (NUSJ): an organization founded in 1935 by Father Charles Coughlin, the "Radio Priest" of Royal Oak, Michigan, who began a strong lobbying effort to influence Congress on the course of the New Deal.

nationalism: a strong loyalty to one's own nation above all others.

naturalization: the process in which an alien can apply to become a U.S. citizen. Requirements include five years of legal residence, literacy in English, and a record of good behavior.

Nazism: a political philosophy based on extreme nationalism, racism, and military expansion; dominated Germany from 1933 to 1945.

neutrality: policy of not becoming involved in war between two other nations.

New Deal: the name given to Franklin Roosevelt's plan to save the nation from the devastating effects of the Great Depression. His programs included direct aid to citizens and a variety of employment and public works opportunities sponsored by the federal government.

nickelodeon: an early movie theater, usually charging a nickel for admission.

non-durable goods: goods that are consumed or destroyed when used. Examples include chemicals, paper, rubber, textile, apparels, and foods.

O

old-age insurance: assurance of cash payments, generally made monthly, to retired workers' pensions.

oral history: the memories of an event or time, captured in the words of the person who lived it.

organized crime: a specialized form of crime with two major characteristics: organized into loosely or rigidly structured networks of gangs with certain territorial boundaries; the networks with rigid structures have bosses and a centralized management; and devoted to producing, protecting, and distributing illegal goods and services.

P

pacifism: opposed to armed conflict or war to settle disputes.

papal encyclical: an official letter from the Pope stating the Catholic Church's position on timely social issues and offering guidance for Catholic living.

parish: a local area or community of the members of a church.

partisan: adhering to a particular political party.

patron: a wealthy or influential supporter of an artist.

patronage: the power of public officials to make appointments to government jobs or grant other favors to their supporters, or the distribution of such jobs or favors.

pension(s): money given to an employee when they retire from a company. Pensions can be funded by the government, an employer, or through employee contributions.

philanthropy: humanitarian gifts to be distributed for the welfare of the fellow man.

photojournalism: emerged in the 1930s as a special filed of print communications. Magazines, newspapers, and movie newsreels tapped talented photographers to document labor, rural and urban settings, nature, warfare, and other subjects.

Photo-Secession: an informal society and a movement among photographers in the United States founded in 1903 by Alfred Stieglitz. The movement pursued pictorial photography and high aesthetic standards.

pictorial photography: using the camera to create artwork and moving photography outside of the studio. The techniques included soft-focus, manipulation of the negative and print in the dark room, and production of photographs to mimic paintings, watercolors, and other works of art.

pluralism: a situation in a nation when diverse ethnic, racial, or social groups participate in a common political and economic system.

pogrom: planned massacres of groups of people as the massacres experienced by the Jewish people.

pope: the bishop of Rome and head of the worldwide Roman Catholic Church.

pocket veto: a means by which the president of the United States can prevent a bill passed by Congress from becoming law by delaying the signing of the bill within the 10-day time limit required by the Constitution while the Congress is not in session. In contrast should the president fail to sign the bill while the Congress is in session, it would automatically become law.

Ponzi scheme: a fraud racket in which innocent profit-seeking investors pay their money only to discover the company has few assets and no potential to make a profit. Most such schemes collapsed with a few investors running off with the money of many unhappy people.

popular culture: popular culture consists of expressive forms widely available in society. Such forms include, but are not limited to, theater, television, festivals, architecture, furniture, film, the Internet, books, magazines, toys, clothing, travel souvenirs, music, dance, and body customization. Popular culture can also include folk culture and most of what is thought of as elite culture (i.e. the fine arts).

Popular Front: at the direction of the communist leadership in the Soviet Union, the Communist Party, USA, waged strong opposition from 1935 to 1939 against fascism. Part of its strategy was to support the New Deal and President Roosevelt.

populist: to represent the concerns of common people in political matters.

preference hiring: to legally favor members of a particular racial or ethnic group over other people in hiring for work.

protectionism: adoption of policies that protect a nation's economy from foreign competition.

price supports: a government financial aid program for farmers in which commodity prices are set at a certain level at or above current market values. If the market value is less than the set value, the government will pay the farmer the difference. Usually price supports are combined with limitations on production and with the storing of surpluses.

principal: the actual amount of money loaned that must be repaid.

private sector: business not subsidized or directed by the government.

progressive: one who believes in political change, especially social improvement through government programs.

progressive education: educational approach based on child-centered activities that involve hands-on learning in contrast to the highly structured traditional classroom setting focused on memorization.

prohibition: legal prevention of the manufacture, sale, or distribution of alcoholic beverages. The goal of Prohibition is partial or total abstinence from alcoholic drinks. Prohibition officially began on January 16, 1920, when the Eighteenth Amendment took effect, and ended December 5, 1933, when the amendment was repealed.

proletariat: a low social or economic group of society generally referring to the working class who must sell their labor to earn a living.

protestant work ethic: a code of morals based on the principles of thrift, discipline, hard work, and individualism.

public utility: a business that provides an essential public service, such as electricity, and is government regulated.

public works: government funded projects that are intended to benefit the public such as libraries, government buildings, public roads, and hydro-power dams.

pump priming: an economic theory as applied by the New Dealers that if enough people received paychecks once again, that they would once again buy goods and services, and the economy would eventually come back into balance.

Q

quotas: the number of people of a certain kind, such as a race or nation, allowed to legally immigrate into a country.

R

racketeering: engaging in a pattern of criminal offenses. Examples of racketeering include gambling, robbery, loan sharking, drug trafficking, pornography, murder, prostitution, money laundering, kidnapping, extortion, fraud, counterfeiting, obstruction of justice, and many more.

ratify: approve.

reactionary: a strongly conservative response or a strong resistance to change.

receiver: a device, such as part of a radio, that receives incoming signals and translates them into something perceptible, such as sound.

recession: an economic slowdown of relatively short duration. During a recession, unemployment rises and purchasing power drops temporarily.

reconversion: to change something, such as industry production, back to what it was before its more recent changes.

refinance: arrange new loan terms so that regular payments can be more affordable. This usually involves adjustment of the interest rate and the length of the repayment period.

regionalism: an artistic movement primarily associated with the 1920s and 1930s in which artists chose to represent facets of American rural and urban life.

relief: when a needy person or family receives money, food, or vouchers from the government for support. This term is not commonly used in the United States anymore, it is currently called welfare.

render: to cook and thereby melt out fat from fatty animal tissue. The cooked fat is then put into a press and the lard squeezed out The remaining product is called crackling.

reorganization: refers to the Indian Reorganization Act of 1934 and a major shift in federal policy toward American Indians during the New Deal. Under Reorganization, the federal government encouraged native arts and crafts, tribalism, and protection of native lands and resources.

repatriation: return to the country of origin.

republic: a government in which political power is primarily held by the citizens who vote for elected officials to represent them.

Republican Party: one of the two major political parties in the United States. The Republican Party emerged in the 1850s as an antislavery party. In the twentieth century, the Republican Party represents conservative fiscal and social policies and advocates a more limited role for federal government.

retrenchment: cutting of expenses from budgets; school retrenchment of the 1930s also included cutbacks in instruction, teacher salaries, number of teachers, and resulted in larger class size.

rhetoric: the use of language effectively toward influencing the conduct of others.

rumrunner: an individual bringing illegal liquor across a border; rumrunners often use boats and sometimes airplanes for the illegal transportation.

S

scabs: non-union laborers brought in to replace striking laborers.

screwball comedy: comedies with sophisticated plots and characters.

scrip: coupons or certificates, usually paper, issued as substitutes for cash in retail establishments to be used for goods and services. The coupons are assigned a specific value and are used as temporary money.

securities: stocks and bonds.

securities loan: a bank loan that uses stocks or bonds as collateral; or a bank's loan to a stockbroker.

segregation: maintaining a separation of the races, normally in public facilities such as restaurants, hotels, theaters, and other public places.

seminary: an institution of higher learning for the religious training for ministers, priests, or rabbis.

Senate: one of the two bodies with specific functions that make up the legislative branch of the United States government. Each state is allocated two sènators. (*See also* Congress; House of Representatives)

sensationalism: arousing interest or emotions with shocking, exaggerated treatments and presentation of the news.

separate but equal: an early Supreme Court doctrine established in 1897 held that racial segregation in public facilities did not violate equal protection of the law if equal facilities are available.

separation of powers: the constitutional division of responsibilities between the three independent branches of government—executive, judicial, and legislative.

serial drama: a drama that takes place over a series of episodes, such as a soap opera.

Share-Our-Wealth Plan: Huey Long, senator from Louisiana, promoted the idea of wealth distribution by heavy government taxation of the rich and guaranteeing every family an average wage of $2,000 to $3,000 per year. This concept was carried starting in 1935 by the Share-Our-Wealth Society.

sharecroppers: farm workers who worked the land of a landowner and often could keep half the value of their crops; for the other half they received from the landowner land to farm, housing, fuel, seed, tools, and other necessities in return for part of the crops raised.

shyster: a slick, smart movie character, usually portraying a lawyer, politician, or newspaperman, who was professionally unscrupulous in their dealings.

silver screen: nickname for motion pictures based on the color of the projection screen in a theater where images of adventure and romance entertained viewers.

sit-down strike: a strike where workers remain in the workplace but decline to work. This action effectively blocked the employer from replacing them with other workers. The Supreme Court outlawed this practice in 1939.

slapstick: films employing comedy and farce to entertain viewers.

slums: severely overcrowded urban areas characterized by the most extreme conditions of poverty, dilapidated housing, and crime-ridden neighborhoods.

soap opera: a drama that takes place over a series of episodes. Takes its name from the early sponsorship of radio serial dramas by soap manufacturers.

social insurance: a broad term referring to government sponsored social welfare programs of old age assistance and old age pensions, unemployment supports, worker's compensation, and healthcare programs. The term has two elements: (1) the social element meaning its programs applied to groups not just individual self-interests;

and, (2) the insurance principle under which people are protected in some way against a risk.

social legislation: a bill or legislative proposal sent to Congress which addresses social issues such as old age assistance, pensions, unemployment supports, worker's compensation, and healthcare programs.

social reconstructionism: a more radical form of progressive education; calls for the establishment of a new, more equitable social order accomplished through instruction by teachers in the schools.

Social Security: a public program that provides economic aid and social welfare for individuals and their families through social insurance or assistance. In the United States, Social Security was passed into law in 1935, as a life and disability insurance and old age pension for workers. It is paid for by employers, employees, and the government.

socialism: various political and economic theories calling for collective ownership and administration either by the people or government of the means of production and distribution of goods; sometimes thought of an in-between step between capitalism and communism.

speakeasy: a place where alcoholic beverages were sold illegally during Prohibition; patrons gained admission by giving a simple password, thus the name "speakeasy."

speculation: high risk investments such as buying stocks and/or bonds in hopes of realizing a large profit.

stalemate: a situation in which the two sides in a contest are evenly matched and neither is able to win.

standard of living: basic necessities of food, clothing, and shelter, plus any other conveniences or luxuries the family is unwilling to do without.

stock: certificate of ownership in a company also known as shares.

stock market: a market where shares of stock, or certificates of ownership in a company, are bought and sold.

strike: a labor stoppage where workers, usually through the action of their union, refuse to work until management addresses their complaints or requests about wages, hours, working conditions, and benefits.

strip plowing or strip cropping: to till an agricultural field in strips leaving untilled areas between the tilled strips.

studio system: operating between 1930 and 1945 to produce over 7,500 feature films, eight "studios" or major companies dominated film production, distribution, and exhibition. Studios not only made films, they owned theaters that projected their products. They also secured exclusive contracts with actors and actresses.

substantive due process of law: pertaining to the purpose of the act such as limitations put on someone.

suburb: a community on the outskirts, but within commuting distance, of a city.

suburbanization: to create suburbs around a central city.

suffrage: the right to vote especially in a political election.

survivors' insurance: monthly cash benefits paid to the surviving family members of a worker who has died. Survivors may include the wife, dependent children under eighteen years of age, and a dependent parent age 62 or older.

swashbuckler: movies generally set among pirates and knights with melodrama, sword play, and cannon fire.

swing: a type of rhythm driven jazz that became very popular during the depression era. Like other forms of jazz, swing incorporates improvisation. Swing is also associated with "big bands" of sixteen musicians or more. Vocalists were also associated with swing and big bands. The term swing is often credited to Duke Ellington and the 1932 song "It Don't Mean a Thing (if it ain't got that swing);" the dance craze of the mid- to late 1930s.

syndicate: an association or network of groups of individuals who cooperate to carry out activities of an enterprise. The groups may be formal or informal and may carry out legal or illegal activities.

syndicated: to sell a piece or column written by one journalist to many newspapers across the country for publication at the same time. The column is generally signed by the author.

synthetic: something made by artificially combining components, unlike a process which occurs naturally.

T

talkie: a motion picture with sound accompaniment.

tariff: a tax on items imported, often in the form of duties or customs. It is intended to make foreign-made goods more expensive than goods made in the United States.

tenant farming: an agricultural system in which farmers rented farmland and provided their own tools. They received two-thirds to three-fourths of the value of their crops. Often they purchased tools, clothing, and food with loans against crops they expected to grow the following season. The landlord kept records and computed earnings.

tenement: large housing structures containing apartment dwellings that barely meet or do not meet minimum standards of sanitation and comfort.

tenure: an assurance of job stability.

temperance: the use of alcoholic beverages in moderation or abstinence from their use.

terracing: changing a sloped hillside into a series of flat planting areas.

totalitarianism: a political system in which the government exercises complete control over its citizens.

Townsend Plan: proposal of Dr. Francis E. Townsend of Long Beach, CA., in 1933, calling for the federal government to give a pension of $200 a month to every U.S. citizen on the condition that the money be spent within 30 days.

Townsendites: advocates of the Townsend Plan who pressed hard for their version of old-age pension benefits between 1933 and 1940.

*Townsend Weekly***:** a publication of the supporters of the Townsend Plan which articulated their views and discontent with the Social Security Act.

transcription show: in early radio, a show that was recorded on disc for distribution to radio stations for later transmission.

transients: a person traveling around, usually in search of work.

transmitter: a device that generates a carrier wave encapsulating a signal derived from speech or music or other sources, and radiates the results from an antenna.

trespass: to unlawfully enter the land of another person.

tribalism: maintaining the social integrity of a traditional Indian tribe through support of its customs and beliefs.

trilogy: a series of three artistic works such as three musical pieces or books.

trust: the fiduciary (legal and monetary) responsibility of the federal government is known as trust or "trust responsibility." This concept was guaran-

teed by treaties and supported by the findings of the U.S. Supreme Court in the case of *Cherokee Nation v. Georgia* (1831). The trust responsibility compels the federal government to act in the best interest of tribes when setting policy or passing laws.

trustee: one to whom property is entrusted to be administered for the benefit of another, or one of a number of persons appointed to manage the affairs of an institution.

U

unconstitutional: to determine that a federal or state law is not in agreement with the Constitution.

underworld: the world of organized crime.

underwrite: to guarantee financial support of a company or program, assuming financial responsibility.

unemployment insurance: cash payments made for a certain period of time to a worker who involuntarily loses their job. The worker must be able and willing to work when a new job is available.

unionism: a belief in the right of workers to organize and bargain collectively with employers over work conditions.

urban: relating to a city.

urbanization: people moving from farms and small rural communities to large cities.

V

vaccine: any preparation introduced into the body to prevent a disease by stimulating antibodies against it.

vagrant: a person wandering about with no permanent address and no visible or permanent means of financial support.

variety show: a form of entertainment, usually consisting of a series of acts, such as songs, comedy, and dances.

Vaudeville: emerged out of burlesque in the early twentieth century for family audiences. Vaudeville consists of musical acts, short plays, comedy acts, and skits. Vaudeville, unable to compete with the movies, virtually disappeared in the early 1930s with many vaudeville theaters converted to movie houses.

venereal disease: contagious disease acquired through sexual intercourse.

ventriloquist: the art of projecting one's voice, often into a wooden dummy. A form of entertainment that includes a dialogue between the dummy and the ventriloquist.

vivisection: the action of cutting into or dissecting a living body; the practice of subjecting living animals to cutting operations in order to advance physiological and pathological knowledge.

volunteer: carrying out a service out of one's own free will and without payment for the action.

W

Wall Street: the location in New York City of the New York Stock Exchange.

welfare: when a needy person or family receives money, food, or vouchers from the government for support. Traditionally called "going on the dole," or relief.

welfare-to-work: term used in the late twentieth century in the United States to describe programs that seek to move welfare recipients from welfare to private employment.

western: a film genre which became popular in the 1930s and despite some criticism remained popular through the years.

wets: those who opposed Prohibition.

wildcat strike: a locally organized work stoppage, not necessarily endorsed by a labor union, to try to achieve worker goals.

workers' compensation: programs designed to provide cash benefits and medical care to workers who sustain a work-related illness or injury.

work relief: when the government provides a needy person with a paying job instead of simply giving them money for support. Different from the current term, welfare-to-work, in that the "work" in work relief is on a government-sponsored project; the "work" in welfare-to-work is in the private sector. The term is not commonly used anymore in the United States.

Y

yardstick: in a sense like a real yardstick, a standard by which to measure. As used by Franklin D. Roosevelt, the term refers to a government program or agency set up to perform a task normally done by private industry in order to assess whether that private industry is charging a fair price for its services.

yellow dog contract: a signed agreement in which an employee promises not to join a labor union.

yellow journalism: an extreme form of sensationalism taking real life events and twisting and turning stories to catch the public's attention. Stories are not only exaggerated but misrepresented.

Young Communist League: An organization focused on teenagers and Americans in their twenties promoting the philosophy and politics of the Communist Party, USA; active in the 1920s and 1930s.

Z

Zionism: the movement to established a national homeland for the Jewish people in Palestine.

General Bibliography

This bibliography contains a list of sources, including books, periodicals, novels, and websites, that will assist the reader in pursuing additional information about the topics contained in this volume.

Books

Adams, Henry H. *Harry Hopkins: A Biography.* New York: G.P. Putnam's Sons, 1977.

Agee, James, and Walker Evans. *Let Us Now Praise Famous Men: Three Tenant Families.* Boston: Houghton Mifflin Co., 2000.

Altmeyer, Arthur J. *The Formative Years of Social Security.* Madison: The University of Wisconsin Press, 1968.

Andersen, Kristi. *The Creation of a Democratic Majority, 1928–1936.* Chicago: University of Chicago Press, 1979.

Anderson, James D. *The Education of Blacks in the South, 1860–1935.* Chapel Hill: University of North Carolina Press, 1988.

Appel, Benjamin. *The People Talk: American Voices from the Great Depression.* New York: Simon & Schuster, 1982.

Balderrama, Francisco E., and Raymond Rodríguez. *Decade of Betrayal: Mexican Repatriation in the 1930s.* Albuquerque: University of New Mexico Press, 1995.

Barber, William J. *Designs within Disorder: Franklin D. Roosevelt, the Economists, and the Shaping of American Economic Policy, 1933–1945.* New York: Cambridge University Press, 1996.

———. *From New Era to New Deal: Herbert Hoover, the Economists, and American Economic Policy, 1921–1933.* New York: Cambridge University Press, 1985.

Bauman, John F., and Thomas H. Goode. *In the Eye of the Great Depression: New Deal Reporters and the Agony of the American People.* DeKalb: Northern Illinois University Press, 1988.

Bentley, Joanne. *Hallie Flanagan: A Life in the American Theatre.* New York: Alfred A. Knopf, 1988.

Bergman, Andrew. *We're in the Money: Depression America and Its Films.* New York: New York University Press, 1971.

Bernstein, Irving. *A Caring Society: The New Deal, the Worker, and the Great Depression.* Boston: Houghton Mifflin Co., 1985.

———. *Turbulent Years: A History of the American Worker, 1933–1941.* Boston: Houghton Mifflin Co., 1970.

Best, Gary D. *The Critical Press and the New Deal: The Press Versus Presidential Power, 1933–1938.* Westport: Praeger, 1993.

Bindas, Kenneth J. *All of This Music Belongs to the Nation: The WPA's Federal Music Project and American Society.* Knoxville: University of Tennessee Press, 1995.

Black, Gregory D. *Hollywood Censored: Morality Codes, Catholics, and the Movies.* New York: Cambridge University Press, 1994.

Bloomfield, Maxwell H. *Peaceful Revolution: Constitutional Change and American Culture from Progressivism to the New Deal.* Cambridge, MA: Harvard University Press, 2000.

Brinkley, Alan. *Culture and Politics in the Great Depression.* Waco, TX: Markham Press Fund, 1999.

———. *The End of Reform: New Deal Liberalism in Recession and War.* New York: Alfred A. Knopf, 1995.

———. *Voices of Protest: Huey Long, Father Coughlin, and the Great Depression.* New York: Knopf, 1982.

Brown, Lorraine, and John O'Connor. *Free, Adult, Uncensored: The Living History of the Federal Theatre Project.* Washington, DC: New Republic Books, 1978.

Brown, Robert J. *Manipulating the Ether: The Power of Broadcast Radio in Thirties America.* Jefferson, NC: McFarland & Co., 1998.

Buhite, Russell D., and David W. Levy, eds. *FDR's Fireside Chats.* Norman: University of Oklahoma Press, 1992.

Burns, Helen M. *The American Banking Community and New Deal Banking Reforms.* Westport: Greenwood Press, 1974.

Bustard, Bruce I. *A New Deal for the Arts.* Seattle: University of Washington Press, 1997.

Caldwell, Erskine, and Margaret Bourke-White. *You Have Seen Their Faces (1937).* New York: Derbibooks, 1975.

Ciment, James. *Encyclopedia of the Great Depression and New Deal.* Armonk: M.E. Sharpe, Inc., 2001.

Clarke, Jeanne N. *Roosevelt's Warriors: Harold L. Ickes and the New Deal.* Baltimore: Johns Hopkins University Press, 1996.

Clavin, Patricia. *The Failure of Economic Diplomacy: Britain, Germany, France and the United States, 1931–36.* New York: St. Martin's Press, 1996.

Cole, Olen, R., Jr. *The African American Experience in the Civilian Conservation Corps.* Gainesville: University Press of Florida, 1999.

Cole, Wayne S. *Roosevelt and the Isolationists, 1932–1945.* Lincoln: University of Nebraska Press, 1983.

Conkin, Paul Keith *The New Deal.* Arlington Heights: Harlan Davidson, 1992.

Cook, Blanche W. *Eleanor Roosevelt: Vol. 2, The Defining Years, 1933–1938.* New York: Penguin, 2000.

Crouse, Joan M. *The Homeless Transient in the Great Depression: New York State, 1929–1941.* Albany: State University of New York Press, 1986.

Cushman, Barry. *Rethinking the New Deal Court: The Structure of a Constitutional Revolution.* New York: Oxford University Press, 1998.

Davis, Kenneth S. *FDR: The New Deal Years, 1933–1937.* New York: Random House, 1986.

DeNoon, Christopher. *Posters of the WPA.* Los Angeles: Wheatley Press, 1987.

Dickinson, Matthew J. *Bitter Harvest: FDR, Presidential Power, and the Growth of the Presidential Branch.* New York: Cambridge University Press, 1997.

Dubofsky, Melvyn. *Hard Work: The Making of Labor History.* Urbana: University of Illinois Press, 2000.

Dubofsky, Melvin, and Stephen Burnwood, eds. *Women and Minorities During the Great Depression.* New York: Garland Publishing, 1990.

Edsforth, Ronald. *The New Deal: America's Response to the Great Depression.* Malden, MA: Blackwell Publishers, 2000.

Eliot, Thomas H. *Recollections of the New Deal: When the People Mattered.* Boston: Northeastern University Press, 1992.

Fausold, Martin L. *The Presidency of Herbert C. Hoover.* Lawrence: University Press of Kansas, 1985.

Federal Writers Project. *These Are Our Lives.* New York: W.W. Norton & Company, Inc., 1939.

Fine, Sidney. *Sit-Down: The General Motors Strike of 1936–1937.* Ann Arbor: University of Michigan Press, 1969.

Flanagan, Hallie. *Arena: The Story of the Federal Theatre.* New York: Duell, Sloan and Pearce, 1940.

Flynn, George Q. *American Catholics and the Roosevelt Presidency, 1932–1936.* Lexington: University Press of Kentucky, 1968.

Fraser, Steve, and Gary Gerstle, eds. *The Rise and Fall of the New Deal Order, 1930–1980.* Princeton: Princeton University Press, 1989.

Freidel, Frank. *Franklin D. Roosevelt: Launching the New Deal.* Boston: Little, Brown, 1973.

———. *Franklin D. Roosevelt: A Rendezvous with Destiny.* New York: Little, Brown & Co., 1990.

French, Warren, Ed. *A Companion to the "The Grapes of Wrath."* New York: Penguin Books, 1989.

Fried, Albert. *FDR and His Enemies.* New York: Palgrave, 1999.

Galbraith, John Kenneth. *The Great Crash, 1929.* Boston: Houghton Mifflin Company, 1997.

Gall, Gilbert J. *Pursuing Justice: Lee Pressman, the New Deal, and the CIO.* Albany: State University of New York Press, 1999.

Graham, Maury, and Robert J. Hemming. *Tales of the Iron Road: My Life as King of the Hobos.* New York: Paragon House, 1990.

Greenberg, Cheryl Lynn. *"Or Does It Explode?": Harlem in the Great Depression.* New York: Oxford University Press, 1991.

Gregory, James N. *American Exodus: The Dust Bowl Migration and Okie Culture in California.* New York: Oxford University Press, 1989.

Guerin-Gonzales, Camille. *Mexican Workers and American Dreams: Immigration, Repatriation, and California Farm Labor, 1900–1939.* New Brunswick: Rutgers University Press, 1994.

Hall, Thomas E., and J. David Ferguson. *The Great Depression: An International Disaster of Perverse Economic Policies.* Ann Arbor: University of Michigan Press, 1998.

Hamilton, David E. *From New Day to New Deal: American Farm Policy from Hoover to Roosevelt, 1928–1933.* Chapel Hill: University of North Carolina Press, 1991.

Harris, Jonathan. *Federal Art and National Culture: The Politics of Identity in New Deal America.* New York: Cambridge University Press, 1995.

Hastings, Robert J. *A Nickel's Worth of Skim Milk: A Boy's View of the Great Depression.* Carbondale: Southern Illinois University Press, 1986.

Healey, Dorothy, and Maurice Isserman. *Dorothy Healy Remembers: A Life in the Communist Party.* New York: Oxford University Press, 1990.

Hill, Edwin G. *In the Shadow of the Mountain: The Spirit of the CCC.* Pullman, WA: Washington State University Press, 1990.

Himmelberg, Robert F. *The Origins of the National Recovery Administration.* New York: Fordham University Press, 1976.

Hockett, Jeffrey D. *New Deal Justice: The Constitutional Jurisprudence of Hugo L. Black, Felix Frankfurter, and Robert H. Jackson.* Lanham: Rowman & Littlefield Publishers, 1996.

Horan, James D. *The Desperate Years: A Pictorial History of the Thirties.* New York: Bonanza Books, 1962.

Hurt, Douglas. *American Agriculture: A Brief History.* Ames: Iowa State University Press, 1994.

Hurt, R. Douglas. *The Dust Bowl: An Agricultural and Social History.* Chicago: Nelson-Hall, 1981.

Ickes, Harold L. *The Secret Diary of Harold L. Ickes: The First Thousand Days, 1933–1936; The Inside Struggle, 1936–1939; The Lowering Clouds, 1939–1941.* 3 vols. New York: Simon & Schuster, 1952–54.

Jeansonne, Glen. *Messiah of the Masses: Huey P. Long and the Great Depression.* New York: HarperCollins College Publishers, 1993.

Jellison, Charles A. *Tomatoes Were Cheaper: Tales from the Thirties.* Syracuse, NY: Syracuse University Press, 1977.

Jonas, Manfred. *Isolationism in America, 1935–1941.* Ithaca: Cornell University Press, 1966.

Kalfatovic, Martin R. *The New Deal Fine Arts Projects: A Bibliography, 1933–1992.* Metuchen: Scarecrow Press, 1994.

Kennedy, David M. *Freedom From Fear: The American People in Depression and War, 1929–1945.* New York: Oxford University Press, 1999.

Kindleberger, Charles P. *The World in Depression, 1929–1939.* Berkeley: University of California Press, 1986.

Kirby, John B. *Black Americans in the Roosevelt Era: Liberalism and Race.* Knoxville: University of Tennessee Press, 1980.

Klein, Maury. *Rainbow's End, The Crash of 1929.* New York: Oxford University Press, 2001.

Kornbluh, Joyce L. *A New Deal for Workers' Education: The Workers' Service Program, 1933–1942.* Urbana: University of Illinois Press, 1987.

Lacy, Leslie A. *The Soil Soldiers: The Civilian Conservation Corps in the Great Depression.* Radnor: Chilton Book Company, 1976.

Leuchtenberg, William E. *The FDR Years: On Roosevelt and His Legacy.* New York: Columbia University Press, 1995.

———. *Franklin D. Roosevelt and the New Deal, 1932–1940.* New York: Harper & Row, 1963.

———. *New Deal and Global War.* New York: Time-Life Books, 1964.

Lindley, Betty, and Ernest K. Lindley. *A New Deal for Youth: The Story of the National Youth Administration.* New York: Viking, 1938.

Long, Huey P. *Every Man a King: The Autobiography of Huey P. Long.* New Orleans: National Book Company, Inc., 1933.

Low, Ann Marie. *Dust Bowl Diary.* Lincoln: University of Nebraska Press, 1984.

Lowitt, Richard. *The New Deal and the West.* Bloomington: Indiana University Press, 1984.

Lubov, Roy. *The Struggle for Social Security, 1900–1935.* 2nd ed. Pittsburgh: University of Pittsburgh Press, 1986.

Maidment, Richard A. *The Judicial Response to the New Deal.* New York: Manchester University Press, 1991.

Martin, George. *Madam Secretary: Frances Perkins.* Boston: Houghton Mifflin, 1976.

McElvaine, Robert S. *The Great Depression: America, 1929–1941.* New York: Times Books, 1993.

McJimsey, George. *Harry Hopkins: Ally of the Poor and Defender of Democracy.* Cambridge: Harvard University Press, 1983.

———. *The Presidency of Franklin Delano Roosevelt.* Lawrence: University of Kansas Press, 2000.

Meltzer, Milton. *Brother, Can You Spare a Dime? The Great Depression, 1929–1933.* New York: New American Library, 1977.

———. *Driven From the Land: The Story of the Dust Bowl.* New York: Benchmark Books, 2000.

Melzer, Richard. *Coming of Age in the Great Depression: The Civilian Conservation Corps in New Mexico.* Las Cruces: Yucca Tree Press, 2000.

Mettler, Suzanne. *Dividing Citizens: Gender and Federalism in New Deal Public Policy.* Ithaca: Cornell University Press, 1998.

Milner, E.R. *The Lives and Times of Bonnie and Clyde.* Carbondale, IL: Southern Illinois University Press, 1996.

Moley, Raymond, and Eliot A. Rosen. *The First New Deal.* New York: Harcourt, Brace & World, Inc., 1966.

Nye, David E. *Electrifying America: Social Meanings of a New Technology.* Cambridge: The MIT Press, 1990.

Ohl, John K. *Hugh S. Johnson and the New Deal.* De Kally: Northerna Illinois University Press, 1985.

Olson, James S., ed. *Historical Dictionary of the 1920s: From World War I to the New Deal, 1919–1933.* Westport: Greenwood, 1988.

———, ed. *Historical Dictionary of the New Deal: From Inauguration to Preparation for War.* Westport: Greenwood, 1985.

———. *Saving Capitalism: The Reconstruction Finance Corporation and the New Deal, 1933–1940.* Princeton: Princeton University Press, 1988.

Parker, Stamford. *FDR: The Words That Reshaped America.* New York: Quill, 2000.

Parrish, Michael E. *Anxious Decades: America in Prosperity and Depression, 1920–1941.* New York: W.W. Norton, 1992.

———. *Securities Regulation and the New Deal.* New Haven: Yale University Press, 1970.

Perkins, Frances. *The Roosevelt I Knew.* New York: The Viking Press, 1946.

Perkins, Van L. *Crisis in Agriculture: The Agricultural Adjustment Administration and the New Deal, 1933.* Berkeley: University of California Press, 1969.

Philip, Kenneth R. *John Collier's Crusade for Indian Reform, 1920–1954.* Tucson: University of Arizona Press, 1977.

Phillips, Cabell. *From the Crash to the Blitz, 1929–1939.* New York: Macmillan, 1969.

Potter, Claire Bond. *War on Crime: Bandits, G-Men, and the Politics of Mass Culture.* New Brunswick, NJ: Rutgers University Press, 1998.

Powers, Richard Gid. *G-Men, Hoover's FBI in American Popular Culture.* Carbondale: Southern Illinois University Press, 1983.

Radford, Gail. *Modern Housing for America: Policy Struggles in the New Deal Era.* Chicago: University of Chicago Press, 1996.

Reagan, Patrick D. *Designing a New America: The Origins of New Deal Planning, 1890–1943.* Amherst: University of Massachusetts Press, 1999.

Reiman, Richard A. *The New Deal and American Youth: Ideas and Ideals in a Depression Decade.* Athens: University of Georgia Press, 1992.

Reisler, Mark. *By the Sweat of Their Brow: Mexican Immigrant Labor in the United States, 1900–1940.* Westport, CN: Greenwood Press, 1976.

Rogers, Agnes. *I Remember Distinctly: A Family Album of the American People, 1918–1941.* New York: Harper & Brothers Publishers, 1947.

Roosevelt, Eleanor. *The Autobiography of Eleanor Roosevelt.* New York: Da Capo Press, 2000.

———. *The Autobiography of Eleanor Roosevelt.* New York: Harper and Brothers Publishers, 1958.

Roosevelt, Franklin D. *The Public Papers and Addresses of Franklin D. Roosevelt.* 5 vols. New York: Random House, 1938-1950.

Rose, Nancy E. *Put to Work: Relief Programs in the Great Depression.* New York: Monthly Review Press, 1994.

Rothermund, Dietmar. *The Global Impact of the Great Depression, 1929–1939.* New York: Routledge, 1996.

Rozell, Mark J., and William D. Pederson. *FDR and the Modern Presidency: Leadership and Legacy.* Westport, CN: Praeger, 1997.

Ruth, David E. *Inventing the Public Enemy: The Gangster in American Culture, 1918–1934.* Chicago: University of Chicago Press, 1996.

Rutland, Richard A. *A Boyhood in the Dust Bowl, 1926–1934.* Boulder: University Press of Colorado, 1997.

———. *The Democrats: From Jefferson to Clinton.* Columbia: University of Missouri Press, 1995.

Salmond, John A. *The Civilian Conservation Corps, 1933–1942: A New Deal Case Study.* Durham: Duke University Press, 1967.

Schieber, Sylvester J., and John B. Shoven. *The Real Deal: The History and Future of Social Security.* New Haven: Yale University Press, 1999.

Schlesinger, Arthur M., Jr. *The Coming of the New Deal: The Age of Roosevelt.* Boston: Houghton Mifflin Company, 1988.

Schwartz, Jordan A. *The New Dealers: Power Politics in the Age of Roosevelt.* New York: Alfred A. Knopf, 1993.

Sennett, Ted. *This Fabulous Century: The Thirties.* New York: Time-Life Books, 1967.

Shindo, Charles J. *Dust Bowl Migrants in the American Imagination.* Lawrence: University Press of Kansas, 1997.

Sitkoff, Harvard. *A New Deal for Blacks: The Emergence of Civil Rights as a National Issue, the Depression Years.* New York: Oxford University Press, 1978.

Skidelsky, Robert. *John Maynard Keynes: The Economist as Saviour, 1920–1937.* New York: Viking Penguin, 1994.

Smith, Page. *Redeeming the Time: A People's History of the 1920s and the New Deal.* 8 vols. New York: Penguin, 1987.

Smith, Wendy. *Real Life: The Group Theatre and America, 1931–1940.* New York: Knopf, 1990.

Sobel, Robert. *The Great Bull Market: Wall Street in the 1920s.* New York: Norton, 1968.

Sternsher, Bernard. *Rexford Tugwell and the New Deal.* New Brunswick Rutgers University Press, 1964.

Stevens, J .E. *Hoover Dam: An American Adventure.* Norman: University of Oklahoma Press, 1988.

Storrs, Landon R.Y. *Civilizing Capitalism: The National Consumers' League, Women's Activism, and Labor Standards in the New Deal Era.* Chapel Hill: University of North Carolina Press, 2000.

Svobida, Lawrence. *Farming in the Dust Bowl.* University Press of Kansas, 1986.

Swados, Harvey, ed. *The American Writers and the Great Depression.* New York: Bobbs-Merrill Company, Inc., 1966.

Swain, Martha H. *Ellen S. Woodward: New Deal Advocate for Women.* Jackson: University Press of Mississippi, 1995.

Szostak, Rick. *Technological Innovation and the Great Depression.* Boulder: Westview Press, 1995.

Terkel, Studs. *Hard Times: An Oral History of the Great Depression.* New York: Pantheon Books, 1986.

Thompson, Kathleen, and Hilary MacAustin, eds. *Children of the Depression.* Bloomington: Indiana University Press, 2001.

Tobey, Ronald C. *Technology as Freedom: The New Deal and the Electrical Modernization of the American Home.* Berkeley: University of California Press, 1996.

Toland, John. *The Dillinger Days.* New York: Da Capo Press, 1995.

Tugwell, R. G. *The Brain Trust.* New York: Viking Press, 1968.

Tyack, David, Robert Lowe, and Elisabeth Hansot. *Public Schools in Hard Times: The Great Depression and Recent Years.* Cambridge: Harvard University Press, 1984.

Uys, Errol Lincoln. *Riding the Rails: Teenagers on the Move During the Great Depression.* New York: TV Books, 2000.

Ware, Susan. *Beyond Suffrage: Women and the New Deal.* Cambridge: Harvard University Press, 1981.

————. *Partner and I: Molly Deson, Feminism, and New Deal Politics.* New Haven: Yale University Press, 1987.

Watkins, T. H. *The Hungry Years: A Narrative History of the Great Depression in America.* New York: Henry Holt and Company, 1999.

————. *Righteous Pilgrim: The Life and Times of Harold L. Ickes, 1874–1952.* New York: Henry Holt & Co., 1990.

Wicker, Elmus. *The Banking Panics of the Great Depression.* New York: Cambridge University Press, 1996.

Wigginton, Eliot, ed. *Refuse to Stand Silently By: An Oral History of Grass Roots Social Activism in America, 1921–1964.* New York: Doubleday, 1992.

Winfield, Betty H. *FDR and the News Media.* New York: Columbia University Press, 1994.

Winslow, Susan. *Brother, Can You Spare a Dime? America From the Wall Street Crash to Pearl Harbor: An Illustrated Documentary.* New York: Paddington Press, 1979.

Worster, Donald. *Dust Bowl: The Southern Plaines in the 1930s.* New York: Oxford University Press ,1982.

Zieger, Robert H. *The CIO, 1930–1935.* Chapel Hill: University of North Carolina Press, 1995.

Periodicals

Adamic, Louis. "John L. Lewis's Push to Power," *Forum,* March 1937.

Amberson, W.R. "The New Deal for Share-Croppers," *Nation,* February 13, 1935.

Ballantine, A.A. "When All the Banks Closed," *Harvard Business Review,* March 1948.

Berle, A.A., Jr. "What's Behind the Recovery Laws," *Scribner's,* September 1933.

Broun, Heywood. "Labor and the Liberals," *Nation,* May 1, 1935.

Cannon, Brian Q. "Power Relations: Western Rural Electric Cooperatives and the New Deal," *Western Historical Quarterly,* vol. 31, Number 2 (2000).

Childs, M.W. "The President's Best Friend," *Saturday Evening Post,* April 26, 1941.

Cole, Olen, Jr. "The African-American Experience in the Civilian Conservation Corps," *Western Historical Quarterly,* vol. 31, no. 4 (2000).

Daniels, Jonathan. "Three Men in a Valley," *New Republic,* August 17, 1938.

Don Passos, John. "Washington: The Big Tent," *New Republic,* March 14, 1934.

Epstein, Abraham. "Social Security Under the New Deal," *Nation,* September 4, 1935.

Fleck, Robert K. "Population, Land, Economic Conditions, and the Allocation of New Deal Spending," *Explorations in Economic History,* Volume 38, Number 2 (2001).

Flynn, J.T. "The New Capitalism," *Collier's,* March 18, 1933.

Fogel, Jared A., and Robert L. Stevens. "The Cavas Mirror: Painting as Politics in the New Deal," *Magazine of History,* vol. 16, no. 1 (2001).

Garraty, John A. "Unemployment During the Great Depression," *Labor History,* Spring 1976.

Hirsch, Arnold R. "'Containment' on the Homefront: Race and Federal Housing Policy From the New Deal to the Cold War," *Journal of Urban History,* vol. 26, no. 2 (2000).

Hopkins, Harry L. "Beyond Relief," *New York Times Magazine,* August 19, 1934.

Ickes, Harold L. "My Twelve Years with F.D.R.," *Saturday Evening Post,* June 12, 1948.

Lord, Russell. "Madame Secretary," *The New Yorker,* September 2 and 9, 1933.

McCormick, Anne O'Hare. "The Great Dam of Controversy," *New York Times Magazine,* April 20, 1930.

McWilliams, Carey. "A Man, a Place, and a Time: John Steinbeck and the Long Agony of the Great Valley in an Age of Depression, Oppression, and Hope," *The American West,* May 1970.

Metzer, Richard. "Coming of Age in the Great Depression: The Civilian Conservation Corps Experience in New Mexico, 1933–1942," *Western Historical Quarterly,* vol. 32, no. 3 (2001).

Morgenthau, Henry, Jr. "The Paradox of Poverty and Plenty," *Collier's,* October 25, 1947.

Naison, Mark D. "Communism and Black Nationalism in the Depression: The Case of Harlem," *Journal of Ethnic Studies,* Summer 1974.

Nelson, Daniel. "Origins of the Sit-Down Era: Worker Militancy and Innovation in the Rubber Industry, 1934–1938," *Labor History,* Spring 1982.

Ohanian, Lee E. "Why Did Productivity Fall So Much During the Great Depression?," *American Economic Review,* vol. 91, no. 2 (2001).

Perkins, Frances. "Eight Years as Madame Secretary," *Fortune,* September 1941.

Poe, J.C. "The Morgan-Lilienthal Feud," *Nation,* October 3, 1936.

Pringle, H.F. "The President," *The New Yorker,* June 16–23, 1934.

Richberg, Donald. "The Future of the NRA," *Fortune,* October 1934.

Sherwood, Robert E. "Harry Hopkins," *Fortune,* July 1935.

Shover, John L., ed. "Depression Letters From American Farmers," *Agricultural History,* July 1962.

Stevens, Robert L., and Jared A. Fogel. "Images of the Great Depression: A Photogrpahic Essay," *Magazine of History,* vol. 16, no. 1 (2001).

Summers, Mary. "The New Deal Farm Programs: Looking for Reconstruction in American Agriculture," *Agricultural History,* vol. 74, no. 2 (2000).

Swing, R.G. "Father Coughlin," *Nation,* January 2, 1935.

Swing, R.G. "The Purge at the AAA," *Nation,* February 20, 1935.

Tugwell, Rexford. "The Price Also Rises," *Fortune,* January 1934.

Tugwell, Rexford. "America Takes Hold of Its Destiny," *Today,* April 28, 1934.

Webbink, Paul. "Unemployment in the United States, 1930–40," *American Economic Review,* February 1941.

White, Edward G. "The Constitution and the New Deal," *Journal of Interdisciplinary History,* vol. 32, no. 2 (2001).

Novels

Adamic, Louis. *My America (1938).* New York: Da Capo Press, 1976.

Caldwell, Erskine. *Tobacco Road.* Thorndike, ME: G.K. Hall, 1995.

Cantwell, Robert. *The Land of Plenty.* Carbondale: Southern Illinois University Press, 1971.

Dos Passos, John. *U.S.A.* New York: Penguin Books, 1996.

Farrell, James T. *Studs Lonigan: A Trilogy.* New York: The Modern Library, 1938.

Hurston, Zora Neale. *Their Eyes Were Watching God (1937).* New York: Harper & Row, 1990.

Lee, Harper *To Kill a Mockingbird.* Philadelphia: Chelsea House Publishers, 1998.

Steinbeck, John. *The Grapes of Wrath.* New York: The Viking Press, 1939.

Wright, Richard. *Uncle Tom's Children.* New York: The World Publishing Company, 1938.

———. *Native Son.* New York: Harper & Row, 1940.

Websites

Bonneville Power Administration. http://www.bpa.gov

Civilian Conservation Corps Alumni. http://www.cccalumni.org

Franklin D. Roosevelt Library and Museum. http://www.fdr library.marist.edu

Roosvelt University. Center for New Deal Studies. http://www .roosevelt.edu/newdeal.htm

Library of Congress. American Memory. http://memory.loc .gov/ammem/fsowhome.html

New Deal Network. http://newdeal.feri.org

Riding the Rails. The American Experience. Public Broadcast System. Website: http://www.pbs.org/wgbh/amex/rails/

Social Security Administration. http://www.ssa.gov

Tennessee Valley Authority. http://www.tva.gov

Index

Bold page numbers indicate a primary article about a topic. Italic page numbers indicate illustrations. Tables and charts are indicated by a t *following the page number. The index is sorted in word-by-word order.*

A

AAA. *See* Agricultural Adjustment Administration (AAA)
AALL (American Association for Labor Legislation), 3:47–48, 181, 191
AAPA (Association Against the Prohibition Amendment), 3:6–7, 31
Abbott, Edith, 3:89
Abbott, Grace, 3:53, 291, 298–99
Abbott, Robert, 2:181
Abstract expressionism, 1:36
ACLU (American Civil Liberties Union), 1:140, 178–79
ACTU (Association of Catholic Trade Unionists), 3:132–33
Adamic, Louis, 2:211, 213, 225
Adams, Ansel, 2:123
ADC (Aid to Dependent Children), 3:187
Addams, Jane, 1:209, 2:130, 150, *294*, 3:293
Adjustable rate mortgages (ARM), 1:61
Adventist, 3:128
Advertising
    agriculture and, 1:95

anti-Sinclairism advertisement, 2:331–32
    electric appliances, 3:259
    growth of, 2:127, 131–32
    newspaper, 2:159, 164, 175, 180
    radio, 1:266, 3:59–60, 70
    regulation of, 2:130
    Spam advertisement, 2:*32*
AFC (America First Committee), 2:144–45, 149
Affirmative action, 1:218, 225
AFI (American Film Institute), 1:268, 2:85
AFL. *See* American Federation of Labor (AFL)
AFT (American Federation of Teachers), 1:193, 194, 205
Agee, James, 2:15, 170, 213, 300
Agricultural Adjustment Act, 2:279
Agricultural Adjustment Administration (AAA)
    benefits of, 2:9–10
    black Americans and, 1:81
    creation of, 2:6–7, 258
    farmer relief, 2:258–59
    food processing tax, 2:6, 9, 14, 279
    hunger relief and, 2:25
    isolationists support of, 2:141
    Mexican Americans and, 1:293
    Supreme Court ruling, 1:174, 2:9, 279, 3:210–11
    See also Agricultural relief programs
Agricultural Marketing Act, 1:95
Agricultural relief programs, 2:**1–20**
    benefits checks for, 1:*246*
    CCC and, 1:9, 115, 2:7

Commodity Credit Corporation loans, 2:8, 261, 3:109
    Emergency Farm Mortgage Act, 1:172–73, 2:6, 101, 258
    Farm Credit Administration, 1:173, 2:6, 257, 260, 3:108–9
    Farm Mortgage Moratorium Act, 1:173, 183, 184, 2:263
    Farm Mortgage Refinancing Act, 2:101, 261
    Federal Farm Bankruptcy Act, 2:262
    FSA loans, 2:301
    grazing regulations, 1:182, 2:7
    impact of, 2:15–16
    land laws, 2:3
    New Deal and, 1:172–74, 2:277–79, 3:108–9
    perspectives on, 2:13–15
    price-control issues, 2:4, 8, 9, 11–12, 279
    Resettlement Administration loans, 1:76, 83, 174, 2:297
    See also Agricultural Adjustment Administration (AAA); Conservation
Agriculture
    agricultural colleges, 2:3
    bank failures and, 2:11
    crop surplus, 1:95, 98, 99, 2:11, 25, 26, 279
    drought, 1:168–69, 177, 178, *182*, 2:7
    economic decline, 1:56, 95, 99, 2:3–4
    economic prosperity, 1:98–99, 2:1, 2–3

Agriculture (continued)
electricity and, 2:9, 3:172
farming cooperatives, 2:9, 12
government role in, 2:1, 14
Hoover, Herbert and, 1:95, 98, 2:3,
12, 16, 18
international competition, 1:95, 2:11
land reclamation and, 1:99
marketing and, 1:95
migrant workers, 1:27, 2:13, 15,
3:*38*, 78
overgrazing problems, 1:182, 2:7
prohibition and, 1:99
Roosevelt, Franklin and, 2:4–7,
8–9, *14*
soil conservation, 1:169, 174–76,
181–82, 183, 2:278
World War I and, 1:56, 95, 98–99,
2:1, 11
World's fairs and, 3:355
See also Agricultural relief
programs; Crops; Dust Bowl;
Farmers
Agriculture Department, U.S., 1:31,
112, 2:27, 3:173, 261
Aid to Dependent Children (ADC),
3:187
AIDS/HIV, 3:52, 53
Air Quality Control Regions (AQCR),
1:233
Airline industry, 2:121
Airplanes, 3:339
Alabama Power Company, 3:237, 238
Alcatraz prison, 3:8
Alcorn County Electric Cooperative,
3:157, 159
Alexander, Will, 1:83
Algar, James, 1:280
Algren, Nelson, 2:35, 211
ALL (American Liberty League),
1:105–6, 2:267, 286–87
All the King's Men (film), 2:327
All the King's Men (Warren), 2:331
Allen, Florence, 3:285
Allen, Gracie, 3:63
Allen, Hervey, 2:214, 222
Allen, Robert, 2:163, 3:219
Alliance for Progress, 1:217
Allied forces, 3:325
Alsberg, Henry, 1:30
Alsop, Stewart, 1:237
Altmeyer, Arthur, 3:197
AMA. *See* American Medical
Association
America Eats (Algren), 2:35
America First Committee (AFC),
2:144–45, 149
America for Americans Club, 1:288
American Association for Labor
Legislation (AALL), 3:47–48,
181, 191
American Association of University
Women, 3:291

American Bankers Association, 1:188
*The American Banking Community and
New Deal Banking Reforms,
1933-1935* (Burns), 1:64–65
American Birth Control League, 2:393
American Catholic Bishops, 2:87
American Chamber of Horrors,
(Lamb), 3:53
American Child Health Association,
3:48–49
American Civil Liberties Union
(ACLU), 1:140, 178–79
American Council on Education, 1:212,
2:83
American Creed, 2:23–34, 37
American culture, 2:126, 132
American Cyanamid Company, 3:246
American Decades: 1930-39 (Bondi),
1:208, 213
*An American Dilemma: The Negro
Problem and Modern
Democracy* (Myrdal), 1:75
The American Experience: Huey Long
(film), 2:327
American Farm Bureau Federation,
3:156, 160
American Federation of Labor (AFL)
American Federation of Teachers
and, 1:194
black Americans and, 1:66, 72
Committee of Industrial
Organization and, 2:191,
194–95, 3:336
discrimination in, 1:66, 2:199
membership of, 1:160
minimum wage opposed by, 2:231
Prohibition opposed by, 3:6
repatriation of Mexican Americans,
1:288
skilled *vs.* unskilled workers, 2:191,
194, 199
See also Congress of Industrial
Organizations (CIO)
American Federation of Teachers
(AFT), 1:193, 194, 205
American Federation of Women's
Clubs, 1:13
American Film Institute (AFI), 1:268,
2:85
American Gothic (Wood), 2:4
American Guide Series, 1:31, 2:35,
213–14, 3:311
American Independent Party, 1:227
American Indian Defense Association,
1:13–14
American Indian Life (Collier), 1:3
American Indians, 1:**1–23**
arts and crafts legislation, 1:5, 7–8,
15, 19, 118
assimilation attempts, 1:10, 17,
18–19
CCC-ID and, 1:9, 18, 110, 112,
117, 118, 251

citizenship, 1:10, 12
cultural suppression, 1:12, 15
discrimination against, 1:7, 17
documentary photos of, 2:304–5
education, 1:6–7, 12, 14–15, 20,
117
employment, 1:12, 15, 18, 21, 117
farming, 1:1, 9, 10, 12
in films, 2:86
government policy toward, 1:2,
10–12, 17
health, 1:12, 15, 17, 117
Hoover, Herbert and, 1:11
illiteracy rates, 1:117
Indian law, 1:8–9, 19
land allotment, 1:6, 9, 10, 12, *14*,
22, 29
landownership as individual *vs.*
tribal, 1:1, 5, 17, 19
multiculturalism and, 1:7, 10, 18
Native Americans *vs.*, 1:20
notable people, 1:21–22
perspectives on, 1:15–19
poverty, 1:17, 117
Pueblo Lands issue, 1:12–14
religion, 1:5, 17, 19
Roosevelt, Franklin and, 1:8, 9
self-determination era, 1:20–21
tribalism, 1:3–4, 11
trust responsibility, 1:19–20
See also Collier, John; Office of
Indian Affairs
American Institute of Public Opinion
surveys, 2:163, 3:52
American Jitters: A Year of the Slump
(Wilson), 2:213
American Legion, 1:186–87, 196–97,
204, 206
American Liberty League (ALL),
1:105–6, 2:267, 286–87
American Medical Association (AMA)
birth control and, 3:292
food and drug standards and, 2:43,
3:37
health insurance opposed by, 3:39,
40, 48, 51
Sheppard Towner Act *vs.*, 3:48, 49
American Memory Project, 2:302, 307
American Mercury, 2:178
American Municipal Association
(AMA), 2:114
American National Theater and
Academy (ANTA), 1:36
American Newspaper Guild, 2:180,
181
American Quarterly (Kuznick), 3:363
American Red Cross, 1:259, 2:24, 3:36
American Relief Administration
(ARA), 3:99
American Socialism, 2:219–20
American Society of Composers,
Authors, and Publishers
(ASCAP), 3:62, 71

American Stock Exchange, 1:97

American Telegraph and Telephone (AT&T), 2:167

The American Writer and the Great Depression (Swados), 2:212

American Youth Act, 3:83

American Youth Commission, 3:83

American Youth Congress, 3:83

Americanization. *See* Popular culture

America's Capacity to Consume (Brookings Institution), 1:93

Ames, Champion v. (1903), 3:217

Amos 'n' Andy, 1:78, 266, 277, 3:72, 73–74

Anarchism, 2:315–16

Anderson, Marian, 1:83–184

Anderson, Mary, 3:291–92, 297, 299

Anderson, Sherwood, 2:170, 207, 213, 219, 3:103

Andrews, John, 3:191, 197

Andrews, Lincoln, 3:5

Angels with Dirty Faces (film), 1:131, 142

Animals, 1:115, 171–72, 173, 2:7, 3:52

Annual Report of the Secretary of the Interior, 1:22–23

Annual Reports (Rural Electrification Administration), 3:175–76

Annunciation (Le Sueur), 2:321

Anthony Adverse (Allen), 2:215, 222

Anti-Saloon League (ASL), 3:14–15, 17, 18, 25

Anti-Semitism, 2:318, 3:135, 136–37, 142, 246

Antioch College, 3:252

Antitrust laws, 2:230, 232, 243–44, 245, 280

Antiwar demonstrations, 1:231

AP (Associated Press), 2:175, 180

Appalachian Regional Development Act, 1:220

Applause (film), 2:73

Appliances
electrical, 3:166, 172
loans for, 2:9, 262, 3:157, 165, 260, 271
phonographic record players, 3:59
radios, 1:22, 93, 264, 2:177, 3:59, 68, 73
refrigerators, 2:37, 3:172, 239, 271
stoves, 2:37, 3:*158*, 167, 239

Aquacade, 3:361

Architecture
Bay Bridge, San Francisco, 3:356–57
Broadacre City, 1:32, 33
Chicago World's Fair, 1:17, 2:122, 126, 3:352, *354*, 355–56, 365
Chrysler Building, 1:32, 2:122, 131
Egyptian Revival Architecture, 2:87
Empire State Building, 1:32, 2:122
Golden Gate Bridge, 2:120, *121*, 3:356

Gothic Revival style, 2:123–24
of interwar era, 2:121–22
New York World's Fair, 1:264, 277, 3:353, 359–61
Prairie School movement, 2:135
Rockefeller Center, 1:32–33, 2:122
San Francisco World's Fair, 3:353, 356–59
skyscrapers, 2:122
Woolworth Building, 2:122

Arena (Flanagan), 1:37, 38

ARM (Adjustable rate mortgages), 1:61

Armaments
arms race, 2:153
atomic bomb, 3:338
bomber planes, 3:339
munitions industry, 2:142–43, 3:229–30, 245
nitrates for, 3:229–30, 245
produced during World War II, 2:145, 3:326
radar system, 3:341–42
sold to foreign nations, 2:145
submarines, 3:340, 344–45
tanks, 3:339, *345*
voluntary ban on, 2:143–44

Armistice Day, 2:*147*, 149

Arms race, 2:153

Armstrong, Edwin, 3:68

Armstrong, Jack, 1:313

Armstrong, Louis, 1:79, 325

Army, U.S.
black Americans in, 3:355
Bonus Army, 1:126, 144, 148, 3:102–3
CCC and, 1:110, 111–12, 118
sanitation efforts, 3:48

Army Corps of Engineers, U.S., 3:231, 248, 262, 265, 267, 271

Arrowsmith (Lewis), 2:219

Art Deco, 2:121, 3:353, 359

Arts, 1:**24–39**
black Americans and, 1:35, 75–76, 79
celebrating American life, 1:34
community art centers, 1:28, 35
contributing forces, 1:34
CWA public work projects, 1:26–27
documenting life, 1:31
Federal Art Project, 1:28, 29, 76, 292, 2:277, 287, 3:312
fine arts, 1:279–80, 2:128
folk and domestic, 1:33–34, 2:123
Great Depression's effect on, 1:34
Harlem Renaissance, 1:35, 79, 2:123, 128
high *vs.* low art, 1:279–80, 2:132, 3:316
impact of, 1:35–36
Mexican American cultural revival, 1:292
Modernism style, 2:128

National Endowment for the Arts (NEA), 1:36, 221, 233
nationalism and, 1:35
notable people, 1:36–37
patrons and teaching institutions, 1:32
perspectives on, 1:34–35, 2:287, 3:311, 318
Public Works Art Project, 1:26, 292, 2:262, 3:311
Realism style, 2:123, 128
Treasury Relief Art Project, 1:26
work relief programs for artists, 1:24–31
World's fairs and, 3:357–58, 364
See also Architecture; Literature; Music; Resettlement Administration; Theater

Arts and crafts movement, 2:126, 131

Asbury, Herbert, 3:2

ASCAP (American Society of Composers, Authors, and Publishers), 3:62, 71

Ashcake, 2:28

Ashwander v. Tennessee Valley Authority (1936), 3:261

Asian America: Chinese and Japanese in the United States Since 1850 (Daniels), 1:303

Asian Americans, 1:290–91, 297–98, 301

ASL (Anti-Saloon League), 3:14–15, 17, 18, 25

Assembly line, 2:119, 120, 130, 3:163, 164–65

Associated Farmers of California, 2:13

Associated Press (AP), 2:175, 180

Association Against the Prohibition Amendment (AAPA), 3:6–7, 31

Association for Improving the Condition of the Poor, 1:259

Association of American Painters and Sculptors, 1:34

Association of Catholic Trade Unionists (ACTU), 3:132–33

Astaire, Fred, 1:270, 2:78–79, 90

AT&T (American Telegraph and Telephone), 2:167

Atget, Eugene, 2:306

Atlantic Charter, 2:148

Atlantic Monthly, 2:178

Atomic bomb, 3:338

Attaway, William, 1:76

Aunt Mame (film), 2:90

Aunt Sammy, 2:27

Austin, Mary, 1:13

Australia, 2:15, 59

Austria, 2:50, 52

The Autobiography of Alice B. Toklas (Stein), 2:219

Automobile industry, 1:72, 2:196–97, 205, 233. *See also* Ford Motor Company

Index

Automobiles, 1:*309*
    driving for pleasure, 1:275, *276*,
        314
    emission standards, 1:223, 233
    increased use of, 1:321, 2:106
    Model T Ford, 2:106, 119, 204
    number of, 1:264, 2:119, 120
    Oldsmobile, 2:106
    overview, 1:308
    payment plans, 1:93
    safety standards, 1:223, 229, 2:130
    as status symbol, 2:131
Axis powers, 3:325

B

Babbit (Lewis), 2:219
Babes in Arms (film), 2:82
Baby Face (film), 3:296
Bach, Emily, 2:150
Back to the land movement, 2:31,
    3:131, 258, 276
Bailey v. Drexel Furniture Co. (1922),
    3:219
Baker, George, 3:138
Balderrama, Francisco, 1:303
Baldwin, C.B. (Beanie), 1:261
Ballantine, Arthur, 1:49
Bambi (film), 2:73
Bank failures
    in 1920s, 1:41–42, 52, 56, 95,
        2:256
    in 1930s, 1:47, 94, 2:256
    in 1980s, 1:61, 102
    agriculture and, 1:95
    causes of, 1:40–43, 60, 61
    in Europe, 2:50, 52
    FDIC and, 1:46, 103
    home loan defaults and, 2:98, 101
    RFC and, 3:101, 103–5
    in rural areas, 3:110
    stock market crash and, 1:94
Bank Nights, 1:268, 2:73, 95
Bank of United States, 1:43
Bank runs, 1:*44, 101*
    bank closures caused by, 1:43,
        2:256
    FDIC and, 1:46, 48, 59
    psychology of, 1:48
    reopening banks, 1:50
Bankhead, Tullulah, 2:77
Bankhead-Jones Farm Tenancy Act,
    2:297, 301
Banking, 1:**40–65**
    1980s crisis, 1:61, 102
    bank holiday, 1:40, 41, 47–51, 64,
        103–4, 2:255, 3:107–8
    branch banking, 1:41, 51, 53–54, 57
    commercial banks, 1:45, 52–53, *54*,
        60, 62
    commercial loans decline, 3:96,
        108, 110

credit cards, 1:60
dual banking system, 1:46, 54, 56,
    57
Emergency Banking Relief Act,
    1:41, 49–50, 57, 2:256, 3:105,
    107
federal investigations, 1:44–45, 51
federal regulations, 1:46–47
fraud and mismanagement, 1:45,
    51, 104
Glass-Steagall Act, 1:46, 48, 51–52,
    59–60, 62, 103, 2:260
Hoover, Herbert and, 1:44–45, 46,
    47–48, 57, 89
interest rates, 1:60, 61, 93
loan speculations, 1:56–57
lost of confidence in, 2:256,
    3:106–7
money market fund introduced, 1:61
notable people, 1:62–64
perspectives on, 1:57–59
reforms, 2:280
Roosevelt, Franklin and, 1:47,
    48–50, 51, 57, 64, 102–3
Roosevelt, Franklin fireside chats
    on, 1:50, *58*, 64, 2:256, 3:108
savings and loan associations
    (S&Ls), 1:53, 61
savings campaigns, 1:188
stock speculations of, 1:45, 53, 60,
    94, 3:110
unit banks, 1:41, 52–54, 60
See also Bank failures; Bank runs;
    Federal Deposit Insurance
    Corporation (FDIC); Federal
    Reserve System; Gold standard
Banking Act of 1933, 1:46, 48, 51–52,
    59–60, 62, 103, 2:260
Banking Act of 1935, 1:41, 52, 2:280
Baptists, 3:124
The Barbershop (film), 2:77
Barbershop Blues (film), 2:84
Barnes, Harry, 2:146
Barrow, Clyde, 1:132, 134–35
Barton, Bruce, 1:91
Baruch, Bernard, 2:245
Baseball, 1:264, 274, 2:124
Bathtub gin, 3:23
Bauer, Catherine, 2:114
Bay Bridge, San Francisco, 3:356–57
Beard, Charles, 1:209, 2:216
Beard, Mary, 2:216
Bearle, Adolph, 2:230
Beatty, Warren, 2:90
Beaumont,, 2:308
The Beautiful and the Damned (Lewis),
    2:219
Beer, 2:257, 3:11, 17, 22
Beer Tax Act, 2:256–57
Bell, Elliott, 1:107
Bell, Fred, 1:*90*
Belmont, Alva, 3:295

Bennett, Hugh, 1:175, 183
Bennett, Robert, 1:11
Bennington College, 1:197, 198
Benny, Jack, 3:63, 71
Berg, Gertrude, 1:266
Bergen, Edgar, 1:268
Bergman, Andrew, 1:281, 2:75, 78, 94
Bergreen, Laurence, 1:144
Berkeley, Busby, 2:78, 90, 94
Berle, Adolph
    about, 2:247–48
    as Brain Trust member, 2:254, 255
    *The Modern Corporation and
        Private Property,* 2:230, 248,
        250, 271
    Supreme Court and, 3:219
Berlin-Rome Axis, 2:152
*The Best American Sports Writing of
    the Century* (Halberstam), 2:136
Bestseller book lists, 2:212, 215, 222
Bethune, Mary McLeod
    about, 1:209, 3:299
    on "Black Cabinet," 3:288, 299
    as Negro Affairs Director for NYA,
        1:252, 3:288, 314
    Roosevelt, Eleanor and, 1:73, 209
Betters, Paul, 2:114
Betty Crocker Cooking School of the
    Air, 1:311, 2:41
Betty Crocker's Picture Cookbook
    (General Mills), 2:41
Between Two Wars (Golby), 2:68
Beyer, Clara, 3:285, 299–300
Big Thompson Project, 3:265
Bilbo, Theodore, 1:82
Billy the Kid, 1:135
Bingo, 2:73
Bird, Caroline, 1:318–19
Birds Eye Frozen Food, 2:33
Birdseye, Clarence, 2:33
Birth Control Clinical Research
    Bureau, 3:292
Birth Control Federation of America,
    3:292
Birth control movement, 3:292
The Birth of a Nation (film), 2:86, 88
Birth rate, 1:191, 317, 318
"Bishops Program for Social
    Reconstruction," 3:129
Bisquick, 2:35
The Bitter Years: 1935-1941
    (Steichen), 2:302, 312
Bituminous Coal Labor Board, 2:247
Black, Eugene, 1:57, 62
Black, Hugo, 2:223–24, 231, 3:212,
    221, *222*
Black Americans, 1:**66–86**
    activism of, 1:73, 75, 83, 226, 326
    affirmative action and, 1:218
    American Federation of Labor and,
        1:66, 72
    Amos 'n' Andy depiction, 1:78, 266,
        277, 3:72, 73–74

arts and, 1:35, 75–76, 79
"Black Cabinet," 1:73, 84, 85, 152, 3:288, 319
black churches, 3:119, 137–38
CCC work relief for, 1:75, 113, 250–51
civil rights and, 1:70–71
communism and, 1:72, 76
Democratic Coalition and, 1:73
discrimination against, 1:66, 70, 77, 81
education, 1:190, 203, 207–8, 213, 252, 318
employment, 1:77, 81
everyday life, 1:68, 318–20, 2:226
as farmers, 1:67, 70, 81, 318, 2:12
in Federal Writers' Project (FWP), 1:76, 3:312
in films, 2:83–84
ghettos, 1:75, 78, 131, 226
Great Society and, 1:225–26, 231–32
Hoover, Herbert and, 1:69
housing and, 1:75, 318–19
illiteracy, 1:69, 76
Jim Crow laws and, 1:77–78, 3:335
legal rights, 1:78, 79
life expectancy, 1:76
Macbeth all-black production, 1:29, *30*, 76, 3:314
migrating North, 1:68–69, 78
military and, 1:77, 3:335, 346
"New Negro" era, 1:35
notable people, 1:83–85
NYA work relief for, 2:277, 3:314
oral histories of, 3:311, 312
perspectives on, 1:80–82
popular culture and, 2:132
population statistics, 1:69, 81
poverty, 1:230
racism toward, 1:66, 78–79, 199, 203, 210
Reconstruction Finance Corporation (RFC) and, 1:69
retrenchment and, 1:193
Roosevelt, Eleanor and, 1:67, 71–72
Roosevelt, Franklin and, 1:75, 76, 82, 152
in rural South, 1:67–68
in sports, 2:125
TVA and, 1:70, 3:234
unemployment, 1:66, 67, 68, 69, 193, 318
unions, 1:68, 72, 75
violence toward, 1:66, 68, 318
voting patterns, 1:73, 79–80, 83, 152, 2:282
voting rights, 1:83, 161, 221, 235
wages, 1:68, 70, 81, 193, 247
work relief for black American women, 1:244, 3:315
World War II mobilization and, 3:335
WPA work relief programs, 1:75
See also Hughes, Langston; King, Martin Luther; Lynching; Wright, Richard
Black Boy (Wright), 2:222, 224
"Black Cabinet," 1:73, 84, 85, 152, 3:288, 319
Black movement, 1:226, 326
Black Panther Party, 1:226
Black Worker, 1:75
Blackfoot Indians, 1:*4*
Blair, Emily, 3:300
Blaisdell, Home Building and Loan Association v. (1934), 3:204
Blaisdell, John, 3:204
Blind Americans, 3:187
Blitzkriegs, 3:339
Blitzstein, Marc, 1:29–30, 36
Blonde Venus (film), 2:77
Blood on the Forge (Attaway), 1:76
Bloodbird (Burton), 3:275
Blue, Rupert, 3:48
Blue Cross, 3:51
Blue Eagle symbol, 2:78, 82, 233, *237, 249*
Blue Shield, 3:51
Bly, Nellie (Elizabeth Seaman), 2:173
Board of Education, Brown v. (1954), 1:83, 228
Boas, Franz, 2:123
Bobbs-Merrill Company, 2:34
Bomber planes, 3:339
Bond, Horace Mann, 1:209–10
Bondi, Victor, 1:208, 213
Bonfils, Winifred (Annie Laurie), 2:173
Bonneville Dam, 1:257, 3:265–66, 280–81
Bonneville Power Administration (BPA), 1:257, 3:258, 268
Bonnie and Clyde (film), 2:90
Bonus Army, 1:126, 144, 148, 3:102–3
Boole, Ella, 3:8, 27
"Boondoggling," 1:257
Bootlegging
    by early settlers, 3:12
    liquor deaths, 1:125, 3:3, 20
    by organized crime, 1:124–25, 131, 137, 3:21–22
    public attitude toward, 1:138, 139
Borah, William, 2:141–42, 153–54
Border Patrol, 1:287, 3:5
Borsodi, Ralph, 3:276
Boston Cooking School Cookbook (Farmer), 2:22, 33, 44, 45
Boulder Canyon Project Act, 3:263
Boulder City, 3:264, 277
Boulder Dam. *See* Hoover Dam
Bourke-White, Margaret, 2:*171*, 210, 223, 303
Bowery Savings Bank, 1:*44*
Bracero Program, 1:300
Bradley, Charles, 2:13
Brady, Matthew, 2:304
Brain Trust group, 2:254, 255
Brandeis, Louis, 1:156, 3:204, 208–9, 218
Bread, 2:28, 36, 47
Breadlines, 2:21–22, 23, 24, 45–46
Breakfast, 2:29
Breedlove v. Suttles (1937), 1:80
Breen, Joseph, 3:140
Bridge games, 1:265
Bridges, Harry, 2:322, 3:287
Brinkley, Alan, 1:278
Broadacre City, 1:32, 33
Brodie, Maurice, 3:45
Brookings Institution, 1:93. *See also* Meriam Report
Brophy, John, 2:202–4
Brother, Can You Spare a Dime? America from the Wall Street Crash to Pearl Harbor: An Illustrated Documentary (Winslow), 1:64, 2:45–46
"Brother Can you Spare a Dime" (song), 1:280
Brotherhood of Sleeping Car Porters union, 1:75, 3:335
Broun, Heywood, 2:161–62, 164, 181
Browder, Earl, 2:321, *328*
Brown, D. Clayton, 3:176
Brown, Edgar, 1:73
Brown, Lorrain, 1:38
Brown v. Board of Education (1954), 1:83, 228
Brownell, Baker, 1:36
Brunnette, Harry, 1:135
Bryan, William Jennings, 1:155, 3:15, 18
Buchanan v. Warley (1917), 1:78
Buck, Pearl, 2:214, 218, 222
Buckley, Corrigan v. (1926), 1:78
Buckley, Robert, 3:212
Buckner, Mortimer, 3:96
Budget. *See* Federal budget
Building A Democratic Political Order (Plotke), 1:146
Bullets or Ballots (film), 2:80, 95
Bunche, Ralph, 1:75, 76, 82
Bungalow style homes, 2:106–207
Bureau of Immigration and Naturalization, 1:287
Bureau of Indian Affairs (BIA), 1:2, 11. *See also* Office of Indian Affairs
Bureau of Internal Revenue, 3:4
Bureau of International Expositions, 3:364
Bureau of Land Management. *See* U.S. Grazing Service
Bureau of Motion Pictures, 2:89
Bureau of Reclamation, 1:99, 3:261–62, 270, 273
Burke, Clifford, 1:80
Burns, George, 3:63, 64, 71
Burns, Helen, 1:64–65
Burns, Lucy, 3:295

Bursum, Holm, 1:12
Bursum Bill, 1:3, 12–13
Burton, Thomas, 3:275
Busby Berkeley: Going Through the Roof (film), 2:94
Bush, George, 1:301, 3:71, 200
Business
    antitrust laws, 2:230, 232, 243–44, 245, 280
    business cycles, 1:89–90, 98*t*
    business failures, 1:94
    cartels, 2:235, 237, 243, 246
    cooperating with government, 2:230–31, 244–45, 246, 247
    Democratic Party and, 1:147
    Depression blamed on, 1:147, 202
    education funded by, 1:193, 194, 202–3, 205
    government regulation of, 1:88, 148, 2:242, 247
    income, 1:208, 2:119
    isolationists view toward, 2:142
    journalism and, 1:263
    laissez-faire economics, 1:148, 2:229–30, 246
    large *vs.* small companies, 1:89, 93, 2:239
    New Deal and, 3:336
    NIRA and, 2:233
    Prohibition opposed by, 3:26–27
    reconversion to pre-war production, 3:346
    relocations to Third World countries, 2:202
    Roosevelt, Franklin and, 1:151, 159, 2:228, 247, 276, 285
    Second New Deal and, 2:284–85
    Social Security and, 3:193–94
    teachers *vs.,* 1:194–96, 205, 208
    trade associations, 2:236–37
    World War II mobilization and, 3:334, 336, 338
    World's fairs and, 3:355
    See also Corporations; Holding companies; Industry; Monopolies; National Industrial Recovery Act (NIRA)
Business and Professional Women's Federation, 3:291
Business Week, 2:170, 272–73
Butler, United States v. (1936), 2:9, 279, 3:210
Byrnes, James, 3:221

C

C & S Corporation (Commonwealth and Southern Corporation), 3:236, 237, 238–39
Café Society, 1:314–16
Cagney, James, 1:130, 135, 142, 2:75, 80

Cahill, Holger, 1:27, 3:312, 319
Caldwell, Erskine, 2:210, 222, 223
California
    Associated Farmers of California, 2:13
    "End Poverty in California" campaign, 1:150, 2:317, 330
    Los Angeles border blockades, 1:178–79
    Los Angeles Summer Olympic Games, 1932, 3:354
    Panama-California Exposition, 3:356
    San Francisco, 2:120, *121,* 3:353, 356–59
    Water and power projects, 3:268–69
    See also Hollywood
"California, Here We Come" (Davenport), 1:184
California Central Valley development, 3:268–69
California League Against Sinclairism, 2:331–32
California real estate speculation, 1:92
California Red: A Life in the American Communist Party (Healey and Isserman), 2:321, 332
California Sanitary Canning Company strike, 2:201
California State-Fullerton, 1:121
California Teacher's Association (CTA), 1:196
Call It Sleep (Roth), 2:211
Camera Club of New York, 2:304
Campbell, Walter, 3:53
Campell's Soup, 2:34
Canada, 2:15, 3:167, 168
Canada, Missouri ex rel Gaines v., 3:227
Cancer, 3:33, 40, 42
Canned food, 2:31, 34, 40, 41, 42
Cannery and Agricultural Workers Industrial Union (CAWIU), 2:322
Cannon, James, 3:7
Cantor, Eddie., 1:266
Cantwell, Robert, 2:211
Capitalism
    as cause of Great Depression, 2:208
    Christians and, 3:124, 125, 126–27, 132
    defined, 3:119
    failure of, 1:3
    laissez-faire system of, 2:246
    social reconstructionism *vs.,* 1:205
Capone: The Man and the Era (Bergreen), 1:144
Capone, Alphonse "Al," 1:128–29, 137–38, 139, 140, 141, 2:75
Capra, Frank, 2:80, 90–91
Captain Blood (film), 1:271
Card games, 1:265, 279, 310

Cardozo, Benjamin, 3:204, 206–7, 210, 223
Carmichael, Stokely, 1:226
Carmody, John, 3:163, 172–73, 175
Carnegie, Dale, 2:215
Carnegie, Hattie, 1:325
Carnegie Foundation, 1:198
Carson, Rachel, 1:223, 229
Cartels, 2:235, 237, 243, 246
Carter, Boake, 2:168, 181
Carter, Jimmy, 1:11, 163
Carter v. Carter Coal Company (1936), 3:210
Catholic Bishops' Committee on Motion Pictures, 2:78
Catholic Herald, 3:131
Catholic Rural Life Conference, 3:131–32
Catholic Worker Movement, 3:144
Catholicism
    against birth control, 3:292
    agriculture and, 3:131–32
    anti-Catholicism, 3:141, 143, 145
    charities of, 3:141–42
    film censorship, 3:140
    finance and, 3:130–31
    government and, 3:132, 139, 143
    New Deal and, 3:118, 130
    NRA and, 3:132
    organized labor and, 3:132–33
    perspectives on, 3:143
    Protestants *vs.,* 3:14
    Roman Catholic Church, 3:141, 145
    Roosevelt, Franklin and, 3:130, 133–34, 143
    school system of, 3:141
    social ideals, 3:118, 129–30
    Social Security and, 3:133
    See also Coughlin, Charles
Catt, Carrie, 3:295
CAWIU (Cannery and Agricultural Workers Industrial Union), 2:322
CBS (Columbia Broadcasting System), 2:167, 3:59, 60
CBS Mercury Theater on the Air, 1:266–67
CCC. *See* Civilian Conservation Corps (CCC)
CCC-ID. *See* Civilian Conservation Corps-Indian Division (CCC-ID)
CCMC (Committee on the Costs of Medical Care), 3:36–37
Cedar Bill, 3:289
Censorship, of radio, 3:60–61
Census, 1:22, 301, 2:106
Centennial International Exhibition, 3:362
Central Conference of Jewish Rabbis, 2:78, 87
Central Republic Bank of Chicago, 3:101, 113

Central Valley Project Act, 3:269

Century of Progress Exposition, 1:17, 2:122, 126, 3:352, *354*, 355–56, 365

Chain stores, 1:321, 2:36–37

Chamberlain, Neville, 2:151, 3:340

"Chambers of Horrors" exhibit, 3:46

Champion v. Ames (1903), 3:217

Chaplin, Charlie, 1:270, 2:77, 91, 199, *200*

Charity
    beliefs about, 2:24, 3:191, 193
    Catholic, 3:130, 131, 141–42
    charitable groups, 1:253
    homelessness and, 3:122
    Hoover, Herbert and, 2:24, 39
    Jewish Americans and, 3:134
    settlement houses, 2:130–31, 3:293
    for transients, 3:77
    wealthy Americans and, 2:39
    See also Hunger relief; Social
        workers; Volunteerism; Welfare

A Charter for the Social Sciences in the Schools (Beard), 1:209

Chavez, Cesar, 1:284, 302

Cherokee Nation v. Georgia (1831), 1:19

"The Chevrolet Chronicles," 3:60

Chicago (poem), 2:217

Chicago and Downstate: Illinois as seen by the Farm Security Administration Photographers, 1936-1943 (Reid and Vickochil), 2:313

Chicago Defender, 2:181

Chicago School writers, 2:217

Chicago Tribune, 2:163, 178

Chicago World's fair, Century of Progress Exposition, 1:17, 2:122, 126, 3:352, *354*, 355–56, 365

Chickamauga Dam, 3:250

The Child and the Curriculum (Dewey), 1:210

Child labor, 2:197, 233, 3:219, 285

Child Labor Act, 1:156

Child Protection Act, 1:224

Children
    Abbott, Grace and, 3:298, 299
    child labor, 1:156, 2:197, 233, 3:219, 285
    childhood diseases, 3:33
    daily activities, 1:313–14, 327
    malnutrition in, 1:205, 239, 319, 321
    radio and, 3:59, 69
    social security aid, 3:187
    sports for, 1:314
    as transients, 3:85
    See also Games; Youth

Children Discover Arithmetic: An Introduction to Structural Arithmetic (Stern), 1:211

The Children of Light and the Children of Darkness (Niebuhr), 3:148

Children's Bureau, 1:22

China, 2:58, 153, 3:342

Chinatowns, 1:290, 303

Chinese Americans, 1:290, 297, 303

Chinese Exclusion Act, 1:286, 290, 297, 300

Christian Century, 3:128, 141

Christian Register, 3:124

Christian Science Monitor, 2:173

Christianity and the Social Crisis (Rauschenbusch), 3:139

Christmas Seals, 3:36

A Christmas Story (film), 3:64

Chrysler, 2:119–20, 3:105

Chrysler Building, 1:32, 2:122, 131

Churchill, Winston, 1:242, 3:340, 344

The Chute (Halper), 2:210

Cincinnatti Post, 2:172

CIO. *See* Congress of Industrial Organizations (CIO)

Citizen Kane (Welles), 1:37, 279, 3:73

Citizen's League for Fair Play, 1:81

City Chickens, 2:28

City Lights (film), 2:77, 91

Civil rights
    American Legion and, 1:186–87
    Black, Hugo and, 3:224
    civil liberties infractions, 3:213
    Committee for Industrial Organization and, 1:72
    communism and, 1:76, 186–87
    defined, 1:217
    Equal Rights Amendment, 3:291, 295, 297–98
    ethnic groups and, 1:300
    FBI violations, 1:146
    goals of, 1:74
    Great Society and, 1:217–18, 231–32, 233
    New Deal and, 1:69, 218
    poll tax as violation of, 1:74, 80
    racial equality, 1:73
    "red rider" as violation of, 1:197
    Roosevelt, Eleanor and, 1:67, 71–72
    Roosevelt, Franklin and, 1:70–71, 73, 152, 218
    Stone, Harlan and, 3:222
    viewed as Communism, 1:186–87
    See also Civil rights movement;
        Discrimination; Lynching;
        Racism; Segregation

Civil Rights Act of 1964, 1:83, 217, 219, 230, 235

Civil Rights Act of 1968, 1:223

Civil Rights Congress, 1:76. *See also*
    National Negro Congress (NNC)

Civil rights movement
    march on Washington, DC, 1:75, 83
    nonviolent approach, 1:83, *226*, 235
    religious groups and, 3:146

violence during, 1:83, 140, 226

See also King, Martin Luther

Civil War
    Army Corps of Engineers and, 3:267
    reconstruction period, 1:73, 77, 152, 253
    as Republican Party crossroad, 1:146
    stock exchanges and, 1:97

Civil Works Administration (CWA)
    aid checks, 1:260–61
    budget for, 1:247
    farmers aided by, 1:245
    projects of, 1:245, 2:262
    purpose of, 1:120, 3:308
    transients and, 3:82–83
    wage rates of, 1:246–47
    work relief program, 1:26–27, 245, 246–47, 2:262, 3:308
    See also Public Works Art Project
        (PWAP); Works Progress
        Administration (WPA)

Civilian Conservation Corps (CCC), **1:109–22**
    achievements, 1:110, 114–15, 118–19, 250
    agricultural relief programs, 1:9, 115, 2:7
    black Americans employed by, 1:75, 113, 250–51
    criticisms of, 1:110, 111–12, 118
    Dust Bowl aided by, 1:174
    education programs, 1:113, 200–201, 211, 251
    ethnic groups and, 1:292–93
    Federal agency status, 1:115
    federal land improvements, 1:114–15, 117, 118, 250
    goals of, 1:109, 112–13, 200, 250, 2:258, 3:308
    history resources, 1:115
    life in, 1:121
    literacy programs, 1:251
    Local Experienced Men (LEM) used by, 1:112, 117
    notable people, 1:119–21
    perspectives on, 1:118
    as Public Service Camps, 1:117, 119
    recruit requirements, 1:112, 114, 121, 251
    Roosevelt, Franklin and, 1:9, 109, 110, 111, 112, *113*
    segregation in, 1:250
    "Striking a Chord: Loveless CCC" (song), 1:111
    termination, 1:112, 115–16, 3:337
    transients and, 3:82, 87
    U.S. Army and, 1:110, 111–12, 118
    veterans employed by, 1:112–13, 250
    web sites, 1:115, 121

Civilian Conservation Corps
(continued)
World War II and, 1:115, 116
youth employed in, 1:9–11, 116–17,
250–51
See also New Deal
Civilian Conservation Corps-Indian
Division (CCC-ID), 1:9, 18,
110, 112, 117, 118, 251
Civilian Conservation Corps Museum,
1:115
Civilian Conservation Corps
Reforestation Relief Act, 1:250,
2:258
Clapper, Raymond, 2:161, 181–82
Clarens, Carlos, 1:131
Clark, Bennett, 2:156, 3:186
Clayton Act, 2:244
Clean Air Act Amendments, 1:223, 233
Cleveland Press, 2:172
Clinton, Bill, 1:164, 3:196, 200
Close, Upton, 2:168
Clothing, 1:321, 322, 2:121
Cloud, Henry Roe, 1:15, 18
Cloward, Richard, 1:229
Coal-miners, 2:46–67, 247, *283,* 3:210,
334
Coast Guard, 3:6
Coca-Cola salad, 2:34
Cocktail parties, 2:220–21
Cody, Buffalo Bill, 1:7
Cody, Frank, 1:196
Coffee, 2:27
Coffin, Jo, 3:285
Cohen, Benjamin, 2:289
Cohen, Felix, 1:8, 9, 19, 21
Cohen, Wilbur, 3:197
Coiner, C.T., 2:*249*
Coin's Financial School (Harvey), 2:317
COLAs (Cost-of-Living Adjustments),
3:196
Colbert, Claudette, 2:80, 3:350
Colbert, David, 1:107, 281
Colbert, Jean, 3:71
Cold War, 2:148, 152, 3:346
Collectivism, 1:196
College attendance, 1:317–18
Collier, John
about, 1:3, 15
American Indian culture supported
by, 1:7, 13, 18
American Indian Defense
Association founded by,
1:13–14
American Indian Life, 1:3
Bursum Bill opposed by, 1:3,
12–13
CCC-ID established by, 1:9
as Commissioner of Indian Affairs,
1:2–3, 4–5, 6, 9, 11
Indian Reorganization Act (IRA)
and, 1:21, 22–23
Indian rights supported by, 1:8, 13

Indians at Work, 1:18
Office of Indian Affairs criticized
by, 1:15, 22
reforms supported by, 1:9–10
Collier, John, Jr., 1:209, 2:298, 301, 309
Collier's magazine, 1:184, 3:219
Colorado River development, 3:258,
263–65, 274, 277
Columbia Broadcasting System (CBS),
2:167, 3:59, 60
Columbia Construction Company,
3:266
Columbia Pictures, 2:73
Columbia River basin project, 1:257,
3:258, 265–68, 270, 278,
280–81
Comedy
anarchist, 2:76–77
censorship of, 3:61
films, 1:269–70, 2:76–77, 80
radio, 1:266, 3:59
Comic books, 1:272
Comic strips, 1:272, 313, 3:64
*The Coming of the New Deal: The Age
of Roosevelt* (Schlesinger), 2:5,
7, 20
Commercial banks, 1:45, 52–53, *54,*
60, 62
Commission of Indian Affairs, 1:15
Commission on Human Rights, 1:72
Commission on Interracial
Cooperation, 1:83
Commission on the Status of Women,
3:297
Committee for Economic
Development, 3:346
Committee for Industrial Organization,
1:72, 2:194, 320
Committee on Economic Security,
3:186
Committee on the Costs of Medical
Care (CCMC), 3:36–37
Committee on the Relation of
Electricity to Agriculture
(CREA), 3:166
Committee to Defend America by
Aiding the Allies, 2:145, 150
Commodity Credit Corporation, 2:8,
261, 3:109
Commons, John, 3:197
Commonweal, 3:131, 144
Commonwealth and Southern
Corporation (C & S), 3:236,
237, 238–39
Communications Act, 1:266, 3:62
Communism
American Indians and, 1:17
black Americans and, 1:72, 76
civil rights activities viewed as,
1:186–87
defined, 2:315, 3:120
educators accused of, 1:196–97,
204, 205, 206

FBI focus on, 1:135, 139–40
Great Depression blamed on, 1:28
Hearst, William Randolph and,
1:197, 206, 2:163, 182
in Latin America, 2:58
loss of interest in, 2:212, 324
loyalty oaths and, 1:197, 204–5
Marxism and, 2:208–9, 220, 321
progressive education viewed as,
1:204, 206
proletarian literature and, 2:207,
208–12, 219–20, 221
"red rider" statement and, 1:197
Roosevelt, Franklin on, 2:332
social activists viewed as, 1:302
social reconstructionism viewed as,
1:196, 210
Socialism and, 2:219
in Soviet Union, 2:152–53, 320
strikes and, 1:28
theaters viewed as, 1:38
unions and, 1:28, 31, 186–87
youth and, 2:332
See also Communist Party (CP);
House Un-American Activities
Committee (HUAC)
Communist Party (CP)
black Americans and, 1:76
labor unions and, 1:127, 135, 2:201,
326
protest marches by, 1:126
work relief and, 3:318
Communist Party of the United States
of America (CPUSA), 2:320–21,
324, 325, 326
Community Development Block Grant,
2:114
Competition, 1:153–54, 2:230, 244
Comstock Law, 3:292
Conchies, 1:116, 117
Confederation of Mexican Farmers and
Workers Union, 1:289
Conference of Women in Industry,
3:291
Conference on Unemployment, 1:254
Congress of Industrial Organizations
(CIO)
American Federation of Labor and,
2:191, 194–95, 3:336
American Federation of Teachers
and, 1:194
Communist Party of the United
States of America and, 2:320,
326
growth of, 2:191
industrial unions, 2:191, 194, 202
unskilled workers in, 2:191, 199
women and, 2:199–200
Congressional Union, 3:295
Connally Act, 3:207
Conquest of Arid America (Smythe),
3:276
Conroy, Jack, 2:211

Conscientious objectors, 1:116, 117
Conservation
    Civilian Conservation Corps
        Reforestation Relief Act, 1:250,
        2:258
    conservation districts, 1:183
    Dust Bowl and, 1:174–76, 181,
        182–83, 184, 2:7
    livestock grazing regulations, 1:182,
        2:7
    soil conservation, 1:169, 174–76,
        181–82, 183, 2:278
    soil-conserving crops, 1:174, 181,
        2:9, 279
    Taylor Grazing Act, 1:115, 117,
        118, 182, 2:7
    U.S. Grazing Service, 1:115, 117,
        182
    water conservation, 1:183
    See also Civilian Conservation
        Corps (CCC)
Conservation Recipes (Mobilized
    Women's Organization), 2:36
Conservatives
    American Legion, 1:186–87,
        196–97, 204, 206
    beliefs of, 3:119, 120–21, 170, 217
    communism feared by, 1:206
    Daughters of the American
        Revolution, 1:83–84, 85,
        196–97, 204, 206
    New Deal and, 1:112, 2:267, 286,
        3:121, 336
    poverty and, 1:230
    progressive education and, 1:206
    REA and, 3:161, 170
    role of government and, 2:286, 326,
        3:336
    social reconstructionism vs., 1:196
    Social Security and, 3:194
    in Supreme Court, 3:203, 215,
        217–19
    WPA and, 3:317–18
    See also Political "right"
Considine, Bob, 2:136
Constitution, U.S.
    Congress' authority over business,
        2:232
    due process clause of, 3:204, 205,
        208
    NIRA and, 2:232
    public education and, 1:198, 202
    "red rider" as violation of, 1:197
    separation of powers, 3:205–6, 208,
        217
    Stone, Harlan and, 3:222
    Warren Court changes to, 1:228,
        237
    Web site for, 3:228
    See also Constitutional amendments
Constitutional amendments
    Fifteenth Amendment, 1:79, 80
    Fifth Amendment, 3:207–8

First Amendment, 3:213
Fourteenth Amendment, 1:78,
    3:204, 205, 211, 214
Nineteenth Amendment, 1:156,
    2:149, 395
Tenth Amendment, 3:216, 217
Twentieth Amendment, 2:254–55
Twenty-first Amendment, 1:131,
    2:257, 3:10, 13
Twenty-fourth Amendment, 1:80
Twenty-second Amendment, 1:158
See also Eighteenth Amendment
Construction companies, 3:264–65,
    266, 277–78
Consumer protection
    automobile safety, 1:223, 229,
        2:130
    experimental medicine and, 3:45
    Federal Food, Drug and Cosmetic
        Act, 1:223, 2:43–44, 284, 3:46,
        49, 52
    Highway Safety Act, 1:223
    See also Federal Trade Commission
        (FTC); Food and Drug
        Administration (FDA)
Consumerism. *See* Materialism
Consumers League, 3:291
Cook, Maurice, 3:278
Cook, Nancy, 2:*231*
Cookbooks
    Betty Crocker's Picture Cookbook
        (General Mills), 2:41
    Boston Cooking School Cookbook
        (Farmer), 2:22, 33, 44, 45
    Conservation Recipes (Mobilized
        Women's Organization), 2:36
    The Joy of Cooking (Rombauer),
        2:22, 33–34, 44, 45
    101 Delicious Bisquick Creations
        (General Mills), 2:35
    *Ruth Wakefield's Toll House Cook
        Book* (Wakefield), 2:33
    What You Can Do with Jell-O
        (General Foods), 2:34
    Your Share (Betty Crocker),
        2:40–41
Cooke, Morris
    about, 3:173
    New York Power Authority trustee,
        3:155
    Philadelphia Electric Company
        lawsuit, 3:168, 170
    PWA consultant, 3:155
    rural electrification and, 3:154,
        157–58, 163, 168, 169, 170
    TVA and, 3:242
Coolidge, Calvin, 1:87, 89, 100, 2:12,
    3:6, 248
Cooper, Jack, 1:280
Cooperative movement, 2:230–31,
    244–45, 246, 247
Cooperatives, 2:9, 12, 3:157–60,
    167–68, 275

Copeland, Royal, 2:44
Corcoran, Thomas, 2:289
Corell, Charles, 3:72, 73
Corporate Bankruptcy act, 2:264
Corporate internationalism, 3:346–47
Corporation for Public Broadcasting,
    1:221
Corporations
    defined, 1:97
    New Deal and, 2:228–29
    new products, 2:119
    power companies and, 3:170
    rebuilding European economies,
        3:346–47
    Republican Party supported by,
        1:234
    rise of, 1:97–98, 157, 2:250
    small companies *vs.*, 1:89, 93,
        2:239
    unions *vs.*, 1:234
    wealth of, 1:93, 2:119, 126, 128
    World War I mobilization lead by,
        3:338, 343–44
    World War II mobilization and,
        3:329
    World's fairs exhibits, 3:354–55,
        359
    See also Holding companies;
        Industry-military alliance
Corporatism philosophy, 2:229, 244,
    245, 246, 3:170
Corrigan v. Buckley (1926), 1:78
Cort, John, 3:132
Corwin, Norman, 3:68
Cost-of-Living Adjustments (COLAs),
    3:196
Costigan, Edward, 1:247
Cott, Nancy, 2:201
Coughlin, Charles
    about, 3:71, 146
    anti-Semitism of, 3:71
    New Deal and, 2:267
    radio program of, 3:68
    Roosevelt, Franklin and, 3:130,
        133–34, 143, 146
    social justice and, 3:218–19
Council of Economic Advisors, 1:230
Country music, 1:273–74
Counts, George, 1:196, 205, 210
Couzens, James, 2:39
Covarrubias, Miguel, 3:357–58
Cowles, Gardner, 2:170, 304
Cowley, Malcolm, 2:212
Cox, James, 2:154
CPUSA. *See* Communist Party of the
    United States of America
    (CPUSA)
Crabgrass Frontier (Jackson), 2:103,
    116
Cracklings, 2:27
The Cradle Will Rock, 1:29–30, 36,
    3:316
Craft industries *vs.* corporations, 1:89

Craig, May, 2:168
Cravens, Kathryn, 2:168
Crawford, Joan, 3:296
CREA (Committee on the Relation of
    Electricity to Agriculture), 3:166
Credit unions, 1:53
Creditor nation, 1:96
Crime, 1:**123–45**
    American mafia, 1:130–31, 140
    American public and, 1:138
    FBI and, 1:142
    in film, 1:129–30, 131
    gangster films, 1:129–31, 142,
        268–69, 277, 2:74–75
    Great Depression and, 1:124–25
    immigrants and, 1:135–36
    impact of, 1:140–42
    juvenile delinquents, 1:131
    labor strikes, 1:126–28, 136
    notable people, 1:142–44
    outlaws, 1:132, 134–35, 139
    overview, 1:123–24
    perspectives on, 1:139–40
    Prohibition and, 1:137, 138
    protest marches, 1:126
    Roosevelt, Franklin and, 1:133
    Scottsboro 9 case, 1:76, 2:*206*
    war against, 1:132–35, 142
    See also Bootlegging; Organized
        crime; Violence
Crime Control Act, 1:61
Crime Movies: An Illustrated History
    (Clarens), 1:131
Crocker, Betty, 1:311, 2:40–41
Croly, Herbert, 2:169
Crops
    destroyed, 2:6–7, *10*
    federal distribution of, 1:173, 2:7,
        25, 37
    planting reduced, 1:172, 2:5–6, 7, 9,
        16, 17, 258
    soil-conserving, 1:174, 181, 2:9,
        279
    surplus, 1:95, 98, 99, 2:11, 25, 26,
        279
    World War II and, 2:26
Crosby, Bill, 3:63
Crosby, Bing, 1:266
Crosby, Washburn, 2:41
Crowley, Leo, 1:62
Crowley, Malcolm, 2:221
Cuddihy, R.J., 2:167
Cullen, Countee, 1:79
Culture
    American culture, 2:126, 132
    commercialization of, 1:276
    for the common good, 1:276
    cultural activities, 1:276
    cultural democracy, 1:28–29,
        3:316–17
    cultural pluralism, 2:288
    democracy's relationship to, 1:264,
        275–76

electricity and, 3:172
    multiculturalism, 1:2, 7, 15, 18
    radio and, 3:58, 69
    WPA cultural projects, 3:309
    youth and, 1:279
    See also Popular culture
*Culture and Politics in the Great
    Depression* (Brinkley), 1:278
The Culture of Cities (Mumford),
    2:119
Cumming, Hugh, 3:41, 42, 53
Cummings, E.E., 2:216, 219
Cummings, Homer, 1:133–34, 135,
    142, 143
Cunningham, Al, 1:281
Currie, Lauchlin, 2:289–90
Curtis, Charles, 1:*148*
Curtis, Edward, 2:304
Cushman, David, 3:323
Customs Service's Boarder patrol, 3:5
Czechoslovakia (poem), 2:217

D

Daché, Lilly, 1:325
Dagenhart, Hammer v. (1918), 3:217
Dalberg, Edward, 2:211
Dali, Salvador, 3:361
Dall, Curtis "Buzzie," 1:*299*
Dams
    Bonneville Dam, 1:257, 3:265–66,
        280–81
    Chickamauga Dam, 3:250
    Folsom River Dam, 3:271
    Fort Peck Dam, 3:269
    Grand Coulee Dam, 1:257, 3:258,
        265, 266–68, 270
    Hetch Hetchy Dam, 3:274, 275
    history of, 3:271
    Hiwassee Dam, 3:*244*
    Hoover Dam, 3:258, *263*
    Imperial Diversion Dam, 3:265
    Laguna Dam, 3:272
    list of, 3:270
    map of, 3:*251*, *277*
    Norris Dam, 3:*233*, 239–40, *247*
    Parker Dam, 3:265
    Pine View Dam, 3:269, 270
    Shasta Dam, 3:269
    TVA and, 3:261
    Wheeler Dam, 3:240
    Wilson Dam, 3:239, 245–46,
        247–48
    as work relief projects, 3:257
Dance
    dance marathons, 1:265, 312–13,
        2:222–23
    swing, 1:264, 273, 279, 312, 3:67
Dance Fools Dance (film), 3:296
Daniels, Roger, 1:304
Darby Lumber Co., United States v.
    (1941), 3:219

Dark Victory, 1:271
Darrow, Clarence, 2:239, 241, 248
Darwell, Jane, 2:15
Darwinism, 3:217
Daughters of the American Revolution
    (DAR), 1:83–84, 85, 196–97,
    204, 206
Davenport, Walter, 1:184
Davis, Bette, 1:271, 3:296
Davis, Helvering v. (1937), 3:220
Davis, John, 1:75, 76
Davis, Kingsley, 1:212–13, 3:89–90
Davis, Steward Machine Co. v. (1937),
    2:9
Davy, Martin, 1:244–45
Dawes, Charles, 3:101, 113
Dawes Act, 1:10, 3:113
Day, Dorothy, 3:144, 145–46
The Day of the Locust (West), 2:214
De Saible, Jean Baptiste Pont, 3:356
Dead End, 1:131
Debs, Eugene, 2:126
Débutante balls, 1:314, *315*, 328
*Decade of Betrayal: Mexican
    Repatriation in the 1930s*
    (Balderrama and Rodriguez),
    1:303
Delano, Jack, 2:300–301, 307, 308,
    309
DeLeath, Vaughn, 1:280
Delinquency and Opportunity (Cloward
    and Ohlin), 1:229
DeMille, Cecil B., 2:91
Democracity, 3:359
Democracy
    art of, 1:38
    cultural democracy, 1:28–29,
        3:316–17
    Facism as threat to, 1:135
    relationship to culture, 1:264,
        275–76
Democratic coalition, 1:**146–67**
    after World War II, 1:228
    black Americans in, 1:73
    contributing forces, 1:154–57
    decline of, 1:228–29
    Democratic National Convention,
        1:148
    described, 1:147, 150, 228
    election of 1936, 1:150–52
    election of 1938, 1:152–54, 3:339
    end of, 1:163–65
    Fair Deal of, 1:161–62, 3:338
    Great Society and, 1:228–29
    impact of, 1:161–65, 2:288
    international relations and,
        1:159–61
    labor movement and, 1:159, 160
    mass political movement and,
        1:157–58
    New Dealers and, 1:148–49
    notable people, 1:165–66
    perspectives on, 1:157, 158–61

progressivism of, 1:148–49
Roosevelt, Franklin and, 1:146–47, 150–51, 158
social reform movements and, 1:150
special interest groups and, 1:151, 153–54, 158–59, 163, 234
vulnerablity of, 1:230
See also Democratic Party
Democratic National Committee (DNC), 3:284, 288–89, 297
Democratic Party
beginnings of, 1:154
big business opposed by, 1:155
black Americans and, 1:73
decline of, 1:154–55
Democratic Coalition and, 1:159
free-silver and, 1:155
Great Depression as crossroad, 1:146
internationalism of, 1:156
membership rules, 1:80
New Freedom programs, 1:155–56
organization of, 1:158–59
as party of the people, 1:234
political machines, 1:159
progressive income tax of, 1:155–56
racial discrimination in, 1:69
racism in, 1:81
Republican Party decline and, 1:147–48
slavery issues and, 1:154
Social Security and, 3:194
Supreme Court reorganization plan and, 3:220
Vietnam War and, 1:163
women's right to vote and, 1:156
Demonstration Cities and Metropolitan Area Redevelopment Act, 1:223
Demonstration Farm Equipment Tour, 3:163
Dempsey, Jack, 2:132–33
Denman, William, 3:212
Denver Post, 2:173
Department of Agriculture, 1:31, 112, 2:27, 3:173, 261
Department of Commerce, 2:245, 3:109–10
Department of Education, 1:207
Department of Health, Education, and Welfare, 1:207
Department of Housing and Urban Development (HUD), 1:223, 2:113–14
Department of Interior, 1:112, 207
Department of Justice, 1:75
Department of Labor, 1:112, 250, 251
Department of transportation, 1:232
Deportation
Hoover, Herbert and, 1:288
of Mexican Americans, 1:286–88, 292, 300, 303

raids by government agents, 1:287, 288, 298
Roosevelt, Franklin and, 1:288, 292
social activists targeted, 1:302
World War II and, 1:294
Depository Institution's Deregulation and Monetary Control Act (DIDMCA), 1:61
Depression Era Recipes (Wagner), 2:28
DePriest, Oscar, 1:250
Desegregation, 1:193, 207, 208, 212
Design for Living (film), 2:77
Dewey, John, 1:158, 196, 204, 210–11
Dewey, Thomas, "Lucky" Luciano and, 1:144
Dewson, Molly
about, 3:300–301
educating women on political issues, 3:288
Gas Money Plan, 3:284
on Kennedy, John F., 3:297
Perkins, Frances and, 3:284, 295
placing women in government, 3:284, 285, 288–89
Reporter Plan, 3:288–89, 293
on Roosevelt, Franklin, 3:295
suffrage campaign, 3:295
DIDMCA (Depository Institution's Deregulation and Monetary Control Act), 1:61
Dies, Martin, 1:303, 3:313, 316
Dies Committee. *See* House Un-American Activities Committee (HUAC)
Diet. *See* Food
Dill-Connery Bill, 3:181
Dillinger, John, 1:132, 134, 139, 142–43
Dining During the Depression (Thibodeau), 2:38, 47
Dionne Quintuplets, 1:323
Disabled Americans, 1:207, 3:187, 196
Disarmament conferences, 2:142, 149
Discrimination
in American Federation of Labor, 1:66, 2:199
American Indians and, 1:7, 17
black Americans and, 1:66, 70, 77–78, 81
Civil Rights Act prohibiting, 1:83, 217, 219, 230, 235
Democratic Party and, 1:69
Department of Labor antidiscrimination efforts, 1:250, 251
housing and, 1:223, 2:102–3, 112, 114
investigations, 1:260, 3:335
Jewish Americans and, 3:135
married persons and, 3:289
Mexican Americans and, 3:334
in New Deal programs, 1:69–70, 85, 152, 250

Roosevelt, Franklin and, 1:67, 69, 75, 81, 3:335
small business and, 2:239, 241
Socialist Party against, 1:72
women and, 1:250, *255*, 2:199, 3:309, 326, 332–33, 346
See also Racism; Segregation
Dish Nights, 2:73
The Disinherited (Conroy), 2:211
Disney, Walt, 1:270, 311, 2:70, 72–73, 91–92
Division of Rural Rehabilitation, 1:242, 294
Divorce rate, 1:317
Dix, Dorothy (Elizabeth Gilmer), 2:173, 182
DNC (Democratic National Committee), 3:284, 288–89, 297
"Do the Rich Give to Charity?" (Mackey), 2:39
Do We Need a Dictator (The Nation), 2:272
Doak, William, 1:287, 288, 302, 3:298
Dodsworth (Lewis), 2:219
Doolin, Elmer, 2:31–32
Dorothy Healey: An American Red (film), 2:327
Dorsey, Tommy, 1:267
Dos Passos, John, 2:210, 219, 223
Douais, Adolf, 2:219
Doughton, Robert, 3:197–98
Douglas, Stephen, 1:154
Douglas, William, 3:220–21
Dow Jones industrial average, 1:93
Draft, Selective Service Act, 2:144
Drexel Furniture Co., Bailey v. (1922), 3:219
Drought, 1:168–69, 177, 178, *182*, 2:7, 277
Drought Relief Service (DRS), 1:173
Drugs, 2:43, 3:25
Drying foods, 2:31
du Pont brothers, 3:27–28
Dubin, Al, 2:94
DuBois, W.E.B., 2:174, 182
Duck Soup (film), 2:76–77
Due process, 3:204, 205, 208
Dumbo (film), 2:73
Dunaway, Faye, 2:90
DuPont Company, 2:150
Dust Bowl, 1:**168–85**, 2:*209*
conservation efforts, 1:174–76, 181, 182–83, 184, 2:7
defined, 2:277
drought, 1:168–69, 177, 178, *182*, 2:7
Guthrie's songs about, 1:179
health problems, 1:171–72
impact of, 1:181–83
jackrabbit "plague," 1:171
media resources, 1:173, 175
migration from, 1:172, 178–80, 184
notable people, 1:183–84

Dust Bowl (continued)
    overview, 1:168–69, 176–78,
        2:210–11
    perspectives on, 1:178–80
    soil erosion and, 2:7, 12–13
    See also Agricultural relief
        programs; Conservation; Dust
        storms; *The Grapes of Wrath*
        (Steinbeck)
Dust Bowl Ballads (Guthrie), 1:179
Dust Bowl Diary (Low), 1:184
Dust Storm, Cimarron Country, 1936
    (photo), 2:299
Dust storms
    in 1950s, 1:182
    causes of, 1:168, 169, 2:12–13
    crops and livestock lost in, 1:172
    described, 1:169, 170–71, *176*,
        184–85
    drought and, 1:169, 177–78
Dynamics of the Party System:
    Alignment and Realignment of
    Political Parties in the United
    States (Sundquist), 1:228
Dynamite (Adamic), 2:211

E

Earhart, Amelia, 2:124, 3:291
East India Company, 1:98
Eastman, Joseph, 3:100
E.C. Knight Company, United States v.
    (1895), 2:244, 3:218
Eccles, Marriner, 1:52, 62–63, 2:114,
    290, 3:265
Economic and monetary union (EMU),
    2:67
Economic Community (EC), 2:66–67
The Economic Consequences of the
    Peace (Keynes), 1:259
Economic Opportunity Act (EOA),
    1:119, 219
Economy
    of 1980s, 1:102
    business cycles, 1:89–90, 98*t*
    CCC benefits for, 1:112
    classical theory of, 1:259
    education budget, 1:187
    ethnic groups blamed for, 1:285,
        286, 298, 303
    free-silver, 1:155, 2:316
    global economic crisis, 2:52
    Gold Reserve Act, 2:262
    government deficit spending, 1:217,
        242, 2:281, 285–86, 326–27
    gross national product, 3:185*t*, 326,
        334
    growth rate, 2:287
    industrialization and, 1:253, 275,
        284, 2:171
    industry-military alliance and,
        3:338, 345

inflation safeguards, 3:331
    international relations and, 1:96
    Keynesian economics, 1:259–60,
        2:276, 281, 289
    national planning lacking, 1:87
    postwar, 3:346
    priming the pump, 1:247, 249,
        2:326–27
    recession of 1937, 2:282, 292
    Roosevelt, Franklin and, 1:149,
        2:282
    stock market crash and, 1:147, 188
    tax cuts for stimulating, 1:217
    U.S. dollar devalued, 2:284–85
    World War II benefits for, 2:18,
        284, 3:330–31
    See also Federal budget; Gold stan-
        dard; Price-control; World trade
Economy Act, 2:256, 3:289–91
Eddy, Mary Baker, 2:173
Ederle, Gertrude, 2:124
Edison, Thomas, 1:84, 2:92, 3:166, 242
Edsforth, Ronald, 2:252
Education, 1:**186–214**
    American Indians and, 1:6–7, 12,
        14–15, 20, 117
    American's faith in, 1:202, 207
    art education, 1:28
    bilingual education, 1:211
    Black Americans and, 1:190, 203,
        207–8, 213, 252, 318
    business community and, 1:193,
        194, 202–3, 205
    business community *vs.* teachers,
        1:194–96, 205, 208
    CCC programs, 1:113, 200–201,
        211, 251
    college
    attendance, 1:317–18
    conservatives *vs.* progressives,
        1:205–6
    cost per student, 1:192–93, 203, 207
    curriculum study, 1:198
    drop-out rate, 1:212
    educational experiments, 1:197–98
    experimental schools, 1:186, 211
    funding for, 1:186, 188–90, 198–99,
        202–3
    Great Society and, 1:207, 221
    intelligence of students and, 1:207,
        212
    Johnson-O'Malley Act (JOM),
        1:6–7, 9, 20–21
    militant teachers, 1:194, 195, 205,
        208
    music education, 1:29
    new dealers *vs.* conservative
        educators, 1:202, 206–7
    notable people, 1:209–12
    in NYA, 1:188, 201–2, 252
    private school, 3:141
    progressive education, 1:191–92,
        196, 197–98, 203–4, 208, 211

Roosevelt, Eleanor and, 1:199
    Roosevelt, Franklin education
        policy, 1:199–200, 206
    rural *vs.* city schools, 1:190, 203
    school attendance, 1:188, 190, 202,
        203, 207, 2:171
    in science and technology, 2:119
    social reconstructionism, 1:196–97,
        205, 206, 210
    traditional *vs.* progressive
        schooling, 1:191, 198
    trends in, 1:207
    views toward, 1:190
    vocational, 1:208
    See also Educators; Retrenchment;
        Schools; Teachers
Educational Equality League of
    Philadelphia, 1:193
Educators
    American Legion and, 1:196–97, 204
    communism and, 1:196–97, 204,
        205, 206
    new dealers *vs.* conservative
        educators, 1:202, 206–7
    racism of, 1:199, 203, 210, 211
    retrenchment and, 1:193–96
    See also Teachers
Egyptian Revival Architecture, 2:87
EHFA. *See* Electric Home and Farm
    Authority (EHFA)
Eiffel Tower, 3:362
Eighteenth Amendment
    bootlegging and, 1:125
    described, 3:5
    farmers affected by, 1:99
    flaw in, 3:18
    liquor prohibited, 1:136, 2:256–57
    New York Times article, 3:30–31
    ratification of, 3:17–18
    Rockefeller, John D. and, 3:30–31
    women's committee for repeal of,
        3:8
    See also Twenty-first Amendment;
        Volstead Act
Eimi (Cummings), 2:216
Einstein, Izzy, 3:20
Eisenhower, Dwight, 1:126, 162
Eisenstaedt, Alfred, 2:304
Elderly Americans
    everyday life, 1:320
    health care for, 1:232–33
    pension plan, 2:267
    poverty of, 1:230, 322–23, 3:177,
        190, 196
    Senior Citizen's Freedom to Work
        Act of 2000, 3:196
    Townsend Plan for, 2:267, 317–18,
        325, 3:39, 182
    See also Social Security
Elections
    1928, 1:157, 3:7–8, 141
    1932, 1:47, 2:254, 3:103, 127, 130,
        155, 192, 259

1936, 1:146, 150–52, 2:281–82, 3:128, 133–34, 188
1938, 1:152–54, 3:40, 339
1940, 1:158
1944, 1:158
1960, 1:162
1964, 2:230
1968, 1:226–28
1972, 1:163
Electric Home and Farm Authority (EHFA), 2:9, 262, 3:157, 259, 271
Electric motors, 3:172
Electricity
    benefits of, 3:171–72, 175
    cost issues, 3:153, 155, 157, 167, 260, 275
    demonstrations, 3:163, 166
    early days of, 3:153, 166, 229, 242–43
    in Europe and Canada, 3:167–68
    farmers and, 3:172, 259, 272
    film series on, 3:275
    first central power plant, 3:166, 242
    first experience of, 3:165, 175
    health benefits, 3:35–36, 167, 172
    Hoover, Herbert, electrical power and, 3:155, 169, 175, 243
    life without, 3:167, 175
    modernization and, 3:258–60
    national campaign for, 3:160
    power shortages, 3:172
    private *vs.* public power, 3:249–50, 274, 275–76
    progress and, 3:242
    regulation of, 2:247, 3:260
    Roosevelt, Franklin and, 3:154, 156, 258
    "spite lines," 3:161
    standardization of electrical systems, 3:273
    See also Power companies; Rural Electrification Administration (REA); Tennessee Valley Authority (TVA); Water and power
Electricity for Rural America: The Fight for the REA (Brown), 3:176
Elementary and Secondary Education Act, 1:209, 221
Eliot, Thomas, 3:198
Eliot, T.S., 2:148
Elixir-Sulfanilamide deaths, 3:46
Ellington, Duke, 1:79, 278, 279, 281, 2:*129*
Elmer Gantry (Lewis), 2:219
Emergency Banking Relief Act, 1:41, 49–50, 57, 2:256, 3:105, 107
Emergency Cattle Purchase Program, 1:173
Emergency Conservation Work Act, 1:110, 112, 113

Emergency Education Program, 1:200, 209
Emergency Farm Mortgage Act, 1:172–73, 2:6, 101, 258
Emergency Railroad Transportation Act, 2:261
Emergency Relief and Construction Act, 2:100, 259
Emergency Relief Appropriation Act (ERAA), 1:173, 249, 2:275, 276–77, 3:157
Emerson, Peter, 2:304
Emery, Edwin, 2:168
Emery, Michael, 2:168
The Emperor Jones (film), 2:83, 84
Empire State Building, 1:32, 2:122
Employment, 1:**239–61**
    American Indians and, 1:12, 15, 18, 21, 117
    artists and, 1:26–31
    black Americans and, 1:66, 77, 81
    CCC work relief, 1:9, 109–10, 112, 112–13
    CWA work relief, 1:26–27, 245, 246–47, 2:262
    education needs for, 1:212
    employed *vs.* unemployed, 1:306
    extra wage earners, 1:307
    Fair Labor Standards Act, 2:197, 280, 3:285, 334
    Federal Housing Administration and, 2:103
    FERA work relief, 1:241–45
    married persons in government and, 3:289–91
    married women and, 1:102, 307, 323, 3:332–33
    middle class families and, 1:326
    nation-wide employment service, 2:259–60
    notable people, 1:258–60
    perspectives on, 2:254–56
    PWA work relief, 1:247–49
    racial hiring quota system, 1:74–75, 82
    RFC relief loans, 1:241
    Roosevelt, Franklin and, 1:75, 77, 249
    as servants for the wealthy, 1:314
    United States Housing Authority and, 2:105
    working conditions, 2:191, 326
    workweek, 1:275, 2:128, 164, 191, 3:342–43
    World War II and, 1:115, 3:333–34, 342–43
    WPA work relief, 1:26–27, 75, 200, 249–50, 2:276–77
    yellow dog contracts, 2:192
    for youth, 1:110–11, 116–17, 250–51, 2:275, 277
    See also National Youth Administration (NYA); Reconstruction

Finance Corporation; Unemployment; Unions; Wages; Workweek
Employment Act of 1946, 1:161
EMU (Economic and monetary union), 2:67
"End Poverty in California" campaign, 1:150, 2:317, 330
Endurance contests, 1:265, 312–13, 2:222–23
Englebrecht, H.C., 2:142
Entertainment. *See* Leisure time
Entrepreneurs, 2:23, 31–33, 47
Environmentalism
    automobiles emission standards, 1:223, 233
    environmental films, 1:173
    influential book on, 1:229
    Silent Spring (Carson), 1:223, 229
    water and power project concerns, 3:278
    Water conservation, 1:183
    Water Quality Act, 1:223
    See also Conservation
EOA (Economic Opportunity Act), 1:119, 219
EPIC (End Poverty in California) campaign, 1:150, 2:317, 330
Epstein, Abraham, 2:192, 3:180–81, 185, 198
Equal protection clause, 3:205
Equal Rights Amendment (ERA), 3:291, 295, 297–98
ERA (Equal Rights Amendment), 3:291, 295, 297–98
ERAA *See* Emergency Relief Appropriation Act
Escapism, 1:263, 275, 276–78, 281–82, 2:84
    See also Leisure
Ethiopia, 1:82
Ethnic groups, 1:**284–304**
    anti-minority sentiment, 1:286, 298
    Asian Americans, 1:290–91, 297–98, 301
    Census 2000, 1:301
    cultural pluralism and, 2:288
    education and, 1:190, 199, 211
    in films, 2:88
    Hoover, Herbert and, 1:287
    human rights violations, 1:300
    New Deal programs, 1:292–94, 298–99
    notable people, 1:302–3
    overview, 1:284–86
    riding the rails, 3:81
    support organizations, 1:291–92
    World War II and, 1:294
    World's fairs and, 3:363, 364
    See also American Indians; Black Americans; Immigration; Mexican Americans
Eucharistic Congress, 3:141

Euro monetary unit, 2:67
Europe
    American popular culture and, 1:278
    bank collapse, 2:50, 52
    corporatism philosophy, 2:244
    economic and monetary union
      (EMU), 2:67
    Economic Community (EC),
      2:66–67
    economic rebuilding, 3:346–47
    electricity in, 3:167–68, 276
    euro currency, 2:67
    European Union (EU), 2:66, 67
    films in, 2:88
    fragmentation of, 2:61–62, 67
    gold standard and, 2:55, 56, 268
    import tariffs and, 1:96, 100, 101,
      2:3–4, 15, 52, 55
    opinion of Roosevelt, Franklin, 2:64
    perspectives on the U.S., 1:100
    political instability in, 2:51, 57, 58,
      61
    post World War I economy, 1:100,
      2:61–62
    public housing, 2:109
    racism in, 1:81–82
    seeking European unity, 2:62,
      64–67
    selling war materials and, 2:143–44
    social insurance in, 3:190–91
    transients in, 3:88
    unemployment rates, 2:51, 63t
    U.S. investment capital in,
      1:100–101, 2:52, 54, 63, 268
    U.S. isolationism and, 1:101–2,
      2:15, 3:344
    welfare programs, 1:225
    women and, 3:297
    World War II and, 3:339–42,
      344–45
    World's fairs in, 3:362
    See also Global impact of the Great
      Depression; *specific countries;*
      World trade
European Federal Union, 2:62
European Recovery Program, 3:347
European Relief Council, 3:99
European Union (EU), 2:66, 67
Evans, Luther, 3:312, 319
Evans, Walker
    Let Us Now Praise Famous Men,
      2:15, 170, 213, 300, 309
    in *Masters of Photography,* 2:308
    Stryker, Roy and, 2:299–300, 307
Every Man a King (Long), 2:329, 331
"Everybody Ought to be Rich"
    (Raskob), 1:91, 105
Everyday life, 1:**305–29**
    birth, marriage, divorce, 1:317
    black Americans, 1:68, 318–20,
      2:226
    Café Society, 1:314–16
    children's activities, 1:313–14, 327

college, 2:317–18
dance marathons, 1:265, 312–13,
    2:222–23
documenting, 1:31
elderly Americans, 1:320
family budget, 1:307t
farmers, 1:321, 2:18–20, 3:167, 175
home ownership, 1:308–9
homeless Americans, 1:320–21, 327
"keeping up appearances," 1:305,
    306, 308, 323
leisure time, 1:309–10
maintaining normality, 1:305, 306
making do, 1:307–8, 2:22, 26–27,
    39, 47
married working women, 1:102,
    307, 323
middle class families, 1:306–7, 323,
    326–27
news sources, 1:309
notable people, 1:325–26
riding the rails, 2:225–26, 3:87
vacations, 1:314
wealthy Americans, 1:306–7, 314,
    327–28, 2:39–40
youth activities, 1:212–13, 317,
    2:*278*
See also Automobiles; Leisure time
Executive orders, 3:157
Export-Import Bank, 3:107
Eyewitness to America (Colbert),
    1:107, 281, 3:350
Ezekiel, Mordecai, 2:16

F

Facism, 1:135, 278
Factories, 2:197–98, 199
Fads, 1:265–66
Fahey, John, 2:114
Fair Deal, 1:161–62, 3:338
Fair Employment Practices Committee
    (FEPC), 1:74–75, 77, 82, 260,
    3:335
Fair Housing Act, 1:83
Fair Labor Standards Act, 2:197, 280,
    3:285, 334
Fairfax, Beatrice (Marie Manning),
    2:168, 173, 184
Faithless (film), 2:77
Falk, Isidore, 3:37, 40, 53–54
Fall, Albert, 2:176–77
Family Limitation (Sanger), 3:292
Fannie Mae mortgages, 2:104, 111–12
Fantasia (film), 2:73
Far East. *See* China; Japan
Farley, James, 1:149, *164,* 165
Farley, Jim, 3:285
Farm Credit Administration (FCA),
    1:173, 2:6, 257, 260, 3:108–9
Farm Mortgage Moratorium Act,
    1:173, 183, 184, 2:263

Farm Mortgage Refinancing Act,
    2:101, 261
Farm Security Administration (FSA)
    aid to Dust Bowl refugees, 1:180
    documentary photographs, 2:31,
      297–301, 303, 306–7, 309–10,
      312–13
    home rehabilitation loans, 3:271
    housing for migrants, 1:180
    irrigation projects, 3:271
    Lange, Dorothea on, 2:307
    photojournalism of, 2:170, 308
    public opinion of, 2:306
    Resettlement Administration (RA)
      and, 1:174, 2:8
Farm Workers' Union, 1:68
Farmer, Fannie, 2:22, 33, 44, 45
Farmers
    black Americans as, 1:67, 70, 81,
      318, 2:12
    decrease in, 2:42, 3:343
    electricity for, 2:278–79, 3:157,
      165, 172, 175, 272
    everyday life, 1:321, 2:18–20,
      3:167, 175
    farmer rebellion, 1:126, 2:4, 13,
      18–20
    film series for, 3:275
    free-silver supported by, 1:155
    ideals *vs.* reality, 3:274–75
    income, 1:93, 319t, 2:4, 8, 9, 3:343
    as isolationists, 2:151
    poverty, 1:230
    price control issues, 2:4, 8, 9,
      11–12, 279
    REA and, 2:278–79, 3:160, 163, 169
    relocating, 1:176, 2:275, 297
    strikes, 1:287–88, 289
    tax on, 2:8
    in Tennessee Valley, 3:245
    World War II and, 3:343
    See also Agricultural relief
      programs; Farms; Mortgages;
      Sharecroppers; Tenant farmers
Farmers' Holiday Association, 2:4, 17,
    18, 19–20
Farming cooperatives, 2:9, 12
Farming the Dust Bowl: A First-Hand
    Account from Kansas (Svobida),
    1:184–85
Farms
    commercial v. small farms, 2:2, 8,
      11, 13, 14, 15–16
    farm modernization, 2:8, 11, 15–16
    foreclosures, 1:172, 2:4, 8, 19–20
    number and value, 2:3t
    relief for, 2:**1–20**
    small farm problems, 2:8, 14–15,
      17, 20
Farrell, James T., 2:210, 223
Fashion, 1:322
Fata Morgana (Douais), 2:219
The Fatal Glass of Beer (film), 2:77

Fatal Interview (Millay), 2:217
Father Divine's Peace Mission, 3:138
Faulkner, William, 2:214, 219
Fawcett, John, 3:90–91
FBI. *See* Federal Bureau of
    Investigation (FBI)
FCC (Federal Communications
    Commission), 1:266, 3:62
FDA. *See* Food and Drug
    Administration (FDA)
FDIC. *See* Federal Deposit Insurance
    Corporation
Fechner, Robert
    about, 1:119, 258
    budget cuts and, 1:114
    as CCC director, 1:112, 211, 258
    CCC segregation and, 1:250, 251
    death of, 1:115
Federal Art Project, 1:28, 29, 76, 292,
    2:277, 287, 3:312
Federal budget
    deficit spending, 1:217, 242, 2:281,
        285–86, 326–27
    Keynesian economics and, 2:276
    national debt, 2:327
    public program expenditures, 1:234,
        3:185t
    retrenchment, 1:*189*, 190–96
    Roosevelt, Franklin and, 1:114, 2:256
    statistics, 1:242t
    tax cuts and, 1:217
    World War II and, 3:326
Federal Bureau of Investigation (FBI),
    1:133, 135, 139–40, 142, 146
Federal Charter for a National Theater,
    1:36
Federal Communications Commission
    (FCC), 1:266, 3:62
Federal Council of Churches of Christ,
    3:121, 124, 127, 150
Federal Council on Negro Affairs
    ("Black Cabinet"), 1:73, 84, 85,
    152, 3:288, 319
Federal Dance Project (FDP), 2:277
Federal Deposit Insurance Corporation
    (FDIC)
    bank failures and, 1:46, 103
    bank runs and, 1:46, 48, 59
    creation of, 1:51
    impact of, 1:59–61
    opposition to, 1:58
    support for, 1:59, 65
Federal Emergency Relief Act, 2:259
Federal Emergency Relief
    Administration (FERA)
    divisions of, 1:242
    drawbacks of, 1:244
    education and, 1:200
    financial aid from, 1:243–44, 3:308
    funding for, 1:245
    "Health Inventory" study, 3:37, 50
    Hickock, Lorena as writer for, 3:288
    hunger relief projects, 2:25

medical relief program, 3:37–38
    resistance to, 1:244
    transients and, 3:81, 82
    wage rates for, 1:246
    work relief program, 1:241–42,
        245, 2:259
Federal Fair Housing laws, 2:114
Federal Farm Bankruptcy Act, 2:262
Federal Farm Board, 1:95, 2:3, 266
Federal Food, Drug and Cosmetic Act,
    1:223, 2:43–44, 284, 3:46, 49, 52
Federal Home Loan Act, 1:46
Federal Home Loan Bank Act,
    2:99–100
Federal Home Loan Board, 1:46, 61
Federal Housing Act, 1:256
Federal Housing Administration (FHA)
    benefits of, 2:103–4, 114
    home loans refinanced, 1:309
    impact of, 2:111
    modernizing homes and, 3:258,
        259, 260
    mortgages insured by, 1:47, 2:103
    property appraisal methods, 2:102,
        103
    Roosevelt, Franklin, on, 2:115–16
    suburb dwellings favored by, 2:103,
        109, 112
Federal Meat Inspection Act, 1:224
Federal Music Project (FMP), 1:29, 76,
    292, 3:311
Federal National Mortgage
    Association. *See* Fannie Mae
Federal One, 1:26–28, 34–35, 36, 37,
    3:210–311, 316–17
Federal Open Market Committee
    (FOMC), 1:55
Federal Power Commission, 2:247,
    3:260, 273
Federal Radio Commission, 2:177
Federal Reclamation Act, 3:262
Federal Reserve Act, 1:54
Federal Reserve Banks, 1:55, 56, *60*
Federal Reserve Board, 1:45, 46, 54,
    55, 2:280, 292
Federal Reserve System
    bank failures and, 1:59
    bank holiday and, 1:50
    bank loans and, 1:45
    centralized control of banking,
        1:156, 2:280
    described, 1:54, 55, *56*
    development of, 1:54, 55
    disadvantages, 1:54
    FDIC and, 1:51
    loan speculation and, 1:57
    locations of banks, 1:*60*
    opposition to, 1:58
    restructuring of, 1:52
    value of U.S. money and, 2:55
Federal Savings and Loan Insurance
    Corporation (FSLIC), 1:47, 61,
    2:104

Federal Securities Act, 2:259, 263
Federal Security Agency (FSA), 1:115,
    3:46–47
Federal Surplus Commodies
    Corporation (FSCC), 2:25, 42
Federal Surplus Relief Corporation
    (FSRC), 1:173, 2:7, 25, 37–38,
    42
Federal Theater Project (FTP)
    achievements, 1:29–30, 2:277
    described, 3:312–14
    "Federal Theater of the Air," 1:29
    Flanagan, Hallie as director, 3:288,
        312–14, 320
    impact of, 1:36, 37–38, 3:314
    Living Newspapers, 3:243, 313
    racial equality in, 1:75–76
    shut down by House Un-American
        Activities Committee, 1:32,
        3:314, 316
Federal Trade Commission (FTC)
    business regulated by, 2:259
    Humphrey, William ruling, 3:208–9
    natural gas shipments regulated,
        2:247
    package labeling regulated, 2:130
    power companies investigated,
        3:248–49
    prevention of unfair competition,
        2:244
Federal Transient Relief Service, 3:82,
    83, 88
Federal Water Power Act, 3:246
Federal Works Agency, 1:249
Federal Writers' Project (FWP)
    American Guide Series, 1:31, 2:35,
        213–14, 3:311
    black Americans and, 1:76, 3:312
    documenting American life, 3:311,
        312
    employment for writers, 1:30–31,
        2:208, 213–14
    Historical Records Survey (HRS),
        1:31, 3:312
    Mexican American folklore revival,
        1:292
    public perspectives on, 2:287
    purpose of, 2:225
    Slave Narratives, 3:311, 312
    Steinbeck's writings about, 2:222
    These Are Our Lives, 1:327, 2:214,
        225–26
    World War II and, 3:312
Federalists Party, 1:154
Fellowship of Reconciliation (FOR),
    3:145
Ferguson, Plessy v., 1:77–78
Fertilizer, 3:229–30, 239
FHA. *See* Federal Housing
    Administration (FHA)
Fiction, 1:272–73
Field, Sally, 2:90
Fields, W.C., 1:268, 2:76, 77

Fifteenth Amendment, 1:79, 80
Fifth Amendment, 3:207–8
Fight for Freedom Committee, 2:145
Filburn, Wickard v. (1941), 2:9
Filipino Americans, 1:291
Films, 1:268–72, 2:**70–96**
　　American Film Institute list, 2:85
　　animated, 1:270, 2:72–73
　　attendance, 1:129, 2:70, 71, 72, 79*t*,
　　　89, 3:59
　　attracting audiences, 2:73–74
　　black Americans in, 2:83–84
　　box office receipts, 2:87*t*
　　comedies, 1:269–70, 2:76–77, 80
　　contributing forces, 2:84
　　costume dramas, 1:271
　　crime, 1:129–30, 131, 133
　　Depression era films, 2:307
　　development of, 2:84
　　documentary, 2:167, 186, 307, 310,
　　　327
　　environmental, 1:173
　　as escapism, 2:84
　　in Europe, 1:278, 2:88
　　everyday life and, 1:310–12
　　G-men, 2:79–80
　　home films, 1:266
　　horror, 1:271, 2:82
　　impact of, 2:88–90
　　juvenile delinquents, 1:131
　　law enforcement in, 2:80, 95
　　literary adaptations, 1:272, 2:82
　　on the medical profession, 3:47
　　melodrama, 1:271
　　messages of, 1:277
　　Movie Palaces, 2:87, 88–89
　　musicals, 1:270–71, 2:78–79
　　newsreels, 1:309, 2:186
　　notable people, 2:90–94
　　overview, 1:311–12, 2:70–71
　　perspectives on, 2:86–88
　　on the Political "Left," 2:327
　　popularity of, 2:123
　　post-depression era, 2:89–90
　　power of, 2:88
　　production codes, 2:78, 87, 88,
　　　3:140
　　race films, 2:83–84
　　Shirley Temple films, 1:270, 311,
　　　313–14, 2:79
　　shyster films, 2:75–76
　　social conscious films, 2:81–82
　　sound and color techniques, 2:73
　　swashbuckler, 1:271, 2:82
　　"talkies," 1:129, 321, 2:71, 73, 76,
　　　86
　　television series, 2:90
　　themes for, 1:268
　　thrillers, 1:271–72, 2:82
　　by TVA, 3:241
　　Westerns, 1:271, 2:80
　　women in, 2:77–78, 3:296
　　World War I and, 2:89, 96

　　See also Gangster films;
　　　Hollywood; Movie theaters
Filne, Edward, 1:250
Financial Institutions Reform,
　　Recovery and Enforcement Act
　　(FIRREA), 1:61
Finland, 2:57, 3:27, 340
Finn, Evelyn, 1:85
Fireside chats, 1:*153*, 3:*72*
　　author of, 2:270
　　on the banking crisis, 1:50, *58*, 64,
　　　2:256, 3:108
　　fighting German expansion,
　　　2:156–57
　　instilling public confidence, 1:326,
　　　3:57, 65
　　popularity of, 1:121, 2:267, 3:65
　　reorganizing the Supreme Court,
　　　2:74, 3:226–27
　　on U.S. involvement in World War
　　　II, 3:344, 349–50
　　warmth and charm in, 2:163
Firestone, 2:235–36
FIRREA (Financial Institutions
　　Reform, Recovery and
　　Enforcement Act), 1:61
First Amendment, 3:213
First hundred days, 2:25, 255–56, 257,
　　268–69, 272–73
Fisher, Boyd, 3:160
Fitzgerald, Ella, 1:280
Fitzgerald, Scott F., 2:131, 214, 219
Five-Power Treaty, 2:149
Flammable Fabrics Act, 1:224
Flanagan, Hallie
　　about, 1:36
　　Arena, 1:37, 38
　　as Federal Theater Project director,
　　　3:288, 312–14, 320
　　Hopkins, Harry and, 1:37
　　House Un-American Activities
　　　Committee and, 1:38
Flanigan, Fan, 1:327
Flash Gordon, 1:313, 3:359
Fletcher, Duncan, 1:51, 62
Flight from the City (Borsodi), 3:276
Flood control, 3:271, 272
Florida League for Better Schools,
　　1:196
Florida real estate speculation, 1:92
Floyd, Charles "Pretty Boy," 1:132,
　　134
Flynn, John, 2:145, 154–55
FMP. *See* Federal Music Project (FMP)
Folk and domestic art, 1:33–34, 2:123
Folk music, 1:31, 273–74, 279
Folk schools, 1:197, 208
Folsom, Marion, 3:193
Folsom River Dam, 3:271
Fonda, Henry, 2:15
Food, 2:**21–49**
　　basics, 2:26–28, 29, 31, 34, 40
　　canned food, 2:31, 34, 40, 41, 42

chain stores, 1:321, 2:36–37
cost of, 1:307–8, 2:40*t*
desserts, 2:29–33, 34, 35, 36, 48
during World War II, 2:40–41
food distribution, 2:25, 37–38, 42
food entrepreneurs, 2:23, 31–33, 47
food riots, 1:126, 2:24, 37
frozen food, 2:33, 42
from gardens, 2:29, 30–31, 36, 47
genetically modified, 2:42
making do, 1:307–8, 2:22, 26–27,
　　39, 47
malnutrition and, 1:205, 239, 319,
　　321, 2:23, 24
new foods, 2:40
nutrition, 2:36, 40
organic, 2:42
overview, 2:21–22
packaging and labeling standards,
　　3:46, 49
preserving, 2:31
processed food, 2:34–35, 42
rationing, 2:40, 3:331
safety issues, 1:223, 224, 2:43–44,
　　284
starvation, 2:24, 40
stealing, 2:24
storage, 3:167
vitamins A and B, 2:36
WPA student lunches, 1:200
　　See also Consumer protection;
　　　Cookbooks; Crops; Hunger
　　　relief; Recipes
Food Administration, 2:36
Food and Drink in America: A History
　　(Hooker), 2:46–47
Food and Drug Administration (FDA),
　　1:223, 2:44, 3:35, 46
Food coupons, 1:244
Food riots, 1:126, 2:24, 37
Food Stamp Act, 1:224, 2:43
Food stamps, 1:224, 2:25–26, 42–43
Food store chains, 1:321, 2:36–37
Football, 1:274
Footlight Parade (film), 2:78
For Whom the Bell Tolls
　　(Hemingway), 2:212, 214
Forbidden (film), 3:296
Ford, Gerald, on Social Security, 3:200
Ford, Henry
　　about, 2:204
　　anti-Semitism of, 3:136, 246
　　Muscle Shoals bid of, 3:246, 248
　　outdoor museum of, 2:124
Ford, John, 2:15, 82, 92, 307
Ford Motor Company
　　anti-union tactics, 2:205
　　assembly line of, 2:120, 199
　　banking crisis and, 3:104–5
　　Chicago World's Fair exhibit, 3:355
　　electricity film series, 3:275
　　labor unions opposed by, 2:234
　　Model T's, 2:106, 119, 204

refusal to join NRA, 2:233
strikes, 2:*235*
union representation, 2:*244*
Forgotten People: A Study of New Mexicans (Sanchez), 1:294
Forrestal, James, 3:347
Fort Peck Dam, 3:269
Fortune magazine, 1:328, 2:169, 178–79, 184, 300, 310
42nd Street (musical), 1:270
Fosdick, Harry, 3:125, 140, 145, 146–47
Foster, William, 2:321, 328–29
The Foundry (Halper), 2:210
"Four Horsemen of Reaction," 3:203, 215
Four-Power Treaty, 2:149
Fourteenth Amendment, 3:204, 205, 211, 214
France
  anti-war sentiment, 2:151–52
  electricity in, 3:167
  films by, 1:278
  gold standard suspended by, 2:60
  Great Depression and, 2:57
  political instability of, 2:57, 61
  surrender to Germany, 3:*329*, 340, *341*
  unemployment in, 2:57
  war debts of, 2:56–57
  war on Germany, 2:151, 3:327
Franco, Francisco, 2:61
Frank, Glenn, 1:211
Frank, Jerome, 2:16, 44, 3:218
Frankenstein (film), 1:271
Frankenstein, Richard, 2:*198*
Frankfurter, Felix, 2:290, 3:211, 220
Frazier, Brenda, 1:315–16
Frazier, Lynn, 1:183
Frazier-Lemke Bankruptcy Act, 1:173, 183, 184, 2:101–2, 3:108, 208–9
Free, Adult, Uncensored: The Living History of the Federal Theatre Project, (O'Connor), 1:38
Free enterprise
  government ownership and, 3:249–50
  New Deal and, 1:151, 2:246, 286, 287
  Progressives view of, 3:170, 249
  REA and, 3:169
  TVA and, 3:249, 250
Free Silver Movement, 1:155
"Freedom of the Press" statue, 3:*360*
Fritos, 2:31–32
From the Crash to the Blitz: 1929-39 (Phillips), 1:326
Frost, Robert, 2:216
Frozen food, 2:33, 42
FSA. *See* Farm Security Administration (FSA)
FSLIC (Federal Savings and Loan Insurance Corporation), 1:47, 61

FTC. *See* Federal Trade Commission (FTC)
FTP. *See* Federal Theater Project (FTP)
Furman, Bess, 2:168
A Further Range (Frost), 2:216
Fury (film), 2:82
Futurama exhibit, 3:359, 364
Future Outlook League, 1:81

G

G-Men (film), 1:131, 135, 139, 142, 2:80
Gable, Clark, 2:80, 82, 92
Gabler, Neal, 1:278
Gabriel over the White House (film), 1:133, 2:80, 88
Gadsden Purchase (1853), 1:296
Gaines, Lloyd, 3:227
Galbraith, John Kenneth, 1:249
Gallup, George, 1:163
Games
  bingo, 2:73
  card games, 1:265, 279, 310
  for children, 1:279, 314
  jacks, 1:279
  jigsaw puzzles, 1:264, 265, *324*, *325*
  jumprope, 1:279
  Kick the Can, 1:279
Gangster films, 1:129–31, 142, 268–69, 277, 2:74–75, 86
Gangsters, 1:125, 139
Garbo, Greta, 2:77, 92–93, 94
Gardening, 2:29, 30–31, 36, 41, 47
Garland, Judy, 2:7, 82, 83
Garment industry, 1:290, 2:127, 199–200, 3:301
Garn-It (German Depository Institutions Act), 1:61
Garner, John Nance, 1:*151*
Garver, Thomas, 2:313
Gasoline, 2:120, 3:331
Gasoline engines, 3:167
Geary Act, 1:297
Geddes, Norman, 3:359, 361, 364, 365
Gehrig, Lou, 1:325–26, 2:*134*
Geiger, Robert, 1:158
Gelfand, Mark, 2:113
General Allotment Act, 1:5, 10, 11, 12, 18
General Electric, 3:271, 272
General Federation of Women's Clubs, 3:291, 295
General Foods, 2:33, 34, 42
General Mills, 2:35, 40, 41
General Motors, 2:196–97, 3:213
  banking crisis and, 3:105
  car models produced, 2:119–20
  labor strike, 1:128
  Women's Emergency Brigade and, 3:*290*

The General Theory of Employment, Interest and Money (Keynes), 1:259, 2:290
Generation gap, 1:325
The Genesis of World War (Barnes), 2:146
Genetically modified food, 2:42
Georgia, Cherokee Nation v. (1831), 1:19
German Depository Institutions Act (Garn-It), 1:61
Germany
  armed forces and armaments, 3:339–40, 341
  bank failures, 2:51
  dependency on U.S. investments and loans, 2:63
  economy, 1:101, 2:54, 268
  electricity in, 3:167
  expansion through Europe, 3:327, *328*, 340
  health care system, 3:48, 51–52
  impact of the Great Depression, 2:52–54, 64
  social insurance in, 3:191
  social welfare programs, 1:225
  surrender of, 3:330
  tariff on imported goods, 2:15
  transients in, 3:88
  Treaty of Versailles and, 2:148
  unemployment in, 2:51, 52, 53, 54
  war debts of, 2:52–53, 56, 63, 3:113
  war declared on the U.S., 2:145
  World War I and, 2:54, 63, 146
  See also Hitler, Adolf
Gershwin, George, 3:359
Gervais, C.H., 3:30
Get rich quick mentality, 1:91–92, 100
Ghettos, 1:75, 78, 131, 226
GI Bill (Servicemen's Readjustment Act), 3:338
Giant Power Board, 3:168–69, 242
Gibbons, Clyde, 2:167
Gibbons, Mary, 3:133
Gibson, Josh, 2:125
Gilded Age, 2:126
Gilkey, Gordon, 3:364–65
Gilmer, Elizabeth (Dorothy Dix), 2:173, 182
Ginnie Mae, 2:111
Glass, Carter, 1:45, 51, 52, 63
Glass-Steagall Act, 1:46, 48, 51–52, 59–60, 62, 103, 2:260
Global impact of the Great Depression, 2:**50–69**
  Australia and, 2:59
  Austria and, 2:51
  Economic Community (EC), 2:66–67
  European Union (EU), 2:66, 67
  failure in international cooperation, 2:61, 64

Global impact of the Great Depression
    (continued)
    Far East and, 2:58–59
    France and, 2:57, 60, 61
    Germany and, 2:52–54, 63–64
    gold standard suspended, 2:51, 55,
        56, 62
    Great Britain and, 2:54–57
    growth of nationalism, 2:51
    Hoover, Herbert and, 2:52
    Latin America and, 2:52, 58, 62
    League of Nations and, 1:156, 2:62,
        146, 148, 3:297
    notable people, 2:67–68
    perspectives on, 2:50, 64
    rise of political instability, 2:61
    Roosevelt, Franklin and, 2:52,
        59–60
    Russia and, 2:57–58
    seeking European unity, 2:62,
        64–67
    Sweden and, 2:52, 3:27
    U.S. blamed for, 2:50, 51
    U.S. investment capital withdrawn,
        2:52, 54
    World Economic Conference,
        2:59–61, *65*, 68–69
    world trade collapse, 2:50, 52, 55,
        57
    World War II and, 2:64
    See also Tariffs; War debts
The Godfather, 1:140
God's Little Acre (Caldwell), 2:210
Goebbels, Joseph, 3:67, 68
Golby, John, 2:68
Gold, 1:44, 50, 3:207
    See also Gold standard
Gold, Michael, 2:209–10, 221
Gold diggers (film), 2:78, 94
Gold Reserve Act, 2:262
Gold standard, 2:57, 62, 268
    currency stabilization and, 2:59–60
    described, 2:55
    suspension of, 2:51, 55, 56
Gold Standard Act, 1:155
"The Goldberg's" (radio), 1:266
Golden Age of Hollywood, 1:268,
    2:70, 88–89
Golden Gate Bridge, 2:120, *121*, 3:356
Goldwater, Barry, 1:219, 220
Golf, 1:311
Gone with the Wind (film)
    black Americans in, 2:84, 88
    as costume drama, 1:271
    moral codes and, 1:281
    photograph, 2:*92*
    premiere, 2:*74*
    racism and, 2:82
    Technicolor in, 2:73
Gone with the Wind (Mitchell),
    1:272–73, 2:82, 215, 222
Gonorrhea, 3:43, 46
Gonzalez, Pedro, 1:302

The Good Earth (Buck), 2:214, 218,
    222
Good Neighbor Policy, 2:58, 145–46
Goodhue, Bertram, 3:356
Goodman, Benny, 1:273, 280, 312, 326
Goodrich, NRA and, 2:236
Goodyear Tire Corporation, 1:128,
    2:*195*, 196, 235, 236
Gore, John, 3:238
Gosden, Freeman, 3:72, 73
Government
    business regulated by, 1:88, 148,
        2:247
    Catholics in, 3:130
    centralized power of, 1:218, 242
    changing role of, 1:256–58, 2:270,
        287–88
    cooperation with business,
        2:230–31, 244–45, 246, 247
    during national crisis, 3:204
    government records archived, 1:8
    increased role for, 2:264, 328
    industry-military alliance and,
        3:336, 344, 345–46
    Laissez-faire administration, 1:87,
        88, 98, 100, 2:325
    limited *vs.* large role for, 1:155,
        2:325–26
    national security and, 3:347
    New Deal and, 2:163
    public attitude toward, 1:256
    public education and, 1:198, 202,
        207
    public interest in, 2:163
    regulation of power companies,
        3:169
    revenue of, 3:1
    specialized news coverage, 2:161
    state governments *vs.,* 1:241–42,
        3:216–17
    stock market regulation, 1:92, 104,
        105, 3:131
    unemployment and, 1:256–58
    women in, 2:287–88, 3:285, 293,
        297
Gramm-Leach-Bliley Financial
        Services Modernization Act,
        1:62
Grand Canyon, 1:118
Grand Coulee Dam, 1:257, 3:258, 265,
    266–68, 270
Grand Hotel (film), 3:296
The Grapes of Wrath (film), 1:268,
    2:15, 82, 307
The Grapes of Wrath (Steinbeck)
    as bestseller, 2:214, 222
    Dust Bowl refugees described,
        1:179, 181, 2:226
    as proletarian literature, 2:212, 222
    Pulitzer Prize for, 2:15, 210, 224
    Realism style of, 2:128
Grassroots activism, 1:230
Gray, Harold, 1:313

Great Atlantic and Pacific Tea
        Company, 2:36
Great Britain
    appeasement policy, 2:151
    armed forces and weapons, 3:341–42
    economy, 1:100, 2:268
    gold standard suspended, 2:51, 55,
        56
    health care system, 3:48, 51–52
    impact of the Great Depression on,
        2:54–57
    New York World's Fair and,
        3:360–61
    social insurance in, 3:191
    tariffs on foreign goods, 2:55
    unemployment, 2:56
    U.S. assistance to, 2:145, 3:344
    war debts of, 2:55, 56–57, 62
    war declared on Germany, 2:151,
        3:327, 341–42
    war materials of, 3:339
The Great Depression: America
    (McElvaine), 1:71, 81, 2:75,
    81–82, 197
The Great Gatsby (Fitzgerald), 2:131,
    219
Great Illusion (Asbury), 3:2
Great Plains. *See* Dust Bowl
Great Plains Committee, 1:182
Great Plains Conservation Program,
    1:183
Great Plains Drought Area Committee,
    2:7
Great Society, 1:**215–38**
    achievements, 1:224
    American Indians and, 1:11
    Appalachian Regional Development
        Act, 1:220
    black Americans and, 1:226,
        231–32
    civil rights, 1:217–18, 231–32, 233
    consumer protection, 1:223–24
    contributing forces, 1:228–29
    Corporation for Public
        Broadcasting, 1:221
    Democratic Coalition and, 1:228–29
    Department of Transportation,
        1:232
    economic affluence and, 1:217
    education and, 1:207, 221
    election of 1968, 1:226–28
    environmentalism, 1:223
    Food Stamp Act, 1:224, 2:43
    health care, 1:232–33
    housing, 1:221–23
    immigration, 1:223
    impact of, 1:230–32
    influential books, 1:229
    labor movement and, 1:232, 234
    National Endowment for the Arts
        (NEA), 1:36, 221, 233
    New Deal and, 1:162, 224, 228,
        230–32, 2:289

notable people, 1:234–37
opposition to, 1:224–26
overview, 1:215–16, 217, 239
perspectives on, 1:229–30
poverty and, 1:3, 218–19, 233–34, 2:113
supporters and critics, 1:229–30
tax cuts, 1:217
Vietnam war, 1:231
voting rights, 1:220–21, 235
Warren Court, 1:228, 237
welfare state, 1:225
See also Social security
The Great Train Robbery (film), 2:86
Greenfield Village outdoor museum of, 2:124
Greenhalgh, Paul, 3:359
Greta Garbo: The Mysterious Lady (film), 2:94
Griffith, D.W., 2:86
Griffiths, Martha, 3:297
Grocery store chains, 1:321, 2:36–37
Gropius, Walter, 2:122
Gross, Louise, 3:6, 8
Gross national product, 3:185*t*, 326, 334
Grovey v. Townsend (1935), 1:80
Gruenberg, Benjamin, 3:363
Guffey-Snyder Bituminous Coal Stabilization Act, 2:247, 3:210
Guiding Light (radio and television), 3:64
Guinn v. United states (1915), 1:80
Guthrie, Woody, 1:179, 257, 273, 280, 3:268

H

Haas, Francis, 3:130, 132, 147
HABS (Historic American Buildings Survey), 2:302, 303
Hadden, Briton, 2:178
HAER (Historic American Engineering Record), 2:302, 303
Hairstyles, 1:321
Halberstam, David, 2:136
Hall, Gus, 2:315, 321, 329
Halper, Albert, 2:210
Hamilton, Walton, 3:37, 39
Hammer v. Dagenhart (1918), 3:217
Hammett, Dashiell, 2:215
Handbook of Federal Indian Law (Cohen), 1:9, 19, 21
Hanighen, F.C., 2:142
Hansen, Alvin, 2:290, 292
The Happiest Man on Earth (Maltz), 2:210
Harburg, E.Y. "Yip," 1:280
Hard, William, 2:182
Hard Times; An Oral History of the Great Depression (Terkel), 1:85, 106–7, 2:205

Harding, Warren, 1:87, 89
Harding, William, 3:6, 246
Hare-Hawes-Cutting Act, 2:151
Harlem, 1:35
Harlem Renaissance, 1:35, 79, 2:123, 128
Harper, Lee, 1:67
Harper's Magazine, 2:156, 178, 210
Harring, Michael, 1:229
Harrison, Byron, 3:198
Harrison, George, 1:49, 63
Hartman, Ben, 1:33
Harvest Gypsies (Steinbeck), 1:179, 181
Harvey, William, 2:317, 330
Hastie, William, 1:73, 75, 84, *84*, 152
Hawley-Smoot Tariff Act, 1:96, 100, 101, 2:3–4, 15, 52
Hayes, Patrick, 3:139, 143
Haynes, George, 3:137
Haynes, Roy, 3:4–5
Hays, William, 1:281, 2:78, 87, 3:140
Hays Commission, 1:281
Head Start Program, 1:209, 219, 234, 2:328
Healey, Dorothy (Rosenblum), 2:201, 321–22, 327, 330, 332
Health care. *See* Public health
Health insurance, 3:34, 37, 39–40, 47–48, 50, 51, 53
Hearst, William Randolph
    about, 2:172, 182–83
    communism and, 1:197, 206, 2:163, 182
    movie studio of, 2:88
    New Deal and, 2:163, 182
    newspaper consolidations, 1:174
    Prohibition opposed by, 3:26
    public power supported by, 3:275
Heart disease, 3:33, 40
Heart of Atlanta Motel v. United States (1964), 1:217
Heline, Oscar, 2:18
Helvering v. Davis (1937), 3:220
Hemingway, Ernest, 2:22, 214, 219
Henderson, Leon, 3:331, 347–48
Henie, Sonja, 2:124
Hepburn, Katherine, 3:296
Her Fall and Rise (film), 2:77
Herald Tribune, 2:186–87
Heroes (film), 2:82
Herring, Clyde, 2:13
Hersch, John, 1:106
Hertzberg, Sidney, 2:145
Hesse, Karen, 1:175
Hetch Hetchy Dam, 3:274, 275
Heyl, Helen Hay, 1:191
Hickock, Lorena
    as Associated Press reporter, 2:168, 3:287
    CWA wages report, 1:246–47
    reports by, 2:44–45
    Roosevelt, Eleanor and, 3:287

work relief report, 2:38
    as writer for FERA, 3:241, 287–88
Higher Education Act of 1965, 1:221
Highlander Folk School, 1:197, 208
Highway Beautification Bill, 1:234
Highway Safety Act, 1:223
Hilliard, Harriet, 3:63
Hilliers, John, 2:304
The Hindenburg (Mooney), 1:281
Hindenburg crash, 1:266, 281, 3:67
Hine, Lewis, 2:306
Historic American Buildings Survey (HABS), 2:302, 303
Historic American Engineering Record (HAER), 2:302, 303
Historic preservation of photographs, 2:302
Historical Records Survey (HRS), 1:31, 3:312
A History of Urban America (Glaab and Brown), 2:97, 116
Hitchcock, Alfred, 1:101, 271, 2:82, 88
Hitchhiking, 3:79
Hitler, Adolf
    about, 2:67–68, 3:*340*
    conquest of Europe, 2:61
    goals of, 2:54
    I Saw Hitler!, 2:186
    Jews persecuted by, 3:135
    Mein Kampf, 2:216
    music banned by, 3:67–68
    Mussolini, Benito and, 2:*61, 157*
    New Order of, 2:54, 67, 268
    preaching racial and religious hatred, 1:81–82
    propaganda of, 1:275
    radio and, 3:70
    rearming Germany, 2:143
    youth influenced by, 1:250
HIV/AIDS, 3:52, 53
A Hobo Memoir (Fawcett), 3:90–91
Hoboes. *See* Transients
Hoeme, Fred, 1:174
Hoey, Jane, 3:301
HOLC. *See* Home Owners' Loan Corporation (HOLC)
Holding companies
    Commonwealth and Southern Corporation (C & S), 3:236, 237, 238–39
    as monopolies, 3:159
    overview, 1:89, 106
    power companies and, 3:159, 236, 237, 238–39, 274
    Public Utilities Holding Companies Act, 2:247, 280–81, 3:260, 271
Hollywood, 2:**70–96**
    Columbia Pictures, 2:73
    golden age, 1:268, 2:70, 88–89, 132
    golden year of 1939, 2:82–83
    Great Depression and, 2:71–72
    House Un-American Activities Committee and, 1:32

Hollywood (continued)
    major studies, 2:72
    "Movie Palaces," 2:87, 88–89
    overview, 2:70–71
    Paramount Studios, 2:72, 76
    production codes, 2:78, 87, 88
    profit statistics, 2:72, 87t
    prosperity of, 2:132
    southern California and, 2:84, 86
    Warner Brothers Pictures, 2:78, 82,
        93–94, 95
    See also Films; Movie theaters
"Hollywood Hotel" radio program, 3:64
Holmes, John, 3:145, 147
Holmes, Oliver Wendell, 3:216, 218,
    219
"Holy rollers," 3:138
*Home Building and Loan Association
    v. Blaisdell* (1934), 3:204
Home modernization, 3:259–60, 271,
    278
Home Owners Loan Act (1934), 2:101
Home Owners' Loan Corporation
    (HOLC)
    amortized mortgages introduced,
        2:102
    appraisal methods, 2:102, 112
    creation of, 2:260
    impact of, 2:111
    mortgages refinanced, 1:309, 2:101,
        260, 3:259
    redlining and, 2:102–3, 112
Home Owners' Refinancing Act,
    2:101, 260
Homelessness
    of 1980s, 1:102, 3:88
    caused by unemployment, 2:192
    CCC and, 1:118
    charities and, 3:122
    churches and, 3:122
    everyday life of, 1:320–21, 327
    "Hoovervilles," 1:241, 320–21, 327,
        2:265, 3:95, 106
    kindness toward, 1:308
    National Committee on Care for
        Transients and Homeless
        (NCCTH), 3:77, 83
    in New York City, 2:104–5
    statistics, 3:77–78
    See also Riding the rails; Transients
Homestead Act, 2:3
Hooker, Richard, 2:46–47
Hoover, Herbert, 3:*114*
    about, 1:105, 2:16
    as Commerce secretary, 3:109–10
    foreign policy, 2:52
    Great Depression and, 2:264–66
    "hands-off" government policy,
        1:241–42, 2:264, 266, 316–17
    Hoover Dam and, 3:263
    journalism and, 2:163, 178
    laissez-faire administration, 1:87,
        89

nomination speech, 3:30
    political philosophy, 3:94
    recovery plans, 3:94–97, 112–13
    Roosevelt, Franklin and, 3:*104*
    State of the Union address (1931),
        3:115–16
    See also specific topics
Hoover, J. Edgar
    about, 1:143
    Capone, Al and, 1:137–38
    as FBI director, 1:133, *134*, 139,
        142
    G-Men film and, 2:80
    organized crime and, 1:135
    popularity of, 1:135, 139, 140
Hoover, Lou Henry, 2:36
Hoover Dam, 3:258, 263–64, 274
"Hoover Hogs," 2:28
"Hoovervilles," 1:241, 320–21, 327,
    2:265, 3:*95, 106*
Hope, Bob, 3:63
Hopi Snake Dance, 1:12, 17
Hopkins, Harry, 3:*308*
    about, 1:119, 258–59, 2:45, 290,
        3:320
    art advocate, 1:26, 36
    CCC recruiting and, 1:114
    CWA and, 1:245, 246
    as FERA director, 1:242, 244–45
    fighting unemployment, 1:37, 261
    transients and, 3:87
    on unemployed Americans, 3:306–7
    Williams, Aubrey and, 1:212
    on work relief, 1:37, 3:322
    WPA and, 1:249, 250, 3:309, 322
Horizons (Geddes), 3:356, 364
Hormel Company, 2:32, 42
Hostess Twinkies, 2:30
Houghton-Mifflin, 2:300
House Committee on Banking and
    Currency, 1:45
House Un-American Activities
    Committee (HUAC), 1:31–32,
    38, 76, 3:313–14, 316
Houseman, John, 3:316
Houses of Hospitality, 3:144
Housing, 2:**97–116**
    automobiles and, 2:106
    black Americans and, 1:75, 318–19
    building statistics, 2:103
    bungalow style homes, 2:106–207
    census on, 2:106
    cost of, 1:318, 326, 2:111
    Department of Housing and Urban
        Development (HUD), 1:223,
        2:113–14
    discrimination in, 1:223, 2:102–3,
        112, 114
    eviction protests, 2:192
    foreclosures, 1:241, 2:97–98, 99
    Great Society and, 1:221–23
    greenbelt towns, 2:113
    home ownership, 1:308–9

home values, 2:99, 100
    Hoover, Herbert and, 2:97, 99–101
    impact of New Deal programs,
        2:111–14
    low-income inner-city housing,
        2:104–5, 107–8, 110, 305–6
    of middle class families, 1:326
    National Housing Act, 1:46–47, 61,
        2:264
    notable people, 2:114–15
    perspectives on, 2:109–10
    public housing programs, 2:105,
        109, 112–13, 283
    public transportation and, 2:106
    PWA housing program, 1:74, 246,
        2:104
    redlining property and, 2:102–3
    Roosevelt, Franklin and, 2:101,
        103, 109, 115–16
    segregation and, 1:78, 2:105
    in slums, 2:104–6, *110*
    unsuccessful programs, 2:99–101
    Wagner-Steagall Housing Act,
        2:105, 109, 116, 283
    for World War I workers, 2:108–9
    See also Federal Housing
        Administration (FHA); Home
        Owners' Loan Corporation
        (HOLC); Mortgages; Slums
Housing Act of 1949, 2:112–13
Housing and Urban Development Act,
    1:223
Houston, Charles, 3:227
How Green Was My Valley (film), 2:82
How I Came to Love the Classics
    (Cunningham), 1:281
How the Other Half Lives (Riis), 2:108
*How to Win Friends and Influence
    People* (Carnegie), 2:215
Howard, Edgar, 1:21
Howard, Roy, 2:163–64, 183
Howe, Louis, 1:165
Hubbard, Preston, 3:232, 254
HUD (Department of Housing and
    Urban Development), 1:223,
    2:113–14
Hudson's Bay Company, 1:98
Huff, William, 3:357
Hughes, Charles
    about, 3:221–22
    Carter v. Carter Coal Company
        (1936) ruling and, 3:210
    Gold Clause Cases and, 3:207
    minimum wage ruling and, 3:214
    National Labor Relations Act ruling
        and, 3:214–15
    NIRA ruling, 3:210
    oil legislation ruling and, 3:205,
        206
    price regulation ruling and, 3:205, 206
    private contracts ruling and, 3:204
    Railroad Retirement Act ruling and,
        3:208

Hughes, Langston, 1:79, 2:216, 217
Hull, Cordell, 1:158, 2:*65*, 68, 114,
    143–44
Hull House, 1:209, 2:130–31, 3:293
Humanitarianism, 2:39
Humanities Act, 1:221
Hume, David, 1:106
Humphrey, Hubert, 1:227
Humphrey, William, 3:208
Humphrey's Executor v. United States,
    3:208
Hunger relief
    American Relief Administration
        (ARA) and, 3:99
    attitude toward, 2:23–24
    breadlines, 2:21–22, 23, 24, 45–46
    Federal Surplus Relief Corporation
        (FSRC), 1:173, 2:7, 25, 37–38, 42
    food coupons, 1:244
    food stamps, 1:224, 2:25–26, 42–43
    Hoover, Herbert and, 2:24, 36, 3:99
    hunger march, 3:308
    soup kitchens, 1:102, 2:23, 24
    See also Charity
*The Hungry Years: A Narrative History
    of the Great Depression in
    America* (Watkins), 1:307, 314,
    2:38, 39
Hurley, Jack, 2:313
Hurston, Zora, 1:76, 2:214
Husted, Marjorie, 2:41
Hydropower. *See* Water and power

I

I Am A Fugitive From a Chain Gang
    (film), 2:81–82
I Saw Hitler! (Thompson), 2:186
I Was Marching (Le Sueur), 2:321
ICC (Interstate Commerce
    Commission), 3:100
Ickes, Harold
    about, 2:114, 3:279
    American Indian law and, 1:8
    black Americans and, 1:82, 84
    election of 1936 and, 1:146
    Fort Peck Dam and, 3:269
    Indian New Deal and, 1:9
    NRA and, 2:238
    petroleum embargo of, 2:144
    PWA administered by, 1:247, 249
    racial hiring quota system of,
        1:74–75, 82
    as secretary of the interior, 1:2
IGR (Institute for Government
    Research), 1:15, 22
ILBWU. *See* International Ladies'
    Garment Workers' Union
    (ILGWU)
I'm No Angel (film), 2:78, 84
IMF (International Monetary Fund),
    2:64, 65

Immigration, 1:294–98
    Asian, 1:297–98, 301
    Chinese Exclusion Act, 1:286, 290,
        297, 300
    citizenship requirements, 1:295
    decline in, 1:300, 2:127
    fears about, 2:131
    Great Society programs for, 1:223
    head tax, 1:297
    Hoover, Herbert and, 3:136
    increase in, 1:295
    international relations and, 1:298
    Japanese, 1:298
    of Jewish refugees, 3:136, 137
    literacy tests, 1:297
    Mexican, 1:289, 290*t*, 295, 296–97
    Naturalization Act, 1:295
    Prohibition and, 3:14, 26
    quotas for, 1:223, 297, 298,
        300–301, 3:136
    resentment toward, 1:298, 301–2,
        303–4
    Roosevelt, Franklin and, 3:136
    transients and, 3:85
Immigration Acts, 1:223, 287, 297,
    298, 301
Immigration and Naturalization Service
    (INS), 1:287, 288
The Immigration Crisis (Dies), 1:303
Immigration Reform and Control Act
    (IRCA), 1:302
Imperial Diversion Dam, 3:265
In Dubious Battle (Steinbeck), 1:303,
    2:14–15, 210, 224
In the Land of Head Hunters (film), 2:86
Inauguration date change, 2:254–55
Income
    black Americans, 1:318
    businessmen *vs.* teachers, 1:208
    farmers, 1:93, 319*t*, 2:4, 8, 9, 3:343
    Mexican Americans, 1:285, 289
    middle class families, 1:93, 306, 326
    national per capita income, 2:191
    physicians, 1:319*t*, 3:51
    by profession, 1:319*t*
    of wealthy Americans, 1:93, 306
    for women, 3:296
    See also Wages
Income tax, 1:155–56, 3:318, 332
Index of American Design (Federal Art
    Project), 3:312
Indian Arts and Crafts Board, 1:8, 19
Indian Citizenship Act, 1:12
Indian Health Service (IHS), 1:11
Indian Law, 1:8–9, 19
Indian New Deal, 1:2–3, 8–10, 18–19
Indian Reorganization Act (IRA),
    1:4–6, 17, 19, 22–23
Indian Self-Determination and Educa
    tional Assistance Act, 1:20
Indians at Work (Collier), 1:18
Indoor plumbing, 3:172
Industrial Mobilization Plan, 3:327

Industrial unions, 2:191, 194
Industrial Valley (McKenney), 2:211
Industrial Workers of the World
    (IWW), 2:322, 324
Industrialization
    agricultural economy *vs.,* 1:253
    arts and crafts movement and,
        2:126, 131
    critics of, 2:129–30
    economic boon from, 1:275, 284,
        2:171
    growth of, 2:126, 128
    industrial revolution, 2:220
    rural electrification and, 3:172
    social insurance and, 3:189–90, 193
    social problems and, 2:130–31
    transients and, 3:84–85
Industry
    fair competition and, 2:230
    industry-military alliance, 3:329,
        336, 338, 344, 346
    mass production in, 2:119, 120, 130
    military-industrial complex,
        3:346–47
    monopolies, 2:230, 238
    New Deal and, 2:228–29
    reconversion to pre-war production,
        3:346
    relocations to Third World
        countries, 2:202
    See also Business; Corporations;
        Industrialization; National
        Industrial Recovery Act (NIRA)
Industry-military alliance, 3:329, 336,
    338, 344, 346
*Inquiry into the Effects of Spirituous
    Liquors on the Human Body and
    Mind* (Rush), 3:13
INS (Immigration and Naturalization
    Service), 1:287, 288
INS (International News Service),
    1:175, 2:180
Institute for Government Research
    (IGR), 1:15, 22
Insull, Samuel, 1:89, 3:272, 274, 279
Insurance industry, 1:62
Intellectual elite, 2:220–22
Interdepartmental Committee to
    Coordinate Health and Welfare
    Activities, 3:39
Interest rates, 1:60, 61, 93
Internal Revenue Service, 1:129
International Association of
    Machinists, 1:77
International Brotherhood of Red Caps,
    2:194
International Ladies' Garment
    Workers' Union (ILGWU),
    1:290, 2:127, 199–200
International Longshoreman's
    Association, strike, 1:128
International Monetary Fund (IMF),
    2:64, 65

International News Service (INS), 2:175, 180
Internationalism *vs.* isolationism, 1:161, 2:139
Interpretations: 1933-1935 (Lippmann), 2:186–87
Interstate Commerce Commission (ICC), 3:100
Interstate Freeway system, 2:328
Interstate Liquor Act, 3:17
Interstate Migration report, 1:179
Interwar era, 2:**117–37**
   architecture, 2:121–22
   contributing forces, 2:126–29
   golden age of sports, 2:124–25
   impact of, 2:132
   media, 2:122–23
   notable people, 2:132–35
   overview, 2:117–18
   perspectives on, 2:64, 129–32
   preserving the past, 2:123–24
   science, business and technology, 2:119
   transportation, 2:119–21
   See also World War II; World War II mobilization
Investment banks, 1:45, 53, 62
The Invisible Man (film), 1:272
The Invisible Scar (Bird), 1:318–19
IRA. *See* Indian Reorganization Act (IRA)
IRCA (Immigration Reform and Control Act), 1:302
Irrigation, 3:262, 264, 266, 271
Irrigation pumps, 3:271
Islam, 3:138
Isolationism, 2:**138–58**
   American economic concerns and, 2:149
   contributing forces, 2:146–49
   Hawley-Smoot Tariff Act and, 2:15
   Hoover, Herbert and, 2:151
   impact of, 2:152–53
   international perspectives on, 2:151–52
   internationalism *vs.*, 1:159–61, 2:139
   national perspectives on, 2:149–51
   Neutrality Acts, 2:143–44, 150, 156
   New Deal and, 2:138–39, 140–42, 143
   notable people, 2:153–56
   Nye Committee investigations, 2:142–43, 150–51
   overview, 1:96, 2:138–40
   peace movement and, 2:149
   political and cultural, 1:34
   responses against, 2:145–46
   shifting away from, 2:150
   support for, 2:138–39, 140–41, 144–45, 149
   World War I and, 1:96, 101–2, 2:15
Israel, Edward, 3:129–30, 149, 150

Isserman, Maurice, 2:321, 332
It Can't Happen Here (Lewis), 2:212, 214, 219, 222
It Happened One Night (film), 2:80
Italy, 2:145
IWW (Industrial Workers of the World), 2:322, 324

J

Jacks, 1:279
Jackson, Andrew, 1:17, 154
Jackson, Kenneth, 2:103, 116
Jackson, Robert, 3:221
Japan
   Great Depression and, 2:56, 59
   Pearl Harbor bombed, 2:145, 146, 3:67, 328–29
   U.S. bombing of, 3:338
   World War II expansion, 3:328, 342
Japanese American Citizens League (JACL), 1:292
Japanese Americans
   immigration to U.S., 1:298
   overview, 1:290–91
   relocation during World War II, 1:117, 294, 300, 3:331
   support organizations, 1:292
Jazz, 1:79, 266, 278, 312, 2:84, 3:67–68. *See also* Swing
The Jazz Singer (film), 2:73, 86
Jefferson, Thomas, 1:17, 154, 3:259, 274
Jell-O, 2:34–35
Jewish Americans
   American culture and, 2:126, 132
   anti-Semitism, 2:318, 3:135, 136–37, 142, 246
   charities of, 3:134
   concerns about European Jews, 3:118–19
   education and, 3:134–35
   Great Depression and, 3:134–35
   immigration of Jewish refugees, 3:136, 137, 145
   New Deal and, 3:145
   perspectives on, 3:145
   prominence of, 2:126
   in sports, 2:125
   on Supreme Court, 1:156
   Zionist movement, 3:137, 142
Jews, Movies, Hollywoodism and the American Dream (film), 2:94
Jews Without Money (Gold), 2:210
J.F. Shea Company, 3:266
Jigsaw puzzles, 1:264, 265, *324*, 325
Jim Crow Concert Hall, 1:85
Jim Crow laws, 1:77–78, 83, 3:335
Jive talk, 1:312, 313
Job Corps, 1:119, 219
Johnny cakes, 2:28

Johnson, Hiram, 1:7, 2:144
Johnson, Hugh
   about, 2:248–49, 271
   "Buy Now" program, 2:237
   Ford, Henry and, 2:234
   Ickes, Harold and, 2:238
   "Memorandum 228" and, 2:241
   NRA conflicts and, 2:233, 237–39, 246, 248–49
   NRA production controls and, 2:236
Johnson, James, 1:79
Johnson, Lady Bird, 1:234
Johnson, Lyndon B.
   about, 1:222
   affirmative action and, 1:217–18
   centralizing governmental powers, 1:218
   civil rights and, 1:217
   Economic Opportunity Act, 1:119
   education and, 1:221
   environmentalism of, 1:223
   on the Great Society, 1:215
   Great Society programs, 1:11, 162
   Great Society speech, 1:237
   New Deal and, 1:218, 222
   program of social reform, 1:215
   Public Law, 1:36
   Roosevelt, Franklin and, 1:*220*
   segregation and, 1:217
   social reform and, 1:229
   special task force groups, 1:218–19
   State of the Union address, 1:216
   unemployment program, 1:256–57
   Vietnam War and, 1:163, 231
   voting rights speech, 1:237–38
Johnson, Lyndon B, *See also* Great Society
Johnson, William, 1:36, 3:16–17
Johnson Act, 2:56–57, 142
Johnson-O'Malley Act (JOM), 1:6–7, 9, 20–21
Joint Commission of the Emergency in Education, 1:196
Jolson, Al, 2:73, 86
Jones, Jesse, 1:46, 63, 3:105–6, 108, 111, 114–15
Jones, Mary Harris "Mother," 2:322
Jones & Laughlin Steel Corp., NLRB v. (1937), 1:159, 3:213–15, 220
Jones & Laughlin Steel Corporation, 3:213–14
Journal of Education, 1:191
Journal of the American Medical Association, 3:47
Journalism, 2:**159–88**
   1920s, 2:176–77
   business and, 2:178
   conservatism of, 2:163
   criticisms of, 2:163
   documentary journalism, 2:207
   everyday reporters, 2:164
   impact of, 2:179–81

investigative reporting, 2:179
leaders, 2:163–64, 171–73
literary journalism, 2:170
major news stories, 2:165
muckraking in, 2:177
New Deal and, 2:151, 178
news service agencies, 2:172, 175, 180
notable people, 2:181–86
overview, 2:159–61
perspectives on, 2:178–79
photojournalism, 2:170, 184, 303–4, 308
radio journalism, 2:177
Roosevelt, Franklin and, 2:164–66
Roper media survey, 2:178–79
specialized news coverage, 2:161
syndicated columnists, 2:161–62
women in, 2:168–69, 173–75
yellow journalism, 2:172
See also Magazines; Newspapers
The Joy of Cooking (Rombauer), 2:22, 33–34, 44, 45
Jumprope, 1:279
Jung, Theo, 2:299, 309–10
The Jungle (Sinclair), 2:317, 330
Just Before the War: Urban America From 1935 to 1941 As Seen By Photographers of the Farm Security Administration (Garver), 2:313
Juvenile delinquents, 1:131, 229

K

Kaltenborn, Hans von, 2:167, 183, 3:67, 72–73
Karloff, Boris, 1:*271*
Kearns, Doris, 1:216
Keating-Owen Child Labor Act, 3:219
Keeping up appearances, 1:305, 306, 308, 323
Keller v. United States (1909), 3:217
Kelley, Florence, 3:293, 301
Kellogg-Briand Pact, 2:149
Kennedy, John F.
    Democratic coalition and, 1:162
    election victory of 1960, 1:162
    food stamp program, 2:43
    social reform plans, 1:217, 2:289
    on Social Security, 3:100
    television and, 3:71
    unemployment program, 1:256
    women and, 3:297
Kennedy, Joseph, 1:104
Kennedy, Robert, 1:227
Kent, Frank, 2:161, 183
Keynes, John
    about, 1:259–60, 2:290
    on economics, 1:255, 259–60, 2:276, 281, 289
    on the Great Depression, 2:68

Keynesian economics, 1:255, 259–60, 2:276, 281, 289
Kick the Can, 1:279
King, Martin Luther, Jr.
    about, 1:234–35
    assassination, 1:227
    civil rights march, 1:75, 83, 235
    nonviolent civil disobedience, 1:83, 226, 235
    religious organizations and, 3:146
    voting rights march, 1:221
King, Peter, 1:92
King Kong (film), 1:271, 2:*81*, 82
Kingston steam plant, 3:*235*
Kitchens, 2:37, 3:*156*, *158*, 260
Knox gelatin, 2:34–35
Kodak Camera, 3:193
Kolmer, John, 3:45
Kool Aid, 2:32
Korean War, 2:153, 3:347
Korematsu v. United States (1944), 3:224
Kraft Foods, 2:27
Kristallnacht (Night of Broken Glass), 3:135, 136
Krock, Arthur, 2:183
Kromer, Tom, 2:211
Ku Klux Klan (KKK), 1:79–80, 157, 2:82, 3:136. *See also* White supremists
Kuznick, Peter, 3:363

L

La Follette, Robert, 1:247
La Guardia, Fiorello, 2:104–5, 114–15
La Placita raid, 1:288
Labor colleges, 1:197
Labor movement, 2:**189–206**
    child labor, 1:156, 2:197, 233, 3:217, 219, 285
    civil liberties infractions, 3:213
    communists support of, 2:321–22
    contributing forces, 2:197–99
    Fair Labor Standards Act, 2:197, 280, 3:285, 334
    Great Society and, 1:232, 234
    impact of, 1:201–2
    increase in unrest, 1:148
    Memorial Day Massacre, 1:*127*, 128, 2:197, 3:213
    "Mother" Jones and, 2:322
    New Deal support for, 1:159, 166
    notable people, 2:202–5
    overview, 2:189–91
    perspectives on, 2:199–201
    protective labor legislation, 3:291, 292, 293
    rebuilding, 2:191–92
    working conditions and, 2:191, 197–98

See also Labor unions; National Industrial Recovery Act (NIRA); Strikes
Labor unions
    American Legion and, 1:186–87
    anti-labor bills, 1:161
    decline of, 1:163–64, 234, 2:191, 198–99, 202
    distrust of, 2:323
    growth of, 2:194, 195–96, 197
    industrial unions, 2:191, 194, 202, 324
    influence of, 1:160
    labor strikes, 1:126–28, 136, 2:282
    lack of recognition, 1:126–27
    NRA and, 2:241
    pro-labor laws, 1:126
    Prohibition opposed by, 3:9
    right to organize, 1:159, 160, 2:192, 279, 326
    Roosevelt, Franklin and, 1:160, 2:142, 261, 3:339
    skill *vs.* unskilled workers, 2:194
    Social Security and, 3:194
    unfair labor practices and, 2:193–94, 247, 280
    World War II mobilization and, 3:334
    See also Labor movement; Unions
The Ladies Home Journal, 1:91, 105, 2:106–207
LaFollete, Robert, 2:141, 3:275
LaGuardia, Fiorello, 1:268
Laguna Dam, 3:272
Laissez-faire philosophy
    capitalism and, 2:246
    Catholicism and, 3:129, 132
    constitutionalism, 3:217, 218
    economic theories, 1:148, 2:229–30, 246
    government and, 1:87, 88, 98, 100, 2:325
    Hoover, Herbert and, 1:87, 89
    Republican Party and, 1:148, 157
    Spencer, Herbert and, 1:99–100
    Supreme Court and, 3:204, 217, 218, 220
Lake Mead, 3:264
Lake Roosevelt, 3:268
Lamb, Ruth, 3:46, 53
Lamb, William, 2:122
The Land of Plenty (Cantwell), 2:211
Land of the Spotten Eagle (Standing Bear), 1:7
Landon, Alfred, 1:151, 165–66, 2:178, 3:133, 188
Lange, Dorothea
    books by, 2:307
    camera used by, 2:301
    John Vachon, John described by, 2:300
    Ma Burnham, 2:310
    in *Masters of Photography,* 2:308

Lange, Dorothea (continued)
  Migrant Mother, 1:174, 2:299, *301,*
    310
  Migratory Cotton Picker, 1:*27*
  opinion on FSA, 2:307
  as RA photographer, 1:31
  transients and, 3:87
Lanksy, Meyer, 1:143
Latin America, 2:52, 58, 62
Laurie, Annie (Winifred Bonfils),
    2:173
Law and the Modern Mind (Frank),
    3:218
Law enforcement
  during Prohibition, 3:5
  in films, 2:80, 95
  public confidence in, 1:133–34, 135
  public opinion of, 1:138–39, 2:75
  violence of, 1:*226*
  See also Federal Bureau of
    Investigation (FBI)
Lawrence, David, 2:161, 183–84
Lawyer Man (film), 2:75, 76
Lay, Herman, 2:32
Le Sueur, Meridel, 2:24, 321, 322, 330
League Against War, 3:145
League of American Writers, 2:212
League of Decency, 2:78
League of Nations, 1:156, 2:62, 146,
    148, 3:297
League of United Latin American
    Citizens (LULAC), 1:291
League of Women Voters, 3:288–89,
    291, 295
Lee, Harper, 1:67
Lee, John C.H., 1:245
Lee, Russell, 2:300, 308, 310
Legal philosophy, 3:218
Legion of Decency, 3:140
Leigh, Vivien, 2:82, 85, *92*
Leisure time, 1:**262–83**
  Café Society, 1:314–16
  dance marathons, 1:265, 312–13,
    2:222–23
  democratization of entertainment,
    1:264
  electricity and, 3:171
  escapism and, 1:263, 275, 276–78,
    281–82
  in everyday life, 1:309–10
  fads, 1:265–66
  increased time for, 1:262, 275
  for middle-class families, 1:327
  notable people, 1:280–81
  popular music, 1:273–74
  print media, 1:272–73
  public well being and, 1:263
  radio, 1:266–68
  sports, 1:274–75, 310
  travel, 1:275
  unemployment and, 1:264
  See also Dance; Films; Games;
    Radio; World's Fairs

Lemke, William, 1:183–84
Lend-Lease Act, 2:145, 3:344
LeNoir, John, 2:187
Lenroot, Katharine, 3:301
Leo XIII, (Pope), 3:129
LeSueur, Meridel, 2:211
Let Us Now Praise Famous Men (Agee
    and Evans), 2:15, 170, 213, 300,
    309
Level measurements for cooking, 2:33,
    44
Lewis, David, 3:198
Lewis, Fulton, 2:168
Lewis, John, 1:72, 2:192, 194, 195,
    204, 320
Lewis, Sinclair, 2:212, 214, 219, 222
Lewis & Clark Centennial Exposition,
    3:363
Liberals, 2:267, 286, 326, 3:119–20.
    See also Political "left";
    Progressives
"Liberty at the Crossroads," 3:67
Liberty bonds, 3:332
Liberty Party, 2:317
Library of Congress, 2:307, 308
Liebmann, New State Ice Co. v. (1932),
    3:204
Life expectancy, 1:76, 2:127, 3:34, 190
Life magazine, 2:170, 184, 303, 310
*Life the Movie: How Entertainment
    Conquered Reality* (Gabler),
    1:278
Lifestyle. *See* Everyday life
Lilienthal, David, 3:236, 237, 251–52,
    255
Lincoln, Abraham, 1:149, 154, 3:13
Lindbergh, Charles, 2:*176*
  America First Committee supported
    by, 2:145
  as isolationism advocate, 2:145,
    155, 157
  Neutrality and War speech, 2:157
  son kidnapped, 1:132, 2:165, 3:67
Lippmann, Walter, 2:136, 161, 184,
    186–87
Lipshitz, Isidore, 1:*33*
Liquor
  beer, 3:11, 17, 22
  consumption, 3:19*t,* 25
  cost of, 3:3
  drinking customs, 3:12
  early colonists and, 3:1
  government control of, 3:24
  homemade, 3:22–24, 26
  industrial alcohol in, 3:20
  near beer, 3:22
  rum, 3:1, 12, 21, 22
  sources, 3:20–22
  as symbol of independence, 3:24
  thefts, 3:19
  whiskey, 3:12, 20
Literacy
  American Indians and, 1:117

black Americans and, 1:69, 76
immigration and, 1:297
increase in, 1:76
voting and, 1:80
WPA program for, 1:76, 200
Literary adaptation films, 1:272
Literary Digest, 2:170, 177
Literary journalism, 2:170
Literary magazines, 2:221
Literature, 2:**207–27**
  anti-fascist, 2:212–13
  biographies, 2:217–18
  by black Americans, 1:76
  book clubs, 2:218
  bourgeois (ruling class) and, 2:220
  contributing forces, 2:218–20
  documentary journalism, 2:207
  Great Depression's effect on,
    2:220–22
  histories, 2:216
  impact of, 2:222–23
  individualistic, 2:214–15
  League of American Writers, 2:212
  literary magazines, 2:221
  modernism style, 2:208
  nationalistic, 2:207, 213
  notable people, 2:223–25
  novels describing the South, 2:222
  paperback books, 2:123, 218
  perspectives on, 2:220–22
  poets, 2:216–18
  post–World War I, 2:218–19
  proletarian literature, 2:207,
    208–12, 219–20, 221
  publishing industry, 2:212, 215,
    218, 220*t,* 222
  pulp fiction, 1:263
  realism in, 2:128, 208, 222
  self-improvement books, 2:215
  war novels, 2:222
  See also Federal Writers' Project
    (FWP); Journalism
Little, Brown Publishing Company,
    2:44
Little Big Books, 1:272
Little Caesar (film), 1:129–30, 140,
    268–69, 2:75, 80
Little House in the Big Woods
    (Wilder), 2:214
"Little Orphan Annie," 1:272, 313,
    3:64
Livestock destruction, 1:173
Living Newspapers, 3:243, 313
"Living Pictures" (Dali), 3:361
*A Living Wage: Its Ethical and
    Economic Aspects* (Ryan), 3:148
Llewellyn, Karl, 3:218
Llewellyn, Richard, 2:82
Local Experienced Men (LEM), 1:112,
    117
Lomax, John, 1:280
Long, Huey
  about, 2:329, 3:198

Every Man a King, 2:329, 331
  films about, 2:327
  Share-Our-Wealth plan, 1:150,
    2:267, 319, 320, 325, 329
  Social Security Bill and, 3:185
*The Long Range Planning of Public
    Works* (Mallery), 1:247
Look Homeward, Angel (Wolfe), 2:214
Look magazine, 2:170, 304
Lorentz, Pare, 1:173, 2:306, 307
Los Angeles Times, 2:173
Louis, Joe, 1:84–85, 274, 2:125, 136
Louisiana Purchase Exposition,
  3:362–63
Louisville Joint Stock Bank v. Radford,
  3:208
Love Me Tonight (film), 2:73
Low, Ann Marie, 1:184
Loyalty oaths, 1:32, 197, 204–5
Lubitsch, Ernst, 2:77, 93
Luce, Henry
  about, 2:184, 310–11
  Fortune, 2:310
  Life, 2:170, 303, 310
  March of Time documentary film
    series, 2:167, 186, 310
  March of Time radio program, 2:167
  Time magazine, 2:169, 178, 310
Luciano, Charles "Lucky," 1:131,
  143–44
Lumpkin, Grace, 2:210
Luna, Maria, 1:303
Lutherans, 3:141
Lynching
  anti-lynching bills, 1:71, 72, 74
  anti-lynching films, 2:82
  of black Americans, 1:68, 78
  NAACP anti-lynching Committee,
    1:78
  NNC opposition to, 1:76
*Lyndon Johnson and the American
    Dream* (Kearns), 1:216
Lyon, Leverett, 2:241

M

Ma Burnham (Lange), 2:310
MacArthur, Douglas, 1:126, 3:103
MacBeth (Shakespeare), 1:29, *30,* 76,
  3:314
Mackey, Harry, 2:39
MacLeish, Archibald, 2:308, 3:68
Macon County Public Health
  Department, 3:42
Mafia, 1:130–31, 135, 136, 138
Magazines
  literary magazines, 2:221
  muckraking in, 2:177
  overview, 1:272, 2:169–70, 177–78
  photojournalism magazines,
    2:303–4
  popularity of, 2:123

Main Street (Lewis), 2:219
Maine, 3:1, 13
Making do, 1:307–8, 2:22, 26–27, 39,
  47
Mallery, Otto, 1:247
Malnutrition, 1:205, 239, 319, 321,
  2:40
The Maltese Falcon (film), 1:271–72
The Maltese Falcon (Hammett), 2:215
Maltz, Albert, 2:210
Mamoulian, Rouben, 2:73, 93
*The Man Nobody Knows: The
    Discovery of the Real Jesus*
    (Barton), 1:91
"Man of La Mancha," 1:38
Manhattan Melodrama, 1:132
Manning, Marie (aka Beatrice Fairfax),
  2:168, 173, 184
March of Dimes Campaign, 3:45
The March of Time, 1:266, 309
March of Time (film), 2:167, 186, 310
Marching! Marching! (Weatherwax),
  2:211
Marconi, Guglielmo, 3:59, 68
Marconi Console, 3:59
Margold, Nathan, 1:8, 21
Marriage during the Great Depression,
  1:317
Marsh, Clarence, 1:201
Marshall, George, 3:347
Marshall, Thurgood, 1:232
Marshall Plan, 2:153, 3:347
Martin, Charles, 1:244
Martyn, Thomas, 2:169
Marx, Karl, 2:209
Marx Brothers, 1:270, 2:76–77
Marxism, 1:208–9, 2:220, 321
Marzolf, Marian, 2:169
Mass political movement, 1:157–58
Mass production, 2:119, 120, 130,
  3:110, 163, 164–65
The Masses, 2:177
Masters of Photography (Beaumont
  and Newhall), 2:308
Matching grants system, 1:243–44
Materialism, 1:91–92, 100, 321, 2:130,
  147–48, 3:139
Maurin, Peter, 3:144
Mayer, Grace, 2:302
McAvoy, Thomas, 2:304
McCarran Act, 1:301
McCarty, John, 1:180
McClure's magazine, 2:177
McConnell, Francis, 3:125, 145, 147
McCormick, Anne O'Hare, 2:168, 252
McCormick, Robert, 2:163, 184
McCoy, Bill, 3:22
McCoy, Horace, 1:313, 2:222
McCraw, Thomas, 3:232
McDaniel, Hattie, 2:93, 94
McElvaine, Robert, 1:71, 81, 2:75,
  81–82, 197
McEntee, John, 1:115, 120

McFadden Act, 1:54
McGovern, George, 1:163
McKay, Claude, 1:79
McKenney, Ruth, 2:211
McMurtrie, Douglas, 3:312
McNary-Haugen Bill, 2:11
McNickle, Darcy, 1:21
McReynolds, James, 3:203, 207
Mead, Elwood, 3:264, 276
Meade, Margaret, 2:123
Means, Gardiner, 2:230, 271
Means test, 3:309
Meat, 1:224, 2:28, 40
Mechanical jurisprudence, 3:218
Medical Care Act, 1:232, 2:328
Medical cooperative societies, 3:51
Medical poisoning, 3:45, 46
Medical researchers, 3:47
Medicare/Medicaid, 1:232–33, 3:53
Mein Kampf (Hitler), 2:216
Mellon, Andrew, 1:51, 105
Melodrama films, 1:271
Meltzer, Milton, 1:37
Memorial Day Massacre, 1:*127,* 128,
  2:197, 3:213
Men, 1:317, 320, 323
Mencken, H.D., 2:219
Mencken, Henry, 2:178
Mental illness, 3:43
Mercer, Lucy, 3:286
Merchants of Death (Englebrecht and
  Hanighen), 2:142
Meriam, Lewis M., 1:15, 21–22
Meriam Report, 1:2, 3, 11, 15, 22
Merriam, Charles, 2:115
Methodists, 3:123, 124–25, 126–27,
  140
Metropolitan Insurance Company, 3:34,
  36
Mexican Americans
  assimilation, 1:294
  cultural heritage preservation, 1:292
  deportation, 1:286–88, 292, 300,
    303
  economic hardships, 1:285, 289,
    294, 296, 300
  immigration to U.S., 1:289, 290*t,
    295,* 296–97
  new deal and, 1:292–94
  repatriation, 1:288, 300
  support organizations, 1:291
  women's employment, 1:289–90
  World War II mobilization and,
    3:334
Mexican Farm Labor Union, 1:289
Mexican Mutual Aid Association,
  2:322
Meyer, Eugene, 3:96, 100, 113–14
Mickey Mouse, 2:72, 92
Middle class families
  budgets, 1:306, 307
  employment and, 1:326
  everyday life, 1:306–7, 323, 326–27

Middle class families (continued)
　Great Society opposed by, 1:225,
　　226, 232
　housing, 1:326
　humanitarianism of, 2:39
　income, 1:93, 306, 326
Midget Village, 3:356
Migrant Mother (Lange), 1:174, 2:299,
　301, 310
Migrant workers
　FSA housing for, 1:180
　living conditions, 2:13
　medical care, 3:*38*
　Migratory Cotton Picker, 1:27
　Steinbeck's writings on, 2:15
　transients as, 3:78
　See also The Grapes of Wrath
　　(Steinbeck)
Migratory Birds' Act, 1:133
Migratory Cotton Picker, (Lange), 1:*27*
Military
　black Americans in, 3:335, 346
　Industrial Mobilization Plan, 3:327
　industry-military alliance, 3:329,
　　336, 338, 344, 346
　inter-war mobilization planning,
　　3:338–39
　military-industrial complex,
　　3:346–47
　rebuilding European economies
　　and, 3:346–47
　segregation in, 1:75, 77
　See also Army, U.S.
Milk, 3:34, 44
Milk Control Board, 3:205
Millay, Edna St. Vincent, 2:217, 219
Millis, Walter, 2:143
Mills, Ogden, 1:49, 63, 3:114
Mills Brothers, 1:280–81
*The Miner's Fight for American
　standards* (Lewis), 2:204
Minimum wage
　during World War II, 2:280, 3:334
　established by Fair Labor Standards
　　Act, 2:197, 280, 3:334
　NIRA recommendations, 2:232, 233
　NRA standard rates, 1:70.1.81
　opposed by American Federal of
　　Labor, 2:231
　Supreme Court ruling on, 3:214
　for women, 3:293
Minorities. *See* Ethnic groups
Minstrel shows, 2:88
Miranda rights, 1:228
Mirror Show, (Geddes), 3:361
Miss Evers' Boys (television), 2:90
Miss Lonely Hearts (West), 2:214
Mississippi River Valley, 3:272
Missouri ex rel Gaines v. Canada.,
　3:227
Missouri-Pacific Railroad loan
　controversy, 3:100–101
Mitchell, Arthur, 1:73

Mitchell, Charles, 1:51, 93
Mitchell, Harry, 2:16–17
Mitchell, Jonathan, 3:318
Mitchell, Margaret, 1:272–73, 2:82,
　222
Mix, Tom, 1:313
Model T Ford, 2:106, 119, 204
*The Modern Corporation and Private
　Property* (Berle and Means),
　2:230, 248, 250, 271
*The Modern Reader: Essays on
　Present-Day Life and Culture*
　(Lippman), 2:136
Modern Times (film), 2:77, 91, 199,
　200
Modernization, 3:258–60, 271, 278
Moley, Raymond, 1:49, 63, 64, 2:11,
　254, 270
Molly Pitcher Club, 3:6, 8
Money
　gold and cash hoarded, 1:44, 50
　See also Gold standard; Silver
Money market fund, 1:61
Mongole soup, 2:34
Monkey Trial, 3:362
Monopolies
　antitrust laws and, 2:243
　business, 2:230
　holding companies as, 3:159
　industry and, 2:230, 238
　New State Ice Co. v. Liebmann
　　(1932) and, 3:204
　NRA and, 2:232, 238, 241
Montella, Frank "Bo," 1:121
Montezuma, Carlos, 1:18
Montgomery bus boycott, 1:260
Moody, Helen, 2:124
Moore, Harry, 3:54
Moore v. Dempsey, 1:78
Morality, 1:139, 2:78, 87
Morehead v. Tipaldo, 3:211
Morgan, Arthur, 3:234, 235, 236–37,
　252
Morgan, Harcourt, 3:235, 253
Morgan, John P., 1:51, 63, 314
Morgenthau, Henry, Jr, 1:*63*, 3:185,
　198
Morrison, Herb, 1:266, 281
Morrison Knudsen Company, 3:264
Mortgages
　in 1920s, 2:107
　adjustable rate, 1:61
　amortized, 2:102, 103, 111
　bank mortgages, 1:60
　defaulting on, 2:97–98
　Emergency Farm Mortgage Act,
　　1:172–73, 2:6, 101, 258
　Fannie Mae mortgages, 2:104,
　　111–12
　Farm Mortgage Moratorium Act,
　　1:173, 183, 184, 2:263
　Farm Mortgage Refinancing Act,
　　2:101, 261

Home Owners' Loan Corporation
　refinancing, 1:309, 2:101, 260,
　　261, 3:259
　insured by Federal Housing
　　Administration, 1:47, 2:103
　mortgage associations, 2:103–4
　statistics, 2:98, 260
　Veteran's Administration program,
　　2:111
Motion Picture Producers and
　Distributors of America
　(MPPDA), 2:78, 87, 3:140
Motion Pictures Association of
　America (MPAA), 3:140
Mouthpiece (film), 2:75–76
Movie Palaces, 2:87, 88–89
Movie theaters
　attendance, 1:129, 2:70, 71, 72, 79*t*,
　　3:59
　Bank Nights, 1:268, 2:73, 95
　as Movie Palaces, 2:87, 88–89
　number of, 1:264
　prosperity of, 2:132
Mowrer, Edgar, 2:184
Mowrer, Paul, 2:185
MPAA (Motion Pictures Association of
　America), 3:140
MPPDA (Motion Picture Producers
　and Distributors of America),
　2:78, 87, 3:140
Mr. Dees Goes to Town (film), 2:80
Mr. Smith goes to Washington (film),
　1:269–70, 2:80
Muckraking, 2:177
Muhammad, Elijah, 3:138
Muhammad, W.D. Farad, 3:138
Muller v. Oregon (1908), 3:218
Multiculturalism, 1:2, 7, 15, 16–17, 18
Mumford, Alice, 3:*359*
Mumford, Lewis, 2:119, 133–34, 135,
　221
Municipal utility companies, 3:159,
　166
Munitions industry, 2:142–43,
　3:229–30, 245
Murals, 1:*33*, 3:312, 357–58
Murphy, Frank, 1:166, 196, 2:196, 197,
　3:130, 221
Murphy, Louis, 2:5
Murrow, Edward, 2:168, 185, 3:67, 73
Muscle Shoals, 3:229–30, 239, 244–49
Muscle Shoals bill, 3:231–32, 247–48,
　254
Museum of Modern Art, 2:308
Music
　country music, 1:273–74
　"crooning" singing style, 1:280
　Federal Music Project (FMP), 1:29,
　　76, 292, 3:311
　folk music, 1:31, 273–74, 279
　Jazz, 1:79, 266, 278, 312, 2:84
　in movie theaters, 2:87
　music education, 1:29

musicals, 1:30, 270–71, 2:78–79
popular, 1:273
radio, 1:266, 3:62
record industry, 1:264, 2:128
singing commercials, 3:60
songwriters, 3:62
swing, 1:264, 273, 279, 312, 3:67
Musicals, 1:30, 270–71, 2:78–79
Mussolini, Benito, 2:*61*, 68, 77, 143, *157*
Mutiny on the Bounty (film), 1:271
Mutual Broadcasting Group, 3:59
Mutual Broadcasting System, 2:167
Mutual funds, 1:91
Muybridge, Eadweard, 2:84
My America (Adamic), 2:213, 225
My Pedagogic Creed (Dewey), 1:210
Mydans, Carl, 2:299, 308, 311
Myers, James, 3:129–30
Myers, Norman, 1:121
Myrdal, Gunnar, 1:75
Myth of a Guilty Nation (Nock), 2:146

N

NAACP. *See* National Association for
the Advancement of Colored
People
Nabisco Company, 2:34
NACCA (National Association of
Civilian Conservation Corps
Alumni), 1:115
NACD (National Association of
Conservation Districts), 1:183
Nader, Ralph, 1:224, 229, 2:130
Nash, Frank, 1:133
Nathan, Robert, 1:239
The Nation, 2:272
Nation, Carry, 3:15–16
*A Nation of Cities: The Federal
Government and Urban
America, 1933-65* (Gelfand),
2:113
National Advisory Commission on
Civil Disorders, 1:226
National American Woman Suffrage
Association (NAWSA), 3:295
National Association for the
Advancement of Colored People
(NAACP), 1:21, 78, 207, 3:227,
234
National Association of Broadcasters,
3:62
National Association of Civilian
Conservation Corps Alumni
(NACCCA), 1:115
National Association of Conservation
Districts (NACD), 1:183
National Association of Home
Builders, 2:99
National Broadcasting Corporation
(NBC), 2:167, 3:59, 60
National Cancer Institute, 3:43

National Commission on Law
Observance and Enforcement.
See Wickersham Commission
National Committee for Economy in
Government, 1:190
National Committee on Care for
Transients and Homeless
(NCCTH), 3:77, 83
National Committee on Federal
Legislation for Birth Control,
3:292
National Conference of Catholic
Charities (NCCC), 3:130, 131,
142
National Conference on Organized
Crime, 1:141
National Congress of American Indians
(NCAI), 1:20, 21
National Consumers' League (NCL),
3:293
National Council of Negro Women
(NCNW), 1:73, 209
National Credit Association (NCA),
1:94
National Credit Corporation (NCC),
3:93, 96–97
National Defense Act, 3:245
National Defense Advisory
Commission (NDAC), 3:327,
338
National Education Association (NEA),
1:188, 193, 194, 196
National Electric Light Association
(NELA), 3:166
National Electrical Code, 3:260
National Employment Act, 2:259–60
National Endowment for the Arts
(NEA), 1:36, 221, 233
National Endowment for the
Humanities (NEH), 1:36
National forests, 1:117, 250
National Foundation on the Arts, 1:221
National Grange, 3:156, 160
National Guard, 1:126, 128, 136, 2:197
National Health Conference, 3:40
National Health Survey, 3:39
National Highway Traffic
Administration, 2:130
National Housing Act, 1:46–47, 61,
2:103, 104, 115, 264, 3:259. *See
also* Wagner-Steagall Housing
Act
National Hunger March, 3:308
National Industrial Recovery Act
(NIRA), 2:**228–51**
agriculture excluded, 2:232
big business favored by, 2:236–37,
239
cartels and, 2:246
Catholics support of, 3:132
central planning and, 2:247
codes of fair practice, 2:229,
233–35, 237, 238, 261

compliance problems, 2:237–38
conflict over, 2:237–39, 242
contributing forces, 2:243–45
cooperative movement, 2:230–31,
247
corporate influence, 2:230, 246
economic reform sections, 2:232–33
fixing, 2:239–41
free enterprise and, 1:151
impact of, 2:246–47
interstate commerce regulation, 2:232
journalism and, 2:178
labor standards and, 2:232
laissez-faire economic theories and,
2:229–30
minimum wage provision, 2:232,
233, 3:291
National Industrial Recovery Board
and, 2:241–42
National Recovery Review Board
created, 2:239
National Resources Board created,
1:5
notable people, 2:247–50
NRA created, 2:192, 229, 233
overview, 2:228–29, 260–61
perspectives on, 2:246
price control regulations, 2:238–39,
246
price of goods *vs.* wages, 2:237
promoting, 2:223
purpose of, 2:104, 192
PWA established, 2:104, 192, 232
as regulatory agency, 2:246
renewal considerations, 2:242
Section 7, 1:159, 160, 2:192, 232
Special Industrial Recovery Board,
2:238
Supreme Court ruling on, 1:159,
160, 2:192, 242–43, 268,
3:209–10
unions and, 1:159, 160, 2:192, 261
women discriminated against,
3:285, 291
See also National Recovery
Administration (NRA)
National Institute of Health (NIH),
3:40–43
National Labor Relations Act (NLRA)
legal support for unions, 1:159,
160, 2:247, 291, 328, 3:132
National Labor Relations Board
created by, 2:193, 280
Supreme Court ruling, 3:214–15
unfair labor practices specified by,
2:247, 280
workers rights and, 3:213
National Labor Relations Board
(NLRB)
creation of, 2:193, 280
defense team, 3:226
Fahy, Charles as general counsel,
3:226

National Labor Relations Board
(NLRB) (continued)
*NLRB v. Jones & Laughlin Steel
Corp.* (1937), 1:159, 3:213–15,
220
unfair labor practices prevented by,
2:193–94
National Munitions Board, 2:143
National Negro Congress (NNC), 1:75,
76. *See also* Civil Rights
Congress
National Organization of Women
(NOW), 3:297
National Origins Quota Act, 1:223,
297, 298, 301, 3:136
National parks, 1:118, 3:274, 275
National Planning Board. *See* National
Resources Planning Board
(NRPB)
National Power Policy Committee,
3:271, 279–80
National Prohibition Act. *See* Volstead
Act
National Recovery Administration
(NRA)
advisory council for, 2:241
black Americans and, 1:70, 81
Blue Eagle symbol, 2:78, 82, 233,
237, 249
enforcing NIRA codes, 2:236
Industrial Emergency Committee
created, 2:240
isolationist opponents of, 2:142
"Memorandum 228," 2:241
monopolies and, 2:232, 238, 241
National Industrial Recovery Board
and, 2:241–42
National Planning Board created,
2:240
policy changes in, 2:240
price controls, 2:236–37
purpose of, 2:261
reform measures, 2:239–40
reorganization, 2:241–42
Roosevelt, Franklin and, 2:240,
241, 242, 247
rubber tire industry and, 2:235–36
ruled unconstitutional, 2:192, 243,
268, 270
small business discriminated
against, 2:239, 241
standard wage rates established,
1:70, 81
structure of, 2:233
unpopularity of, 2:271
women and, 3:291
National Recovery Council, 2:238
National Recreation Association,
1:264–65
National Research Council (NRC),
3:362
National Resources Committee,
2:116

National Resources Planning Board
(NRPB), 1:5, 2:240, 241, 3:337
National security, 3:338, 346
National Service Board for Religious
Objectors (NSBRO), 1:117
National Socialist Party. *See* Nazi Party
National Traffic Motor Vehicle Act,
1:223
National Tuberculosis Association,
3:36
National Union for Social Justice
(NUSJ), 2:319
National Venereal Disease Act, 3:44
National War Labor Board, 3:336
National Women's Party (NWP),
3:291, 292, 295, 297
National Youth Administration (NYA)
achievements, 1:252, 2:277
black Americans in, 2:277, 3:314
CCC influence on, 1:112
desegregation in, 1:212
Division of Negro Affairs, 1:73,
201, 252
education through, 1:188, 201–2, 252
ethnic groups and, 1:292–93, 294
goals of, 1:200, 252
termination, 3:337
transients and, 3:82
work relief programs, 1:201, 212,
252, 2:275, 277, 3:314–15
Nationalism
defined, 1:156, 2:51
growth of, 2:51
in Latin America, 2:58, 62
overview, 1:35
spirit of, 2:207
World's fairs and, 3:352
Nationality Act. *See* McCarran Act
Native Americans. *See* American
Indians
Native Son (Wright), 1:76, 2:211, 214,
222, 224
Natural resources
Civilian Conservation Corps (CCC)
and, 1:110, 112
conservation of, 1:112
New Deal achievements, 2:270
See also Civilian Conservation
Corps (CCC); Conservation
*Naturalistic Photography for Students
of the Art* (Emerson), 2:304
Naturalization Act, 1:295
NAWSA (National American Woman
Suffrage Association), 3:295
Nazi Party, 1:82, 101, 278, 2:53, 268
NBC (National Broadcasting
Corporation), 2:167, 3:59, 60
NCA (National Credit Association),
1:94
NCAI (National Congress of American
Indians), 1:20, 21
NCC (National Credit Corporation),
3:93, 96–97

NCCC (National Conference of
Catholic Charities), 3:130, 131,
142
NCCTH (National Committee on Care
for Transients and Homeless),
3:77, 83
NCL (National Consumers' League),
3:293
NCNW (National Council of Negro
Women), 1:73, 209
NDAC (National Defense Advisory
Commission), 3:327, 338
NEA (National Education Association),
1:188, 193, 194, 196
NEA (National Endowment for the
Arts), 1:36, 221, 233
Near beer, 3:22
Nebbia, Leo, 3:205
Nebbia v. New York (1934), 3:205
Nebraska-Kansas Act, 1:154
NEH (National Endowment for the
Humanities), 1:36
Neighborhood councils, homelessness
and, 1:241
NELA (National Electric Light
Association), 3:166
Nelson, Donald, 3:346
Nelson, Ozzie, 3:63
Ness, Eliot, 1:129, 138, 141
Nestlé, 2:33
Neutrality Acts, 2:143–44, 150, 156
New American Caravan, 2:216
New Deal, 2:**252–73**
banking relief, 2:256, 260
boards and councils for, 2:261
corporate relief, 2:264
criticisms of, 1:211, 255, 2:262,
264, 266–68
development of, 1:26, 2:253–54
Economy Act, 2:256, 3:289–91
farmer relief, 2:257, 258, 260, 261,
262–63
first hundred days, 2:25, 255–56,
257, 268–69, 272–73
goals of, 1:292
Gold Reserve Act, 2:262
Great Society and, 1:162, 224, 228,
230–32
Hoover, Herbert and, 2:264–66
housing relief, 2:260, 264
impact of, 2:268–69
industrial recovery, 2:260–61
list of programs, 2:266, 269*t*
notable people, 2:270–72
overview, 1:199, 2:252–53, 266,
269*t*
Prohibition ended, 2:256–57
public opinion of, 2:272, 287
public support for, 2:267–68
railroad recovery, 2:261
stock market reform, 2:259, 263–64
Supreme Court and, 2:268, 270
work relief, 2:258, 259–60, 262

See also New Deal, second; *specific programs*

New Deal: America's Response to the Great Depression (Edsforth), 2:252

New Deal, second, 2:**274–94**
  assessment of, 2:290–91
  banking and business reform, 2:280–81
  business and, 2:284–85
  development of, 2:275–76
  economic recovery, 2:284
  end of, 2:284
  farmer relief, 2:277–79
  First New Deal and, 2:284–86
  goals of, 2:276
  government deficit spending, 2:281, 285–86
  housing, 2:282–84
  impact of, 2:284, 287–89
  labor reform, 2:279–80
  list of key legislation, 2:287
  notable people, 2:289–90
  opportunities lost, 2:281–82
  overview, 2:269–70, 274–76
  perspectives on, 2:286–87
  Roosevelt, Franklin and, 2:292–93
  social security, 2:280
  tax reform, 2:281
  work relief programs, 2:276–77
  See also specific programs

The New Deal in Review (*New Republic*), 2:290–91

New Masses, 2:45, 217, 221

New Negro Movement, 1:79

New Order, 2:54, 67, 268

The New President (Alsop), 1:237

The New Republic, 2:157–58, 169, 177, 290–91

The New Republic (Gold), 2:221

New School of Social Research, 1:209

New State Ice Co. v. Liebmann (1932), 3:204

New York, Nebbia v. (1934), 3:205

New York City, 2:132, 220–21, 222. *See also* New York World's Fair

New York City Housing Authority (NYCHA), 2:104–5

New York Daily Mirror, 3:29, 31

New York Stock Exchange, 1:*94*, 97

New York Times
  bestseller list, 2:212, 215
  Eighteenth Amendment article, 3:30–31
  on the New Deal, 2:252
  rescued from bankruptcy, 2:172–73
  research-related deaths and, 3:47

New York World, 2:171–72, 175

New York World's Fair, 1:264, 277, 3:353, 359–61

The New Yorker, 2:170

Newhall, Nancy, 2:308

News sources
  newspapers, 1:309
  newsreels, 1:309, 2:186
  Roper survey on, 2:178–79
  statistics, 2:164*t*, 179
  See also Newspapers; Radio; Television

Newspaper Guild, 2:164

Newspapers
  advertising revenue, 2:159, 164, 175, 180
  big business and, 2:178
  circulation statistics, 2:171, 176, 180
  criticisms of, 2:163
  daily newspapers, 2:176, 180
  Great Depression's effect on, 2:164
  Labor unions, American Newspaper Guild, 2:180, 181
  modern newspaper, 2:175
  newspaper chains, 2:175–76, 180
  radio stations owned by, 3:60
  Roosevelt, Franklin and, 2:178
  tabloids, 2:176–77
  unions, 2:164, 180, 181
  women in, 2:168

Newsreels, 1:309, 2:186

Newsweek, 2:169

Niagara Falls hydropower plant, 3:271

Nickelodeons, 2:86

Niebuhr, Reinhold, 3:125, 145, 147–48

"Night of Broken Glass" (*Kristallnacht*), 3:135, 136

NIH (National Institute of Health), 3:40–43

Nine Old Men (Allen), 3:219

Nine-Power Treaty, 2:149

Nineteenth Amendment, 1:156, 2:149, 3:295

NIRA. *See* National Industrial Recovery Act (NIRA)

Nitrates, 3:229–30, 245

Nixon, Richard, 1:20, 163, 257–58, 3:195–96

NLRA. *See* National Labor Relations Act (NLRA)

NLRB. *See* National Labor Relations Board (NLRB)

NLRB v. Jones & Laughlin Steel Corp. (1937), 1:159, 3:213–15, 220

NNC (National Negro Congress), 1:75, 76

No Small Courage: A History of Women in the United States (Cott), 2:201

No thanks (Cummings), 2:216

Nock, Albert, 2:146

Norman A. Myers Letters to Home: Life in C.C.C. Camps, Douglas County, Oregon, 1:121

Norris, George
  about, 3:173–74, 253, 279
  electric power legislation of, 3:250–51

Muscle Shoals and, 3:231–32, 246–48, 254
  power companies *vs.,* 3:249, 274
  rural electrification and, 3:160, 162, 169
  TVA and, 2:140–41, 3:236, 255

Norris-Rayburn bill, 3:161–62

The North American Indian, (Curtis), 2:304

North Atlantic Treaty Organization (NATO), 2:153

NOW (National Organization of Women), 3:297

NRA. *See* National Recovery Administration (NRA)

NRPB (National Resources Planning Board), 1:5, 2:240, 241, 3:337

NSBRO (National Service Board for Religious Objectors), 1:117

Nuclear power plants, 3:250

Nuremberg Laws, 3:135

Nutrition, 2:36, 40

Nye, Gerald, 2:141–43, 150–51, 155–56

Nye Committee investigations, 2:142–43, 150–51

Nylon, 2:119

O

O'Connor, Basil, 2:254

O'Connor, James, 1:63

O'Connor, John, 1:38

Odets, Clifford, 2:322, 330

Oettinger, Hank, 1:260

Of Mice and Men (Steinbeck), 1:303, 2:15, 224

Of Time and the River (Wolfe), 2:214

Office for Price Administration and Civilian Supply (OPACS), 3:331

Office of Economic Opportunity (OEO), 1:219

Office of Education, 1:207, 212. *See also* Department of Health, Education, and Welfare

Office of Indian Affairs
  as Bureau of Indian Affairs, 1:2, 11
  CCC-ID established by, 1:9
  competency commissions, 1:10
  creation of, 1:11
  duties of, 1:19
  Indian culture suppressed by, 1:12
  Indian education and, 1:14
  Indians employed in, 1:21
  inefficiency and corruption in, 1:13, 15, 19
  influence on Indian life, 1:10

Office of Production Management (OPM), 3:327–28

Office of Thrift Supervision (OTS), 1:61

Office of War Information (OWI), 2:303, 307–8

Office of War Mobilization (OWM), 3:330

Office of War Mobilization and Reconversion, 3:346

Official Guide Book of the Fair 1933, 3:365

Oglethorpe, James, 3:12

Ohio Emergency Relief Administration, 1:244

Ohio unemployment insurance plan, 3:180

Ohlin, Lloyd, 1:229

Oil discoveries on Indian land, 1:19

Oil prices, 1:61

O'Keefe, Georgia, 2:123

Old-Age Insurance (OAI), 3:186–87, 188–89

Olds, Ransom, 2:106

Oldsmobile automobile, 2:106

Olson, Floyd, 2:317

Olympic Games, Los Angeles, 1:275, 3:354

O'Malley, Thomas, 1:7

One Flew Over the Cuckoo's Nest (film), 1:38

One Hour With You (film), 2:77

100,000,000 Million Guinea Pigs, 3:46

One Third of a Nation: Lorena Hickock Reports on the Great Depression, 1:247

Oral histories, 3:311, 312

Oregon, Muller v. (1908), 3:218

An Organic Architecture (Wright), 2:135

Organized crime
  business ventures of, 1:128
  drug trafficking, 1:128, 142, 3:25
  end of gangster period, 1:128–29
  FBI and, 1:135
  gambling operations, 1:137
  growth of, 1:135, 138
  labor racketeering, 1:128, 131
  mafia, 1:130–31, 135, 136, 138
  overview, 1:137–38, 140–42
  racketeering, 1:141
  See also Bootlegging; Capone, Alphonse "Al"

Organized Crime Control Act, 1:140

Origins of the TVA: The Muscle Shoals Controversy, 1920-1932, (Hubbard), 3:232, 254

Orphanages, 1:321

The Other America (Harrington), 1:229

Otis, Harrison Gray, 2:173

OTS (Office of Thrift Supervision), 1:61

Out of the Dust (Hesse), 1:175

The Outline of History (Wells), 2:216

Owen, Ruth Bryan, 3:285

Owens, Jesse, 1:82, 275, 2:125

Oxley, Lawrence, 1:73

"Ozzie and Harriet" show, 3:63

P

Pacifica statue, 3:357

Pacifism, 3:145–46

Page, Kirby, 3:125

Paige, Leroy "Satchel," 2:125

Paley, William, 3:73

Palmer, A. Mitchell, 1:143

"Palmer raids," 1:143

Panama-California Exposition, 3:356

Panama-Pacific International Exposition, 3:356, 363

Panama Refining Company v. Ryan (1935), 3:205–7, 226

Pankhust, Emmaline, 3:301

Pankhust, Genevieve, 3:291

Papal encyclicals, 3:118, 129

Paper dolls, 1:279

Paramount Studios, 2:72, 76

Parker, Bonnie, 1:132, 134–35

Parker Dam, 3:265

Parks, Rosa, 1:83

Parran, Thomas, 3:43–44, 52, 54

Parrish, West Coast Hotel v. (1937), 3:214

Parsons, Louella, 3:64

Partisan, 3:202

Partisan Review, 2:216

Pastime. *See* Leisure time

Pastures of Heaven (Steinbeck), 2:224

Patterson, Eleanor, 2:185

Patterson, Robert, 3:348

Paul, Alice, 3:301

Paul, Nancy, 3:291, 295

Peace advocates, 2:142, 145, 149, 150

Peace Corps, 1:217

Pearl Harbor bombed, 2:145, 146, 3:67, 328–29

Pearson, Drew, 2:163

Pecora, Ferdinand, 1:51, 63, 104

Pecora hearings, 1:51, 104

Peek, George, 2:17

Pegler, Westbrook, 2:161, 185

Penicillin, 3:42, 44

Pentecostal churches, 3:128, 138

The People, Yes (Sandburg), 2:218

People's Party, 2:316, 323–24

Pepperidge Farm, 2:32

Perisphere structure, 3:359, *360*

Perkins, Edwin, 2:32

Perkins, Frances
  about, 2:204–5, 3:179, 301–2
  child labor and, 3:285
  Dewson, Molly and, 3:284
  as first women cabinet member, 3:302
  Kelley, Florence and, 3:301
  on the National Consumers' League, 3:293
  protective labor legislation and, 3:291
  Roosevelt, Franklin and, 3:*180,* 183, 193, 295, 296

as Secretary of Labor, 3:283–84, 285–87
  social insurance speeches, 3:181–82
  Social Security and, 3:183, 187, 199

Pershing, John, 3:338

Personal Responsibility and Work Opportunity Reconciliation Act, 3:88

Pesotta, Rosa, 1:289–90

Petroleum Administration Board, 3:205, 226

Philadelphia Electric Company, 3:168, 170

Philippines, 2:151, 3:328

Phillips, Cabell, 1:326

Phonographic record player, 3:59

Photo-Secession Movement, 2:304

Photography, 2:**295–314**
  as art form, 2:308
  color, 2:307
  commercial photography, 2:308
  contributing forces, 2:304–6
  documentary, 1:31, 174, 2:295, 296–301, 303, 304, 307–8
  First International Photographic Exposition, 2:302
  historic photographs, 2:302
  impact of, 2:301, 307–8
  New Deal agencies use of, 2:303
  notable people, 2:309–12
  overview, 2:295–96
  as pastime, 1:265–66
  perspectives on, 2:306–7
  photojournalism, 2:170, 184, 303–4, 308
  small cameras, 2:301
  for TVA, 3:241
  web sites, 2:302, 307
  WPA photography projects, 2:302–3
  See also Farm Security Administration (FSA); Resettlement Administration (RA)

Photojournalism, 2:170, 184, 303–4, 308

Phylon journal, 2:182

Physicians, 1:319*t,* 3:48, 51, 52

Pickling foods, 2:31

Pie Town photographs (Lee), 2:300

Pierce v. Society of Sisters (1925), 3:141

Piggly Wiggly, 2:36

Pinchot, Gillford, 3:168, 169, 174, 175, 242, 249

Pine View Dam, 3:269, 270

Pinocchio (film), 2:73

Pittsburgh Courier, 2:174

Pius XI (Pope), 3:118, 129, 140

"A Place to Lie Down" (Algren), 2:211

Places in the Heart, (film), 1:175, 2:90

Planned Parenthood Federation of
America, 3:292
Plastics, 2:119
Plessy v. Ferguson, 1:77–78
Plotke, David, 1:146
The Plow That Broke the Plain (film),
1:173, 2:306
Pluralism, 2:288
Poison Squad, 3:49
Poland, 2:64, 3:339, 340
Polio, 3:40, 44–45, 52, 53
Political action committees (PACs),
1:163, 234
Political instability, 2:51, 57, 58, 61
Political "left," 3:**315–33**
    Americans distrust of, 2:323
    anarchism, 2:315–16
    beliefs of, 2:315, 323
    Communist Party of the United
        States of America, 2:320–21,
        324, 325, 326
    Coughlin, Charles and, 2:318–19
    defined, 2:209, 3:119, 120
    End Poverty in California, 1:150,
        2:317, 330
    impact of, 2:323, 326–28
    leftist voices, 2:321–23
    as liberals, 2:209
    Liberty Party, 2:317
    "Mother" Jones, 2:322
    overview, 2:315–16
    People's Party, 2:316, 323–24
    perspectives on, 2:324–26
    progressivism, 2:324
    Share-Our-Wealth plan, 2:319–20
    susceptibility to, 2:54
    Townsend Plan, 2:267, 317–18,
        325, 3:39, 182
    views on poverty, 2:316
    WPA and, 3:318
    See also Communist Party;
        Socialism; Unionism
Political "right," 2:315, 3:119
Politics, 1:234, 3:58, 62, 67
Poll tax, 1:74, 80
Pollock, Jackson, 2:287
"Ponzi schemes," 1:94
Poole, Elijah, 3:138
Poole, John, 1:*101*
Popsicles, 2:30
Popular culture
    escapism and, 1:263, 275, 276–78,
        281–82
    ethnic groups and, 2:132
    fads, 1:265–66
    high *vs.* low art, 1:279–80
    impact of, 1:278–80
    international, 1:278
    society integrated by, 1:279
    socio-economic class tensions, 1:277
    technology and, 1:263–64
    in urban *vs.* rural areas, 1:277
    See also Films; Radio; Sports

Popular Front, 1:278, 2:320, 325
Popular music, 1:273–74, 279, 312
Population
    in 1930, 1:264, 2:180
    Asian Americans, 1:297, 298, 301
    black Americans, 1:69, 81
    census 2000, 1:301
    Chinese Americans, 1:290
    of cities *vs.* urban areas, 1:275, 2:16
    growth rate, 2:127
    Mexican Americans, 1:285–86,
        296–97, 300
    statistics, 2:171, 176
    in urban areas, 1:264, 275, 2:3
Populists. *See* People's Party
Porterfield, Bob, 1:37
Portland Oregonian, 2:179
*Portrait of a Decade: Roy Stryker and
    the Development of
    Documentary Photography in
    the Thirties* (Hurley), 2:313
Post-Dispatch, 2:171
Postal Service, U.S., 3:187–88
Pound, Roscoe, 3:218
Poverty
    American Creed and, 2:23–34, 37
    attitudes toward, 1:244
    beliefs about, 1:27, 229, 230, 2:37,
        39, 306
    declining voice of the poor,
        1:233–34
    education and, 1:203, 221
    of elderly Americans, 1:230,
        322–23, 3:177, 190, 196
    "End Poverty in California"
        campaign, 1:150, 2:317, 330
    Great Depression and, 3:38
    Great Society's war on, 1:3,
        218–19, 233–34, 2:113
    health care for the poor, 1:232–33
    of Mexican Americans, 1:294
    sanitation and hygiene, 3:33
    social programs decreased,
        1:233–34
    as social *vs.* economic problem,
        1:229–30
    stigma of, 1:323–25, 2:23–24
    See also Charity; Welfare
Power (Federal Theater Project), 3:243
Power companies
    antitrust actions against, 2:280
    electric cooperatives *vs.,* 2:9, 3:275
    excessive charges of, 3:160, 242,
        274
    Federal Trade Commission
        investigations, 3:248–49
    Giant Power Board *vs.,* 3:168–69
    holding companies and, 3:159, 236,
        237, 238–39, 272, 274
    impact of water and power projects,
        3:277
    profit issues, 3:155, 157, 167,
        169–70

public perspectives on, 3:242, 249,
    260
    REA and, 3:158–59
    regulating, 3:260
    ruralization and, 3:259, 273–74
    "spite lines," 3:161
    SuperPower plan, 3:169, 243
Prairie States Forestry Project, 1:174
Presbyterians, 3:124, 140, 141
Preservation of food, 2:31, 33, 34, 40,
    41, 42
President's National Conference on
    Home Building and Home
    Ownership, 2:99
*The Press and America: An Interpre-
    tive History of the Mass Media*
    (Emery and Emery), 2:168
Price-control
    for agriculture, 2:4, 8, 9, 11–12,
        279
    for consumer goods, 3:331
    "Memorandum 228" and, 2:241
    NIRA and, 2:236–37, 238–39, 246
Price wars, 2:235
Priming the pump, 2:326–27
"Primitive and Modern Medicine"
    (mural), 1:*33*
Primitivism, 2:123
Prisons, 3:8
Private enterprise. *See* Free enterprise
*The Problem of Indian Administration.
    See* Meriam Report
Processed foods, 2:34–35, 36–37, 42
"A Program of Medical Care for the
    United States" (Winslow), 3:37
Progressive Education Association
    (PEA), 1:196, 198
Progressive Party, creation of, 1:155
Progressives
    antitrust tradition of, 2:230
    beliefs of, 3:170
    corporations and, 2:230
    Democratic coalition and,
        1:148–49
    free enterprise and, 3:170, 249
    progressive era, 2:126
    progressive Republicans, 2:138–39,
        140–41, 3:194
    REA and, 3:155, 161, 170
    role of government and, 1:148–49,
        155, 2:230, 316, 324
Prohibition, 3:**1–32**
    advocates, 3:14–17, 18, 25
    agriculture affected by, 1:99
    "Alcoholic Blues" (song), 3:26
    American Federation of Labor
        opposition to, 3:6
    beer legalized, 2:257, 3:11
    Beer Tax Act, 2:256–57
    beginning of, 3:18–20
    costs, 2:4, 3:2
    Eighteenth Amendment, 1:99, 125,
        136, 2:256–57, 3:5, 17–18

Prohibition (continued)
  election of 1928, 3:7–8
  end of, 2:256–57, 3:2–3, 10–12, *29,*
    31
  enforcement, 3:3, 4–6, 19, 20
  first attempts, 3:1, 12, 13
  Great Depression and, 3:2, 9–10
  Hoover, Herbert and, 3:8, 10, 30
  impact of, 3:24–25
  international prohibition, 3:27
  Interstate Liquor Act, 3:17
  liquor consumed during, 3:*19*
  liquor sources, 3:17, 20–24
  Maine as first prohibition state, 3:1,
    13
  notable people, 3:27–30
  opponents, 3:4, 6–7, 8–9, 26–27
  as patriotic, 3:10, 17
  penalties, 3:8, 19
  perspectives on, 3:25–27
  Presidential Convention of 1932,
    3:10, 27
  public attitude toward, 1:138, 3:6,
    24
  repeal coalition, 3:9
  repealed, 1:125, 3:1–32
  results of, 3:3–4, 7
  Roosevelt, Franklin and, 3:10–11, 12
  speakeasies, 1:136–37, 3:24, 25
  states acceptance of, 3:17
  temperance movements, 3:1, 12, 13,
    14
  Twenty-first Amendment, 1:131,
    2:257, 3:10, 13
  "the untouchables," 1:129, 141
  violations, 3:19–20
  Wickersham Commission, 1:288,
    3:8, 31
  women and, 3:4, 8–9, 14, 25–36
  World War I and, 3:17–18
  youth and, 3:24, 26
  See also Bootlegging; Volstead Act
Prohibition Bureau, 3:4, 5
Prohibition Party, 3:14
Proletarian literature, 2:207, 208–12,
    219–20, 221
Property taxes, 1:186, 188, 189, 199,
    202
Prosperity
  of 1920s, 1:87, 91, 96, 102
  following World War II, 1:325
  of interwar era, 2:131
  stock market crash and, 1:240
Protestant Council of Churches, 2:78,
    87
Protestants
  anti-Semitism of, 3:137
  business and, 3:139–41
  congregation *vs.* clergy, 3:126, 128,
    145
  conservatism of, 3:126–27
  described, 3:121
  election of 1928, 3:141

  election of 1932, 3:127
  election of 1936, 3:128, 133–34
  end of Protestant era, 3:128–30
  Federal Council of Churches of
    Christ, 3:121, 124, 127, 150
  Great Depression and, 2:121, 3:118
  leftist views of, 3:124, 125
  local church efforts, 3:122–23
  Methodists, 3:123, 124–25, 126–27,
    140
  New Deal and, 3:123, 128
  organized labor and, 3:127
  pacifism in, 3:145
  perspectives on, 3:142–43
  Prohibition and, 3:121, 128, 139
  Social Creed of the Churches,
    3:139–40, 149, 150
  social service issues, 3:121, 122,
    123, 139
Protests
  antiwar demonstrations, 1:231
  "Don't Buy Where You Can't
    Work," 2:192
  eviction protests, 2:192
  hunger march, 3:308
  protest marches, 1:126, 235
Public Broadcasting Act, 1:221
Public Enemy (film), 1:130, 131, 142,
    2:75, 80
Public health, 3:**33–56**
  AIDS/HIV, 3:52, 53
  anti-vaccine and anti-vivisection
    societies, 3:52
  beliefs about, 3:35, 36
  bootlegged liquor and, 1:125, 3:3,
    20
  British and German systems, 3:48,
    51–52
  cancer, 3:33, 40, 42
  Children's Bureau, 3:35
  costs of, 3:36–37
  diet and, 3:34, 40
  disease reductions, 3:33–34
  Dust Bowl illnesses, 1:171–72
  for elderly Americans, 1:232–33
  Federal Food, Drug and Cosmetic
    Act, 1:223, 2:43–44, 284, 3:46,
    49, 52
  FSA and, 1:115, 3:46–47
  Great Society and, 1:232–33
  health insurance, 3:34, 37, 39–40,
    47–48, 50, 51, 53
  heart disease, 3:33, 40
  Hoover, Herbert and, 3:48–49, 50
  impact of, 3:52–53
  leading causes of death, 3:33, 40
  legislative reform, 3:36–37
  maternal and child health, 3:35, 39,
    48–49, 293, 298
  medical cooperative societies, 3:51
  medical poisoning, 3:45, 46
  medical relief, 3:37–39
  medical researchers, 3:47

  Medicare/Medicaid, 1:232–33, 3:53
  National Institute of Health (NIH),
    3:40–43
  New Deal programs, 3:33, 34–35, 37
  notable people, 3:53–54
  operating room, 3:*41*
  polio, 3:40, 44–45, 52, 53
  preventive services, 3:36–37
  private money for, 3:35, 36
  public safety issues, 3:46–47, 49–50
  riding the rails and, 3:80–81
  Roosevelt, Franklin and, 3:39, 50
  Social Security Act, 3:35, 39, 43,
    50, 186–87
  tuberculosis, 3:34, 36, 44
  in urban *vs.* rural areas, 3:34, 36, 37
  venereal disease, 3:35, 43–44, 46, 48
  See also American Medical
    Association
Public Health Service (PHS), 3:35–36,
    40, 47, 53, 54
Public housing, 2:105, 109, 112–13,
    283
Public opinion surveys, 2:163
*Public Schools in Hard Times: The
    Great Depression and Recent
    Years* (Tyack), 1:191, 193
Public Service Commission, 3:168
Public Speech (MacLeish), 2:215
Public Utilities Holding Company Act
    (PUHCA), 2:247, 280–81,
    3:260, 271
Public Works Administration (PWA)
  achievements, 1:249, 256, 3:308
  aid to schools, 1:200
  black Americans employed in, 1:74
  construction projects, 2:232, 3:308
  creation of, 2:232
  economic growth and, 1:249
  funding water and power projects,
    3:266, 270–71
  housing program, 1:74, 246, 2:104
  impact of, 1:256
  racial hiring quota system, 1:74–75,
    82
  work relief program, 1:247–49,
    3:308
  See also Federal Works Agency
Public Works Art Project (PWAP),
    1:26, 292, 2:262, 3:311
Publishing industry, 2:212, 215, 218,
    220*t*, 222
  See also Journalism; Literature
Pueblo Lands Act, 1:9, 12, 13
PUHCA. *See* Public Utilities Holding
    Company Act (PUHCA)
Pulitzer, Joseph, 2:171–72, 173
Pulitzer Prize, 2:171
Pulp fiction, 1:263, 272
Pure Food and Drug Act, 3:46, 49, 50
Puzzled America (Anderson), 2:170, 213
PWAP. *See* Public Works Art Project
    (PWAP)

Q

Quadragesimo Anno (Pope Pius XI), 3:118, 129, 131, 149–50

The Quest for Security (Rubinow), 3:199

Quest of Truth and Justice (Barnes), 2:146

Quilt-making, 1:34

R

RA. *See* Resettlement Administration (RA)

Race quotas, 1:74–75, 300–301

Race riots, 1:72, 78, 83, 227

Racial equality, 1:83

Racism

of Adolf Hitler, 1:81–82

black arts and, 1:79

deportation and, 1:288

of educators, 1:199, 203, 210, 211

employment and, 1:78

in Europe, 1:81–82

Hoover Dam project and, 3:264

in public relief programs, 1:320

racial equality ideals, 1:82, 83

reactions against, 1:83–84

Roosevelt, Eleanor and, 1:81

study about, 1:75

voting and, 1:79–80

See also Discrimination

Racketeer Influenced and Corrupt Organizations Act (RICO), 1:140–41

Racketeering, 1:141

Radar system, 3:341–42

Radford, Louisville Joint Stock Bank v., 3:208

Radical politics. *See* Political "Left"

Radio, 3:**57–75**

actors on, 1:267, 3:58, 64

advertising, 1:266, 3:59–60, 70

American Society of Composers, Authors, and Publishers and, 3:62, 71

Amos 'n' Andy, 1:78, 266, 277, 3:72, 73–74

Aunt Sammy home economics program, 2:27

beginnings of, 2:222–23

censorship of, 3:60–61

comic strip characters on, 3:64

commentators, 2:167–68

contributing forces, 3:68

drama, 1:266–67, 3:63–64

educational, 1:221

as escapism, 3:57, 63, 69

golden age of, 2:132, 3:59

Great Depression and, 2:167, 3:68

impact of, 3:70–71

listeners, 3:62–63

misuse of, 3:69

music on, 1:266, 3:62

networks, 3:59–61

as news source, 3:65–67, 70

notable people, 3:71–73

perspectives on, 3:69–70

politics and, 3:67–68

popularity of, 1:266, 310–11, 321, 3:57

radio journalism, 2:177

radio signals (AM/FM), 3:68, 71

regulating, 3:61–62

Roper Survey, 2:178–79

rural electrification and, 2:166–67, 3:172

soap operas, 1:264, 267, 311, 3:63

sound effects, 3:58, 70

stunt broadcasts, 3:67

theater on, 1:29, 266–67, 3:64–65

types of programming, 1:266–68, 2:123

"War of the Worlds" broadcast, 1:267, 311, 3:64–65, 68, 73

war reports, 3:66–67, 68, 69

women in, 2:168–69

See also Fireside chats

Radio Addresses of Col. Charles A. Lindbergh, 2:157

Radio Corporation of America (RCA), 1:100, 3:68

Radio stations, 2:167

Radiola console, 3:68, 73

Radios, 1:22, 93, 264, 2:177, 3:59, 68, 73

Railroad

American Indians and, 1:15

decline of, 2:121

Emergency Railroad Transportation Act, 2:261

expansion of, 1:296

improvements, 3:109–10

Missouri-Pacific Railroad loan controversy, 3:100–101

Railroad Retirement Act, 3:207–8

tourism and, 1:15

transcontinental railroad, 3:273

transient riding, 3:**76–91**

See also Riding the rails

Railroad Retirement Act, 3:207–8

Railway Mediation Act, 3:110

Randolph, A. Philip, 1:75, 76, 77, 3:335

Rangelands, 1:117, 250

Rankin, Jeanette, 2:150, 154

Raskob, John, 1:91, 105, 3:28, 30

Rationing food and gas, 2:40, 3:331

Rauschenbusch, Walter, 3:139

Rayburn, Sam, 3:161, 174

Razzias, 1:287, 288

REA *See* Rural Electrification Administration (REA)

Reaching For The Stars (Waln), 2:216

Reader's Digest, 2:39, 169

Reagan, Ronald

economic crisis of 1980s, 1:102

homelessness and, 3:88

labor unions unsupported by, 2:202

pro-business & cuts in social programs, 1:164

as sports announcer, 3:67

tax cuts of, 1:233

television and, 3:71

Recession of 1937, 2:282, 292

Recipes

Baking Powder Biscuits, 2:47–48

Bread, Baking Powder Biscuits recipe, 2:47

Cakes: milkless, eggless, butterless, 2:48

Depression Era Recipes (Wagner), 2:28

meatloaf, 2:28

product driven, 2:34–35

Recipes and Remembrances of the Great Depression (Thacker), 2:31, 44, 47

seven-minute icing, 2:30

Spam Stew, 2:47

Stories and Recipes of the Great Depression of the 1930s, (Van Amber), 1:327, 2:47–48

substitute ingredients, 2:48

vegetable soup, 2:48

Reclamation Service. *See* Bureau of Reclamation

Reconstruction Finance Corporation (RFC), 3:**92–117**

aid to schools, 1:200

banking crisis and, 1:46, 50

black Americans and, 1:69

Central Republic Bank controversy, 3:101, 113

creation of, 3:97–98

financing New Deal agencies, 3:105–6, 108–9

Hoover, Herbert and, 2:100, 3:97–98, 100–102, 111, 115–16

impact on U.S. loan system, 3:111

loan requirements of, 3:99–100

loans to banks, 3:105, 108

Missouri-Pacific Railroad loan controversy, 3:100–101

perspectives on, 3:111–13

Roosevelt, Franklin and, 3:105–9

unemployment relief loans from, 1:241

War Finance Corporation and, 3:109

World War II defense efforts, 3:110–11

Reconstructionism, 1:196–97, 205, 206, 210

Record industry, 2:128

Record players, 3:59

Red Berets, 3:*290*

Red Cross, 1:259, 2:24, 3:36

"Red Ivory Tower," 2:221

"Red rider," 1:197

Redcaps union, 2:194
Reed, Stanley, 3:214, 220
Reed College, 1:197, 198
Refrigerators, 2:37, 3:172, 239, 271
Reid, Robert, 2:313
Religion, 3:**118–52**
    Adventist, 3:128
    of American Indians, 1:5, 17, 19
    Baptists, 3:124
    black churches, 3:119, 137–38
    civil rights movement and, 3:146
    contributing forces, 3:139–42
    Disciples of Christ, 3:124
    election of 1932 and, 3:127
    election of 1936 and, 3:128, 133–34
    Episcopalian, 3:124
    film censorship, 3:140
    Great Depression and, 3:121
    Holiness movement, 3:138
    inter-faith cooperation, 3:143
    leftist views, 3:124–26
    local church efforts, 3:122–23
    New Deal and, 3:123–24, 127
    notable people, 3:146
    organized labor and, 3:127
    Pacifism, 3:145–46
    Pentecostal churches, 3:128, 138
    perspectives on, 3:142–46
    post World War I, 3:139
    post World War II, 3:146
    Presbyterians, 3:124, 140, 141
    Social Gospel movement, 3:139
    social services of, 3:121–23
    Unitarians, 3:124
    See also Catholicism; Jewish
        Americans; Protestants
Reno, Milo, 2:17
Repatriation, 1:286, 288, 300
*Report of the Commissioner of Indian
    Affairs* (Collier), 1:22–23
Report on the Survey of Hopi Crafts
    (Whiting), 1:8
Reporter Plan, 3:288–389
Republic Steel, 1:*127*, 128, 2:197,
    3:213
Republican Party
    anti-slavery viewpoint, 1:149, 154
    big business and, 1:155, 157
    black voters and, 1:80
    Bonus Army and, 1:148
    business ideas, 1:147–48
    conservative movement, 1:227, 228
    decline of, 1:148, 155
    election of 1938 and, 1:152
    government role limited by, 1:155,
        2:253
    laissez-faire approach, 1:148, 157
    as minority party, 1:148, 150, 155
    Muscle Shoals project and, 3:246
    nationalism of, 1:156
    New Deal programs and, 1:150
    origins of, 1:149
    policies of, 1:162

progressive Republicans, 2:138–39,
    140–41, 3:194
push for tax cuts, 1:233
radio used by, 3:67
return of, 1:156–57, 163
Roosevelt, Franklin and, 1:151
Social Security and, 3:185, 194
supply-side economics, 1:164
TVA and, 3:246
values of, 1:149
Rerum Novarum (Pope Leo XIII),
    3:129
Reserve banks, 1:55
Resettlement Administration (RA)
    agricultural relief programs, 1:31
    American Indians and, 1:9
    creation of, 1:174, 2:8
    documentary photos, 2:296–97, 303
    FSA and, 1:174, 2:8
    Historical Section, 1:31, 174, 2:297,
        303
    loans to farmers, 1:76, 83, 174,
        2:297
    medical
    plans, 3:51
    purpose of, 1:174, 2:297
    relocating farmers, 1:176, 2:275,
        297
    Special Skills Division, 1:31
    See also Farm Security
        Administration (FSA)
Resolution Thrift Corporation (RTC),
    1:61
Resources. *See* Natural resources
Retirement pensions, 1:43
Retrenchment, 1:*189*, 190–96
Reuther, Walter, 2:*198*, 205
Revenue Act of 1942, 3:332
Reynolds, George, 3:96
RFC. *See* Reconstruction Finance
    Corporation (RFC)
Rhoads, Charles, 1:251
Richard Wright—Black Boy (film),
    2:327
Richberg, Donald, 2:241, 242, 249,
    3:212
Riding the rails, 3:**76–91**
    dangers of, 3:79–81
    Davis, Kingsley on, 3:89–90
    everyday life of, 2:225–26, 3:87
    film on, 2:82, 3:81
    language of, 3:84
    public perspectives on, 3:85–87
    reasons for, 3:76
    web sites on, 1:111
    women, 3:81
    youth and, 1:111, 116–17, 275,
        3:*78, 86, 90*
    See also Homelessness; Transients
*Riding the Rails: Teenagers on the
    Move During the Great
    Depression* (Uys), 3:91
Rigby, Cora, 2:174–75

Right wing. *See* Conservatives
Riis, Jacob, 2:108, 305–6
Riots
    food riots, 1:126, 2:24, 37
    race riots, 1:72, 78, 83, 227
    Watts riot, 1:326
The Rise of American Civilization
    (Beard), 1:209, 2:216
Ritz Crackers, 2:30, 34
The River (film), 1:173
River and Harbor Act, 3:266, 267
Rivera, Diego, 1:32–33, 3:357–58
The Road to War: America, 1914-1917
    (Millis), 2:143
Roadside Americana, 2:120
Roberts, Owen, 3:204, 205, 207, 208
Robeson, Paul, 2:83–84
Robinson, Bill, 2:84, 93
Robinson, Edward G., 1:129, 2:75, 80,
    95
Robinson, Joseph, 3:212, 215–16
Roche, Josephine, 3:302
Rockefeller, John D., 3:30–31
Rockefeller Center, 1:32–33, 2:122
Rockefeller Foundation, 1:15, 22, 198,
    3:35, 36
Rocky Mountain spotted fever, 3:41
Rodriguez, Raymond, 1:303
Rogers, Ginger, 1:270, 2:79
Rogers, Jimmie, 1:274
Rogers, Will, 1:64, 2:165
Rombauer, Irma, 2:22, 33–34, 44, 45
Rooney, Mickey, 2:82, 93
Roosevelt, Eleanor
    about, 1:85, 326, 3:286
    Antioch College and, 3:252
    "Chambers of Horrors" exhibit and,
        3:46
    at Chicago World's Fair, 3:*354*
    coal-mine workers and, 2:*283*
    Dewson, Molly and, 3:284
    Hickock, Lorena and, 3:287
    Kennedy, John F. and, 3:297
    marriage of, 1:121, 3:286
    "My Day" newspaper column,
        2:183, 3:286
    NRA supported by, 2:*168*
    press conferences, 2:168
    public attitude toward, 2:39
    radio broadcasts, 1:268, 3:286
    serving food, 2:*42*
    victory garden of, 2:41
    Woodward, Ellen and, 3:*302*
Roosevelt, Franklin, Jr., 3:46
Roosevelt, Franklin Delano, 3:*211*
    about, 1:120–21, 326, 2:18, 252
    belief in work relief, 3:308
    Bonneville Dam dedication speech,
        1:257, 3:280–81
    at Boulder Dam, 3:*263*
    campaign speech, 1932, 3:259
    Chicago World's Fair address,
        3:352

cooperative economic movement of, 2:230–31
Coughlin, Charles and, 3:133–34, 146
"cradle to grave" statement, 3:183, 199–200
death of, 3:338
election campaign speech, 1:166
electrical power speech, 3:232
extramarital affair, 3:286
first hundred days, 2:25, 255–56, 257, 268–69, 272–73
foreign policy, 1:161, 2:58, 144, 145–46
health of, 1:121, 3:44–45
Hoover, Herbert and, 3:*104*
inaugural address, 1:48, 258, 2:228, 272, 292–93
inauguration of, 3:105
Johnson, Lyndon B. and, 1:*220*
labor and industry speech, 2:205–6
modernization ideals, 3:258–59
Muscle Shoals speech, 3:234
on National Power Policy Committee, 3:279–80
national social insurance speech, 3:199
New York World's Fair address, 3:353
newspaper coverage on, 2:163, 186–87
nomination acceptance speech, 2:253–54
Norris, George and, 3:233–34
Perkins, Frances and, 3:*180*, 296, 304
Philosophy of Social Justice Through Social Action speech, 3:149–50
press conferences, 2:164–66
public attitude toward, 1:323, 2:39, 178*t*, 272, 281, 291–92
public support of, 2:267–68, 281, 3:219
radio skills, 3:67
religion of, 3:125
on religious charities, 3:150–51
rural life favored by, 2:31, 3:258, 276
on signing the Social Security Act, 3:200
Supreme Court appointments/"Roosevelt Court," 3:220–21
television appearance, 2:180
"The only thing we have to fear is fear itself," 1:240
Timberline Lodge dedication, 3:320–22
war against Japan, 3:*350*
on work relief programs, 3:322
See also Fireside chats; *specific topics*

Roosevelt, Theodore, 1:155, 3:221
"Roosevelt Court," 3:220–21
The Roosevelt I Knew (Perkins), 3:193, 304
Roper, Elmo, 2:178
Roper media survey, 2:178–79
Rorty, James, 2:213
Rose, Billy, 3:361
Rosefield, J.L., 2:32
Rosenman, Samuel, 1:64, 109, 242, 2:254
Rosie the Riveter, 3:*298*
Ross, Barney, 2:125
Ross, Ben, 1:244
Ross, Harold, 2:170
Ross, Nellie, 3:285, 302–3
Roth, Henry, 2:211
Rothstein, Arthur, 2:*298*, 299, 307, 308, 311, 313
RTC (Resolution Thrift Corporation), 1:61
Rubber tire industry, 2:235–36
Rubenstein, Helena, 3:291
Rubinow, Isaac, 3:191, 198–99
Rudkin, Margaret, 2:32
Rugg, Harold, 1:200
Rum, 3:1, 12, 21, 22
The Rumrunners: A Prohibition Scrapbook (Gervais), 3:30
Runaway Youth Program, 3:88
Rural areas
    back to the land movement, 2:31, 3:131, 258, 276
    electricity for, 2:3, 262, 3:169, *171*, 272
    farming in, 2:3
    health care in, 3:34, 36, 37, 51
    poverty in, 1:277
    See also Farmers; Rural Electrification Administration (REA)
Rural Electrification Act, 1:277, 3:162
Rural Electrification Administration (REA), 3:**153–76**
    conservatives *vs.* progressives, 2:170
    cooperatives and, 3:157–60
    cost issues, 3:165
    Department of Agriculture and, 3:173, 261
    development of, 3:155–57, 162–65
    discontinued, 3:171
    farmers and, 2:278–79, 3:160, 163, 169
    Giant Power *vs.* SuperPower, 3:168–69
    goals of, 3:154, 258
    hands on involvement, 3:163
    impact of, 3:170–72
    as lending agency, 3:157–58
    loans from, 3:157, 163–64, 165, 170
    municipal utility companies and, 3:159

notable people, 3:172–74
    overview, 3:153–55
    as permanent agency, 3:160–62, 261
    perspectives on, 3:169–70
    "spite lines" and, 3:161
    transmission line innovations, 3:164–65
    work relief and, 3:157, 163
    See also Electricity; Power companies; Water and power
Rush, Benjamin, 3:13
Russell, Howard, 3:14
Russell, Rosalind, 3:296
Russia, 2:57–58, 3:88, 99, 340
Russo, Anthony, 1:144
Ruth, Babe, 1:264
Ruth, George "Babe," 2:134–35
Ruth Wakefield's Toll House Cook Book (Wakefield), 2:33
Ryan, John, 3:129, 132, 134, 148
Ryan, Panama Refining Company v. (1935), 3:205–7, 226
Rydell, Robert, 3:361–62

S

S&Ls (savings and loan associations), 1:53, 61
Sabin, Pauline, 3:9, 28
Sacramento River Valley, 3:272
SAIF (Savings Association Insurance Fund), 1:46, 61
Salvation Army, 1:102, 2:24, 3:79
Salzman, Jack, 2:212
San Francisco, 2:120, *121*, 3:353, 356–59
Sanchez, George, 1:294
Sandburg, Carl, 2:217–18
Sanger, Margaret, 3:*48*, 292
Sarnoff, David, 3:68, 73
Saturday Evening Post, 1:237, 2:95, 170, 177, 3:313
Savings and loan associations (S&Ls), 1:53, 61
Savings Association Insurance Fund (SAIF), 1:46, 61
Scarface (film), 2:75
Schechter Poultry v. United States (1935), 2:192, 243, 268, 270, 3:209–10
Schlesinger, Arthur, 2:5, 7, 20
Schneiderman, Rose, 3:303
The School and Society (Dewey), 1:210
Schools
    American Legion and, 1:206
    black schools, 1:203, 213
    closing of, 1:190, 191, 3:77, 85
    cost-cutting measures, 1:190–91
    desegregation in, 1:193, 207, 208
    folk schools, 1:197, 208
    rural *vs.* city, 1:190, 203
    segregation in, 1:83, 203, 3:227

Science
    advancements in, 2:119
    progress of, 2:135, 136
    scientific research, 2:119
    World's fairs and, 1:17, 3:352,
        355–56, 363
Science Advisory Committee, 3:362
Science and the Public Mind
    (Gruenberg), 3:363
Science for the World of Tomorrow
    (Wendt), 3:363
Scottsboro 9 case, 1:76, 2:*206*
Scripps, Edward, 2:172, 183
Scripps-Howard, 2:163–64, 172, 175
SCS. *See* Soil Conservation Service
    (SCS)
Schwartz, Bonnie, 1:245
SDS (Students for a Democratic
    Society), 1:229
Seaman, Elizabeth (Nellie Bly), 2:173
SEC (Securities and Exchange
    Commission), 1:104, 105, 2:264
Section 7 (NIRA), 1:159, 160, 2:192,
    232
Section 8 (HUD), 2:113
Securities and Exchange Commission
    (SEC), 1:104, 105, 2:264
Securities Exchange Act, 1:104, 105,
    2:259, 263–64
Seeger, Charles, 1:31
Seeing Red (film), 2:327
Segregation
    in CCC, 1:212
    intelligence testing and, 1:210
    Jim Crow laws for, 1:77–78, 3:335
    Johnson, Lyndon and, 1:217–81
    King, Martin Luther and, 1:234, 235
    in the military, 1:69, 75, 77, 3:335
    in music bands, 1:273
    in schools, 1:83, 203, 3:227
    Supreme Court cases, 1:77–78, 83,
        228, 3:227
    in theater groups, 1:76
    TVA and, 3:234
    as unconstitutional, 1:83, 228
    Wallace, George and, 1:236, 237
    in the workplace, 3:315
    See also Desegregation
Selective Service Act, 2:144
Self-reliance, 1:322, 3:191
Selznick, David O., 1:281
Senate Indian Affairs Committee, 1:6,
    22
Senior Citizen's Freedom to Work Act
    of 2000, 3:196
Servicemen's Readjustment Act (GI
    Bill), 3:338
SES (Soil Erosion Service), 1:175, 176,
    183
Settlement houses, 2:130–31, 3:293
Seven-minute icing, 2:30
Shadow on the Land (Parran), 3:43–44,
    54

Shahn, Ben, 2:299, 307, 308, 311
Shall It Be Again? (Turner), 2:146
Share-Our-Wealth movement, 1:150,
    2:267, 320, 325, 3:182, 184
Sharecroppers
    black Americans as, 1:81, 318,
        2:12
    described, 1:318, 2:8, 12
    Let Us Now Praise Famous Men,
        2:15, 170, 213, 300, 309
    New Deal programs for, 2:8, 13–14,
        17, 258, 297
    unions for, 1:68, 2:201
Shasta Dam, 3:269
She Done Him Wrong (film), 2:78
Shelterbelt Project, 1:250
Sheppard-Towner Act, 3:48, 49, 50,
    293, 298
Sherman Anti-Trust Act, 2:243–44
Sherman Silver Purchase Act (1890),
    1:155
Shirer, William, 3:67
Shouse, Jouett, 2:286, 287
Shreveport Rates Cases (1914), 3:216
Shyster films, 2:75–76
Siedenborg, Frederic, 3:132
Silent Spring (Carson), 1:223, 229
Silver, 1:155, 2:58, 62, 316
Sinatra, Frank, 1:273
Sinclair, Upton, 1:150, 2:317, 325,
    330–32
Six Companies, 3:264–65
Skippy peanut butter, 2:32
"The Skull" (photo), 2:299
Skyscrapers, 2:122
Slang, 1:273, 313
Slaughterhouse Cases (1873), 3:217
Slave Narratives (Federal Writers'
    Project), 3:311, 312
Slavery, 3:311, 312
Slums
    documentary photos of, 2:104–6,
        305–6
    Federal Housing Administration
        and, 2:103, 112
    ghettos, 1:74, 78, 131, 226
    housing in, 2:104–6, *110*
    poor sanitary conditions, 2:23
    public housing programs, 2:105,
        109, 112–13, 283
Small business
    big business *vs.,* 1:89, 93, 2:239,
        3:344
    discrimination against, 2:239, 241
    mass production and, 2:120
    World War II and, 3:344, 346
Smallpox epidemic, 3:52, 53
Smith, Adam, 1:88, 96, 106–7
Smith, Alfred
    about, 1:*156,* 3:28–29
    election of 1928 and, 1:157, 3:7–8,
        141
    election of 1932 and, 3:130

electric power policy, 3:248
    Prohibition opposed by, 3:141
    Roosevelt, Franklin and, 3:133
Smith, Hilda, 3:295
Smith, Kate, 1:266, 280, 311
Smith, Moe, 3:20
Smith, Mulford v. (1939), 2:9
Smith-Connally War Labor Disputes
    Act, 3:334
Smuggling liquor, 3:21, 30
Smythe, William, 3:276
Snake River hydroelectric dam, 3:262
SNCC (Student Nonviolent
    Coordinating Committee), 1:226
Snow White and the Seven Dwarfs
    (film), 1:270, 280, 2:73
Soap operas, 1:264, 267, 311, 3:63
Social Creed of the Churches,
    3:139–40, 149, 150
Social Frontier, 1:208
Social Gospel movement, 3:139
Social Ideals of the churches, 3:150
Social insurance, 3:189–93, 199. *See
    also* Social Security
Social Justice, 3:146
Social reconstructionism, 1:196–97,
    205, 206, 210
Social reform, 1:150, 2:130–31, 304.
    See also New Deal, second;
    Social Security
Social Security, 3:**177–201**
    in 2000, 3:196
    academics and, 3:194
    advisory councils for, 3:194
    amendments to, 3:189, 195
    American Association for Labor
        Legislation and, 3:191
    beneficiaries of, 3:192*t,* 193, 196
    benefit payments, 2:318, 327, 3:195
    Bush, George on, 3:200
    business and, 3:193–94
    Carter, Jimmy on, 3:200
    Clinton, Bill on, 3:200
    Committee on Economic Security,
        3:183–84
    congressional hearings on,
        3:181–82
    contributing forces, 3:189–93
    Cost-of-Living Adjustments, 3:196
    creation of, 2:280
    described, 2:280, 3:178
    Dill-Connery Bill, 3:181
    disability amendments, 3:195
    for disabled Americans, 3:187
    early years, 3:179, 188–89
    economic recovery and, 2:280,
        3:189
    impact of, 3:194–97
    labor and, 3:194
    Medicare/Medicaid, 1:232–33, 3:53,
        195
    old-age pension plans, 2:202, 3:179,
        181, 184, 195

overview, 3:177–78
Perkins, Frances on, 3:304
perspectives on, 3:193–94
public attitude toward, 3:191, 193
retirement age and, 3:196
Roosevelt, Franklin and, 3:39, 178, 182–83, 184, 193, 198
social insurance and, 3:190–91
Social Security Bill, 3:184–86
Social Security Board, 3:*186*, 187–88, 196
Supplemental Security Income (SSI), 3:195–96
Supreme Court ruling, 3:220
taxes for, 2:280, 3:187, 189
unemployment insurance, 2:196, 280, 3:39, 179–81, 183–84, 187, 196
Wagner-Lewis Bill, 3:179–81, 182
See also Social Security Act
Social Security Act
Aid to Dependent Children, 3:187
eleven titles of, 3:186–87
federal health standards established, 3:39
health insurance and, 3:39, 50, 53
Old-Age Insurance, 3:186–87, 188–89
Perkins, Frances and, 3:285
public health services funded by, 3:35, 39, 43
Social Security board, 3:*186*, 187–88, 196
Social services, 3:121–23, 139
Social workers, 1:253–54, 3:285, 289, 293
Socialism
American Socialism, 2:219–20
communism and, 2:219
defined, 2:219, 315, 3:120
fear of, 1:73
New Deal criticized by, 2:286
public relief viewed as, 1:253
REA and, 3:161
Socialist Party, 1:72, 2:126, 3:295
Socialist Worker's Alliance, 1:241
Society of Sisters, Pierce v. (1925), 3:141
Sociological jurisprudence, 3:218
Soil Conservation Act, 1:175, 181, 183
Soil Conservation and Domestic Allotment Act, 1:174, 2:9
Soil Conservation Service (SCS), 1:175–76, 181, 2:7, 278
Soil-conserving crops, 1:174, 181, 2:9, 279
Soil erosion, 1:168–69, 171, 175, 182, 183, 2:7, 12–13
Soil Erosion: A National Menace (Bennett), 1:183
Soil Erosion Service (SES), 1:175, 176, 183
Sokoloff, Nikolai, 1:29, 3:311

"Somewhere Over the Rainbow" (song), 1:280, 2:71, 83
"Song of a New Day" (song), 3:359
Songwriters, 3:62
The Sound and the Fury (Faulkner), 2:214, 219
Sound effects, 3:58, 70
Soup kitchens, 1:102, 2:23, 24
Southern Christian Leadership Conference (SCLC), 1:83, 235
Southern Tenant Farmers' Union, 1:81, 2:17
Soviet Union
anti-fascism of, 2:320
Cold War, 2:148, 152–53, 3:346
communism of, 2:152–53, 320
Sputnik I satellite launching, 1:208
Spain, 2:61, 152, 3:66–67
Spam, 2:32, 42, 47
Spanish Americans, 1:211
Speakeasies, 1:136–37, 3:24, 25
Special Committee on Investigation of the Munitions Industry. *See* Nye Committee
Special Committee to Investigate Un-American Activities and Propaganda. *See* House Un-American Activities Committee (HUAC)
Special interest groups, 1:151, 153–54, 158–59, 163, 234
Special Problems of Negro Education (Wilkerson), 1:213
Speech From a Forthcoming Play (Cummings), 2:216
Spencer, Herbert, 1:99–100
The Spirit of St. Louis (Lindbergh), 2:155
Sports
baseball, 1:264, 274, 2:124
black American athletes, 2:125
for children, 1:314
football, 1:274
golden age of, 2:124–25
Jewish athletes, 2:125
miniature golf, 1:311
Olympic Games, 1:275, 3:354
radio broadcasts, 1:268, 274, 311, 3:67
synchronized swimming, 3:361
types of, 1:274–75
women in, 2:124–25
Sports Illustrated, 2:184
Sputnik I satellite launching, 1:208
SSI (Supplemental Security Income), 3:195–96
Stackpole, Peter, 2:304
Stackpole, Ralph, 3:357
Stagecoach (film), 1:271, 2:82
Stalin, Joseph, 2:57, 68, 152
Standard of living, 1:275, 306, 307, 321
Standard Oil Company, 1:98, 156

Standard State Solid Conservation District Law, 1:176
Standing Bear, Luther, 1:*6*, 7
Stanwyck, Barbara, 3:296
Starvation, 2:24, 40
Stayton, William, 3:6, 27, 29
Steagall, Henry, 1:45, 46, 51, 63, 2:115
Steamboat Willie (animation), 2:92
Steichen, Edward, 2:302, 312
Stein, Gertrude, 2:219
Steinbeck, John
about, 1:303, 2:223–24
Harvest Gypsies, 1:179, 181
In Dubious Battle, 1:303, 2:14–15, 210, 224
Of Mice and Men, 1:303, 2:15, 224
Pastures of Heaven, 2:224
realism style, 2:128
Tortilla Flat, 1:303, 2:210, 224
Travels with Charley, 2:222
See also The Grapes of Wrath (Steinbeck)
Stern, Catherine Brieger, 1:211
Steward Machine Co. v. Davis (1937), 2:9
Stewart, James, 1:269, 2:80
Stieglitz, Alfred, 2:304, *305*
Stimson, Henry, 3:325, 335, 344, 348–49
Stock market
"buying on the margin," 1:92–93, 94
Federal Securities Act, 2:259, 263
fraud and hype, 1:93, 94
government regulation of, 1:92, 104, 105, 3:131
impact of the crash, 1:87, 94, 102–5, 3:92–93
New Deal reform, 2:259, 263
Securities Exchange Act, 1:104, 105, 2:259, 263–64
stock exchanges, 1:*94*, 97
stock prices, 1:89*t*, 97*t*, 2:*60*
U.S. international investments, 1:100–101, 2:52, 54, 63, 268
See also Reconstruction Finance Corporation (RFC); Stock market crash
Stock market crash, 1:**87–108**
agricultural crisis, 1:95, 98–99, 3:92
"Black Thursday," 1:88, 3:92
business cycles and, 1:89–90, 98*t*
get rich quick mentality, 1:91–92, 100
government regulation lacking, 1:88–89
Hoover, Herbert and, 1:125, 188, 3:93
international conditions, 1:96
lack of national planning, 1:96, 99–100
lacking information, 3:93
materialism and, 1:91–92, 100, 321
notable people, 1:105–6

Stock market crash (continued)
overview, 1:87–88
perspectives on, 1:100–102
real estate boom and bust, 1:92
rise of corporations and, 1:89,
97–98, 106
safeguards lacking, 1:96
stock market craze, 1:88, 92–95,
106–7
volunteer approach to recovery,
3:94–96
warning signs ignored, 1:96, 3:92
wealth distribution and, 1:90–91,
102, 2:325
See also Reconstruction Finance
Corporation; Stock market
Stockard, George, 1:327
Stone, Harlan, 3:203, 204, 222–23
*Stories and Recipes of the Great
Depression of the 1930s,* (Van
Amber), 1:327, 2:47
The Story of Utopias (Mumford), 2:135
Stoves, 2:37, 3:*158*, 167, 239
Strand, Paul, 2:306
Stranded (film), 3:87
Strauss, Nathan, 2:115
Strayhorn, Billy, 1:281
Streamline Moderne, 2:121
Strike (Vorse), 2:211
Strikes
canning industry, 2:201, 322
Democratic Coalition and, 1:166
farmer, 1:287–88, 289
garment industry, 1:290, 2:127,
199–200
labor, 1:126–28, 136, 2:282
laundry workers, 2:*323*
Memorial Day Massacre, 1:*127*,
128, 2:197, 3:213
Mexican Americans, 1:289
newspaper, 2:164, *166*
rent, 2:192
sit-down, 2:*195*, 196–97, 3:213
teamsters, 2:*193*
United Mine Workers strike, 3:334
wildcat, 2:196
See also Protests
"Striking a Chord: Loveless CCC"
(song), 1:111
Stryker, Roy
about, 2:311
Evans, Walker and, 2:299–300, 307
instructions from, 2:313
Office of War Mobilization and,
2:307–8
RA/FSA photographers and, 1:37,
2:31, 297–301, 306–7, 309–10
Studebaker, John, 1:199
Student Nonviolent Coordinating
Committee (SNCC), 1:226
Student Work Councils, 1:252
Students for a Democratic Society
(SDS), 1:229

Studs Lonigan trilogy (Farrell), 2:210,
223
Sturdevant, William, 3:240
Submarines, 3:340, 344–45
Suicide, 1:102, 107, 322, 3:42–43
Sulfa drugs, 3:42, 44, 46
Sullivan, Mark, 2:161, 185
Sullivan's Travels (film), 1:268
The Sun Also Rises (Hemingway),
2:219
Sunday, Billy, 3:15, 18
Sunday World, 2:172
Sundquist, James, 1:228
Super heroes, 1:313
SuperPower plan, 3:169, 243
Supplemental Security Income (SSI),
3:195–96
Supreme Court, 3:**202–28**, *215*
AAA and, 1:174, 2:9, 279,
3:210–11
black American justices, 1:82, 232
"Black Monday," 3:208–10
change of direction, 3:213–16
civil liberties and, 3:213
conflicts with New Deal, 3:205–8,
220
conservatives on, 3:203, 215,
217–19
contributing forces, 3:213–19
first Jewish Court justice, 1:156
"Four Horsemen of Reaction,"
3:203, 215
freedom of contract rulings, 3:204,
217
impact of, 3:220–21
laissez-faire philosophy and, 3:204,
217, 218, 220
liberals on, 3:203
minimum wage ruling, 3:214
notable people, 3:221–24
overview, 3:202–4
partisan leanings, 3:202, 203
perspectives on, 3:219–20
Railroad Retirement Act ruling,
3:207–8
reorganization plan, 3:203–4,
212–13, 215–16, 219–20,
224–25
Roosevelt, Franklin and, 2:270,
282, 3:210, 339
"Roosevelt Court," 3:220–21
state *vs.* federal power and, 3:216–17
Supreme Court reform bill, 2:282
Warren Court decisions, 1:228, 237
Web site for, 3:228
Supreme Court cases
*Ashwander v. Tennessee Valley
Authority* (1936), 3:261
Bailey v. Drexel Furniture Co.
(1922), 3:219
Breedlove v. Suttles (1937), 1:80
Brown v. Board of Education
(1954), 1:83, 228

Buchanan v. Warley (1917), 1:78
Carter v. Carter Coal Company
(1936), 3:210
Champion v. Ames (1903), 3:217
Cherokee Nation v. Georgia (1831),
1:19
Corrigan v. Buckley (1926), 1:78
Gold Clause Cases, 3:207
Grovey v. Townsend (1935), 1:80
Guinn v. United states (1915), 1:80
Hammer v. Dagenhart (1918),
3:217
*Heart of Atlanta Motel v. United
States* (1964), 1:217
Helvering v. Davis (1937), 3:220
*Home Building and Loan
Association v. Blaisdell* (1934),
3:204
*Humphrey's Executor v. United
States,* 3:208
Keller v. United States (1909),
3:217
Korematsu v. United States (1944),
3:224
*Louisville Joint Stock Bank v.
Radford,* 3:208
Missouri ex rel Gaines v. Canada.,
3:227
Morehead v. Tipaldo, 3:211
Mulford v. Smith (1939), 2:9
Muller v. Oregon (1908), 3:218
Nebbia v. New York (1934), 3:205
New State Ice Co. v. Liebmann
(1932), 3:204
*NLRB v. Jones & Laughlin Steel
Corp.* (1937), 1:159, 3:213–15,
220
Panama Refining Company v. Ryan
(1935), 3:205–7, 226
Pierce v. Society of Sisters (1925),
3:141
Plessy v. Ferguson, 1:77–78
Schechter Poultry v. United States
(1935), 2:192, 243, 268, 270,
3:209–10
Shreveport Rates Cases (1914),
3:216
Slaughterhouse Cases (1873), 3:217
Steward Machine Co. v. Davis
(1937), 2:9
Swift & Co. v. United States (1905),
3:216
United States v. Butler (1936), 2:9,
279, 3:210
United States v. Darby Lumber Co.
(1941), 3:219
*United States v. E.C. Knight
Company* (1895), 2:244, 3:218
West Coast Hotel v. Parrish (1937),
3:214
Wickard v. Filburn (1941), 2:9
Survey of Indian Affairs, 1:15
Surviving the Dust Bowl (film), 1:175

Susan Lenox (film), 2:77
Sutherland, George, 3:204, 208, 210
Suttles, Breedlove v. (1937), 1:80
Svobida, Lawrence, 1:184–85
Swados, Harvey, 2:212
Swarthmore College, 1:197, 198
Sweden, 2:52, 56, 3:27, 167
Swift & Co. v. United States (1905),
    3:216
Swimming, 3:361
Swing, 1:264, 273, 279, 312, 3:67
Swing, Raymond, 2:168
Swope, Gerard, 2:245, 246, 249–50
Sydenstricker, Edgar, 3:37, 39
Syphilis, 3:42, 43, 48

T

Tacker, Emily, 2:31
Taft, William, 1:155, 3:19, 217
Taft-Hartley Act, 1:161
Take a Letter Darling (film), 3:296
Tammany Hall, 1:253
Tanks, 3:339, *345*
Tarbell, Ida, 2:173, 174, 177
Tariffs, 1:96, 100, 101, 2:3–4, 15, 52,
    55
Tarzan, 1:313
Tax leagues, 1:189
Tax Reduction Act, 1:217
Taxation
    Beer Tax Act, 2:256–57
    corporate taxes, 3:332
    of farmers, 2:8
    food processing, 2:6, 9, 14, 279
    Great Society and, 1:225
    head tax, 1:297
    import tariffs, 1:96, 100, 101,
        2:3–4, 15, 52, 55
    inability to pay, 1:189–90
    income tax, 1:155–56, 3:318, 332
    liquor tax, 1:125, 3:1, 2, 4, 12,
        13–14
    poll tax, 1:74, 80
    property taxes, 1:186, 188, 189,
        199, 202
    Social Security tax, 2:280, 3:187,
        189, 196–97
    tax cuts, 1:90, 217, 233
    wealthy Americans and, 1:90,
        2:281, 3:196–98
    for World War II mobilization,
        3:332
Taylor, Paul, 2:307
Taylor Grazing Act, 1:115, 117, 118,
    182, 2:7
Teachers
    business community *vs.*, 1:194–96,
        205, 208
    as communists, 1:205
    income, 1:208, 319*t*
    loyalty oaths, 1:197, 204–5

    as militants, 1:194, 195, 205, 208
    New Dealers *vs.,* 1:199
    protests, 1:195
    "red rider" statement, 1:197
    retrenchment and, 1:193–96
    unions, 1:193, 194, 205, 208
    See also Education
Teapot Dome oil-lease scandal,
    2:176–77
Technical Committee on Medical Care
    (TCMC), 3:39–40
Technology
    advances in, 2:127, 136
    assembly line, 2:119, 120, 130,
        3:110, 163, 164–65
    farm modernization, 2:8, 11, 15–16
    Golden Gate Bridge and, 2:120,
        121, 3:356
    for kitchens, 2:37
    popular culture and, 1:263–64
    research, 2:119
    social problems solved by, 2:130
    World's fairs and, 3:352
Technology and service industries, 2:202
Television, 2:90, 180–81, 3:71
Temperance movements, 3:1, 12, 13,
    14
Temple, Shirley, 1:270, 311, 313–14,
    2:79, 93
Temporary Emergency Relief
    Administration, 1:120. *See also*
    Federal Emergency Relief
    Administration (FERA)
Tenant farmers
    black Americans as, 1:318
    defined, 1:318, 2:4
    documentary photography and, 2:306
    New Deal and, 2:13–14, 17, 258
    Southern Tenant Farmers' Union,
        1:81, 2:17
    Steinbeck's writing on, 2:15
Tender Is The Night (Fitzgerald), 2:214
Tennessee Electric Power Company
    (TEPCO), 3:238–39, 254
Tennessee River, 3:229, 230, 231,
    243–45, 248
Tennessee River Valley, 3:230,
    243–45, 260–61
Tennessee Valley Authority (TVA),
    3:229–56
    achievements, 2:259, 270,
        3:239–42, 250, 261, 277
    agricultural experiments, 3:239, *240*
    Alabama Power Company and,
        3:237, 238
    Alcorn County Electric Cooperative
        and, 3:157, 159
    benefits of, 2:270
    black Americans and, 1:70, 3:234
    Board of Directors, 3:235–37, 261
    Commonwealth and Southern
        Corporation (C & S) and, 3:236,
        237, 238–39

    contributing forces, 3:242–50
    dam construction, 2:*251*, 3:239–40,
        250*t*
    experimental cooperative, 3:156–57
    farmers in, 3:230
    Federal Theater Project play on,
        3:243
    fertilizer production, 3:229–30, 239,
        240
    Giant Power Board, 2:168–69,
        3:242
    goals, 1:200, 208, 3:156, 230, 239
    Hiwassee Dam, 3:*244*
    impact of, 3:250–51
    Lilienthal, David and, 3:236, 252,
        255
    Morgan, Arthur and, 3:234, 235,
        236–37, 252
    Morgan, Harcourt and, 3:235, 253
    Muscle Shoals and, 3:229–30, 239,
        244–49
    Muscle Shoals bill, 3:231–33,
        247–48, 254
    Norris Dam, 3:*233*, 239–40, *247*
    notable people, 3:251–54
    perspectives on, 3:249–50
    politics and, 3:231–33
    power companies *vs.,* 3:234,
        237–39
    public perspectives on, 3:239, 241,
        243
    publicity campaign, 3:240–41
    REA and, 3:261
    Republican Party and, 3:246
    Roosevelt, Franklin and, 3:234,
        249, 254–55
    Supreme Court ruling on, 3:238,
        261
    Tennessee Valley Authority Act,
        3:234, 237
    TEPCO purchase, 3:238–39, 254
    Tupelo experiment, 3:239, 261
    U.S. Army Corps of Engineers
        report, 3:231, 248
    Wheeler Dam, 3:240
    Willkie, Wendell and, 3:236, 237,
        238–39, 250, 255
    Wilson Dam, 3:239, 245–46,
        247–48
    World War II and, 3:261
    World's Fair exhibit, 3:241
    as yardstick, 3:237, 249, 250, 276
    See also Electricity; Norris, George;
        Power companies
*Tennessee Valley Authority, Ashwander
    v.* (1936), 3:261
Tennessee Valley economy, 3:230
Tenth Amendment, 3:216, 217
TEPCO (Tennessee Electric Power
    Company), 3:238–39, 254
Terkel, Studs, 1:85, 106–7, 2:205
Terrell, Harry, 2:5, 19–20
Texas annexation, 1:296

Thacker, Emily, 2:31, 44, 47
Theater
    Barter Theater, 1:37
    black Americans in, 1:75–76
    Communism, theaters viewed as,
        1:38
    Federal Charter for a National
        Theater, 1:36
    musicals, 1:30
    on radio, 1:29, 266–67, 3:64–65
    segregation in, 1:76
    white supremacists and, 1:76
    See also Federal Theater Project
        (FTP)
Their Eyes Were Watching God
    (Hurston), 1:76, 2:214
These Are Our Lives (Federal Writers'
    Project), 1:327, 2:214, 225–26
*They Fly through the Air with the
    Greatest of Ease* (Corwin), 3:68
They Shoot Horses, Don't They?
    (McCoy), 1:313, 2:222
They Won't Forget (film), 2:82
Thibodeau, Karen, 2:38, 47
The 39 Steps, (film), 1:271, 2:82
*Thirty Years of Lynching in the United
    States, 1889-1918* (NAACP),
    1:78
"This Land is Your Land" (song),
    1:273, 280
This Side of Paradise (Lewis), 2:219
This Ugly Civilization (Borsodi), 3:276
Thomas, Lowell, 1:326, 2:167, 184
Thomas, Norman, 3:145
Thomas, T. Parnell, 3:313, 316
Thompson, Dorothy, 2:162, 168, 186,
    187–88
Thomson, Virgil, 3:316
Thorgersen, Ed, 3:66
Three Little Pigs (film), 2:70, 72
The $3,000,000 Machine (*Fortune*),
    1:328
Three Soldiers (Dos Passos), 2:223
Thurman, Wallace, 1:79
Timberline Lodge, 3:320–22
Time magazine
    about, 2:169, 178
    Jim Crow Concert Hall, 1:85
    Krock, Arthur article, 2:183
    on law enforcement in films, 2:95
    Luce, Henry and, 2:169, 178, 310
    Thompson, Dorothy article,
        2:187–88
Times-Herald, 2:185
Tipaldo, Morehead v., 3:211
Tireman, Loyd S., 1:211
To Kill a Mockingbird (Lee), 1:67
To Make My Bread (Lumpkin), 2:210
Tobacco Road (Caldwell), 2:210, 222,
    223
Toll House Chocolate Chip Cookies,
    2:32–33
Toll of the Sea (film), 2:73

Toomer, Jean, 1:79
Tortilla Flat (Steinbeck), 1:303, 2:210,
    224
Tourism, 1:12, 314
Tower of the Sun, 3:357
Townsend, Francis
    about, 2:331, 3:182, 199
    Democratic Coalition and, 1:150
    old-age pension plan, 2:267,
        317–18, 325, 3:39, 182
    Social Security Bill and, 3:184
Townsend, Grovey v. (1935), 1:80
Townsend, Willard, 2:194
Townsend Clubs, 1:150, 3:182
Toys, 1:314
Trade Associations, 2:236–37
Transcontinental railroad, 3:273
Transients, 3:76–91
    attitudes toward, 3:86, 88
    contributing forces, 3:84
    defined, 3:79
    in Europe, 3:88
    Guthrie, Woody as, 1:280
    Hoover, Herbert and, 3:78
    New Deal programs for, 3:77,
        81–83, 87, 88
    notable people, 3:89
    private programs, 3:83
    public perspectives on, 3:85–87
    reasons for, 3:78
    youth as, 1:111, 116–17, 3:78, *86*
    See also Homelessness; Riding the
        Rails
Transportation
    electric trolleys, 2:106
    growth of aviation, 2:121
    Highway Safety Act, 1:223
    interstate Freeway system, 2:328
    National Traffic Motor Vehicle Act,
        1:223
    road building, 2:120
    truck and bus traffic, 2:120–21
    See also Automobiles; Railroad
Travelers Aid, 3:83
Travels with Charley (Steinbeck),
    2:222
Traylor, Bill, 1:33
Treasure Island, San Francisco, 3:356,
    357
Treasury Relief Art Project, 1:26
Treaties of disarmament, 2:149
Treaty of Guadalupe Hidalgo, 1:296
Treaty of Versailles, 2:143, 147, 148,
    152
Triangle Fire, 3:301
Triple-A Plowed Under (Federal
    Theater Project), 3:313
Trouble in Paradise (film), 2:77
Truman, Harry
    bombing Japan, 3:338
    desegregation order, 1:75
    electric power and, 3:277
    Fair Deal policy, 1:161–62, 3:338

    New Deal and, 1:161, 2:228
    women and, 3:297
Truth in Packaging Act, 1:223
Trylon structure, 3:359, *360*
Tuberculosis, 3:34, 36, 44
Tugwell, Rexford
    about, 2:18, 45, 115, 271
    as Brain Trust member, 2:254, 255
    food and drug safety bill of, 2:43
    on Greenbelt towns, 2:113
    NRA and, 2:238
    on photography, 2:312
    preference for rural life, 1:33
    as RA director, 1:174, 2:296–97
    small farms and, 2:8
Tunney, Gene, 2:132–33
Tupelo, Mississippi, 3:239, 261
Turner, Kenneth, 2:146
Tuskegee Syphilis Study, 3:42
TVA. *See* Tennessee Valley Authority
    (TVA)
TVA and the Power Fight (McCraw),
    3:232
12 Million Black Voices (Wright),
    2:224, 226
Twentieth Amendment, 2:254–55
Twenty-first Amendment, 1:131, 2:257,
    3:10, 13
Twenty-fourth Amendment, 1:80
Twenty-second Amendent, 1:158
The Two Extremes (Heyl), 1:191
Tyack, David, *Public Schools in Hard
    Times: The Great Depression
    and Recent Years,* 1:191, 193,
    203, 213
Tydings-McDuffie Independence Act,
    1:291, 2:151

U

UAW (United Automobile Workers),
    1:72, 2:196–97
Un-American Activities Committee,
    1:76
Uncensored (Writer's Anti-War
    Bureau), 2:145
Uncle Tom's Children (Wright), 1:76,
    2:211, 224, 226
Unemployed Teachers' Association,
    1:193
Unemployment
    in 1932, 1:147, 2:189–90
    in 1980s, 1:102
    attitude toward, 1:252–54, 256, 258,
        323
    black Americans and, 1:66, 67, 68,
        69, 193, 244, 318
    CWA and, 2:262
    homelessness caused by, 2:192
    Hoover, Herbert and, 1:249, 254
    immigration blamed for, 1:302,
        303–4

impact of New Deal programs, 1:256–58

inadequate relief for, 1:241

increase in, 2:23

insurance, 2:196, 280, 3:39, 179–81, 183–84, 187, 196

leisure and, 1:264

New Deal relief programs, 1:241, 248–49

overview, 1:254, 2:189, 266

protest marches, 1:126

Social Security compensation, 3:187

statistics, 1:67, 147, 149, 239–41, 276, 318, 2:128

white *vs.* black women, 1:244

youth, 1:109–10, 111, 2:277, 3:76, 77

See also Employment; Reconstruction Finance Corporation (RFC)

Union square (Halper), 2:210

Unionism, 2:316

Unions

anti-union activities, 2:17

black Americans and, 1:72, 2:101, 194

businesses resistance to, 2:199

communism and, 1:28, 31, 186–87

company unions, 2:192, 193, 199

decline of, 1:163–64, 234, 2:191, 198–99, 202

defined, 1:275, 2:190

free-trade and, 2:202

government opposition to, 1:90–91, 2:190

growth of, 2:194, 195–96, 197, 199, 328

leadership, 2:16–17

legal support, 1:159, 160, 2:291

Mexican Americans and, 1:289

NIRA and, 1:159, 160, 2:192, 232, 261, 279

racketeering in, 1:128, 131

right to organize, 1:159, 160, 2:192, 279, 326

women and, 1:290, 2:199–200, 201

workers' gains, 2:199–200

yellow dog contracts, 2:192, 199

See also American Federation of Labor (AFL); Labor movement; Labor unions

Unit banks, 1:41, 52–54

Unitarian church, 3:124

United Automobile Workers (UAW), 1:72, 2:196–97

United Cannery, Agricultural, Packing and Allied Workers of America (UCA-PAWA), 2:13, 201

United Farm Workers of America, 1:302

United Jewish Appeal for Refugees and Overseas Needs, 3:137

United Mine Workers of America, 1:72, 2:192, 204, 3:334

United Nations (UN), 1:72, 2:64–65, 148

United Nations Declaration of Human Rights, 1:72

United Press Association (UP), 2:172, 175, 180

United States, Guinn v. (1915), 1:80

United States, Heart of Atlanta Motel v. (1964), 1:217

United States, Humphrey's Executor v., 3:208

United States, Keller v. (1909), 3:217

United States, Korematsu v. (1944), 3:224

United States, Schechter Poultry v. (1935), 2:192, 243, 268, 270, 3:209–10

United States, Swift & Co. v. (1905), 3:216

United States Daily, 2:183

United States Film Service, 1:173, 2:307

United States Housing Authority (USHA), 2:105, 109, 112, 283

United States News, 2:183–84

United States Steel, 1:98

United States v. Butler (1936), 2:9, 279, 3:210

United States v. Darby Lumber Co. (1941), 3:219

United States v. E.C. Knight Company (1895), 2:244, 3:218

Unsafe at Any Speed (Nader), 1:229

Untemeyer, Samuel, 3:145

"The Untouchables," 1:129, 141

The Untouchables (film), 1:141

Up From the Footnote: A History of Women Journalists (Marzolf), 2:169

Urban areas

electricity for, 3:166, 272

growth of, 1:277, 2:35

health care in, 3:34, 36, 37

industrialization and, 3:189–90

popular culture in, 1:277

population of, 1:264, 275, 2:3, 16

urban renewal programs, 2:112–13

See also Farms

U.S. Camera, 2:300

U.S. Chamber of Commerce, 1:190, 196, 205, 3:169

U.S. Children's Bureau, 3:293

U.S. Conference of Mayors (USCM), 2:114

U.S. Forest Service, 1:117, 119

U.S. Grazing Service, 1:115, 117, 182. *See also* Taylor Grazing Act

U.S. Navy, 1:69

U.S. News and World Report, 2:184

U.S. Rubber, 2:236

USA trilogy (Dos Passos), 2:210, 223

USCM (U.S. Conference of Mayors), 2:114

USHA. *See* United States Housing Authority (USHA)

"Usonian" house, 1:33

Utah State Historical Society, 1:121

Utility companies. *See* Power companies

Utopians, 2:130

Uys, Errol, 3:91

V

Vacations, 1:314

Vaccines, 3:45, 52

Vachon, John, 2:300, 307, 308, 311–12, 313

Vagrant, 3:79

Vallee, Rudy, 1:266, 268

Van Amber, Rita, 1:327, 2:47–48

Vann, Robert, 1:73, 2:174

Variety shows, 1:268

Vaudeville, 2:88, 3:58, 63

Vegetables, 2:29, 31, 40, 41

Venereal disease, 3:35, 43–44, 46, 48

Vespucci, Amerigo, 1:20

Veterans

Bonus Army march, 1:126, 144, 148, 3:102–3

CCC veteran interviews, 1:121

CCC work relief, 1:112–13, 250

GI Bill benefits, 3:338

mortgage program, 2:111

Veteran's Administration (VA), 2:111

Vickochil, Larry, 2:313

Victory gardens, 2:41

Vietnam War, 1:163, *224,* 231, 2:153, 3:146

Vigilante Cura (Pope Pius XI), 3:140

Violence

anti-union activities, 2:17

anti-war protests, 1:140

Bonus Army march and, 1:126, 144, 3:103

civil rights movement and, 1:83, 140, 266

crowd violence, 1:125–26

farmer rebellion, 1:126, 2:4, 13, 18–20

sit-down strikes and, 3:213

street violence, 1:140

toward black Americans, 1:66, 68, 318

toward farm workers, 1:68

See also Crime; Protests; Riots; Strikes

Violins and Shovels (Meltzer), 1:37

Visel, Charles, 1:303

VISTA (Volunteers in Service to America), 1:219

Vivisection societies, 3:52

Voices From the Dust Bowl: The Charles L. Todd and Robert Sonkin Migrant Worker Collection, 1940-41, 1:175

Volstead Act
  described, 1:136, 3:18
  industrial alcohol and, 3:20
  movement for modification of, 3:6, 26
  as too restricting, 3:24
  violations, 3:19
  See also Eighteenth Amendment
Voluntary Committee of Lawyers, 3:7
Volunteerism, 3:193
Volunteers in Service to America (VISTA), 1:219
Vorse, Mary Heaton, 2:211
Voting
  black Americans and, 1:73, 79–80, 83, 152
  grandfather clause, 1:80
  Great Society programs, 1:220–21, 235
  Johnson, Lyndon voting rights speech, 1:237–38
  protest marches for, 1:235
  suffrage movement, 3:295
  Voting Rights Act, 1:83, 221, 235
  white-only primaries, 1:80
  women's voting rights, 1:156, 2:149, 3:295
Voting Rights Act, 1:83, 221, 235
Vroman, Adam, 2:304–5

W

Wadsworth, James, 3:29–30
Wages
  average weekly salary, 1:275
  black Americans and, 1:70, 81
  CCC workers, 1:251
  CWA workers, 1:246–47
  during World War II, 3:334–36, 342, 343
  Hoover Dam project and, 3:264
  increase in, 1:90
  industrial workers, 2:128
  price of goods and, 2:237
  by profession, 1:319*t*
  wage-rate controls, 3:336
  women *vs.* men, 3:296
  WPA workers, 3:309, 318
  See also Income; Minimum wage
Wagner, Patricia, 2:28
Wagner, Robert, 1:247, 2:105, 115, 271–72, 3:40, 199
Wagner Bill, 3:40
Wagner-Connery Act. *See* National Labor Relations Act (NLRA)
Wagner-Lewis Bill, 3:179–81, 182
Wagner-Peyser Act. *See* National Employment Act
Wagner-Steagall Housing Act, 2:105, 109, 116, 283
Waiting for Lefty (Odets), 2:322
Waiting for Nothing (Kromer), 2:211

Wakefield, Ruth, 2:32–33
Wallace, DeWitt, 2:169
Wallace, George, 1:221, 225, 227, 235–64, 3:220
Wallace, Henry, 2:4, 5, 6, 7, 17, 19, 238
Wallace, Lila Acheson, 2:169
Waln, Nora, 2:216
Walsh, Edmund, 3:130
The Waltons (television), 2:90
War bonds, 3:331
A War Congress (*Business Week*), 2:272–73
War debts
  effect of the Johnson Act, 2:56–57, 142
  France, 2:56–57
  Germany, 2:52–53, 56, 63, 3:113
  Great Britain, 2:55, 56–57, 62
  Hoover, Herbert and, 2:52–53
  lend-lease payment plan, 2:145, 3:344
  Roosevelt, Franklin and, 2:56
  suspension of, 2:52–53, 56
War Finance Corporation (WFC), 3:109
War Industries Board (WIB), 2:231, 244, 3:338
War Manpower Commission (WMC), 3:331–32
War materials. *See* Arms
"War of the Worlds" (Wells), 1:267, 311, 3:64–65, 68, 73
War Production Board (WPB), 3:329, 346
War pudding, 2:36
War Relocation Authority (WRA), 3:331
War Resources Board (WRB), 2:432, 3:327–28
Ward, Harry, 3:148, 150
Ward, Henry, 3:145
Warhol, Andy, 1:280
Warley, Buchanan v. (1917), 1:78
Warner, Jack, 2:93–94
Warner Brothers Pictures, 2:78, 82, 93–94, 95, 3:87
Warren, Earl, 1:228, 237
Warren, Harry, 2:94
Warren, Robert, 2:327, 331
Warren Court, 1:228, 237
Washing Conference treaties, 2:149
Washington, George, 3:359
Washington State, 1:257, 3:258, 265, 266–68, 270
Wasserman, Dale, 1:38
The Waste Land (Eliot), 2:148
Water and power projects, 3:**257–81**
  back to the land movement and, 3:276
  Bonneville Power Administration (BPA), 1:257, 3:258, 268
  Bureau of Reclamation, funding water and power projects, 3:270

California Central Valley, 3:268–69
Colorado River, 3:258, 263–65, 274, 277
Columbia River basin, 1:257, 3:258, 265–68, 270, 278, 280–81
contributing forces, 3:271–74
developing the West, 3:261–63, 272–74
electrical modernization, 3:258–60
environmental concerns, 3:278
flood control, 3:271, 272
funding for, 3:266, 270–71
impact of, 3:276–78
notable people, 3:278–79
perspectives on, 3:271, 274–76
power companies and, 3:260, 271–72, 274
Roosevelt, Franklin and, 3:262–63
rural America and, 3:272
Tennessee River Valley, 3:230, 243–45, 260–61
See also Power companies; Tennessee Valley Authority (TVA)
Water conservation, 1:183
Water Facilities Act, 3:262
Water Power Act, 3:273
Water Quality Act, 1:223
Watkins, Harold C., 3:46
Watkins, T.H., 1:306–7, 314, 2:38, 39
Watts riot, 1:226
Wealth distribution
  American values and, 3:170
  changes in, 3:278
  Share-Our-Wealth movement, 1:150, 2:267, 320, 325, 3:182, 184
  stock market crash and, 1:90–91, 102, 2:325
  wealthy Americans and, 1:90–91, 102, 2:208, 3:184
The Wealth of Nations (Smith), 1:106
Wealth Tax Act, 2:281
Wealthy Americans
  attitude towards poverty, 2:39
  beliefs about unemployment, 1:323
  budgets, 1:307
  charity and, 2:39
  comedy about, 2:80
  culture and, 1:276
  everyday life, 1:306–7, 314, 327–28, 2:39–40
  income of, 1:90
  Republican Party supported by, 1:234
  taxing, 1:90, 3:196–98
  wealth distribution and, 1:90–91, 102, 2:208, 3:184
Weatherwax, Clara, 2:211
Weaver, Robert, 1:73, 85
Web sites
  American Memory Project historic photographs, 2:302, 307

Barter Theater, 1:37

California League Against Sinclair-
    ism advertisement, 2:331–32

Chicago World's Fair guide book,
    3:365

Civilian Conservation Corps (CCC),
    1:115, 121
    on the Dust Bowl, 1:175
    on Gus Hall, 2:315
    National Association of Civilian
        Conservation Corps Alumni,
        1:115
    on railroad "wanderers," 1:111
    U.S. Constitution, 3:228
    veteran interviews, 1:121

Welfare
    attitude toward, 2:37–38, 3:191,
        192, 319
    as demoralizing, 3:309
    factors of, 1:225
    food stamps, 1:224, 2:25–26, 42–43
    Roosevelt, Franklin and, 3:309
    work relief *vs.*, 3:308, 309

Welles, Orson
    about, 1:37, 3:73
    Citizen Kane, 1:37, 279, 3:73
    The Cradle Will Rock, 1:29–30, 36,
        3:316
    Macbeth, 1:29, 30, 76, 3:314
    "War of the Worlds" radio
        broadcast, 1:267, 311, 3:64–65,
        68, 73

Wells, H.G., 1:272, 311, 2:216

Wells-Barnett, Ida, 2:173

Wendt, Gerald, 3:363

*We're in the Money: Depression
    America and its Films*
    (Bergman), 1:281, 2:75, 78, 94

"We're in the Money" (song), 2:78,
    94–95

West (United States)
    California Central Valley
        development, 3:268–69
    Colorado River development, 3:258,
        263–65, 274, 277
    Columbia Basin project, 3:265–68
    developing, 3:261–63, 272–74
    New Deal and, 3:277

West, Mae, 1:281, 2:78

West, Nathanael, 2:214

West Coast Hotel v. Parrish (1937),
    3:214

Westinghouse, 3:271, *361*

WFC (War Finance Corporation),
    3:109

Whale, James, 1:272

Whalen, Grover, 3:365

What You Can Do with Jell-O (General
    Foods), 2:34

Wheeler, Burton, 1:22, 2:*141*, 3:220

Wheeler, Wayne, 3:7, 18, 30

Wheeler-Howard Act. *See* Indian
    Reorganization Act (IRA)

*Where Life Is Better: An Unsentimental
    American Journey* (Rorty),
    2:213

Whiskey, 3:12, 20

White, Minor, 2:312

White, Sue, 3:303

White, Walter, 1:71, 85

White, William, 2:145, 150

White Label program, 3:293

White supremacists
    about, 1:231
    decreased acceptance of, 1:82,
        2:288
    Ku Klux Klan, 1:79–80, 157, 2:82,
        3:136
    lynchings by, 1:78
    theater and writing opposed by,
        1:76

Whiting, Alfred, 1:8

Wholesome Meat Act, 1:224

Wholesome Poultry Products Act,
    1:224

"Who's Afraid of the Big Bad Wolf"
    (song), 2:70, 72

WIB (War Industries Board), 2:231,
    244, 3:338

Wickard v. Filburn (1941), 2:9

Wickenden, Elizabeth, 3:82, 89

Wickersham Commission, 1:288, 3:8,
    31

Wild Boys of the Road (film), 2:82,
    3:81

Wild West Show, 1:7

Wilder, Laura Ingalls, 2:214–15

Wilderness Preservation Act, 1:223

Wiley, Harvey, 3:49

Wilkerson, Dopey, 1:213

Willard, Daniel, 2:39

Williams, Aubrey, 1:201, 211–12, 252,
    260, 3:89, 320

Williams, Claude, 3:125

Williams, R.C., 3:35

Williams, William, 2:135

Williard, Frances, 3:14

Willkie, Wendell, 1:158, 3:236,
    237–39, 250, 254, 255

Wilson, Edmund, 2:213

Wilson, Woodrow
    food programs of, 2:36
    League of Nations and, 2:62, 146
    nitrogen plants and, 3:245
    Peace Industries Board proposed
        by, 2:245
    progressivism of, 1:155
    radio stations shut down, 3:68
    segregation and, 1:69
    women and, 3:294
    World War I and, 2:146

Wilson Dam, 3:239, 245–46

Winant, John, 3:187, 199

Winchell, Walter, 2:168, 186, 3:67, 73

Winslow, C.E.A., 3:36–37

Winslow, Susan, 1:64, 2:45–46

Wisconsin Labor Market (Altmeyer),
    3:197

Wise, Stephen, 3:135, 149

Withington, Lothrop, 1:317

Witte, Edwin, 3:183, 194, 199

The Wizard of Oz (film)
    collector's edition, 2:94
    described, 2:7, 83
    as musical, 1:270–71
    photograph, 2:*89*
    "Somewhere Over the Rainbow"
        (song), 1:280, 2:71, 83
    in technicolor, 2:73

WMU (Women's Moderation Union),
    3:8–9

Wolcott, Marion, 2:300, 312

Wolfe, Thomas, 2:212–13, 214

Woman of the Year (film), 3:296

Woman's Crusade, 3:14

Women, 3:**282–305**
    birth control movement, 3:292
    black American women, 1:244,
        3:315
    breadlines avoided by, 2:24
    clothing, 1:322
    as community, 3:295
    discrimination against, 1:250, *255*,
        2:199, 3:309, 326, 332–33, 346
    educating on political issues,
        3:288–89
    education, 1:252
    employment and, 1:102, 307, 323,
        3:285, 332–33
    Equal Rights Amendment, 3:291,
        297–98
    in film, 2:77–78, 3:296
    first woman governor, 3:302–3
    first women cabinet member, 3:302
    in government, 2:287–88, 3:285,
        293, 297
    as home economists, 2:37
    homeless, 3:88
    income of, 3:296
    in journalism, 2:168–69, 173–75
    life without electricity, 3:167
    married and working, 1:102, 307,
        323, 3:289, 292
    Mexican American women,
        1:289–90
    National Consumers' League
        (NCL), 3:293
    New Deal and, 3:285, 287–88, 293
    peace movement of, 2:149
    perspectives on, 3:296–97
    Prohibition and, 3:4, 8–9, 14,
        25–26, 27
    protective labor legislation for,
        3:291, 292, 293
    in radio, 2:168–69
    riding the rails, 3:81
    role in society, 2:126, 3:346
    Roosevelt, Eleanor and, 2:168, 389,
        3:285, 286, 293

Women (continued)
Roosevelt, Franklin and, 3:285, 289, 295–96, 297
sewing, 1:308, 3:315
speakeasies and, 1:136–37, 3:24
in sports, 2:124–25
unemployment and, 1:244
unions and, 1:289–90, 2:199–200, 201
voting rights, 1:156, 2:149, 3:295
war mobilization and, 3:332–33
Women's Charter, 3:291–92, 299
Women's Trade Union League (WTUL), 2:293–94
work relief programs, 2:277, 3:287, 303–4, 315
Women in Industry (Abbott), 3:89
Women in Industry Service (WIIS), 3:294
Women on the Breadlines (LeSueur), 2:24, 211
Women Rebel (Sanger), 3:292
Women's Army Auxiliary Corps, 3:288
Women's Bureau, 3:291, 297
Women's Charter, 3:291–92, 299
Women's Christian Temperance Union (WCTU), 3:1, 12, 14, 18, 25
Women's Committee for Repeal of the Eighteenth Amendment, 3:8
Women's Division of the Democratic National Committee (DNC), 3:284, 297
Women's Emergency Brigade, 3:*290*
Women's International League for Peace and Freedom, 2:142, 149, 150
Women's Moderation Union (WMU), 3:8–9
Women's Organization for National Prohibition Reform (WONPR), 3:9, 27
Women's Trade Union League (WTUL), 2:293–94
WONPR (Women's Organization for National Prohibition Reform), 3:9, 27
Wood, Edith, 2:115
Wood, Elmer, 2:110
Wood, Grant, 2:4, 255
Wood, Robert, 2:144
Woodard, Alfie, 2:90
Woodin, William, 1:49, 57, 63–64
Woodon, William, 2:254, 255
Woodward, Ellen, 3:285, 287, *302*, 303–4, 315, 320
Woolworth Building, 2:122
Work ethic, 1:225, 322, 3:191
Works Progress Administration (WPA), 3:**306–24**
achievements, 2:276–77, 289, 3:310
adult education program, 1:200, 208–9
American Indians and, 1:8

article in defense of, 3:323
CCC and, 1:112
churches and, 3:123
construction projects, 3:309–10
cultural democracy and, 1:28–29, 3:316–17
discrimination in, 1:250
ethnic group programs, 1:294
Federal Art Project, 1:28, 29, 76, 292, 2:277, 287, 3:312
Federal Dance Project (FDP), 2:277
Federal Music Project (FMP), 1:29, 76, 292, 3:311
Federal One, 1:26–28, 34–35, 36, 37, 3:210–311, 316–17
goals of, 1:26, 120, 188, 249
Head Start Program and, 1:209
health programs, 3:54–55
Hopkins, Harry and, 1:249, 250, 3:309, 322
impact of, 3:319
large-scale projects, 1:249
lunch program, 1:200, 209
notable people, 3:319–20
NYA supervised by, 3:314
perspectives on, 3:317–18
photography projects, 2:302–3
public perspectives on, 2:287, 3:318
Roosevelt, Franklin and, 3:309
termination, 3:337
Timberline Lodge project, 3:320–22
transients and, 3:82, 83
women and, 3:315
as work relief, 3:306, 309
work relief programs, 1:26–27, 75, 200, 249–50, 2:276, 3:306, 309
World's fair construction projects, 3:356–57
See also Federal Theater Project (FTP); Federal Writers' Project (FWP); National Youth Administration (NYA)
Workweek, 1:275, 2:128, 164, 191, 3:342–43
World, 2:172
World Economic Conference, 2:59–61, *65,* 68–69
World trade
collapse of, 2:50, 52, 55, 57
import tariffs, 1:96, 100, 101, 2:3–4, 15, 52, 55
overview, 2:50, 268
World Trade Organization (WTO), 2:202
World War I
agriculture and, 1:56, 95, 98–99, 2:1, 11
American involvement in, 2:146–48
Armistice Day, 2:*147,* 149
disillusionment with, 2:146, 147, 148
economy and, 1:96, 188
Germany and, 2:54, 63, 146

hunger relief efforts, 3:99
isolationism after, 1:34, 96, 101–2, 2:15
planning and mobilization, 3:338–39
Treaty of Versailles, 2:143, 147, 148, 152
See also War debts
World War II
economic boon of, 1:77, 325, 2:18, 284, 3:330–31, 342–43
electricity needs during, 3:266, 277
ethnic groups and, 1:300
food conservation, 2:40–41
impact of, 2:64
industry-military alliance, 3:329, 336, 338, 344, 346
isolationism during, 2:146, 3:342
Japanese Americans relocated, 1:117, 294, 300, 3:331
New Deal and, 1:112
Office of War Information (OWI), 2:303, 307–8
Pearl Harbor bombed, 2:145, 146, 3:67, 328–29, 342
race issues, 1:82
U.S. neutrality during, 2:143–44, 150, 156, 3:327, 344
war declared on Germany, 2:61, 3:327
See also Armaments; Interwar era; World War II mobilization
World War II mobilization, 3:**325–51**
America's workers, 3:342–43
black Americans in, 3:335
delays, 3:325, 326, 327
employment and, 3:330, 331–32
end of Great Depression and, 3:338
Europe at war, 3:339–42, 344–45
expenses, 3:326, 332, 334
impact of, 3:345–47
interwar mobilization planning, 2:145, 3:338–39
labor unions and, 3:334
Mexicans and Mexican Americans in, 3:334
mobilization agencies, 3:327–30
national perspectives on, 3:343–44
New Dealers and, 3:336–38, 339, 343
notable people, 3:347–49
overview, 3:325–26
political developments, 3:339
producing war materials, 2:145
wartime wages, 3:332, 334, 342–43
women in, 3:332–33
workforce changes, 3:333–34
See also Armaments; Interwar era; World War II
World Woman's Party, 3:297, 301
World's fairs, 3:**352–66**
Art Deco, 3:353, 359

Century of Progress Exposition, Chicago, 1:17, 3:352, *354*, 355–56, 365
    employment opportunities at, 3:353
    ethnic groups and, 3:363, 364
    Golden Gate International Exposition, San Francisco, 3:353, 356–59
    impact of, 3:364
    international, 3:364
    New York World's Fair, New York City, 1:264, 277, 3:353, 359–61
    notable people, 3:364–65
    progressiveness of, 3:365
    public perspectives on, 3:363
    purpose of, 3:352
    science and, 3:352, 355–56, 361–62, 363
    social and economic roles of, 3:362–63
    TVA exhibit, 3:241
    videos on, 3:364
    women and, 3:358, 361
World's Industrial Cotton Centennial Exposition, 3:362
WPA. *See* Works Progress Administration (WPA)
The WPA—Loafers or Workers? (Cushman), 3:323
WPB (War Production Board), 3:329, 346
WRA (War Relocation Authority), 3:331
WRB (War Resources Board), 2:432, 3:327–28

Wright, Frank Lloyd, 1:33, 2:122, 126, 135, 3:276
Wright, Richard
    about, 1:*79*, 2:224–25, 322–23, 331
    Black Boy, 2:222, 224
    Communist Party and, 2:322, 323
    Native Son, 1:76, 2:211, 214, 222, 224
    Richard Wright—Black Boy (film), 2:327
    12 Million Black Voices, 2:224, 226
    Uncle Tom's Children (Wright), 1:76, 2:211, 224, 226
Writer's Anti-War Bureau, 2:145
WTO (World Trade Organization), 2:202
Wuthering Heights (film), 2:82
Wyler, John, 2:82
Wyler, William, 2:94

Y

Yea or Nay? (*The Economist*), 2:68–69
Yellow fever, 3:47
Yellow Jack, 3:47
Yellowstone National Park, 1:118
Yosemite National Park, 3:274, 275
You Can't Go Home Again (Wolfe), 2:213
You Have Seen Their Faces (Caldwell and Bourke-White), 2:210, 223, 303
Young Communist League, 2:332
Young Mr. Lincoln (film), 2:82

Your Share (Betty Crocker), 2:40–41
Youth
    CCC work relief programs, 1:110–11, 116–17, 250–51
    communism and, 2:332
    drinking and, 3:24, 25
    everyday life, 1:212–13, 317, 2:*278*
    as extra wage earners, 1:307
    fair labor standards, 2:280
    games and activities of, 1:279
    juvenile delinquents, 1:131
    NYA work relief programs, 1:201, 212, 252, 2:275, 277, 3:314–15
    Prohibition and, 3:24, 26
    Roosevelt, Eleanor and, 1:250, 3:315
    Roosevelt, Franklin and, 1:250, 2:277
    as transients, 1:111, 116–17, 3:78, *86*, *90*
    unemployment, 1:109–10, 111, 2:277, 3:76, 77
    See also Children; Games; National Youth Administration (NYA); Riding the rails
Youth in the Depression (Davis), 1:212–13, 3:89–90

Z

Zaharias, Mildred "Babe," 2:124–25
Zanuck, Darryl, 2:94
Zionists, 3:137, 142
Zoster, William, 1:126